PRACTICAL THEOLOGY

SPIRITUAL DIRECTION
FROM ST. THOMAS AQUINAS

PETER KREEFT

PRACTICAL THEOLOGY
SPIRITUAL DIRECTION
FROM ST. THOMAS AQUINAS

358 Ways Your Mind Can Help You to Become a Saint
from the *Summa Theologiae*

IGNATIUS PRESS   SAN FRANCISCO

Cover art: *St. Thomas Aquinas* by Carlo Crivelli, 1476
National Gallery, London
Courtesy of Wikimedia Commons

Cover design by Enrique Javier Aguilar Pinto

© 2014 by Ignatius Press, San Francisco
All rights reserved
ISBN 978-1-58617-968-7
Library of Congress Control Number 2014943996
Printed in the United States of America ∞

CONTENTS

INTRODUCTION

St. Thomas wrote a very short preface to his very long (4,000-page) *Summa Theologiae*. In it he says he wrote his *Summa* "for beginners"! I too will give you a fairly short preface (though not as short as his) to tell you why I wrote this fairly long book (though not as long as his), and why "beginners" should read it.

In a lifetime of browsing through Aquinas, my amazement has continually increased not only at his theoretical, philosophical brilliance and sanity but equally at his personal, practical wisdom, his "existential bite". Yet this second dimension of St. Thomas has usually been eclipsed by the other. I wrote this book to help bring that sun out from its eclipse. Since I already wrote an annotated anthology of St. Thomas' purely rational, philosophical wisdom, *Summa of the Summa*, extracting it from its larger theological context of faith and divine revelation. I here try to redress the balance with an easily digestible sample of his much larger distinctively religious wisdom.

Here are 358 pieces of wisdom from St. Thomas' masterpiece the *Summa,* which are literally more valuable than all the kingdoms of this world because they will help you to attain "the one thing needful", the *summum bonum* or "greatest good", the ultimate end and purpose and meaning of life, which has many names but which is the same reality. Three of its names are "being a saint", "beatitude" (supreme happiness) and "union with God". That was my principle for choosing which passages to use: do they help you to attain your ultimate end, i.e., sanctity, happiness, union with God?

St. Thomas would have agreed with Léon Bloy, who often wrote that in the end there is only one tragedy in life: not to have been a saint.

This is the same thing as attaining true happiness. St. Thomas, like Aristotle, meant by "happiness" not merely "subjective contentment" but "real perfection", attaining the end or "final cause" or purpose of your very existence.

This is the same thing as union with God, the source of all holiness and all happiness. St. Thomas knew that union with God begins not after death but now. If this real union does *not* begin now, as a seed—if you are not "born again of the Spirit"—then that life cannot and will not grow, as a flower, in eternity.

This book is a selection of St. Thomas' fertilizers to make that seed grow.

There are four kinds of fertilizer. They are the four dimensions of every religion. The word "religion" (from *religare*) means "a binding-back relationship", a "tying-to"; and there are four ways every religion ties us to God, or something like God. (These four ways are also the four parts of *The Catechism of the Catholic Church*.) They are (1) theology, (2) morality, (3) public liturgy, and (4) private prayer. Condensing the last two into one, they are (1) creed, (2) code, and (3) cult; or (1) words, (2) works, and (3) worship; or (1) the spiritually true, (2) the spiritually good, and (3) the spiritually beautiful. They are the three ways to become a saint, the three highways to Heaven, and they all begin in the heart, for "in the heart are the highways to Zion (Heaven)" (Ps 84:5). St. Thomas was a master of all three.

The ultimate reason we must become *holy* is that that is the only way to become *real*. For becoming holy is becoming what reality ultimately is, i.e., what God, the ultimate reality and the touchstone for all reality, is: true, good, and beautiful; real, loving, and joyful. "You must be holy because I the Lord your God am holy" was His ultimate explanation of His law to His chosen people, who were His collective prophet to the world.

Attaining this end depends on the will—the will to attain it, the will's choice to believe God, to hope in God, and above all, to love God and that which God is (truth, goodness, beauty).

But the will depends on the mind. Each truth about God known by the mind is a new motive for loving Him with the will. It also works the other way around: the more you love any person (human or divine), the more you want to know him (or Him) better, and the more you do. And this always causes deep joy.

But we simply can't jump-start our will by a simple command: "Go to now, love God more!" When we give this command to ourselves, we immediately find, like St. Augustine in the *Confessions,* that the very same self that commands sanctity also disobeys its own commandment! We have divided selves. The self that wants above all things to be forever bound to God and His will in eternity also wants to be free from Him at the present moment to do its own will. Our wills are divided. We love our Father in Heaven, yet we are rebellious kids. We are stubborn, silly, stupid, selfish, and sinful. That is the "bad news". Without it the "good news" makes no sense. A free heart transplant is not good news unless your old heart is in bad shape. "Sin" means our hearts are in bad shape. "Sin" means "separation"—from God and from our neighbors and even from our deepest selves.

We need the mind to educate and enlighten the will, as a traveler needs a map.

No one in history has ever supplied that map more brilliantly and profoundly than St. Thomas.

Therefore, reading St. Thomas is a powerful aid to happiness, to sanctity.

It has been that to me. I have found more personal spiritual nourishment, more motivation to be holy, in the dry, abstract pages of the *Summa* than in most other "spiritual" writers.

But reading the *Summa* all by yourself is difficult, unless someone makes it easy. It's not likely that you will read all 4,000 pages of the *Summa,* so I give you here a kind of *Reader's Digest* version. By chopping up the meat into small, bite-sized pieces, as Mommy does for Baby—or, to change the image to something less insulting, I do the preliminary work of going down into the 4,000-page tunnels of this labyrinth, as into a deep mine, extract a few choice gold nuggets from this rich lode, bring them to the surface, and give them to you to wear as jewelry.

I tried to type the next sentence "The *Summa* is a gold mine", and it came out "The *Summa* is a gold mind." I think this was my guardian angel playing a providential joke on me. The typo is the truth.

Here are 358 gold nuggets that have helped me enormously in the struggle of real life, the struggle to live in the real world, to be sane, or in the words of the classic Anglican prayer, "to know Thee more clearly, to love Thee more dearly, and to follow Thee more nearly". They will help you too.

This is St. Thomas' book, not mine. I am only one hungry, homeless bum calling to my friends: "Look! Free steak dinners over there!" He supplies the steak, I supply only the sauces. Thus his words are in boldface type, mine are not. My comments that follow each quotation do not mean to *add* to what St. Thomas says but only (1) explain it, (2) apply it, and (3) festoon it, like a Christmas tree. Or, better, they unwrap the Christmas presents St. Thomas gives us. They are not scholarly theological commentaries but more like what the Jews call *midrash:* spiritual commentaries: practical, personal, existential, "livable" thoughts. I have formatted these readings as answers to questions that real people actually ask their spiritual directors.

I used the old, literal, faithful Dominican Blackfriars translation. The style is old-fashioned, like the King James Bible, i.e., arresting and formal and proper. It gets your attention. It is memorable. It is "different", because the subject matter is different. It is about the most important thing in the world, not about advertisements or news reports or gossip; so since it *is* more important, it deserves a style that *sounds* more important.

The style of the translation is also literal. It tells you exactly what Aquinas actually wrote, word for word, rather than what some translator thinks he would have written if he had to write in twenty-first century American vernacular. Yet it is totally clear: you don't have to be a scholar to understand it. Whenever there is a technical term that means something different in Aquinas than it does in contemporary English, I added the contemporary translation or explanation in parentheses.

The numerical references after each quotation tell you three things: first, the "part" of the *Summa* (I, I-II, II-II, III, or S [supplement]), then the number of the "Question", then the number of the "Article". For an account of how the *Summa* as a whole is organized (it's a mirror image of how all reality is organized!) and how each part of each "Article" functions (it's the five most basic and necessary steps in a complete logical analysis), see the Introduction to my *Summa of the Summa.*

I follow the order of the *Summa.* Often, I treat and repeat the same point two or three times, in a somewhat different way, or a different context, because that is what St. Thomas did; and the justification for both of us doing that is the intrinsic importance of these issues.

I. RELIGION

Isn't organized religion a crutch? Why do we need the Bible and the Church? Can't we know God by our own reason and common sense and experience instead of "divine revelation"?

It was necessary for man's salvation that there should be a knowledge revealed by God besides philosophical science (wisdom) **built up by human reason ... because man is directed to God as to an end that surpasses the grasp of his reason:** *"The eye has not seen, O God ... what things Thou hast prepared for them that wait for Thee"* (Is 66:4). **But the end must first be known by men who are to direct their ... actions to the end. Hence it was necessary for the salvation of man that certain truths about God which exceed human reason should be made known to him by divine revelation** (I,1,1).

Life is a road. The most important thing about a road is its end, where it goes. If the road of life has no real end and goal, it is meaningless. It is a circle or a swamp or a wilderness, not a road.

What is our end? Not ourselves. Our end is to know God—not just to know *about* Him but to *know* Him. *"This is eternal life: to know Thee, the one true God"* (Jn 17:3).

But even if we had not fallen into sin and error, our knowledge of God would have been less adequate than a worm's knowledge of us. For the distance between the finitude of the worm and the finitude of man is only finite, while the distance between finite man and infinite God is infinite.

Only God can bridge that gap, by acting "down" with His power; we cannot bridge it by moving "up" with our power. A worm cannot climb Mount Everest. This was so from the beginning, even before we fell. How much more do we need divinely revealed truth now that we are fallen and foolish.

We need it not just to satisfy our natural curiosity but to actually get us to God, **for man's salvation.** We are half-blind and lost in a haunted forest. Without a road map, we will not get Home. The purpose of divinely revealed theology is not just theoretical but utterly practical.

That is why you should read St. Thomas. The ultimate reason for studying theology is the same as the ultimate reason for your existence. It is "Salvation", that is, it is Heaven, Happiness, Holiness (three words for the very same thing).

Yes, we can know much about God by the proper use of our natural human reason: e.g., that He exists, that He is one, that He is perfect. But since we are fallen fools, most of our philosophy is *not* "the proper use of human reason" but the *improper* use of human reason. Just look at the history of modern philosophy if you doubt that! That is why Aquinas adds:

Even as regards those truths about God which human reason could have discovered, it was necessary that man should be taught by a divine revelation; because the truth about God such as reason could discover would only be known by a few (how many Aristotles were there in ancient Greece?), **and that after a long time** (how many die before they get even that far?), **and with the admixture of many errors** (how many mistakes do philosophers make?). **Whereas man's whole salvation, which is in God, depends upon the knowledge of this truth. Therefore, in order that the salvation of men might be brought about more fitly and more surely, it was necessary that they should be taught divine truths by divine revelation** (I,1,1).

Yes, organized religion is a crutch. You mean you didn't know that you are a cripple? If you don't know that, then you are a very serious cripple indeed, mentally and spiritually. Go back to Socrates: "Know thyself." For Socrates, there are only two kinds of people: the wise, who know they are fools; and fools, who think they are wise. Similarly, for Christ and all the prophets, there are only two kinds of people: saints, who know they are sinners; and sinners, who think they are saints. Which are you? You can tell which class you fit into by whether or not you accept the "crutch", the road map. Maybe the Jews were lost forty years in the wilderness because Moses was too proud to stop and ask for directions. (It's a guy thing.)

2. THE NEED FOR THEOLOGY

Is theology really the most important thing I need to know?

Since this science (theology) **is partly speculative** (truth for the sake of truth) **and partly practical** (truth for the sake of practice), **it transcends all others** (both) **speculative and practical. Now one speculative science is said to be nobler** (higher, more valuable) **than another either by reason of its greater certitude or by reason of the higher worth of its subject-matter. In both these respects this science surpasses other speculative sciences: in point of greater certitude, because other sciences derive their certitude from the natural light of human reason, which can err, whereas this derives its certitude from the light of the divine knowledge, which cannot be misled; in point of the higher worth of its subject-matter because this science treats chiefly of those things which by their sublimity transcend human reason, while other sciences consider only those things which are within reason's grasp.**

Of the practical sciences, that one is nobler which is not ordained to a further purpose, as political science is nobler than military science, for the good of the army is directed to the good of the State. But the purpose of this science (theology), **in so far as it is practical, is eternal bliss, to which as to an ultimate end the purposes of every practical science are directed.**

Hence it is clear that from every standpoint it is nobler than other sciences (I,1,5).

Good theology is not the knowledge of theology but the knowledge of God. Bad theology is the theology of the theologian who died and went to Heaven and at the gates of Heaven God offered him the choice between Heaven and a theology lecture on Heaven, and he chose the lecture.

Theology has two ends, which Thomas calls "speculative" (or contemplative) and practical (or active). It seeks truth as an end in itself and also as a means to a life of acts that both lead to and stem from salvation.

"Theology" means "the science (*logos*) of God (*theos*)"—"science" in the old, broad, pre-modern sense of "knowledge of the truth ordered by *logos* (reason and language)".

There are two factors that make one truth (and therefore one science) higher or more valuable than another: *certainty* and *importance*. Theology is #1 in both. For if there is "revealed theology"; if there is a wisdom not just *about* God but *from* God; if there is not just man's thoughts about God but also God's thoughts about man; then this is the most certain knowledge we have, because God, unlike man, can never deceive or be deceived. And it is also the most important knowledge we have; because if God exists, then knowing God is the most important knowledge there is, because God is the most important reality there is. He is the most important because He is our ultimate End. (That should be obvious!)

Why then is there more controversy in theology than in other sciences, if it is the most certain? It certainly seems less certain than, say, physics. Isn't it dependent on personal opinion or faith, while other sciences are objective and certain?

St. Thomas answers this objection too, and explains why the most certain seems least certain:

It may well happen that what is in itself the more certain may seem to us the less certain on account of the weakness of our intelligence, *"which is dazzled by the clearest objects in nature, as the owl is dazzled by the light of the sun"* (Aristotle). **Hence the fact that some happen to doubt about articles of faith is not due to the uncertain nature of the truths, but to the weakness of human intelligence. Yet the slenderest knowledge that may be obtained of the highest things is more desirable than the most certain knowledge obtained of lesser things** (I,1,5).

We must choose between (1) more perfect (clear, adequate, certain-to-us) knowledge of imperfect things (the things of this world) and (2) less perfect knowledge of more perfect things (the things of God). Which is more important to you: a tiny, imperfect little insight into the heart of the person you love the most, or a mathematically complete and certain formula for a better paper clip?

Isn't the knowledge of God that a simple saint has, by experience and love and intimate personal relationship, a much higher kind of knowledge than the knowledge that the world's most brilliant theologian has only by reason and study and thinking?

Yes it is; and St. Thomas explicitly says that:

Since judgment pertains to wisdom, the twofold manner of judging produces a twofold wisdom. A man may judge in one way by (personal) **inclination, as whoever has the habit of a** (particular) **virtue judges rightly of what concerns that virtue, by his very inclination towards it.... In another way, by knowledge** (*scientia*, science), **just as a man learned** (educated) **in moral science might be able to judge rightly about virtuous acts even though he had not the virtue. The first manner of judging divine things belongs to that wisdom which is set down among the gifts of the Holy Ghost:** *"The spiritual man judgeth all things"* (1 Cor 2:15).... **The second manner of judging belongs to this doctrine, which is acquired by study, though its principles are obtained by revelation** (I,1,6).

St. Thomas himself had both kinds of knowledge. When God gave him an intimate mystical experience of Himself, shortly before he died, he stopped writing. (The *Summa*, his masterpiece, is unfinished—like life itself.) He said, "I can write no more, for compared with what I have seen, everything I have ever written is only straw."

Even before this experience, he showed that he had the higher knowledge. One of his fellow monks saw him alone on the floor of the chapel, and heard the voice of Christ speaking to him from the crucifix: "You have written well of Me, Thomas; what will you have as your reward?" And his answer was the very definition of a saint, and of the whole meaning of life: "Only Yourself, Lord." In those three words he said more than he said in the 4,000 pages of the greatest work of theology ever written.

But the lower kind of knowledge can be a significant help to the higher. Even a book like this one can take you some small but significant steps toward St. Thomas' wisdom and holiness, since it is based on St. Thomas' own masterpiece, which in turn is based on God's own Book of revelation, the Bible. A book is not a person, but it can help us to understand a person better—especially if the primary author of the Book is the very Person we seek to understand, and if when we read His books (He wrote two, nature and Scripture) we read with the person-loving heart as well as the truth-loving head.

4. How to interpret the Bible

If the Bible is our primary source of theology, which is the knowledge of God, how should we interpret it? Literally or symbolically?

St. Thomas' answer to that question, like his answer to many others, is: "Both." Here's why:

The author of Holy Writ is God, in Whose power it is to signify His meaning not by words only (as man also can do) but also by things themselves. So whereas in every other science things are signified by words, this science has the property that the things signified by the words have themselves also a signification.

Therefore that first signification, whereby words signify things, belongs to the first sense, the historical and literal. That signification whereby things signified by words have themselves also a signification is called the spiritual sense, which is based on the literal, and presupposes it (I,1,10).

Words are signs—signs of real things or events. Words point beyond themselves.

Real things and events can also be words, that point to God, since divine providence orders all things and events as writers order their words. This is why we often learn more about God from real events and people and history than we do from words in books. It is because these *things* are words too. God wrote two books, not just one: the Bible and nature, which includes people and history and events. The actual events are "words" (meaningful signs) in the book of divine providence. They point beyond themselves; they are signs of other things—above all, of God Himself, the Author of both books.

That is the justification for a symbolic interpretation of the things, events, and persons in the Bible. It is not an alternative to a literal interpretation, but a rich addition, another layer of meaning, looking-along these signs instead of just looking-at them. We have largely lost this art of sign reading, since it is not "scientific" in the modern sense. But it is a rich mine with many gold nuggets in it.

Take, for instance, the story of the Exodus. A real Moses really led real Jews from real oppression in real Egypt under real Pharaoh, really crossing the real Red Sea and really wandering through a real wilderness, past real Mount Sinai, really receiving a real Law, and really entering a real Promised Land. Yet all these real things and events were deliberately designed by God as symbols, signs pointing beyond themselves to deeper, more spiritual things. The Exodus also = salvation; Egypt = sin; Pharoah = Satan; Moses = Christ; the Jews = the Church; the Red Sea = death; the wilderness = Purgatory; the Old Law = the New Law; the gospel; the old Mount (Sinai) = the new mount from which Jesus preached His "sermon on the mount" (Mt 5-7); and the Promised Land = Heaven. The "=" is not mathematical but symbolic.

St. Thomas distinguishes three kinds of symbolic interpretation:

Now this spiritual sense has a threefold division.

(1) **For as the Apostle says** (Heb 10:1), **the Old Law** (Old Testament) **is a figure** (symbol, image) **of the New Law** (New Testament, Gospel);

(2) **And ... the New Law itself is a figure of future glory** (Heaven).

(3) **Again, in the New Law, whatever our Head has done is a type** (symbol, image, model) **of what we ought to do** (I,1,10).

So many passages in the Bible invite a fourfold interpretation:

(1) the literal, historical sense, **on which all the others are based**;

(2) the allegorical sense (the example of the Exodus, above);

(3) the moral sense ("the imitation of Christ");

(4) the eschatological sense: thus Jesus' physical miracles of healing are signs of spiritual healing from spiritual deafness, blindness, paralysis, etc. in Heaven.

5. The (a) reality and (b) inadequacy of our innate knowledge of God

Even if we need divine revelation to know more about God, and to know Him better, as St. Thomas explained in point #1, don't we already know there is a God by innate common sense? Isn't it part of human nature to believe in some God or other? All cultures in history have religion. Isn't the gospel like a seed planted in a soil (human nature) that is already fertilized from within?

Yes:

(a) **To know that God exists in a general and confused way is implanted in human nature, inasmuch as God is man's beatitude** (ultimate good, perfection and happiness). **For man naturally desires happiness, and what is naturally desired by man must be naturally known by him.**

(b) **This, however, is not to know absolutely** (explicitly, clearly) **that God exists; just as to know that someone is approaching is not the same as to know that Peter is approaching even though it is Peter who is approaching. For there are many who imagine that man's perfect good, which is happiness, consists in riches, and others in pleasures, and others in something else** (I,2,I).

Everyone has some God, some ultimate end, some *summum bonum* ("greatest good"). In this sense there are no simply non-religious human beings. An atheist too has a god: it is usually himself or his own pleasures, comforts, or joys.

If this were not so—if we did not innately seek beatitude—then the gospel, the revelation of the true God as our true beatitude, would not even be understandable or desirable; just as the offer of real, nourishing food would not be either understandable or desirable to an entity like a robot without hunger and without a digestive system.

Therefore, when talking with "non-religious" people, do not accept their false belief that there are two kinds of people: "religious people" and "non-religious people". Don't talk to the false mask they wear; talk to the real hunger within. It is always there.

As St. Augustine famously said, "Thou hast made us for Thyself, and [therefore] our hearts are restless until they rest in Thee." There are no exceptions to that.

Once someone recognizes and admits this vague yet sharp hunger in themselves, this "lover's quarrel with the world", this desire for a truer, deeper, more real happiness than we have in this world, for this "something more" that we cannot define yet cannot avoid yearning for because it is suggested in all the deepest joys in this world (human love, sex, music, sunsets, babies, storms, mountains, waves, poetry)—once this is admitted, the most direct and effective road for evangelism opens up: the evangelism of the heart. St. Thomas is the all-time master of the head, but he begins and ends in the heart. He enables your philosophy and your prayer to be one.

6. THE "PROBLEM OF EVIL"

Why does God allow evil? This is the strongest argument for atheism.

St. Thomas formulates the argument. He says, **If one of two contraries** (opposites) **be infinite, the other would be altogether destroyed. But the word "God" means that He is infinite goodness. If, therefore, God existed, there would be no evil discoverable. But there is evil in the world. Therefore God does not exist** (I,2,3).

If God is infinitely good, He does not will any evil. And if He is infinitely powerful, He gets all that He wills and only what He wills. So why is there evil? Does God lack goodness or power?

Here is St. Thomas' answer:

As Augustine says, *"Since God is the highest good, He would not allow any evil to exist in His works unless His omnipotence and goodness were such as to bring good even out of evil."* **This is part of the infinite goodness of God, that He should allow evil to exist and out of it produce good** (I,2,3).

The clearest example of this is the crucifixion of Christ, the most evil deed ever done, the murder of God. And out of this greatest evil came the greatest good, our salvation. If God can pull off that trick there, He can do that anywhere. Every tragedy can be a "Good Friday".

So when you see something evil, whether a physical evil (like death) or a moral evil (like the oppression of the innocent), know that God in His infinite wisdom knows infinitely more than you do about it and does not prevent it even though He could, because He is bringing some greater good out of it, usually a good that we cannot yet see, except by the eyes of faith and trust.

St. Thomas' answer to the problem of evil is not just good philosophy; it is good spiritual direction, it is powerfully practical. Because it enables us to say to God "Even though I do not understand why You allowed this, I trust you", not just when we see little evils like hemorrhoids but even when we see horrible evils like Holocausts. Job said, "Though He slay me, yet will I trust Him" (Job 13:15). We cannot prove it, and we cannot fully understand it, but we are always free to make the choice to trust Him. The atheist tries to take that freedom from us. St. Thomas defends us against that assault.

Neither St. Thomas nor any other human being can give the atheist what he demands: a reason why God allows this or that particular evil (e.g., the death of a child, or the power of a Hitler). But he can give the atheist a reason why it is irrational and unfair for him to demand to know such reasons. For *if there is* a God, Whose wisdom is infinitely greater than ours, *then we would not* be able to understand the reasons why He allows many things to happen, any more than a dog or an infant can understand why adults do what they do. For the difference between our finite minds and God's infinite mind is at least as great as the difference between a dog's or an infant's finite mind and our own. We are not God. Why is it so hard for us to remember that?

In a vision, God summarized all of divine revelation to St. Catherine in two two-word sentences: "I'm God. You're not." Why is it so easy for us to forget that second thing?

There is therefore infinite room to trust Him even—especially—when we are shocked, surprised, and scandalized by some evil whose good result we simply do not see. We do not have divine eyes. But there is One Who does. Those are the two most salient facts of our existence.

If we *did* understand the reasons why God allowed every evil He allows, if we understood "the big picture", we would be as wise as God; and in that case there would be no God above ourselves, and this would not disprove atheism, this would prove atheism.

7. GOD'S NECESSITY: "HIS ESSENCE IS EXISTENCE"

Who made God? No one, of course, but how is that possible? Why is it so natural for us to ask that question?

We ask that question because we do not understand that God is not just one of many beings, *a* being, the first and greatest being, but a different *kind* of being than everything else. He exists from within His own essence (His essential nature); everything else needs an external cause to exist.

That is why God alone is to be adored absolutely, in Himself and from Himself and for Himself: because He alone exists absolutely, in Himself and from Himself and for Himself.

If the existence of a thing differs from its essence, this existence must be caused either by some exterior agent or by its own essential principles (sources). **Now it is impossible for a thing's existence to be caused** (efficient cause, agent, origin) **by its own essential constituent principles, for nothing can be the sufficient cause of its own existence, if its existence is caused. Therefore that thing whose existence differs from its essence must have its existence caused by another.**

But this cannot be true of God, because we call God the first efficient cause. Therefore it is impossible that in God His existence should differ from His essence....

... [J]ust as that which *has* fire but *is* not itself fire (by its essence) **is on fire by participation** (in fire), **so that which *has* existence but *is* not existence is a being by participation** (in existence).... **If therefore He is not His own existence, He will be not essential being but participated being. He would not then be the first being—which is absurd. Therefore God is His own existence** (I,3,4).

This very abstract language about essence and existence is really quite easy to understand. The "essence" of a thing is its nature, *what* it is; its existence is *whether* it is. Unicorns have an essence but no existence; horses have both; square circles have neither.

Everything in the universe, everything except God, exists because it is caused, brought into existence by something else. Parents cause children, factories cause cars, the sun causes light, tectonic plate movements cause earthquakes. God alone has no cause, needs no cause; God alone exists from within rather than from without, by His essence rather than from a cause. Thus only God is necessary; everything else is a contingent might-not-have-been. And only God is eternal; everything else has a beginning.

What does this theological point have to do with the practical problem of becoming a saint? Everything. It most sharply distinguishes God the Creator from all creatures, no matter how great. (Even the greatest angel exists only because it is brought into existence by God.) And it is thus the reason for the first and greatest commandment, "Thou shalt have no other gods before Me", or, in Jesus' formulation of the same commandment, "Thou shalt love the Lord thy God with thy whole heart, soul, mind, and strength." Why is this the first commandment? Because it is the first truth, the first reality; and the commandments define what it is to live in reality rather than in fantasy, in truth rather than error or lies.

Sanctity is sanity. Being a saint is living in reality. Worshipping a creature, having a false God, is a lie. Not worshipping God, treating God as a creature, as a means to your own ends, as a finite thing, is a lie. Why? Because "only God is God." This is the true heart of Islam. It is the *Shahadah* that every Muslim recites many times a day to remember the unforgettable wisdom that we so easily forget.

St. Thomas gives us the philosophical principles, the essence and existence language, that explains why God alone is the fullness of being. His essence is existence, and therefore He does not receive any being, any perfection, any essence, or any existence, from any other being, any creature. We are all dependent and interdependent; God alone is absolutely independent. To accept these two facts in our daily lives, to live as if this were true (since it is!), is the beginning of both sanity and sanctity.

8. ALL PERFECTIONS ARE IN GOD

Why do we sin? Most sins—perhaps all—are idolatries, preferring something else to God, some creature to the Creator. But creatures are temptingly good. We can't help loving good wherever we find it. How can we avoid idolizing creatures, placing our love and hope and happiness in them instead of God?

By realizing that every good thing we seek is in God more perfectly than it is in any creatures. "Seek what you seek, but it is not where you seek it", says Augustine. St. Thomas says:

All created perfections are in God. Hence He is spoken of as universally perfect ("all-perfect"), because He lacks not any excellence which may be found in creatures.

This may be seen from two considerations.

First, because whatever perfection exists in an effect must also be found in the effective cause ... Since therefore God is the first effective cause of things, the perfection of all things must pre-exist in God in a more eminent way ...

Second, from what has already been proved, God is existence (being) itself. Consequently, He must contain within Himself the whole perfection of being ... Since therefore God is subsisting being itself, nothing of the perfection of being can be wanting to Him. Now all created perfections are included in the perfection of being, for things are perfect only insofar as they have being after some fashion. It follows therefore that the perfection of no being is wanting to God (I,4,2).

Whatever is desirable, in whatsoever beatitude (happiness, joy), whether true (beatitude) or (even) false (i.e., merely apparent beatitude), pre-exists wholly and in a more eminent degree in the divine beatitude.

As to contemplative happiness, God possesses a continual and most certain contemplation of Himself and of all things else.

And as to that which is active, He has the governance of the whole universe.

As to earthly happiness, which consists in delight, riches, power, dignity, and fame, according to Boethius (The Consolation of Philosophy III,10), He possesses joy in Himself and all things else for His delight:

Instead of riches, He has that complete self-sufficiency which is promised by riches;

In place of power, He has omnipotence;

For dignities, the government of all things;

And in place of fame, He possesses the admiration of all creatures (I,26,4, "Whether All Beatitude is Included in the Beatitude of God?").

To paraphrase Augustine, when the john knocks on the door of the whorehouse he is looking for a cathedral. Every sin is a desire for some forbidden fruit, some invitingly fat, wiggly worm that the devil puts on his hook. If the fruit, or the worm, had no goodness, we would not desire it. Even stupid fish don't bite bare hooks.

But everything, every good without exception, that we seek in forbidden fruit, or in worms on hooks, is to be found in God, in pure, perfect form. "Seek what you seek, but it is not where you seek it", says Augustine. "You seek Life in the place of death."

All sin, therefore, comes from a lack of faith—faith in this very fact, that God contains all perfections, not just some. God is not an option for "religious people", whoever they are. God is the only game in town.

God, out of sheer love and generosity, has put all sorts of delightful "perfections" (desirable qualities, "good stuff") into His creation—seas, stars, sunsets, babies, music, food, sex—and especially into His creation of persons, who are made in His image. And the Creator has even shared with us His creativity, so that we can create many more beauties of art, discoveries of science, powers of technology, and delights of society and culture. We naturally and rightly fall in love with them. The gifts of culture are God's gifts too, indirectly, just as much as the gifts of nature are His gifts directly. But it is hard to avoid idolizing them, overdoing them and underdoing God.

Here, in St. Thomas, is a powerful aid to obeying the first and greatest commandment. It is the realization that every finite perfection we love and seek in the creation is to be found in an infinitely perfect form in God. What are we seeking in human love, in nature, in creativity, in thought? It's desirable only because it's a little like God. All that we love in creatures is a reflection of the Creator. There, and there alone, in Him, can we find everything we are seeking in them. The reflections of His perfections in the mirror of creation should send us away from the mirror, not into it. And when we run into the mirror, seeking our happiness there, the mirror breaks and our happiness shatters. For every truth is a reflection of His truth, every good is a reflection of His good, every beauty is a reflection of His beauty. The reflections are real, but they are only real *reflections*. They point back to the Reality they reflect. All truth is God's truth. All goodness is God's goodness. All beauty is God's beauty. **He must contain in Himself the whole perfection of being.**

And therefore *He* is what we need, He is *all* of what we need, and He is the *only* One we need. For if we need something else besides God, something in addition to God, then God is not God.

There is a mystery about our desires: they have no limit! We are never totally and absolutely satisfied. Why? Because they are about God.

"The form (nature) of the Desired is in the desire." St. Thomas means by that saying that there is no such thing as desire simply, desire with no specific object, desire for nothing, or for everything in general, for an abstraction. There is only desire for food, drink, sleep, truth, goodness, beauty, sex, love, friendship, etc. The form of the object of each desire is in the desire itself, and gives it its nature: desire for sex is sexual desire, desire for knowledge is curiosity, desire for friendship is loneliness.

And thus since the form of its object is in the desire itself, and since what we most deeply desire is God, the infinite source of all finite perfections, therefore the infinite nature of God is "in" this infinite desire for God, like a negative photograph, or like a silhouette. When your mother dies, your grief is a mother-shaped grief; when you lack God it is a God-shaped lack, a God-shaped (and God-sized) vacuum. The desire for God has no limit because its object (God) has no limit.

St. Thomas here simply explains, in philosophical language, St. Augustine's beloved and famous saying that summarizes the whole meaning of life: "Thou hast made us for Thyself, and [that is why] our hearts are restless until they rest in Thee" (*Confessions* I,1).

How this frees us from worry! Jesus tells foolish, fussing Martha the startling good news that "There is only one thing needful!" (Lk 10:38-42). It's Him. Mary knew that, and Martha didn't, even though both loved Him. No thought more liberating, more simplifying, more unifying than that thought has ever entered into a human mind. Your life can be one. You can be one. You do not need to be torn apart, harried and hassled, bothered and bewildered. You can become one great person by having one great love.

For you are what you love. Your love is your destiny. Augustine says your love is your gravity (*amor meus, pondus meum*).

In speaking to Martha, Christ speaks to all of us. He sees us in her, and he wants to liberate us out of her confusions, her illusions, and her worries, and into Mary's "one thing needful". He is the One we need to seek, and find, and meet, and love, and serve in all things. Because everything we seek, every good, every happiness, every joy, every perfection, is There.

(You see now why I took two pages instead of one for this simplest of all lessons. It is really all we need to know to become saints, if we only live it.)

If God made all things, did He make bad things too?

Every being that is not God, is God's creature. Now every creature of God is good (1 Tim 4:4), and God is the greatest good, therefore every being is good.... No being can be spoken of as evil ... as being, but only insofar as it lacks being. Thus a man is said to be evil because he lacks some virtue, and an eye is said to be evil because it lacks the power to see well (I,5,3).

St. Thomas was once invited to a dinner with King Louis and his court. The absent-minded professor did not join the conversation at the meal but was thinking through some theological problem. Suddenly he banged his fist on the table and muttered, "*That* will settle the Manichees!" The court held their breaths at this absent-minded breach of etiquette in front of the king, but the wise king called for his secretary to write down St. Thomas' argument before he forgot it. What was the argument? It was probably the very quotation above. Manicheeism claimed that since there were good things and bad things, there were two gods: the good one made good things and the bad one made bad things, which the Manichees identified with material things.

St. Augustine was held back from Christianity, and suckered into Manicheeism, for years by the problem of evil. He wondered: If God is the maker of all things, mustn't He be the maker of ill things? Why did the good God make evil? Why did God create mosquitoes and volcanoes and hemorrhoids? Then one day he realized that he did not need another, evil God to make these things, as the Manichees said, but that these things are not *evil*.

Augustine said, "I sought for the cause of evil, but I sought in an evil way." He was looking everywhere else but in the mirror. Evil is in our sins, which come from us, not in our being, which comes from God. We love to blame matter, or our bodies, or others, or "society", or our parents, or chance, or evolution, or genetics, or our ancestors, or the Devil, or even God, for the evil in our lives. But God is all-good, so we can't blame God; and all that God made is good, so we can't blame any of that. God made even the Devil good in the beginning; the Devil corrupted himself by his own rebellion. The devil can only tempt us, not force us. So we are left with nothing to blame but ourselves.

There have always been heresies that blamed evil on matter: Manicheeism, Gnosticism, and Neoplatonism in ancient times, various "spiritualities" or spiritualisms in ours. These isms are not only an insult to God and His creation, but also a convenient but dishonest excuse for our own sins. "My hormones made me do it" is no better an excuse than "the Devil made me do it."

When St. Thomas says that "**no being can be spoken of as evil ... as being, but only insofar as it lacks being**", he does not mean that evil is unreal, illusory, or fantasy. Blindness is a real physical evil, but it is not a *thing*, an entity, a being; it is a defect or lack or privation in a thing: the privation (deprivation) of sight in the thing we call an eye. The eye is good, the blindness is not. The soul is good, the sin is not. God made the eye and its sight but not the sightlessness, the privation of sight; God made the soul and its virtues, and its love (for "God *is* love"), but not the sins, the vices, the lack of virtue, the lovelessness.

All the being, all the positive "stuff", is good, for it all came from God before we turned it against Him. God made the metal in the earth that we made into the nails that we hammered into His Son's hands and feet, and He made the flies that buzzed around His bleeding head on the Cross. And God made our strength of mind and will that we used to command the hands and hammers.

He said, after each day's work of creation, "It's good!" Let us dare to agree with Him. Let us love everything He loved into being. All that is, is good; all being is good; being as such is good, *ens est bonum*. It is better to be than not to be; that's why God said, "Let there be!" He's just got this *thing* about being. We should too!

10. Only three kinds of goods

How can I simplify my life? It's not lacking in good things, it's too full of them. How can I find space, and time, and simplicity?

The answer is: By realizing that the only things you need are good things, and that there are not as many good things as you think, because there are only three kinds of goods:

Goodness is rightly divided into (1) the virtuous, (2) the useful, and (3) the pleasant.... Goodness is not divided into these three as something univocal to be predicated equally of them all, but as something analogical to be predicated of them according to priority and posteriority. Hence it is predicated chiefly of the virtuous, then of the pleasant, and lastly of the useful (I,5,6).

What is "virtuous" is good in itself. The reason to be virtuous, to do right and not wrong, is simply because it's right and not wrong. What is "pleasant" is simply what makes you happy. And what is "useful" is whatever is a means to either what is virtuous or what is pleasant.

These are three *different kinds* of goods. They are good analogically, good in different ways, different senses. They are not the same in rank. They are in a hierarchy. (1) The virtuous good is the "good-est" because it is good absolutely, in itself. (2) The pleasant is next because it is also an end in itself (we seek pleasure for no other reason than pleasure), but it is not absolute but relative ("different strokes for different folks"). Also, not all pleasures are virtuous, though all virtues are pleasant. And the deepest pleasure is an effect of virtue, not vice versa. (3) Finally, the useful is good only as a means to either virtue or pleasure.

Hedonists are fools who seek only pleasure. But these people are never really deeply happy, deeply pleased. Pleasure comes only as a by-product. Pleasure-addicts are like hypochondriacs. They destroy the very thing they seek by idolizing it.

Pragmatists and utilitarians are fools who seek only utility. But as Chesterton says, "man's most pragmatic need is to be more than a pragmatist", to have some end to justify all these means, some absolute that all these things are relative to, something all these useful things are useful *for*.

Most of us are semi-hedonists and semi-utilitarians because we fill up our lives and our thoughts with useful goods first of all, then pleasant goods, then virtue last of all, as a kind of last-minute check. We invert the hierarchy. Especially in modern America, where we idolize our feelings (pleasures) and treat everything else (even unborn babies) as utilitarian, disposable consumer goods.

How can we find more room and time in our lives and our thoughts for the higher goods? By simplifying and minimizing the lower goods, and above all by eliminating everything else that is not really good at all. St. Thomas' classification gives us a road map for a wonderful simplification of our lives. Everyone needs that today. Everyone complains that their lives are too complex, that there is not enough time, not enough leisure—even though (or perhaps *because*) we have all these technological time-saving devices, our hundreds of mechanical slaves. We are slaves to our slaves. St. Thomas' simple common sense can free us from this slavery.

For there are only three kinds of good. So if a thing is not virtuous, useful, or pleasant, it's not really good. So fagetaboutit! Simplify your life by throwing out all the things you have that you don't need, all that's not virtuous, useful, or pleasant. Don't do anything for any other reason, e.g., because "everybody's doing it" or "everybody has one" or just because it's "expected", or because you feel a spontaneous desire for it once you see a commercial for it. Do you really *need* to buy that expensive sneaker or super cell phone, or to read that book that's on the best-seller list, or go to that dull meeting? Is it your moral duty? Does it give you happiness, or even pleasure? If the answer to all three questions is no, then dump it! A house without a garbage can becomes cluttered and smelly. The same is true of a life.

Our lives need a "Thoreau" simplification.

Where can I find God?

The answer is literally everywhere.

God is in all things; not, indeed, as part of their essence, nor as an accident, but as an agent is present to that upon which it works. For an agent must be joined to that wherein it acts immediately, and touch it by its power; hence ... the thing moved and the mover must be joined together.

Now since God is very being by His own essence, created being must be His proper effect, as to ignite is the proper effect of fire.

Now God causes this effect (being, existence) **in things not only when they first begin to be, but as long as they are preserved in being, as light is caused in the air by the sun as long as the air remains illuminated. Therefore as long as a thing has being, God must be present to it according to its mode of being. But being is innermost in each thing and most fundamentally inherent in all things ... Hence it must be that God is in all things, and innermostly.**

Objection 1. **It seems that God is not in all things, for what is above all things is not in all things, but God is above all things.**

Reply to Objection 1. **God is above all things by the excellence of His nature ... (but) He is in all things as the cause of the being of all things....**

Objection 2. **Further, what is in anything is thereby contained. Now God is not contained by things, but rather does He contain them....**

Reply to Objection 2. **Although corporeal things are said to be in another as in that which contains them, nevertheless spiritual things contain those things in which they are, as the soul contains the body.** (The soul contains the body, not vice versa, as the spiritual meaning of a play contains its physical setting, not vice versa.) **Hence also God is in things as containing them.**

Objection 4. **Further, the demons are beings. But God is not in the demons, for there is no fellowship between light and darkness ...**

Reply to Objection 4. **In the demons there is their nature, which is from God, and also the deformity of sin, which is not from Him; therefore it is not to be absolutely conceded that God is in the demons except with the addition** *inasmuch as they are beings.* **But in beings not deformed in their nature, we must say absolutely that God is** (I,8,1).

This point is so important that it will take two pages to explore it. It is important because it can directly help you to become a saint. The easiest and most effective way to become a saint is to "practice the presence of God," which is to get just a little bit closer to the Beatific Vision which we will have in Heaven, the Vision which will make it impossible for us to sin because we will be in the presence of the One Who is so supremely beautiful and good and lovable that sin will no longer be attractive, and because "we will see Him as He is." Then we will know by direct sight and experience rather than by faith that nothing can ever be more attractive than Him. We can get only a little bit closer to that Vision in this life, but even the tiniest bit of progress on that road is worth infinitely more than spectacular success on any other road.

St. Thomas here gives us the philosophical basis for practicing the presence of God everywhere. He explains how God *is* everywhere, **in all things.** If we see this "big picture", the whole world will light up like a stained glass window when the rising sun (the rising Son!) suddenly shines on it, all the colors bursting into life with one and the same light.

This is not pantheism, but it is not deism either. Pantheism sees God as a sea and us as waves: He's only all of us. Deism sees God as a deadbeat dad Who left His kids after fathering them. He's gone. For St. Thomas, God is in all things, present rather than absent; but He also transcends all things. In fact, He is in all things only *because* He transcends them all—like light: only because it transcends all colors, can it be present to all colors. Or like mind: only because it transcends matter can it be present to all matter by knowing it all. So with God: because He is infinite existence itself, transcending all finite, limited essences or natures, He can be present to all of them in giving them existence.

The essence of a rock, a dog, or a man, does not include God. But their existence is caused by God, not just in the past, by creation, but also in the present, by preservation. God preserves them in being, He continues to give them the act of existence.

Everything gives what it has, and God is the fullness of being itself, so God gives being, i.e., He creates being and preserves in being. To say that God is the fullness of being is to say that God does not *have* existence, from any outside source or cause; He *is* existence by His own essence, therefore He can give it; and this is what creation of being and preservation in being means.

Pantheism grasps half the truth: that God is not one being among others, but the fullness of being. But pantheism forgets His transcendence. Deism grasps the other half of the truth: that God is the transcendent Creator; that He is not any creature, nor the sum total of all creatures, but transcends creatures. But deism forgets His immanence, His presence.

St. Thomas explains that presence by the nature of causality. For A to cause B, A must touch B, A must meet B. Since God causes creatures, He must touch them. Men do not impregnate women without touching them, and women do not give birth to children without touching them, and baseball bats do not move baseballs through the air without touching them. And minds do not solve problems without touching them mentally, i.e., thinking about them. The "touch" may be physical or mental, but all causality involves some touch, i.e., some presence of the cause to the effect.

But creatures touch other creatures only externally, from without. God touches creatures internally, at their ultimate center: their act of existing. He "turns them all on" from within. Hot things give heat, and dogs give dogginess, and God, Infinite Being, gives being. And therefore we can find Him in every being, in every grain of sand.

Gilson calls this "the great syllogism":

(1) **Being is innermost in each thing.**

(2) **God is very being, by His own essence.**

(3) Therefore **God is in all things, and innermostly.**

Think of a thing as a series of concentric circles. From the outer to the inner, they are: (1) external relations to other things, (2) accidental actions, (3) accidental qualities or properties, (4) essential properties, and (5) the essence itself.

For instance, there is (1) your superiority to your cat (relation), (2) your eating steak (action), (3) your being hungry (accidental quality), (4) your ability to speak (essential property), and (5) your being human, being a rational animal (your essence).

Or for Bambi there is (1) being in the forest (relation), (2) running (action), (3) being skinny (accidental property), (4) having senses (essential property), and (5) being a deer (essence).

What makes all five of these aspects *actual* is existence, the point at the center of all five circles. A unicorn has these other five aspects too, but none of them is actual, or real, because unicorns don't exist, even though they have perfectly good essences and the other four dimensions. When God gives existence to a deer but not to a unicorn, He "turns on" the whole of the deer, and is therefore present to the whole concrete substance, all of the deer, at once.

And because He is not in time, He is not past or future but present, present *now,* creating us *now,* not just in the past. God has no dead past and no unborn future; He is "the living God", not the dead or unborn God; He is everything that He is, and does everything that He does, in the present. He is always *now.* He is right now saying: "fiat", "let it be" to you. That is why you exist. And your cat too.

Meet Him there. For "all real living is meeting" (Rabbi Martin Buber in *I and Thou*).

How can our ultimate end be "the Beatific Vision" of God Himself? Isn't that too high and holy and distant for us to hope for? We are like worms and God is like Mount Everest. Doesn't it make more sense to say, in the words of the famous Vermont farmer joke, that "you can't get there from here"?

Whether any created intellect can see the essence of God?

It is written: *We shall see Him as He is* (1 Jn 2:2).

God is in Himself supremely knowable. But what is in itself supremely knowable may not be knowable to a particular intellect on account of the excess of the intelligible object above the intellect, as, for example, the sun, which is supremely visible, cannot be seen by the bat by reason of its excess of light. Therefore some who considered this held that no created intellect can see the essence of God.

This opinion, however, is not tenable. For as the ultimate beatitude of man consists in the use of his highest function, which is the operation of the intellect (mind, understanding), **if we suppose the created intellect could never see God, it would either never attain to beatitude, or its beatitude would consist in something else besides God; which is opposed to faith.... Further, the same opinion is also against reason. For there resides in every man a natural desire to know the cause** (reason, explanation) **of any effect which he sees, and thence arises wonder in men. But if the intellect of the rational creature could not reach so far as to the first cause of things, the natural desire would remain void.**

Hence it must be absolutely granted that the blessed see the essence of God (I, 12, 1).

How can we see God? How can we get there from here? The question is legitimate, and stems from a profoundly true understanding of the infinity of the gap between us and God. Only someone who vastly overestimates humanity, or vastly underestimates divinity, or both, can be insensitive to this question, or unworried about it.

("Seeing" Him, of course, means not just "perceiving" Him with the eyes, or even with the abstract reason, but above all with the heart; "knowing" Him personally, not just impersonally; as Father, not just Explanation. The I AM is not just AM (being) but also I (person).)

But the question is answerable, for God has planted the desire to see Him in our very nature, which remains in all of us, even the most sinful. We find in our very nature the desire to know the ultimate explanation for everything, which is in the Mind that designed everything, the Author of the story we are all in. For we desire to know all that can be known about all that is. (We also desire to attain and enjoy all the good that is and all the beauty that is, but we first have to know it in order to appreciate and enjoy it.) This is not a religious dogma that requires faith to believe; it is a fact anyone can find simply by introspection. Whether or not there is a God, our hearts are in fact restless until they rest in God. It takes only honesty, not faith, to discover that.

So whether God exists or not, we have a natural desire for God. But "nature makes nothing in vain." All natural desires correspond to real beings that can satisfy them: hunger, thirst, eros, tiredness, loneliness, boredom, ugliness, injustice, and pain point to food, drink, sex, rest, friends, interest, beauty, justice, and pleasure. Unless this one desire—the greatest one of all—is the one and only exception.

But if that is the case, if this is the one exception to the law that runs through everything else, then the correspondence between desires and satisfactions in everything else is not caused by a good God, nor by random chance (it is far too coincidental for that) but by a bad God, or the Devil, who lures us with a thousand appetizers and then starves us of the main course.

Perhaps that cannot be *proved* to be false, as St. Thomas thinks it can; but why would anyone choose to believe that rather than believe, hope and trust the alternative explanation, that God (and therefore the nature He gave us) is good and trustable? Why bet on what you can't win even if you win?

13. REASON'S POWER TO KNOW GOD

If we can know God by reason, why do we need faith and revelation? If we *can't* know God by reason, how can faith be intelligent and intelligible? What is the role of reason in our faith life?

Whether God can be known in this life by natural reason?

It is written (Rom 1:19), *That which is known of God ... is manifest in them ...*

Our natural knowledge begins from sense. Hence our natural knowledge can go as far as it can be led by sensible things. But our mind cannot be led by sense so far as to know the essence of God because the sensible effects of God do not equal the power of God as their cause. Hence from sensible things the whole power of God cannot be known, nor ... can His essence be seen.

But because they are His effects and depend on their cause, we can be led from them so far as to know of God *whether He exists* and to know of Him what must necessarily belong to Him as the first cause of all things, exceeding all things created by Him. Hence we know His relationship with creatures so far as to be the cause of them all; also that ... He superexceeds them all (I,12,12).

We can know by faith as well as reason that we can know God by reason as well as faith. The Bible (Rom 1–2) and the Church (Vatican Council I) clearly tell us that everyone, even unbelievers, can know that there is a God by nature ("sensible things") and by conscience. If there is design, there is a Designer; and if there is a moral law, there is a moral Lawgiver. Reason can lead us that far—to a Mind behind nature and a Will behind the moral law—though it cannot tell us the *essence* of this Being.

So our own reason, if honestly and commonsensically followed, will do two things: it will begin our journey to God by assuring us that there is indeed a God at the end; and it will confess its inadequacy to finish the journey, and will send us looking for the higher vehicle that can finish it: for divine revelation, which gives us the road map, and for divine grace, which gives us the fuel.

At the end of the journey is total truth (the understanding of the ultimate reason for all things), total goodness (perfect holiness, and the model for all holiness), and total beatitude (infinite, unending, ecstatic, incomprehensible joy). If we honestly admit our need and desire for these three things at the beginning of the journey, we will eventually arrive at the end; that is a solemn promise from God himself: "All who seek [Me] will find (Me)" (Mt 7:7–11). Only those who are not honest with their own nature, and do not seek, will fail to come to know the divine nature; only those who refuse their own humanity will fail to reach the divinity; only those who suppress these three clues God has put into their deepest heart will find misery rather than happiness in their heart at the end.

How much can reason tell us about God? Enough to begin but not enough to end. St. Thomas lists three things about God that we can know by reason alone: (1) that He exists, (2) that He is the first cause and ultimate explanation of all things, of their existence as well as of their design and intelligibility; and (3) that He is mysterious to us not because He is less real, true, good, or beautiful than all His creatures, but more. He is to our mind as the sun is to the eyes of a bat or an owl.

Thus St. Thomas avoids the two opposite extremes of theological skepticism and rationalism, intellectual despair and intellectual pride. Like Aristotle, his habit is always to seek out and avoid two extremes on nearly every issue. For there is usually one angle for standing upright and two angles for falling, to the right or to the left.

In Norse mythology there is a "rainbow bridge" from earth to Heaven (Asgard). What is the real "rainbow bridge" from man to God? In objective reality it's Christ, of course; but what is it in subjective reality, in our souls, in our minds? It's faith, of course; but mustn't there must be a bridge from reason too, for those who don't yet have faith?—a bridge from reason to faith as well as from reason to God? But there's a problem with any bridge from reason: our words and our concepts are finite, and made for finite things: dogs, atoms, galaxies. How can we label God? If we can't label Him, how can we identify Him? When the mystics get close to Him, they all say that words utterly fail. How far can words (and the concepts they express) go? Can they help at all? How can our language about God be meaningful?

No name belongs to God in the same sense as it belongs to creatures; for instance, wisdom in creatures is a quality (an "accident", or property, of the creature's essence)**, but not in God** (where nothing is accident but all is substance, essential nature) ... (and therefore) **what is said of God and creatures is not univocally** (with one and the same meaning) **predicated of them ...**

God (Who is infinite) **is more distant from creatures than any** (finite) **creatures are from each other; but the distance of some creatures** (from each other) **makes univocal predication of** (even) **them impossible ... therefore much less can anything be predicated univocally of God and creatures....**

The term *wise,* **applied to man, in some degree circumscribes and comprehends the thing signified; whereas this is not the case when it is applied to God.... Hence it is evident that the term** *wise* **is not applied in the same way to God and to man. The same rule applies to other terms. Hence no name is predicated univocally of God and creatures.**

Neither, on the other hand, are names applied to God and creatures in a purely equivocal sense, as some have said. Because if that were so, it follows that from creatures nothing could be known or demonstrated about God at all, for the reasoning would always be exposed to the fallacy of equivocation. Such a view is against ... what the Apostle said: *The invisible things of God are clearly seen through the things that are made* (Rom 1:20).

Therefore it must be said that these names are said of God and creatures in an analogous sense.... For in analogies the idea is not one and the same, as it is in univocals, yet it is not totally diverse, as it is in equivocals; but a term which is thus used in a multiple sense signifies various proportions to one thing; thus *healthy* **applied to urine signifies the sign of animal health, and applied to medicine signifies the cause of the same health** (I,13,5).

St. Thomas, as usual, rejects two opposite errors here: rationalism and skepticism. Rationalism is far too optimistic about the power of our words to tell Who God is; for only God's Word (Christ), and not our words, can fully express God. But skepticism is far too pessimistic; for since God designed man with a rational soul, with a mind that is dependent on and dimly reflecting the divine mind, words can help—a little. He has not left Himself without witness in our minds.

Rationalism thinks human reason can do more than it really can, in insisting that our words about God must apply to God as our words for creatures apply to creatures: univocally, with one and the same meaning. Skepticism thinks human reason can do less than it can, in insisting that our words about the infinite God can refer to nothing real in God, since our words are taken from our experience of finite creatures. Skepticism says our words about God are equivocal, that they have a wholly different meaning when applied to God than they do when applied to creatures. Thus there is no "rainbow bridge" for reason to get to God.

St. Thomas steers clear of both extremes. Our positive words for God ("good", "wise", etc.) are neither univocal—wholly the same—nor equivocal—wholly different—but analogical—partly the same and partly different.

And these two "parts" cannot be separated, like two quantities, into a univocal part and an equivocal part. God's goodness (and His wisdom, His power, and all His other perfections) is not *the same as* man's goodness; nor is it *totally unlike* man's goodness; but it is *a little bit like* man's goodness. Or rather, man's goodness is a little bit like God's. A good man is more like God than a good dog is, and a good man is more like God than a bad man is. Thus we can begin to move forward in the right direction on the rainbow bridge, to a significant and helpful extent.

But our words and concepts cannot take us all the way to the other side of the river. We cannot know God's essence; we cannot know *what He is*. But we can know, by analogy, what He is *like* (or rather, what is like Him: for a person is not like his picture, a picture is like a person). Thus created things (*all* created things!) do give us clues and signs to their (and our) Creator.

We can also know what He is *not*, and here our words can be univocal, and perfectly clear. God is not an angel, or a man, or a dragon, or a lion, or a galaxy (though all these things resemble Him in some at least metaphorical way). By this clear, univocal negative knowledge we can avoid idolatry.

This is not just a theoretical, philosophical point. It affects our lives. Analogy means that we can know God by means of all things, in all things, but imperfectly. Our reason, like our faith, sees "through a glass, darkly". The whole world consists of divine footprints, fingerprints, clues, pointing fingers. Look along them, not just at them, and you will be looking toward God. And looking toward Him is both a cause and an effect of longing toward Him and living toward Him and loving toward Him, i.e., being a saint.

The name "Michael" means "Who is like God?" The implied answer to this rhetorical question is, of course, "No one." But doesn't that mean St. Thomas is wrong when he says we can think and speak of God by analogies with earthly things? God is not like anything else at all.

The answer to this question depends on whether analogy means that God is like creatures or vice versa. St. Thomas says it is vice versa. God is indeed not like anything else; but everything else is like Him. He is the standard, the touchstone, the "prime analogate", and we creatures are the analogies. That is what St. Thomas means by saying that the positive names for God, all of which are analogical, are predicated (said) not primarily of creatures but of God.

It seems that names are predicated primarily of creatures rather than of God....

On the contrary, it is written: *I bow my knees to the Father of our Lord Jesus Christ, of Whom all paternity in heaven and on earth is named* (Eph 3:14–15); **and the same applies to other names applied to (both) God and creatures....**

In names predicated of many in an analogical sense, all are predicated because they have reference to one same thing ... such a name must be applied primarily to that which is (first) ... and secondarily to those others as they approach more or less to that first. Thus, for instance, *healthy* **(is first) applied to animals (and then secondly it also) comes into the definition of** *healthy* **applied to medicine, which is called healthy as being the cause of health in the animal, and also into the definition of** *healthy* **which is applied to urine, which is called healthy in so far as it is the sign and effect of the animal's health....**

The words *God is good*, **or** *wise*, **signify ... that these (properties) exist in Him in a more excellent way.... These names are applied primarily to God rather than to creatures because these perfections flow from God to creatures....**

The same rule does not apply to metaphorical ... names ... all names applied meta-phorically to God are applied to creatures primarily rather than to God ... so the name *lion* **applied to God means only that God manifests strength in His works, as a lion in his** (I,13,6).

Scripture uses many earthly analogies for God. But the analogies work only one way: everything is in some way a little bit like God (that is why they can lead us to God: the "rainbow bridge"), but God is not like them. He made us in His image, not vice versa. He is not called "our Father" because His fatherhood is named after ours, but because ours is named after His. (That's the point of the passage from Ephesians that St. Thomas quotes above.) When Christ said to His disciples, "I have food to eat of which you do not know", they interpreted it literally; and He corrected them: "My food is to do the will of him who sent me" (Jn 4: 31–34). They did not understand that this "soul food" is real food, and that body food is only an image or analogy of that. That which nourishes spiritual life—namely, doing the will of the Father, loving and trusting surrender to His will—is not an image of the bread that nourishes physical life; bread is an instructive image of it. Everything is. God's world is a cathedral full of icons.

Some of these icons are metaphors: God can be called a lion not because He really is a lion. Other icons are not mere metaphors: God is called *good*, and *Father*, and *love* because He really is good, and Father, and love. The analogical use of the word is applied to creatures and the literal use is applied to God. We are the analogy, not Him. In metaphors, the analogical use is applied to God and the literal use to creatures.

What makes a lion a lion is its finite form, its lion-ness, and this is the shape of those particular *limits* on being, truth, goodness, and beauty that God designed the lion to have. For instance, to be a lion is not to be as big as an elephant or as gentle as a pussycat. These limits are not in God, so God is not a lion. But all the perfections these limits limit—all the being, truth, goodness, and beauty that are in a lion—are in God without limit. All the perfections of a pussycat are in God too. Thus God is simultaneously maximally strong and maximally gentle. He is the standard for the "gentle-man".

The philosophical principle in St. Thomas that explains and justifies this one-way analogy (a principle we will see later) is that essence limits existence (being), and that God is infinite, unlimited existence, Being itself rather than *a* being. If you don't understand that, don't worry. Just remember that being, for St. Thomas, is not an abstraction. If it's only an abstraction to you, leave it alone; it will do you no good and much harm to think of God as an abstraction. That's like thinking of a volcano as an abstraction.

16. GOD'S KNOWING IS CREATIVE

In one of Christ's parables, God says to the damned, "Depart from Me, I never knew you" (Mt 7:23). How can God not know anything? Mustn't He know everything real?

Augustine says, *Not because they are, does God know all creatures spiritual and temporal, but because He knows them, therefore they are.* **The knowledge of God is the cause of things. For the knowledge of God is to all creatures what the knowledge of the artificer is to things made by his art** ... (I,14,8).

In one sense the damned are real (and in that sense God knows them) but in another sense they are not real *because* He does not know them. He knows *of* them ("wissen") but He does not personally *know* them ("kennen"). He says to them: "I never knew you; depart from me, you evildoers" (Mt 7:23).

He created the world by thinking it into being, by knowing it into existence. He is a creative artist, we are scientists; He thought up and designed and created what we discover. The world is our science but God's art. (See #17.) He knows it into being, as Tolkien knew hobbits into being.

God's knowing and willing are one: He wills us into being by knowing us into being. In us, knowing and willing are two, and we have to know something (real or imagined) *before* we will it.

We have earthly existence, earthly life (*bios*), because He knew us into being as *bios* when He said "Let there be this person." And we have eternal existence because He knew us into eternal existence, eternal life (*zoe*), in Christ, in Whom He knew us (*kennen*) and prepared His Kingdom for us to inherit "from the foundation of the world" (Mt 25:34).

But to the damned He will say "I never knew you; depart from me" (Mt 7:23). Thus Psalm 1 describes the difference between eternal happiness and unhappiness this way: "The Lord knows the way of the righteous, but the way of the wicked shall perish" (Ps 1:6).

A consequence of this principle about divine knowing is the vanity of earthly glory:

Man's happiness cannot consist in human fame or glory. For glory consists in *being well* *known and praised* ... Now the thing known is related to human knowledge otherwise than to God's knowledge: for human knowledge is caused by the things known, whereas God's knowledge is the cause of the things known. Wherefore the perfection of human good, which is called happiness, cannot be caused by human knowledge, but rather human knowledge of another's happiness proceeds from and in a fashion is caused by human happiness itself, imperfect or perfect. And therefore man's happiness depends, as on its cause, on the glory which man has with God (I-II,2,3).

A significant part of our joy in Heaven will be to know that God knows us and is pleased by us, as a father knows, and pays attention to, and is pleased by, his tiny infant's first clumsy walking steps, or first attempt to draw Daddy a picture birthday card. What a joy to be recognized by Daddy! That is why we will have, and now rightly desire, rewards in Heaven: not because our Heavenly Father is a cosmic Santa, a means to the rewards He gives, but because the rewards are Himself, His "well done, good and faithful servant; enter into the joy of your master" (Mt 25:21). What is that joy? It *is* that very recognition and approval.

It does not enter into us, we enter into it. It is not in us, we are in it, because we are in Him. We *are* real, and good, and joy-filled, because God *says* so. He makes it so by knowing it.

He spoke the universe into being, and He does the same to us, first in our creation and then in our redemption, and He does all three creative acts by His creative Word: (1) His Word "let there be" created the universe. (2) He only "made" our bodies out of some "stuff," but He *created* our souls out of nothing, as He had created the "stuff" out of nothing by His Word. (3) And that same Word died to redeem us and remake us, to "create" new hearts (Ps 51:10). Making saints out of sinners was even greater than making something out of nothing. For nothingness put up no resistance to Him, as we did.

How much resistance? Look at a crucifix to see what He had to do to conquer that resistance.

17. Human science = the knowledge of God's art

Is science an honorable and holy occupation, or is it only a means for satisfying human curiosity and for the creature comforts and conveniences of technology? Is our serious study of creatures a kind of idolatry or infidelity, or is it pleasing to the Creator? Is it somehow ultimately about Him?

Natural things are midway between the knowledge of God and our knowledge; for we receive knowledge from natural things, of which God is the cause by His knowledge. Hence, as the natural objects of knowledge are prior to our knowledge, and are its measure, so the knowledge of God (the knowledge God has of things) **is prior to natural things and is the measure of them; as, for instance, a house is midway between the knowledge of the builder who made it and the knowledge of the one who gathers his knowledge of the house from the house already built** (I,14,8).

Truth in science is discovered; truth in art is created. God is an artist, not a scientist; He designed and created the world, which is first of all the product of His art and then becomes the object of our science. Therefore all human science—in all senses of "science", ancient (broad) and modern (narrow)—is really an appreciation of the divine art. And since all art reveals something about its artist, the knowledge of creatures, by its very nature, leads us in the direction of the knowledge of the Creator, if we are only fair and honest and open-minded toward it.

This is why many great scientists have in fact been led closer to God by the discoveries of their science. There is no such thing as "the conflict between science and religion". It is as mythical as a zombie. Insofar as it does exist, that conflict is as unnatural as "the war between the sexes": an unnatural, fallen, abnormal situation that is mistakenly taken as the norm. Or it is like the Marxists' "class conflict", the supposedly necessary power struggle between the haves and the have-nots: it is an ideological contrivance, a piece of propaganda. It is either unnatural or unreal. The very idea of it comes into history not from a good mind but from a bad will. The ultimate origin or first cause of this lie is envy or pride or greed or arrogance, not honest love and truth-seeking. (That does not mean, of course, that individuals cannot be honestly conned and confused by its propaganda.)

Science is an honorable and even a holy occupation. It is a kind of remote and indirect mental telepathy with God, the reading of some of God's thoughts after Him, however dimly. The greatest of scientists (e.g., Copernicus, Galileo, Kepler, Newton and Einstein) were all quite clear about that.

But you don't have to be a professional scientist to appreciate science. Science is for everyone. Science is not elitist. Science is only methodologically refined common sense. Take science courses. Read science books. (Just be aware of the difference between science and ideology.) Learn more about the divine creativity. Everything you learn about Him is a new reason to adore and love Him. He is amazing and wonderful, and therefore so is His creation.

18. Is God alive?

Is God alive, or is He just an idea, an ideal, an essence, a nature, a Platonic Form, a principle, a formula, something abstract? Is He more like the Idea of an alligator or more like an alligator? Is God something that would act on you and interrupt you and interfere with you and creep up on you and *surprise* you, like a live alligator? Can you meet Him? Can you say "Look out! It's alive!"?

Life in the highest degree belongs to God. In proof of which it must be considered that since a thing is said to live in so far as it operates of itself and not as moved by another, the more perfectly this power is found in anything, the more perfect is the life of that thing ... But although our intellect (too) **moves itself to some things, yet others** (things) **are supplied** (to it) **by nature,** (through sensation and by) **first principles** (like the law of non-contradiction) **which it cannot doubt, and** (by) **the last end, which it cannot but will. Hence, although with respect to some things it** (our intellect) **moves itself, yet with regard to other things it must be moved by another.** (But) **that Being whose act of understanding is Its very nature, and which ... is not determined by another, must have life in the most perfect degree. Such is God; and hence in Him principally is life** (I,18,3).

We tend to reduce "life" to "biological life" or at least "human life". But what is essential to life, and common to all life, is not necessarily molecules, or mortality, but self-movement, movement from within rather than merely from without. Even plants grow from within, unlike rocks.

There are various levels of life: plants, animals, men, angels, God. All are active from their own nature, all *do* something. When we say to a rock "Don't just stand there, do something", it does not obey. But even a plant does: it grows. And an animal moves around and desires things. And a human being makes free choices. And an angel contemplates God. God too, in the supreme sense, acts, *does* things. He is more like an alligator than a rock, or an idea. Ideas can't act; only real things can act.

C.S. Lewis says that speaking about "man's search for God" is like speaking about the mouse's search for the cat. We don't creep up on the Hound of Heaven; He follows us. (But He has gentle feet, withdrawn claws, and merciful eyes.) Here is Lewis' unforgettable description:

"Men are reluctant to pass over from the notion of an abstract ... deity to the living God. I do not wonder. Here lies the deepest tap-root of Pantheism and of the objection to traditional imagery. It was hated not, at bottom, because it pictured Him as man but because it pictured Him as king, or even as warrior. The Pantheist's God does nothing, demands nothing. He is there if you wish for Him, like a book on a shelf. He will not pursue you. There is no danger that at any time heaven and earth should flee away at His glance. If He were the truth, then we could really say that all the Christian images of kingship were a historical accident of which our religion ought to be purged. It is with a shock that we discover them to be indispensable. You have had a shock like that before, in connection with smaller matters—when the line pulls at your hand, when something breathes beside you in the darkness. So here; the shock comes at the precise moment when the thrill of *life* is communicated to us along the clue we have been following. It is always shocking to meet life where we thought we were alone. 'Look out!' we cry, 'it's *alive.*' And therefore this is the very point at which so many draw back—I would have done so myself if I could—and proceed no further with Christianity. An 'impersonal God'—well and good. A subjective God of beauty, truth and goodness, inside our own heads—better still. A formless life-force surging through us, a vast power which we can tap—best of all. But God Himself, alive, pulling at the other end of the cord, perhaps approaching at an infinite speed, the hunter, king, husband—that is quite another matter. There comes a moment when people who have been dabbling in religion ('Man's search for God!') suddenly draw back. Supposing we really found Him? We never meant it to come to *that!* Worse still, supposing He had found us?" (*Miracles*, 11).

19. PREDESTINATION AND FREE WILL

The Bible teaches predestination (Rom 8). But if God eternally predestines everything that happens, including my life, then it seems that everything is necessary, everything has to be, "whatever will be, will be." In that case, how can I be free and responsible? It seems I'm just one of God's puppets, or chess pieces, or characters in a novel which He writes. So why does He hold me responsible for my choices?

(Objection:) **All good things that exist God wills to be. If therefore His will imposes necessity on things willed, it follows that all good happens of necessity; and thus there is an end to free will, counsel, and all other such things** (commands, rewards, punishment, praise, blame, duty, responsibility—in fact, "there is an end to" the meaningfulness of all moral language!).

(Reply:) **The divine will imposes necessity on some things willed but not all ... this happens** (not on account of the *lack* of omnipotent power and efficacy of the divine will, but precisely) **on account of the efficacy of the divine will. For when a cause is efficacious ... the effect follows upon the cause not only as to the thing done, but also as to its manner of being done.... Since then the divine will is perfectly efficacious, it follows not only that things are done which God wills to be done, but also that they are done in the way that He wills. Now God wills some things to be done necessarily, some contingently, to the right ordering of things, for the building up of the universe. Therefore to some effects He has attached necessary causes, that cannot fail; but to others, defective and contingent causes, from which arise contingent effects** (I,19,8).

The effect of divine providence is not only that things should happen somehow, but that they should happen by necessity or by contingency. Therefore whatsoever divine providence ordains to happen infallibly and of necessity happens infallibly and of necessity; and that happens from contingency which the plan of divine providence conceives to happen from contingency (I,22,4).

There is no distinction between what flows from free will and what is of predestination, as there is no distinction between what flows from a secondary cause and from a first cause. For the providence of God produces effects through the operation of secondary causes ... wherefore that which flows from free will is also of predestination (I,23,5).

Predestination does not remove free will, it establishes it. For *to corrupt nature is not the work of providence.* And free will is an aspect our nature, our essence. If a thing lacks free will, it's not a human being. Therefore God's grace and providence perfects rather than undermines our free will. He turns it on, not off. The First Cause establishes second causes rather than undermining them. Grace perfects nature.

Therefore we can trust God for everything, as if everything is His predestinating providence, for everything *really is* His providence; and at the same time we can make choices as if we are truly free and really responsible for our own good and evil, and our own salvation or damnation, *since we really are.* Thus the Apostle tells us to "work out your own salvation with fear and trembling, for God is at work in you" (Phil 2:12-13). It is another both/and rather than an either/or.

All good human acts are co-operative: ours *and* God's at the same time, not ours alone or God's alone. They are not ours *rather than* God's, for we cannot do good without His grace; and they are not His *rather than* ours, for He will not do our moral good for us without our free choice. Thus it is correct to say that we should pray as if it all depended on God and work as if it all depended on us, because both parts of that saying are not an "as if"; both parts are true. But since the cooperation is not 50-50 but 100-100, it is *not* correct to say or think that we should pray as if it did not depend on us or to work as if it did not depend on God, because that is not true.

Truth is our ultimate standard for all practice. That is why St. Thomas is so practical.

20. Does God love mosquitoes?

I hate mosquitoes. Does God hate mosquitoes too?

It is said (Wis 11:25): *Thou lovest all things that are, and hatest none of the things which thou hast made.*

I answer that **God loves all existing things. For all existing things, in so far as they exist, are good, since the existence of a thing is itself a good; and likewise, whatever perfection it possesses. Now it has been shown above (I,19,4) that God's will is the cause of all things. It must needs be, therefore, that a thing has existence, or any kind of good, only inasmuch as it is willed by God. To every existing thing, then, God wills some good. Hence, since to love anything is nothing else than to will good to that thing, it is manifest that God loves everything that exists.**

Yet not as we love. Because since our will is not the cause of the goodness of things, but is moved by it as its object, our love, whereby we will good to anything, is not the cause of its goodness; but conversely, its goodness, whether real or imaginary, calls forth our love, by which we will that it should preserve the good it has and receive besides the good it has not, and to this end we direct our actions; whereas the love of God infuses and creates goodness (I,20,2).

We know that God loves all things because all things are made by Him and He is love, so they are made by His love: He loved them into existence. Just as our mind conforms to the truth of things while His mind designs and creates it (point #16, above), so our love responds to goodness while His love creates it.

All things are (ontologically) good. God said so, after creating them (Gen 1). Neither moral evil (sin) nor physical evil (defect, disease, death) are *things* (point #9, above). We should therefore love these things (which are good) more and evil less; love sinners more and sins less; love souls more and vices less; love bodies more and their diseases less; love the virtue of trustful endurance of pain more

and the vice of cruel infliction of pain less. The "therefore" above means that ethics (the science of what ought to be) is always based on metaphysics (the science of what is); for what really ought to be is based on what really is. That is why St. Thomas the metaphysician is such a good guide to ethics.

We should strive and contrive to creatively distinguish the good from the bad in all things; and therefore we can and should find ways to love even mosquitoes. Look at one under a microscope and admire its delicate design. When walking in a snowstorm, stop looking down and complaining: look up and admire even the cold, whipping wind on your face, and stop only when it really harms you. You can love God in every thing because you can find God in every thing. If you are put in solitary confinement in a tiny cell without food or light, you can find God in the stones in the wall. If that is true, then you can certainly find God in a mosquito.

If you are in love with someone, you want to learn to know and love everything your beloved loves. If you love God, you will want to learn to know and love everything He loves. And God loves mosquitoes. Therefore if you love God, learn to love mosquitoes.

(That does not necessarily mean you do not fulfill your human destiny by swatting them dead. But respect them, and their divine design, as you swat them, as a traditional bullfighter respects his enemy the bull even as he defeats it. You are all playing your parts in a single drama, a dance.)

The question about mosquitoes may seem silly. But this is really a spinoff from a much more profound question, the question about creation: Why did God create so many different things? Eastern religions are fascinated by unity, by the oneness of ultimate reality, and they seek a mystical experience of this oneness as their ultimate end. But Western religions believe the distinctively Jewish idea of God creating a real universe of many things out of nothing. The deeper part of the question about mosquitoes involves the reason for creation. The next question is the natural extension of this one.

21. WHY GOD LOVES ALL THE DIFFERENT THINGS IN THE UNIVERSE AND WHY WE SHOULD TOO

Throughout the Church's history, her saints, like the prophets in the Bible, have warned us against violating the first and greatest commandment, the commandment against idolatry, against giving our whole heart to anything except God. This "anything" means any creatures, created things, since these are the only things that exist except God. But if God created all these things, and declared them "good" (Gen 1), doesn't it follow that we should love them too, as God does, and appreciate them more than we usually do rather than less?—not as if they were our God, of course, but as our God-given gifts. What does St. Thomas say about God's attitude toward the amazingly manifold universe of things that He created? Why did God make so many things different from Himself and from each other?

The distinction and multitude of things come from the intention of the first agent, Who is God. For He brought things into being in order that His goodness might be communicated to creatures and be represented by them; and because His goodness could not be adequately represented by one creature alone, He produced many and diverse creatures, so that what was wanting to one in representing the divine goodness might be supplied by another. For goodness, which in God is simple and uniform, in creatures is manifold and divided; and hence the whole universe together participates the divine goodness more perfectly, and represents it better, than any single creature whatever (I,47,2).

Like St. Thomas in thinking about God's creation—and like God in creating—we must make distinctions. (a) In one way we love creatures too much, and we should love them less, for we are commanded, by God incarnate Himself, as "the first and greatest commandment", to "love the Lord your God with your whole heart and soul and mind and strength" (Mk 12:30), and therefore to avoid a divided heart which gives to God only *some* of itself, its love and devotion, and gives the other part to creatures. We should not love

creatures *as God*, because they *are* not God. We should love everything as what it really is; our love should be realistic, should conform to reality. (b) But for this very same reason, we love creatures too little, and we should love creatures more, *as creatures of God,* i.e., as what they are. God loved them into existence; who are we to quarrel with God's loves?

This applies even to fallen creatures, evil people. God made the people, and loves them, but not the evil in them. We should love all persons, even monsters like Hitler, as God does, *because* God does; and we should hate the sins that deface them as God does, that is, precisely because we love the persons that are being defaced by sin. This applies to ourselves as well as others; for there is in each of us a potential "Hitler in Ourselves" (the shocking but accurate title of a book written after World War II by the German philosopher Max Picard) as well as a potential Mother Teresa in ourselves. (So we have no excuse for not being Mother Teresas!)

Why did God create so many different creatures? Because everything has a unique task: to represent some one of the infinitely many aspects of God, or dimensions of God, or facets in the infinite divine diamond. Men show something about God that women do not, and women show something about God that men do not, and therefore the whole "image of God" in mankind is only "male *and* female" together, according to the Bible itself (Gen 2:7). The same is true of dogs and cats, empty space and burning stars, proud lions and meek lambs, white people and black people, things in nature like eagles and man-made things like airplanes, which also show something about God, something that natural things do not—which is one reason why God made mankind: so that mankind could make all sorts of other things that also show some aspects of the goodness of God, indirectly.

The universe is a work of art, in fact the greatest of all works of art. The greater the work of art, the more it has both unity and diversity. The Bible, *The Lord of the Rings* and *The Divine Comedy* have both more unity and more diversity than smaller, lesser works of art. The universe is God's other Bible.

22. INEQUALITY IS GOOD

Is God an egalitarian? Does He love all these many things He created equally?

Augustine says: *God loves all things that He has made, and amongst them rational creatures more, and of these especially those who are members of His only-begotten Son; and much more than all, His only-begotten Son Himself.*

I answer that ... in a twofold way anything may be loved more or less. In one way on the part of the act of the will itself, which is more or less intense. In this way God does not love some things more than others, because He loves all things by an act of the will that is one, simple, and always the same. In another way, on the part of the good itself that a person wills for the beloved. In this way, we are said to love that one more than another for whom we will a greater good, though our will is not more intense. In this way we must needs say that God loves some things more than others. For since God's love is the cause of goodness in things, as has been said, no one thing would be better than another if God did not will greater good for one than for another (I,20,3).

We will find this diversity and inequality and hierarchy even in Heaven (perhaps *especially* in Heaven): **Of those who see the essence of God, one sees Him more perfectly than another ... because one intellect will have a greater power or faculty to see God than another. The faculty of seeing God ... does not belong to the created intellect naturally, but is given to it by the light of glory, which establishes the intellect in a kind of** *deiformity* (Godlikeness).... **Hence the intellect which has more of the light of glory will see God more perfectly.**

And he will have a fuller participation in the light of glory who has more charity; because where there is more charity, there is the more desire, and desire in a certain degree makes the one desiring apt and prepared to receive the object desired. Hence he who possesses the more charity will see God **the more perfectly, and will be the more beatified** (I,12,6).

God is our standard. What God wills, we should will. What God loves, we should love.

And God loves inequality, hierarchy, the superiority of one thing over another. For that is the natural order, and He designed and willed and created that order.

Therefore we should accept, and will, and love this order too. Not in politics—that's our invention—but in nature—that's God's invention. God loved natural inequality into being. He made it.

God is just. Justice consists in two things, not just one: it consists in equality *and* inequality. Justice means giving each his due, and that means treating equals equally *and* unequals unequally.

How do we apply this principle? In three ways:

(1) All men are equal in essence, in sharing essential human nature; therefore humans have equal rights and equal value in everything essential.

(2) All men are also unequal in properties connected with the human essence, properties that are in all human beings but in different degrees, such as IQ, strength, wisdom, virtue, beauty, health, etc. Therefore the wiser, e.g., have more right to rule than the less wise, and the virtuous have more right to be admired and imitated than the vicious.

(3) And all men are also unequal in accidents, such as wealth, political power, good luck, and success in sports. These therefore are also naturally and rightly unequal and to be treated unequally. When Boston beats Vancouver in hockey, Vancouver should not be given half the Stanley Cup.

But even here there is always the essentially human, and therefore the essentially equal, dimension that deserves respect; and it is always the more important dimension since it flows from the essence and the essence is always more important than the accidents or properties.

Above all, the reason for egalitarianism should never be envy. There is no envy in Heaven, even though there is inequality. There, you will rejoice that another is more blessed than you.

Be Heavenly here.

23. Do men or angels rank higher in God's love?

This last point (#22) says that the reason some things are better than others is that God loves them more, since His love does not respond to and conform to the goodness of things, as our love does, but *creates* the goodness of things, in various degrees or grades (i.e., hierarchy). Therefore, since angels are superior to humans, it seems that God must love them more, just as He loves man more than animals, and animals more than minerals. If this is so, then why then did He do more for us, in Christ, than He did for the angels?

God loves the human nature assumed by the Word of God in the person of Christ more than He loves all the angels; for that nature is better, especially on the ground of union with the Godhead. But as to natural condition, an angel is better than a man.... Hence it is said of man: *Thou hast made him a little less than the angels* **(Ps 8:6).... God therefore did not assume human nature because He loved man, absolutely speaking, more, but because the needs of man were greater; just as the master of a house may give some costly delicacy to a sick servant that he does not give to his own son in sound health** (I,20,4).

There are two kinds of love: eros and agape. Eros is desire, agape is charity. Eros is getting, agape is giving. Eros, in itself and rightly ordered, is good and natural and necessary, but agape is better and higher, for God is agape, not eros. God is the pure and total gift-of-self of each of the Persons of the Trinity to each other, out of pure charity, not need. God needs nothing and loves everything.

Agape does not passively conform to the value of its object in the way that eros does. Rightly ordered eros does just that; it loves each thing as it deserves. This is justice. In eros, love should conform to justice. Wrongly ordered eros is injustice, loving lesser things more than greater things, e.g., things more than people, pleasure more than virtue, or self more than God. But agape goes beyond justice because it responds to need, not deservingness. Agape is not justice, nor is it sub-justice, but it is super-justice.

The Good Shepherd spent all His time searching for the one "black sheep" that got lost, while the 99 good sheep who more deserved His attention remained faithfully at home without His extra attention—not because He loved the evil sheep more than the good but because the "black sheep of the family" needed Him more than the others. When He designed and created the world, He loved angels into a higher existence than He loved men into; but when He came into the world as the Great Physician, He came to search out and save the needy, the lost, the sinners: us.

We should do the same. We should practice both justice (rightly ordered eros) and charity (agape). We should not treat animals better than men, or reward sinners more than saints, because that is unjust; but we should seek out those who need us most, and those who will most benefit from us (and that always means our own families first), not necessarily those who deserve us most, because that is what charity does. Charity is spiritual triage.

The saints are God's water: they go to the lowest and driest places. Do you live in a society, or a situation, that is full of evil? Don't complain; practice nursing. That's why He put you there.

24. RECONCILING JUSTICE AND MERCY

Since justice gives to each his due, but mercy gives more than what is due, how can God be both just and merciful at the same time without contradiction? If He does that, can we do it too?

(1) God acts mercifully not ... by going against His justice but by doing something more than justice. Thus a man who pays another 200 pieces of money, though owing him only 100, does nothing against justice, but acts liberally or mercifully. **The case is the same with one who pardons an offence committed against him, for in remitting it he may be said to bestow a gift. Hence the Apostle calls remission a forgiving:** *Forgive one another, as Christ has forgiven you* (Eph 4:32). **Hence it is clear that mercy does not destroy justice but in a sense is the fullness thereof. And thus it is said:** *Mercy exalteth itself above judgment* (Jas 2:13).

(2) Justice must exist in all God's works (but) **the work of divine justice always presupposes the work of mercy, and is founded thereon. For nothing is due** (by justice) **to creatures except for something pre-existing in them.... And since we cannot go on to infinity** (in pre-existing causes), **we must come to something that depends only on the goodness of the divine will** (viz. our own very existence) (I,22,3–4).

Since both justice and mercy are true of God, since this is the nature of ultimate reality, therefore it ought to be true of us too, if we live in conformity with reality. The reason we should be both just and merciful is that God is: "Be ye holy for I the Lord your God am holy" (see Lev 11:44).

(1) In one way justice takes priority—mercy must presuppose justice in order to *define* itself as going beyond justice.

(2) But in other ways, mercy takes priority. First, in *time*. Mercy came first. Since we were created, our very existence is a gift, and we were not there to deserve the gift before we got it (we didn't exist before we received the gift of existence)—therefore mercy comes first. God's motive for creation is not justice, it is mercy (or, more exactly, it is *like* mercy in that it is pure charity).

And everything God does after creation is grace. "Everything is a grace", said St. Thérèse of Lisieux. And grace is gift, and that means mercy, not justice.

The ultimate foundation for grace (gift) is the very life of the Trinity. God is pure gift to us because He is pure gift to Himself: the Father gives Himself eternally to the Son, and the Son to the Father, and the Holy Spirit of love eternally proceeds from that giving. To be real is to be like that. The alternative is to be phony, unreal. That is the ultimate difference between sin and sanctity, and between Hell and Heaven.

This eternal life of the Trinity is both perfect justice (since each of the divine Persons deserves infinite love, and receives it from the others) and perfect mercy (since each freely gives Himself as pure grace, pure gift, pure agape).

Because both justice and mercy exist in God, that is why both justice and mercy must exist in all God's works, and why they should exist in ours.

If those I love are predestined by God to be saved, they will be saved, so why should I pray for them? And if they are not, there is nothing I can do to change God's will. So why pray for others' salvation?

(As regards not God's predestinating act itself but men's salvation as the effect of predestination,) **predestination is said to be helped by the prayers of the saints, and by other good works, because providence, of which predestination is a part, does not do away with secondary causes but so provides effects that the order of secondary causes falls also under providence. So as natural effects are provided by God in such a way that natural causes are directed to bring about those natural effects, without which those effects would not happen, so the salvation of a person is predestined by God in such a way that whatever helps that person towards salvation falls under the order of predestination, whether it be one's own prayers or those of another, or other good works and suchlike, without which one would not attain to salvation. Whence, the predestined must strive after good works and prayer because through these means predestination is most certainly fulfilled** (I,23,8).

As Pascal said, "God established prayer in order to give to creatures the dignity of causality." Every prayer and every good work makes a difference, possibly an eternal difference, *without which those effects would not happen.*

It is a fallacy to think that since God has predestined all things, and since "whatever will be, will be", that therefore our prayers cannot make a real difference to the future. We cannot change God's predestination but we can change the future because that is one of the things God has predestined: our free choices that cause the future to be one thing rather than another.

God knows whether X will be saved or not, so why should I pray for X? Because perhaps God has predestined that the salvation of X depends partly on your prayers, and if you do not supply them, X will not be saved. Every vote counts.

We do not see these details because God deliberately hides them from us. For if we saw all the effects of our prayers and good works, if we saw the difference we make—like Jimmy Stewart in *It's A Wonderful Life*—we would be overwhelmed and paralyzed with responsibility.

Nothing changes God's will. But "prayer changes things" because God changes things through our prayers. For God has willed that causal order of things; God has willed that His will be fulfilled only through the instrumentality of our prayers. He often refuses to give us the things we need until we pray for them because He sees that we need prayer even more than we need the things we pray for. Prayer is like work: God could have given us everything without our work (food, for instance), but He knew that we need to work even more than we need the things we work for. We co-operate, i.e., we work-with, God—not as equals, not side by side, like two soldiers on a battlefield, but like a general and his infantryman, or like an author and his character. He will not do it without us and we cannot do it without Him.

By the way, St. Thomas, unlike classical Calvinists, does not believe in two equal and parallel predestinations, to Hell as well as to Heaven, to damnation as well as salvation. "Predestination" means predestination to Heaven, for "God is not willing that any should perish but that all should come to salvation" (2 Pet 3:9). God knows that not all will come to salvation, and allows this, by allowing our free choice, and in that sense and that sense only He wills (allows) damnation. He writes the whole story, its eternal tragedies as well as its divine comedies, but He acts in the story only in one way, for the comedy, for the salvation. "For God sent the Son into the world not to condemn the world, but that the world might be saved through Him" (Jn 3:17).

26. Personalism

Relative to the whole universe, we are extremely tiny and extremely temporary. How can we believe that we are so important? Isn't that arrogant and provincial?

The answer is that we are important because we are important to God, Who is the *standard* of "importance". And we are important to God because, unlike everything else in the universe, we are persons. And persons are supremely great because *God* is (three) Persons. We are made in His image. He is "I AM" and that is why we too can say "I am." Animals can't. Only persons are "I's". Animals have eyes but no I's. That is why they are not immortal, rational, moral, or religious.

Person **signifies what is most perfect in all nature** (i.e., in all reality)—**that is, a subsistent individual of a rational nature. Hence, since everything that is perfect must be attributed to God, forasmuch as His own essence contains every perfection, this name** *person* **is fittingly applied to God; not, however, as it is applied to creatures, but in a more excellent way** (I,29,3).

That first sentence of St. Thomas' quote constitutes a philosophical revolution: **"***Person* **signifies what is most perfect in all nature."** That is the essential metaphysical premise of Personalism, a modern philosophy often unfairly associated with subjectivism, anthropocentrism, and a prejudice against objective metaphysics, especially Thomism. Yet the essential foundation of Personalism is right here in St. Thomas, though he does not develop it. He opens the door to it but goes only a few feet inside. Pope St. John Paul II and others followed this lead many feet further, but on Thomistic metaphysical principles, not on anti-Thomistic, anti-metaphysical, anti-traditional, anti-objectivist, anti-intellectual principles, as many modern "Personalist" philosophers did. This marriage of medieval Thomism with modern Personalism is pregnant with possibilities, and begs to become the cutting edge of Catholic philosophy for the next century, even the next millennium.

Nearly everyone agrees with the morality of Personalism, i.e., with respect for persons and their rights, with the love of persons; with treating persons as ends and not means (Kant's famous second formulation of the "categorical imperative", which has become almost a universal moral consensus throughout the free world); and with Christ's second great commandment and the second table of the Mosaic Law ("love your neighbor as yourself"), which is essentially the first formulation of Kant's "categorical imperative". But why? What is its foundation? Is it true because we say so, or because we will it? Do we will it into existence? Do we create it, as Kant says we do? Or do we discover it, so that first of all it is true, it is so, and then we say so *because* it is so? Obviously, the second, objective, alternative is a stronger foundation than the first, which is only subjective. Personalism requires a metaphysical foundation. And St. Thomas provides it.

Ultimately, *God* provides it by being a Trinity of Persons. Non-Christians do not know that, of course; but Jews and Muslims too know that man is great because he is immortal spirit created by God, not mere mortal animal emerging from slime by blind evolution; that we are the King's kids, not King Kong's kids. And even non-theists know that man is great, though they do not know God as the ultimate reason for that. But they too can agree with St. Thomas' principle that persons are the most perfect things in all of reality, whether there are any divine Persons or not.

This is the strongest reason for love and cooperation with all other persons in the world, even those who appear to be your enemies, and for working against whatever dis-respects persons and working for whatever respects persons. This is not a merely pragmatic, tactical cooperation with those who seem to be less total opponents (e.g., Muslims) against more total opponents (e.g., atheists); it is a genuine, principled, enthusiastic "yes" to the image of God, and thus implicitly to God; for "as you did it to one of the least of these my brethren, you did it to me" (Mt 25:40).

27. Pain or sin: Which is worse?

Is pain and suffering the worst thing in the world?

A wise workman chooses a less evil in order to prevent a greater, as the surgeon cuts off a limb to save the whole body. But divine wisdom inflicts pain to prevent (moral) fault. Therefore fault is a greater evil than pain. There is a twofold reason for this. The first is that one becomes evil by the evil of fault, but not by the evil of pain, as Dionysius says: *To be punished is not an evil, but it is an evil to be ... worthy of punishment....* Because the fault itself consists in the disordered act of the will, and the pain consists in the privation of something used by the will, fault has more of evil in it than pain has. The second reason can be taken from the fact that God is the author of the evil of pain but not of the evil of fault (I,48,6).

"Evil" is ambiguous: it may mean the evil we suffer, physical or emotional, or the evil we do (sin). The *essence* of Heaven and our beatitude is moral goodness, not physical goodness: charity, not pleasure. Pleasure, and happiness, which is deeper, and joy, which is deeper still, are its byproducts. And the *essence* of Hell is the absence of moral goodness, not the absence of physical goodness, not the absence of pleasure and the presence of pain. Martyrs experience physical pains, but they are not in Hell. Tyrants, addicts, and playboys experience momentary physical and emotional pleasures, but they are not in Heaven.

We all instinctively know that spiritual evil (sin) is worse than physical or emotional evil (pain or depression), because when we truly and deeply love someone—e.g., our own children—we deem it even worse that they become voluntarily wicked than that they suffer involuntary pain. If your son was in the army and captured by the enemy and forced to choose between collaborating with the wicked enemy by torturing his fellow prisoners, or being tortured himself, his choosing the first evil would be even more horrible to you than the

second. A live coward is *not* better than a dead hero.

Suffering is an evil, and we are obligated to relieve it; but deliberately chosen evil is far worse, and we are obligated to have no mercy on it. We must hate sin *because* we love sinners. The more you love the patient, the more you hate the disease, whether "the patient" is a body or a soul. Bodies are good and holy and precious, but souls even more so. Sin is soul-disease. Therefore sin is a worse evil than body-disease, pain or suffering.

God is not less moral, less heroic, or less idealistic than we are. He too would rather see us endure pain than inflict it. Even pagan Socrates knew that, and taught that "it is better to suffer evil than to do it" (*Gorgias*). When we agree with that, we are agreeing with God.

This has religious as well as ethical implications. Nothing more powerfully helps us to bear pain than the realization that God wills it. We can bear it out of trust and faith and love for our Heavenly Father. We can even rejoice in the opportunity for a little heroism, in the opportunity to exercise our faith and trust and love, to love Him for His own sake and not just for the sake of the pleasures and comforts He gives us. True love is content with nothing less than that.

Even if He only *allows* suffering rather than directly inflicting it, He allows it *deliberately*; and whatever He does deliberately He does out of love for us; and love always gives the beloved the good the beloved needs; and therefore God in His wisdom (which is bound to be mysterious to us because He sees so much more than we do) wills that we suffer because He sees that we need it for our own deepest, truest, most lasting good, or the good of someone else, or both. As Rabbi Abraham Heschel said, "The man who has not suffered— what can he possibly know, anyway?"

We are more sensitive to pain than to sin. We major in minors. We are upside down, we are standing on our heads. God is right side up. We need to start judging things God's way.

28. GOD AND EVIL

I don't understand how to get God off the hook for all kinds of evil in the world He created. How can we trust Him completely if He is implicit in evil?

Augustine says that *God is not the author of evil* *because He is not the cause of tending to non-being.* (a) **The order of the universe requires ... that there should be some things that can and do sometimes fail.... (b) The order of justice ... requires that penalty should be dealt out to sinners. And so God is the author of the evil which is penalty, (c) but not of the evil which is fault** (I,49,2).

There are three kinds of evil: (a) the evil of physical imperfection or failure or emotional suffering (e.g., death, disease, or depression), (b) the evil of punishment, or penalty for moral evil, and (c) the evil of fault, or sin. All three have this in common: they all destroy something good.

God is the author of being, not nonbeing. Therefore God is not the author of evil. But He (a) allows physical imperfections for the sake of preserving the order of the universe, (b) wills the punishment of sins for the sake of preserving justice, and (c) allows sin to be chosen for the sake of preserving free will. In all three ways He is perfectly good, and perfectly trustable.

It is possible, but not easy, for us to accept and love these three things God does.

(a) We wish He would instantly re-create the universe and make all of it physically perfect and pain-free.

(b) And we wish He would let us get away with sin without punishing us; that there would be no punishment and no justice, only mercy.

(c) And we wish He would make us instant saints by force and zap us into the Beatific Vision in Heaven rather than tolerating our slow and sinful, twisting and turning earthly roads to Heaven.

But (a) would mean the end of pain and therefore also the end of compassion and courage; we would become flabby, amoral, lazy, spoiled, and inhuman, like the people in *Brave New World*.

And (b) would mean that He, and therefore we too, would cease to be moral at all, for justice is presupposed by all virtues, especially mercy: If there is no justice, how can mercy go beyond justice? And justice requires punishments.

Temporal (temporary) punishment is necessary not only for justice but also for our rehabilitation, to make us good; and goodness is necessary to make us perfectly happy; therefore it is His desire for our happiness, that is, it is His mercy and compassion and love for us, that demands that we be punished because that is what is best for us, that is what we need, even when it is not what we want. The very tenderness of His tender love requires "tough love".

And (c) would make us zombies or robots. A Heaven we entered without our own will and free choice would be like an A on a test that our father took for us instead of our taking it ourselves.

So in all these ways in which He tolerates evil, He does so only out of His goodness. The practical "bottom line" of this theology is that we can totally trust Him and love Him, for He is the author of only good and not evil in all three of these ways.

This means that we can pray, "Thanks, I needed that" when we experience pains, even when we don't see or feel that we needed it. That's called faith.

If we don't have that kind of faith, but want it, we can pray, "Lord, I believe; help my unbelief."

I *believe* that good is stronger than evil, but can I *prove* this? I *hope* that good will triumph over evil in the end, but can I be *certain* of this? Is this triumph necessary because of the very essential and unchangeable nature of evil?

The first principle of good (God) is essentially good ... But nothing can be essentially bad. For it was shown above that every being, as such, is good, and that evil can exist only in good as in its subject.

Secondly, because the first principle of good is the highest and perfect good which pre-contains in itself all goodness.... But there cannot be a supreme evil, because ... although evil always lessens good, yet it never wholly consumes it; and thus, while good ever remains, nothing can be wholly and perfectly bad.... *if the wholly evil could be, it would destroy itself* (I,49,3).

We tend to think of "good" and "evil" as equal and opposite forces, like an angel and a devil, or a cloud of light and a cloud of darkness, or pleasures and pains. But that is granting too much to evil. Evil is always a parasite; it can only exist in something good, as a parasite can live only on a host; and if it ever did destroy the good it lives on, it would also destroy itself. It can't win.

The ultimate reason for this is because God is God. He is not *a* god. He is not *a* being that happens to be good, fighting *another* being that is evil. He is the fullness of Being. Evil is not another *being* any more than darkness is another light or blindness is another power like sight.

And therefore we can fight with total confidence. It's a fixed fight. Evil cannot possibly win in the end, even though Gods' victory may leave a terrible body count and loss of blood—both ours and God's.

30. Do angels know the future?

Isn't knowledge of the future a privilege of God alone? But if our guardian angels can't know the future, how can they be wiser than us and guide us?

The future can be known in two ways. First, it can be known in its cause. And thus, future events which proceed necessarily from their causes are known with sure knowledge, as that the sun will rise tomorrow. But events which proceed from the causes in the majority of cases are not known for certain, but conjecturally; thus the doctor knows beforehand the health of the patient. This manner of knowing future events exists in the angels, and by so much the more than it does in us, as they understand the causes of things both more universally and more perfectly; thus doctors who penetrate more deeply into the causes of an ailment can pronounce a surer verdict on the future issue thereof. But events which proceed from their causes in the minority of cases are quite unknown, such as casual and chance events.

In another way future events are known in themselves. To know the future in this way belongs to God alone ... for God sees all things in His eternity, which, being simple, is present to all time and embraces all time. And therefore God's one glance is cast over all things which happen in all time as present before Him, and He beholds all things as they are in themselves.... Men cannot know future things except in their causes or by God's revelation. The angels know the future in the same way but much more distinctly (I,57,3).

Angels live in time too, as we do—though it is purely spiritual time, *kairos*, not material time, *kronos*—and therefore they, like us, can often know the future before it happens, in a partial and fallible way, but not *as* it happens, in a total and infallible way, as God does. God knows all times at once.

Angels know the future in the same way that we do, only better than we do. Think of the story of creation as two novels written by the same Author. The first is about angels and the second is about us and the material universe we live in. The universe is a very big setting, but we are the characters (the only ones, as far as we know) in the second novel; and the characters are more important than the setting. The Author transcends both novels, and knows events which to the characters are past or future but which to Him are present, since everything in his novels is present to the all-knowing mind of the Author.

Sometimes He brings the characters in his first novel, the angel novel, into the second novel, the human one, somewhat as Tolkien had some of the elves from *The Silmarillion* interact with the hobbits in *The Lord of the Rings*.

Having angels interact with humans is in some ways like having humans interact with animals, for we can understand the animals in many ways better than they can understand themselves, and we can know their future better than they do (especially if we are veterenarians), to help them and tame them and make them better and happier. Think of the angels as our veterenarians. As we know animals' future better than animals do, angels know our future better than we do—but not infallibly, as only God does.

Or, to use an alternative analogy, they are like our big brothers (we have the same Heavenly Father), and we can trust them because they are much wiser and stronger than we are.

By the way, Aquinas was scientifically wrong in classifying as "sure knowledge" our knowledge "that the sun will rise tomorrow". One day, it will *not* rise because it will explode or implode, some billions of years from now.

31. HOW IS THE HUMAN HEART KNOWN BY GOD, MEN, ANGELS, AND DEMONS?

Do angels know the secrets of my mind even if I don't want them to? What about demons?

What is proper to God (alone) **does not belong to angels. But it is proper to God to read the secrets of hearts, according to Jer 17:9:** *The heart is perverse above all things, and unsearchable; who can know it? I am the Lord, Who search the heart.* **Therefore angels do not know the secrets of hearts.**

A secret thought can be known in two ways: (1) first, by its effect. In this way it can be known not only by an angel but also by man ... for thought is sometimes discovered not merely by outward act but also by change of countenance; and doctors can tell some passions of the soul by the mere pulse. Much more then can angels, or even demons ... (2) In another way thoughts can be known as they are in the mind, and affections as they are in the will; and thus God alone can know the thoughts of hearts and affections of wills ... (I,57,4).

Owing to their upright will ... the good angels form no judgments ... save under the divine ordinance; hence there can be no error or falsehood in them. But since the minds of demons are utterly perverted from the divine wisdom, they at times form their opinions of things simply according to the natural conditions of the same. They are not deceived as to the natural properties of anything, but they can be misled with regard to supernatural mysteries; for example, on seeing a dead man they may suppose that he will not rise again, or on beholding Christ they may judge Him not to be God (I,58,5).

Angels are stronger and wiser than demons, especially regarding spiritual things and regarding God's plans and God's strategies for us. Angels never err; demons often do.

Both angels and demons are smarter and cleverer than we are regarding "the natural properties of anything".

Neither angels nor demons can read our secret thoughts if we don't want them to. Only God can do that.

But angels can read us, or hear us, or know us, when we want them to, when we pray. They will gently and respectfully enter our minds and inspire us with good thoughts when we open the door for them, but not before. They are gentlemen. Demons want to knock the door down (the door of our permission, our free will), but they can't.

Our demonic opponents are formidable and fearsome (see 1 Pet 5:8), but our angelic allies are even more so. It's a fixed fight.

So jump in and swing your spiritual sword with confidence and joy. But carefully. There are going to be casualties even in a winning war.

Why doesn't God just zap us into Heaven now? Why does He make us wait?

Man's soul and an angel are ordained alike for beatitude; consequently equality with angels (equality in a common end, not in a common nature) **is promised to the saints.... Now the soul separated** (at death) **from the body, if ... deserving beatitude, enters at once into beatitude, unless there be some obstacle** (which needs to be removed in Purgatory). **Therefore so does an angel. Now an angel instantly, in his first act of charity, had the merit of beatitude. Therefore, since there was no obstacle within him, he passed at once into beatitude by only one meritorious act... because grace perfects nature according to the manner of nature.... Man was not intended to secure his ultimate perfection at once, like the angel. Hence a longer way was assigned to man than to the angel for securing beatitude.... It is of the nature of an angel** (but not of the nature of a man) **instantly to attain the perfection unto which he is ordained** (I,62,5).

When we wish we were angels, we deny our human nature. Three ways to do this are (1) the wish to have mental telepathy, (2) the wish to be without bodies and bodily pains and death, and (3) the wish to attain beatitude instantly rather than gradually.

We are in a material and temporal universe, with material and temporal bodies, because God chose to create us that way. We are ontological amphibians, with part of our being in water and part on land. Our souls know eternal truths and seek eternal joys because they live in spiritual time, *kairos,* which touches eternity and is not dependent on matter and space. This we have in common with the angels. But unlike the angels we also live and think and choose in the material space-time continuum that we call the universe, because our souls are the life of our bodies, and our bodies are in matter and the time that is measured by matter and space, *kronos.* We are the only spirits that have bodies and the only animals that have spiritual souls. We are the lowest and stupidest angel and the highest and smartest animal, or rather, we are neither; we are ourselves.

A necessary property of having a material body is gradual movement. A necessary property of having a spiritual soul is awareness of something above movement, something eternal. This combination makes patience hard for us, unlike either angels or animals. But it also makes patience necessary.

The best kind of impatience is impatience for sanctity. "Blessed are those who hunger and thirst for righteousness." But we must also accept our slowness, and be patient with ourselves and our slowness and stupidity. Why? Because God is! At AA they tell you not to expect instant cures. As Brother Lawrence says in *The Practice of the Presence of God,* we must not demand to go faster than grace.

33. THE GREATEST SIN

How was it possible for some of the angels to fall, if they were created in Heaven? What sin can exist in a pure spirit?

Only the sin of pride and envy can exist in an angel.... Augustine says that the devil *is not a fornicator nor a drunkard nor anything of the like sort, yet he is proud and envious.... As to guilt, all sins are in the demons, since by leading men to sin they incur the guilt of all sins. But as to affection, only those sins can be in the demons which can belong to a spiritual nature. Now a spiritual nature cannot be affected by such pleasures as appertain to bodies, but only by such as are in keeping with spiritual things.... Under envy and pride as found in the demons are comprised all other sins derived from them (I,63,2).

It is said, in the person of the devil (Is 14:13–14): *I will ascend into heaven ... I will be like the Most High.* **And Augustine says that being *inflated with pride, he wished to be called God*** (I,63,3).

Pride is the Devil's sin. It is a purely spiritual sin.

Don't seek "spirituality". The Devil is a pure spirit. Cold spiritual sins are worse than hot carnal sins because there is more free will in them. When we lust we act like animals but when we hate or envy or, above all, have competitive pride and arrogance—e.g., when we sneer—we are acting like devils.

That is why humility, which opposes pride, is a prerequisite for salvation. Jesus warned the Pharisees they were heading for Hell because they didn't have humility.

The only other sin that could have been part of the Devil's fall is envy. Envy also does not require a body.

Envy is also the stupidest of all sins because it is the only sin that never once caused anyone even a false feeling of pleasure.

To avoid pride and envy, just remember God's four-word summary of the Bible to St. Catherine: "I'm God; you're not." We forget the second point so easily that God has to make that reminder the very first and greatest commandment. How do we violate it if we are not polytheists? We *are*. The ancients worshipped thousands of gods but we worship millions of gods: ourselves.

To worship yourself is *not* to love yourself. It is to lack real, proper self-love. To love what is, what God created, and what we really are, is proper self-love. To want to be like God (the first temptation, in Eden: Gen 3:6) is to love what is not, what God did not make, and what we really are not.

We are commanded to "love your neighbor as yourself", so we are therefore also implicitly commanded to love ourselves as our neighbor. We are not junk; we are the King's kids.

Believing that is not pride. In fact, it's part of humility. If we believe we're apes, we will be proud, because we are very great apes, very good and smart and civilized apes. But if we believe we are made in the image of God, we will be humbled by our sins and follies, by our acting like apes when we are princes and princesses. Are we designed to be apes or saints? If apes, we are more than successes; if saints, we are more than failures. We are rebels.

By the way, beware the pride that masks as humility: "Look at me. How horribly evil I am!" Humility does not say "Look at me" at all.

34. Do creatures withdraw us from God?

The old spiritual writers emphasize detachment from creatures, and asceticism. But why is this necessary? Why would God create a universe that's so full of temptations?

Corporeal creatures according to their nature are good, though this good is not universal but partial and limited ... Creatures of themselves do not withdraw us from God, but lead us to Him; for *the invisible things of God are clearly seen, being understood by the things that are made* **(Rom 1:20). If, then, they withdraw men from God, it is the fault of those who use them foolishly.... And the very fact that they can thus withdraw us from God proves that they came from Him, for they cannot lead the foolish away from God except by the allurements of some good that they have from Him** (I,65,1).

We have only our own wrong attitudes to God's good creatures to blame, never God's creatures. It's as wrong to blame the apple as it was wrong for Adam to blame Eve (and God for giving him Eve) and for Eve to blame the Devil. God tempts no one (Jas 1:13). We make ourselves into addicts and idolaters, but the good things that we become addicted to or that we idolize remain good, for God made them. When we are free from addiction to anything, we appreciate it more, not less. For instance, wine. The psalmist praises God for making wine "to gladden the heart of man" (Ps 104:15), not to sadden it or to tempt us to alcoholism. He gladdens, we sadden.

Many spiritual writers warn us against loving creatures too much. That's true, but that "too much" is relative to God and our neighbors, which are ends whom we are to love for their own sakes, while things are only means, to use for their sakes. We reverse that order when we use people and love things instead of using things and loving people. In one sense we cannot love people too much, only too little (as means instead of ends). In another sense, we can, for we can treat them as God, as our final end.

"I gotta have those things" is a dangerous and wrong kind of love of creatures. But "They are God's beautiful and desirable works of art" is not. "I gotta have them" starts with "I"; "They are God's works of art" starts with them and with God. The first kind of love is greed, the second kind of love is appreciation. Grateful appreciation never led anyone astray. In fact it is a necessary ingredient in sanctity. Listening to a bird or a thunderstorm or gazing at the sunset or the stars is a cure for atheism, not a temptation to it.

God put us into a beautiful cathedral called the universe. Everything in it speaks of Him. Every creature is to be trusted. The only thing to be mistrusted is sin.

When the New Testament says "Do not love the world" (1 Jn 2:15), the word for "the world" is not *gaia* but *aion*. *Gaia* is a space word, the material planet. That is good. God made it. *Aion* is a time word: the fallen world-order, the fallen relations between men and things that was orchestrated by the Devil, not by God.

35. Why is it important that we have only one soul, not many?

Why is the human body sacred? Why is even an embryo sacred?

Nor do we say that there are two souls in one man ... one, animal, by which the body is animated and which is mingled with the blood; the other, spiritual, which obeys the reason; but we say that it is one and the same soul in man that both gives life to the body by being united to it and orders itself by its own reasoning....

If man were *living* by one form, the vegetative soul, and *animal* by another form, the sensitive soul, and *man* by another form, the intellectual soul, it would follow that man is not absolutely one. Thus Aristotle argues ... against those who hold that there are several souls in the body, he asks, *What contains them?*—that is, what makes them one? It cannot be said that they are united by the one body, because rather does the soul contain the body and make it one, than the reverse (I,76,3) ... a proof of which is that on the withdrawal of the soul, no part of the body retains its proper action (I,76,8).

The same soul that keeps our cells alive also thinks. When we die, our soul leaves our body, and we can neither keep the cells alive nor think. It's one and the same soul that does both. We are not angels added onto animals.

That is why the body is sacred: because we do not have two souls but one; because the same soul that is going to Heaven to see God and be united to Him forever is the soul that is now giving physical life to our physical body. The soul that makes our eternal dwelling in Heaven sacred also makes our temporal dwelling of the earthly body sacred. If a great prince who is destined to rule in a great palace is now living in a humble hut, that hut is made kingly by the one who lives in it.

St. Thomas' technical philosophical points almost always have practical payoffs like this one. Because there can be only one essential form in the single substance that is a man, our bodies are holy. This is also why even a one-celled zygote is holy. The soul is already in it, giving it human life, dividing and replicating rapidly in amazing order, forming itself into a human brain and nervous system. Only a human soul can do that.

What does St. Thomas mean by saying that the body does not contain the soul but the soul contains the body?

Descartes tried to find the soul in the pineal gland at the base of the brain. Many today say mind *is* brain. St. Thomas was much more sophisticated than that. Descartes did not know that the soul cannot be contained in the body because it contains the body. It is the body's form or unity or meaning, as the message of a book is the meaning of its physical words. Spiritual souls contain bodies. They contain them spiritually, not physically, for only physical bodies contain other physical bodies physically and materially: organs, tissues, cells, atoms, molecules. You will never find the soul in any one bodily organ, any more than you will find the meaning or theme of a play in any one act or character alone; the meaning is what holds everything together. The play is not contained in the physical setting; the physical setting is contained in the play, is part of the play, is one dimension of the play.

That is what exalts the setting: that it is the setting of this great play. The stones that make up the castle walls in *Hamlet* are given greatness and dignity by the greatness of the play they are in. Other stones lack that greatness. The setting of the play shares in the play and its greatness. So our bodies share in our souls' greatness.

No other bodies in the universe have that greatness. In fact the whole universe lacks that greatness. One human zygote is greater than the whole physical universe. It will live forever, for it is *you* at a very early stage (you were once a zygote). It (*you*) will see God; the galaxies will not.

Why can't we blame our bodies for our sins of the flesh?

As the Philosopher (Aristotle) **says:** *We observe ... despotic and a politic principle; for the soul dominates the body by a despotic power, but the intellect dominates the appetite by a politic and royal power.* **For a power is called despotic whereby a man rules his slaves, who have not the right to resist in any way the orders of the one that commands them, since they have nothing of their own. But that power is called politic and royal by which a man rules over free subjects, who, though subject to the government of the ruler, have nevertheless something of their own by reason of which they can resist the orders of him who commands. And so the soul is said to rule the body by a despotic power because the members of the body cannot in any way resist the sway of the soul, but at the soul's command both hand and foot, and whatever member is naturally moved by voluntary movement, are moved at once. But the intellect or reason is said to rule the irascible and concupiscible** (appetites) **by a politic power, because the sensitive appetite has something of its own by virtue of which it can resist the commands of reason. For the sensitive appetite is naturally moved not only by ... the cognitive power which the universal reason guides, but also by the imagination and sense. Whence it is that we experience that the irascible and concupiscible powers do resist reason, inasmuch as we sense or imagine something pleasant which reason forbids, or unpleasant which reason commands ...** (I,81,3).

Augustine, in the *Confessions,* marvels at the same thing St. Paul marvels at in Romans 7: "The good that I will, I do not do; the evil that I will not, that I do." He blames his "flesh", but this is *not* his body. His body obeys his will perfectly: if he is not paralyzed or chained, his arm rises every time he commands it to rise. But his will does not obey itself; it is a divided will. Part of it is enslaved, not to his body but to his selfish passions. It disobeys both its navigator, the reason, and itself. The captain of the starship Soul is a schizophrenic.

Aristotle explains this by the political analogy: the passions, being of the soul, are free to rebel against the rightful rule of the reason and against the rational will. The body is not.

So we do not need to hate, fear, resent, oppose, harm, or chain the body. We need to tame the passions, that is, the emotions.

But the emotions are precisely what we take with the greatest seriousness today! Pop psychology virtually worships them. Ever since Rousseau, they have swapped place with the reason: reason is looked down on as cold and inhuman, while the passions of the heart are assumed to be innocent and natural and unfallen. In fact they are treated as authoritative, having rights over the reason. Part of the problem is that we have demoted "reason" to "calculation".

Contrast all the saints. They do not *hate* the emotions, but they *ignore* them, and tell us to do the same, especially when making moral choices, praying, and contemplating.

They are like dogs. We must often say "Down, boy!" as Christ said to the storm on the Sea of Galilee. He will help us. It's not easy. But it is liberating and rewarding.

They are not our enemies. That is Stoicism. They are like our dogs, "man's best friend", but we need to tame them.

37. Why practicing the presence of God is the key to sanctity

What can we do about our moral insanity: choosing misery (sin), not happiness (virtue)?

Augustine says that *all desire happiness with one will* ... **as the intellect of necessity adheres to the first principles** (e.g., the Law of Non-contradiction, X is not non-X), **the will must of necessity adhere to the last end, which is happiness, since the end is in practical matters what the principle is in speculative matters ... But** (this) **natural necessity** *does not take away the freedom of the will* ... (For) **we are masters of our own actions by reason of our being able to choose this or that. But choice regards not the end but** *the means to the end,* **as the Philosopher says** ... (I,82,1) (These "means" are) **individual goods which have not a necessary connection with happiness, because without them a man can be happy; and to such the will does not adhere of necessity.**

But there are some things (faith, hope, charity) **which have a necessary connection with happiness, by means of which things man adheres to God, in Whom alone true happiness consists. Nevertheless, until through the certitude of the Divine Vision the necessity of such connection be shown, the will does not adhere to God of necessity, nor to those things which are of God** (faith, hope, charity). **But the will of the man who sees God in His essence of necessity adheres to God, just as now we desire of necessity to be happy** (I,82,2).

Plato taught us an important half-truth when he said that all evil comes from ignorance. (It is only a half-truth because he forgot that ignorance also comes from evil, and that the will moves the reason as well as the reason moving the will.) The truth of his "half-truth" is that if we truly knew and totally understood, without a doubt, that choosing good (which ultimately means choosing obedience to God's will) always made us happy, deep down and in the long run, and that choosing the opposite (evil) always infallibly made us miserable, we would never choose evil. We will see this clearly in the Beatific Vision, face to face with God in Heaven. But we do not see this clearly now.

As St. Thomas says, all desire happiness, necessarily. But not all desire virtue as the means to happiness. We are free to choose different means, different roads to the end we all seek. So if we could glue "happiness" to "virtue" with a mental glue that did not become unstuck, we would always desire virtue as we desire happiness. What glues happiness to virtue in this way? Wisdom.

Therefore the key to being good and choosing good is wisdom, the wisdom that sees the good as it is, i.e., as desirable, and sees the evil as it is, i.e., as undesirable; the wisdom that sees through the Devil's deceptive worm wiggling invitingly on his concealed hook.

How do we acquire the X-ray vision that sees through this deception? It's crucially important, because if sin didn't seem like fun, we'd all be saints! The answer is that we must first choose to practice the truth, i.e., the presence of God and the goodness of God and the trustability of God and the beauty of God. Make it a habit to say many times a day, "Father, I trust you." Especially when He (through your conscience) tells you to make some sacrifice that seems painful instead of pleasant.

In other words, get as close to the Beatific Vision as you can. In this life we do not clearly see the necessity of the connection between virtue and happiness. But we can believe it. Faith = wisdom.

Wisdom comes in four ways: experience, reasoning, seeing, and believing (faith). We know from experience that every time we have chosen virtue, it has made us deeply happy, and every time we have chosen sin, it has made us deeply miserable. But this experience is not enough, for we still choose sin. (We are quite insane. We choose misery over joy. That is part of Original Sin.) Reasoning can prove it to us, as in Plato. But this moves us even less than experience does. What about vision, just seeing it, just knowing it? Some have more of this gift than others, but no one has much of it this side of Heaven. Pray for this vision, though; it is a great grace. There remains faith: "If God said it, it must be true."

God did more than say it: He showed it, He did it, on the Cross.

Knowledge and love, intellect and will, truth and goodness, are the two things that raise us above the animals, the two powers of the soul that image God the best. Which is the greatest of these?

... we find that the will is sometimes higher than the intellect from the fact that the object of the will occurs in something higher than ... the object of the intellect ... For ... the action of the intellect consists in this—that the *idea of* the thing understood is in the one who understands; while the act of the will consists in this—that the will is inclined to *the thing itself* as existing in itself ... When, therefore, the thing in which there is good is nobler than the soul ... the will is higher than the intellect. But when the thing which is good is less noble than the soul, then ... the intellect is higher than the will. Wherefore the love of God is better than the knowledge of God, but on the contrary the knowledge of corporeal things is better than the love thereof (I,82,3).

Knowledge is greater than love regarding everything less than ourselves, because knowledge makes the thing known more like the knower: it makes material things spiritual, makes them into ideas, makes them into things known, things in our mind. By knowing a thing we raise it up to our own level, so to speak. The star or tree or dog cannot enter our mind physically, only spiritually, as our idea of it. We give it a second life, so to speak, by knowing it. It is mortal but we are immortal, so we make its memory in us immortal. And even during its mortal life, the dog or the tree that we know has the privilege of being a part of our lives, entering into human relationships and human meanings. This is a remote image or analogy of

how we enter into God's own life by divine grace. We humanize the world; God divinizes us.

But since knowledge makes the thing known more like the knower, therefore when we know God we drag Him down to our level, just as we raise physical things up to our level when we know them. We can only know God in human terms, which are radically inadequate.

But love is greater than knowledge regarding what is greater than ourselves, because whereas knowledge makes the thing known more like the soul that knows it (knowing it "spiritualizes" it), love does the opposite: it makes the soul that loves more like the thing loved. The more you love a good or evil person, the more good or evil you become. The more you love God, the more you become like God.

This is why we can love God more than we can know Him. We can reach out in love to the whole God, the independently real God, God as He is in Himself; but we can know only those few aspects of God that we can comprehend, we can know only the God that can fit into our human mind somehow, we can know God only as He makes Himself appear to us.

That's the point of C.S. Lewis' poem "On a Theme from Nicholas of Cusa":

"When soul and body feed, one sees / Their differing physiologies. / Firmness of apple, fluted shape / Of celery, or tight-skinned grape / I grind and mangle when I eat, / Then in dark, salt, internal heat, / Annihilate their natures by / The very act that makes them I. / But when the soul partakes of good / Or truth, which are her savoury food, / By some far subtler chemistry / It is not they that change, but she, / Who feels them enter with the state / Of conquerors her opened gate, / Or, mirror-like, digests their ray / By turning luminous as they."

39. Proof that we have free will

Many philosophers and scientists are determinists. How can we prove they are wrong? How can we prove that we really have free will?

Man has free-will; otherwise counsels, exhortations, commands, prohibitions, rewards and punishments would be in vain (I,83,1).

If we have no free will, all our moral language is meaningless and based on an illusion. It is meaningless to counsel, command, prohibit, praise, or punish a machine. When the soda machine fails to deliver a soda in response to the money we put into it, we do not expect it to feel guilty and go to Confession; we just kick it. (Behaviorist psychologists call this "operant conditioning", and claim that that's really all we do to each other too, but in a more sophisticated way. Yes, they actually say that. They are quite insane.)

If we have no free will, the entire spiritual life is meaningless. Machines cannot become saints. If, on the other hand, we do have free will, then the ultimate responsibility is on our shoulders; for God wills for us to become saints, so the only force in the universe that can prevent us from attaining that ultimate end and joy is our own will, our own choices, our own sins. Even the Devil can only tempt us, not force us. And even God cannot force our freedom, for that is a self-contradiction, "forced freedom". He can only give us grace, to aid and "egg us on". And even if grace is the first cause of our free choices of good, we are responsible because grace does not turn off, but turns on, nature, and therefore our nature, and therefore our souls, and therefore our souls' wills, and therefore their freedom.

The practical point about free will is personal responsibility. We are morally responsible for whatever we freely choose, but not for what we do not freely choose. If our choices are determined by our social and economic system, as Marx says, or by our ape ancestry and genes, as materialistic Darwinian philosophers who claim to be only biologists say, or by our animal id rather than by

our rational ego, as Freud says, then we are not responsible for sin. There is no sin, and therefore no salvation.

St. Thomas did not know the modern pseudo-scientific arguments for determinism, of course. But they amount to nothing more than a more sophisticated, detailed version of the second argument against the existence of God in ST I,2,3: that natural science claims to be able to explain all human behavior without free will, just as it claims to be able to explain all that exists without God.

So the refutation of this argument from science, in order to convince the scientist, would have to produce some phenomenon that even the determinist admits, but which cannot be explained by determinism.

St. Thomas finds this in the fact that we all assume the meaningfulness of moral language: praising and blaming, counseling and advising, commanding and prohibiting, exhorting and warning, rewarding and punishing. Remember the analogy of the soda machine. Determinists must either stop treating human beings as if they were anything other than machines—in other words, practice the awful philosophy they preach—or else stop preaching it, stop thinking that men are only complex machines. Determinists disprove determinism by their behavior.

This is a dangerous argument, because a purely logical determinist with weak human instincts, confronted with this argument, may embrace the change in behavior rather than the change in thought; may start practicing the insanity he preaches rather than preaching the sanity he practices. St. Thomas is so optimistic about human common sense that he takes for granted the implied premise, which is that we not only do all these things in fact (praising, blaming, rewarding, punishing, etc.) but that we rightly do them; that they are attitudes justified by their objects, i.e., persons; that they are not "in vain", i.e., not meaningless and pointless, like trying to teach a stone to talk. And this can be only if persons have free will. And only if we have free will can we become saints.

Reason seems to confine us. How can free will be based on reason?

(1) **Some things act without judgment, as a stone moves downwards, and in like manner all things which lack knowledge.**

(2) **And some act from judgment but not a free judgment, as brute animals. For the sheep, seeing the wolf, judges it a thing to be shunned, from a natural** (instinctive) **and not a free judgment, because it judges not from reason but from natural instinct. And the same thing is to be said of any judgment of brute animals.**

(3) **But man acts from judgment.... But because this judgment, in the case of some particular act, is not from a natural instinct but from some act of comparison in the reason, therefore he acts from free judgment and retains the power of being inclined to various things ... and therefore in such matters the judgment of reason may follow opposite courses, and is not determinate to one. And** (thus) **forasmuch as man is rational it is necessary that man have a free-will** (I,83,1).

St. Thomas uses "judgment" here in a broader sense than we usually do today, as something animals also share. And he uses the term "natural" here in a narrower sense than we usually do, as contrasted to "free" and "rational". Thus animals have judgment, but not free judgment.

His point is that our reason, unlike animal instinct or sense perception, knows not just concrete particulars but abstract universals, and this is why we are free. Animal instinct knows "the good" only in the form of food or sex or sleep, and whichever concrete, particular good is stronger will always move the animal. If it is more tired than hungry, it will sleep; if it is more hungry than tired, it will eat. But human reason knows "the good" in general, and that is why we can choose between different concrete, particular goods. We can compare one concrete good with another only because we have an abstract and universal standard for this judgment, as animals do not. Even if we are more tired than hungry, we may refuse to sleep if we are on sentry duty, and we may eat even if we are not hungry if we know we need the strength the food will give us.

Why then do we so often think reason *confines* us rather than frees us? Why do we think that free will is not really free if it conforms to reason? We think that reason confines us because we think of it in materialistic and even mechanistic ways, like a computer. It is, in fact, more like light: it frees us to make choices. Or perhaps we complain that reason confines us because moral reason commands us to do things that require sacrifice. But these things too liberate us—from an addiction, in fact from our master addiction to selfishness. We are never free by violating reason, especially moral reason, any more than we are free when we put our eyes out.

Therefore, if we want to be saints, we must listen to reason. That is the practical payoff of this theoretical point. (Needless to say, "reason" means far more than "cleverness" or "logical consistency" or even "scholarly sophistication"—it means knowing the truth.) Training our will by habit to obey reason is an essential preliminary to training our passions to obey. If we do not see, or understand, by reason, the attractiveness and rightness of will obeying reason instead of passions, we will not be able to control our passions freely. "Reason" is a holy thing, or at least something tremendously helpful to holiness; for it sees through the Devil's most effective lie, that sin is fun.

That is why we are commanded to "take every *thought* captive to obey Christ" (2 Cor 10:5), like taming wild beasts. Buddhists often understand the importance of thought better than modern Christians do. The first line of the most popular Buddhist book, the *Dhammapada*, is: "All that we are is determined by what we think." That is why Buddhists meditate so much, and why we should too. It works!

Does God cause me to choose what I seem to choose by my own free will, or not? If so, how can I be free? If not, how can His grace make a difference to my choices?

Free-will is the cause of its own movement because by his free-will man moves himself to act.

But it does not of necessity belong to liberty that what is free should be the *first* cause of itself, as for one thing to be cause of another it does not need to be the first cause. God, therefore, is the first cause, Who moves (other) **causes both natural** (involuntary) **and voluntary. And just as by moving natural causes** (e.g., winds, and dogs) **He does not prevent their acts being natural** (windy and doggy)**, so by moving voluntary causes** (our free will) **He does not deprive their actions of being voluntary** (free). **But rather He is the cause of this very thing in them, for He operates in each thing according to its nature** (I,83,1).

Two kinds of determinism threaten free will: from below (by material forces, as in Marx, Darwin, and Freud) and from above (by a Calvinist rather than Catholic God). We must avoid both deterministic philosophies.

Two errors are possible about the relationship between God's grace and our free will. We can deny either the sovereignty and sufficiency and primacy of grace, or the reality of free will. This dilemma is not easy to solve, because we must reconcile rather than deny the two things that here seem to exclude each other. If God pulls my strings, I seem to be a mere puppet. If He does not, He seems no longer to be the universal First Cause.

St. Thomas strongly affirms both halves of this dilemma and reconciles them by the principle that grace perfects the nature it created rather than destroying it, reducing it, or opposing it. God **operates in each thing according to its nature.** He is the friend, not the enemy, of all nature and therefore especially of our nature and its perfection, especially its moral perfection, which necessarily and essentially includes free choice.

Here are three analogies for the relation between grace and nature. God is like light, salt, or knowledge. Light does not rival any color but reveals all colors. Salt does not destroy food but preserves it and brings out the flavor of each. Knowledge does not destroy its material objects, as one material object destroys another, but gives all its objects a second life, a spiritual life, in the mind. So God's grace moves our free will to freely choose the good, not as one domino moves another but as a playwright moves his characters. Puppets do not make good characters, and God is a perfect author.

It is therefore foolish to fear the loss of our liberty and freedom and self-mastery when we surrender totally to God. For God is not a slave master but a creative author. Our surrender to Him is in fact the only way we can be totally free. He is not our rival in the same universe, like Zeus; He is the Creator. Sometimes we need to get free from our imperfect fathers on earth, but never from our perfect Father in Heaven.

This is not just a clever solution to a tricky theological and philosophical problem. It makes a great difference to our lives, because it preserves both our total personal responsibility (we really are free, therefore we really are responsible for our choices) *and* our reliance on divine grace (we really are dependent on it, we really do receive it, and it really makes a difference: an eternal difference).

It's not either/or, it's both/and.

And it's not 50% ours and 50% His; it's 100% ours and 100% His.

It's like love.

It *is* love.

"Dogmatism"—that's the attitude of the Catholic Church that the modern world simply can't stomach. How can we justify the claim that we can have knowledge, real knowledge, even certain knowledge, and not just opinion or belief, about objective reality—about any objective reality, much less about God?

This is a religious and practical question as well as a theoretical, philosophical question. For if the standard view among modern academics and intellectuals is true—that we must be tolerant and "non-judgmental" about everything, including religion, because all we can know, really, is our own feelings and opinions—then all religion, especially the Catholic religion, are doomed and dead.

The most controversial specific area of this battle is sex. We used to talk about "natural" vs. "unnatural" sex (e.g., sodomy and contraception) because we assumed that our intellects could know what the nature of things really is. In order to stop this "offensive" and "judgmental" language, typically modern intellectuals are skeptical of all such talk about the "nature of things".

In the following crucial passage St. Thomas uses the very technical term "the intelligible species" to mean not the real nature of the real thing as it is in reality but the correct concept or image of that nature of the thing. The question is: Do we know real things or only our own concepts? Can we know the real nature of things, or only our own ideas of them, for sure?

Here is St. Thomas' simple refutation of today's subjectivism:

Some have asserted that our intellectual faculties know only the impression made on them, as, for example, that sense is cognizant only of the impression made on its own organ. Therefore the intellect knows only the intelligible species which it has received, so that this species is what is understood.

This is, however, manifestly false for two reasons. First, because the things we understand are the objects of science; therefore, if what we understand is merely the intelligible species in the soul, it would follow that every science would not be concerned with objects outside the soul (and thus all sciences would be included under psychology)....

Secondly, it is untrue because it would lead to the opinion of the ancients (the Sophists) **who maintained that *Whatever seems, is true,* and that consequently contradictories are true simultaneously.... Thus every opinion would be equally true ...** (including the opinion that *that* opinion was false!) (I,85,2).

St. Thomas' two arguments are what logicians call a "reduction to absurdity": if this subjectivist and skeptical theory is true, obviously absurd consequences follow. Alas, the modern mind no longer considers it absurd to reduce all sciences to psychology or to say that truth = nothing more than whatever seems true to you; that appearance cannot be distinguished from reality with certainty, only as an opinion.

This is an extremely useful philosophy for two classes of persons: salesmen and demons. (The Devil invented advertising; he founded the first Apple store back in the Garden of Eden.)

If all we know are our own concepts, we are like prisoners in a cave staring at images on the wall. (Does that sound familiar?) Or like people who watch only TV and media, not the real world. (Does that sound eerily familiar?) And even though we do not usually believe that about the things our senses perceive, if we believe that about the things our mind believes, including religion, then all we can do is to believe in ourselves, hope in ourselves, love ourselves, pray to ourselves, obey ourselves, and trust ourselves for our own salvation. That is a perfect definition of the philosophy of Hell.

Philosophy is important because a really bad philosophy, like subjectivism, can endanger our salvation.

43. HUMAN EQUALITY AND INEQUALITY

(1) What's the ultimate basis of human equality? (2) What's the ultimate basis for human inequality?

The image of God is in man in three ways.

First, inasmuch as man possesses a natural aptitude for understanding and loving God; and this aptitude consists in the very nature of the mind, which is common to all men.

Secondly, inasmuch as man actually or habitually knows and loves God, though imperfectly; and this image consists in the conformity of (man to) **grace** (in this life).

Thirdly, inasmuch as man knows and loves God perfectly (in the next life); **and this image consists in the likeness of glory ...**

The first (human nature) **is found in all men, the second** (grace) **only in the just, the third** (glory) **only in the blessed** (I,93,4).

(1) We all have the same Ultimate Origin and the same Ultimate End because we were all created by the same God in His image. And that image is centered in our mind and will, our spiritual soul, by which we can know and love Him and thus attain our Ultimate End, spiritual union with Him in Heaven. That is everyone's ultimate (a) origin, (b) nature, and (c) destiny. (Those three always hang together.) We have a common essence because we have a common Creator. If we stop believing in the Cause of our equality, we will eventually stop believing in our equality, and we will start treating each other as inferiors instead of equals, like the Nazis, or *Brave New World*. We may keep believing in equality for a while for other reasons, like the ideology of political correctness, or simply because we happen to feel like it or agree about it in "consensus"; but these things will not remain forever; only Truth, not Ideology or Opinion or Consensus, will remain forever. Only God will remain forever, for God is Truth itself.

(2) Inequality is rooted in free will. Because we have free will, we all have the ability to say Yes to God, by faith and hope and love, or to say No. And even those who say Yes do not all do it equally. So we can classify all human beings, by the standard of their positive response to God, into four categories. (The categories are divided gradually rather than sharply, but they are really divided, they are really unequal.) Some respond to God not at all, some weakly, some moderately, and some strongly. All receive grace, but not all respond to it. And those who do, do not respond equally to it.

That's why you're reading this book: you're not yet a saint and you want to be. You hunger and thirst for righteousness—and therefore you are blessed, and you will be filled, according to the highest and most reliable of all authorities.

The ultimate inequality is between the saved and the damned. The saved fulfill their humanity; the damned lose it. Among the saved, even in Heaven there will be inequality, not only hierarchically, in quantity of glory, but also in quality. Because although all will know and love the same God perfectly, they will do this in uniquely personal ways, so that they will look up to each other and admire each other and learn from each other, as they do here. Everyone will have heroes in Heaven. The Blessed Virgin Mary will not be on the same level as Aunt Bertha, who barely squeaked into Heaven by the skin of her teeth.

Why do you suppose God created so many persons rather than just one? Surely one reason is so that each one will be able to know and love some one aspect of God in a way no one else can. That is our ultimate and glorious inequality. We will not all be the same in Heaven. (How dull would that be?) Our individual differences will be perfected, not set aside. Yet we will also all be unified by our common love of God, far more unified than we ever were on earth. Our differences will no longer divide us by war, misunderstanding, hate, scorn, lovelessness, and selfishness.

How wonderfully unequal are the saints, and how tediously equal the sinners!

If we truly have equal human dignity, then why should one man ever be master of another? Why should I be told what to believe and do by popes, bishops, and priests? Wasn't there equality, and therefore no need for authority, in the state of innocence in the Garden of Eden? And won't that be restored in Heaven? Hierarchy, rule, authority, and obedience came only with sin, isn't that right?

No, it is not.

The condition of man in the state of innocence was not more exalted than the condition of the angels. But among the angels some rule over others. Therefore it was not beneath the dignity of the state of innocence that one man should be subject to another.

Mastership has a twofold meaning. First, as opposed to slavery ... (And this is due only to sin.) **In another sense ... he who has the office of governing and directing** *free* **men can** (also) **be called a master. In the state of innocence man could have been a master of men, not in the former but in the latter sense ...**

But a man is the master of a free subject (e.g., parents over a child, or civil authorities over a citizen) **by directing him either towards his proper welfare or to the common good. Such a kind of mastership would have existed in the state of innocence between man and man for two reasons.**

First, because man is naturally a social being, and so in the state of innocence he would have led a social life. Now a social life cannot exist among a number of people unless under the presidency of one to look after the common good; for many, as such, seek many things, whereas one attends only to one. Wherefore the Philosopher says, in the beginning of the *Politics,* **that wherever many things are directed to one, we shall always find one at the head directing them.**

Secondly, if one man surpassed another in knowledge and virtue, this would not have been fitting unless these gifts conduced to the benefit of others, according to I Pet 4:10: *As every man hath received grace, ministering the same one to another.* **Wherefore Augustine says:** *Just men command not by the love of domineering but by the service of counsel;* **and:** *The natural order of things requires this, and thus did God make man* (I,96,4).

So don't resent authority and rule and obedience. They are not bad words, "sin words". They are good words. They go all the way up into the Trinity: even God the Son, though equal to His Father, submits to the will of His Father. When He did that on earth, He did not contradict what He did in eternity, but manifested it.

And its fruit is not just goodness but also joy. We are made for surrender and obedience, and whenever we attain and live what our very nature is made for, we find joy. Whenever we twist it or ignore it, we find misery.

St. Thomas' last point is that the rule of those who are superior in wisdom and virtue is not for the benefit of the rulers but for the benefit of the ruled. To rule is to sacrifice. When Karol Woytilya was elected Pope, he didn't say, "Now I can eat great Italian food." He said, "My life is finished."

Good parents understand that. They don't have kids so that their kids can serve them; they have kids so that they can serve their kids—by their authority. Authority is for service, not for privilege. Authority *over* someone is always based on being *under* a higher authority. The only exception is God, the Author of all authority.

And even within the Trinity the Son obeys the Father's will, though He is equally divine. To obey is not to be inferior, and to command is not to be superior, in nature.

Authority means right, not might. Be grateful that you are under authority most of the time on earth and forever in Heaven, where God does not abdicate.

45. CHANCE

Does anything happen by chance?

It is written (Wis 14:3): *But Thou, O Father, governest all things by Thy Providence* ...

Certain ancient philosophers denied the government of the world, saying that all things happened by chance. But such an opinion can be refuted as impossible in two ways.

First, by observation of things themselves; for we observe that in nature things happen always or nearly always for the best; which would not be the case unless some sort of providence directed nature towards good as an end—which is to govern. Wherefore the unfailing order we observe in things is a sign of their being governed; for instance, if we enter a well-ordered house we gather therefrom the intention of him that put it in order.

Secondly, this is clear from a consideration of divine goodness, which ... was the cause of the production of things in existence. For as *it belongs to the best to produce the best,* **it is not fitting that the supreme goodness of God should produce things without giving them their perfection. Now a thing's ultimate perfection consists in the attainment of its end. Therefore it belongs to the divine goodness, as it brought things into existence, so to lead them to their end; and this is to govern** (I,103,1).

When Christianity came into the pagan world, it added many categories, many ideas that the pagans never had: for instance, the creation of the whole universe out of nothing, the Incarnation of God in Christ, the Trinity, a God of perfect love, and every man as created in His image and intrinsically valuable. But there was one pagan category that Christianity subtracted: chance. In a universe in which God knows literally every hair that falls from our head and every sparrow that falls from the sky, nothing, not the slightest motion of the slightest subatomic particle in the farthest galaxy, is unknown and left to chance. "Chance" is nothing but an expression of human ignorance. We don't know the reasons and causes and design of all things, because we are not God. But God does, because He is!

Therefore everything, including your reading this book at this very moment, is designed and planned by God. Trust Him absolutely and totally with every detail; He is the storyteller and you are one of His beloved characters in His story, which is history.

St. Thomas deduces the reality of a universal divine providence both from below and from above. First he deduces it from sense observation of the many examples of it in the universe, the many ways it is ordered (and modern science multiplies these things by the millions). (This is technically induction, not deduction.) Second, he deduces it from the revealed dogma that God is perfectly good.

God is even now governing all things. This is more than just keeping them in order, conserving their order. He does that too, as a "cosmic conservative." But He also is moving them forward to their end, their fulfillment. He is also a "cosmic progressive". The fulfillment and end and purpose of all the other things God created in the universe is to aid you to attain eternal life with Him. The universe is like a womb, or a placenta: it exists to produce us. And then it is like a cathedral: it exists to sanctify us. God didn't make galaxies for the sake of galaxies but for us. Galaxies can't marry God. We can. The universe is just the temporary house God made for His bride. The permanent house will be even bigger and more wonderful.

46. THE CONNECTION BETWEEN MONOTHEISM AND PEACE

What practical difference does it make to the world, and specifically to world peace, that there is one God, not many?

We must of necessity say that the world is governed by one.

For since the end of the government of the world is ... the greatest good, the government of the world must be the best kind of government.

Now the best government is government by one.

The reason for this is that government is nothing but the directing of the things governed to the end, which consists in some good. But unity belongs to the idea of goodness ... as all things desire good, so do they desire unity, without which they would cease to exist. For a thing so far exists as it is one. Whence we observe that things resist division as far as they can, and the dissolution of a thing arises from some defect therein (e.g., disease, death, civil war).

Therefore the intention of a ruler over a multitude is unity, or peace.

Now the proper cause of unity is one. For it is clear that several cannot be the cause of unity or concord except so far as they are united ...

From this it follows that the government of the world, being the best form of government, must be by one (I,103,3).

If we have many gods, we cannot have peace, whether these gods are supernatural (like Zeus) or natural (like money, sex, or power), because peace comes only from unity, and unity comes from rule, and rule comes from God or gods.

Let's go through that again, step by step.

Augustine defines peace as "the tranquility of order."

Order requires unity in diversity, a unified whole of many diverse parts, a uni-verse.

In every one-and-many order, the one governs the many. This is true in every work of art, including yourself. Your soul governs your body. Your heart governs your blood circulation. Your DNA governs your cell growth. Your reason governs your passions. All of this manyness is governed by one "you", one "I". You have two eyes but not two I's.

Heaven is perfect peace because it is perfect unity.

It is perfect unity because it is governed by one God.

Earth gets closer to Heaven, and to peace, and to unity, in so far as it worships the one God, freely chooses to be governed by the one God.

Therefore missionaries and evangelists are the most important causes of world peace.

And therefore religious wars are the most scandalous of all wars, and religious divisions the most scandalous of all divisions. How does the one God feel, how does our Father feel, when He sees His beloved children hating and murdering each other? How do you feel? Does He care less than you do?

He has told us how He feels: "Whatever you do to one of the least of these [My family], you do to Me" (Mt 25:40). He never exaggerated. He meant that literally. He didn't say "it is *as if* you did it to Me."

Saints don't start wars. They end them. To end wars, stockpile the most powerful of weapons: saints. "Blessed are the peacemakers, for they shall be called the children of God" (Mt 5:9). The children of God make peace because that is God's nature, and "like Father, like son." The children of the Devil make wars because that is their nature and the nature of their father.

We have one power that even God does not have: we can choose our own nature. For we get our nature from our father, and we can choose our own supernatural father, God or the Devil (Jn 8:44).

47. How our free choices share in God's sovereign government

If the governor of all things is God and we are not God, doesn't that reduce us to passivity?

As to the *design* of government, God governs all things immediately; whereas in its *execution* He governs some things by means of others....

It is a greater perfection for a thing to be good in itself and also the cause of goodness in others, than only to be good in itself. Therefore God so governs things that He makes some of them to be causes of others in government, as a master who not only imparts knowledge to his pupils but gives also the faculty of teaching others....

If God governed alone, things would be deprived of the perfection of causality (I,103,6).

God does not micromanage. He exalts His subordinates, as a good parent does to his children, a good CEO to his middle management and a good President to his cabinet. Like a good teacher, He teaches His students to teach themselves and each other.

Therefore divine grace exalts, perfects, and uses human beings and human nature rather than demeaning it, rivaling it, or ignoring it. It even does this to sub-human nature: the more God has His way in a dog, the doggier it is. The more grace, the more nature, as the more light, the more color. One color may exclude and rival another (or they may blend), but light is no rival to any color. It transcends all color, therefore rivals none, as God transcends all creatures and therefore rivals none.

Therefore we are truly free when God is most active in our lives. We are tempted to think the opposite: that when we are free, we are free from God's influence; that when *we* have clearly and consciously chosen freely some good thing (any good thing, physical or moral), *God* has not done anything. It is exactly the opposite: that is when God is most present in us. Our divine destiny and our human freedom, our conformity to God and our liberty from idolatry and addiction, are two sides of the same life, just as the destiny of the plot and the free will of the characters are two sides of the same story in every good story ever told.

Why is this? Because God governs by reason and love, not by force; by gentle persuasion and winsome love. When Elijah met Him, He was not in the fire or the earthquake or the hurricane, but in the still, small voice. We meet Him there too. (That's why He put that story in His book for us.)

The closest pre-Christian thinking ever came to this remarkable and revolutionary idea is probably the *Tao Te Ching*. (See *Christ the Eternal Tao* by Hieromonk Damascine.) God, like the nature He created, acts most powerfully when He is most invisible.

48. GOD'S ACTION AND PRESENCE IN ALL THINGS

How can I find God in all things? Where is He?

Both reason and faith bind us to say that creatures are kept in being by God ... For the being of every creature depends on God, so that not for a moment could it subsist, but would fall into nothingness, were it not kept in being by the operation of the divine power ...

This is made clear as follows: Every effect depends on its cause ... the air does not continue to be lit up, even for a moment, when the sun ceases to act upon it.... Now every creature may be compared to God as the air is to the sun which enlightens it. For as the sun possesses light by its nature, and as the air is enlightened by sharing the sun's nature (as light)**, so God alone is Being by virtue of His own essence, since His essence is His existence; whereas every creature has being** (existence) **by participation, so that its essence is not its existence.**

Therefore, as Augustine says, *If the ruling power of God were withdrawn from His creatures, their nature would at once cease (to exist) and all nature would collapse* (I,104,1).

Therefore we can find God everywhere, because being is everywhere.

Human beings are not everywhere, and we can find God more richly in human beings than in sub-human beings. Living things are not everywhere, and we can find God more richly in living beings than in beings that lack life. But being is everywhere, in every grain of sand and subatomic particle. So we can find God in every grain of sand—because He is really there, acting, keeping it in being, saying "Be!" to it right now, in this present moment. To our human consciousness in time, God created the universe almost 14 billion years ago (the "Big Bang"); but in the mind of the timeless God, He is creating it right now. When an author says "Let it be!" to his novel, he says that to every event in the novel, to the whole novel. He is outside it, as God is outside the universe; but the author is also in every word of his story, as God is in every grain of sand.

In one version of Hindu theology, Brahman, the supreme God, falls asleep every *kalpa* cycle (every 28 billion years), and the whole universe is created, as He manifest Himself as Vishnu the Creator, because it is only His dream. Then, He wakes up and manifests Himself as Shiva the Destroyer, and the whole universe ceases to exist, because it is only His dream. In Christian theology, the universe is real: God does not dream it; He creates it out of nothing. But there too, everything would disappear if God stopped loving it into existence.

We can love all things that exist, just because they exist, because God does. We can meet Him in a grain of sand, because He is really there, giving being to it. We are never alone. We share humanity with all humans, animal feelings with all animals, life with all plants, and existence with all existing things. And God is the source of all these things. We are never alone, unless we are in Hell. Sartre is exactly wrong when he famously says "Hell is other people." Hell is precisely the absence of all others, beginning with God. We are always part of the community of creatures, the communion of saints. Even grains of sand are something like tiny saints, because they are His.

49. How God is in His creatures

When I meet God in His creatures, should I see them as mirrors or as paintings? Do I find His light by looking away from them or by looking at them? Do I find God more by seeing through them and leaving them behind, or by seeing into them, by entering more into the nature and operation of each creature?

Some have understood God to work in every agent in such a way that no created power has any effect in things, but that God alone is the immediate cause of everything wrought—for instance, that it is not fire that gives heat, but God in the fire, and so forth.

But this is impossible. First, because the order of cause and effect would be taken away from created things, and this would imply lack of power in the Creator; for it is due to the power of the cause that it bestows active power on its effect.

Secondly, because the active powers which are seen to exist in things would be bestowed on things to no purpose if these wrought nothing through them....

We must therefore understand that God works in things in such a manner that things have their proper operation (I,105,5).

The error St. Thomas opposes here is the error of the Asharites among Muslim philosophers: the denial of secondary causality, the denial of creatures' own identity and power. In Western philosophy this is called "occasionalism" because it sees creatures as incapable of acting themselves; they are mere "occasions" for God to act. The Hindu Upanishads also see God in this way, as "the Thinker of every thought, the Doer of every deed".

But a God Who envied creatures their own identity and power would be a weak God, not a strong one. The God Who lovingly lavishes identities and powers throughout His creation is the strong God, not the weak one. "I'm going to beat you up" is the word of the bully, who tries to compensate for his own perceived weakness. The bully has to fill his own inner emptiness. "I love you and I want to win your love" is the word of the self-assured one, who has extra fullness to give. That is why love is the supreme power.

God is really present in all things in their own unique natures and actions. God's greatness is revealed in the fact that He does not shout so that the voices of creatures cannot be heard. He speaks in a still, small voice. Like light, He is Himself invisible and makes all things visible. He is anonymous: He hides in things, He lets things be themselves. Even God is humble; how can we be proud?

The knowledge of creatures does not distract from the knowledge of God, but reveals it. All truth is God's truth.

But the love of creatures can distract us from the love of God if it is a disordered love, a love that is not for God's sake, a love of a creature *instead of* God. In other words, it can be idolatry, the violation of the first and greatest commandment. But it can also be an ordered love, a love of His creatures that is motivated by the love of God and that leads to a greater appreciation of God. Loving the Artist and loving His art naturally reinforce each other. They do not by nature rival each other.

Does God use angels to teach us? When I get to Heaven and meet my guardian angel, will I see all the occasions in my life when he inspired me to think rightly, even though I thought at the time that it was only me that was responsible for the thought?

Since the order of divine Providence disposes that lower things be subject to the actions of higher ... as the inferior angels are enlightened by the superior, so men, who are inferior to angels, are enlightened by them.

(1) *The revelation of divine things* **reaches men through the ministry of the angels....**

(2) **The human intellect is strengthened by the action of the angelic intellect....** *Natural reason*, **which is immediately from God** (in His act of creating each human soul), **can be strengthened by an angel.**

(3) **Again, the more the human intellect is strengthened, so much higher an intelligible truth can be elicited ... from creatures....** Angels *propose the intelligible truth to men under the similitudes of sensible things....* **Thus man is assisted by an angel so that he may obtain from creatures a more perfect knowledge of God** (I,111,1).

(4) **To change the will belongs to God alone, according to Prov. 21:1:** *The heart of the king is in the hand of the Lord; whithersoever He will He shall turn it.* (But the will can be moved indirectly from without by another human or an angel.) **As regards an angel, this can be only in one way—by the good apprehended by the intellect ...** (thus both) **an angel and a man** (can) *move the will by way of persuasion ...* (I,111,2).

(5) **... the angels** *reveal things in dreams,* **as appears from Mt. 1:20, 2:13, 19....**

(6) **Both a good and a bad angel by their own natural power can** *move the human imagination* (I,111,3).

(1) Just about every important event in divine revelation (the Bible) is surrounded by angels.

(2) Angels can increase your mental energy.

(3) Angels can help you see the presence of God in creatures.

(4) Angels cannot directly move your will, but they can indirectly persuade your will through proposing truth to your mind.

(5) Angels can speak in dreams (this is rare). They can also make your ordinary dreams "good dreams" rather than "bad dreams".

(6) Angels can pop ideas into your imagination. Didn't you ever wonder where that great creative idea, prompted by "your" imagination, ever came from?

They can do all this because they are *His* angels. Their very name means "messengers". They do not write the letters, they only deliver them. They are invisible not only because they are pure spirits, without bodies (unless they take them on) but also because they are transparent to His will and action. They are signs, they are pointing fingers. Like Mary, their whole life and joy is to point to Him; therefore they tell us exactly what she did, at Cana: "Do whatever He tells you." And that is the one simple and adequate secret of all sanctity and all perfect joy.

Are "guardian angels" nice, comforting myths, like Santa Claus? Or are they as real as radiators?

And why do we need them?

On the text, *Their angels in heaven do always behold the face of My Father which is in heaven,* **Jerome says:** *Great is the dignity of souls, for each one to have an angel deputed to guard it from its birth.*

Each man has an angel guardian appointed to him.... For men are not only incorruptible (immortal) **in the common species but also in ... each individual.... Now it is manifest that the providence of God is chiefly exercised towards what remains for ever, whereas as regards those things which pass away, the providence of God acts so as to order their existence** (as means) **to the things which are perpetual** (as ends) (I,113,2).

The demons are ever assailing us ... (1 Pet 5:8).... **Much more, therefore, do the good angels ever guard us** (I,113,6).

We need angels' help because we are at war. Wake up and smell the gunpowder.

War is horrible, but it is at least *interesting*. (Indeed, it is very likely that one of the main sources of war is boredom. You're never bored when you're planning to kill or be killed.) And since angels and demons are real, life is war. Therefore life is interesting.

The theme of spiritual warfare is on nearly every page of the Bible. If it's mythology, so is the whole Bible, including all the upbeat stuff about love and mercy and salvation. It's a package deal; it all stands on the same foundation, it comes to us with the same authority: "Thus says the Lord."

It is "the Word of God", after all, and according to the Word of God in print, Christ is the Word of God in the flesh, Who fulfills "the Word of God" in print, i.e., "the Law and the Prophets"; so that Scripture partakes of the same authority as Christ Himself, though less clearly and completely. "The Word of God" is always singular. It is ontologically one. To deny Scripture is, therefore, ontologically

and objectively speaking, to deny Christ, even if that is not one's psychological and subjective intention.

We seldom realize the incredible privilege it is to have these Heavenly warriors fighting for us, guarding us, caring for us. A dog or a cat is privileged to be brought into the life of a human family and to have that immensely superior species, human beings, paying them so much attention, loving and caring for them. For the very same reason, we are privileged to be brought into the life of angels. We are their pets.

We are more than that, of course. Unlike animals, our lives are immortal. In this way we are closer to angels than to animals, and we will share the life of the angels in Heaven forever: their joy, their praise, their music (of which our most moving music is an echo). But it is also true that unlike angels, our lives are not only immortal but also mortal; for we have animal bodies, and in this way we are closer to animals than to angels. We are quasi-animals with immortal souls and we are quasi-angels with mortal bodies. So when we are kind to our pets, this helps us to understand a little better what the angels are to us. When we realize how humble and unselfish the angels are to care about us, we understand a little better how we should treat our pets; and also the other way round: when we care for our pets we better understand how angels care for us.

Angels and demons are not equal, as good and evil, light and darkness, truth and error, love of being and hatred of being, are not equal. **The demons are ever assailing us....** *Much more,* **therefore, do the good angels ever guard us.** It's not an "equally" but a "much more". It's a fixed fight.

Just be sure you're fighting on the winning side every moment. Be sure you keep listening to the angel who's whispering into your right ear instead of the demon who's whispering into your left ear. You have one vote cast for you (your guardian angel's vote) and one vote cast against you (your tempting demon's vote), and you cast the deciding vote.

52. Why evil spirits assault us

Why do demons assault us? And why does God allow them to?

The Apostle says (Eph 6:12): *Our wrestling is not against flesh and blood but against Principalities and Powers, against the rulers of the world of this darkness, against the spirits of wickedness in the high places.*

Two things may be considered in the assault of the demons: the assault itself and the ordering thereof. The assault itself is due to the malice of the demons, who through envy endeavor to hinder man's progress, and through pride usurp a semblance of divine power by deputing certain ministers to assail man, as the angels of God in their various offices minister to man's salvation. But the ordering of this assault is from God, Who knows how to make orderly use of evil by ordering it to good (I,114,1).

Demons assault us out of pride and envy, which are the worst of all sins because they are purely spiritual, not physical, not due to weakness. And God providentially allows this evil, as He allows other evils, because He loves us and knows what is best for us in the long run, as we do not. (Late-breaking news: We're not God!)

And that is the most essential part of the answer to the strongest argument against God, the "problem of evil", why bad things happen to good people. *We don't know* why God allows this or that apparently pointless and useless evil to happen. But we do know that God is God and we are not, and that He is in control, as we are not, and that He is infinitely wise, as we are not, and infinitely more loving than we are. If we don't know that, we don't know God. If we do know that, we know why He allows demons and lesser evils: because He is infinitely powerful, wise, and good.

God's providence can use the worst of human or demonic evil for good. God's plans include and use the evil plans of His evil and rebellious creatures for the strengthening of His good ones. He does it in the lives of His saints, repeatedly. Not a one of them lived a life of pure peace and comfort, free from sorrows, sufferings, sacrifices, doubts, and temptations. He did it in choosing Judas Iscariot for one of the Twelve. He did it on the Cross, when He allowed the Devil his greatest triumph— for our salvation. And He does it in your life too. He is even more totally trustable than the Devil is totally untrustable.

In light of that trust, we can laugh at the Devil. He hates it when you laugh at him in light of that trust, though he loves it when you laugh at him in light of your own naïveté and overconfidence.

53. How "everything has a purpose" changes the meaning of life

"Everything has a purpose" is part of the wisdom and world view of every ancient culture, but not of modern culture, because it is not scientifically, but only philosophically and commonsensically, verifiable. How important is it for my life and my practical wisdom today? What difference does it make?

(1. Its universality.) **Every agent of necessity acts for an end. For ... the first of all causes** (real reasons) **is the final cause** (end, purpose, goal). **The reason of which is that matter** (the "material cause") **does not receive form** (the "formal cause") **save in so far as it is moved by an agent** (the "efficient cause").... **But an agent does not move except out of** (conscious or unconscious) **intention** (movement in a specific direction) **to an end** (the "final cause"). **For if the agent were not determinate to some particular effect** (as its end), **it would not do one thing rather than another....**

(2. Its distinctively human form.) **This determination is effected in the rational nature by the rational appetite, which is called the will ... in other things, it is caused by their natural inclination, which is called the natural appetite.... [A] thing tends toward an end by its action or movement in two ways: first, as a thing moving itself to the end, as man; secondly, as a thing moved by another to the end, as an arrow tends to a determinate end through being moved by the archer, who directs his action to the end. Therefore those things that are possessed of reason move themselves to an end because they have dominion over their actions through their free-will, which is the faculty of will and reason. But those things that lack reason tend to an end by natural inclination, as being moved by another and not by themselves, since they do not know the nature of an end as such and consequently cannot ordain anything to an end, but can be ordained to an end only by another.**

(3. The ultimate cause and unity of both forms of final causality, or purpose.) **For the entire irrational nature is in comparison to God as an instrument ...** (I-II,1,2).

The point here is very abstract but very important. Don't be put off by the unfashionable, old, abstract words. The point is simple: an ordered universe, like an ordered life, must include order to *ends*. In this universe everything moves, everything changes. But nothing changes unless moved both from behind and from ahead, so to speak: both from an agent ("efficient cause") and for a determinate goal or end (the "final cause"). Acorns become oaks, not tulips; tulip bulbs become tulips, not oaks. Puppies become dogs, not cats; kittens become cats, not dogs. Heavy objects fall and hot air rises. Everything moves in determinate, specified *directions*.

Therefore our human lives, which include *conscious* purposes, fit into this purpose-filled universe. We are not freaks. Something analogous to our conscious purposes exists everywhere, for the universe is the effect of conscious purposes too: not ours but God's. The world is no accident; it is created and designed by an Intelligence. Therefore there are universal laws, laws that are true both for humans and for everything else. And one of these is that everything has a purpose. And to be realistic we must acknowledge and respect that purpose, that natural end—of every thing and every person, especially ourselves.

I call this "realism" because we must live in the real world, the world of God's design, not in an imaginary world of our own design, if we want to be sane. Being sane and being saintly are ultimately the same thing: conforming our thoughts and our lives to the nature of reality, which is ultimately God, His nature *and His designs*.

And that includes sex. (Your reaction to this is probably either "Oops!" or " Aha!") The natural end of sex is both personal love and babies. To hate and refuse either one of these ends is a sin against the essential nature of sex. That's why both deliberate love-prevention and baby-prevention are sins.

That is only one corollary of this principle of universal teleology. There are many, many others. But this is the one that modern man resists the most.

What's wrong with "different strokes for different folks" and "Don't impose your values on me"? Why must all human lives have the same single ultimate end?

... it is not possible to proceed indefinitely in the matter of ends ... for in whatsoever things there is an essential order of one to another, if the first be removed, those that are ordained to the first must of necessity be removed also. Wherefore the Philosopher proves that we cannot proceed to infinitude in causes of movement, because then there would be no first mover, without which neither can the others move, since they move only through being moved by the first mover ... (and similarly,) **if there were no last end, nothing would be desired** (I-II,1,4).

That in which a man rests as in his last end is master of his affections, since he takes therefrom his entire rule of life ... according to Matthew 6:24, *No man can serve two masters*.

It is therefore necessary for the last end so to fill man's appetite that nothing is left besides it for man to desire.... [T]he will of an individual man must be fixed on one last end (I-II,1,5).

The argument for a single ultimate efficient cause, an Uncaused Cause, a First Cause (which is a "thin slice" of what we mean by God), is the same as the argument for a single ultimate End or Final Cause. If you take away the cause, you take away the effect. If there were no first domino, the whole chain would not fall; and the universe is a very large set of falling domino chains. Similarly, if there were no final end, the whole chain of means to that end, steps to that end, would not move. If you did not want a better job, you would not be taking courses; if you were not taking courses, you would not be reading the textbook; if you were not reading the textbook you would not be putting your glasses on; if you were not putting your glasses on, you would not be moving your hand to your face. If there were no ultimate efficient cause, no First Cause, then nothing would move in the objective world of the universe; and if there

were no ultimate Final Cause, no one Final End of all desire, then nothing would ever move in the subjective world of your soul, nothing would be desired.

Therefore everything you do every day is for God, for union with God, for your last end, for your Heavenly perfection—from the first movement of your arm in shutting off the alarm clock to the closing of your eyes as you fall asleep; from the first thought of your day in offering it all up to God (let that be your first thought every day: it takes only seconds!) to the last thought of your day, asking God to send your guardian angel to guard your sleep—and from the miracle of your soul entering your body at the moment of your conception to the moment of your soul leaving your body at death.

Everything is connected by the Last End. There is a connection between your use of toilet paper and your participation in the Beatific Vision. Nothing is simply secular. That is because God is God, not Zeus. As He is the one Creator of *all* things, He is the one final End of *all* things.

Therefore offer up *everything* to Him, everything you do and everything you see and everything you think and everything you love. For everything you do is to be done for Him, and everything you see is a preparation for seeing Him, and everything you think is a tiny truth that is part of His whole Truth, and everything you love is loved only because it resembles Him in some way Who is the only Totally Lovable One. He left some of His perfume in the things He made, as He passed by; and you can't help falling in love as you smell it.

As a Christian you are privileged to know Who it is that you are always falling in love with. You have been given the secret of this universal riddle; you have been given the great gift of faith: both your personal subjective faith and *The* Faith, the truth of divine revelation. You know Who is the one love in every love of your life. You know your last end.

That kind of love has to be one. It is simply impossible to give your whole heart to two. "No man can serve two masters" (Mt 6:24).

Even toilet paper?

It would seem that man does not will whatsoever he wills for the last end. For ... man does not always think of the last end in all that he desires or does....

On the contrary.... Man must of necessity desire all, whatsoever he desires, for the last end ... because the last end stands in the same relation in moving the appetite as the first mover in other movements. Now it is clear that secondary moving causes do not move save inasmuch as they are moved by the first mover. Therefore secondary objects of the appetite do not move the appetite except as ordained to the first object of the appetite, which is the last end.

One need not always be thinking of the last end whenever one desires or does something, but the virtue (effective power) of the first intention, which was in respect of the last end, remains in every desire directed to any object whatever, even though one's thoughts be not actually directed to the last end. Thus while walking along the road one needs not to be thinking of the end at every step (I–II,1,7).

All schools of modern psychology teach us (as Plato did in Book 9 of the *Republic*) that there are great depths of unconscious thought and desire as well as the surface level that we are aware of, our conscious thoughts and desires.

On the conscious level, none of us can honestly say that God is in every thought of the mind and every desire of the heart.

How then can Christ expect us to obey the first and greatest commandment, to love God with our whole heart and mind (and soul and strength) (Mt 22:37)? He does not give us impossible commands.

The answer is that He knows the power of the unconscious because He is the world's best psychologist, since He is the Mind (*Logos*) of God, Who designed us.

On this level, which is unconscious but real, we *can* and should will all that we will for God, for our last end. And not just as a kind of pious postscript or afterthought to what we do, but as the moving force and energy of our lives, and of our conscious desires and thoughts, even if this force is unconscious most of the time.

For the end moves the means, and the last end is that which moves all the things that are means to it. If we are monotheists and not polytheists, if we believe in the one God as God, and hope in God as God, and love God as God—i.e., as our one Truth and Good and Beauty, not just as one among many—then we will dedicate to Him our whole desire and thought, our whole heart and mind, and our whole lives, both inner (heart and soul and mind) and outer ("strength"); and this dedication will "work", will "count", will make a real difference *to everything in our lives*, in God's eyes and therefore in reality (for those are only two ways of saying the same thing).

Renewing this consecration each morning, in your Morning Offering, is an essential and foundational prayer. It is like making love to your spouse not just once but repeatedly: a sacramental making-really-present of the reality that is signified and symbolized by its sign. Life's greatest secret is incredibly simple. It is just repeating two magic syllables each day to God: the same syllables you said in your wedding vow: "I do."

And that includes everything in your life. Including toilet paper. If your spouse needs some, you share that too. Nothing is outside your marriage. Nothing is simply secular any more.

Remind yourself of that tremendous and transforming truth many times a day; repeat your Morning Offering, by whatever means works best: perhaps just a gesture, a one-second *salute* to remind yourself that you are under His command in absolutely everything you do, and you are doing it for Him.

I know it's shallow to think of money and the things money can buy as the secret of happiness; but is there a good, solid, objective, logical proof that this is shallow, or is it just a good sermon? Most people, after all, have some doubts about this. If they didn't, they wouldn't worry so much about money, If you see a friend with a new smile on his face today, what's the first thing you think of to say? Probably something like: "What happened to you? Did you just win the lottery?"

It is impossible for man's happiness to consist in wealth.

For wealth is twofold, as the Philosopher says, viz. natural and artificial. Natural wealth is that which serves man as a remedy for his natural wants, such as food, drink, clothing, cars, dwellings, and such like, while artificial wealth is that which is not a direct help to nature, as money, but is invented by the art of man for the convenience of exchange and as a measure of things saleable.

Now it is evident that man's happiness cannot consist in natural wealth. For wealth of this kind is sought for the sake of something else, viz. as a support of human nature; consequently it cannot be man's last end, rather is it ordained to man as to its end. Wherefore in the order of nature, all such things are below man and made for him, according to Psalm 8:8: *Thou hast subjected all things under his feet.* And as to artificial wealth, it is not sought save for the sake of natural wealth, since man would not seek it except because by its means he procures for himself the necessaries of life. Consequently much less can it be considered in the light of the last end....

The desire for natural riches is not infinite, because they suffice for nature ... But the desire for artificial wealth is infinite, for it is the servant of disordered concupiscence, which is not curbed....

... [T]he more perfectly the sovereign good is possessed, the more it is loved ... whereas in the desire for wealth ... the contrary is the case; for when we already possess them, we despise them and seek others ... Hence it is written (Sir 24:29): *They that eat *me shall yet hunger ...* **which is the sense of Our Lord's words** (Jn 4:13): *Whosoever drinketh of this water,* **by which temporal goods are signified,** *shall thirst again.* **The reason of this is that we realize more their insufficiency when we possess them; and this very fact shows that they are imperfect and that the sovereign good does not consist therein** (I-II, 2,1).

First of all, nobody loves money itself. Money is only dirty paper. They love the power money gives them to buy things, or the things themselves. Money is only a means—"a means of exchange". It can't be the final end. If it had no purchasing power, it would be no better than any other dirty paper.

We love money so much because it can buy *anything*—anything money can buy: houses, cars, good food, police protection, the best medical services, political influence. It can buy even sex, though not love (i.e., prostitutes); and even the fake ecstasy of drugs, though not real ecstasy. Money is like the sky; it's spread over everything, i.e., every *thing*.

But "what does it profit a man if he gain the whole world but lose his own soul?" To sell your soul, your self, to the Devil for the sake of world—it's not only wicked, it's really, really stupid. For *who* has that whole world that you sold your self to the Devil for now, if you have sold your very self to the Devil? Answer: Not you, for there is no "you" there any more to have anything. You've sold your "you" to "the ruler of this world" (Jn 12:31). If you sell yourself to him for money, you belong to him, and so does all your money and all it can buy. A rich slave is still a slave. His master actually prefers a rich slave, because it is the master, not the slave, who controls all the slave's riches.

The Devil walks into a lawyer's office. "What can I do for you?" asks the lawyer, politely. "Ah, but it's what I can do for you", replies the Devil. "I can make you richer than Bill Gates. All you have to do is sign this little contract giving me your soul and the souls of all your descendants forever." "So what's the catch?" asks the lawyer. Why do we laugh at that? Because we're laughing at ourselves.

Honor, love, and respect—everyone wants it. Isn't that the secret of happiness? Doesn't being loved and honored and respected make you happier than anything else, even more than loving and honoring and respecting someone else?

Happiness is in the happy. But honor is not in the honored, but rather in him who honors and who offers deference to the person honored, as the Philosopher says. Therefore happiness does not consist in honor.

It is impossible for happiness to consist in honor. For honor is given to a man on account of some excellence in him, and consequently it is a sign and attestation of the excellence that is in the person honored ...

As the Philosopher says, honor is not the reward of virtue for which the virtuous work; but they receive honor from men by way of reward, *as from those who have nothing greater to offer.* **But virtue's true reward is happiness itself.... [I]f they worked for honor, it would no longer be a virtue, but** (the vice of worldly) **ambition (I-II,2,3).**

Many sociologists and psychologists (e.g., David Riesman and Nathan Glaser in the classic *The Lonely Crowd)* tell us that we moderns typically live outside ourselves; we have little or no inner life. We follow fads and fashions. We tell the truth with a clock. We worry about other people's opinions about us and about everything else. We are conformists. Even nonconformists conform to the fads and fashions of their nonconformity. "Rebellious" teenagers talk the same, dress the same. They voluntarily don the same uniforms—to express their nonconformity! They demand to be honored by their peers above all things.

Honor is prized in every society. But the premodern version of honor was *excellence*: being better than anyone else at something. This is still prized, but only in the worlds of entertainment and sports, the theaters that we erect to distract ourselves from ourselves. What we prize in our real lives is honor for *not* being different, for being the same, for being one of the lonely crowd. We prize "consensus" over truth.

But the new modern version of honor is just as subject to St. Thomas' two arguments against it as the ancient version is, and probably much more so.

The first point is incredibly simple: honor is not in you, it's in someone else's mind. Your happiness, in contrast, is yours. Happiness is inside you, honor is outside you and inside someone else.

And the second point is just as simple: What is it that you want to be honored for? For nothing? Do you want to be a fake? For something, then. For what? For something truly good? Or for something not truly good? That would again be a fake. Then it is not honor itself but the truly good thing that you are honored for, that is your true good and happiness and last end.

But what is that? You still have not found it, no matter how much you are honored, because it must be something more than honor itself.

Fame or glory seems to be just honor multiplied, and St. Thomas already refuted honor as a candidate for happiness: it's external, not internal. So fame or glory is obviously the wrong answer for the same reason. Is there anything else, any other profound and practical lesson, that we can learn from his rejection of fame or glory as our last end and the thing happiness consists in?

(Fame or) **glory consists *in being well known and praised*.... Now the thing known is related to human knowledge otherwise than to God's knowledge; for human knowledge is caused by the things known, whereas God's knowledge is the cause of the things known. Wherefore the perfection of human good which is called happiness cannot be caused by human knowledge, but rather human knowledge of another's happiness proceeds from and in a fashion is caused by human happiness itself.... Consequently man's happiness cannot consist in fame or glory. On the other hand, man's good depends on God's knowledge as its cause. And therefore man's beatitude depends, as on its cause, on the glory which man has with God** (I-II,2,3) (Cf. Ps 1:6; Mt 7:23; Jn 10:14).

C.S. Lewis writes somewhere that he read in a religious periodical the statement that the most important thing is what we think of God. By God Himself, says Lewis, it is not. What God thinks of us is not only more important but infinitely more important.

Why? Because what we think does not determine reality; reality determines what we think, if we think truly. For that is what truth *is*: conformity of thought to reality. But what *God* thinks *does* determine reality, for God is the Designer and Creator of all reality except Himself. God's knowledge does not conform to any pre-existing reality, as ours does. There *is* no pre-existing reality. He does not bow down to anything outside Himself, to any creature. That would be idolatry. Imagine God Himself committing idolatry! He is not a cosmic hypocrite who does not practice what He preaches to us.

In other words, God is an artist, not a scientist. A scientist is wrong if he says that mayflies live longer than elephants. But an artist could create a story in which mayflies live longer than elephants. Scientists *discover* the world of science, the world they did not create; but artists *design* the worlds of art, for they create those worlds. Shakespeare defines Hamlet, not Hamlet Shakespeare.

The practical payoff of this theological point is that while it is very important to be intellectually right in *conforming your thoughts to reality*, and most especially your thoughts about God, it is even more important to be morally and religiously right, i.e., *to conform your reality to what God thinks* and reveals, especially what He reveals about His will for you.

For to obey His will is to become more real. To disobey is to lose your reality, your humanity, your you-ness. You can lose your very self, your very identity, in Hell. That is why the demon-possessed man in the Gospels cannot say "I" any more but only "we." He has disappeared into the demons that are possessing him, so when Christ asks him his name, he replies, "My name is Legion, for we are many" (Mk 5:9). That is what is at stake in every moral decision we make: we become more real or less real, more Heavenly or more Hellish, more true or more false, more "I" or "Legion," by conforming our wills and lives to God's will for us or to the Devil's will. For that divine will and Mind is our very identity. Hamlet has no identity outside Shakespeare or in opposition to Shakespeare. Nor have we outside of or in opposition to God.

Those fools (yes, there are fools!) who say that truth is created by our minds, that truth is "my truth" or "your truth", and that you can "create your own reality", are not just confused: they are maximally confused, they are falling into the greatest possible confusion: they are confusing themselves with God. Human minds can't make other human beings happy because human minds cannot make anything objectively real. Only God can. What others think of you can do nothing to you, only to them.

Power obviously makes you more like "Almighty God." So why doesn't it make us happy?

It would seem that happiness consists in power. For all things desire to become like to God ... (and) men who are in power seem ... to be most like to God....

(But) **God's power is** (identical with, one with, inseparable from) **His goodness; hence He cannot use His power otherwise than well. But it is not so with men. Consequently it is not enough for man's happiness that he become like God in power, unless he become like Him in goodness also.**

It is impossible for happiness to consist in power, and this for two reasons. First because power has the nature of principle (beginning) ... while happiness has the nature of last end. Secondly because power has relation to (is open to both) **good and evil, whereas happiness is man's proper and perfect good** (I-II,2,4).

Power, St. Thomas reminds us, is a means, not an end. It is something we begin with, something we use, something that is potential to its good use (e.g., nuclear power, or a sharp mind). But happiness is our end, our goal, our attainment, our actuality, not just our potentiality. That is his first argument against power as what happiness consists in.

And his second argument is that happiness is our supreme good, and therefore it excludes all evil. But power does not exclude all evil: it can exist in evil men, and often does.

We think too highly of power. "Almighty God"—it's almost His middle name for us. It's the first thing we think of when we say "God". We use "Good God" not as His middle name but as a swear word!

But nowhere in His revelation does it say "God is power." It does, however, say that "God is love" (1 Jn 4:8).

Love is not power. Power struggles ruin love, or show that love is already ruined. Love does not seek power, nor does it seek the freedom that consists in power. (There is also another, higher freedom than that.) Lovers don't want to be free; they want to be bound to their beloved. They never talk about freedom. Why? Because they are already free, in a much higher sense. They are free because love is the truth of our being, love is our true destiny, and "the truth will set you free" (Jn 8:32).

Truth became incarnate. Right after saying "the truth will set you free", Christ says, "So if the Son makes you free, you are free indeed" (Jn 8:36). The Son of God is truth (Jn 14:6), for He is the *Logos* (Jn 1:1, 9, 14), the very Mind of God. If you have Him—if He has you—you are free indeed.

That is why the martyrs laugh and sing and joke and forgive as they die. They have found the higher freedom, they are free—not from their bodies or from pain or from death, but from sin, from selfishness, from lovelessness, which is the ultimate slave-driver. They are not happy *because* they are suffering the loss of their lower freedom, their natural human powers, but *despite* that. They are not masochists, they are lovers. They are happy because they have attained their higher freedom and are free even from their need for the lower freedom now.

Most of us would not be so stupid as to say that happiness consists in power. But many of us would say that it consists in freedom, and what most of us mean by "freedom" is usually only power. You might think that you're not free if you are in jail, or chained, or paralyzed, or enslaved. But you would be wrong if you think that, for "stone walls do not a prison make / Nor iron bars a cage."

If freedom is only power, and if "all power tends to corrupt", then so does freedom. There's something wrong with that, something missing there, some other kind of freedom that's being forgotten when freedom is confused with power. For Christ came to set us free, and He did not say that power will make you free, but that truth will. Obviously, He has a different concept of freedom.

Ghandi understood that concept of freedom. He wrote: "God is not in strength but in truth."

"If you have your health, you have everything." Isn't that true? What else do we need?

Bodily health is internal, unlike money, things, honor, fame, glory, or power. So it's closer to true happiness than any of those things. What's still missing?

Man surpasses all other animals in regard to happiness. But in bodily goods he is surpassed by many animals: for instance, by the elephant in longevity, by the lion in strength, by the stag in fleetness. Therefore man's happiness does not consist in goods of the body.

... all goods of the body are ordained to the goods of the soul as to their end.... Just as the body is ordained to the soul as its end, so are external goods ordained to the body itself. And therefore it is with reason that the good of the body is preferred to external goods ... (I–II,2,5).

Who is it who typically says "If you have your health you have everything?" Only old people, not young people. Only those who have lost their health, not those who have it. Those who have it know by experience that it is not "everything", for even if they have perfect health, they do not have perfect happiness.

Why? For an embarrassingly obvious reason: because we are not mere animals. A trip to the zoo refutes this candidate for happiness. Look at the logic of St. Thomas' simple syllogism in his first paragraph.

No animal can be as happy (or unhappy) as man. But animals can excel men in any bodily good. Therefore man's happiness cannot consist in bodily goods.

Then look at the reason for it in his second paragraph. The body is indeed important—because it is the matter for the soul, the means for the soul. You do not "have" a soul in the same sense as you "have" a body; you are a soul. And even though you are a body too (it is not just something you have as you have clothing), yet you "are" not a body in the same sense as you "are" a soul. Your soul is like your meaning and your body is like your words. Your soul is like the music and your body is like the notes. Your body is your outside and your soul is your inside. And that is why health cannot be the whole of happiness. In fact, health is an inadequate answer for the very same reason why it is a more adequate answer than any of the external goods, or "goods of fortune": it is not internal enough. Soul-health is a better answer than body-health because it is more internal.

We reverse the order of reality when we use our mind only to serve our body and when we use our body only to get external things. We harmonize with the order of reality only when we use our body to serve our soul and when we use the things of the world to serve our body. Things are to be used as means, and people (including ourselves) are to be loved as ends, not vice versa. Our bodies are halfway in between: bodies are parts of our personhood and also parts of the material world. They are both subjects and objects.

Thus there are three degrees of interiority, or internality, or I-ness: (1) my stuff, (2) my body, and (3) my soul; (1) mine, (2) me, and (3) I; (1) the objects of the self, (2) the objectifiable self, and (3) the non-objectifiable self.

But there is something even more internal than the goods of the soul, as we will find out a few pages later. It is God, Who, as St. Augustine profoundly says, "is more intimate to me than I am to myself".

Everybody wants pleasure, just as everybody wants to avoid pain, and not just as a means to any further end. Pleasure is sought as an end in itself. So why isn't pleasure or delight the same as happiness?

Because bodily delights are more generally known, *the name of pleasure has been appropriated to them,* **although other delights excel them; and yet happiness does not consist in them ...** (I-II,2,6).

"Other delights excel them." Everyone who has experienced both bodily pleasures and spiritual pleasures agrees. The pleasures of the soul are deeper, better, profounder, more variously and lastingly and truly delightful than the pleasures of the body. That is why love is not only more moral than lust but also more joyful. That is why sex with strangers or prostitutes is not joyful, just pleasurable. If you don't agree, that only proves that you have never really tried both kinds of pleasure. Try it, you'll like it!

The questioner might continue: If I'm not just my body, I understand why physical pleasures alone can't make all of me happy, can't make the innermost "me" happy. But "pleasure" means more than just physical pleasures. Isn't pleasure the same as happiness if we mean spiritual pleasures? What's the difference between pleasure and happiness if we always seek both as ends, never as means?

It would seem that man's happiness consists in pleasure, for since happiness is the last end, it is not desired for something else, for other things for it. But this answers to pleasure more than to anything else....

(However, pleasure or) **delight is desirable for something else, i.e., for the good which is the object of that delight and ... gives it its form** (I-II,2,6).

St. Thomas does not mean here that we seek pleasure as a *means* to this "something else", this true good, but that we are pleased *because of* this "something else". Something must *cause* us to be

pleased with it, and that something is our true good. "Happinesss" does not mean merely "subjective contentment". It means "our true good". We should not confine "happiness" to a feeling, nor "good" to "morally obedient". If we do that, we narrow and misunderstand both, and put them in opposition. In reality, happiness and our true good are identical. Our true good is the rose, and happiness is the smell it gives off. Or happiness is the rose and pleasure the smell. We smell the rose, not the smell.

St. Thomas makes this point in two ways. (The two are not alternatives but two dimensions of the very same point.) Pleasure is a "proper accident" of happiness, not its essence; and it is an effect of happiness, not its cause:

... every delight is a proper accident (natural property) **resulting from** (caused by) **happiness or from some part of happiness, since the reason that a man is delighted is that he has some fitting good, either in reality or in hope or at least in memory. Now a fitting good, if indeed it be the perfect good, is precisely man's happiness; and if it is imperfect, it is a share of happiness ... at least apparent. Therefore it is evident that ... delight, which results from the perfect good, (is not) the very essence of happiness, but something resulting from it as its proper accident ...** (I-II,2,6).

St. Thomas' point is very simple, and you don't need to be a saint to see it. We are pleased, i.e., we experience pleasure, only when something causes it. Something that is really there, something objectively real, causes in us the subjective feeling of being pleased. We are pleased *at this,* not just "pleased". So it is the "this" that is our true good and the cause of our subjective happiness. We have not yet found out what that "this" is merely by saying that we are pleased, or experience pleasure, whenever we are truly happy and blessed. What blesses us? What causes our pleasure?

62. WHY EVEN MORAL VIRTUE ALONE CAN'T MAKE YOU HAPPY

The typically modern mind identifies religion with morality. Isn't that the heart of it, and the most important thing of all? Isn't that the ultimate end and point of life: to be morally good? So happiness would then consist in the good of the soul, which would be intellectual and moral virtue.

If ... we speak of man's last end as to the thing itself which we desire as last end, it is impossible for man's last end to be the soul itself or something belonging to it. Because the soul, considered in itself, is as something existing in potentiality, for it becomes knowing actually from being potentially knowing, and actually virtuous from being potentially virtuous. Now since potentiality is for the sake of act as for its fulfillment, that which in itself is in potentiality cannot be the last end. Therefore the soul itself cannot be its own last end (I-II,2,7).

Could you be happy without God if you were good enough? If so, there is no God. God is not God if He is not your ultimate meaning and end and happiness. *You* are not that—your own end—not even a morally perfect you. God did not design you to be perfect alone. Even God is not alone; He is together, He is a family, a society, a Trinity. That is why "it is not good for man to be alone" (Gen. 2:18): because he is created in the image of the Trinitarian God.

Your own virtue, even genuine and perfect virtue, is not your happiness. God is your happiness. In fact, perfect virtue consists ultimately in this: forgetting yourself and your virtue and caring only about God, knowing and loving God.

In fact, when virtue makes itself its own end, it becomes the worst of vices, Pharisaical pride. The alternative, humility, is not a low self-image, it is *no* self-image, it is blissful self-forgetfulness. Even earthly pleasures teach us that lesson: as soon as we turn from the thing we are pleased with, the sunset or symphony or sex or scotch, to think of ourselves, the pleasure is gone. The deepest pleasures are always self-forgetful. That is why the word "ecstasy" has two related meanings: "standing-outside-yourself", which is the literal meaning, and "highest joy". "Oh what a good boy am I!" makes you a bad boy, a proud one. "I am now having a religious experience; how interesting!" makes any religious experience you had disappear like a bubble being pricked by the knife of self-conscious analysis.

St. Thomas gives us the metaphysical principle behind this experiential fact: the soul is not complete, not finished; it is in potentiality, in process. It is not the golden castle, it is the golden chariot journeying to the golden castle along the golden road. God is the castle, and the road is the world.

To put the point in more abstract and literal terms, although the soul is not in space and matter, as the body is, it is in time. In fact, it is in two kinds of time: the time that is relative to material bodies passing through space, which is *kronos,* and the time of mind and will and spirit, the time of meaning and purpose, which is *kairos.* But both are time. Souls grow, minds mature, humanity lives through a history of consciousness as well as a history of material civilization, both collectively and individually. The soul is not its own end, as the flying arrow is not its own target. The arrow of our souls flies to God as the target—unless the arrow is so badly bent that it flies backwards, in which case it pierces the eye of the archer and makes him blind as a Pharisee.

63. WHY NOTHING BUT GOD CAN POSSIBLY
EVER MAKE YOU COMPLETELY HAPPY

I know St. Thomas says that only God can make you happy. But isn't that a matter of faith, not reason? And isn't that true just for the saints, or for religious people? Why does he have to impose his values on everyone else? Is there a logical, necessary, universal reason for this exclusivism?

It is impossible for any created good to constitute man's happiness. For happiness is the perfect good, which satisfies the appetite altogether; else it would not be the last end, if something yet remained to be desired. Now the object of the will, i.e., of man's appetite, is the universal good, just as the object of the intellect is the universal true. Hence it is evident that nothing can satisfy man's will except the universal good. This is to be found not in any creature but in God alone, because every creature has goodness by participation. Wherefore God alone can satisfy the will of man.... Therefore God alone constitutes man's happiness.

Augustine says: *As the soul is the life of the body, so God is man's life of happiness* (I-II,2,8).

Your body is much smaller than the universe, but your heart is much bigger—infinitely bigger. Your heart is that which loves, that which desires, that which seeks, that which hunts and hungers for happiness. Your heart has a hole in it, like a keyhole. It is a very strangely shaped hole, but, then, Christianity is a very strangely shaped religion. Neither of these two shapes is obvious, both seem at first sight surprising, even incredible, but *they match.*

They match in size as well as shape. The keyhole is bigger than the universe. The entire universe isn't a big enough key to turn that lock and open the secret of your heart. You are a God-sized keyhole, a God-shaped vacuum, an infinitely deep canyon that you keep trying to fill with finite rocks.

Either *nothing* fills it, and life's deepest desire, unlike all other desires, is meaningless because it points to nothing real; or else God alone can fill it. Take your choice. Choose ultimate meaninglessness if you wish. Perhaps you can't be definitively proved to be wrong. But what a stupid choice it is!

What do you get out of that? What can you possibly gain? Or choose ultimate meaningfulness if you wish. Perhaps you can't be definitively proved to be right. But what can you lose? And what a glorious choice it is! What an adventure, what a hope, what a meaning and light and love and purpose that choice infuses into life! If you love life, why not believe, surrender, accept God's marriage proposal to your soul? You have nothing to lose but your pride and your misery. (They always go together.)

St. Thomas does not claim to prove here that God *will* satisfy your soul. But he does prove that "God *alone can* satisfy." That is, he proves (1) that *nothing but* God (the true God, the real God, the God of love, not the gods of paganism or modernism or Phariseeism) can satisfy your deepest longing, and (2) that God *can*. Whether He *will* or not is up to His will and yours: His will to give and yours to accept. Gifts must be freely given and freely received. In fact He will make love to your soul and make it spiritually pregnant, but He will not rape you. He leaves you free to say No. You just have to trust Him for the first part, His willingness to give. But the second part, your willingness to receive, is up to you.

God is not an option for "religious people" (whoever they are). God is the only game in town. God is the very life of your soul as the soul is the life of your body. That's the point St. Thomas makes in quoting St. Augustine. (All of St. Thomas is really only an enormous elaboration and explanation of St. Augustine, especially his most famous saying, "Thou hast made us for Thyself, and (therefore, that's why) our hearts are restless until they rest in Thee.") The point is simple: Your body isn't happy without your soul. A body without a soul is a corpse. And your soul isn't happy without God. A soul without God is a spiritual corpse, a zombie. There are real zombies: spiritual zombies, not physical zombies. Jesus came to earth to save the zombies. Jesus died so that He could put life—His life—into your soul.

He does this in an astonishing way: you drink His blood. Really. (I warned you it was a very strangely shaped key!) That's what He said (Jn 6:53). Salvation is a blood transfusion.

Since neither external goods, nor goods of the body, nor goods of the soul, constitute happiness, but only God, does that mean that our body and our senses play no part in our true happiness except to distract us and tempt us? Why did God give them to us? What is their role in our attaining happiness?

A thing may belong to happiness in three ways: (1) essentially, (2) antecedently (before, as cause), **(3) consequently** (after, as effect). **Now the operation of sense cannot belong to man's happiness essentially. For happiness consists essentially in his being united to the Uncreated Good, Which is his last end, as shown above, to which man cannot be united by an operation of his senses** ... (and also) **because, as shown above, man's happiness does not consist in goods of the body, which goods alone we attain through the operation of the senses. Nevertheless the operations of the senses can belong to happiness both (2) antecedently and (3) consequently.**

(2) Antecedently, in respect of imperfect happiness such as can be had in this life, since the operation of the intellect demands a previous operation of the sense. (Your senses feed your mind and heart; if you sense nothing at all, you can know nothing and can desire nothing.)

(3) Consequently, in that perfect happiness which we await in heaven, because at the resurrection, *from the very happiness of the soul,* **as Augustine says,** *the body and the bodily sense will receive a certain overflow, so as to be perfected in their operations....*

In perfect happiness the entire man is perfected in the lower part of his nature by an overflow from the higher (point (3)). **But in the imperfect happiness of this life, it is otherwise: we advance from the perfection of the lower part to the perfection of the higher part** (point (2)) (I-II,3,3).

But speaking of perfect happiness, some (heretics) **have maintained that ... it is necessary for the soul to be entirely separated from the body.... But this is unreasonable. For since it is natural for the soul to be united to the body, it is not possible for the perfection of the soul to exclude its** (the body's) **natural perfection.**

Consequently, we must say that perfect disposition of the body is necessary, both (2) antecedently and (3) consequently, for that happiness which is in all ways perfect.

Antecendently, (a perfect body is necessary) **because, as Augustine says,** *if the body be such that the governance thereof is difficult and burdensome ... the mind is turned away from that vision of the highest heaven.* **Whence he concludes that** *when this body will no longer be 'natural' but 'spiritual,' then will be its glory which erstwhile was its burden.*

Consequently, because from the happiness of the soul there will be an overflow on to the body so that this too will obtain its perfection (I-II,4,6).

Heaven is not bodiless, a place for angels only. It includes a resurrected body, without which we are not complete human beings. God did not make a mistake in making us embodied creatures, and He will not undo His perfect plan. We alone are both spirit and matter; we alone hold all creation together.

And the pilgrim road to Heaven is not bodiless either, a road fit for angels. It includes bodily joys and sufferings, both of which we can and should offer to God in trust. It includes learning to ride these beautiful but unruly horses. C. S. Lewis says, in *Miracles,* "The old field of space, time, matter, and the senses is to be weeded, dug and sown for a new crop. We may be tired of that old field; God is not.... These small and perishable bodies we now have were given to us as ponies are given to schoolboys. We must learn to manage: not that we may some day be free of horses altogether, but that some day we may ride bare-back, confident and rejoicing, those greater mounts, those winged, shining and world-shaking horses which perhaps even now expect us with impatience, pawing and snorting in the King's stables."

65. Happiness is the "Beatific Vision"

Isn't St. Thomas too intellectualistic when he says that the essence of our happiness is an intellectual vision of God? He makes our ultimate end and happiness center on contemplation rather than action, knowing rather than loving. Doesn't that demote love from the highest place, and isn't that pagan Greek philosophy rather than Christian religion? Isn't that Aristotle rather than Christ?

Our Lord said (Jn 17:3): *This is eternal life: that they may know Thee, the only true God.* Now eternal life is the last end.... Therefore man's happiness consists in the knowledge of God, which is an act of the intellect.

As stated above, two things are needed for happiness: one, which is the essence of happiness; the other, that is as it were its proper accident, i.e., the delight connected with it.

I say then that as to the very essence of happiness, it is impossible for it to consist in an act of the will.... For the will is directed to the end, both (1) absent, when it desires it, and (2) present, when it is delighted by resting therein. (1) Now it is evident that the desire itself of the end is not the attainment of the end, but is a movement towards the end; while (2) delight comes to the will from the end being present, and not conversely: a thing is not made present by the fact that the will delights in it. Therefore, that the end be present to him who desires it, must be due to something else than an act of the will.

This is evidently the case in regard to sensible ends. For if the acquisition of money were through an act of the will, the covetous man would have it from the very moment that he wished for it. But (1) at that moment it is far from him, and (2) he attains it by grasping it in his hand, or in some like manner, and (3) then he delights in the money got. And so it is with the intelligible end. For (1) at first we desire to attain an intelligible end; (2) we attain it, through it being made present to us by an act of the intellect; and (3) then the delighted will rests in the end when attained.

So therefore the essence of happiness consists in an act of the intellect, but the delight that results from happiness pertains to the will. In this sense Augustine says that happiness is *joy in truth* (I-II,3,4).

The cause is greater than its effect. But vision is the cause of delight. Therefore vision ranks before delight (I-II,4,2).

Now man's highest operation is that of his highest power in respect of its highest object; and his highest power is the intellect whose highest object is the divine good (I-II,3,5).

It is written (1 Jn 3:2): *When He shall appear we shall be like to Him because we shall see Him as He is.* Final and perfect happiness can consist in nothing else than the vision of the divine essence (I-II,3,8).

Love (desire) is the only vehicle that can get us there, and love (joy) is the song we will sing forever when we get there, but the glue that actually sticks us to God is knowing, seeing Him face to face. Christ Himself tells us that: "This is eternal life, that they know you the only true God" (Jn 17:3). It's personal knowledge, of course, not theory; acquaintance, not description; experience, not expertise; God, not theology. But it's knowledge: the kind of knowledge Adam had of Eve (Gen 4:1).

If all that is not convincing to you, then let's just say that when we get to Heaven we will all laugh at the very question whether our ultimate eternal joy is a matter of the knowing intellect or the loving will. For it may well be that that question is like whether we bought twelve eggs or a dozen, or like the question whether the moon is smaller than the sun or the sun is bigger than the moon. Ultimate knowing *is* the highest kind of loving and ultimate loving *is* the highest kind of knowing.

66. How we can get there from here

The old Vermont farmer joke about the lost driver concludes with the punch line: "You can't get there from here." Why isn't that true of Heavenly perfection? The ideal seems as far beyond our reach and capacity as flying would be to a tree sloth or climbing Mount Everest to a worm.

Since happiness consists in gaining the last end, those things that are required for happiness must be gathered from the way in which man is ordered to an end.

Now man is ordered to an intelligible end partly through his intellect and partly through his will: through his intellect in so far as a certain imperfect knowledge of the end pre-exists in the intellect; through the will, first by love, which is the will's first movement toward anything; secondly, by a real relation of the lover to the thing beloved ... (I–II,4,3).

The better analogy would be not the tree sloth or the worm but the caterpillar. We are programmed to fly, to be transformed.

St. Thomas mentions the three things necessary to attain any end, earthly or Heavenly: knowledge, love, and presence; our conceiving what to desire, our subjective desire moving to it, and it being or becoming really present. Applied to God as our last end, this means (1) moving toward Him with our minds, knowing God, which in this life is by faith; (2) moving toward Him with our will, our desire, which is hope, and (3) God's objective reality that is known and loved coming to us, moving toward us, letting Himself be united to us, which is love (divine charity).

Our divine life, our *theosis,* is like a plant. Faith roots the plant in the truth, hope makes it grow up into the heavens, and love is the flower or fruit it produces.

God has given us all we need to get us to Himself. He put the wings in the caterpillar.

God designed us to need and love each other. He will surely perfect that design in Heaven. Life without friendship is not a human life. How then can God alone suffice for our eternal happiness? Isn't that selfish and lonely? Won't we need human friends as well as God in Heaven to be happy? But if we need something besides God, wouldn't that make God only *part* of our true good, and thus something less than God?

(In the following answer, please keep clearly in mind that St. Thomas is not saying that we will not *have* friends in Heaven, only that we will not *need* them, for indeed if God alone is not enough to make us perfectly happy, then God is not God.)

Charity is perfected in happiness. But charity includes the love of God and of our neighbor. Therefore it seems that fellowship of friends is necessary for happiness.

If we speak of the happiness of this life, the happy man needs friends ... that he may do good to them; that he may delight in seeing them do good; and also that he may be helped by them in his good work....

But if we speak of perfect happiness which will be in our heavenly Fatherland ... man has the entire fullness of his perfection in God.... the fellowship of friends conduces to the well-being of happiness ... (yet) if there were but one soul enjoying God, it would be happy, though having no neighbor to love.

But supposing one neighbor to be there, love of him results from perfect love of God. Consequently, friendship is, as it were, concomitant with perfect happiness (I-II,4,8).

Just as our spirit's happiness will "flow over" into our glorified body, from its essential place in our soul to its additional place in our body, as a glorious "extra", so our love of God will "flow over" into our love of neighbor in Heaven, as it does on earth.

But not out of need. Our "horizontal" loves of each other in Heaven will be based on pure charity, not on need. We will love each other as God loves us: out of pure "overflow".

And even though it is right and good and necessary for us to need each other here, and to express that need-love, we also need to learn more of the pure gift-love, the pure charity, that is the nature of God, because that is the love we will give and receive in Heaven. That's the relevance of Heaven to our daily lives: life in this world is dress rehearsal for opening night on the stage of eternity. To say the same thing in another analogy, God gave us time, and space, and matter, and the universe to be our spiritual gymnasium, and we need to work out every day. To use still another image, this world is our elementary school, and we need to learn its lessons so that we can graduate to high school and university when we die. Purgatory is high school, and Heaven is the university where we keep learning to love more and more forever.

68. Don't Expect Perfect Happiness in This Life

Can we be really happy in this world? How does St. Thomas avoid both the cynical pessimism of saying no and the naïve optimism of saying yes?

A certain participation in happiness can be had in this life, but perfect and true happiness cannot be had in this life. This can be seen from a twofold consideration.

First, from the general notion of happiness. For since happiness is a perfect and sufficient good, it (1) excludes every evil and (2) fulfills every desire. (1) But in this life every evil cannot be excluded. For this present life is subject to many unavoidable evils: to ignorance on the part of the intellect, to inordinate affection on the part of the appetite, and to many penalties on the part of the body.... (2) Likewise neither can the desire for good be satiated in this life. For man naturally desires the good which he has to be abiding. Now the goods of the present life pass away, since life itself passes away, which we naturally desire to have and would wish to hold abidingly, for man naturally shrinks from death. Wherefore it is impossible to have true happiness in this life.

Secondly, from a consideration of the specific nature of happiness, viz. the vision of the divine essence, which man cannot obtain in this life (I-II,5,3).

I've always had basset hounds because they look so sad that they make me feel happy. They do that by reminding me that this world is indeed a vale of tears, though it's both beautiful, in its own way, and hilariously funny.

If we expect this world to be a palace, we will be constantly complaining, and miserable; if we expect it to be boot camp, we will be amazed at how comfortable it is and will be constantly thanking God for all the fun we have. We are, after all, supposed to offer Him all our "prayers, works, *joys,* and sufferings" in our Morning Offering. I think the joys are the hardest item of the four to offer up, because they tend to make us forget Him instead of making us remember Him with thanksgiving, which is what they're supposed to do, and why they exist and why God gives them to us. Maybe that's why He doesn't give us more. Maybe the more grateful we are, the more things we will get to be grateful about. God will say: "Good; you've learned that lesson. I can trust you to learn another one."

Pre-modern cultures had far fewer creature comforts than we do. They didn't have science and technology to remake the world in the image of our own desires. They didn't even have anesthetics! Think for a moment about the physical pains in the average life of a medieval peasant. And yet they were *happier* than we are—as the people in poor societies, like the Caribbean, are often happier than the people in the richest societies (Europe and North America). Want hard proof of that? Compare the suicide rates. What is the poorest continent in the world? The same one that smiles the most: Africa. Compare photos of Africans with photos of everyone else, and compare the smile count.

Expect the world to be Heaven, and it will feel like Hell. Expect it to be Purgatory, and it will feel like Heaven. The two most salient facts about Purgatory are pain and hope, suffering and meaning. It's labor, travail, childbirth. It's hard work, but it's much more meaningful and fulfilling than pointless leisure. It's even *happier,* even though it's not more *comfortable.*

This world is a big womb, a giant nursery, an elaborate nativity set, a cosmic crèche. What the angel said to Mary, God says to us too, and in these words is the meaning of life—of our life as well as Mary's: "The Holy Spirit will come upon you, and the power of the Most High will overshadow you; therefore the child to be born will be called holy, the Son of God" (Lk 1:35). Christ wants to be born in us too. He wants to become really present in our souls, as He becomes really present on the altars of all the Catholic churches in the world. In these two places, the extensions of the Incarnation keep happening again and again. We're in labor. Come on now, push!

69. ETERNAL SECURITY?

Protestant fundamentalists usually insist that we can and should be certain of our salvation; and Calvinists usually say that we have "eternal security": "once saved, always saved." Are they right?

(1) **Now it is impossible for anyone seeing the divine essence to wish not to see it.... It is thus evident that** (once he attains this Heavenly vision) **the happy man cannot forsake happiness of his own accord. (2) Moreover, neither can he lose happiness through God taking it away from him. Because, since the withdrawal of happiness is a punishment, it cannot be enforced by God, the just Judge, except for some fault; and he that sees God cannot fall into a fault, since rectitude of the will of necessity results from that vision. (3) Nor again can it be withdrawn by any other agent, because the mind that is united to God is raised above all other things, and consequently no other agent can sever the mind from that union.... (4)** (And) **it seems unreasonable that as time goes on man should pass from** (this) **happiness to misery** ... (because perfect) **happiness is consummate perfection, which excludes every defect from the happy. And therefore whoever has happiness has it altogether unchangeably. This is done by the divine power, which raises man to the participation of eternity** ... (I-II,5,4).

The fundamentalists and Calvinists are profoundly right in a sense: they're right about Heaven though not about earth. Our faith here can only be in God, not in our faith (that's presumption). He will never abandon us, but we can abandon Him. That's why we must be vigilant.

St. Thomas gives us the reason both for "eternal security" in Heaven and the lack of it on earth. What gives us this security, what makes it impossible for us to abandon God, is the Beatific Vision. When we see God as He really is, it will be psychologically impossible for us not to love Him, or to love anything else more than Him. But without that vision, it is possible for us to be as insane as we are, and to prefer something else to God, to succumb to the Devil's advertisements. We are suckers.

Everyone always wants happiness, whether they're good or evil, whether they're on the road to Heaven or to Hell, whether they're on earth or already in Heaven. But on earth our will can be selfish and stubborn, and our reason can be blinded by our passions, or by its own choice to be guided by blind passions rather than by true reason. In Heaven, not.

In other words, here our minds are not so filled with light that they move our wills infallibly. Here, our wills can move our minds. Here, we are still at sea and not in our home port, and here the captain of our soul, the will, can be willful and say to the navigator, who is reason, when the navigator presents to the captain the charts that tell the ship where to go and where not to go, "Shut up. Go below. I don't want to look at your charts." But in Heaven, the captain will *see* where the ship is: in the dock, in Heaven, in Paradise. He won't need faith. It won't be a choice. In other words, in Heaven the captain (the will) and the navigator (the reason) will be one, with no room for opposition between them.

When you're in a burning building looking out of the twentieth story window down to the street and all you see is clouds of billowing smoke, you have to choose to believe the firemen below who tell you they have a safety net and it's safe to jump. When the clouds of smoke disappear, you don't have to believe any more: you see it. In this world, it's a leap in the dark; in the next world, it's a leap in the light.

That's why it's so important to get our reason and will in order here: because of the smoke. Many leaps are needed. Virtue doesn't always look like joy and vice doesn't always look like misery, so we have to choose to listen to God, not Satan. We have to keep doing the opposite of what Eve did.

We can do that because that's what Mary did, because her doing *that* ("fiat!") brought to us our Savior, and we can do that only because He is in us, He is the one Who does it in us. But we have to let Him. He won't force us, as He didn't force her: He's big on freedom, He's a gentleman, He says "Please."

Shouldn't human happiness and fulfillment be attainable by human nature, just as the happiness and fulfillment and end of any other creature—dog or angel or bird or even plant—is attainable by its nature?

It would seem that man can attain happiness by his natural powers. For nature does not fail in necessary things.

Just as nature does not fail man in necessaries, although it has not provided him with weapons and clothing, as it provided other animals, because it gave him reason and hands, with which he is able to get these things for himself; so neither did it fail man in things necessary although it gave him not the wherewithal to attain (perfect) **happiness, since this it could not do. But it did give him free-will, with which he can turn to God, that He may make him happy.**

Imperfect happiness that can be had in this life can be acquired by man by his natural powers.... But man's perfect happiness, as stated above, consists in the vision of the divine essence. Now the vision of God's essence surpasses the nature not only of man but also of every creature (I-II, 5, 5).

Man is different. There is nothing in the nature of a dog that demands anything more than doggy satisfactions. A dog does not, by nature, desire to become a human being, or even to be adopted into a human family—although when it *is* adopted into a good human family it is happier than it was in its mere doggy life. A plant does not want to become an animal, nor is there anything to suggest that it could. In fact, the only way this happens is by the animal eating the plant; but then the plant loses its plant life. The dog, on the other hand, when adopted into a human family and allowed to share a little bit of our human life, does not lose anything doggy. So our adopting a dog is a better

image or analogy than an animal eating a plant for God adopting us into His life, into the divine family of the Trinity.

Man is different because God put into him Augustine's "restless heart", which cannot find its rest anywhere except in Him. There has never existed, and never will exist, any such thing as a purely natural human being, a man in his merely natural state, with no relation to the supernatural. Man is the only creature that transcends his own nature. He is more than he is.

The "imperfect happiness" that "can be had in this life" does not satisfy us, as it does to every animal. We are the only animal that simply *cannot,* deep down, obey the first and greatest commandment of our modern-day prophets, the pop psychologists, viz. to "accept yourself as you are". We are the ones who are blessed not when we are satisfied but only when we are dissatisfied, only when we "hunger and thirst for righteousness", a perfect righteousness that cannot be attained in this life. And without that true righteousness we can never be our true selves and truly happy.

You are the King of Heaven's kid, not King Kong's kid. You are destined to sit on the lap of the King of Kings. Don't settle for less. You are a Prince of Heaven; if you have true self-respect, you will say "Hmph!" or "Pooh!" to the toys of earth. (St. Paul dared to use an even stronger epithet for them in Philippians 3:8: "*skubala.*" It's the s-word in English. Look it up.)

You see, detachment from worldly goods isn't onerous but fun once you *see* truly. It can become a game. We can take all the gold-plated *skubala* as a joke if we know the perfect happiness we are being readied for.

Don't grovel. Don't grovel to the pretty toys the Devil dangles on the string for you. Your Heavenly Father doesn't even want you to grovel to *Him,* but to love Him. Grovelers don't smile; lovers do.

Since happiness is in the will (attaining its true end), and secondly in the feelings (the feeling of satisfaction that results from the presence of the end), why is the *reason* so important for the attainment of happiness? Isn't St. Thomas too intellectualistic?

Happiness can be considered in two ways. First, according to the general notion of happiness; and thus of necessity every man desires happiness ... (for in this sense) to desire happiness is nothing else than to desire that one's will be satisfied. And this everyone desires. Secondly we may speak of happiness according to its specific notion, as to that in which it consists. And thus not all know happiness, because they know not in what thing the general notion of happiness is found ...

Since therefore happiness is to be gained by means of certain acts, we must ... know by what acts we may obtain happiness, and by what acts we are prevented from obtaining it (I-II,5,8;6).

If we don't know the road, we cannot attain the goal, no matter how much we desire it. The way to perfect happiness is Christ, Who said "I am the way, the truth, and the life" (Jn 14:6). And the "acts" by which we attain Him and happiness are faith, hope, and love.

St. Augustine imagined God speaking to him while he was vainly searching for happiness in sin: "Seek what you seek, but it is not where you seek it."

Reason, discernment, discrimination between the real good and the apparent good, between objective reality and subjective feeling—this is essential for happiness, and for salvation.

Pascal explains the nobility of reason in *Pensee* #347: "Man is only a reed, the weakest in nature, but he is a thinking reed. There is no need for the whole universe to take up arms to crush him: a vapor, a drop of water is enough to kill him. But even if the universe were to crush him, man would still be nobler than his slayer, because he knows that he is dying and the advantage the universe has over him. The universe knows nothing of this. Thus all our dignity consists in thought. It is on thought that we must depend for our recovery, not on space and time, which we could never fill. Let us then strive to think well; that is the basic principle of morality."

This "thinking well" has very little to do with IQ. It requires simplicity, not complexity. Simplicity or singleness of mind comes from simplicity or singleness or purity of heart: "Blessed are the pure of heart for they shall see God" (Mt 5:5). The heart (will) leads the mind here. "If your will were to do the will of My Father, you would understand My teaching" (Jn 7:17). Blessed Mother Teresa rarely used words of more than one syllable, but she understood life and love and God far better than any mere theologian.

St. Thomas is great because he is not a mere theologian, he is also a saint. His answer to Christ when He asked him what he wanted as his reward for writing the *Summa*, was "only Yourself, Lord". That's true intelligence.

Karl Barth was asked this question after his final lecture: "Professor Barth, we all believe you are the greatest theologian of the twentieth century. Tell us, please, what is the profoundest idea you have ever had." His answer came instantly: "Jesus loves me."

That kind of wisdom is the apex of reason and the secret of happiness. It's hard only because it's so simple.

Are there things the omnipotent God can't do? Is this one of them?

If it's *not* impossible for God to force us to will the good, why doesn't He do it?.

Violence can prevent the exterior members from executing the will's command. But as to the will's own proper act, violence cannot be done to the will ... (For) what is compelled or violent is from an exterior principle ...

God, Who is more powerful than the human will, can move the will of man, according to Prov. 21:1: *The heart of the king is in the hand of the Lord; whithersoever He will, He shall turn it.* **But if this were by compulsion, it would no longer be by an act of the will, nor would the will itself be moved, but something else against the will.... In like manner, a man may be dragged by force, but it is contrary to the very nature of violence that he be thus dragged of his own will....**

Violence is directly opposed to the voluntary, as likewise to the natural. For the voluntary and the natural have this in common, that both are from an intrinsic principle, whereas violence is from an extrinsic principle. And for this reason, just as in things devoid of knowledge violence effects something against nature, so in things endowed with knowledge it effects something against the will. Now that which is against nature is said to be *unnatural* **and in like manner that which is against the will is said to be** *involuntary* **(I-II,4,5-6).**

A meaningless self-contradiction does not suddenly become meaningful just because you say God can do it. "A free choice that is forced or compelled" is a meaningless self-contradiction. It means "a choice that is both voluntary and involuntary at the same time". What is voluntary comes *from* the will; what is forced comes *to* the will from outside and prevents it from doing what it will.

You may think you are being reverent or pious by saying that God can do what is in itself self-contradictory and therefore meaningless, but all you are saying is that God can do nonsense, which is like saying that God can do smrvvmff ffrvvmm. It does not even rise to the dignity of error or heresy. It says literally nothing.

God cannot and does not move the will from the outside, by violence (that is the meaningless self-contradiction), but only from inside, voluntarily; by love, not by force. When we choose to love, that is God operating on and in and through our will, our free will. God turns our freedom on, not off.

This is a necessary part of the answer to the atheist's No. 1 argument against God, the "problem of evil": if God is all-powerful and all-good, why doesn't He wipe out all evil? The hardest part of this question to answer is the deepest evil of all: Hell. Why doesn't God eradicate Hell? Because that would eradicate free choice. If we were forced into Heaven against our will, we would not be happy because we would not get what we will. Scratch the surface of free will and you find, necessarily, underneath it, the possibility of moral evil and even Hell, in the end.

If God respects our freedom that much, how dare we respect each other's freedom less? How dare we try to compel one another's will, override another's will, by violence? It is not only wicked, it is stupid, because it is impossible.

On the other hand, God can and does influence our will—freely, not violently; from within, not from without; by appeal to love, not force. We can and should do the same to each other.

73. IS THERE SUCH A THING AS PARTIAL FREEDOM AND RESPONSIBILITY?

Most human actions seem less than totally free, and therefore we seem to be less than totally responsible for them. Is this true?

Yes. That's why one of the three requirements for a mortal sin is full consent of the will. If we sincerely struggle, if we have a divided will, it is a sin of weakness, and venial, not mortal. (In fact, the struggle is a sort of anticipated repentance.)

Such things as are done through fear are of a mixed character, being partly voluntary and partly involuntary ... (for instance) **the throwing of the cargo into the sea ... during the storm, through fear of the danger ...** (I-II,6,7).

Does this mean that the sins of the flesh, sins of lust, sins of passion, are not sins then because they are partly involuntary? No. If we struggle against them, we have a double will. (It is actually a double will*ing*, not a double will; each individual has only one will.) The will to obey the sinful passion is an evil will, and the will to overcome the sinful passion is a good will. But the will to do a sinful act out of concupiscence is voluntary, not involuntary. Without that will, the act would not be done. We are responsible for sins of the flesh, just as we are responsible for any other sins. There is no such thing as an involuntary sin.

The involuntary act deserves mercy or indulgence, and is done with regret. **But none of these can be said of that which is done out of concupiscence** (disordered passion). **Therefore concupiscence does not cause involuntariness ... but on the contrary makes something to be voluntary. For a thing is said to be voluntary from the fact that the will is moved to it ...**

If concupiscence were to destroy knowledge altogether, as happens with those whom concupiscence has rendered mad, it would follow that concupiscence would take away voluntariness.... But sometimes in those actions which are done from concupiscence, knowledge is not completely destroyed, because the power of knowing is not taken away completely ... this is voluntary ... for the will can resist the passion (I-II,6,7).

It is a convenient but dishonest excuse to claim that passion is irresistible, or that the will is not free. But we know from experience that this is not so. Conscience also informs us of this fact, though we try to suppress that information, and sometimes succeed.

But it is only suppressed, not destroyed. If we imagine the soul as something like a computer, we can refuse to press the keys that make the information appear on the screen, but the information is still there inside the central processing unit. We cannot change our hardware; we cannot rip up our moral motherboard.

Plato thinks it is. He argues that if we were *not* ignorant—of the fact that choosing evil always makes us miserable and choosing good always makes us happy—we would never choose evil, because no one ever chooses to be unhappy. Even sulking resentment is chosen because it makes us feel good by feeling self-righteous. If sin didn't feel like fun, we'd all be saints.

Yet we all know from experience that we often sin not because we are ignorant of this fact—because we're not! We also know that education, which lessens ignorance, does not necessarily lessen sin. In fact, educated people can justify sins more easily than uneducated people can, because they are clever enough to rationalize their sins away.

But how can we sin knowing, as we do, that sin will always make us miserable? Are we insane?

St. Thomas, as usual, gives us the bigger picture, in which both of the above truths, which apparently contradict each other, are reconciled. He shows that Plato is right but only half right.

If ignorance causes a choice to be involuntary, then it excuses the choice. And sometimes this happens. But sometimes it does not. St. Thomas explains the difference by distinguishing three kinds of ignorance: (1) "antecedent" ignorance, before the choice, that influences the choice (this is the most complex case); (2) "concomitant" ignorance, during the choice, and (3) "consequent" ignorance, after and caused by the choice. Only the first makes the choice involuntary.

If ignorance causes involuntariness, it is in so far as it deprives one of knowledge, which is a necessary condition of voluntariness.... But it is not every ignorance that deprives one of this knowledge. Accordingly, we must take note that ignorance has a threefold relationship to the act of the will: in one way, *concomitantly*; in another, *consequently*; in a third way, *antecedently*.

***Concomitantly*, when there is ignorance of what is done ... [when] even if it were known, it would be done ... thus in the example given, a man did indeed wish to kill his foe but killed him in ignorance, thinking to kill a stag. And ignorance of this kind, as the Philosopher states, does not cause**

involuntariness, since it is not the cause of anything that is repugnant to the will ...

Ignorance is *consequent* to the act of will in so far as ignorance itself is voluntary ... as when a man wishes not to know, so that he may have an excuse for sin, or that he may not be withheld from sin; according to Job 21:14: *We desire not the knowledge of Thy ways*. And this is called *affected ignorance*.... Ignorance is [also] said to be voluntary when it regards that which one can and ought to know ... when does not take the trouble to acquire the knowledge which one ought to have....

Ignorance is *antecedent* to the act of will when it is not voluntary and yet is the cause of the man's willing what he would not will otherwise ... for instance, a man, after taking proper precaution, may not know that someone is coming along the road, so that he shoots an arrow and slays a passer-by. Such ignorance causes involuntariness ... (I–II,6,8).

An immensely practical conclusion follows: When we sin, we must first blind our mind to the truth. We do this voluntarily, by our free will, even if it is done subconsciously rather than consciously, i.e., even if we are not consciously aware of it as we are doing it. We are still doing it, and we are responsible for this. This is what Plato forgot: that the will can move the mind as well as the mind moving the will. The will can slap the mind's lips shut.

St. Thomas explains how this works, in his usual very practical and commonsensical psychology:

The will moves the intellect as to the exercise of its act. But as to the determination (content, meaning, information) **of the act ... the intellect moves the will** (I–II,9,1 ad 3).

The will, like a ship's captain, commands the intellect, which is like the navigator, to speak and to show him the maps and charts or to go away and shut up. The will is the "efficient cause", the mover, of the mind. The mind is the "formal cause", the designer, of the act. The mind informs the will about what is good and what is evil. But the mind does this only if the will allows it or commands it. We can make ourselves morally deaf. We can shut the lips of our own conscience. But we cannot kill it. There is always a moral navigator on board.

That explains the negative half: that we can blind our own minds. Here is the positive half: We can always choose to begin by listening to our conscience, our moral reason.

That is why Brother Lawrence's classic *The Practice of the Presence of God* is so deservedly popular. It is a very simple and effective aid to becoming a saint. Our very first choice is whether or not to "practice the presence of God", to look at the truth of God's reality and presence and will rather than only at our own desires. As Buddha said, "All that we are is determined by our thoughts." Let Christ be their Lord too.

Plato was right when he said that all evil comes from ignorance. He forgot that ignorance also comes from evil. He also forgot that we are not in Heaven yet. In Heaven there will be no sin because there will be no ignorance, and there will be no ignorance because all will practice the presence of God perfectly, and all will do this because all will see God's beauty face to face in the Beatific Vision. There will be no sin because there will be no temptation; the beauty of holiness will shine forth clearly as the sun, and never be dimmed by the deceptions of the Devil.

The Devil is a clever fisherman: he fishes for human souls by baiting his horrible hook with delicious-looking worms. In Heaven we will see through all the worms. We will see through his two main deceptions: that sin is fun and that sanctity is boring.

So the closer we can get to that Heavenly wisdom here on earth, the easier holiness will be for us, the more effortlessly we will choose the good. But it takes lifelong effort to get to that effortlessness.

Isn't passion just strong will? Isn't will just another name for passion?

Or is passion just another name for bodily desires?

No to both questions. Passions are neither acts of will nor acts of the body. Passions are feelings or desires. They are in the soul, not the body. But they are not acts of will. Will is an aspect of reason rather than passion. St. Thomas makes this clear by distinguishing the way the soul rules the body and the way the will and reason rule the passions:

As The Philosopher (Aristotle) **says, the reason, in which resides the will, moves, by its command, the irascible and concupiscible powers, not, indeed,** *by a despotic sovereignty,* **as a slave is moved by his master, but by a** *royal and politic sovereignty,* **as free men are ruled by their governor, and can nevertheless act counter to his commands. Hence both irascible and concupiscible powers can move counter to the will; and accordingly nothing hinders the will from being moved by them at times** (I-II,9,2).

St. Thomas divides the passions (feelings, emotions) into "irascible" and "concupiscible". Irascible passions hate or fear their object and desire to move away from it. Concupiscible passions love and desire their object and desire to move toward it.

Plato believed that the will had to obey the reason because there was no other source of guidance for it. But St. Thomas notes, commonsensically, that the will can obey the passions instead of the reason, and this accounts for the fact that we often know what is good and what is evil—even what is good for us, what is truly best for us, for our own ultimate happiness—and yet choose evil over good, choose what we know is not in our own best interests. We can choose misery over joy if our will, led by our passions, commands our mind to focus on the short-range pleasures and ignore the long-run miseries.

The passions are neither impotent nor omnipotent; they are potent. Plato's rationalism treated the passions as impotent. Emotionalism (probably the single most popular and most common psychological error of popular modern thought) treats them as omnipotent.

This not only explains, in theory, why Plato was wrong but also, more importantly, in practice, shows us how to avoid sin: subject the passions to the reason. The passions are not evil but they are stupid. They need a teacher. They are like horses who need a rider for their own good. Or, to change the analogy, the soul is like a school: the will is like the headmaster of the school; the reason is the teacher; and the passions are the students. The headmaster should always send the students to the teacher and send the teacher to the students. When the master (the will) allows those two powers (the reason and the passions) to go their separate ways, chaos results.

It is Christ, the *Logos*, the Word of God, the Mind of God, Who is the ultimate source of all teaching. So the "bottom line" of this point, as of the previous one, is to surrender all our students, all our passions, to Christ. Trust the Teacher: He loves you even (especially!) when He gives you hard lessons.

76. Does God move my will or do I?

If we are not pantheists, we distinguish ourselves from God (Duh!), so we naturally ask the question: when God gives me grace, does He move my will or do I? How can it be both? How can grace preserve my freedom of will?

It is written (Sir 15:14): *God made man from the beginning, and left him in the hand of his own counsel.* **Therefore He does not of necessity move man's will.... As Dionysius says,** *it belongs to Divine providence not to destroy but to preserve the nature of things.* **Wherefore it moves all things in accordance with their conditions, so that from necessary causes, through Divine motion, effects follow of necessity; but from contingent** (not-necessary) **causes effects follow contingently** (I-II,10,4).

This is a fundamental mystery of religion. "Religion" means, literally, "binding relationship". Religion is essentially the relationship between man and God. Both man and God are free. So religion is the mystery of the relationship between these two freedoms, these two free wills. God freely offers us grace, offers us His very self, and we freely choose to accept it or to reject it.

But how do these two wills meet? How can God move me without making me less free rather than more?

He does not move us without our free choice. And when both He and we move freely into a relationship (*both* move freely into a relationship—that's almost the very definition of love), it's not 50-50, or 100% and 0 or 0 and 100% but 100% and 100%. Every happily married couple knows that that's possible; for that's what happens when the two become "one flesh" without ceasing to be two. "One flesh" means one person, one embodied person, one body—as Christ has one body, not two, He being the Head. That's the image St. Paul used for marriage: Christ's relation to the Church: see Ephesians 5:32.

It's God's transcendence, as our Creator, that preserves our freedom. We are free because God is not Brahman, the pantheistic One and Only; we are not mere parts of Him. Parts are not free to choose their relationship with the Whole. And we are free because God is not a pagan god like Zeus either, not one of the many beings that exist in the universe. If He were, then when He moved us, He would move us from without, as Zeus supposedly moved the Greeks to cower in fear by throwing down his thunder and lightning. Rather, God is the transcendent Creator and Designer of everything in the universe, including us and our free choices, as an author is the transcendent creator and designer of everything in his novel, including the characters and their free choices. One character can compel another (e.g., Laertes compels Hamlet to die, Laertes kills Hamlet), but Shakespeare does not compel any of his characters. He does not take away their freedom (that is what *compulsion* does), he *gives* them their freedom. He decrees that some things (the choices of his characters) take place freely, by the characters' free choice rather than by necessity; and he decrees that other things (the setting, like falling leaves or rain) take place unfreely and by natural necessity (leaves and rain have no free will). God is our Author, and also the Author of the natural setting that is the universe. He is the Author of both freedom, in us, and unfreedom, in nature.

The great mystery of Christianity is that the Author has a relationship with His characters; that He steps into His book and says "Hello" to His characters. All divine revelation is a little bit like the Incarnation. Christ is the fulfillment of what God did throughout the Old Testament: the Author, without ceasing to be the transcendent, divine Author, steps into His own story and eventually even becomes one of His characters. He first speaks many words (plural) to His characters, and then becomes the Word (singular), the main Character of the whole story.

What's the difference? Is it a matter of degree? Are we just a little smarter? Do we just have more and different instincts, like a religious instinct?

Gregory of Nyssa says that *irrational animals act willingly but not from choice* ... **the difference between the sensitive appetite** (animal instinct) **and the** (free) **will is that ... the sensitive appetite is determinative to one particular thing ... whereas the will ... is indeterminate in respect of particular goods. Consequently choice properly belongs to the** (human free) **will, and not to the sensitive appetite which is all that irrational animals have. Wherefore irrational animals are not competent to choose.... An irrational animal takes one thing in preference to another because its appetite is naturally determinate to that thing. Wherefore as soon as an animal, by its sense or its imagination, is offered something to which its appetite is naturally inclined, it is moved to that alone, without making any choice** (I-II,13,2).

The difference between humans and animals is in two powers that we have that the animal does not: reason and free will, or free choice. These powers are not instincts. Instincts are unfree. They are necessarily determined to one thing only, as we are hungry only for food and thirsty only for drink and tired only for sleep and have sexual desire only for sex. We are like the animals in having animal instincts. But we are more. Animals see and will only the concrete particular good. We understand the universal good, and therefore are free to choose between various particular goods. That is why we have free choice.

Only free choice is meritorious, praiseworthy, or blameworthy. God does not praise or blame us for our animal instincts. That's why it doesn't matter morally how you *feel* when you pray or when you choose (although good feelings *help*), only your free choice to believe God, hope in God, and love God, counts.

How often we act like animals! How often we let instinct determine behavior.

(1) Sometimes this is both good and necessary, like breathing or eating.

(2) Sometimes it is neither necessary nor good, like sinning by following our passions contrary to our reason.

(3) And sometimes it is not necessary—the instinct, once recognized, is freely followed—but it is good, like choosing to do for God what our natural instincts incline us to do anyway, like helping the suffering out of instinctive compassion, or giving thanks out of instinctive gratitude. Our instincts can help us as well as hinder us. Most of our life is lived on the animal level; we can use our instincts as we tame animals; we can transform that part of ourselves into the raw material (the "material causes") for good choices. In fact much of moral character-building consists in forming and educating the instincts.

This is less onerous than it seems, since we have more good instincts than evil ones. Most of the things we do out of a combination of natural instinct *and* some free choice to follow the instinct have positive moral value—eating, reading, working, conversing, caring for our own and others' welfare—because they are acts that are natural and rightly directed to good ends. (See point #81, below.) That is the refutation of pessimism. The refutation of optimism is the fact that our instincts are not unfallen, so that all of the things we do and all of our instincts are prone to infection by some evil, especially the master evil of selfishness.

(4) And we can also act contrary to an instinct or animal passion, as animals cannot. For instance we can fast, as animals cannot; we can choose to offer up an innocent, orderly passion (hunger) for a higher good (God).

(5) We can also avoid sin by choosing to offer up and "mortify" a disordered passion instead of obeying it.

Aren't these two things contraries? Doesn't reason restrict our will and our freedom?

It is exactly the opposite: reason *creates* our freedom:

Man does not choose of necessity.... The reason for this is seated in the very power of the reason. For the will can tend to whatever the reason can apprehend as good.... And in all particular goods the reason can consider an aspect of some good *and* the lack of some good, which has the aspect of evil, and in this respect it can apprehend any single one of such goods as to be chosen or to be avoided. The perfect good alone, which is Happiness, cannot be apprehended by the reason as an evil or as lacking in any way. Consequently man wills Happiness of necessity, nor can he will not to be happy, or to be unhappy. Now since choice is not of the end but of the means, it is not of the perfect good, which is Happiness, but of other particular goods. Therefore man chooses not of necessity but freely (I-II,13,6).

Senses and sense appetites perceive only particular goods, like this particular piece of delicious food. Reason perceives good in general, and therefore—because of our reason—we can freely choose between different concrete particular goods, as animals cannot. They always act according to the strongest instinct that is driving them at the time: if they are more tired than hungry, they will sleep; if more hungry than tired, they will eat. They always see and respond to whatever particular good looms largest in their view, like train travelers passing telephone poles. They always play the piano keys that are closest to their hand rather than reading the sheet music. But we can follow the sheet music and choose which keys to play. Their life is only noise, while ours can be music, precisely because we have reason, which can understand universals.

God loves to hear the music His children play.

Our music can be ordered—when it is played in obedience to reason's sheet music—or disordered—as when an infant in a rage pounds on the keys. This is not freedom. The infant is not free to make beautiful music. Freedom requires the discipline, or discipleship, of reason, not just to regulate it from without, but to create it in the first place. We are not free unless we are good, and we are not good unless we listen to reason.

Hilary says: *It is an unruly will that persists in its desires in opposition to reason.* **But the goodness of the will consists in not being unruly. Therefore the goodness of the will depends on its being subject to reason.**

As stated above, the goodness of the will depends properly on the object (*what* is willed). **Now the will's object is proposed to it by the reason.... Therefore the goodness of the will depends on reason, in the same way as it depends on the object (I-II,19,3).**

If that title is true, then evil has no being; since all being is good; or else evil is good, if it has being.

We must speak of good and evil in actions as of good and evil in things: because just as a thing *is*, so is the act that it produces. Now in things, each one has so much good as it has being, since good and being are convertible (i.e., all that has being, has goodness and all that has goodness, has being).... But God alone has the whole plenitude of His Being in a certain unity, whereas every other thing has its proper fullness of being in a certain multiplicity. Wherefore it happens with some things that they have being in some respect and yet they are lacking in the fullness of being due to them. Thus the fullness of human being requires a compound of soul and body, having all the powers and instruments of knowledge and movement; wherefore if any may be lacking in any of these, he is lacking in something due to the fullness of his being. So that as much as he has of being, so much has he of goodness, while so far as he is lacking in the fullness of his being, so far is he lacking in goodness, and is said to be evil: thus a blind man is possessed of goodness inasmuch as he lives, and of evil inasmuch as he lacks sight.... Evil acts in virtue of deficient goodness. For if there were nothing of good there, there would be neither being nor possibility of action. On the other hand if good were not deficient, there would be no evil (I-II,18,1).

St. Thomas speaks of physical evil here, but also of sin. Insofar as sin *is*, insofar as it has some kind of being, there has to be some goodness even in sin. If there is no being in it, there is nothing that can be twisted and perverted. If there is no good, there can be no evil; if there is no being, there can be no non-being, or anti-being, or lack of being. What is evil about it is precisely that it is a lack of being that it should have. Evil is real, but it is a real lack of being, as blindness is a lack of the power of sight.

The better you are, the more real you are. The more evil you are, the less real you are. This is true of moral evil as of physical evil. Just as losing a limb by amputation, or losing your body by death, makes you less physically real, so losing virtue by sin makes you less spiritually real. Your soul can get sick and die just as your body can. Venial sin sickens it, mortal sin kills it. (Mortal sin does not kill its power to give biological life to its body, but it does kill its power to receive spiritual life, the life of grace, from God.) Heaven, and the people in Heaven, are far more real, unimaginably more real, than we are. Hell, and the people in Hell (if they are still people rather than ex-persons), are far less real, unimaginably less real, than we are.

Therefore whenever you see evil, look for the good behind it, the good that it is perverting. When you see a parasite, look for its host. When God saw the hate-filled persecutor of Christians, Saul of Tarsus, He saw a powerful mind and will that had been twisted by hate; and He untwisted it and filled it with His love; and thus Saul became Paul, the most powerful missionary in history. If Hitler had been a saint, how wonderfully he could have used his "charisma", his psychological power, and his strong will. Poor Chamberlain was not a fanatic of either hate or love; Hitler was a fanatic of hate; a saint is a fanatic of love. Hitler, like Paul of Tarsus, was closer to being a great saint than Chamberlain was. It's easier to change the direction of a speeding car by turning it around 180 degrees than it is to start up a stalled one. Alternatively, suppose St. Thomas Aquinas had used his astonishing mental powers in the service of atheism, or even Satanism. The world of thought would be in even deeper trouble, far deeper trouble, than it is.

The next time you meet someone with deep hate, fear, pride, or despair, ask God to show you the being behind the non-being, the man or woman behind the perversion of humanity, the healthy cells that are hiding behind the cancer cells. Sin is cancer; it only feeds on healthy cells. Rescue them.

What makes anything good or evil?

A fourfold goodness may be considered in a human action.

First ... as much as it has of action and being, so much has it of goodness. (This is the goodness of its being, or ontological goodness, that point #79, above, speaks of.)

Second, it has goodness ... which is derived from its suitable object. The "object" of an act means *what is done* by it. Is it a robbery or a payment? Is it taking an innocent life or saving one? Is it telling truth or telling lies? The moral law, summarized in the Ten Commandments, defines which objects (acts) are morally good and which are morally evil.

Thirdly, it has goodness from its circumstances. When one is hungry, eating is physically good and feeding is morally good; when one is full, not so. Married lovemaking is good, but not when medically dangerous. Sugar is good, but not to a diabetic. The moral law cannot define all the possible changing circumstances, so our reason and imagination and cleverness must play a major part in our moral judgment of concrete cases, in applying general principles to particular circumstances.

Fourthly, it has goodness from its end. The end is what we seek; thus it is our motive. It is in our motive and our desire before it is achieved in the world. This existence in our desires, this "motive", is subjective and psychological. Giving money to the poor, though objectively good, is not subjectively good if its motive is pride and vanity (I-II,18,4).

Thus for any act to be good it must be both ontologically good (the first point), and morally good, which includes doing the right thing (the second point), in the right way (the third point), and for the right reason and motive (the fourth point).

The second of these four dimensions (the rightness or wrongness of the act itself) is objective and absolute, the third (the circumstances or situation) is objective and relative, the fourth (the end or motive) is subjective and absolute. Thus morality is both objective and subjective, both relative and absolute, not at the same time in the same dimension but in its different dimensions.

Legalism sees only the second dimension, doing the right thing. Relativism sees only the third dimension, changing circumstances. Subjectivism sees only the fourth dimension, subjective motive. Every error sees a part of the truth, but fails to see another part. This is what makes St. Thomas so great: his synoptic vision of the whole.

A human act must be whole to be good, as the human body must have a whole set of working organs to be healthy. Any one malfunctioning organ can kill you; thus defect in any one of the three dimensions of morality can make the act wrong. Or, to use another analogy for the same point, a moral act is like a work of art. If a piece of music is too loud, or too long, or too sweet, or too sour, it is defective. Or if a story has unbelievable characters, or theme, or plot, or style, it is a bad story even if its other dimensions are good. Everything counts.

Is ethics a kind of "Remember your umbrella and boots" sort of thing, a P.S., an afterthought? Or does it color most of the things we do? How many moral choices do we make during an average day? Aren't most of our actions neither morally good nor evil?

... [E]very individual action must needs have some circumstance that makes it good or bad, at least in respect of the intention of the end. For since it belongs to the reason to direct, if an action that proceeds from deliberate reason be not directed to the due end, it is by that fact alone repugnant to reason, and has the character of evil. But if it be directed to a due end, it is in accord with reason, wherefore it has the character of good. Now it must needs be either directed or not directed to a due end. Consequently every human action that proceeds from deliberate reason, if it be considered in the individual, must be good or bad.

If, however, it does not proceed from deliberate reason but from some act of the (instinctive rather than deliberate) **imagination, as when a man strokes his beard, or moves his hand or foot, such an action, properly speaking, is not moral or human, since this depends on the reason. Hence it will be indifferent, standing apart from the genus of moral actions** (I-II,18,9).

We usually think that our lives, our choices, and our actions are something like 5% bad, 15% good, and 80% neutral. St. Thomas erases the neutral. But what's left is not a 3–1 majority of good over evil, but more like a 95–5 majority, because all those neutral acts are good too!

How do you make eating and falling asleep and getting dressed and driving a car morally good acts? Simply by having the right end, the right ultimate end, to your whole life, and intending them to come under that end. You may not understand or think about how driving your car to the supermarket is a step on the road to God, to Heaven, but it is. Especially if you offered up *all* your prayers, works, joys, and sufferings of each day this morning. God counts that. You may forget the covenant you made with Him this morning, but He doesn't. (See point #55, above.)

Everything that is distinctively human, that is, everything that proceeds from and obeys reason, is good. (There are also, of course, many things that we do without reason, like breathing or scratching an itchy beard.)

St. Thomas is a great optimist. There is far, far more good than evil in life, just as there is far, far more joy than suffering. The glass isn't half full, it's 95% full.

Unless, of course, God is not your God but you are your own God. In that case all these little acts are acts of worship to the wrong God. In that case, St. Thomas says, they are directed to an undue end. They must be either directed to the due end, the right end, the true end, or else a false one. That's St. Augustine's point in *The City of God*: there are only two "cities", two bodies of people: the invisible Body of Christ and the invisible Body of the World. As C.S. Lewis says in *The Great Divorce*, "There are only two kinds of people, in the end: those who say to God 'Thy will be done' and those to whom God says, in the end, '*Thy* will be done.'"

But because of the presence and power of the unconscious, even a conscious atheist or pagan may be directing his actions to the good, though wrongly conceived, like the polytheists in ancient Athens whom St. Paul said were already worshipping the one true God, though in ignorance (Acts 17:23).

Ethics is about good and evil. Everything human, if it's not evil, is good. Ethics is therefore not like an umbrella and boots; it's like food. It's not about a checklist, a postscript; it's about everything.

Should I listen to reason or to God?

Although the eternal law is unknown to us ... as it is in the Divine Mind, nevertheless it becomes known to us somewhat ... by natural reason, which is derived therefrom as its proper image (I-II,19,4).

... it is from the eternal law, which is the Divine Reason, that human reason is the rule of the human will, from which the human will derives its goodness. Hence it is written (Ps. 4:6-7): *Many say: Who showeth us good things? The light of Thy countenance, O Lord, is signed upon us;* **as though to say: "The light of our reason is able to show us good things and guide our will in so far as it is the light of (i.e., derived from) Thy countenance." It is therefore evident that the goodness of the human reason depends on the eternal law ...** (I-II,19,4).

... [T]o scorn the dictate of reason is to scorn the commandment of God (I-II,19,5).

Asking whether you should listen to God or to reason is like asking whether you should listen to Beethoven's Fifth Symphony or to the recording you have of it. It's like asking whether the earth is lit up by the sun or by sunlight. It's like asking whether you should obey your commanding officer or his commands. The natural law of reason is *a participation in* the eternal law of God (I-II,91,2). That means more than "an image of" or "an effect of". It means real sharing, real presence. That is why to disobey reason is to disobey God. Reason is His voice, His interior prophet, in our souls. We call that prophet conscience. (St. Thomas used two terms for it: "synderesis" was the awareness of its reality and truth and authority and rules, and "conscience" was the application of it. We use "conscience" for both.) Conscience is essentially the power of reason to know good and evil. It also gives us feelings of obligation (before an act) and of guilt (after an act), but it is reason before it is feeling.

If there is any one thing in St. Thomas that will probably surprise, and shock, and turn off, and be misunderstood by, the typically modern mind, whether Christian or agnostic or atheist or new-age-secular-humanist-relativist-subjectivist-whatever, it is how often and how highly he speaks of "reason". "Reason" means for him not "argument" or "logic" or "being like Mr. Spock" or "being like a computer". "Reason" means being like a human being. It means everything distinctively human. It means awareness, understanding, consciousness. It means alpha waves (awareness), not just beta waves and theta waves (perturbations). Perhaps the best single image for what "reason" means is *light*. Thus a mystic "seer" is doing something supremely *rational* in mystical experience.

Reason is *sacred* because it is an essential part of the image of God in us. That image changes *everything* in us, as light changes every color in the world it lights up. We share many things with the sub-rational animals: animal instincts, desires, feelings, sex, bodies, eating, communication; but we don't merely add another level by reason; we raise *all those things* up to another level by reason.

Even our bodies and their sexuality is a dimension of the image of God in us, according to Genesis 1:31. (See John Paul II's "Theology of the Body" on this.)

Animal eating becomes an act of community and charity. Sharing a meal is sacramental. The German language even has two different words for animal eating and human eating: *fressen* and *essen*.

The higher animals have feelings—that's why they make good pets and why it's evil to be cruel to them—but when feelings enter the domain of reason, in us, they participate in moral good and evil. Human compassion—the feeling as well as the act—is a moral good, a virtue or a participation in virtue; while doggy compassion, lovable and innocent as it is, is just a pre-moral good, an instinct.

Animals communicate by sounds, we communicate by words. Communication, like everything else, changes when the light of reason shines on it. This is because the light of reason is "the light of Thy countenance, O Lord ... shining upon us" (Ps 4:6).

Why must we always obey our conscience? Why is it sacred?

Since conscience is a kind of dictate of the reason (for it is an application of knowledge to action ...), to inquire whether the will is evil when it is at variance with erring reason is the same as to inquire whether an erring conscience binds....

And since the object of the will is that which is proposed by the reason ... from the very fact that a thing is proposed by the reason as being evil, the will by tending thereto becomes evil (even if reason is in error and the object is not in fact evil) ...

In like manner, to believe in Christ is good in itself, and necessary for salvation; but the will does not tend thereto except inasmuch as it is proposed by the reason. Consequently if it be proposed by the reason as something evil, the will tends to it as to something evil (Thus a belief in Christ that is dishonest or hypocritical is evil, not good, even if its object is in fact true.) ... **to scorn the dictate of reason is to scorn the commandment of God** (I-II,19,5).

Whether the will is good when it abides by erring reason? ... Whereas the previous question is the same as inquiring *whether an erring conscience binds*, **so this question is the same as inquiring** *whether an erring conscience excuses....*

... [W]hen ignorance causes an act to be involuntary, it takes away the character of moral good and evil ... when ignorance is in any way willed, either directly or indirectly ... due to negligence, by reason of a man not wishing to know what he ought to know ... it does not cause the act to be involuntary ... such an error of reason or conscience does not excuse the will.... [I]f a man's reason or conscience err through inexcusable ignorance, then evil must needs result in the will. Nor is this man in a dilemma, because he can lay aside his error, since his ignorance is vincible and voluntary (I-II,19,6).

St. Thomas, like the reason he champions, is soft as light and hard as nails; he will not let us escape our own conscience. If we claim we are not guilty for doing some evil because our conscience did not forbid it, since we did not recognize it as evil, he replies that perhaps our conscience *did* forbid our not wanting to know, our not seeking, honestly and open-mindedly, to know whether the act is in fact evil or not. "If it feels good, do it" is automatically evil, whatever "it" may be, because it means "Don't worry about your reason and conscience; let passion rule reason." And we all know in conscience that that is in itself a dishonest excuse, a rationalization.

Of course, "conscience" does not mean feeling. Feeling is a passion, and one of the things to be made *subject to* reason and conscience. Conscience is *a knowing*.

Do you want to meet God? Do you want to touch Him? Do you want to hear Him speaking to you? Do you want to know His will for you? Do you want to have a "religious experience"? You do this every time your conscience speaks. Seeking mystical experiences instead is a diversion and an excuse for neglecting this hourly, humdrum meeting with the divine will that confronts us, usually in an uncomfortable way. That's why we look for something else. Do you want to be a mystic? Conscience is mystical enough. Do you want to meet Absolute Authority? Listen to your conscience. Do you want God to come closer to you? No you don't; He is already too close for comfort in your conscience.

Ordinary conscience is sacred because it is the very voice of God speaking in your moral reason.

Here's an embarrassing truth for you: **A gloss on Matthew 12:35 says: *A man does as much good as he intends*** (I-II,19,8). Thus William Law tells you (in *A Serious Call to the Devout Life*) the only reason why you are not a saint: "Because you do not thoroughly intend to be." You know you can become a saint if you really wanted to. You have no excuse but your own inexcusable laziness, and no hope but God's mercy.

84. Holy subjective intentions or holy objective deeds?

Which of the two is the key to holiness?

... [F]or a thing to be evil, one single defect suffices, whereas for it to be good ... it is not enough for it to be good in one point only, it must be good in every respect.... [I]f the will be good from its intention of the end, this is not enough to make the external action good ... (I-II,20,2).

To ask whether objective deeds or subjective motives are the key to holiness is like asking which is the key to health, the heart or the lungs?

Morality is like a work of art, or like bodily health: all the dimensions must be good for the work to be good. An otherwise healthy body can die if any one of its systems fail.

... [T]he difference between good and evil is applicable to both the interior and external act.... [T]he interior act of the will and the external action, considered morally, are one act ... these two goodnesses or malices (evils), of the internal and external acts, are ordained to one another (I-II,20,3).

There is an inherent oneness between motive and act, whether good or evil. You can't murder or rape out of love, and you can't give your life for another out of hate. If you do a bad deed out of a good motive, the badness of the deed will pollute your motive too, if not immediately then in its future consequences; and if you do a good deed out of a bad motive, the bad motive will pollute the deed too, and what comes from the deed. No compromise with evil is possible.

We often wonder why a good intention is not enough. "Isn't sincerity of heart the only thing God cares about?" No. And here is the very simple reason why: **If ... by the external action no further goodness or evil be added, it is to no purpose that he who has a good or an evil will does a good deed or refrains from an evil deed—which is unreasonable** (I-II,20,4).

Nobody thinks sincerity alone is enough in his surgeon, his financial advisor, or his airline pilot. Only when we're not dealing with anything objectively real do we reckon good intentions sufficient. If good and evil are objectively real, then good intentions are not sufficient.

They are, of course, necessary—absolutely necessary. Good intentions are like roots: crucial beginnings, but not the whole plant. Good intentions are like babies: we start there, but we don't end there. In fact, it is only babies that we admire when they merely have good intentions, because we don't expect them to be able to do much else yet in the real world.

If you walk off a cliff sincerely believing that it is a swimming pool, you will not find water, you will find death. If you try very, very hard and very sincerely to make an odd number by adding only even numbers, you will not succeed, ever. But there are real moral roads as well as real physical and mathematical roads, and they lead to really different destinations. That's why God cares so much about deeds as well as intentions. Only three of the Ten Commandments (the first one, about adoring, and the last two, about coveting), define subjective intentions; the rest define objective deeds.

Augustine says while speaking of the passions of the soul: *They are evil if our love is evil, good if our love is good.*

We may consider the passions of the soul in two ways: first, in themselves, secondly, as being subject to the command of the reason and will. If then the passions be considered in themselves, to wit, as movements of the irrational appetite (only), then there is no moral good or evil in them, since this (moral good or evil) depends on the reason. If, however, they be considered as subject to the command of the reason and will, then moral good and evil are in them.

For the sensitive appetite is nearer than the outward members to the reason and will, and yet the movements and actions of the outward members are morally good or evil inasmuch as they are voluntary. Much more, therefore, may the passions, in so far as they are voluntary, be called morally good or evil. And they are said to be voluntary either from being commanded by the will or from not being checked by the will (I-II,24,2).

On this question the opinion of the Stoics differed from that of the Peripatetics (Aristotelians); for the Stoics held that all passions are evil, while the Peripatetics maintained that moderate passions are good.... The passions of the soul, in so far as they are contrary to the order of reason, incline us to sin; but in so far as they are controlled by reason, they pertain to virtue (I-II,24,2). ("Moderate" here refers to quality, not quantity. It's not that fewer passions are better, but that passions moderated by reason, formed by reason, in accord with reason, are good while those contrary to reason are bad.)

... [J]ust as it is better that man should both will good and do it in his external act, so also does it belong to the perfection of moral good that man should be moved unto good not only in respect of his will but also in respect of his sensitive appetite, according to Ps. 83:3, *My heart and my flesh have rejoiced in the living God,* where by *heart* we understand the intellectual appetite (will) **and by** *flesh* **the sensitive appetite** (I-II,24,3).

Just as eating is in itself neither good nor bad, but when it becomes a material aspect of a moral deed such as receiving the Eucharist, or eating poison, or gluttony, or cannibalism, it becomes good or evil. Sleeping is in itself neither morally good or evil, but a sentry sleeping on duty is evil.

In the third paragraph St. Thomas uses the analogy between physical deeds and emotions: physical deeds become morally good or evil when reason clicks in and they are consciously chosen. And the same applies a fortiori to the passions or emotions.

"Reason", remember, means not just "calculation" but something almost as broad as "consciousness". "Will" is "rational desire", or "reason plus desire". The "voluntary" is "what is done by the (free) will". Only voluntary acts are morally good or evil.

We should feel less guilty or less proud than we do about the bad or good feelings and emotions we can't help having, and we should feel more guilty or more proud about all the things we will— including the feelings we will. Bad feelings, when they arise spontaneously, are not morally bad; but when we will them, they become morally bad. Good feelings are not virtuous when they arise spontaneously, but when we will them because they are good, and the causes of good deeds, or when we enjoy them because they are the effects of good deeds, they become morally good. Good emotions are part of a saint's soul! The better you are, the more you enjoy being good.

So don't feel either guilty or proud of your feelings in themselves. All the "passions" (i.e., the emotions that just well up in us without our choice) are neutral, neither good nor evil morally (though some may be helpful and others dangerous) until we make rational choices, conscious choices that involve them. We feel aversion to a nasty person, or sexual excitement when we see a nice person. These are not sins. But when we plan or fantasize how we are going to make the nasty person suffer, or how we would seduce the nice person, that is sin. It takes reason and will to sin.

86. "My love is my gravity" (Augustine)

I know love is good, and commanded; but how strong is it? Is it already the strongest desire, the lord of our life, or do we have to struggle to make it that?

Augustine says that all the passions are caused by love, since *love yearning for the beloved object is desire, and having and enjoying it is joy* **(I-II,25,2).... All the other emotions of the soul are caused by love, as Augustine says (I-II,27,4) ... every agent, whatever it be, does every action from love of some kind (I-II,28,6).**

We have to struggle to straighten out our hearts, but not to make the heart first, and central. That's what "heart" means literally: the organ in the very center of the body, at the center of the circulatory system, the center of the body's life. The heart spiritually is the will, not the feelings.

It is under our control. Feelings are not. The love Christ commands is the love we can have simply by choosing it, not the love we can't control. How could what is not under our control be commanded?

Our job is not to make the heart beat, but to make it beat right. It's always the heart, the first. All that we are is determined by what we love. That king is always on the throne; our job is to educate the king. He has the final authority; we have to direct it to good rather than evil.

Thus all good is rightly ordered love. To be good is to *love* (will) the good. And all evil is wrongly ordered love, disordered love. To be evil is to love the evil: to love evil things, or lesser goods more than greater goods: things more than people or self more than God. That wisdom is from Augustine, and St. Thomas is even more Augustinian than he is Aristotelian, on all the most important issues (though not on technical details or terminology).

Augustine writes, "*Amor meus, pondus meum*", which means literally "My love [is] my gravity", or my weight. Love pulls us. We go where our love takes us. Love is our spiritual gravity, our mass, our density—and our destiny. It is earth's destiny to orbit the sun because it is drawn by the sun's gravity into a stable orbit. We must do to God what the earth does to the sun. We must have a stable orbit around God, and not leave Him for the darkness of outer space. We do this by love, which is voluntary, unlike physical gravity.

Since all the other movements of the soul are caused by love, we can educate and convert our emotions by educating and converting our love. If we love God with all our heart and our neighbors as ourselves, everything else will follow. Everything. Hillel was once challenged to say the whole of Jewish law while standing on one foot. He said: "Love and hate in your neighbor what you love and hate in yourself. That is the law. All the rest is commentary."

If our love is right, everything else will be right. Including our emotions. Love is, of course an emotion *too*, though it is more than that: it is first of all an act of the will, a choice. If our love is right, then everything will be right: our physical, external actions, our inner emotions, and our eternal destiny.

Even our thoughts. We think only if we want to, and we think about what we want to think about. Sin always begins with thinking about the fake joy the sin will bring us, thinking about Satan's advertisement instead of God's X ray. Thinking and loving always causally depend on each other. You will understand God and others only if you love them; but you can love them only if you understand them. You can't love x, the totally unknown. The more you love God, the more you will understand Him; and the more you understand Him, the more you will love Him.

What did Dante mean when he spoke of the love that "moves the sun and all the stars" in the last line in his *Divine Comedy*? Didn't he know it was gravity? In #86, above, St. Augustine said that love was a kind of gravity; is gravity also a kind of love?

Love ... differs according to the difference of appetites.... (1) natural things seek what is suitable for them according to their nature, by reason of an apprehension which is not in them but in the Author of their nature.... (2) And there is another appetite arising from an apprehension in the subject of the appetite but from necessity and not from free will. Such is, in irrational animals, the sensitive appetite, which, however, in man has a certain share of liberty in so far as it obeys reason. (3) Again, there is another appetite following freely from an apprehension (by the reason) **in the** (person who is the) **subject of the appetite. And this is the rational or intellectual appetite, which is called the *will*** (I-II,26,1).

We are not freaks. We fit into the universe. We are the keystone of the arch, the last piece of the cosmic jigsaw puzzle, the top creature on the cosmic totem pole. Everything else is a little like us, in a hierarchy of varying degrees—degrees of quality, not just quantity, since the rest of the universe is composed of different species, and species differ in quality, not just quantity. All human beings are a little like God, in a hierarchy of varying degrees of quantity, since we are all one species, and members of a species differ in quantity (quantity of humanity), not in quality. None of us are really apes, even though we try to act like them.

Everything in this hierarchy moves by love.

(1) Physical gravity is a physical form of love. That little rock is falling because it's in love with the big rock called the earth. Electromagnetism is also a physical form of love. That little electron, with its negative charge, is in love with the positive charge on the proton that it's orbiting around, like a man circling around a woman, or a hunter circling around a deer. Of course rocks and electrons don't know what they're doing; they don't know anything at all. But God knew what He was doing when He designed them. Infinite Love created many finite versions of love.

(2) Vegetative growth is another kind of love. That sunflower is growing because it's in love with its own maturity and perfection; and its roots are in love with water, so they're growing toward the water, and its leaves are in love with the sunlight (for photosynthesis), so they're growing toward the sunny side (heliotropism). It too knows nothing, yet it acts from within (as nonliving things don't), so it looks more as if it "knew" where the sunlight or water was.

(3) Animals do know something. Even an invisible microorganism knows where its food is, and where its enemy is, and therefore moves in one direction rather than another. Higher animals know in ways that more and more approximate human knowing.

(4) But only man knows consciously and rationally, and only man's loves can be conscious and rational and responsible through free will. We have in us all four kinds of love. Nothing else does. We are the summit and perfection of all the universe's loves.

88. Loving God more than knowing God

It seems that we can love only what we know, and the more we know, the more we can love. But we can know God very little. Therefore we can love God only very little. But this conclusion seems wrong. Can't our love exceed our knowledge?

(1) ... **knowledge is the cause of love....** **[G]ood ... can be loved only if known ...**

(2) **But some things are loved more than they are known.... [A] thing ... can be loved perfectly even without being perfectly known.... thus in this life God can be loved in Himself but cannot be known in Himself** (I–II,27,2).

Love stretches the lover out into the beloved, conforms the lover to the beloved, transforms the lover into something more like the beloved. Knowledge, on the other hand, in a way does the opposite. Although knowing the truth means conforming our ideas to the reality known rather than vice versa, yet the mode of knowing is determined by the nature of the knower. When we know something greater than ourselves, we can know it only in our terms, we can only drag it down to our level, so to speak. Thus we can only know God by human analogies, and not as He is in Himself, just as a dog can know us only by doggy analogies and in doggy categories. When we know a dog, we know it in a human way, a way superior to the way in which the dog can know itself. We can know a dog scientifically and philosophically, but a dog cannot know itself scientifically or philosophically. So when we know something less than ourselves, we raise it up to our level of comprehension, while when we know

something more than ourselves, we drag it down to our level of comprehension.

It would seem, then, that our limited knowledge of God would limit our love of Him. Yet this is not so. There is a severe limit to our knowledge of God but no limit to our love of Him. Our knowledge of God runs up against a wall, but our love of Him does not. It can expand infinitely.

This is true in Heaven as well as on earth. We will never know God adequately; we will always experience our own limitations in knowing. Yet our love can expand infinitely, both in this world and in Heaven.

Love can exceed understanding on lower levels of the cosmic hierarchy too. A dog can love us more than it knows us. Its affection can exceed its comprehension. And among human beings this is also true: a simpleton can love us more than a genius does, even though he cannot know us as well as the genius can.

To know why this is so—how this principle works, psychologically and ontologically—is less important than to use it. One way to use it is always to be dissatisfied with our love of God, for we can always love God more. Christ blesses this dissatisfaction: "Blessed are those who hunger and thirst after righteousness, for they shall be filled." (For "righteousness" is ultimately love.) Even in Heaven there will be a delightful dissatisfaction, for we will be filled forever by more and more love of the infinitely lovable God. For "all who seek, find", and we will always seek to love God more, and therefore we will always find that we will continually grow in our capacity to love Him more in Heaven. That is why Heaven will never get boring, even though it will never end.

What does love want, will, seek, desire, hope, or long for? What is love *for*?

Union is an effect of love ... every love is a *unitive force*.

... [W]hen a man loves another with the love of friendship, he wills good to him just as he wills good to himself, wherefore he apprehends him as his other self ... Hence a friend is called a man's *other self* (Aristotle) and Augustine says, *Well did one say to his friend: Thou half of my soul....*

... [L]ove moves man to desire and seek the presence of the beloved ... there is a union which is the effect of love. This is real union, which the lover seeks with the object of his love ... the effect of love is that the thing itself which is loved is, in a way united to the lover....*

... [T]he union caused by love is closer than that which is caused by knowledge (I-II,28,1).

It is written (1 Jn 4:16): *He that abideth in charity abideth in God, and God in him.*

... love makes the beloved to be in the lover, and vice versa ... according to Phil. 1:7,... *I have you in my heart....* **the lover is not satisfied with a superficial apprehension of the beloved, but strives to gain an intimate knowledge of everything pertaining to the beloved, so as to penetrate into his very soul....**

... [I]n the love of friendship, the lover is in the beloved inasmuch as he reckons what is good or evil to his friend as being so to himself (I-II,28,2). (See Mt. 25:40.)

What love desires is not just a feeling, something subjective. It would not be satisfied with the most perfect dream. It wants reality. Its goal is metaphysical, ontological. It wants to become really one with the real other that is loved. It wants the two to become one, separation to be overcome, union to really happen.

There are two kinds of love and two kinds of union: selfish and unselfish. In possessive and egotistic love, it wants to eat or swallow its object: if you love ice cream you want to eat it. In what St. Thomas calls the love of friendship, in altruistic love, it wants presence, the real presence of the friend, and wants the good of the friend.

All loves seeks union. And since (in Jesus' words) "all who seek, find"; since (in the words of the Hindu scriptures) "you can have what you want"; therefore love actually *produces* this union, in various ways (marriage, sex, friendship, altruism): it "makes the beloved *to be in* the lover", as St. Thomas says. It gives the lover a new being, a second being. When we love God, God literally comes into us and lives in our soul. For although other human beings often don't reciprocate our love, do not enter our being as we enter theirs, God always does.

When we love a friend, we seek his happiness and ours *at the same time*. For "a friend is the other half of your soul." We are happy when he is happy. We are happy not only for his happiness, be we are happy *in* his happiness. When we love God, we are happy when He is happy with us. We seek His approval, His "well done, good and faithful servant." We are like dogs to God. We are happy only when we make Master happy with us. ("Dog" is only "God" backwards. God loves to make puns.)

We cannot add to God's happiness, we cannot give anything to God—except our love. It is the only thing He cannot give Himself. And He genuinely cares about that—*passionately* cares about that, in fact so passionately that He enters the Enemy's own realm and endures the Enemy's worst on Calvary, the Hell of being forsaken of God—not because He needs us but simply because He loves us.

In Heaven we will do to God what God did to us on earth: we will so forget ourselves that we will "reckon what is good or evil to the friend (God) as being so to himself". The closer we can get to that in this world, the happier we will be. That is "ecstasy", or "standing outside one's self". The next passage is about that.

What is "ecstasy"? How can you "stand outside yourself" (which is what the word means)?

Dionysius says that the *Divine love produces ecstasy*, and that *God Himself suffered ecstasy through love*....

To suffer ecstasy means to be placed outside oneself. This happens as to the apprehensive power and as to the appetitive power. As to the apprehensive power, a man is said to be placed outside himself when he is placed outside the knowledge proper to him. This may be due to his being raised to a higher knowledge.... As to the appetitive power, a man is said to suffer ecstasy when that power is borne towards something else, so that it goes forth out from itself, as it were.... he wills the good of his friend ... (I-II,28,3).

Christ is the Father's eternal ecstasy. The Incarnation practiced this to us. We practice it to each other by unselfconscious love and by self-sacrifice.

The mystics are given the gift of total unselfconsciousness, so they see nothing left of themselves. That is why they say such apparently pantheistic things, like "I looked for myself and I was not there" or "I looked for myself and all I saw was God." Of course they're still there: if they weren't, they wouldn't be having a mystical experience! It takes a real self to forget itself. (Duh!) It takes a real self even to make the mistake that many mystics make (especially Buddhists) when they say that they see that there *is* no real self, that the self is an illusion.

But we non-mystics can approach this state. There is a difference of degree, not a difference of kind, between the total ecstasy of mystical experience and the partial ecstasy of human love, whether of God or of another human person or of some great beauty that blissfully blots out all the inkblots of self-consciousness. When we are engrossed in a work of fiction, we are having a mystical experience, an out-of-body experience. We are not just sitting in a comfortable chair in Boston, we are helping Frodo carry the Ring into Mordor. During the moments when the narrative works its magic on us, we "identify with", or find our identity in, the character in the novel rather than the reader of it. We are given a gift of grace, by the author of the novel (and, ultimately, by the Author of the author of the novel), so that we are "raised to a higher knowledge".

And this always goes together with love. We can separate intellect and will, knowledge and love, only in abstract thought, not in lived reality here. For if we do not love and seek and affirm the God, the human being, or the beauty that elicits our state of cognitive self-forgetfulness, we cannot and do not mentally and spiritually have it. It takes love to change the mind.

(That is the simplest answer, by the way, to the question that troubles many philosophers and scientists, the question whether computers think, whether there is such a thing as "artificial intelligence". The answer is no, because thinking never happens without willing—never, in God, in angels, or in men—and a computer has no will. It never says "No" to its programmer or user, only "Yes." And not freely. It is like a very mobile and flexible book. It knows nothing at all, because it has no will.)

Love and will are the keys to understanding. Thus Jesus says to the Pharisees, "If any man's will is to do his will, he shall know whether the teaching is from God" (Jn 7:17). To be carried out of yourself and "raised to a higher knowledge" by God, you must love God, want God. For He will not come unless He is called. He is a lover, not a tyrant.

Can a "cool" intellectual like St. Thomas be a zealot?

Dionysius says: *God is said to be a zealot, on account of his great love for all things.... Zeal ... arises from the intensity of love. For it is evident that the more intensely a power tends to anything, the more vigorously it withstands oppositions or resistance. Since therefore love is a movement towards the object loved, as Augustine says, an intense love seeks to remove everything that opposes it ... the very fact that a man hates whatever is opposed to the object of his love, is the effect of love* (I-II,28,4).

Zeal is part of love. Zeal includes hate—hate of the enemies of love. Love is intolerant of its enemies. And love has enemies: selfishness, coldness, pride. The Bible is abundantly clear about that.

Love is not soft and squooshy. Love is as hard as a diamond.

But zeal is not violent. It is not a matter of noise or confusion. The quiet light of reason can be zealous: irresistible and intense, like an incoming tide, but not noisy, like a hurricane. Elijah found God in the "still, small voice", not in the fire, the earthquake, or the storm. God's love is more zealous and intense in quiet, humble Mary than in busy Martha or big-mouthed Peter.

But zeal, in its quiet way, is fanatical, adamant, uncompromising. Zeal never gives up. Never. It refuses to be satisfied until all obstacles to its love are removed. That is why God demands Everything. T. S. Eliot calls Christianity "a condition of complete simplicity, / costing not less than / Everything". Jesus says: "You, therefore, must be perfect, as your heavenly Father is perfect" (Mt 5:48). The Bible calls God "Father" but never "Grandfather", for as George MacDonald says, "God is easy to please but hard to satisfy." A grandfather is easy to satisfy and a tyrant is hard to please, but a good father is easy to please (because his love is compassionate) and hard to satisfy (because his love is zealous). Ancient man tended to neglect the first of these truths, modern man the second. We hear little today about zeal, or passion (except, of course, sexual passion), only "compassion". But zeal and compassion are equally necessary. Without zeal there is no sanctity. We cannot comfortably ooze up an eternal growth escalator. We must fight. We have enemies, though they are not of flesh and blood. If this is not true, Jesus and the Bible lie.

Muslims typically have more zeal than Christians. Are we not the Laodicean church that has "lost its first love" and is only "lukewarm"? One of the most shocking verses in the Bible comes next. Read it (Rev 3:16).

Obviously zeal can be badly misplaced into anger, hate, and violence. But remember, "the corruption of the best is the worst." We remember all too easily one half of this principle: when we see a passionate good, we rightly fear its perversion into a passionate evil. But there is also another half: when we see a passionate evil, we must also remember that it is the perversion of a passionate good. We already know that hate is zealous, but we forget that love is even more zealous. God is both compassionate and zealous. He is a lover, not either a fanatic or a wimp. And His love defines what love is.

How do we know that God is a zealot? Jesus. Jesus shows us exactly and totally Who God is (for He came seeking "not my own will but the will of him who sent me": Jn 5:30) and who we must become (for "You, therefore, must be perfect as your heavenly father is perfect": Mt 5:48). If our zeal is so tepid that we would never *dream* of cleansing the temple of our souls by whipping out the money changers by force, then we do not yet understand Jesus, and we do not yet understand what God has in store for us. Just as He will not rest until He finds the cool waters of reason and compassion in fiery Muslims, He will not rest until He finds the hot desert sun of unyielding, adamant will in watery Christians. For He came to kindle a fire upon the earth, and He will not rest until it burns (Lk 12:49). "Our God is a consuming fire" (Heb 12:29). Is that your God? Or do you worship a different one?

If St. Thomas, like his God, is hard as a diamond, is he also soft?

[F]our proximate effects may be ascribed to love, viz. melting (at its presence), **enjoyment** (of its presence), **languor** (sadness at its absence), **and fervor** (zeal to make it present).

Of these, the first is *melting*, which is opposed to freezing. For things that are frozen are closely bound together so as to be hard to pierce; but it belongs to love that the appetite is fitted to receive the good which is loved inasmuch as the object loved is in the lover, as stated above. Consequently the freezing or hardening of the heart is a disposition incompatible with love, while melting denotes a softening of the heart, whereby the heart shows itself to be ready for the entrance of the beloved (I-II,28,5).

St. Thomas is surprisingly poetic, mystical, and even romantic here. He knew the chivalric love poetry of the High Middle Ages, and took from it what he thought was profoundly true about love. (There is hardly any tradition in which St. Thomas did not find something true and worthwhile.)

Every lover experiences something that feels like the melting of the heart at the presence of the beloved, or even at the thought of the beloved. As truth makes heads and wills hard, love makes hearts soft.

"Heart" here refers especially to deep feeling or emotion. "Heart" means not only (1) intuitive reason ("the heart has its reasons") and (2) will but also (3) a certain kind of emotion that distinguishes us from the animals. Animals have many modes of awareness, or thinking, or consciousness, which they share with us: sensation, cleverness, intuition; but not reason. Animals also have something like wills (e.g., a "strong-willed" horse) as we do; but not free choice and moral responsibility. And animals have many human emotions, perhaps even compassion and affection. But not romantic love, which is *personal*. No animal can be Romeo.

A complete saint is sanctified in all aspects of human nature, not just reason and will but emotion as well. (And, of course, the body too: it is "the temple of the Holy Spirit": 1 Cor 6:19.)

Saints are like Jesus, emotionally as well as intellectually and volitionally. And Jesus is both hard as a diamond and soft as a whisper, therefore saints are too.

It may sound strange to call St. Thomas "soft-hearted" right after calling him a zealot. But Christ, and therefore Christians, and the Christian life, are all full of wonderful paradoxes like this. Like the universe.

Of course, "soft-hearted" may mean (a) sentimentalism, (b) cowardice, (c) naïveté, or (d) lack of intelligence, as well as the "melting" of love; but love, at its height, is the opposite of these four other things. Hearts are soft when they are malleable, open, changeable—to the will of God and to the needs of neighbor. Hearts are open when they are available, humble, earthy, not standoffish, penetratable. Like the Persons of the Trinity to each other.

93. Hatred

Hate seems stronger than love. Is it?

Love must needs precede hatred, (for) nothing is hated save through being contrary to a suitable thing which is loved.

And hence it is that every hatred is caused by love ... (I-II,29,2) (In fact,) ... **all emotions are caused by love. Therefore hatred also, since it is an emotion of the soul, is caused by love** ...

It is impossible for an effect to be stronger than its causes.

Now (since) **every hatred arises from some love as its cause, as above stated, therefore it is impossible for hatred to be stronger than love absolutely.**

Furthermore, love must needs be, absolutely speaking, stronger than hatred because a thing is moved to the end more strongly than to the means ... (and) **turning away from evil is directed as a means to the gaining of good (as the end).**

Nevertheless hatred sometimes *seems* to be stronger than love ... because hatred is more keenly felt than love ... (I-II,29,3).

The sum total of all the above teaches us a number of lessons.

Lesson One: St. Thomas is very logical even about the most illogical things, like hate.

Lesson Two: Appearances do not equal reality.

Lesson Three: Feelings are not the touchstone of truth. We often feel hate more keenly than love because we feel more keenly the things that touch our ego more keenly. But our ego is not God. In fact, it is often wrong, because it is fallen, foolish, and faithless. To the two-year-old whose ice cream cone just fell into the mud, nothing in the universe could ever be more important than this tragedy. To the man consumed by hate, the object of hate is the very center of reality, bigger than God or Satan.

Lesson Four: Love is stronger than *anything*, because God is love.

Lesson Five: We can see this even if we confine ourselves to the perspective of human psychology.

Lesson Six: Psychology never contradicts theology.

Lesson Seven: Theology explains psychology. For theology gives us the ultimate reason for the data of psychology (e.g., the relation between means and ends in human motivation).

Lesson Eight: There are always more lessons—everywhere—than we think.

94. Self–hatred?

We're commanded to love our neighbors as we love ourselves, so we must be able to love ourselves. Can we therefore also hate ourselves?

Properly speaking, it is impossible for a man to hate himself. For everything naturally desires good, nor can anyone desire anything for himself save under the aspect of good ... For even they who kill themselves apprehend death as itself a good, considered as putting an end to some unhappiness or pain.

It is impossible for a man to hate himself properly speaking. But accidentally it happens that a man hates himself ... they love themselves according to what they take themselves to be, while they hate that which they really are (I-II,29,4).

We always do love ourselves; that is why we are commanded to love our neighbors as we love ourselves, not to love our neighbors as we *ought* to love ourselves. If we always do love ourselves, and if we cannot at the same time hate and love the same person, then we cannot really hate ourselves.

The practical point of this logical analysis is that we always have a secure, in-place standard for loving others: we are to love them as we always do in fact love ourselves. If we think it is impossible to love stupid, ugly, selfish, bothersome people, we are wrong, because there is one stupid, ugly, selfish, bothersome person that we do succeed in loving all the time: the one in the mirror. Even though we hate some of the things we do or feel, we hate them only because we love ourselves. We feel we are unworthy of such bad stuff. All we have to do is extend that same attitude toward our neighbor: to love the sinner but not the sin, to hate the sin but not the sinner.

God gave us a securely fixed magnetic pole in our very nature: our natural and proper and inevitable and good self-love, our love of our own true good, our own true happiness. As St. Thomas notes, even those who kill themselves do it out of self-love, since the only reason they kill themselves is because they (mistakenly) see death as a better thing than life for themselves.

Since (1) it was absolutely necessary to transform our hearts from selfish hearts into unselfish hearts, hearts full of charity, i.e., full of God (for "God *is* charity"), and (2) since it was impossible for us all to become instant heroes of unselfish charity, great saints and mystics who simply forget ourselves completely, therefore (3) God in His wisdom and mercy made charity easy for us by uniting other-love with self-love ("You shall love your neighbor *as yourself*").

This is easy for two reasons: (1) loving others as you love yourself frees you from feelings. For even when you do not *feel* love for yourself, you always seek your own good; that's all you have to do to your neighbor. You don't have to *feel* love all the time, though that is a very good thing when it happens. God made it easy for you to transcend your feelings: He already put the beginning of charity into your heart, for you already have charity to yourself.

(2) God also made it easy for you by making you one with your neighbor in fact; all you have to do is to acknowledge and affirm that fact. We are all one body, one family. We are not angels. We are biologically one "in" Adam and spiritually one "in" Christ. When we accept this, we can love ourselves and others with the very same act of love: we can love others as parts of ourselves, as others who are also "in" ourselves—because they are!

But we have to be honest. That's why St. Thomas says, in his second paragraph above, that we must will the truth, stand in the light, and seek our own true, real good and not something false. If we seek what is false, we will want to hide from the truth, and we will not get what we wish, for we will only succeed in hiding the truth from ourselves, not ourselves from the truth. For light comes from truth into us, not from us into truth. We must will and love what is, i.e., our true self, not what is not, not a false self. If we will a false self, we hate our true self. We must choose to hate our false self, not our true self, and to love our true self, not our false self. God, our Designer, shows us our true self. It's Christ. Christ shows us perfectly not only who God is but also who we are, "reveals man to himself" as Pope St. John Paul II loved to say.

Honesty is absolutely necessary, as necessary to the mind as food is to the body. But if truth is the food of the mind, how can we be mentally anorexic and hate it? How is dishonesty even possible?

Now it may happen in three ways that some particular truth is repugnant or hurtful to the good we love.

First ... man sometimes hates a particular truth when he wishes that what is true were not true.

Second ... is the case of those who wish not to know the truth of faith, that they may sin freely, in whose person it is said (Job 21:14): *We desire not the knowledge of Thy ways.*

Thirdly, a particular truth is hated as being repugnant inasmuch as it is in the intellect of another man; as, for instance, when a man wishes to remain hidden in his sin, he hates that anyone should know the truth about his sin. In this respect Augustine says in the *Confessions* **that men** *love the truth when it enlightens, they hate it when it reproves* (I-II,29,5).

We cannot hate truth in general, all truth, as we cannot hate food in general, all food. But we can hate a particular truth even though it is good for us, as we can hate a particular food even though it is good for us: because we obey our feelings (St. Thomas usually calls them "passions") instead of our reason, and a particular truth might shock our feelings even though it is good for us to know it, as spinach, yogurt, or bitter medicine may shock our taste buds, even though it is good for us to eat it.

None of us is free of any of the three forms of truth-hating that St. Thomas mentions. This is one of the most pervasive effects of Original Sin, and one of the most dangerous. For without truth, nothing good can be known and therefore willed, just as without light nothing good can be seen and therefore desired. Even the greatest surgeon in the most perfect hospital cannot perform the simplest operation if the lights go out. Satan's first trick is always to dim the lights.

(1) We are all spiritually lazy and self-satisfied: we all wish we were not sinners who have to change. But we are. We wish that all the changes we need could be painless. But they are not. We wish we did not have to "mortify the flesh", i.e., the proud, selfish ego. But we do. We wish we could avoid death. But we can't. We wish Hell was an unreal myth. But it isn't.

(2) We all want to look away from truth, i.e., from God, when we want to sin. This was Nietzsche's explicit motive for atheism: How could I bear that there be a God Who saw my dark side? Every time we sin against God, we sin against ourselves, against our reason, against the truth. The truth is that sin never brings joy and sanctity always does, but we choose not to know this when we want to sin. Whenever we sin, we choose something that we know, deep down, always brings misery instead of joy. To do that, we have to make ourselves temporarily insane. We have to put out the light of reason.

(3) And we don't want other people to know our dark side any more than we want God to know it. (Read *The Brothers Karamazov* for a profound story about this, Fr. Zossima's "midnight visitor".)

There is no way around it: we absolutely need to fall in love with truth, absolutely, unreservedly, totally, "fanatically". We need to pray Psalm 139 over and over. For that is our preparation for Heaven: learning to love the light, loving rather than hating the fact that God has searched us and known us down to every dirty detail. We must learn to stand in the light because that is what Heaven is, standing in the light of God's mind. (Light comes *into* our mind but it comes *from* God's mind, like a searchlight.)

We can do this (loving the fact that God knows everything about us including all our dirty little secrets) if and only if we trust Him to love us as no human being ever can: absolutely, unreservedly, totally, forever, no matter what. It is only because we don't trust Him, only because we don't trust His light to be love, only because we separate Light and Love, that we hate the light. It is faith (trust) that affirms that the light, the ultimate truth, is perfect love. (That's because there is only one God, and He is both.) Therefore faith is the key to this absolute love of truth.

Why are some desires harder to overcome than others? Especially greed and lust?

... concupiscence (unregulated desire) is two-fold; one is natural, the other is not natural. Natural concupiscence cannot be actually infinite, because it is of that which nature requires, and nature ever tends to something finite and fixed. Hence man never desires infinite meat, or infinite drink.... But non-natural concupiscence is altogether infinite ... Hence he that desires riches, may desire to be rich not up to a certain limit but to be simply as rich as possible (I-II,30,4).

Greed for the things money can buy ("natural wealth") is a bad thing, but it is finite. You can only enjoy a finite amount of food or drink, houses or cars, or even sex. But greed for money ("artificial wealth") is infinite. You can always want more. It's like a drug: you have to have higher and higher doses of it to give you the same "buzz" you used to get from little bits of it. And this never stops. It is Hell's false infinite.

It's also essentially competitive. You want not just money but more money than anyone else. Even if you're the second richest person in the world, you are resentful of Number One, as Satan was resentful that God was Number One. Thus this kind of greed is more dangerous because of three things: (1) It is not natural but supernatural, not from the world but from the Devil, from Hell. (2) It is infinite, it has no limit. (3) And it is essentially competitive. The greed here is not for the money but for the power it gives you. You want to be like God, in total control of everything. So it really comes down to competitive pride, in the last analysis, which is the primal sin, the worst sin, the Devil's sin. Ordinary greed for natural wealth is bad enough but it only comes from the world, not from the Devil.

The same is true of lust. Ordinary lust is bad enough, but it only comes from the flesh, not from the Devil. But there is also an unnatural lust that comes from the Devil. Lust for enjoying a woman's or man's body, or for intercourse with that body, is finite. You can only enjoy one body at a time. But lust for your own pleasure as such, pleasure that is under your control, the pleasure of being in control of pleasure—that is infinite, and that is really pride, jealousy of God, resentment at your own finitude. This is Hellish lust; it is really egotism and pride in disguise.

This is the greatest danger of masturbation: it can foster egotism, it can make you actually prefer the fantasy person you create to the real person God created, because it wants to be in control, where there is no other, where you are God, where you create your own dream world. But the whole training of life is to overcome this egotism. (See Charles Williams' terrifying novel *Descent into Hell* on the eternal danger of this egotism, whether it is about sex, or money, or anything else.)

In rejecting the real human other, who is not perfect, and who has free will and thus unpredictability, in favor of one's own fantasies, which are perfectly predictable and totally under your own control, one is really rejecting God. Our neighbor and our world are the two roads out of Hell, i.e., out of pure egotism, that God has put in everyone's path to make salvation as easy as possible. Although *natural* lust misuses neighbors as objects rather than persons, using them rather than loving them; and although *natural* greed misuses things by loving them rather than using them, *unnatural* lust and greed are really forms of pride, which is the sin from Hell, not from the flesh or the world. In Hell there are no neighbors and no world. Sartre is profoundly wrong when he famously says that "Hell is other people." Hell is precisely the lack of other people. I think it is also the lack of other things, real things; that is why many mystics say that the fire in Hell is not material fire, for that is something real outside yourself. It is a companion, an other, though a painful and terrifying one. I think it more likely that Hell is worse than that: it is total aloneness.

When we use others as catalysts for our own selfish lust, we seek, and perhaps even find, some kind of perverse pleasure in this. Is there an even greater pleasure when we treat others rightly, with charity, as is our moral duty? Or is it duty *versus* pleasure, as Kant and the Stoics say?

Whether doing good to another is a cause of pleasure?
... [I]nasmuch as through being united to others by love, we look upon their good as being our own, we take pleasure in the good we do to others, especially to our friends, as in our own good.... Wherefore men take pleasure in their children, and in their own works, as being things on which they bestow a share of their own good.... [F]or whatever we do or suffer for a friend is pleasant, because love is the principal cause of pleasure (I-II,32,6).

Pleasure, of course, is not just physical. It means "being pleased". It is the subjective dimension of happiness—happiness in the classical, old, wise, deep, complete meaning of true blessedness, *eudaimonia*, *makarios*, or *beatitudo*. In other words, St. Thomas means by "pleasure" what we subjectivistic, feeling-oriented moderns mean by "happiness".

The surest way to attain this "happiness", or "pleasure", is through charity. Charity is the will to the good of the other. You know you have this will when you actually do to the other what you think is good for the other. A will is not just a wish or a feeling, it is a command to yourself to act. So it is active charity, acts of charity, that brings pleasure. Kierkegaard says, in *Works of Love,* that for a Christian love *is* the works of love rather than mere feelings. Feelings usually accompany these acts, and they can help to motivate these acts, but the acts are essentially acts of will. The feelings of pleasure they bring are mainly the effects of the works of love. The more you treat someone you hate as if you loved them, the more you will find yourself loving them.

The crucial catalyst of this whole equation is the mind, and what we see, or believe. It is only "inasmuch as ... we *look upon* their good *as being* our own (that) we take pleasure in the good we do to others." We judge our good to *be* their good and their good to *be* our good. It is a judgment of being, a proposition with an "is" verb, not just an imaginative picture or concept. We "look" at a sunset, but we "look upon" it as *being* beautiful, i.e., we judge it to really be beautiful. It is a judgment, not just a concept, whether the basis for that judgment is faith, logical reasoning, or concrete experience. We will love our neighbor as we love ourselves when we look upon our neighbor's good *as being* our own good. It depends on this "big picture", this worldview, this piece of metaphysics. Ethics depends on metaphysics, not only for philosophers but for everybody; not only in argument but in life.

God's tremendous invention of the family is our great teacher here. We all understand (unless we are very, very wicked) how our siblings' good, and our children's good, and our parents' good, gives us pleasure. The next step is to see all men as our brothers, both in Adam and in Christ, both biologically and spiritually. But we will probably never see this, never move from original selfishness to universal charity and unselfishness, without the intermediate step of the family.

All recognize St. Thomas' last statement to be profoundly true, by experience: **"love is the principal cause of pleasure."** Therefore the more love, the more pleasure. This is why the smile on the faces of the saints is the deepest smile in the world. Even when they frown, they smile. You can sense the smile behind the severe frown of the honest moralist or the strict but loving teacher or parent.

So if you want to be truly happy, start in your own home. If you don't love the people you see, you can't love the people you don't see. Try it; you'll like it. It's the world's most reliable experiment: every time you forget yourself and love your neighbor, you find deep joy, deep down. Every time you don't, you find deep doo-doo, deep down.

Does the loving itself bring pleasure? Is the desire itself its own satisfaction? Or does the pleasure come only when the desire is attained or the love is reciprocated?

... the greater the desire for the thing loved, the greater the pleasure when it is attained; *indeed, the very increase of desire brings with it an increase of pleasure,* **according as it gives rise to the hope of obtaining that which is loved, since ... desire resulting from hope is a cause of pleasure. Now wonder is a kind of desire for knowledge, a desire which comes to a man when he sees an effect of which the cause either is unknown to him or surpasses his knowledge or faculty of understanding. Consequently wonder is a cause of pleasure, in so far as it includes a hope of getting the knowledge which one desires to have. For this reason whatever is wonderful is pleasing** (I-II,32,8).

"Blessed are those who hunger and thirst (i.e., those who desire, hope, and wonder) after righteousness, for they shall be filled" (Mt. 5:6)—with pleasure as well as with righteousness. The more we thirst for God and the righteousness that God is, the more pleasure we will be able to experience in Heaven when we attain this righteousness. The degree of Heavenly joy that you will be able to contain will be determined by the intensity and idealism, the aspiration and ambition, of your earthly desire for God, your love for God, and for that which God is (righteousness, holiness, love, peace, truth).

This includes your intellect's desire, your wonder, your holy curiosity, your desire to know Who God is. This is an intellectual desire, but it is not merely a desire for correct concepts but for living presence; not merely a knowledge *about* God but a knowledge *of* God, as you know your friend or your spouse. It is a desire for *kennen,* not *wissen,* for *connaitre,* not *savoir,* for a "knowledge" that is more like sex than like scholarship. Indeed, sex is a pale image of it. The Biblical word for sex is "knowledge" (Gen 4:1). That is not a euphemism or a metaphor.

All who seek, find. Those who seek more, find more. Those who seek less, find less. God satisfies all our desires in Heaven, but if the desire is not there, He cannot fulfill it.

He fills to the brim with His joy, with Himself, whatever receptive places we make in our hearts and lives. That is the ultimate reason why the relationship between virtue and pleasure is an intrinsic necessity. Aristotle knew the proximate, human, psychological reason for that, but not the ultimate, theological reason. But he knew a lot. He knew that the relation between virtue and pleasure was like the relationship between how hungry you are and how much you enjoy your dinner; that happiness is not an extrinsic reward, like a promised payment for a service. It is a necessary causal relationship: the amount of water that can fit into a canyon depends on how deep the canyon is. Rewards are not given by God, in Heaven or on earth, as compensation for lack of pleasure earlier. The reward of happiness is in the very act of virtue, like the joy of surfing (not *having* surfed) a good wave. The reward is the very state itself of the soul (joy) that is caused by zeal in loving God and neighbor.

When you sculpt out a deep God-shaped canyon in your soul by your intense desire (love) to know Him, God will fill it to the brim with what you sought—Himself—and this will bring brimful joy. If you sculpt out only a shallow canyon, He will be able to fill only that—not because of any lack of active power in Him but because of a lack of receptive "weakness" or emptiness in you.

And therefore the purpose of life on earth is to sculpt and dig deeper canyons of desire in our souls for Him to fill. Augustine prays: "Narrow is my heart; enlarge it, that You may fill it." Our hearts are not restless enough; we are too easily contented. That is why the saints counsel us against loving the world too much: not because worldly pleasures are evil but because they are so small, and Heavenly pleasures are so great. The saints are the true hedonists. If you doubt this, visit Mother Teresa's Missionaries of Charity: they are the happiest people you will ever meet on this earth.

Is pleasure inherently dangerous, deceptive and tempting, or is it inherently innocent and good, or is it neither and just neutral?

As is stated in (Aristotle's) *Ethics,* (natural,) **appropriate pleasures increase activity ... whereas pleasures arising from other sources are impediments to activity. Accordingly there is a certain pleasure that is taken in the very act of reason, as when one takes pleasure in contemplating or in reasoning; and such pleasure does not hinder the act of reason but helps it, because we are more attentive in doing that which gives us pleasure, and attention fosters activity.**

On the other hand bodily pleasures hinder the use of reason ... by distracting the reason. Because, as we have just said, we attend much to that which pleases us. Now when the attention is firmly fixed on one thing, it is either weakened in respect of other things or it is entirely withdrawn from them; and thus if the bodily pleasure be great, either it entirely hinders the use of reason by concentrating the mind's attention on itself, or else it hinders is considerably (I-II,33,3).

Pleasure is in itself an inherent good. For "at God's right hand there are pleasures evermore" (Ps 16:11).

Pleasure is good because it motivates good acts. Food tastes pleasant, and that motivates us to eat, and gain strength. Exercise, sports, hunting, writing, puzzle solving, imaginative creativity, music, lovemaking—all these are good for us, and God made them pleasant to motivate us to seek them out.

St. Thomas speaks of a great pleasure that many people in our society never think of: the pleasure of learning, the pleasure in the very act of reasoning (i.e., discovering truth) or, even more, in comprehending and contemplating and appreciating the truth attained.

In Heaven the tremendous *pleasure* of the Beatific Vision will motivate us to enter into it more deeply, and that deeper understanding will produce even more pleasure, which in turn will motivate us to enter into it more deeply, forever. We will never be bored, because God is infinite (literally *infinite!*) and we are forever finite, so there will be new truth and new pleasure at every moment. **"Such pleasure does not hinder the act of reason but helps it."**

Extrinsic, alien pleasures do hinder the use of reason, by distracting it. It is difficult to solve philosophy problems when making love, either rightly, to your spouse, or wrongly, in fornication or adultery.

God invented pleasure. How Satan must enjoy it when he persuades us to feel automatically guilty about it, to think "this feels so good that it must be wrong." That's even stupider than the opposite error, "it feels so right that it can't be wrong." Kant taught that duty and inclination were by nature enemies. The Catholic Church teaches the opposite: it will not canonize a saint without evidence of great joy as well as heroic virtue. Joy is one of the fruits of the Spirit. (You could say that joy is deep pleasure, or that joy is the deepening of happiness as happiness is the deepening of pleasure.)

If Christians had believed that, and lived it, they would have converted the world. For everyone wants joy. Joy sells. (Fake joy sells too, but not for long.)

It's not too late to begin the apostolate of joy.

100. The pleasures of contemplation

How strange it sounds to hear St. Thomas locate the deepest pleasure in the intellect, in contemplation, in philosophical and theological wisdom. Was that just his "thing" because he happened to be "turned on" by philosophy and monasticism? Or is there something universally human about it?

It is written (Wis 8:16): *Her (i.e., wisdom's) conversation hath no bitterness, nor her company any tediousness; but joy and gladness.* **Now the conversation and company of wisdom are found in contemplation. Therefore there is no sorrow contrary to the pleasure of contemplation....**

Nor has it any sorrow annexed to it, as bodily pleasures have, which are like remedies against certain annoyances; thus a man takes pleasure in drinking through being troubled with thirst, but when the thirst is quite driven out, the pleasure of drinking ceases also. Because the pleasure of contemplation is not caused by one's being quit of an annoyance, but by the fact that contemplation is pleasant in itself ... (I-II,35,5).

If you have never experienced "the joy of contemplation", here is a powerful argument for opening your mind to the possibility that you are missing something: divine revelation, not just philosophers like St. Thomas, says so.

Some pleasures are merely physical. They give pleasure to our bodies. Some are emotional: they give pleasure to our desires. These two kinds of pleasures are genuine, and God-designed; but they are "lower". The higher animals share them too.

Three kinds of "higher", uniquely human, pleasures are the pleasures of three powers of the human soul that no animal even approximates: (1) the pleasures of religion, of yielding our whole self to God, (2) the pleasures of morality, of yielding our will and our actions to the true good, true principles, and true virtue, and (3) the pleasures of contemplation, of yielding our mind to truth and beauty.

These higher pleasures are not like oases in the desert, compensations for sorrows, relief from problems, like anesthetics or shopping sprees or escapist entertainment. They do not presuppose pain for us to appreciate them, as most pleasures do. They are good in themselves, and therefore they are among the very few things that we can enjoy forever without boredom. They are Heavenly. Even here they are a faint foretaste of the joys of Heaven. Lovers looking into each other's faces are not bored.

Many people in our poor, sad, hectic world do not even know that such joys exist. And even among those who do know that they exist, many do not know that contemplation is among them.

What should such people do? Simply try it. Practice contemplative prayer. Just practice the presence of God. Do nothing but "look" at Him, with faith. See His perfection and beauty. See His love of you. Just stay there. There is nothing you have to do. Just be in His presence. Nothing else. Just look at Him looking at you and loving you. Try it. You'll like it.

"Contemplation" does not mean something only monks and mystics do. When you enjoy a beautiful piece of music, a painting, a landscape, or a beautiful human face, you are contemplating, and enjoying it. "Contemplation" is not for "intellectuals" only, for it is not the kind of "intellection" that a computer, or a computer geek, does. It is the kind of intellection a lover does when he gazes into the face of his beloved. "I just look at him and He just looks at me" is what the peasant saint told the Curé of Ars when he asked him what he did when he prayed.

You're going to enjoy doing it forever in the "Beatific Vision", so you'd better start practicing here.

Is the fear of pain, sorrow, death, and Hell stronger than the love of pleasure, joy, life, and Heaven?

Good is stronger than evil.... pleasure is desirable for the sake of the good which is its object, whereas the shunning of sorrow is on account of evil. Therefore the desire for pleasure is more eager than the shunning of sorrow.... The reason for this is that the cause of pleasure is a suitable good, while the cause of pain or sorrow is an unsuitable evil. Now it happens that a certain good (the higher goods spoken of in #100) **is suitable without any repugnance at all; but it is not possible for any evil to be so unsuitable as not to be suitable in some way. Wherefore pleasure can be entire and perfect, whereas sorrow is always partial. Therefore desire for pleasure is naturally greater than the shunning of sorrow** (I-II,35,5).

The absence or loss of any good thing, and the sorrow that comes from this, is wholly relative to the goodness of that thing. But the opposite is not true: the good is not relative to the bad. This is the ultimate reason, in the nature of things, why the positive is greater than the negative, why good is greater than evil and why pleasures are greater than pains.

This must be so for a reason of metaphysics. Evil is anti-being; good is pro-being. Evil is the negation of good, but good is not just the negation of evil. Good is absolute; evil is relative (to good). Therefore good is stronger than evil.

And since pleasure is a kind of good, therefore the good of pleasure is stronger than the evil of pain and sorrow.

And therefore the desire for pleasure is greater than the fear of pain. That's why we often take stupid chances, risking great pain, for the sake of an even greater pleasure.

St. Thomas gives the reason for this in the fact that good can be perfect but evil cannot; for the good we seek is perfect goodness, free from all evil, but the evil we fear is not perfect evil, free from all goodness. There *is* no perfect evil, free from all goodness. That would be like a brokenness without a thing that is broken. Perfect pleasure is conceivable, perfect sorrow is not.

Yet we often *feel* the negative (pain, sorrow, fear, death, Hell) more strongly than we feel the positive. That just shows us how unreliable our feelings are as an index to objective reality.

The practical "payoff" in this idea is that we should concentrate much more on good than evil, more on hope than fear, more on virtue than sin, more on love than fear. (In fact, "perfect love casts out fear"—1 Jn 4:18.) St. Thomas says that the most effective way to get rid of a strong evil passion is by an even stronger good passion. So when you are tempted to lust, greed, pride, arrogance, egotism, rage, rebellion, revenge, self-righteousness, or indifference, look at a crucifix. No greater good passion ever existed in this world than Christ's divine-and-human love that manifested itself *there*. Put *that* side by side with your evil and you will get—what? You will get a spiritual battle, a cross, for the Devil will react exactly as Dracula reacts to the crucifix. And then you will get a resurrection.

102. THREE EVILS: SORROW (MISERY) IS WORSE THAN PAIN, AND SIN IS WORSE THAN SORROW (MISERY)

We can distinguish three kinds of good, and three kinds of evil. First, there is external, physical pleasure and pain. Second, there is internal, emotional joy and sorrow. Third, there is moral goodness and badness, virtue and vice, righteousness and wickedness. Do we suffer more from physical, emotional, or moral evil? Which is the greatest evil and the greatest suffering?

Is it better to have joy (good #2) plus suffering (evil #1), or neither? Can we have joy *in* suffering? And is it better to have misery (evil #2) with righteousness (good #3) than joy (good #2) without righteousness? Is it always better to *be* good (good #3) than to *feel* good (goods #1 and 2)?

... sadness of heart (evil #2) **surpasses every outward wound** (evil #1) ...

... inward pain is, simply and of itself, more keen than outward pain, a sign whereof is that one willingly undergoes outward pain in order to avoid inward pain ... Sometimes, however, outward pain is accompanied by inward pain, and then the pain is increased (I-II,35,7).

The very fact of the will being opposed to the evil is a good (good #3, moral good). **And for this reason, sorrow** (evil #2) **or pain** (evil #1) **cannot be the greatest evil, because it has an admixture of the good** (I-II,39,4).

That which is an evil to the soul (evils #2 and 3, sorrow and vice) **is a greater evil than that which is an evil to the body** (evil #1, pain) (I-II,39,4).

(Therefore) **sorrow** (evil #2) **is useful as inducing man to avoid sin** (evil #3) **... just as pleasure** (good #2) **in the good** (#3) **makes one seek the good** (#3) **more earnestly, so sorrow** (evil #2) **for evil** (#3) **makes one avoid evil** (#3) **more eagerly** (I-I,39,3).

Though we may fear pain the most, sorrow second, and sin the least, yet sin is really the worst evil and the most to be feared, with sorrow second and pain least.

Sorrow cuts into us more deeply than pain because it cuts into our very soul, not just our body. Sin cuts even deeper because it harms our very self, not just our feelings.

Modern literature and movies almost always fail to show us this truth. Instead, they reverse it. The most terrible thing is always assumed to be physical suffering, and this typically justifies even the sin of murder. For that is what active euthanasia is, even when motivated by compassion. (It is indeed possible to do a very bad deed for a very good motive, like "mercy killing", just as it is possible to do very good deeds for a very bad motive, as the Pharisees did.)

Our deeper self knows that St. Thomas is right. First of all, we know, deep down, that spiritual suffering is worse than physical suffering because when we are in deep sorrow or despair, we distract ourselves by creating new physical sufferings, like tearing our hair, hitting our head, biting our hands, or banging our head against the wall! (Emotional sufferings are spiritual, of course, not physical; emotions are spiritual feelings.)

Second, we also know, deep down, that sin is worse than suffering because it bothers us deeply and for a long time, often for a lifetime. When we choose sin to avoid sorrow and suffering, we get, in the end, more sorrow and suffering than we get when we choose to endure sorrow and suffering rather than commit sin. Ask women who have chosen abortion. Then ask women who have chosen the opposite. Compare their testimonies when they speak from the heart.

Pain is obviously bad because it hurts. And therefore it is good to relieve it, in others as in ourselves, if some greater good is not avoided by its relief. Is pain also bad for any deeper reason?

Pain deprives one of the power to learn....

Augustine says: *Although during those days I was tormented with a violent toothache, I was not able to turn over in my mind other things than those I had already learnt; and as to learning anything, I was quite unequal to it, because it required undivided attention....*

Now it is evident that sensible pain above all draws the soul's attention to itself.... It is likewise evident that in order to learn anything new, we require study and effort with a strong intention.... Consequently if the pain be acute, man is prevented at the time from learning anything; indeed, it can be so acute that as long as it lasts a man is unable to give his attention even to that which he knew already.

However, a difference is to be observed according to the difference of love that a man has ... because the greater his love, the more will he retain the intention of his mind so as to prevent it from turning entirely to the pain.

Moderate sorrow, that does not cause the mind to wander, can conduce to the acquisition of learning, especially in regard to those things by which a man hopes to be freed from sorrow. And thus *in the tribulation of murmuring* **men are more apt to be taught by God.**

Both pleasure and pain, in so far as they draw upon themselves the soul's intention, hinder the reason from the act of consideration; wherefore it is stated in (Aristotle's) *Ethics* that *in the moment of sexual pleasure, a man cannot understand anything.*

Nevertheless pain attracts the soul's intention more than pleasure does ... (I-II,37,1).

Not only is physical pain not the worst thing in the world, physical pain isn't even the worst thing about physical pain. Pain is an evil, of course, in itself; but its effects on the soul are the worst thing about it. Intense pain is like a tyrant with a whip, demanding the total submission of your mind, your attention. It screams, "Look at me! Look at me!"

The evil of anything is relative to the good that it deprives us of. The goods of our body are great: health, long life, pleasure, and freedom from pain. We willingly and wisely exchange external goods, especially money, to recover these goods of the body. But the goods of the soul are even more important, more internal, more *ours*, than the goods of the body. These are spiritual goods: our freedom of thought, our power to know truth, to learn new truths and remember old ones, and the power to turn our attention to the true, the good, and the beautiful, i.e., the power to "contemplate" the truth. This is the great good that physical pain threatens. That is the main reason it is important to avoid physical pain, especially great physical pain, and to deliver others from this great evil. Jesus' physical healings were not a concession to materialism; they ministered to people's spiritual freedom.

As St. Thomas mentions, however (par. 5), a little pain or sorrow can be conducive to wisdom. Rabbi Abraham Heschel says, "The man who has not suffered—what could he possibly know, anyway?"

If wisdom is a great good, then both too much and too little pain are bad because they are obstacles to wisdom. The same holds for great riches and great poverty, great comfort and great discomfort. God knows how much we need. We do not.

Finally, as St. Thomas explains (par. 4), love can change this. When you love something a little bit, even a little pain will harm or distract you; when you love a lot, even a lot of pain does not harm or distract you. Look at women in childbirth!

Psychoanalysis does not make us holy. It helps us to understand and regulate our emotions, not our religion or our morality. How important is that? How important are well-ordered emotions to the religious and moral life?

(Of the other powers in man) **some obey reason blindly and without any contradiction whatever: such are the limbs of the body, provided they be in a healthy condition; for as soon as reason commands, the hand or the foot proceed to action. Hence the Philosopher says that** *the soul rules the body like a despot,* **i.e., as a master rules his slave, who has no right** (or power) **to rebel. Accordingly some held that all the active principles in man are subordinate to reason in this way. If this were true, for man to act well it would suffice that his reason be perfect.... This was the opinion of Socrates, who said** *every virtue is a kind of prudence* (practical wisdom).... **Hence he maintained that as long as a man is in possession of knowledge, he cannot sin; and that every one who sins, does so through ignorance.**

Now this is based on a false supposition (assumption). Because the appetitive faculty obeys the reason not blindly but with a certain power of opposition; wherefore the Philosopher says that *reason commands the appetitive faculty by a politic power,* **whereby a man rules over subjects that are free and have a certain right** (and power) **of opposition ... in so far as the habits or passions of the appetitive faculty cause the use of reason to be impeded in some particular action. And in this way there is some truth in the saying of Socrates that so long as a man is in possession of knowledge he does not sin, provided, however, that this knowledge is made to include the** *use* **of reason in this individual act of choice.**

Accordingly, for a man to do a good deed it is requisite not only that his reason be well disposed by means of a habit of intellectual virtue, **but also that his appetite be well disposed by means of a habit of moral virtue** (I-II,58,2).

... in order that he be rightly disposed with regard to ... ends, he needs to be perfected by certain habits whereby it becomes connatural, as it were, for man to judge aright of the end. This is done by moral virtue; for the virtuous man judges aright of the end of virtue because *such as a man is, such does the end seem to him* **(Aristotle)** (I-II,58,5).

Two easy errors are possible about emotions, as about nearly anything: to overrate or to underrate their importance; to be an Epicurean or a Stoic; a Rousseau or a Kant. Emotions are to reason and will what soil is to plants, sound to music, and words to literature. They (as well as physical actions and pleasures and pains), are the material, the raw material, the potentialities, that are shaped and formed by the reason and will into who you are, into your personal character. It's like taming a pet.

For this reason, emotions are more important than we usually think. (Well, most *men*, anyway.) Stoics, and people of Stoic tendencies, underestimate them. But people of Epicurean tendencies overestimate them because they know nothing greater, and so they make even morality and religion matters of emotion. Emotions may be the *starting point* for virtue and wisdom, as soil is the starting point for a garden; and good emotions may be the *result* of wisdom and virtue, as fruit and flowers are the result of a garden; but they are not the plants themselves. Good feelings are not good choices, though they make good choices easier and more powerfully motivated. For instance, when you are morally good you will have more interior pleasure, more happiness, and more joy, even while you have pain, sorrow, or misery; and you will certainly have more of these goods afterwards. So cultivating "well-disposed" emotions is important for morality and for happiness. And knowledge is even more important, as St. Thomas explains: Socrates was half right.

If reason is not *sufficient* for morality, is it *necessary*?

Whether there can be moral virtue without intellectual virtue?

(Objection 1.) It would seem that moral virtue can be without intellectual virtue. Because moral virtue, as Cicero says, is *a habit like a second nature* **... as is evident in natural things devoid of knowledge. Therefore in a man there may be a moral virtue like a second nature ...**

(Reply to Objection 1.) The inclination of nature in things devoid of reason is without choice; wherefore such an inclination does not of necessity require reason. But the inclination of moral virtue is with choice; and consequently in order that it may be perfect it requires that reason be perfected by intellectual virtue.

(Objection 2.) Further ... it happens at times that men are virtuous and acceptable to God without being vigorous in the use of reason.

(Reply to Objection 2.) A man may be virtuous without having full use of reason as to everything, provided he have it with regard to those things which have to be done virtuously. In this way all virtuous men have full use of reason. Hence those who seem to be simple, through lack of worldly cunning, may possibly be prudent, according to Mat. 10:16: *Be ye wise as serpents and simple as doves.*

Gregory says that *the other virtues, unless we do prudently what we desire to do, cannot be real virtues.* **But prudence** (practical wisdom) **is an intellectual virtue.... Therefore moral virtues cannot be without intellectual virtues.**

Moral virtue can be without some of the intellectual virtues ... but not without understanding and prudence. (For) in order that a choice may be good, two things are required. First, that the intention be directed to a due end; and this is done by moral virtue, which inclines the appetitive faculty to the good that is in accord with reason, which is a due end. Secondly, that man take rightly the things which have reference to (i.e., those

things which are good means to) **the end; and this he cannot do unless his reason counsel, judge and command aright, which is the function of prudence ...** (I–II,58,4).

On nearly every question, St. Thomas habitually avoids two opposite extremes that other philosophers tend to fall into. The two extremes in morality are intellectualism and anti-intellectualism.

Intellectualists like Plato say reason alone is sufficient for morality; that the cause of moral evil is intellectual ignorance and the cause of moral goodness is reason, with no role for will or feelings. (Plato has a very primitive concept of will: it is little more than the capacity for righteous indignation, which is really a passion rather than the will.) Modern Utilitarians make an error similar to Plato's in identifying morality with rational self-interest, in a much more calculating way. The intellectualism of Aristotle recognizes the will but does not emphasize it as much as Jews and Christians do. No pagans did, since only Jews and Christians believed that the fundamental relationship for human beings, i.e., the relationship to a personal God, was a relationship of will and choice—to trust and obey His will or not to, i.e., faith or sin. These two categories were simply unknown to the pagans. God was not that intimate with them.

Anti-intellectualists make the opposite error. Emotivists like Rousseau say morality is a matter of emotion, not reason or will. Voluntarists like Kant say the opposite: that morality is a matter of will simply, not emotion; that "duty" is not only totally distinct from but even opposed to "inclinations". For Kant the only thing that is good in itself is a good will.

So intellectualists say that reason is sufficient for morality and anti-intellectualists say it is not even necessary; St. Thomas says it is necessary (thus the point of this article: that there cannot be moral virtue without intellectual virtue: wisdom and prudence); but it is not sufficient. The navigator (reason) is necessary, but so is the captain (will), and also well-trained sailors (passions, desires, and emotions).

Stoics say the emotions, passions, or desires are like wild animals: dangerous and bad. They wish they didn't exist. Sentimentalists like the Epicureans, Rousseau, and modern pop psychologists say that emotions are the best thing in us. They think feelings like compassion and empathy, or sexual love, are the highest good. How does St. Thomas stake out a position between these two extremes? What is the role of the passions in the moral life?

(As Aristotle says,) *passions are neither virtues nor vices ... passions are not in themselves good or evil. For man's good or evil is something in reference to reason; wherefore the passions, considered in themselves, can be either good or evil forasmuch as they may accord or disaccord with reason* (I-II,59,1).

Augustine says: *If the will is perverse, these movements*, viz. the passions, *are perverse also; but if it is upright, they are not only blameless but even praiseworthy.* But nothing praiseworthy is incompatible with moral virtue. Therefore moral virtue does not exclude the passions, but is consistent with them.

The Stoics and Peripatetics (Aristotelians) disagreed on this point ... For the Stoics held that the soul's passions cannot be in a wise or virtuous man ... (I-II,59,2).

Christ was perfect in virtue. But there was sorrow in Him, for He said (Mt. 26:38): *My soul is sorrowful even unto death.* Therefore sorrow is compatible with virtue ...

The Stoics ... held that no evil can happen to a wise man, for they thought that just as man's only good is virtue, and bodily goods are no good to man, so man's only evil is vice, which cannot be in a virtuous man. But this is unreasonable. For since man is composed of soul and body, whatever conduces to preserve the life of the body is some good to man, yet not his supreme good, because he can abuse it. Consequently the evil which is contrary to this good can be in a wise man and can cause him moderate sorrow.

Also, although a virtuous man can be without grave sin, yet no man is to be found to live without committing slight sins, according to I Jo 1:8: *If we say that we have no sin, we deceive ourselves ...* And he is to be commended if he sorrow for that sin ...

Wherefore moderate sorrow for an object which ought to make us sorrowful is a mark of virtue, as also the Philosopher says.

Moreover, this proves useful for avoiding evil since, just as good is more readily sought for the sake of pleasure, so is evil more undauntedly shunned on account of sorrow (I-II,59,3).

No man is just who rejoices not in just deeds, as is stated in (Aristotle) ... But joy is a passion ...

If we take the passions as being *inordinate* emotions, as the Stoics did, it is evident that in this sense perfect virtue is without the passions. But if by passions we understand any movement of the sensitive appetite, it is plain that moral virtues, which are about the passions as their proper matter, cannot be without passions. The reasons for this is that otherwise it would follow that moral virtue makes the sensitive appetite altogether idle; whereas it is not the function of virtue to deprive the powers subordinate to reason of their proper activities, but to make them execute the commands of reason by exercising their proper acts ...

Virtue overcomes inordinate passion; it produces ordinate passion. It is inordinate, not ordinate, passion that leads to sin (I-II,59,5).

What St. Thomas says is so clear and complete that commenting on it would be like putting a blanket over a bell.

What is the reason, in the nature of things, for the popularity of the traditional four cardinal virtues of Prudence, Justice, Temperance, and Fortitude?

*The entire structure of good works is built on four virtues.... **The virtue of which we speak now is good as defined by reason, which good can be considered in two ways. First, as existing in the very act of reason: and thus we have one principal virtue, called *Prudence* (practical wisdom); Secondly, according as the reason puts its order into something else, either into operations** (actions), **and then we have *Justice;* or into passions, and then we need two virtues. For the need of putting the order of reason into the passions is due to their thwarting reason; and then the passions need a curb, which we call *Temperance* (moderation, self-control); secondly, by the passions withdrawing us from following the dictate of reason, e.g., through fear of danger or toil; and then man needs to be strengthened for that which reason dictates, lest he turn back; and to this end there is *Fortitude* (courage)....**

For there are four subjects of the virtue we speak of now, viz. the power which is rational in its essence, and this is perfected by *Prudence,* and that which is rational by participation, and this is threefold: the will, subject of *Justice;* the concupiscible (attracting) **faculty, subject of *Temperance;* and the irascible** (repelling) **faculty, subject of *Fortitude*** (I–II,61,2).

St. Thomas is very traditional, both in the sense that he reaffirms and justifies the best of the philosophy he inherits from his philosophical predecessors (Socrates, Plato, Aristotle, Dionysius, Augustine, Boethius) and in the sense that his own philosophy has become an inheritance and a "school" of philosophy that many of his successors have reaffirmed and imbibed as wise and profitable. But he always gives a *reason* for the tradition; tradition serves reason, not vice versa. Here he gives two reasons for the tradition that of all the natural virtues these four are "cardinal," i.e., the hinges ("cardes") on which all other virtues turn,

the foundations on which all the other virtues are built. For they perfect the essential powers of the soul of the person. They are the most personal and internal and substantial: they inhere in our very selves.

It is a useful exercise to make a little map, in outline form, of St. Thomas' explanation of the four cardinal virtues. It is a map of the first floor of the soul of a saint, thus a map of your own future. For the very meaning of life is to become that. And it is much more likely that you will reach the goal at the end of the road if you have a good map of the road to it.

There are higher virtues than these (the three "theological virtues" or God-related virtues of faith, hope and charity), but these four are the foundation of all virtue in the non-supernatural dimensions of man. (There is no such thing as a purely natural man without any relationship to God. It is an abstraction. But abstractions are useful if we remember they are only abstractions.)

The theological virtues are first in value, but the four cardinal natural virtues are known first and must exist first in any person who aspires to the higher virtues. For instance, if prudence (practical wisdom) is not in one's reason, one will have no good reasons to believe the Faith; and if justice is not already in place in the soul, charity will not be able to transcend justice and transform and fulfill it.

All four of these virtues have broader and deeper and more attractive meanings in St. Thomas, and the ancients, than they do in modern parlance. "Prudence" does not mean merely "safety first" but knowing the right thing to do in concrete situations. "Justice" does not mean merely punishment but doing the right thing, giving everyone what is due. "Temperance" does not mean merely not eating too much and not getting drunk, or having fewer or weaker desires, but mastering rather than being mastered by your desires. And "Fortitude" does not mean merely willpower but the inner strength to love something good so much that you will endure the lesser evil of pain for its sake. (And "reason" does not mean merely logical argumentation or calculating, but knowing what really is.)

Why are faith, hope and charity the three greatest things in the world?

... man's happiness is twofold.... One is proportionate to human nature ... which man can obtain by means of his natural principles (powers). The other is a happiness surpassing man's nature and which man can obtain by the power of God alone, by a kind of participation in the Godhead, about which it is written (2 Pet 1:4) that by Christ we are made *partakers of the divine nature*. And because such happiness surpasses the capacity of human nature, man's natural principles which enable him to act well according to his capacity do not suffice to direct man to this same happiness. Hence it is necessary for man to receive from God some additional principles whereby he may be directed to supernatural happiness, even as he is directed to his connatural end by means of his natural principles, albeit not without the divine assistance. Such principles are called *theological virtues*: first because their object is God, inasmuch as they direct us aright to God; secondly, because they are infused in us by God alone; thirdly, because these virtues are not made known to us save by divine revelation ... (I-II,62,1).

First, as regards the intellect, man receives certain supernatural principles which are held by means of a divine light. These are the articles of faith.... Secondly, the will is directed to this end, both as to the movements of intention, which tends to that end as something attainable—and this pertains to hope—and as to a certain spiritual union whereby the will is, so to speak, transformed into that end—and this belongs to charity (I-II,62,3).

When he distinguishes virtues into natural and supernatural, St. Thomas is not saying that there are or ever were any people who actually lived on the natural level alone, without supernatural virtues or vices. It is a conceptual distinction, not a real one. All men who ever lived have both natural and supernatural dimensions, because all were called, from the beginning, to a relationship with the supernatural God—in fact to be "partakers of the divine nature". The distinction between the natural and the supernatural is a distinction between two abstract aspects, not two concrete things. It is like the distinction between body and soul. There is no human body without a human soul; a corpse is what once was a human body but no longer is one. And the human soul without the human body is like a ghost: it is not fully human until it receives its human body in the Resurrection. Ghosts and corpses scare us precisely because they are *not* human.

The four cardinal natural virtues are fertilizer for the spiritual soil in which the three theological virtues are to grow. So even the cardinal virtues are ultimately "theological" in that their ultimate end is God; but the theological virtues are (a) directly and explicitly directed to God, (b) given by God, and (c) revealed by God. (Those are St. Thomas' three distinctions between the two levels of virtues.)

They are for the whole person, not just a part. (True religion is never a specialty.) Since the intellect and will direct the whole person, including the passions and the acts of the body, these crucial virtues exist in the intellect and will and thus determine and give character to the whole person.

Faith is belief in what God has revealed. Faith is intellectual in the sense that it exists in the intellect; however, its motives are not reasons we discovered by ourselves, but personal trust in God. We believe what God has revealed to us because we trust Him personally, not vice versa.

Hope is our anticipatory union with God. We are already united with Him in hope, as an engaged couple is already married in hope.

Charity is like the marriage itself, and it begins in this life.

If God created man in His own image, then man must be innately virtuous, right?

Whether virtue is in us by nature?

Whatever is in man by nature is common to all men and is not taken away by sin.... But virtue is not in all men, and is cast out by sin. Therefore it is not in man by nature....

... [W]ith regard to sciences and virtues, some held that they are wholly from within, so that all virtues and sciences pre-exist in the soul naturally, but that the hindrances to science and virtue, which are due to the soul being weighed down by the body, are removed by study and practice, even as iron is made bright by being polished. This was the opinion of the Platonists. Others said that they are wholly from without.... Others said that sciences and virtues are in us by nature so far as we are adapted to them, but not in their perfection: this is the teaching of the (Aristotelian) Philosophers, and is nearer the truth ... in man's reason are to be found instilled by nature certain naturally known principles of both knowledge and action, which are the nurseries of intellectual and moral virtues ... in so far as there is in the will a natural appetite for good in accordance with reason.... It is therefore evident that all virtues are in us by nature according to aptitude, inchoately, but not according to perfection, except the theological virtues, which are entirely from without (I–II,63,1).

By nature man is *ontologically* good, good in his being, good by his nature, his essence. After each day of creation, God pronounced it "good" (Gen 1:10,12,18,21,25), but after creating man "in His own image" (Gen 1:27) He pronounced His creation "very good" (Gen 1:31).

But man is not by nature *morally* good. Since man has free will, he has to *choose* to be morally good. In this sense of "good", "there is none that (wholly) does good, no, not one" (Ps 14:3; 53:1,3; 1 Jn 1:8)—at least no one who ever lived after the

Fall of Adam and Eve, except (1) Jesus Christ and (2) His mother. For (1) although He was sinless, Christ was a human being as well as God. And (2) God miraculously preserved His mother from both Original Sin and actual sins.

Have you ever met a man without any moral vices or sins, who never made a single less-than-morally-perfect choice? And have you ever met one without any virtues at all, not even "honor among thieves"? Who could be idiotic enough to deny that "there's a little good in the worst of us and a little bad in the best of us?" Only a philosopher.

Some philosophers denied moral evil because they were intellectualists or rationalists like Plato, who said that all evil is due to ignorance; that if we only knew that good was good and evil was evil, we would always choose good and never evil. Some were sentimentalists like Rousseau, who denied moral evil in man and located it all in society or artificial conventions because they reduced all moral good to the easiest one of all: obeying your natural instincts, your desires and feelings, even though they are fallen, including the instinct Rousseau found in himself and followed: the instinct to deceive, rob, and seduce rich ladies and to abandon his own children.

Other philosophers, like Machiavelli, Calvin, and Hobbes, denied moral good in man and reduced all good behavior to external force, whether from a human or divine tyrant.

Both the "optimists" and the "pessimists" forgot that society comes from man, not from something outside man, and therefore cannot make man bad if he is innately good or good if he is innately bad.

St. Thomas, as usual, is the apostle of common sense. Virtue, like reason and language, is in us by nature potentially—we are designed for it—but since the actualization of this potentiality depends on our free choices, there is in us by our own choice both good and evil; and since choices make habits, there are in us both good and evil habits. (Virtues are simply good habits and vices are bad ones.)

If we are not born virtuous or vicious, but have to become virtuous or vicious, how do we do it?

Vicious habits are caused by evil acts. Much more, therefore, can virtuous habits be caused by good acts (I-II,63,2).

... [E]verything that is ... moved by another is disposed by the action of the agent ... if the acts be multiplied, a certain quality is formed in the power which is ... moved, which quality is called a habit ... the habits of moral virtue are caused in the appetitive powers according as they are moved by the reason (I-II,51,2).

... [W]e see that because fire cannot at once overcome the combustible, it does not enkindle at once, but ... gradually.... Now it is clear that ... reason cannot entirely overcome the appetitive power in one act.... Therefore a habit of virtue cannot be caused by one act, but only by many (I-II,51,3).

We become virtuous in the same way we become rich: we invest in the right company and then have patience.

A lost-looking pedestrian with a violin case asked a New York City policeman: "How do I get to Carnegie Hall?" the answer was: "Practice, man, practice."

There's no easier way. You learn to do it by doing it. Repetition creates habits. So begin, already!

It begins in the mind and will, with thinking and deciding. "Sow a thought, reap an act. Sow an act, reap a habit. Sow a habit, reap a character. Sow a character, reap a destiny."

It has to be gradual. Every good choice makes the next one easier and more delightful. Every bad one also makes the next bad one easier and more delightful.

Reason can instantly see a truth, but it cannot instantly convince the will to form a habit of choosing the good, and it cannot instantly tame the appetites. The appetites are like dogs or horses; training takes a long time.

We're lucky it does, for that means there's always hope, always a chance for reform. The angels have no passions, and therefore no hope for change, for reform if they chose evil. They chose good or evil simply and absolutely, once for all, as soon as God gave them a choice, at the moment of their creation. There is no chance that an evil angel (a demon) can ever become good, or that a good angel can ever become bad.

We are not angels. We can't become a saint in one act. And we *must* become saints. That's the meaning of life, and the demand of our Creator (Mt 5:48). That's why there's a Purgatory. He will not give up on us, He will not stop sculpting us, until we are perfect. And He will not do it against our will, only with it. We can't do it without Him and He won't do it without us.

St. Thomas, following Aristotle, says that every moral virtue is a mean between two extremes. That sounds dull and boring. Weren't the saints extremists, absolutists, zealots, and just a little bit wonderfully crazy?

Whether Moral Virtues Observe the Mean?

(Objection 1.) **It would seem that moral virtue does not observe the mean. For the nature of a mean is incompatible with that which is extreme. Now the nature of virtue is to be something extreme....**

(Reply.) **Moral virtue derives goodness from the rule of reason, while its matter** (contents, raw material) **consists in passions** (emotions) **or operations** (external actions). **If therefore we compare moral virtue to reason, it holds the position of one extreme, viz. conformity, while excess and defect** (both) **take the position of the other extreme, viz. deformity. But if we consider moral virtue with respect of its matter, then it holds the position of mean, in so far as it makes the passion conform to the rule of reason. Hence the Philosopher says that** *virtue, as to its essence, is a mean state,* **in so far as the rule of virtue is imposed on its proper matter,** *but it is an extreme in reference to the 'best' and 'the excellent'* ... (I-II,64,1).

Whether Theological Virtues Observe the Mean?

Wherever virtue observes the mean it is possible to sin by excess as well as by deficiency. But there is no sinning by excess against God, Who is the object of theological virtue; for it is written (Sir 43:33 DR): *Bless the Lord, exalt Him as much as you can, for He is above all praise.* **Therefore theological virtue does not observe the mean.... [N]ever can we love God as much as He ought to be loved, nor believe and hope in Him as much as we should.... [T]here can be no excess of hope in comparison with God, Whose goodness is infinite ...** (I-II,64,4).

Even the virtues that do consist in a mean or median, viz. the four cardinal natural moral virtues, consist in a mean only with regard to their matter or raw material, i.e., the bodily actions and emotional passions that the reason and the will rightly order. The order itself, that is, the imposing of order and form on the actions and passions, the forming of *right* actions and passions, is not a mean but **is a matter of "extreme in reference to the 'best'"**. You can do too much or too little "stuff", and you can feel too much or too little of any emotion, but you can't be too virtuous.

Of course you can be too self-consciously virtuous, or too self-righteously virtuous, or too concerned with the apparent virtue of your public persona, but these are not virtues but vices. You can be too sissified, but that is not the virtue of kindness. You can be too conservative and risk-averse, but that is not the virtue of prudence. You can be too bull-headed, but that is not the virtue of courage. You can be a cold-hearted "control freak", but that is not the virtue of self-control. You can refuse to go beyond what is "proper", but that is not the virtue of justice, any more than revenge is.

As for the theological virtues, the more "extremism" the better! You can't ever love God too much, for He is infinitely lovable. You can't ever put too much hope in Him, for He is always more generous than you can imagine or conceive. You can't ever put too much faith in Him, for He is always infallibly true—true to Himself, true to His promises, and true to His love for you. Be an extremist!

There is, however, only one right object for this fanaticism or extremism. For there is only one God. All other absoutes, all other extremisms, are idols. Once we are absolutistic about God, we are freed to be relativistic about everything else. Everything good is good only because it is relative to God, only because it either comes from God or leads to God. So Christianity is also the most relativistic of relativisms, as well as the most absolutistic of absolutisms.

Why is love the greatest thing in the world?

Now since the three theological virtues look at God as their proper object, it cannot be said that any one of them is greater than another by reason of its having a greater object, but only from the fact that it approaches nearer than another to that object; and in this way charity is greater than the others. Because the others, in their very nature, imply a certain distance from the object: since faith is of what is not seen, and hope is of what is not possessed. But the love of charity is of that which is already possessed, since the beloved is, in a manner, in the lover, and, again, the lover is drawn by desire to union with the beloved; hence it is written (1 Jn 4:16): *He that abideth in charity, abideth in God, and God in him* (I-II, 66,6).

The question is a very simple one, and so is the answer. Love is the greatest thing in the world because it is a participation in the very life of God Himself. "God *is* love" (1 Jn 4:8). Faith, hope, desire, aspiration, intention, idealism—these are all very good, and even necessary, but they **imply a certain distance from the object.** Love does not. Love implies the real presence of its object.

Therefore when we choose to exercise an act of agape (unselfish love), we bring the real presence of Christ to the people we love. We become tubes into which Christ comes and through which Christ moves and out of which Christ acts on other people. We are like priests who consecrate the Eucharist in that we help to bring about a real supernatural change, a real presence of Christ. It's not Transubstantiation, but it is a real presence. We become real instrumental causes of His real presence, like Mary at the Annunciation.

These two analogies are only likenesses, of course, but they are real likenesses. We do not become priests and we do not become Mary, but we become like priests and we become like Mary. It's not just a clever poetic conceit that remains in subjective consciousness. It's real. It really happens.

This "love" is not just any kind of love, of course, but agape, charity, unselfish love, the willing of the true good of the other, the gift of self.

When we love in this way, we actually live in God and God in us. That is what Scripture says (1 Jn 4:16). Let's not minimize what Scripture says. It's just as dangerous and just as heretical to under-do as to over-do what Scripture says.

This may seem unduly optimistic about human power, but it presuppoess human fallenness and Original Sin. That is why it is impossible to run the engine of our agape on any other fuel than the very life of the Trinity. There is no other source of it; fallen human nature is incorrigibly selfish.

Therefore whenever anyone truly loves, God is living in them and operating in them. That does not mean that they themselves do not do it. For God is not a rival to man, and His will (which *is* love) does not blot out or set aside man's free will but perfects it, as "grace perfects nature".

This agape certainly seems to be present in the lives of many men and women who do not have faith. We do not know, and should not judge, whether this love-presence of God in their lives is a saving presence, i.e., whether they have the implicit faith that will get them to Heaven. We know that God can work anonymously, and He is far more gracious and tricky than we know. We cannot see faith, because we cannot see into hearts; but we can see love, because we do see deeds; and we should not begrudge or deny the presence of love when we see it anywhere, but rather give praise to both God and man for it.

Mother Teresa frequently spoke of meeting Jesus "in disguise" in other people. This is not just fantasizing or sentimentalism. It is accurate theology. Whenever we see with the eyes of agape, we meet Him.

This is real, not just mental, presence. He is really there. And even though it is not the Eucharist, with His own Body and Blood, it is Eucharis-*tic,* or Eucharist-like in two ways: (1) it is hidden and disguised beneath the appearances; and (2) it is brimming with grace and it therefore calls for thanksgiving.

II3.   THE REASON THERE MUST BE A "*NATURAL* LAW" MORALITY

Since it is God Who created and designed man for virtue, and since the ultimate end of virtue is God—being God-like in this life and united with Him in the next—why do we say moral virtue is "natural" rather than "supernatural"? Why "*natural* moral law?" Why not just "moral law" Most Muslims and Jews, and even many Protestants, are suspicious of "natural law".

Augustine says: *Every vice, simply because it is a vice, is contrary to nature....*

(For) **vice is contrary to virtue. Now the virtue of a thing consists in its being well disposed in a manner befitting its nature.... Hence the vice of any thing consists in its being disposed in a manner not befitting its nature....**

Now man derives his species (essential nature) **from his rational soul; and consequently whatever is contrary to the order of reason is, properly speaking, contrary to the nature of man as man, while whatever is in accord with reason is in accord with the nature of man ...** (I-II,71,2).

What is contrary to God's will is a vice. God willed nature, and human nature, in creating it. Therefore what is contrary to human nature is contrary to God's will.

God's will is expressed not merely in His direct commands, but also in His creating nature, and human nature, with natural ends. The reason there is a natural law is because all nature is teleological, i.e., purposive, designed to move toward natural ends. Puppies grow into dogs, not cats; acorns grow into oaks, not tulips. Birds fly and fish swim. Avalanches fall and fire rises, not vice versa. Eyes are obviously *for* seeing, hands *for* grasping, and sex *for* reproduction (unless you've been brainwashed by modern sex "education"). It's called "the reproductive system"! The denial of a natural moral law and the denial of teleology always go hand in hand.

All the virtues—the four cardinal virtues and the three theological virtues, and all the less important virtues too—make us more perfect, more perfectly like what God designed us to be. All vices deface that design, and deface our very nature. An unjust, unwise, out-of-control, cowardly, faithless, despairing, uncharitable man is less of a *man,* less human, than a saint. He is defacing his own human nature.

St. Thomas mentions reason as the criterion of all the virtues: "whatever is contrary to the order of reason is ... contrary to the nature of man." Reason and capacity for virtue are coextensive: all persons have both, all impersonal things (mere animals, vegetables, or minerals) have neither.

Notice that St. Thomas says not just "reason" but "*the order of* reason". Reason discovers teleology, purposive order, order toward natural ends. This is "reason" in its original, whole-human sense, not "reason" in its truncated, modern, computerlike sense of mere cleverness and calculation, which omits the first and biggest thing of all: understanding the nature of things, seeing what is there. Thus the typically modern denial of design in nature and in human nature, the denial of teleology, is *irrational,* even when it is done in order to be more "scientific". Science does not need to deny the existence of teleology and to assume materialism (i.e., the philosophy that there exist only material and efficient causes, no formal and final causes) any more than it needs to deny religion and assume atheism. It is illogical to assume that the rightful focus on only two of the four causes in science requires us to deny the other two in philosophy. That is as illogical as assuming that biology's focusing on hormones requires psychology to deny romance, or that cybernetics' focusing on brains requires philosophy to deny minds, or that anthropology's focusing on man requires theology to deny God.

So the habitual modern denial or ignoring of teleology is an intellectual *vice.* It is contrary to reason, and therefore contrary to the nature of man, and therefore contrary to natural virtue. To become a *good* man you must know the nature of man and the end of man (your formal and final cause). You cannot become a saint without the natural law.

C. S. Lewis, in *Mere Christianity,* uses the image of humanity as a fleet of ships to explain why ethics has three dimensions. The fleet's sailing orders must tell it three things: First, and most important, what the mission of the fleet is, why it is at sea at all; second, how each ship is to stay shipshape and afloat; and third, how each ship is to cooperate with the others and not hinder or bump into the others. These three things symbolize (1) the ultimate purpose of human life, which in fact is supernatural, is God Himself, (2) individual ethics, and (3) social ethics.

Is that right? Is there a necessary philosophical and theological basis for this classification of all moral good and evil into three parts?

Whether sin (and therefore also sanctity or virtue, sin's opposite) **is fittingly divided into sin against God (#1), against oneself (#2), and against one's neighbor (#3)?**

... there should be a threefold order in man:

One in relation to the rule of reason, in so far as all our actions and passions should be commensurate with the rule of reason;

Another order is in relation to the rule of the divine law, whereby man should be directed in all things;

And if man were a solitary animal, this twofold order would suffice. But since man is naturally a civic and social animal ... hence a third order is necessary, whereby man is directed in relation to other men....

Of these orders the second (the divine) **contains the first** (the individually human) **and surpasses it. For whatever things are comprised under the order of reason are comprised under the order of God Himself. Yet some things are comprised under the order of God which surpass the human reason,** such as matters of faith and things due to God alone....

In like manner, the first order (individual reason) **includes the third** (social ethics) **and surpasses it, because in all things wherein we are directed in reference to our neighbor, we need to be directed according to the order of reason. Yet in some things we are directed according to the order of reason in relation to ourselves only and not in reference to our neighbor....**

... by the theological virtues man is directed to God, by temperance and fortitude to himself, and by justice to his neighbor ...

To sin against God is common to all sins, in so far as the order to God includes every human order, but in so far as order to God surpasses the other two orders, sin against God is a special kind of sin (I–II,72,4).

The most practical consequence of this analysis is that all natural good or evil, virtue or vice, is part of supernatural good or evil; that the natural law, as St. Thomas elsewhere says, is a "participation in" the eternal law; and therefore "to sin against God (and the eternal law) is common to all sin", including sin against yourself and your neighbor. In other words, the "vertical" dimension, the relation to God, is present, at least anonymously, in all "horizontal" choices and acts toward self or neighbor. Thus Christ said, "As you did it to one of the least of these my brothers [including yourself!], you did it to me" (Mt 25:40). Every sin takes the shape of the Cross: every "horizontal" sin against self or others always has the "vertical" dimension of defiling and profaning something holy. Every act of injustice to your neighbor is profaning the Christ of the Eucharist.

Are sins of the flesh more or less serious than spiritual sins?

... [C]arnal sins are of less guilt but of more shame than spiritual sins.... As the Philosopher himself says,... *sins of intemperance are most worthy of reproach because they are about those pleasures which are common to us and irrational animals;* hence by these sins man is, so to speak, brutalized, for which same reason Gregory says that they are more shameful ... (But) spiritual sins are of greater guilt than carnal sins.

Modern people often confuse guilt and shame. This rarely means reducing shame to guilt, but almost always reducing guilt to shame. Shame is social: being seen and disapproved by others. Guilt is individual: being seen and disapproved by God and/or your own conscience. The reason modern people often reduce guilt to shame is that their individual conscience is weak; and the reason it is weak is that their religious conscience is weak. For it is in the face of God that we become most inward and most individuated. We are never so inescapably ourselves as when we are alone with God.

Guilt is in souls, not in bodies: ... the soul can be the subject of guilt while the flesh, of itself, cannot be the subject of guilt ... whatever accrues to the flesh from the corruption of the first sin ... has the character not of guilt but of punishment (I-II,83,1).

Spiritual sins are of greater guilt than carnal sins. Yet this does not mean that each spiritual sin is of greater guilt than each carnal sin, but that ... spiritual sins are more grievous than carnal sins other things being equal ... because carnal sin, as such, is against the sinner's own body, which he ought to love less, in the order of charity, than God and his neighbor, against whom he commits spiritual sins, and consequently spiritual sins, as such, are of greater guilt ...

(Also,) carnal sins have a stronger impulse, viz. our innate concupiscence of the flesh. Therefore spiritual sins, as such, are of greater guilt (being more deliberate)....

The devil is said to rejoice chiefly in the sin of lust because it is of the greatest adhesion and man can with difficulty be withdrawn from it....

(However,) Adultery belongs not only to the sin of lust but also to the sin of injustice ... so that adultery is so much more grievous than theft as a man loves his wife more than his possessions (I-II,73,5).

Adultery is grave not mainly because it occurs when we sink to the level of addicted animals but because it gravely harms the person we promised to love forever. Its spiritual dimension is its worst dimension: it is an injustice, a lie, a betrayal of love, of a person, the most important person in your life, and of your children, and of the very institution of marriage and the family, and thus of human society.

The lusting of the flesh against the spirit, when the reason actually resists it, is not a sin but is matter for the exercise of virtue (I-II,80,3).

We often confuse temptation with sin. This is wrong for two reasons. (1) Satan, not God, tempts. God only allows it (Jas 1:13). (2) Sin produces guilt. Temptation does not. Even Jesus was tempted with all the temptations we are tempted with, since He was wholly human (Heb 4:15). But unlike us, He resisted all temptations. When you are tempted, do not think God has abandoned you. The more virtuous you are, the more the Devil will try to tempt you (Lk 22:31). Look what He did to Christ.

So what, exactly, is the role of ignorance in sin? Does it excuse us?

As the Philosopher states, the opinion of Socrates was that knowledge can never be overcome by passion, wherefore he held every virtue to be a kind of knowledge and every sin a kind of ignorance. In this he was somewhat right because, since the object of the will is a good or an apparent good, it is never moved to an evil unless that which is not good appear good in some respect to the reason, so that the will would never tend to evil unless there were some ignorance or error in the reason....

Experience, however, shows that many act contrary to the knowledge that they have, and this is confirmed by divine authority, according to the words of Luke 12:47: *The servant who knew the will of his lord ... and did not do it ... and James 4:17: To him ... who knoweth to do good and doeth it not, to him it is a sin....*

... [N]othing prevents a thing which is known habitually from not being considered actually, so that it is possible for a man to have correct knowledge ... and yet not to consider his knowledge actually; and in such a case it does not seem difficult for a man to act counter to what he does not actually consider ... in so far as passions hinder him from considering it. How it hinders him in three ways. First, by way of distraction.... Secondly, by way of opposition, because a passion often inclines to something contrary to what man knows in general. Thirdly, by way of bodily transmutation (biological process), **the result of which is that reason is somewhat fettered so as not to exercise its act freely, even as sleep or drunkenness, on account of some change wrought on the body, fetters the use of reason. That this takes place in the passions is evident from the fact that sometimes, when the passions are very intense, man loses the use of reason altogether; for many have gone out of their minds through excess of love or anger** (I-II,77,2).

Socrates rightly identified intellectual knowledge as a necessary cause of moral evil, as St. Thomas points out in the first paragraph above; for the will cannot move to any end unless the intellect first portrays this end as good. Thus we always choose an apparent good, an end that appears to us to be good. All evil consists in wrongly identifying what is in fact an evil as a good, e.g., seeing some sin as pleasant. This is why it is so important to keep our minds pure and right.

But Socrates confused this necessary cause with a sufficient cause, and taught that all evil was caused *only* by ignorance. As St. Thomas points out in the second paragraph, experience and divine revelation both contradict this. Socrates was too much the rationalist to let experience judge his theory rather than vice versa. The explanation for the experienced fact that we do indeed do what we know to be evil is that our knowledge is not merely a *cause* of our willing, it is also an *effect* of our willing. Influenced by our passions, we can command our mind to look or not to look at something.

St. Thomas also sees an ambiguity in "knowing": we may habitually, unconsciously know that a thing is evil—not only morally forbidden but also harmful to ourselves—and yet not allow this knowledge to rise up into consciousness to deter us from the evil because we are so in love with the false pleasure that we attach to the evil. Our passions are disordered. Drug addiction is a clear example. *All* sin is addictive, like a drug: it blinds the mind and rational will. All sin harms the sinner: it gouges out his eyes. In extreme cases, "many have gone out of their minds" through disordered passion; but all sin does this in some degree. It has to, for it if didn't, we could not sin. Socrates is right about that.

St. Thomas also points out, very realistically, that addiction to sin often has a physical, bodily dimension. Almost everything about us is psychosomatic.

117. PASSION AND RESPONSIBILITY

Does passion make us more or less responsible for sin?

The passion of concupiscence is called a temptation of the flesh. But the greater the temptation that overcomes a man, the less grievous his sin, as Augustine states ... if we take passion as preceding the sinful act, it must needs diminish the sin, because the act is a sin in so far as it is voluntary and under our control. Now a thing is said to be under our control through the reason and will, and therefore the more the reason and will do anything of their own accord, and not through the impulse of a passion, the more is it voluntary and under our control. In this respect passion diminishes sin in so far as it diminishes its voluntariness.

On the other hand, a consequent passion does not diminish a sin but increases it; or rather it is a sign of its gravity, in so far as it shows the intensity of the will toward the sinful act (I-II,77,6).

... [O]ne who willfully gets drunk ... is considered to do voluntarily whatever he does through being drunk ... (I-II,77,7).

An act which, in its genus, is evil, cannot be excused from sin altogether unless it be rendered altogether involuntary....

Sometimes the passion is not such as to take away the use of reason altogether, and then reason can drive the passion away by turning to other thoughts ... wherefore such a passion does not excuse from sin altogether ... (I-II,77,7).

The disordered passion that is a cause of sin by blinding the reason has two almost-opposite effects by the very same cause, the blinding of the reason: it both (a) adds to the personal harm of the sin and (b) lessens its personal guilt by lessening freedom and voluntariness.

The more consciously and freely we choose an evil, the more responsible we are for it and the more guilty we are of it; this is why spiritual sins like pride are greater in guilt than carnal sins. Passion that comes *before* the will's choice to sin ("antecedent passion"), and helps to cause it and explain it, diminishes the guilt, by diminishing the freedom and reason. But there is also passion that comes *after* and as a result of the will's choice. This is "consequent passion", willed passion. And this increases the guilt, because we will not only the sin but also the cause of the sin, the disordered passion.

There are important practical, pastoral consequences of this moral principle.

First, since it is reason that disordered passions blind, we must keep our reason clear. "Take every thought captive to obey Christ" (2 Cor 10:5).

Second, we must stop excusing ourselves on the grounds of weakness, for there is always some degree of deliberately willed weakness, as in the case of knowingly getting drunk so that we are "freed" from moral inhibitions. As St. Thomas says, passion usually does not take away reason completely, so as to make the sin wholly involuntary.

Third, we must judge others' sins more leniently, since motives are usually mixed, not pure. For the sinner's reason is usually weak and blinded, as is ours. We habitually are very ready to see the aspect of voluntariness and blameworthiness in others' sins and the aspect of blindness and weakness in our own. To be honest and to see things as they are, we must reverse this habit, and look at the voluntariness and blame in our own sins more, and look at our excuses less, while looking at the (neglected) excuses in others' sins more, and their deliberateness less. For we already see the other half in each case all too readily.

Brother Lawrence, in *The Practice of the Presence of God,* says that every time he sins, and remembers that he sins, and repents, he says to God: "See? Thus shall I always do if You do not give me the grace." This is admirable humility, but it also poses a puzzle: If God *could* give us the grace to avoid any sin, why doesn't He? Obviously we can't blame Him; it is we, not God, who sin. But if He could stop us, what good and loving reason does He have for not stopping us? What good does it do us to be left alone to sin?

God permits some to fall into sin so that by acknowledging their sin they may be humbled and converted, as Augustine states ... through God's mercy temporary blindness is directed medicinally to the spiritual welfare of those who are blinded....

Every evil that God ... permits to be done, is directed to some good ... sometimes to the good of others: thus He directs the sin of tyrants to the good of the martyrs ... (I-II,79,4).

There are two answers to the question of why God deliberately does not give us grace to avoid sin: to deal with our pride and our ignorance. If God prevented us from sinning, we might then sin even more, by pride, which is the worst sin of all. We would also be ignorant of ourselves and our weakness of will, our blindness of mind, and the disorderliness of our passions.

Both reasons come under the reason of *truth.* Humility is an intellectual virtue before it is a moral virtue, for it consists essentially in an accurate knowledge of our own faults and weaknesses. It does not mean having a low opinion of ourselves, but an accurate one.

God is a pragmatist, like a doctor. He tolerates necessary bad side effects in order to cure a worse problem. In order to cure a worse disease, He refuses to cure a lesser one. Trust your Doctor.

This applies not only to the withholding of grace to avoid personal sins, but also to allowing great evils to occur in the world. God never acts arbitrarily, unwisely, unjustly, or unlovingly.

Everything He does, and everything He chooses not to do, is for our good. Even a horrible evil like the Holocaust He must have allowed only to prevent an even greater evil. We seldom see it. Perhaps if Hitler had not erupted into history, the Hitler-like character that lies hidden in all of us (what Max Picard called "the Hitler in ourselves") may have caused the whole world to become Nazi-like in a way that would have been even more harmful because it would have been more disguised and more universal. Sometimes the evil has to rise to the surface to be seen. The addict has to "hit bottom" before he can be cured.

The point is not that we can know such things. We can't. We can only speculate, and the point of such speculation is simply to open our minds and imaginations to possibilities, to give God some "wiggle room". We can know the general principle, that "in everything God works for good, with those who love him" (Rom 8:28), because God has revealed this to us, and God cannot lie. But we cannot understand all the instances or applications of it, because we are not God. (Duh!) That's why faith is needed. We "see through a glass, darkly" (1 Cor 13: 12). We must trust the Great Physician.

That "in everything God works for good, with those who love him, who are called according to his purpose", startling as it is, is the logical conclusion that necessarily follows from the very nature of God, from three of the most basic and essential attributes of God, namely wisdom, power and love. If Rom 8:28 is not true, then God is not God, for He would then be ignorant, weak, or wicked. He is ignorant if He does not know what is ultimately best for us. He is weak if He knows and wills it but cannot do it. And He is wicked if He wills what is for our worst, not for our best.

Therefore all evils that God allows are like dung: they can be used to fertilize some good growth. We can learn from our mistakes. Sin is the very worst thing in the world, worse even than pain (see point #102 above); but even our sins can be made to work for a good end, if only they fall on their faces and creep through the golden door of repentance. We experience this every time we go to Confession.

119. "THE DEVIL MADE ME DO IT"?

Why didn't God accept Eve's excuse that "the Devil made me do it" (Gen. 3:13)?

... the proper principle (origin) of a sinful action is the will, since every sin is voluntary. Consequently nothing can be directly the cause of sin except that which can move the will to act. Now ... that agent which moves the will inwardly to will ... is no other than the will itself, or God.... Now God cannot be the cause of sin.... Therefore it follows that in this respect a man's will alone is directly the cause of his sin ... (I-II,80,1).

... [E]ither the devil or a man may incite to sin, either by offering an object of appetite to the senses or by persuading the reason. But in none of these ... ways can anything be the direct cause of sin because the will is not of necessity moved by any object except the last end ... (I-II,80,1).

Now the intellect, of its very nature, is moved by that which enlightens it in the knowledge of truth, which the devil has no intention of doing in man's regard; rather does he darken man's reason so that it may consent to sin, which darkness is due to the imagination and sensitive appetite. Consequently the operation of the devil seems to be confined to the imagination and sensitive appetite, by moving either of which he can induce man to sin (I-II,80,2).

Further, it is ... written (James 4:7) ... *resist the devil, and he will fly from you,* which would be said neither rightly nor truly if the devil were able to compel us in any way whatever to sin; for then neither would it be possible to resist him, nor would he fly from those who do (I-II,80,3).

No other person, neither the Devil, nor any other evil spirit, nor any human being, can *make* us sin, since sin is voluntary and free; that is why we are responsible for it.

But another can tempt (or "incite") us to sin. (This is why it is so very important to have good friends rather than bad ones, especially at young and formative ages.)

However, no creature can directly move our will. It is free. Even if you are physically forced to act (e.g., if someone stronger than you puts a gun in your hand and then forces your finger to squeeze the trigger), they can force you to shoot but they cannot force you to *will* to shoot. Even when your body is chained, your will is free. "Stone walls do not a prison make, nor iron bars a cage" (Lovelace). God alone can move the will without removing its freedom.

Nor can any evil force, whether human or demonic, directly move the reason to truth, since that would not be a temptation. For truth is the enemy of sin, as light is the enemy of darkness. Temptation does not appeal to reason; reason is its enemy.

What can the Devil do to you, then, if you do not invite him in? (1) Only tempt you to sin, not make you sin. And (2) he cannot directly touch your intellect or will but only the less spiritual powers: he can present tempting images to your imagination and appetites. (This is why it is so important to have a well-trained and well-directed imagination!) It is your choice to look, or listen, or pay attention to these images *or* to refuse to do so. No matter how strong the temptation is, there is always the possibility of overcoming it. (See 1 Cor 10:13: that's a divine promise!) That's why we are responsible and guilty for succumbing to temptation, but not for being tempted. Jesus was tempted too.

Thus St. Thomas gives us a piece of realistic optimism in the last paragraph. The Devil is not like a dragon but like Dracula: he flees from the light. He is actually afraid of you insofar as you have Christ in your soul.

The Devil is also afraid of your guardian angel, who is a "being of light". Darkness fears light. Pray to the angel God has appointed to guard you when you are tempted. Only important people in this world get bodyguards, but each of us is so important to God that He has given each of us a Heavenly soul-guard.

120. WHY THERE IS ALWAYS HOPE FOR CONVERSION EVEN OF THE WORST SINNER

If we have charity, we naturally want to hope for the conversion of everyone without exception, even a monster like Hitler. But isn't this merely wishful thinking? Aren't some people beyond hope? On what objective basis could be founded our subjective hope for the worst of sinners?

Augustine says that *evil does not exist except in some good.* **But the evil of sin cannot be in the good of virtue or of grace, because they are contrary to it. Therefore it must be in the good of nature, and consequently it** (sin) **does not destroy it** (nature) **entirely.... [T]he good of nature that is diminished by sin is the natural inclination to virtue, which is befitting to man** (it is an essential property, and therefore it remains in him) **from the very fact that he is a rational being; for it is due to this that he performs actions in accord with reason, which is to act virtuously. Now sin cannot entirely take away from man the fact that he is a rational being, for then he would no longer be capable of sin. Wherefore it is not possible for this good of nature to be destroyed entirely** (I-II,85,2).

St. Thomas' analysis is totally logical:

1. Evil exists. It is not a substance, a being, but it is real. It exists.

2. If evil exists, it must exist in some being,

3. But all being is good. For God created all things, and declared them good.

4. Therefore evil must exist "in" a good thing. Evil is the perversion of a good thing, the lack of good in a thing that ought to have it: sight in an eye, or love in the will, or order in the passions.

5. What kind of good can evil exist in? There are two kinds of good: natural and supernatural.

6. Supernatural goods are either human (theological virtues) or divine (grace).

7. Evil cannot exist in either supernatural virtues or divine grace, for these are to evil like light to darkness. They are not open to good and evil indifferently, but their very essence is set on good.

8. Therefore, since evil exists and since it cannot exist in any supernatural good, it can exist only in some natural good, some good which is open to both moral good and moral evil.

9. But if evil destroyed all of the goodness in this natural good, it would have nowhere to exist.

10. Therefore there must be some remaining natural good in every thing where we find evil.

11. This also applies to human souls.

12. The good in human souls is virtue, or the inclination to virtue.

13. Therefore this good must remain in a human soul even among the worst vices and evils. This inclination to know and do the good is the very essence of a human soul, and can no more be destroyed, in this life, than the evenness of the number two or the threeness of the sides of a triangle.

14. Another proof of this conclusion is that in order for a man to be capable of sin, he must be capable of virtue, that is, he must know the good and know its goodness, feel the attraction of its goodness. This attraction to the good must exist in order to be overcome by the choice to do evil instead. If not, the choice to do evil is not a free choice.

15. Therefore we can always find this inclination to goodness, however weak and suppressed it is, even in the most wicked soul.

16. This is confirmed by examples in history: e.g., the repentant thief on the cross, Saul of Tarsus, the Gadarene demoniac, and Mary Magdalene, who had "seven devils".

17. Therefore when we speak to a wicked man, we should speak to the good man inside him that is suppressed, the man who is being held prisoner. He is there. He needs someone to acknowledge his existence.

18. Sometimes he responds to fear and severity, sometimes to love and compassion. Use both, as Jesus did.

121. Evidence in our experience for Original Sin

Original Sin is a controversial Christian dogma. Is there evidence in our experience for it?

As a result of original justice (or original righteousness, before the Fall), **the reason had perfect hold over the lower parts of the soul, while reason itself was perfected by God and was subject to Him. Now this same original justice was forfeited through the sin of our first parent ... so that all the powers of the soul are left, as it were,** (at least somewhat) **destitute of their proper order whereby they are naturally directed to virtue, which destitution is called a wounding of nature.**

... [T]here are four of the soul's powers that can be the subject of virtue ... viz. the reason, where prudence resides, the will, where justice is, the irascible (appetite), **the subject of fortitude, and the concupiscible** (appetite), **the subject of temperance. Therefore in so far as the reason is deprived of its order to the true, there is the wound of ignorance; in so far as the will is deprived of its order to the good there is the wound of malice; in so far as the irascible is deprived of its order to the ardous, there is the wound of weakness; and in so far as the concupiscible is deprived of its order to the delectable, moderated by reason, there is the wound of concupiscence....**

But since the inclination to the good of virtue is diminished in each individual on account of actual sin ... these four wounds are also the result of other (actual) **sins, in so far as through sin the reason is obscured, especially in practical matters, the will hardened to evil, good actions become more difficult, and concupiscence more impetuous** (I-II,85,3).

We can see Original Sin by contrast with Original Righteousness, or Rightness, or Justice.

What is right, or proper, or well-ordered is for the higher to rule the lower and for the lower to obey the higher. This means (1) for God to rule the soul, (2) for reason to rule the appetites through the will, (3) for the will to be subject to reason, (4) and for the appetites to obey the rational will, so that we do what is right even when it is painful or hard, and (5) we do not do wrong even when it is pleasant or desirable.

In other words, in this state of innocence we are perfectly regulated by (1) the three theological virtues of faith, hope, and charity, whereby the soul is united to and obedient to God, and the four cardinal natural virtues of (2) prudence, or wisdom, (3) justice, or righteousness, (4) fortitude, or courage, and (5) moderation, or temperance, or self-control.

The opposite vices to the four cardinal natural virtues are (2) ignorance in the reason, (3) injustice in the will, (4) weakness in the irascible (negative, aversive) appetites, and (4) concupiscence (disordered desires) in the concupiscible (positive, attractive) appetites.

Do we now live in the state of innocence or the state of sin? "Know thyself." We're not in Kansas any more, Toto. We are "east of Eden".

How did we get here? It wasn't a tornado. It was the first actual sin of our first parents that brought about the state of Original Sin in human nature and in the whole human race, the state that we were born with. But also it was our own actual sins in our own lives that freely confirmed and strengthened this state of Original Sin that we were born with.

We also choose acts of virtue that oppose and weaken our Original Sin. For our innate inclination to virtue, given to us by God in our very human nature, is not destroyed, only diminished.

With every vice, virtue becomes more difficult, but still possible. With every virtue, additional virtue becomes less difficult, but vice is always still possible. Life is spiritual warfare, and both sides are very much alive. The map of the virtues is a map of a battlefield.

What should I do when there is a conflict between what some human law obligates me to do and what my moral conscience tells me I am obligated to do?--assuming I have made an honest effort to form my conscience. Can obedience to a legitimate human law be evil? Isn't goodness the whole purpose of the law, including human law?

... [T]he definition of law ... is nothing else than an ordinance of reason for the common good, made by him who has care of the community, and promulgated (I-II,90,4).

We are to obey human laws too, but not all human laws are really laws. The practical payoff of St. Thomas' famous definition of law is that if a supposed law lacks any one of the four essential features of law, it is not really a law at all, and need not be obeyed:

(1) if it is not an ordinance of reason: if it is irrational, pointless, meaningless, a mere expression of the will to power;

(2) if it is not for the common good but for harm to the community;

(3) if it is not made by one (or those) who have authority over the community;

(4) or if it is not promulgated (made known).

All God's laws are, by this definition, true laws, but not all human laws are. The Apostles said to the Jewish authorities, "We must obey God rather than man" when they were commanded to stop preaching Christ (Acts 5:29). Divine laws and natural laws always bind; human laws do not always bind.

However, the onus of proof is always on the one who disobeys. The default position, the fallback position, is always obedience. A law, like a person, is to be treated as innocent until proved guilty. For the purpose of law is to habituate us to what is good; and this is true both of human law and of divine law:

... [S]ince law is given for the purpose of directing human acts, as far as human acts conduce to virtue so far does law make men good. Wherefore the Philosopher says ... that *lawgivers make men good by habituating them to good works* (I-II,92,1).

From becoming accustomed to avoid evil and to fulfill what is good through fear of punishment, one is sometimes led on to do so likewise with delight and of one's own accord. Accordingly law, even by punishment, leads men on to being good (I-II,92,2).

The purpose of law is to make men good. It is ignorance of that simple principle that is one of the main causes of all the problems in modern society. A society of moral relativists no longer claims to know what it even means "to make men good".

The purpose of law is not merely to make life more pleasant and peaceful by protecting men from each other's external harms (although that is an attendant benefit). It is also to make men morally good within. Protection, peace and pleasure are only corollaries or properties of law that follow from the essential purpose of law, which is moral goodness. If that essential thing is not there, if law does not make men good, then these corollaries or properties will also be lacking, since the properties of an essence cannot exist without that essence.

That is the fundamental reason why modern societies, which often have superior legal systems to ancient societies, have not eradicated evil from the world. Evil can be eradicated from the world at large only when it is eradicated from the hearts and lives of individual human beings. Only when there is virtue in souls can there be peace and happiness in society.

External laws work through fear of external punishment. The internal law of conscience works through fear of evil itself, and the guilt that comes from committing it. External laws motivate us to obey internal laws, as St. Thomas explains in his last paragraph. (Of course, they also deter and protect.)

123. THE SACREDNESS OF THE NATURAL MORAL LAW

Is natural law less sacred than divine law?

A gloss on Rom 2:14: *When the Gentiles, who have not the* (Mosaic) *law, do by nature those things that are of the law,* **comments as follows:** *Although they have no written law, yet they have the natural law, whereby each one knows, and is conscious of, what is good and what is evil.* . . . **Now among all others the rational creature is subject to divine providence in the most excellent way, in so far as it partakes of a share of providence, by being provident both for itself and for others. Wherefore it has a share of the Eternal Reason ... and this participation of** (in) **the eternal law in** (by) **the rational creature is called the natural law ... the light of natural reason, whereby we discern what is good and what is evil, which is the function of the natural law, is nothing else than an imprint on us of the divine light. . . . [T]he natural law is nothing else than the rational creature's participation in the eternal law** (I-II,91,2).

The natural law is not less sacred than the eternal law: because it *is* the part of the eternal law that is known by natural reason. It is known by conscience. Conscience is (1) an awareness of the whole moral dimension, of the meaning of "good and evil", (2) knowledge of what kinds of things are good (e.g., justice, charity, mercy) and what kinds of things are evil, and (3) a pressure or inducement or feeling of duty or obligation that moves us to do good and avoid evil. It moves us in a unique way, a way that is not merely causal necessity or determinism, yet tells us that obedience to moral law is morally *necessary*.

Even those who are skeptical of any objective, universal moral law—even moral relativists—feel this obligation. No one admires a man who deliberately disobeys his own conscience, nor can anyone admire such disobedience in himself. He does not know it, but this is the Voice of God speaking to him, even if he may be an atheist. It is a real, living participation (sharing) by his human reason

and will in the divine reason and will. This absolute duty can come only from an absolute source, and that can only be God, because ultimately everything else is relative—as the relativist himself dimly perceives (for all error is the misunderstanding of some truth), although he doesn't know that it is relative *to God*.

To say that the natural law is less sacred than the divine law is like saying that your son is less human than you are, or that God's Son is less divine than his Father. For the natural law is not merely an image of the divine law but "has a share of the Eternal Reason", the Mind of God. It is the eternal law incarnate.

Therefore when your natural conscience speaks, that is the Voice of God, though it is heard through your human nature with all its faults, so what you hear is not infallible. You have to form your conscience aright. You can make mistakes in interpreting it, just as those who have private revelations from God, even saints, can make mistakes in interpreting these revelations. Even though they come from God, as sunlight comes from the sun, we can err about them, as sunlight can become clouded when it passes through dirty windows. This is why even saints and mystics can contradict each other. Sincere people of good will who are trying to follow their conscience with all their heart can also contradict each other. Only God Himself is infallible, and the Church and the Book that He Himself guarantees. Nothing else.

We moderns tend to think of our reason from below, so to speak, as a growth of evolution, history, family, human tradition, socialization, etc. It is at least equally accurate to think of it from above, for that is where it came from. (Remember, "reason" = understanding, not just calculation.) Reason did not evolve from biology, it came from God's direct creation of the soul.

Souls can only be created, all at once, not assembled out of previous parts, like bodies, because souls have no parts. They have different powers, but not different parts. You can't have half a soul, or cut off parts of your soul.

How can modern intellectuals deny the existence of a natural moral law?

... [T]he precepts of the natural law are to the practical reason what the first principles of demonstration (like the law of non-contradiction) are to the speculative reason, because both are self-evident principles. Now a thing is said to be self-evident in two ways: first, in itself; secondly, in relation to us. Any proposition is said to be self-evident in itself if its predicate is contained in the notion of the subject; although to one who knows not the definition of the subject it happens that such a proposition is not self-evident. For instance, this proposition, *Man is a rational being*, is in its very nature self-evident, since whoever says *man* says *a rational being;* yet to one who knows not what a man is, this proposition is not self-evident. Hence it is that ... certain axioms or propositions are universally self-evident to all; and such are those propositions whose terms are known to all, such as *Every whole is greater than its part,* and *things equal to one and the same are equal to one another.* But some propositions are self-evident only to the wise, who understand the meaning of the terms of such propositions; thus to one who understands that an angel is not a body, it is self-evident that an angel is not circumscriptively in a place; but this is not certain to the unlearned....

Now as *being* is the first thing that falls under the apprehension simply, so *good* is the first thing that falls under the apprehension of the practical reason, which is directed to action; since every agent acts for an end under the aspect of good. Consequently the first principle in the practical reason is one founded on the notion of good, viz. that *good is that which all things seek after.* Hence this is the first precept of law, that *good is to be done and pursued, and evil is to be avoided.* All other precepts of the natural law are based upon this, so that whatever the practical reason apprehends as man's good or evil belong to the natural law as something to be done or avoided....

... [A]ll those things to which man has a natural inclination are naturally apprehended by reason as being good.... [I]n man there is first of all an inclination to good in accordance with the nature which he has in common with all substances, inasmuch as every substance seeks the preservation of its own being according to its nature, and by reason of this inclination whatever is a means of preserving human life and of warding off its obstacles belongs to the natural law. Secondly, there is in man an inclination to things that pertain in him more specially according to that nature which he has in common with other animals; and in virtue of this inclination those things are said to belong to the natural law which nature has taught to all animals, such as sexual intercourse, education of offspring, and so forth. Thirdly, there is in man an inclination to good according to the nature of his reason, which nature is proper to him; thus man has a natural inclination to know the truth about God, and to live in society; and in this respect whatever pertains to this inclination belongs to the natural law (I-II,94,2).

... [T]here belong to the natural law first certain most general principles that are known to all, and secondly certain secondary and more detailed principles which are, as it were, conclusions following closely from first principles. As to these general principles, the natural law in the abstract can nowise be blotted out from men's hearts. But it is blotted out in the case of a particular action in so far as reason is hindered from applying the general principle to a particular point of practice on account of concupiscence or some other passion ... But as to the other, i.e., the secondary precepts, the natural law can be blotted out from the human heart either by evil persuasions, just as in speculative matters errors occur in respect of necessary conclusions, or by vicious customs and corrupt habits, as among some men theft and even unnatural vices, as the Apostle states (Rom 1) were not esteemed sinful (I-II,94,6).

Of course such extreme foolishness could never be found in our "Christian" civilization! Or are we so "educated" that we can no longer even comprehend St. Thomas' ultra-simple argument above?

What is the relation between moral law and human law? How much of morality does the law cover?

... [T]he same thing is not possible to one who does not have a virtuous habit as is possible to one who has it, as the same thing is not possible to a child as to a full-grown man. For this reason the law for children is not the same as for adults, since many things are permitted to children which in an adult are punished by law or at any rate are open to blame. In like manner many things are permissible to men not perfect in virtue which would be intolerable in a virtuous man.

Now human law is framed for a number of human beings, the majority of whom are not perfect in virtue. Wherefore human laws do not forbid all vices, from which the virtuous abstain, but only the more grievous vices, from which it is possible for the majority to abstain, and chiefly those that are to the hurt of others, without the prohibition of which human society could not be maintained; thus human law prohibits murder, theft and suchlike....

The purpose of human law is to lead men to virtue not suddenly but gradually. Wherefore it does not lay upon the multitude of imperfect men the burdens of those who are already virtuous, viz. that they should abstain from all evil. Otherwise these imperfect ones, being unable to bear such precepts, would break out into yet greater evils. (I-II,96,2) **... [H]uman law does not prescribe concerning all the acts of every virtue, but only in regard to those that are ordainable** (able to be ordained (ordered)) **to the common good** (I-II,96,3).

Habits are crucial to morality because persons are more important than deeds. A good deed is important not only because it helps someone else but also because it manifests a good person, a good character, a good habit, and also because good deeds gradually *form* good habits, good character, good persons. Good deeds are both the effects and the causes of goodness in the doer.

The main purpose of human laws is to induce us to do good deeds and deter us from bad ones, thus making us into good persons, with good habits. A secondary purpose is to protect good people from being harmed by bad people.

If we were already morally perfect, we would need no laws. So laws are only for morally imperfect persons. And therefore laws are only an aid, a help, a second-best thing, a minimum, not a maximum. Laws can't do everything, so they shouldn't try. That's why what's forbidden legally is much less than what's forbidden morally. Human law can't stop pride, selfishness, arrogance, lust, envy, or any of the most serious sins that harm the soul. It can only stop murder, theft, and the like. Human law is like moral kindergarten, not graduate school.

That's why, for instance, there should be laws against pornography but not against masturbation; against abortion but not against sodomy. All four are evil, but only two are preventable by human law. Law should try to do only what law can do.

That principle of minimalism applies to both of the two purposes of law: making people good and protecting them from harm. Human laws can only begin both of those things, not perfect them. It can forbid only the worst public vices and protect us from only the most obvious harms. We need much more than law. We need love, we need forgiveness, we need grace, we need God.

The practical conclusion is twofold: first, since human law is minimal, it should be easy to obey all human laws. "Don't be a criminal" is like "Don't flunk kindergarten." Second, aim much higher than that. Set your sights on being not just a good citizen but a saint.

126. Our obligation to secular human laws
is not just secular but sacred

If human laws are only minimal, does that mean we should not take them very seriously? Do we have a sacred, religious obligation to obey secular, pragmatic human laws?

Laws framed by man are either just or unjust. If they be just, they have the power of binding in conscience, from the eternal law whence they are derived, according to Proverbs 8:15: *By Me kings reign and lawgivers decree just things* (I-II,96,4).

Christians are good citizens, and take human laws very seriously, for religious reasons, not just for secular reasons. That's why they are better citizens than atheists, and certainly better citizens than moral relativists and subjectivists: they have stronger motives for obedience. The very fact that Christians relativize human society, the very fact that they believe in a higher law than human law, means not that they are traitors to secular society because they have a higher love and loyalty, but exactly the opposite: that they take civil obedience *more* seriously than a secularist can. It's like the advertisement for kosher hot dogs: Jews make better hot dogs because "We answer to a higher authority."

This religious reason for obeying secular law is based on a theological and philosophical principle of the distinction among (a) human law, (b) natural law, and (c) eternal law, and the relationship among these three kinds of law. Secular, human law (a), which stems from human reason and will, insofar as it reflects the natural moral law (b), which is based on human nature, is an actual participation in eternal law (c), i.e., God's mind and will. For human society did not just evolve by accident; it was designed by God in accordance with human nature. Man is by nature social and political. Social justice was not merely invented by men, but is an aspect of the eternal will of God.

Therefore social justice is an aspect of the Christian *religion*. The "social gospel" is part of the gospel. The Christian religion is much *more* than just social justice (which is pretty much all it is for theological "liberals"), but it is not *less*. Religious "conservatives" or "traditionalists" should take social justice not less seriously but more seriously than religious "liberals" or "modernists", for the same reason Christians and other supernaturalists can and should take social justice more seriously than naturalists and secularists can.

Obedience to human law is part of our religious obligation (#126); yet disobedience to human law may be part of our religious obligation when that human law is unjust or when it conflicts with God's law, as the Apostles said, "We must obey God rather than men" (Acts 5:29). When does this happen?

... [L]aws may be unjust in two ways: first, by being contrary to human good. (These are) **acts of violence rather than laws, because, as Augustine says,** *a law that is not just seems to be no law at all.* **Wherefore such laws do not bind in conscience except perhaps in order to avoid scandal or disturbance, for which cause a man should even yield his right, according to Matthew 5:40–41:** *If a man ... take away thy coat, let go thy cloak also unto him; and whosoever will force thee one mile, go with him other two ...*

Secondly, laws may be unjust through being opposed to the divine good: such are the laws of tyrants inducing to idolatry or to anything else contrary to the divine law; and laws of this kind must in no wise be observed, because, as stated in Acts 5:29, *we ought to obey God rather than men* (I-II,96,4).

St. Thomas' two moral points here are the following:

(1) We have a moral right to disobey any unjust law, any law that is "contrary to human good", unless there is a weightier moral reason to obey it for the sake of preventing a greater human evil, such as the avoidance of moral scandal or grave public disorder or riot or civil war, or to give a more effective testimony to unbelievers (as in the example from Matthew's Gospel quoted by St. Thomas).

(2) We have not just a right but a moral duty to disobey any law that is unjust because it is directly opposed to the will of God.

This is not a tricky political point, but an absolutely basic, simple one. It follows from the very existence of God. God alone is God; God alone is the absolute; He measures us, we do not measure Him; therefore His law measures our laws, not vice versa. The point is a logical one, not just a theological one, although St. Thomas quotes Scripture to support it theologically. The point is that the very idea of "an unjust human law" makes no sense— is literally meaningless, self-contradictory—unless there is a Justice above the human law. Either God's will, manifested in the natural law, or else man's will, as manifested in human law, is the absolute law. One kind of law must judge the other; it can't be both. You can't have two absolutes.

If, as the majority of intellectuals today believe (especially those who teach in law schools!), there is no higher law than human law (which is called "positive law" today, so that this position is called "legal positivism"); if there no real universal, objective natural law or divine law; or if this "higher law" exists but is allowed only in private and subjectively and individually but not in public; then what St. Thomas says here is nonsense: we can have no right, and a fortiori no duty, to disobey any human law, ever. So to be a modern legal positivist is, logically, to be a "stick in the mud" conservative and to take the existing order as the highest standard. On the other hand, to believe in the traditional "natural law" is the only way to be a principled nonconformist, a rebel, "liberal", or "progressive". "Progress" means "improvement", and improvement means not just change, moving forward in time along the horizontal time axis, but changing for the better, moving upward in value along the vertical axis. Unless there is a vertical axis, unless there is something transcending time and change, unless there is an eternal Good, the very idea of "progress" or "progressivism" is meaningless. That's not religion, that's simple logic.

This is why secularist rulers have always been suspicious of intelligent and committed religious people. (See *A Man for All Seasons* for a classic example of this.) This is why there will always be a tension between a purely secular state and real religion, until the end of time. They are following different drummers, playing different tunes. Their two musics need not always be in conflict, but they can never be identical.

128. THE SPIRIT VS. THE LETTER OF THE LAW

Should the spirit of the law ever trump the letter, the literal?

Hilary says: *The meaning of what is said is according to the motive for saying it; because things are not subject to speech but speech to things.* **Therefore we should take account of the motive of the lawgiver rather than of his very words.... Now it happens often that the observance of some point of law conduces to the common weal in the majority of instances and yet in some cases is very hurtful. Since then the lawgiver cannot have in view every single case, he shapes the law according to what happens most frequently, by directing his attention to the common good. Wherefore if a case arise wherein the observance of that law would be hurtful to the general welfare, it should not be observed. For instance, suppose that in a besieged city it be an established law that the gates are to be kept closed. This is good for public welfare as a general rule, but if it were to happen that the enemy are in pursuit of certain citizens who are defenders of the city, it would be a great loss to the city if the gates were not opened to them; and so in that case the gates ought to be opened, contrary to the letter of the law, in order to maintain the common weal which the lawgiver had in view.**

Nevertheless it must be noted that if the observance of the law according to the letter does not involve any sudden risk needing instant remedy, it is not competent for everyone to expound what is useful and what is not useful to the state; those alone can do this who are in authority, and who on account of such like cases have the power to dispense from the laws. If, however, the peril be so sudden as not to allow of the delay involved by referring the matter to authority, the mere necessity brings with it a dispensation, since necessity knows no law.... He who in a case of necessity acts beside the letter of the law does not judge of the law but of a particular case in which he sees that the letter of the law is not to be observed (I-II,96,6).

The reason the spirit sometimes should trump the letter is that the point of law is to align two wills: the will of the lawgiver and the will of the law-obeyers. If, as sometimes happens, obedience to the letter of the law would violate obedience to the will of the lawgiver, then disobedience to the letter is required by the very spirit or essence of the law, namely obedience to the lawgiver's will.

The clearest and strongest example of this is Jesus' works of healing on the Sabbath, which the legalistic Pharisees opposed because they broke the letter of the law; and His justification for them was that the Sabbath was made for man, not man for the Sabbath. Legalism—the idolatry of worshipping and absolutizing the law instead of the Lawgiver—is a temptation in every age; but the saints are never legalists. They know the Person of God too well.

Our doctor once sped down the Massachusetts Turnpike at ninety miles per hour and crashed through a toll gate to get an infant to a downtown hospital before she died. He was a hero, not a lawbreaker, because the intent of the lawmakers in erecting speed limits and toll gates was to save lives, and his acts fulfilled that intent. The authority of the lawmakers was respected in the very act of disobeying the letter of their law.

This was a rarity: a sudden emergency that justified breaking civil laws. In most cases of religious law, church law, or canon law, there is plenty of time to appeal to proper authority for dispensation from the letter of the law. But both cases are decided out of respect for authority, not disrespect. ("Authority", of course, does not mean "power" but "right". Might does not make right.)

The letter of the law is there precisely to express its spirit, and it usually does. That is why disobedience to the letter must always be exceptional, and it always needs special justification, as obedience does not. If the letter expressed the spirit perfectly and always, no disobedience to the letter would ever be justified; if the letter expressed the spirit rarely, disobedience would often be justified.

Is morality the ultimate end of human life?

... [J]ust as the principal intention of human law is to create friendship (a kind of love) between man and man, so the chief intention of the divine law is to establish man in friendship with God. Now such likeness is the reason of (the motive for) love.... (But) there cannot possibly be any friendship of man to God, Who is supremely good, unless man becomes good; wherefore it is written (Lev 19:2; 11:45): *You shall be holy, for I am holy* (I-II,99,2).

As C.S. Lewis says, "The road to the Promised Land runs past Mount Sinai." The moral law, and the virtues it defines and commands, is a necessary means to our ultimate end; but it is not that end.

God's chosen people, who knew God better than anyone else in the world not because they were superior but because God had chosen them to reveal Himself most intimately to the world, appreciated the importance of morality better than any other people, because they knew that God was good: just, merciful, righteous, loving, perfect. The gods of all the other nations were imperfect and immoral. The Jews united religion and morality more closely than anyone else because they knew morality's ultimate Source was not merely human but divine. To make the same point in the psychological dimension, the Jews uniquely united man's two deepest instincts, the religious instinct to worship and the moral instinct to do good and not evil. The Jews were the world's best psychologists.

Yet they also knew, however obscurely, that God had destined them to another world and another life, after death and the Resurrection. (They came to know this truth of the Resurrection of the body only gradually, the obscurity of their earlier prophets being supplemented by the increasing clarity of the later ones. God usually reveals Himself to man only gradually because man grows gradually, in mind as well as body.) And in that other world and life they would not need the many regulations that are made necessary

by the weaknesses of "the flesh" (which in Scripture means fallen human nature, soul and body together). Their morality was absolute even in this world in the sense that their obligation to obey it was absolute, because it came from the absolute God Himself and it was absolutely true and right; but it was not absolute in the sense of being their ultimate end. Their ultimate end was something "no eye has seen, nor ear heard, nor the heart of man conceived, what God has prepared for those who love Him" (1 Cor 2:9, quoted from Is 64:4). That ultimate destiny was an even more intimate relationship with God than faithful obedience to God's law. It was real presence, union, love, and consequently joy—eternal joy. Morality was a training for *that*.

We can endure the presence of God only if we are like God, not unlike God; that is, if our very character is righteous, just, loving, and holy; if we are light and not darkness. For "God is light, and in Him is no darkness at all" (1 Jn 1:5). In Leviticus, the book of laws, God repeatedly told His people that this was the whole point of morality: "You must be holy because I am holy." The end of morality is Godlikeness. The beginning and end of morality is the divine "I AM."

And God will not let us go until we attain that. Thus Jesus repeats this Godlike demand in his Sermon on the Mount: "You, therefore, must be perfect as your Heavenly Father is perfect" (Mt 5:48). That is why there is a Purgatory.

St. Thomas calls this loving union "friendship." Aristotle noted that "friends have all things in common", first of all their own selves, their nature, their character. In married love the two become one flesh; in friendship the two become one character. We must become Godlike in character to be God's friends; we must become "pure of heart" so that we can "see God," i.e., know Him as our Friend. For that is the end of morality: "This is eternal life, that they know you the only true God" (Jn 17:3). You can know many *things* *about* strangers or enemies but you can only *know* your friends.

The next question about morality is the How question. Can it be taught, and if so how?

As in speculative sciences men are persuaded to assent to the conclusions by means of syllogistic arguments, so too in every law men are persuaded to observe its precepts by means of punishments and rewards. Now it is to be observed that in speculative sciences the means of persuasion are adapted to the conditions of the pupil, wherefore the process of argument in sciences should be ordered becomingly, so that the instruction is based on principles more generally known. And thus also he who would persuade a man to the observance of any precepts needs to move him at first by things for which he has an affection, just as children are induced to do something by means of little childish gifts.

... [T]he Old Law disposed men to the coming of Christ as the imperfect disposes to the perfect, wherefore it was given to a people as yet imperfect in comparison to the perfection which was to result from Christ's coming, and for this reason that people is compared to a child that is still under a pedagogue (Gal 3:24)....

Those who are yet imperfect desire temporal goods, albeit in subordination to God; whereas the perverse place their end in temporal things. It was therefore fitting that the Old Law should conduct men to God by means of temporal goods for which the imperfect have an affection (I-II,99,6).

We are persuaded intellectually, or "taught" (changed from ignorance to knowledge) through arguments. We are persuaded morally (changed from evil to good), not merely by arguments but by rewards and punishments; not merely by educating our intellect but by educating our desires.

When we are persuaded intellectually, two truths are joined: the truth of the premises that we already believe and the truth of the conclusion that follows from them, which we did not believe before we were persuaded by this argument. When we are persuaded morally, by rewards and punishments, two goods, two objects of desire, are joined: the good of the deed we ought to do but do not desire, and the good of the reward we already desire. Thus we are led from presently desired goods to new and harder-to-love goods, as we are led from already-known premises to new, harder-to-know conclusions.

We must correct St. Thomas here in one particular. The Old Law was not merely this-worldly: either in the perfection of its demands, or in the divine source of them, or in the promised rewards for them. It already commanded perfection and revealed the divine reason and rewards for them: "Be ye holy for I am holy." The contrast between the Old Law and the New is a difference in degree, not in kind: an increased clarity about the otherworldly, spiritual rewards, not a new morality. Christ explicitly said that He came not to give a different law, but only to reveal and fulfill the heart of the Old Law: "Do not think that I have come to abolish the law and the prophets; I have come not to abolish them but to fulfill them" (Mt 5:17). The Old Law already commanded perfection: "You shall love the Lord your God with all your heart, and with all your soul, and with all your might" (Deut 6:5).

It is true that among the Chosen People their understanding of their own law progressed from a more primitive stage, where (1) sins and sinners were not clearly distinguished (and therefore God commanded aggressive war against the devil-worshipping Caananites), where (2) justice was clearer than love (as it usually is among children who play "cops and robbers" and who love fairy tales where the villains are killed at the end), and where (3) collective good and evil was clearer than individual good and evil (thus the sins of the fathers are visited upon the children because families are more important than individuals), to a stage where it was seen that (1) the whole reason to hate sins was to love sinners, that (2) the whole reason for justice was to be the necessary foundation for the temple of love, and that (3) personal responsibility was more absolute than collective responsibility, because the whole reason for the temporary earthly community was to instruct and perfect immortal, Heaven-destined persons.

I can pray to God, love God, and love my neighbor anywhere. Why can't I just go into the woods or the desert or the beach to pray? Why should I go to church? I don't get as much out of it as I do out of the world. Church isn't working for me.

The chief purpose of the whole external worship is that man may give (internal) **worship to God. Now man's tendency is to reverence less those things which are common and indistinct from other things, whereas he admires and reveres those things which are distinct from others in some point of excellence. Hence too it is customary among men for kings and princes, who ought to be revered, to be clothed in more precious garments and to possess vaster and more beautiful abodes. And for this reason it behooved special times, a special abode, special vessels, and special ministers to be appointed for the divine worship, so that thereby the soul of man might be brought to greater reverence for God....**

The divine worship regards two things, namely God, Who is worshipped, and men, who worship Him. Now God, Who is worshipped, is confined to no bodily place, wherefore there was no need on His part for a tabernacle or temple to be set up. But men who worship Him are corporeal beings, and for their sake there was need for a special tabernacle or temple to be set up for the worship of God (I-II, 102, 4).

If you "don't get anything out of church", you don't understand the reason for going to church in the first place. We go to church to worship. Worship is not like entertainment: worship is not getting something but giving something. You don't go to church as you go to watch a football game; you go to church as you go to *play* a football game, to *do* something. And that something is worship. It's a form of love: a giving. We *give* God our worship, i.e., our hearts, our promises, our aspirations, our hope, our fidelity. So the reason you're not "getting" anything out of church is that you're not

giving anything. That's what you're supposed to get out of church: the opportunity to give yourself to God.

It's like sex that way: selfish sex is not maximally ecstatic, only unselfish sex is. You get something ecstatic out of sex only when you give your whole self away, only when you forget yourself entirely. It's life's deepest secret: only when you lose yourself can you find it.

Not that church is like sex in that it's supposed to convulse your body, or your emotions. But it is supposed to convulse your will. "Here I am. Take me. Do with me as You will." That's "spiritual sex".

We don't go to church to get away from the world. We go to church to understand the world. We have holy times and places to remind us of the holiness of all times and places. We have the supernaturally extraordinary to remind us of the supernatural value of the ordinary. We leave the world and enter a church not because the world is worth so little but because it is worth so much. It's the church that saves the world. "For God so loved the world that he gave his only begotten Son" (Jn 3:16). We love the world because God does.

St. Thomas' point in his first sentence is that God made us material as well as spiritual. It insults God to ignore the material in us (the body) or outside us (e.g., the walls of a church).

St. Thomas' point in his second sentence is that we appreciate things best by contrast: life by death, pleasure by pain, the supernatural by the natural, the spiritual by the material—and vice versa. The highest things have to be rare for us to appreciate them. That's why Sunday is just one day out of seven.

It's not materialism to dress priests, judges, and kings in beautiful, expensive robes and to house them in beautiful, expensive places (palaces, courts, churches). We express our spiritual loves and loyalties materially, there is no other way. That's what God made matter for: to reveal and express spirit.

We go to church not because God is enclosed in matter but because we are.

Is kindness to animals in the Bible?

(In the Old Testament sacrifices whose elaborate rules God instituted,) **blood was forbidden ... in order to avoid cruelty, that they might abhor the shedding of human blood.... For the same reason they were forbidden to eat animals that had been suffocated or strangled ... because this form of death is very painful to the victim, and the Lord wished to withdraw them from cruelty even in regard to irrational animals, so as to be less inclined to be cruel to other men, through being used to being kind to beasts....**

There seems to be no reason in what is said in Exodus 23:19: *Thou shalt not boil a kid in the milk of its dam* (mother).... (But) **although the kid that is slain has no perception of the manner in which its flesh is cooked, yet it would seem to savor of heartlessness if the dam's milk, which was intended for the nourishment of her offspring, were served up on the same dish** (I-II,102,6).

One of the pieces of evidence that the Bible is divine revelation is its transcendence of human culture and conventions. Merely human books always reflect the ideas of their culture, or of the individuals who write them; a divinely inspired book transcends that. Thus the Bible reflects a very "progressive" view of women and children, and of mercy over justice; it does not share the otherwise universal belief that there must be many gods, that human kings are beyond criticism, that ordinary people are unholy, etc. And it also transcends our ancestors' universal callousness toward animals, as being nothing but mere meat, or useful beasts of burden. Scripture does teach kindness to animals. For God put animals into our world not just to serve us physically, but also spiritually: to teach us lessons like compassion and kindness. Dogs and cats are more compassionate to us than we are to them.

St. Thomas was a keen observer of the material world, especially of animals. (Remember his argument from his observation of animals to prove that human happiness does not consist in the goods of the body: point #60.) He sees symbolic significance, of a moral and religious kind, in specific empirical features of many animals. Just to take flying creatures alone, he mentions eagles, griffons, ospreys, kites, vultures, ravens, ostriches, owls, gulls, hawks, screech-owls, cormorants, ibises, swans, bitterns, coots, herons, falcons, plovers, hoopoes, and bats! (I-II,102,6)

... [M]an's affection ... is moved also in regard to other animals; for since the passion of pity is caused by the afflictions of others, and since it happens that even irrational animals are sensible to pain, it is possible for the affection of pity to arise in a man with regard to the sufferings of animals. Now it is evident that if a man practice a pitiful affection for animals, he is all the more disposed to take pity on his fellow men; wherefore it is written (Prov 12:10): *The just regardeth the lives of his beasts, but the bowels of the wicked are cruel.* Consequently the Lord, in order to inculcate pity to the Jewish people who (like all mankind!) were prone to cruelty, wished them to practice pity even with regard to dumb animals, and forbade them to do certain things savoring of cruelty to animals. Hence He prohibited them to *boil a kid in the milk of its dam;* and to *muzzle the ox that treadeth out the corn;* and to *slay the dam with her young* (I-II,102,6).

God wants us to have kindness, pity, and even a kind of friendship with animals for two reasons: (1) for them and (2) for us. (1) He made them, so He has a proper love for them, and we should too. (2) Above all, He made us to be kind, loving, and friendly to each other and to Him. We are His little children, and animals train us, as toy horses train future cowboys and toy swords train future soldiers.

We can't love God too much, and we can't love sin too little. Everything else, we can love either too much, by idolizing it, or too little, by not appreciating it. In the past, we probably loved and appreciated animals too little. Today, some people love them too much—more than they love other people sometimes, because they give us less trouble!

Sociologists and anthropologists tell us that religion has three dimensions: creed, code, and cult; or words, works, and worship; or theology, morality, and liturgy. Which is the essential dimension of the gospel, or the "new law", or the Christian religion?

Now that which is preponderant in the law of the New Testament, and whereon all its efficacy is based, is the grace of the Holy Ghost (*zoe,* eternal life, supernatural life, sanctifying grace, regeneration, the state of grace, being born again)**, which is given through faith in Christ. Consequently the New Law** (the gospel) **is chiefly the grace itself of the Holy Ghost which is given to those who believe in Christ....**

Nevertheless the New Law contains certain things that dispose us to receive the grace of the Holy Ghost, and pertaining to the use of that grace; such things are of secondary importance, so to speak, in the New Law, and the faithful need to be instructed concerning them, both by word and writing, both as to what they should believe and as to what they should do. Consequently we must say that the New Law is in the first place a law that is inscribed in our hearts, but that secondarily it is a written law (I-II,106,1).

As stated above, there is a twofold element in the Law of the Gospel. There is the chief element, viz. the grace of the Holy Ghost bestowed inwardly. And as to this, the New Law justifies.... The other element of the Evangelical Law is secondary, namely the teachings of faith and those commandments which direct human affections and human actions. And as to this, the New Law does not justify. Hence the Apostle says (2 Cor 3:6): *The letter killeth, but the spirit quickeneth;* **and Augustine explains this by saying that the letter denotes any writing that is external to man, even that of the moral precepts such as are contained in the Gospel. Wherefore the letter even of the Gospel would kill unless there were the inward presence of the healing grace of faith** (I-II,106,2).

Jesus told Nicodemus, the good Pharisee, a teacher of God's own chosen people, that he did not know the very heart of his own God-established religion, which He called "being born again", when He said, "Are you a teacher of Israel and yet you do not understand this?" (Jn 3:10).

Christianity is at its heart extremely simple. (Jesus taught that too, to Martha, who was "worried about many things" and did not know that "one thing is needful": Lk 10:42.) That one thing is called by many names: divine grace, sanctifying grace, regeneration, being born again, the presence of God, salvation, eternal life, *zoe,* supernatural life, the state of grace, agape, sanctification, justification, redemption, *theosis,* the presence of God in the soul, and "the law that is inscribed in our hearts". Each of these terms speaks a different aspect or dimension of that one single reality, which is the only thing that ultimately and absolutely matters. Everything else is a means to that end or a consequence of it. All creeds, codes, and cults are for that, and about that. Everything is good when it is a cause or an effect of that. Everything is bad when it is a cause or an effect of the lack of that. As St. Thomas says, the New Law contains many things "of secondary (yet great) importance" since these all either "dispose us to receive" that "grace of the Holy Ghost" or "pertain to the use of that grace".

St. Thomas was not a legalist, as the Protestant Reformers often thought. Like them, he clearly taught that the Gospel was essentially this "inward" or "spiritual" reality, which "gives life" while the "letter" of the law without the inner spirit "kills" (2 Cor 3:6). Only the real presence of God in the soul, not orthodox beliefs, or moral obedience, or right sacramental worship, is what reconciles us to God. The rest was important only because it was about that, as either its cause or its effect. Luther and Calvin rightly reminded us of that primary fact, a fact the Church had always taught. They were wrong to reject the secondary things but right to emphasize the absolutely primary thing. From the Catholic point of view, therefore, they were more right than wrong.

If there is such a thing as "progressive revelation", if God reveals Himself gradually rather than all at once, in accordance with man's gradual growth and maturity, then does it not follow that in the future He will reveal more than He has in the past, so that there may be a "third testament" beyond the "second testament", i.e., the New Testament, just as the New Testament (the second) is beyond the Old (the first)? And will not that "third testament" be the revelation of the Holy Spirit, as the Old Testament was the revelation of the Father and the New Testament the revelation of the Son? Why was this idea, as taught by Joachim of Flora in the Middle Ages, condemned by the Church as a heresy?

Objection: ... just as the Father is distinct from the Son and the Son from the Father, so is the Holy Ghost distinct from the Father and the Son. But there was a state corresponding with the Person of the Father, viz. the state of the Old Law ... and likewise there is a state corresponding to the Person of the Son, viz. the state of the New Law.... Therefore there will be a third state corresponding to the Holy Ghost....

Reply: The Old Law corresponded not only to the Father but also to the Son, because Christ was foreshadowed in the Old Law. Hence Our Lord said (Jn 5:46): *If you did believe Moses, you would believe me also, for he wrote of Me.* In like manner the New Law corresponds not (only) to Christ but also to the Holy Ghost, according to Romans 8:2: *The Law of the Spirit of life in Christ Jesus*, etc. Hence we are not to look forward to another law corresponding to the Holy Ghost.

The state of the world may change in two ways. In one way, according to a change of law; and thus no other state will succeed this state of the New Law. Because the state of the New Law succeeded the state of the Old Law as a more perfect law (succeeds) a less perfect one. Now no state of the present life can be more perfect than the state of the New Law.... In another way the state of mankind may change according as man stands in relation to one and the same law more or less perfectly. And thus the state of the Old Law

underwent frequent changes, since at times the laws were very well kept and at other times were altogether unheeded. Thus too the state of the New Law is subject to change ... according as the grace of the Holy Ghost dwells in man more or less perfectly. Nevertheless we are not to look forward to a state wherein man (in general) **is to possess the grace of the Holy Ghost more perfectly than he has possessed it hitherto....**

As Dionysius says, there is a threefold state of mankind: the first was under the Old Law, the second is that of the New Law, the third will take place not in this life but in Heaven. But as the first state is figurative and imperfect in comparison with the state of the Gospel, so is the present state figurative and imperfect in comparison with the Heavenly state (I-II,106,4).

There are indeed three ages corresponding to the revelation of the three Persons of the Trinity; but in all three ages all three Persons are active. Every word in the Old Testament is in some way about Christ the Word of God. Each word is an atom in His Face. The Spirit was also active from the beginning, for it was He Who inspired all the prophets. And in the New Testament, Christ reveals not just Himself but His Father. He says His teaching is not His own but His Father's (Jn 7:16), and that He has come into the world only to do the will of His Father, not His own will (Jn 5:30). And it is He Whose prayer to the Father sends the Spirit (Jn 14:16–17). It is the Spirit Who does His work, the work of instilling the very life of Christ—of the whole Trinity—into our souls. It is all one work, for there is only one God.

There is no third law, or third testament because there are only two, the Old and the New, which will be perfected in Heaven. Heaven will do to earth what the New Law did to the Old: not replacement but consummation (Mt 5:17). Really, there is only one covenant, from the beginning. God never abrogates His covenants. Heaven will consummate what the Old Law promised and what the New Law has delivered to us: the real presence of Christ in our souls (—and bodies: Mt 26:26).

Is Christianity hard or easy?

It is written (Mt 11:28): *Come unto Me, all you that labor and are burdened,* **which words are expounded by Hilary thus:** *He calls to Himself all those that labor under the difficulty of observing the Law, and are burdened with the sins of this world.* **And further on He says of the yoke of the Gospel:** *For My yoke is sweet and My burden light.* **Therefore the New Law is a lighter burden than the Old.**

A twofold difficulty may attach to works of virtue with which the precepts of the Law are concerned. One is on the part of the outward works, which of themselves are, in a way, difficult and burdensome. And in this respect the Old Law is a much heavier burden than the New, since the Old Law by its numerous ceremonies prescribed many more outward acts than the New Law.... The other difficulty attaches to works of virtue as to interior acts; for instance, that a virtuous deed be done with promptitude and pleasure. It is this difficulty that virtue solves, because to act thus is difficult for a man without virtue, but through virtue it becomes easy to him.... [T]hus even the Philosopher states that it is easy to do what a righteous man does, but that to do it in the same way, viz. with pleasure and promptitude, is difficult to a man who is not righteous. Accordingly we read also (1 Jn 5:3) **that** *His commandments are not heavy,* **which words Augustine expounds by saying that** *they are not heavy to the man that loveth, whereas they are a burden to him that loveth not.*

Moreover, the tribulations suffered by those who observe the New Law are easily borne, on account of the love in which the same Law consists; since, as Augustine says, *love makes light and nothing of things that seem ardous and beyond our power* (I-II, 107, 4).

Is Christianity hard or easy? The true answer is deeper, more complex, and more paradoxical than a simple yes or no, like all the most important questions about Christianity, and like the most important questions about anything real—e.g., Are we animals or not? Is the universe made of matter or energy? Is light wave or particle? Is truth or love the most absolute? Is God one or many, substance or relationship, essence or person?

On the one hand, Christianity—the very life of Christ in our souls and our lives—is so simple and easy that Christ can say to us—the Christ Who is about to carry the burden of the Cross—that His yoke is easy and His burden is light and we will find in Him rest for our souls (Mt 11:28–30). Once we have Him, nothing can remove or impair or dim that joy, not even torture and death (Rom 8:28–39).

On the other hand, our new marching orders, now that we have enrolled in Christ's army, are much higher and more difficult than those of civilians. We are called to be not just decent citizens but heroes of virtue: saints.

Yet the New Law of the gospel, which is the very presence of Christ in His Church, in His people, in their souls (and in their bodies), makes obedience easy and joyful because it comes from within, from love, and from free choice motivated by love, rather than from without, from obligation and duty. Lovers actually enjoy doing hard things for their beloved—the very things non-lovers complain about. Of course, this transformation from duty to love, and from burden to joy, is usually gradual, like a tide, not sudden, as we grow in grace like a plant. Do not expect instant sanctification by going faster than grace.

As the homily that the Church used to recommend for all wedding ceremonies says, "Married life is a high calling. It imposes many burdens, risks many sufferings, and requires many sacrifices. Only love can make it possible. Only perfect love can make it a joy."

The postage stamp commemorating the founding of Boys' Town orphanage in Nebraska depicts a small boy carrying a larger, crippled one. The caption reads: "He ain't heavy; he's my brother."

Is Christianity internal or external? If both, how are these two dimensions related?

The New Law consists chiefly in the grace of the Holy Ghost, which is shown forth by faith that works through love. Now men become receivers of this grace through God's Son made man, Whose humanity grace filled first, and thence flowed forth to us. Hence it is written ... *Of His fullness we all have received ...*

(But) it was becoming (fitting) that (1) the grace which flows from the incarnate Word should be given to us by means of certain external sensible objects, and that (2) from this inward grace ... certain external works should ensue. Accordingly external acts may have a twofold connection with grace. (1) In the first place, as leading in some way to grace. Such are the sacramental acts which are instituted in the New Law, e.g., Baptism, the Eucharist, and the like. (2) In the second place there are those external acts which ensue from the promptings of grace.

The Kingdom of God consists chiefly in internal acts; but as a consequence, all things that are essential to (those) internal acts belong also to the kingdom of God. Thus if the Kingdom of God is internal righteousness, peace, and spiritual joy, all external acts that are incompatible with righteousness, peace, and spiritual joy are in opposition to the Kingdom of God and consequently should be forbidden in the Gospel of the Kingdom. On the other hand, those things that are indifferent as regards the aforesaid, for instance to eat of this or that food, are not part of the Kingdom of God; wherefore the Apostle says: *The Kingdom of God is not meat and drink* (Rom 14:17).

The New Law is called *the law of perfect liberty* (Jas 1:25) ... in two respects. First, because it does not bind us to do or avoid certain things except such as are of themselves necessary or opposed to salvation and come under the prescription or prohibition of the law. Secondly, because it also makes us comply freely with these precepts and prohibitions inasmuch as we do so through the promptings of grace....

According to the Philosopher what is *free* is cause of itself. Therefore he acts freely who acts of his own accord. Now man does of his own accord that which he does from a habit that is suitable to his nature, since a habit inclines one as a second nature.... Since then the grace of the Holy Ghost is like an interior habit bestowed on us and inclining us to act aright, it makes us to choose freely those things that are becoming to grace and shun what is opposed to it (I-II,108,1).

Christianity is (a) not merely spiritual, invisible, and internal; (b) nor is it primarily material and external; (c) nor is it a hybrid or "balance" of the two. Its essence is spiritual and internal: God's grace, which is His very presence in the soul. But it is material in two ways. (1) Certain material, visible, and external things are the divinely appointed means by which this grace comes to us, viz. the visible Church and the Sacraments. For Christ saved us not by saying "This is My Mind" but "This is My Body", on Calvary and in the Sacraments, which flow from it. (2) Material things are also the necessary *consequences* of this grace, for "(invisible) faith, if it has no (visible) works, is dead" (Jas 2:17); and some visible deeds (sins) are obstacles and enemies to this grace, and are forbidden for this reason.

But the ultimate reason for these physical things is always spiritual, since Christianity is not essentially something physical but something spiritual, since Christianity is essentially the very presence of God in the soul, and both God and the soul are spiritual.

And since spirit alone is free, Christianity in its essence is free. Even the material deeds that are commanded or forbidden are done or avoided *freely*, from within, out of our new spiritual habits or "second nature" that grace creates; out of free faith and hope and love toward God and neighbor rather than out of compulsion and fear of punishment. (See 1 Jn 4:18.) Of course, this purifying and educating of our motives is a gradual process, so that punishments are still needed here in our pilgrim state.

What is the relation between the Ten Commandments of the Old Law and the Beatitudes of the New Law?

... [T]he sermon which Our Lord delivered on the mountain contains the whole process of forming the life of a Christian (I-II,108,3).

The difference between a counsel and a commandment is that a commandment implies obligation, whereas a counsel is left to the option of the one to whom it is given. Consequently in the New Law, which is the law of liberty, counsels are added to the commandments.

... [W]hen a man follows not his (own) **will** (desire) **as to some deed which he might do lawfully, he follows the counsel in that particular case; for instance if he do good to his enemies when he is not bound to, or if he forgive an injury of which he might justly seek to be avenged** (I-II,108,4).

The relation between the Ten Commandments and the Beatitudes is not one of identity, nor is it one of opposition, nor is it one of simple difference. It is one of fulfillment. Christ said, "Do not think I have come to abolish the law and the prophets [the Old Covenant]; I have come not to abolish them but to fulfill them" (Mt 5:17). The Beatitudes are one example of that.

The fulfillment of the old transforms and transcends the old. Therefore Christ's new law, summarized in the Sermon on the Mount (Mt 5–7), the greatest sermon ever preached, goes far beyond the old law in its ideals and expectations, because there is now a new power to attain these higher ideals, viz. Christ Himself, now present in souls and in the Church's sacraments because of the Incarnation.

This New Law is not made up of "commandments" but of "counsels". The difference is freedom. We obey commandments because they morally (not physically) bind us. These binding commandments are not abrogated—all of us are still, and always, under absolute obligation to obey all of them because they directly express the Will of God for all mankind at all times. But "counsels" of perfection are offered to our free choice, not imposed as duties. They are a higher road. They are a maximum; the commandments are a minimum. The motive for obeying the commandments is duty, or obligation. (Thus the ethic of the commandments is Kantian: they are "categorical imperatives.") But the motive for obeying the counsels is love. (Thus Kantian ethics, however honorable, is radically deficient.) Love is by its essence free. This is so even if it is commanded (and it *is*: "*Thou shalt* love"), because love is by its essence a free choice of the will. If love were essentially a feeling, it could not be commanded, for feelings are not free, not directly under our control; but choices of the will are.

The Commandments define obligatory justice. The counsels invite us to freely choose to practice love and mercy and forgiveness to our enemies even when we have just cause to punish them. For that is what God did to us. In fact, in the only prayer Christ gave to us, He made forgiveness so important that He told us to pray for our own damnation if we did not forgive our enemies—to ask God to "forgive us our trespasses *as we forgive* those who trespass against us." And He reiterated and emphasized this one petition after giving us the prayer (Mt 6:14–15).

Paradoxically, the deepest will of the Christian is "Not my will but Thine be done" (Mt 6:10, Mt 26:39). This is the essence of following the higher way (which St. Thomas calls "counsels" as distinct from "commandments"). But "counsels" would be a seriously misleading term if it suggested "take it or leave it", mere "advice". It is nothing less than the meaning of life and the only road to supreme joy. True, it is offered as a road map for us to freely choose to follow rather than imposed as a threat; but it is not one among many roads but "*the* way, *the* truth, and *the* life" (Jn 14:6).

The only way to the supreme joy that Jesus has is to freely embrace His way to that joy, the way of His cross (Heb 12:2).

We usually look for things out in the world, and therefore we tend to look for God there too. And we do find Him, or His fingerprints, everywhere: in nature's beauty and design, in history, in the events of our lives. But when we look within, when we look at our very act of looking-at, or thinking-about, these things, can we find God there too? Is God the First Cause and Unmoved Mover of human reason as well as the First Cause of all the things discovered by our reason?

... [A]ll movements, both corporeal and spiritual, are reduced to the simple First Mover, Who is God. And hence no matter how perfect a corporeal or spiritual nature is supposed to be, it cannot proceed to its act unless it be moved by God.... Hence we must say that for the knowledge of any truth whatsoever man needs divine help that the intellect may be moved by God to its act. But he does not need a new light added to his natural light in order to know the truth in all things, but only in some that surpass his natural knowledge.

... [T]he natural light bestowed upon the soul is God's enlightenment whereby we are enlightened to see what pertains to natural knowledge ... We always need God's help for every thought, inasmuch as He moves the understanding to act (I-II,109,1).

Reason, or Mind, or Thought is not made of matter (though its normal instrument, the brain, is). It has no shape, color, geometrical form, size, or mass. It does not take up space, as matter does. But Reason, or Mind, or Thought in us is just as temporal, just as much in time, as matter is. It takes time to think, just as it takes time to walk. God alone is timeless, eternal.

We can find the eternal God as the First Cause of our reason or intelligence just as we can find Him as the first cause of the material universe. St. Thomas uses the same metaphysical principles in this argument for God's existence that he uses in

his famous "five ways", his cosmological arguments, or arguments from features of the material cosmos. These principles are:

(1) the principle that only a being in act (a being that is actual rather than only potential) can actualize a potentiality in a being that is in potency. Only water can wet, only fire can kindle, only light can lighten;

(2) the fact that our thinking is in fact constantly changed ("reduced") from potency to act—i.e., we grow from not-knowing something to knowing that something;

(3) and therefore there must be a being that is already actually all the things we are potentially: knowledgeable, wise, intelligent, good.

The practical and personal consequences of this abstract theoretical argument are immense, and usually forgotten: whenever we come to know or understand anything whatsoever, God is at work in us. God is the Big Bang Maker of thought just as much as He is the Big Bang Maker of matter. And in the present, not just in the past. And therefore we can find God in, and thank God for, our mental energy just as much as our physical energy.

Every single thing we ever think about has one thing in common: our thinking. Therefore in every single act of thinking God is present, even in false thoughts. Obviously the falsehood is not from Him, but the thought-energy is.

That is why thought, like matter, is holy. For some reason, we rarely think of that. Perhaps we're so busy thinking about external things that we forget that we're *thinking*. Our thoughts about the universe are no more independent of God than the universe is. And we ought to be no less aware of Him there, and no less thankful for His graces and inspirations there, than anywhere else. Where did that bright idea come from? we wonder. From Him. "All truth is God's truth" (Arthur Holmes). Just as all material things are gifts from God, so are all thoughts and inspirations in the soul. Only one kind of light (Gen 1:3) is made of material photons. He is the source of both kinds.

139. GRACE

The most usual fundamental criticism of St. Thomas, and of Catholic theology in general, that you will hear from intelligent and philosophical Muslims and Evangelical and Fundamentalist Protestants is that this theology is just paganism or naturalism with an additional "layer" of supernatural grace; that St. Thomas gives too much credit to fallen human nature and to natural human reason in its ability to know God, and to human free will in its ability to choose good over evil, and to natural human virtue and natural human hopes of Heaven; that St. Thomas' theology is just thinly baptized naturalism.

A fundamental principle of Catholic theology is that grace perfects nature rather than setting it aside; and that means that the Christian life is not a two-layer cake, the supernatural simply added on to the natural. It transforms the natural but by perfecting it, not by demeaning it. The convert's whole natural life is transformed by supernatural grace; so that as he becomes holier he also becomes wiser and happier and even healthier.

But this is what happens to nature *after* grace, and St. Thomas' critics will often agree with him there. But what about nature *before* grace? Doesn't St. Thomas grant too much value and power there to unredeemed nature, pre-graced nature?

(1) **Whether without grace man can know any truth?**

(2) **Whether man can wish or do any good without grace?**

(3) **Whether by his own natural powers and without grace man can love God above all things?**

(4) **Whether man without grace and by his own natural powers can fulfill the commandments of the law?**

(5) **Whether man can merit everlasting life without grace?**

(6) **Whether man by himself and without the external aid of grace can prepare himself for grace?**

(7) **Whether man can rise from sin without the help of grace?**

(8) **Whether man without grace can avoid sin?**

(9) **Whether one who has already obtained grace can, of himself and without any further help of grace, do good and avoid sin?**

(10) **Whether man possessed of grace needs the help of grace in order to persevere?** (I-II, 109)

St. Thomas has a single, one-syllable answer to all of these questions: No.

That answer should guide our attitude in all our prayers and all our good works. This is a matter of realism, not just piety. The reality is that we are totally, not partially, dependent on Him for everything.

That is why humility is the precondition for all virtues and why gratitude is the precondition for all wisdom.

God loved nature and human nature into being. He saved it at an infinite and incomprehensible cost. He continues to love it, use it, and perfect it. Nature *after* grace is indeed raised to a far higher dignity, worth, joy, and power than it is in any non-religious philosophy or in any other religion. But nature *before* grace is nothing. It does not exist. Nature itself is a result of grace, for creation was an act of grace. How could the universe contribute anything at all to its own creation? How could we deserve to be created before we even existed? And how could we possibly take the very first step toward grace, the step of humility and repentance, unless God's grace came first to prompt us? That is the clear teaching of Scripture, shocking and humbling as it is to our natural pride; and St. Thomas is totally scriptural. He never tries to edit and correct divine revelation. Everything positive in the "new" theologies of Luther and Calvin was essentially a rediscovery of elements of Thomistic theology.

St. Thomas is often accused of a "two-layer" theory of man and of virtue. What is the basis for this charge? To what extent is there a real distinction between supernatural and natural virtue?

... [V]irtues acquired by human acts ... are dispositions whereby a man is fittingly disposed with reference to the nature whereby he is a man; whereas infused (supernatural) **virtues dispose man in a higher manner and towards a higher end and in relation to** (God) **... i.e., in relation to a participation in the divine nature, according to Second Peter 1:4:** *He hath given us most great and most precious promises, that by these you may be made partakers of the divine nature.* **And it is in respect of receiving this nature that we are said to be born again as sons of God....**
     Grace ... is a participation of (in) **the divine nature ...** (I-II,110.3).

There are indeed two distinct dimensions in man: nature and grace, what man does from his own created nature and what man does from supernatural grace.

To reduce either one of these to the other constitutes a very basic error. Some, especially the fundamentalists, deny any value to the natural level at all, ignoring creation and focusing only on redemption. Others, especially the "modernists", deny, ignore, or minimize the supernatural and miraculous. Fundamentalists deny nature, which is stupid, but modernists deny grace, which is stupider.

Modernists deny miracles. But grace is not an external gift, like most other miracles. It is the very presence and life (i.e., the "nature" as mentioned in 2 Peter 1:4) of God in the soul, of all three Persons of the Trinity. For God is perfect love, and perfect love is the gift of the lover's very self to the beloved.

It is almost as insulting to God to deny nature as to deny grace, for it is God who created everything in nature with natural dispositions or tendencies: grass grows, fire burns, birds fly, stars shine, all because of their nature. For grass not to grow or for birds not to fly would be unnatural, i.e., against their nature.

"Nature" for pre-modern cultures meant not simply the material universe but the invisible principle or energy-source in each thing that moves it to act in its unique way. A thing's nature is the source of its distinctive activities. It is how we recognize and classify things.

St. Thomas teaches essentially three things about natural virtue: (1) that God created man with natural tendencies to virtues: e.g., to love, to trust, to seek and tell the truth, to be fair, and to regulate his bodily passions by the wisdom of his soul; (2) that all these were perverted and twisted by the Fall into sin and selfishness; and (3) that though they were weakened by their opposite vices, they were not abolished. Some criticize St. Thomas for his pessimism (sentence 2 above) and others for his optimism (sentences 1 and 3), as Christ was criticized theologically by both "fundamentalist" Pharisees and "modernist" Sadduccees, and politically by both Herodian collaborators and Zealot revolutionaries. When you're completely right, both sides think you're wrong.

The natural virtues are distinguished from supernatural or "theological" virtues (faith, hope and charity) by four things: (1) their source is miraculous, supernatural grace; (2) their object is God; (3) they are made known to us only by divine revelation, and (4) their end is our participation in the very divine nature. (This too is scriptural: see the quotation from 2 Peter 1:4 above. But how often do we hear about this, the ultimate divine gift and our ultimate human destiny?)

Here is C. S. Lewis' commentary on 2 Peter 1:4: "The dullest and most uninteresting person you talk to may one day be a creature which, if you saw it now, you would be strongly tempted to worship" (*The Weight of Glory*). "All the rabbit in us is to disappear—the worried, conscientious, ethical rabbit as well as the cowardly and sensual rabbit. We shall bleed and squeal as the handfuls of fur come out; and then, surprisingly, we shall find underneath it all something we never yet imagined: a real Man, an ageless god, a son of God, strong, radiant, wise, beautiful, and drenched in joy" ("Man or Rabbit?").

Some (most Catholics) say that outside of special personal supernatural divine revelations, we can never know whether or not we are in a state of grace, since it would make us presumptuous and proud if we knew we *were,* and if we knew we were *not,* it would make us despairing and hopeless, or else resentful and hateful toward God. Others (mainly Protestants) say we are *supposed* to know, and that that is the point of 1 John 5:13: "I write these things to you who believe in the name of the Son of God that you may know that you have eternal life." What does St. Thomas say?

Whether man can know that he has grace?

There are three ways of knowing a thing: first, by revelation, and thus any one might know that he has grace, for God by a special providence reveals this at times to some....

Secondly, a man may of himself know something, and with certainty; and in this way no one can know that he has grace.... And hence man cannot judge with certainty that he has grace, according to First Corinthians 4:3-4: *But neither do I judge my own self ... but He that judgeth me is the Lord.*

Thirdly, things are known conjecturally (fallibly and without certainty) **by signs; and thus anyone may know that he has grace when he is conscious of delighting in God and of despising worldly things, and inasmuch as a man is not conscious of any mortal sin.... Yet this knowledge is imperfect; hence the Apostle says** (1 Cor 4:4): *I am not conscious to myself of anything, yet am I not hereby justified,* **since, according to Psalms 28:13:** *Who can understand sins? From my secret sins cleanse me, O Lord* (I-II, 112, 5).

Much of what we call knowledge is only probable opinion, or what St. Thomas calls "conjecture" through "signs" (evidence, clues). This is the case here. We must judge whether or not we are in a state of grace before presenting ourselves for Holy Communion; but that judgment, like all merely human judgment, is fallible. It is at best an honest, sincere, thoughtful *opinion.*

God can grant the special grace of certain knowledge that one is in the state of grace. But this is a special grace, not given automatically or universally. (The obvious reason for this is that it would tend to make us proud and lazy, as the knowledge that our teacher has already given us an A on a test we are about to take would quite naturally make most of us lazy in preparing for that test.)

If we cannot even know with certainty that we are presently in a state of grace, all the less can we know that we will persevere until the end and die in that state. So even the rare soul to whom God grants this supernatural knowledge with infallible divine certainty cannot be sure that he is guaranteed Heaven.

We do not have what most Protestant Fundamentalists and Calvinists, for different reasons, claim we do and should and must have, namely, "eternal security". God has this certainty, in His mind; but we cannot because we do not have this eternal, divine point of view. We cannot infallibly foresee the future.

The most serious aspect of this error is that it assumes a kind of 180-degree twist in faith, for it turns our faith away from its proper object, God, and back to itself. We do not have, and should not try to have, total faith in our own faith, only in God and His mercy. The greatest practical and personal danger of this theological error is its natural tendency to make us self-satisfied and comfortable, or even self-righteous and "holier than thou." This is often camouflaged by protestations about how terribly sinful we are: this is why the two apparently opposite self-images are often found in the same people.

We can be sure God will never abandon us. We cannot be sure we will not abandon Him. Our faith is in Him, not in ourselves.

Are we saved by our own free choice or by God's grace? Is grace just "help" to our free will, or is it "sovereign"? If it is sovereign, how can we be free? If God has all the power, how can we have any?

The justification of the ungodly is brought about by God moving man to justice (i.e., the state of grace).... **Now God moves everything in its own manner.... Hence He moves man to justice according to the conditions of his human nature. But it is man's proper nature to have free will. Hence in him who has the use of reason, God's motion to justice does not take place without a movement of the free will; but He so infuses the gift of justifying grace that at the same time He moves the free will to accept the gift of grace ...** (I-II,113,3)

Like all gifts, grace is freely given and freely received. Otherwise it is not a gift. A blow on the head may be freely given but it is not freely received. An accidental hug in a crowded bus may not be freely given but it may be freely received.

Grace turns nature on, not off. Grace perfects nature rather than destroying it or setting it aside. Therefore when God's grace works on man, his human nature is perfected.

But essential to human nature is free will.

Therefore when grace works on man, it works in and with and through free will.

So don't ask the question: Is it grace or free will? That's like asking: Is it Daddy or Mommy who made Baby? Or, better, like asking: Was it Shakespeare or Hamlet who caused Claudius to die?

If A causes B to do some good to C, some good that would not otherwise be done, then both A and B did it.

Grace is unlike other gifts in that the very fact that it is freely received is itself one of the gifts that is given. (Reread St. Thomas' last sentence.) Even complaining about the lack of grace can be a grace, for it can move us to more passionate seeking. "Vertical kvetching" can be a grace, as in the Psalms, which are full of complaints to God. "Seek and you will find", for it is God Who motivated the seeking. In the words of the old hymn, "I sought the Lord and afterwards I knew / He moved my soul to seek Him, seeking me."

This question of reconciling grace and free will is one of the classic questions of religious philosophy, and the simpler and shorter answer (St. Thomas' answer) is better than any of the long, complex, distracting, technical ones that fill the books and articles. Sometimes less is more.

Don't ask how the power is divided between God and yourself. It's not divided. Power is divided only between rivals in the same system. God is not a part of the system of creation but the transcendent Creator. The question is appropriate only regarding gods like Zeus who are immanent parts of the same system as ourselves. Zeus and we are rivals; God and we are not. Hamlet and Claudius are rivals; Shakespeare and Hamlet are not.

143. HOW SALVATION "WORKS" AND WHY FAITH ALONE IS NOT ENOUGH

How does God save us?

If the point of the previous article is true, what we do is done by free choice and what God does is done by grace (which is also free—freely given). What do we do and what does God do? How does salvation work?

The justification (salvation, reconciliation) **of the sinner is a certain movement ... from the state of sin to the state of justice** (grace). **Hence it is necessary for the human mind to regard both extremes** (both terms of this change, the beginning and the ending of it, the state of sin and the state of justice) ... **just as a body in local** (spatial) **movement is related to both terms of the movement. Now it is clear that in local movement the moving body leaves the term** *whence* **and nears the term** *whereto*. **Hence the human mind while it is being justified must by a movement of its free will withdraw from sin and draw near to justice.... Hence in the justification of the ungodly there must be two acts of the free will: one whereby it tends to God's justice, and other whereby it hates sin** (I-II,113,5).

There are four things which are accounted to be necessary for the justification of the ungodly, viz. the infusion of grace, the movement of the free will towards God by faith, the movement of the free will regarding sin, and the remission of sins (I-II,113,6).

The first and last of these four things is God's part. The other two are ours.

(1) "The infusion of grace" is first, because God is first. This causes us to believe. Faith is a gift of God. However, this truth is understood and appreciated only after we believe, not before. After, because it dispels the illusion that we rather than God are the first movers. Not before, because we are so foolish that we will inevitably use this truth as an excuse for laziness, and say: "Well, if God

does not move me to believe, there is nothing I can do, and I am not responsible." This denies our free will.

(2) Our own act of faith opens our soul to God's presence. That is the essence of faith: "believing" = "receiving" (Jn 1:12). There must be intellectual content to faith, of course; we can't "just believe *something*"; but we do not know how adequate, or how clear, that understood content must be, or how efficacious for salvation an "anonymous faith" can be in righteous pagans like Socrates.

(3) The other half of our response is repentance. It is usually simultaneous with faith, since "marrying" God (by faith) and "divorcing" God's opposite, sin (by repentance), imply each other.

(4) The God we embrace by faith is the God Who remits our sin in Christ; so this is the result, or "payoff", of our faith and repentance. We do not cause it but we allow it to be caused in us by God.

So two things, on our part, are required to receive God's saving grace: repentance from sin and faith in God Who saves us (by grace, in Christ). Both are free choices, and both are necessary to allow grace to enter our souls.

Of course "repentance" from sin does not mean instant sanctity. We keep having illicit affairs with our old lover, sin, or the idol of self served as if it were God, even after we are divorced from him. But if we honestly repent, we are no longer married to him, but to God.

This grace also necessarily produces good works (gradually, more and more), which become cooperative agents in our salvation process. Faith always blossoms into love: it's all one plant. It's not that we all by ourselves add good works (the works of love) as a second "layer" to what God all by Himself does in giving us grace in the first "layer". Salvation is not a two-layer cake. It's like a marriage: not 50% + 50% but 100% + 100%. We can do nothing without Him and He will do nothing without us.

What is the greatest work of God? Was it the creation of the angels, man, and the universe?

Augustine ... says that *for a just man to be made from a sinner is greater than to create heaven and earth.*

A work may be called great in two ways: first, on the part of the mode of action, and thus the work of creation is the greatest work, wherein something is made from nothing; secondly, a work may be called great on account of what is made, and thus the justification of the ungodly, which terminates at the eternal good of a share in the Godhead, is greater than the creation of heaven and earth, which terminates in the good of mutable nature. Hence Augustine, after saying that *for a just man to be made from a sinner is greater than to create heaven and earth,* **adds:** *for heaven and earth shall pass away, but the justification of the ungodly shall endure* (I-II, 113,9).

Why is salvation a greater work than creation? To fix a broken product (e.g., a car, a painting, or a book) is not usually a greater work than to make it in the first place.

First of all, the analogy fails because we are not "products" of God but "children" of God.

Second, the effect of creating the universe is something mortal (the universe), but the effect of redemption is immortal. When the stars die we will still be young. That is St. Thomas' point. In terms of modern physics, the universe, and everything in it, is winding down ("entropy") and doomed to death. We, unlike everything in the universe, are being wound *up* forever into increasing circles of divine life. We are not just parts of the universe. Only our mortal bodies are.

Buddha's most certain principle—he called it a "diamond" because it cut through all other elements while nothing, apparently, could cut through it—was the principle of "samsara", or birth-and-death: "Whatever is an arising thing, that is also a ceasing thing." That is true of everything in the universe; but it is not true of the life of God in our souls. For redemption means not merely God's remission of our sin but His sharing with us His own eternal life. All things pass away, but we are not merely things, we are persons, immortal children of an immortal Father.

Third, that out of which God created the universe—non-being—offered no resistance to His omnipotent work. Creation was a "no-sweat" operation; all God had to do was to think and will the universe ("let there be ...") and it was. But we put up resistance to redemption by our sin, our pride, our rebellion.

The "good news" part of this point is that we can cooperate in salvation, as we cannot cooperate in creation. God created us without our consent but He will not redeem us without our consent.

Fourth, it cost God nothing to create us, but it cost Him everything to redeem us. It cost Him His own life, and Heavenly joy: "My God, my God, why have you forsaken me?" (Mt 27:46).

Fifth, the end result of creation is simply natural goodness, which is great but finite; while the end result of redemption is supernatural goodness on our part, "a share in the Godhead", which is infinite. The value of redemption infinitely exceeds the value of creation. "For what does it profit a man to gain the whole world but lose his own soul?" (Mk 8:36).

In many Catholic universities, the theologians seem to believe less than their students. In some parishes, the laity seem to believe more than their priest. Is this normal?

Divine revelation reaches those of lower degree through those who are over them, in a certain order: to men, for instance, through the angels, and to the lower angels through the higher.... In like manner, therefore, the unfolding of faith must needs reach men of lower degree through those of higher degree. Consequently, just as the higher angels, who enlighten those who are below them, have a fuller knowledge of divine things than the lower angels ... so too men of higher degree, whose business it is to teach others, are under obligation to have fuller knowledge in matters of faith, and to believe them more explicitly (II-II,2,6).

Leave it to St. Thomas to say the obvious and commonsensical truths that only PhDs could possibly forget or deny. The first qualification for anyone whose job is to teach the faith is that they have the faith. Because the law of cause and effect says that you can't give what you don't have.

Between 50 and 75% of entering freshmen at large Catholic universities typically identify themselves as believing and practicing Catholics. Only 25–50% of graduating seniors do the same. Obviously, what is being taught most effectively there is unfaith rather than faith, or at least a lesser faith rather than a greater one. When I ask my "Catholic" students what they would say to God if they died tonight and God asked them why He should let them into Heaven, fewer than 5% ever even mention Jesus Christ. This is more scandalous than sex scandals.

The disappearance of these schools would be a tragedy indeed—from the viewpoint of the War Room in Hell.

This current situation is definitely not normal or natural. Yet it has existed and increased ever since the 18th century and the "Enlightenment" (although God certainly does not call it that). However, the tide may be turning in the Church, beginning with the pontificate of John Paul the Great. Catholic teachers are turning to Catholicism, of all things. Instead of editing, correcting, and diminishing the Tradition which was passed on to them from Christ and His apostles, they are increasingly believing it and teaching it.

For of course you can't honestly teach what you don't believe. You can't give what you don't have. The first qualification for religion teachers, then, is faith. If their faith is stronger than that of their students, the result will be an increase in the faith of the students, and in the understanding of that faith. If it is less, the result will be less. For effects come to resemble their causes.

Suppose one of the higher angels, whose task was to enlighten lower angels with some of the light of God, believed and understood less of God than this angel's student. The result of this supposed "enlightening" would be a *diminishing* of the divine light in the mind of the student rather than its amplification. That would be a situation as absurd as me teaching Einstein math, or Josef Stalin teaching virtue to Mother Teresa.

Such an upside down situation is inherently unstable, and must inevitably fall. Darkness cannot conquer light, in the long run.

Isn't faith less certain than science?

On the contrary, the Apostle says (1 Thess. 2:15): *When you had received of us the word . . . you received it not as the word of men but, as it is indeed, the word of God.* **Now nothing is more certain than the word of God. Therefore science is not more certain than faith, nor is anything else. . . .**

A thing which has a more certain cause is itself more certain. In this way faith is more certain than these three (intellectual) **virtues** (wisdom, science, and understanding) **because it is founded on the divine truth whereas the aforesaid three virtues are based on human reason.**

Secondly, certitude may be considered on the part of the subject, and thus the more a man's intellect lays hold of a thing, the more certain it is. In this way faith is less certain because matters of faith are above the human intellect, whereas the objects of the aforesaid virtues are not (II-II,4,8).

Many terms have changed their meaning from pre-modern to modern times; and the most common kind of change has been from the older, more objective sense to a more subjective sense. For instance, "want" used to mean "need", as in "The Lord is my shepherd; I shall not want." Now "need" often means "want," as in "sexual needs". (No one has "sexual needs", only sexual wants, or desires. Many people live quite complete, healthy, happy, and holy human lives without sexual activity, although this is often as incomprehensible to typically modern minds as it was to pre-modern minds how people could possibly live without God.)

One such term is the word "certain", or "certainty". It used to mean something objective: the determination to a specific nature or end, as "triangles are certain to have 180 degrees" or "God exists certainly, i.e., necessarily rather than contingently", or "puppies are certain to become dogs, not cats." Its opposite was randomness or unpredictability. Today "certainty" almost always means something subjective, something predicated not of an objective fact (such as the three examples above) but of a person. In modern usage, "I" am certain that x is y, rather than x itself being certain to be y; so that if you know no geometry, you are *not* certain that all triangles have 180 degrees.

St. Thomas uses the older, objective sense of "certain" when he says that "nothing is more certain than the word of God"—even though many people doubt or disbelieve it. The revealed Faith is the most certain truth knowable, for any man can be deceived or deceive, but God never can.

Thus science is not more certain than faith even though there is no demonstration of the truths of the Faith by the scientific method, as there is of the truths of science.

St. Thomas also admits a second meaning of certitude, "on the part of the subject," i.e., as appearing to a given human intellect; and "in this way faith is less certain." But that concerns appearance (which is relative to a fallible human mind) rather than reality (which is not).

It matters enormously which of these two senses of "certainty" is prior. If we measure the certainty of *the* Faith by that of *our* faith, we are modernists, and we view any claim voiced by any human being to have absolute certainty about any of the doctrines of the Faith as something arrogant, narrow-minded, "fundamentalistic", and thoughtless. If, on the other hand, we measure our own certainty, open as it always is to doubts and misunderstandings, by the certainty of the Faith revealed by God, then it is the most reasonable thing in the world to claim absolute and indubitable certainty even for dogmas like the Trinity that can in no way be proved by any method of human reasoning.

If our faith rests on God's veracity, it has an absolute and eternally unshakable foundation. If it rests on our own mind, it is as secure as sand. Does your faith look like a castle or a sand castle?

What we believe—the content of faith—is from divine revelation, but our choice to believe is from our free will—is that correct?

Two things are necessary for faith. First, that the things which are of faith should be proposed to man: this is necessary in order that man believe anything explicitly. The second thing requisite for faith is the assent of the believer to the things which are proposed to him. Accordingly, as regard the first of these, faith must needs be from God. Because the things which are of faith surpass human reason, hence they do not come to man's knowledge unless God reveal them....

As regards the second, viz. man's assent to the things which are of faith, we may observe a twofold cause, one of external inducement, such as seeing a miracle or being persuaded by someone to embrace the faith, neither of which is a sufficient cause, since of those who see the same miracle or hear the same sermon, some believe and some do not. Hence we must assert another internal cause, which moves man inwardly to assent to matters of faith.

The Pelagians held that this cause was nothing else than man's free will, and consequently they said that the beginning of faith is from ourselves.... But this is false, for, since man, by assenting to matters of faith, is raised above his nature, this must needs accrue to him from some supernatural principle moving him inwardly; and this is God. Therefore faith, as regards the assent which is the chief act of faith, is (ultimately) **from God moving man inwardly by grace** (II-II,6,1).

Our act of faith is both a free choice and a gift of grace. (See #142, above.) For "grace perfects nature", and therefore human nature, and therefore human freedom, which is an essential part of human nature; grace "turns on" our free will rather than turning it off.

Our faith must be a free choice, of course; but it *first* must be "a gift of God" because God is the universal First Cause, not ourselves. Faith is our *response*: to the prior grace of divine revelation without and to the prior grace of a divine movement within. Faith is not something we work up in ourselves by pushing the right psychological buttons. One does not simply "have faith"; one responds to divine revelation and invitation to believe it, either by faith (Yes) or unfaith (No).

If God did not first reveal Himself (in St. Thomas' words, "that the things which are of faith should be proposed to man"), our faith would have no object. That is what St. Thomas calls "the first thing", in the first paragraph above. What he calls "the second thing" is our assent. St. Thomas mentions no less than three causes of this assent. (1) One is the "external inducement, such as seeing a miracle or being persuaded by someone". That is a catalyst, an occasion, for (2) our free choice to assent. (3) But the ultimate mover of both the external catalyst and our internal "reaction" to it is "God moving man inwardly by grace". This was what the Pelagians denied. They thought human freedom had to be absolute.

If God can move us outwardly, by miracles or preaching ("being persuaded by someone"), without destroying or weakening our free will, all the more can He do this inwardly. Just as what comes to us from without—the miracle or the preacher—is no accident but God's gift to us, so also is what comes from us from within, viz. the very act of assenting. For God is within as well as without, and He transcends us, transcends our ego, our self-conscious "I", in both directions equally, though we do not usually attend to the second one. But that transcendence—we may call it the inner transcendence—is just as real as the other one, the outer transcendence. For, as St. Augustine famously observed, God is "nearer to us than we are to ourselves". Human experience has two poles: the subjective ("I") and the objective ("it"). God transcends both. He is not part of our material universe, nor is He part of our spiritual soul. He is neither a galaxy nor a feeling. And therefore He can be present to both, as the playwright is present to both the setting and the characters of his play.

148. Faith and fear

"Faith casts out fear." Yet "the fear of the Lord is the beginning of wisdom." Does faith cast out the beginning of wisdom?

Whether fear is an effect of faith?

... [F]aith is a cause of the fear whereby one dreads to be punished by God; and this is servile fear.

It (faith) is also the cause of filial fear, whereby one dreads to be separated from God, or whereby one shrinks from equaling himself to Him, and holds Him in reverence, inasmuch as faith makes us appreciate God as an unfathomable and supreme good, separation from which is the greatest evil....

Of the first fear, viz. servile fear, lifeless faith is the cause, while living faith is the cause of the second, viz filial fear ... (II-II,7,1).

"Fear" in modern English can mean three different things, which St. Thomas distinguishes.

First, it can be the fear of being punished, whether deservedly or undeservedly. This is a fear of pain. It is called "servile" fear because it is typically found in a slave or servant.

Second, it can be the fear of losing or offending a beloved friend, human or divine. This is "filial fear", the fear proper to a friend or lover.

Third, it can mean deep, wondering reverence, or "awe" at something immeasurably superior. This is an emotion that is much rarer today than ever before in the history of the world, probably because modern life is so full of scientific knowledge and technological power over nature that we live in a dream of arrogant cleverness and a cocoon of predictable comforts. But this old fear still exists. It can arise in the presence of either something tremendously good, like God's love as shown in the Incarnation and the crucifixion, or something tremendously evil, like the Holocaust, or 9/11, or something neither morally good nor evil, like a hurricane or a spectacular sunrise.

This third kind of fear, unlike the other two, is not a fear of losing something. We fear lions and slave drivers because they can hurt us, but we fear ghosts just because they are ghosts. We fear ghosts not because they will harm us but because of what they are: unknowns, from another realm. This is the fear we naturally feel toward angels. (Thus in Scripture when angels appear the first thing they usually say is "Fear not.") The preeminent object of this fear is, of course, God. When John saw Him in Revelations 1:17, he says he "fell at His feet as though dead".

Which "fear of the Lord" is what Scripture speaks of as "the beginning of wisdom" (Prov 9:10)? First of all the third one, awe; and then, as we learn how good God is, it is also the second one, the fear of offending One Who is so good. ("Offending" God means *dishonoring* Him, not getting Him mad.) The first fear, servile fear, is primitive; we are meant to outgrow it. Thus John says that "Perfect love casts out fear. For fear has to do with punishment and he who fears is not perfected in love" (1 Jn 4:18).

St. Thomas connects servile fear with dead faith (loveless faith) and filial fear with living faith. "Dead faith" is merely intellectual and legalistic belief. Thus "Do you believe that God is one? Oh, good for you. The demons also believe that, but shudder with fear" (Jas 2:19).

Yet even this fear is good in its place. As George MacDonald says, "where there are wild beasts about it is better to feel afraid than to feel secure." Thus Christ tells us to fear the Devil: "And do not fear those who kill the body but cannot kill the soul; rather fear him who can destroy both soul and body in hell" (Mt 10:28). St. Peter says the same: 1 Peter 5:8–9.

This fear, of course, does not mean cowardice or running away. It means fighting. The Devil is the coward. He is more afraid of us (or, rather, of Christ in us) than we are of him.

149. How unbelief is a sin

How can God punish anyone for honest, sincere error? How can unbelief be a sin?

Vice (and sin) is opposed to virtue. Now faith is a virtue, and unbelief is opposed to it. Therefore unbelief is a sin.

Unbelief may be taken in two ways: first, by way of pure negation, so that a man is called an unbeliever merely because he does not have the faith. Secondly, unbelief may be taken by way of opposition to the faith, in which sense a man refuses to hear the faith or despises it ... and it is in this sense that unbelief is a sin.

If, however, we take it by way of pure negation, as we find it in those who have heard nothing about the faith, it bears the character not of sin.... [I]f such unbelievers are damned it is on account of other sins ... but not on account of their sin of unbelief. Hence Our Lord said (Jn 15:22): *If I had not come and spoken to them, they would not have sin* (II–II,10,1).

Dishonesty is a sin, whether this is dishonesty to another person in lying to him or dishonesty to yourself in lying to yourself, when you "by ... wickedness suppress the truth" (Rom 1:18, where Paul accuses the whole human race of this sin).

Disbelief is a sin, but honest unbelief is not. But it is a temporary condition on the part of a person who is honestly seeking the truth. It is only temporary because Christ Himself promised that all who seek will eventually find (Mt 7:7–8). It may, however, take a long time—sometimes longer than one's lifetime on earth. That is one reason why there has to be a Purgatory.

St. Thomas says that a pagan who has not heard the Faith does not sin for disbelieving it. You can't believe what you don't know. We can also extend this to those who have heard only a false, unfair, and misleading version of the Faith (e.g., "Catholicism is superstition" or "Christianity is the fairy tale that God is Super Santa"). They are right to reject this. This is rejection of false gods, not the true God.

But when someone is exposed to the true divine revelation and confronts the claims of Christ, and turns away by refusing to hear it, or despises it, hates it, wants the Good News of the gospel to be false—this is serious sin. Wanting the bad news of silly superstitions to be false is a virtue; wanting the good news—that God, Ultimate Reality, is also ultimate goodness and love—to be false is mortal sin because it is refusing the nature of ultimate reality, refusing The Way Things Are. If one dies in this state he cannot go to Heaven because he would hate Heaven. He wills that Heaven be not Heaven and God be not God.

Religious belief is needed for salvation because religious belief means something much more than an intellectual opinion. Remember, "even the demons believe (in this merely intellectual sense), and shudder" (Jas 2:19). "Religious belief" means "faith", and "faith" means "fidelity", and "fidelity" means "faithfulness", the faithfulness of one *person* to another person, not just the acceptance of a *mind* toward an *idea*. Thus St. Thomas elsewhere (ST II–II 1,1) says that the primary object of faith is not just truths but the First Truth, the Person of God; the secondary object of faith is the truths God has revealed. The old Baltimore Catechism defined faith as "an act of the intellect, prompted by the will, by which we believe everything God has revealed on the authority of Him Who has revealed it." Faith is belief in a Person first of all, and only because of that, in what the Person says. This is why we believe the Christian faith: because it is God's mind, not man's.

Faith is *trust*. Banks are called "trust companies" because you actually put your money into them. Insurance companies are often called "fidelity" companies for the same reason. Faith is a real transaction. Something really happens between you and the other person, human or divine. It's not just an attitude. You give something, you invest something, in another person. That something is always at least a part of your very self. This is why faith is necessary for salvation: because that's what Heaven's life *is:* the gift of self in trust and love.

150. THE GOOD DONE BY UNBELIEVERS; AND "IMPLICIT FAITH"

Calvin believed that all the good deeds of unbelievers were worthless to God. Even St. Augustine said that the virtues of the pagans were only "splendid vices." Is that true?

Can unbelievers be saved? There is a serious problem here, for if the answer is yes, then it seems that to be saved you don't need faith, or the gospel, or even Christ, as long as you do good deeds. But if the answer is no, because you do need faith to be saved, then God seems unfair to condemn to Hell pagans who never had the chance to hear the gospel and believe it. Can unbelievers have implicit faith?

It is said of Cornelius, while yet an unbeliever (Acts 10:4,31), that his alms were acceptable to God. Therefore not every action of an unbeliever is a sin, but some of his actions are good....

Unbelief does not wholly destroy natural reason in unbelievers, but some knowledge of the truth remains in them, whereby they are able to do deeds that are generically good. With regard, however, to Cornelius, it is to be observed that he was not an unbeliever, else his works would not have been acceptable to God, Whom none can please without faith. Now he had implicit faith, as the truth of the Gospel was not yet made manifest (II-II,10,4).

St. Thomas assumes in this answer the distinction he made above (#148) between living faith and dead faith. Only living faith can save us. But even implicit faith can be living faith.

Pagans like Cornelius (or Socrates) can be saved because they can have implicit living faith. He was a God-seeker; God was in his heart even though He was not in his head explicitly. We are not saved by how much we know (intellectually) but by the One Whom we know (personally). God does not give us a theology exam at the Last Judgment, with those who get a 60 going to Heaven and those who get a 59 going to Hell.

This only-implicit but still-living faith produces the good works of the righteous pagan like Cornelius, or (probably) Socrates, and these might be called the implicit works of love (agape, charity) even in the absence of the explicit knowledge of the divine love revealed to the Jews and fulfilled by Christ. Thus a living faith and its product, love, can exist among pagans. God does not refuse to enter their souls when they seek Him, even confusedly.

The answer to the "serious problem" above is that Christ as the *Logos,* the Word or Mind or Reason of God, "the true light that enlightens every man who comes into the world" (Jn 1:9), enlightens pagans too, though not as explicitly as Christians because they do not know Him in His Incarnation. Paul makes the same point in Romans 1:19–21. Christ the *Logos* was known not only by the few thousand Jews He met during the three years of His public ministry in Israel, but by "every man who comes into the world". Thus all have a chance of salvation because all know the Savior, the *Logos,* the second Person of the Trinity, even if they do not know His Incarnation as Jesus. For the divine *Logos* and the human Jesus are not two Persons but one and the same Person.

Thus the quintessentially "conservative" dogma of Christ's divinity as the pre-incarnate eternal *Logos* is the basis for the quintessentially "liberal" hope that good pagans can go to Heaven. He is indeed the one and only Way, Truth, and Life, the only Savior. But when Muslims, Buddhists, Hindus, or even honest agnostics give their heart to truth and goodness; when they make the ultimate value and point and purpose and meaning and end of their lives *that which God is,* absolute truth and absolute goodness, they are in fact giving their heart to Jesus even though they do not know it. And He will claim their hearts at the Last Judgment.

So when you find truth and goodness among non-Christians, praise Christ for His gracious, humble, anonymous presence there. And thank Him for revealing Himself more clearly to you, for the more clearly we know the Way, the more likely it is that we will walk in it.

If the sins of the flesh are less blameworthy than spiritual sins, lust can't do much harm, then, right?

... [C]arnal vices, namely gluttony and lust, are concerned with pleasures of touch in matters of food and sex; and these are the most impetuous of all pleasures of the body. For this reason, these vices cause man's attention to be very firmly fixed on corporeal things, so that in consequence man's operation (activity of soul) **in regard to intelligible** (spiritual) **things is weakened—more, however, by lust than by gluttony, forasmuch as sexual pleasures are more vehement than those of the table. Wherefore lust gives rise to blindness of mind, which excludes almost entirely the knowledge of spiritual things.... The flesh acts on the intellective faculties ... by impeding their operation** (II-II,15,3).

One of the reasons lust is bad (not the only reason) is that it makes you stupid. Like any addiction, it blinds your vision to everything else and focuses it on the one thing that is the object of your addiction. St. Thomas often points out that lust harms the reason. This is much more serious if we remember that "reason" meant to him something much more broad, deep, precious, and human than it typically means to us (cold calculation). It is by "reason" that we know "spiritual things".

But he also says that it does harm to the heart, and to love:

Now the fact that spiritual goods taste good to us no more, or seem to be goods of no great account, is chiefly due to our affections being infected with the love of bodily pleasures, among which sexual pleasures hold the first place (II-II,20,4).

St. Thomas was supernaturally preserved from all lust by a miraculous gift given to him after he refused to succumb to the prostitute his brothers put in his room when they imprisoned him to attempt to stop him from becoming a Dominican monk. St. Augustine, on the other hand, was "the playboy of the Western world" before his conversion. Yet both know and say the same thing about lust. Both the constantly sober person and the ex-drunk know the harm of drunkenness, in opposite ways.

Our reason, which is the only power in us that knows Truth, and our heart, which is the only power in us that loves, are thus both harmed by lust. Lust takes away clarity and reason from our mind and freedom from our will. And these two powers, mind and will, are the two most precious powers of the soul, and their objects—truth and goodness—are the only two things we absolutely and eternally need. That is why lust is no casual and relatively harmless sin.

Another reason is that lust is the most addictive of all sins. Love frees us, lust enslaves us. Its glue is the stickiest, and it is harder to free the soul from its clutches than from the clutches of the less attractive, cold-hearted sins like pride or idolatry or envy, because those sins are no fun at all. Yet the cold-hearted sins are in themselves more serious because they are more freely and deliberately chosen. So paradoxically, even though the sins of the flesh, especially lust, are less serious than spiritual sins in that they are less free and responsible, and have in them more of the element of addiction (though all sin is addictive; we are all sinaholics) and less of the element of free choice (though all sin is a free choice; otherwise we would not be responsible for it), yet this same fact explains why they are in another way *more* serious, more harmful, harder to purge. Their cause may be less (less free) but their attractions are greater.

Our world, far more than St. Thomas', is chock full of lustaholilcs. The very word "lust" is typically treated as a joke, or else the alternative is assumed to be unattainable, undesirable, and incomprehensible. When everyone has a fever, a fever seems normal and 98.6 seems abnormally cool. Yet, as C. S. Lewis says, "when poisons become fashionable they do not cease to kill".

Is fear good or evil? What are the different kinds of fear?

(1) **Since the object of fear is an evil** (we love only good things, or at least apparently good things, and we fear only bad things, or at least apparently bad things), **sometimes on account of the evils he fears man withdraws from God; and this is called human fear.**

(2) **Sometimes, on account of the evils he fears he turns to God and adheres to Him. The latter evil** (what is feared here) **is twofold, viz. evil of punishment and evil of fault. Accordingly, if a man turn to God and adhere to Him through fear of punishment, it will be servile fear.**

(3) **But if it be on account of fear of committing a fault, it will be filial fear, for it becomes a child to fear offending its father** (II-II,19,2).

Nothing evil is from the Holy Ghost. But servile fear is from the Holy Ghost.... Therefore servile fear is not evil.... It is (only) **owing to its servility that servile fear may be evil. For servitude is opposed to freedom. Since, then,** *what is free is cause of itself* (Aristotle)**, a slave is one who does not act as cause of his own action but as though moved from without. Now whoever does a thing through love does it of himself ... so that it is contrary to the very notion of servility that one should act from love. Consequently servile fear as such is contrary to charity; so that if servility were essential to fear, servile fear would be evil simply.... Consequently servile fear is substantially good but its servility is evil** (II-II,19,4).

The first kind of fear (human fear that turns us from God) is simply evil, for anything that turns us away from God, the source of all good, is evil. God is the only absolute; everything is relative to Him. "Human fear" is the fear of some apparent evil that is involved in our turning to God, such as the sacrifices we would have to make, or the unpleasant nature of honestly confessing and repenting of our sins. (These things are not really evil, since they lead us to God; but they are apparently evil, and therefore they can be feared, if we lack wisdom, which is the habit of distinguishing appearance from reality.)

But anything that leads us to God is good. And therefore servile fear as well as filial fear is good. Filial fear stems from the love of God and is the desire, because of that love, not to offend the God we know and love as our Father. Servile fear lacks that filial, trusting love—and that lack is evil—but servile fear also leads us to God through fear of punishment. It is a low motive, but it works, and God "stoops to conquer" us by appealing, if necessary, to even low motives. He is easy to please though hard to satisfy. He treats us as patient parents treat intellectually disabled children. For that is what He really is and that is what we really are.

Thus "the (servile) fear of the Lord is the (primitive) beginning of wisdom" but it is not the (mature) end. But the beginning of a good thing is a good thing; and moving closer to God is a good thing; and servile fear moves us closer to God; therefore servile fear is a good thing, as a concrete whole, though the abstract aspect of its servility is not good, because it is opposed to freedom and lacking in love. The noun is good but its adjective is not. It is substantially good and accidentally bad. A man may be a good man yet have some bad habits or ugly features. Imagine the *Mona Lisa* being defaced by an ugly rip in its canvas. A broken masterpiece is not just a *broken* masterpiece, it is also a broken *masterpiece*.

If "perfect love casts out fear" (1 Jn 4:18), does it cast out all servile fear and allow only filial fear? If it does, then does the fact that I fear God's punishment mean I do not have love? How can that be if I am to honestly confess, in the confessional, that I am sorry to have offended God by sin because I fear the loss of Heaven and the pains of Hell (= servile fear) as well as because He deserves all my love (= filial fear)?

Servile fear is not driven out when charity comes.

Servile fear proceeds from self-love, because it is fear of punishment which is detrimental to one's own good. Hence the fear of punishment is consistent with charity in the same way as self-love is: because it comes to the same thing that a man love his own good and that he fear to be deprived of it.

Now self-love may stand in a threefold relationship to charity.

(1) In one way it is contrary to charity, when a man places his end in the love of his own good.

(2) In another way it is included in charity, when a man loves himself for the sake of God and in God.

(3) In a third way, it is indeed distinct from charity, but is not contrary to charity, as when a man loves himself from the point of view of his own good yet not so as to place his end in this his own good (II-II,19,6).

... filial fear must needs increase when charity increases ... for the more one loves a man, the more one fears to offend him and to be separated from him. On the other hand, servile fear ... decreases as charity increases ... since the more a man loves God, the less he fears punishment: first, because he thinks less of his own good, to which punishment is opposed; secondly, because the faster he clings, the more confident he is of the reward and consequently the less fearful of punishment (II-II,19,10).

"Perfect love casts out (servile) fear" indeed, but by a process. It is gradual. Thus as charity (perfect love) increases, servile fear (of punishment) decreases (last paragraph). But the two are not opposed simply and absolutely, like good and evil or light and darkness; they are compatible.

St. Thomas explains why they are compatible: the fear of being punished is of course the fear of suffering some loss to your own happpiness. (One is punished by being fined, not by being given money; by being whipped, not kissed.) We love our own happiness because we love ourselves. And self-love, the root of this servile fear of punishment, is not necessarily contrary to charity. (1) It can be, if it means that you deny that your good is ultimately in God, and make yourself your only or ultimate good. (2) But it is not, if it means that you love yourself for God's sake. Loving God means loving whatever God loves, so if God loves you, you must love yourself—for God's sake. ("God don't make no junk.") (3) In itself, self-love is neutral: to love yourself can become either bad (#1) or good (#2).

The most well-known and universally acknowledged rule of morality is "the Golden Rule", "Do unto others what you would have them do unto you." This is the same principle, in different words, as "Love your neighbor as yourself," i.e., as you already love yourself. But if self-love were evil by its essence, if it were always evil, then "love your neighbor as yourself" would mean "love your neighbor evilly, as you love yourself evilly." If self-love were like a disease, loving your neighbor as you love yourself would only spread that disease.

Filial fear and servile fear are opposites. Therefore although charity and filial fear are directly proportional, while charity and servile fear are inversely proportional. In other words, as charity increases, filial fear increases *and* servile fear decreases. This is the process of spiritual maturing.

Presumption and despair are opposite deadly sins. We hear a lot about despair, and the need for hope; but what is presumption?

Many people seem to be in despair today, which manifests itself in depression; is presumption just as common?

There may be presumption ... in the fact that a man tends to some good as though it were possible by the power and mercy of God whereas it is not possible, for instance if a man hope to obtain pardon without repenting (II-II,21,1). **For just as it is false that God does not pardon the repentant, or that He does not turn sinners to repentance, so it is false that He grants forgiveness to those who persevere in their sins** (II-II,21,2).

"Opposites attract." This is true of evil as well as good. Hedonism and Puritanism, for instance, often go together. So do collectivism and individualism, once the sense of community is lost. So we find in modern Western civilization great presumption and great despair together. For instance the presumption that we can by our science and technology make ourselves unlimitedly intelligent and create a Heaven on earth—this presumption naturally begets a despairing disappointment and resentment against the few physical pains that remain in our lives, and the naïve optimism of this presumption begets a pessimism when it fails to deliver. Thus the "Enlightenment" begets the Existentialists' despair.

It all comes from a denial of divine grace. St. Thomas thus detects a primary source of presumption in seeking genuinely good things, like human happiness on earth, as if we did not need divine grace to attain them; and in the hope that we can obtain God's pardon and mercy without our confessing and repenting of sin. This was prophetic. That attitude was very rare in St. Thomas' day; it is very common in ours. We hear of God's free love and compassion and mercy on sinners all the time, but almost never about His necessary justice and wrath against sin.

St. Thomas thus mentions two apparently opposite falsehoods, both of which stem from the denial of the same truth, the truth of grace, redemption, salvation, and forgiveness: first, the despair that admits divine justice on sin but not the divine grace to convert sinners; and second, the presumption that admits divine grace but denies that there is any sin to forgive.

Thus we often hear people say, in response to "Forgive me", "There's nothing to forgive"—which is almost always false! If there is nothing to forgive, there is no sin. But there is. And the Devil is equally pleased at our embracing either of two alternatives to salvation, forgiveness, and redemption: either the Bad News without the Good News, justice without mercy, sin without salvation (an error more typical of the past), or the Good News without the Bad News, mercy without justice, salvation without sin (an error more typical of the present).

Thus one author described the presumption of typically modern Christianity as a religion in which "a God without wrath saves a man without sin by mercy without judgment for a Heaven without a Hell through a Christ without a cross." God does not and cannot forgive a man who does not accept forgiveness because he does not admit his sin but justifies it. If we justify ourselves, how can God justify us? If we believe "there is nothing to forgive", how can we receive forgiveness? Christ clearly said that we needed repentance as well as faith to be saved. Faith and hope without repentance (which is presumptuous) can no more save us than repentance without faith and hope (which is despairing, like Judas' repentance). The God-glue is a two-part epoxy.

155. IS LOVE IN US FROM GOD OR FROM OUR OWN ACTIVE CHOICE?

Do I decide to love, or does God make me love? Is charity my work or is it God's?

When the Holy Ghost moves the human mind (soul, heart, spirit), **the movement of charity does not proceed from this motion in such a way that the human mind be merely moved without being the principle** (source, origin, cause) **of this movement as when a body is moved by some extrinsic motive power. For this is contrary to the nature of a voluntary act, whose principle needs to be in itself; so that it would follow that to love is not a voluntary act, which involves a contradiction, since love of its very nature implies an act of the will.**

Likewise, neither can it be said that the Holy Ghost moves the will in such a way to the act of loving as though the will were (merely) **an instrument, for an instrument ... has not the power to act or not to act; for then again the act would cease to be voluntary and meritorious....**

Given that the will is moved by the Holy Ghost to the act of love, it is necessary that the will also should be the efficient cause of that act ... (II-II,23,2).

God does not give us charity without our willing it. He does not do it *instead of* us doing it. He turns our free wills on, not off. He, the First Cause, causes us to be the originating cause of our own choice to love, as a parent is the cause of the child yet causes the child to be human and therefore free and therefore to have the power of being the cause of its own choices.

It is not that our will to receive God's grace causes God to give it. As the child's will does not cause the parent's will, but vice versa, so our will does not cause God's will but vice versa. Our willing charity is not the cause of God giving us that gift; God's gift is the cause of our willing it.

Selfish love, eros, is within our natural power. Unselfish love, agape, is not. It is a gift of God. If you have it, thank God for it, not yourself. If you don't have it, ask God for it, not yourself.

But it is evident that the act of charity surpasses the nature of the power of the will ... unless some form be superadded to the natural power, inclining it to the act of love, this same act would not be ... easy and pleasurable to perform. And this is evidently untrue, since no virtue has such a strong inclination to its act as charity has, nor does any virtue perform its act with so great pleasure ...

The Divine Essence Itself is charity, even as It is wisdom and goodness. Wherefore just as we are said to be good with the goodness which is God, and wise with the wisdom which is God (since the goodness whereby we are good is a participation of divine goodness, and the wisdom whereby we are wise is a share of divine wisdom), so too the charity whereby we love our neighbor is a participation of divine charity....

God is effectively the life both of the soul by charity and of the body by the soul ... charity is the life of the soul even as the soul is the life of the body ... just as the soul is immediately united to the body, so is charity to the soul (II-II,23,2).

Human nature by itself without God is hopelessly egotistic, even though it can temper its egotism with justice and kindness and politeness. Charity is the main work of the life of God in the soul (*zoe*, supernatural life, sanctifying grace, the new birth—there are many names for it). Yet we have by nature a need and aptitude for supernatural charity; for when it comes, it makes us supremely happy.

Charity is not only a gift given by God, like a miracle, or creation, or the soul itself; but it is the very life of God Himself, it is God's gift of Himself. We actually "participate in", or share, or have a finite part of, the infinite reality of divine charity. Charity is not only the *effect* of union with God, charity *is* real union with God, as drinking is union with water.

Does charity in us increase more and more forever, without limit? Will we never be bored in Heaven to all eternity because there will always be new and exciting ways to love, new things to love, new increases in love? And if in Heaven, here too?

Whether charity increases indefinitely?
... let none of the faithful say: "Enough."
... **the wayfarer's charity can ever increase more and more.... [C]harity has no limit to its increase, since it is a participation in the infinite charity which is the Holy Ghost....**
The capacity of the rational creature is increased by charity because the heart is enlarged thereby ... so that it still remains capable of receiving a further increase (II-II,24,7).

St. Thomas is a rational, logical, judicious, careful, thoughtful, conservative kind of intellectual, not naturally given to exaggeration, fanaticism, passionate outbursts, Romanticist exuberance, poetic extremes, or Existentialist impatience with limits. Those who know only this dimension of him may be surprised to find this other dimension in him too. It is his "vertical", not "horizontal", dimension. The word for limits and finitude, the word "enough", expresses a primary "horizontal" virtue regarding all things human and natural. It is the virtue of moderation. "Nothing too much", or "moderation in all things", was one of the two virtues (the other was "know thyself") inscribed over the door of the temples to Apollo, especially that of the Delphic oracle, in ancient Greece; and St. Thomas wisely approves this. But when it comes to the relationship with God, with the supernatural, he is an "extremist". All the natural virtues are means between two opposite extremes, as Aristotle said; but the three theological, or supernatural, virtues do not follow this formula. No one can have too much faith (trust in God), too much hope in God's generosity, or too much love for God. "Enough" is one of the two legitimate earthly words that no one pronounces in Heaven. (The other is "mine". Remember the seagulls in *Finding Nemo*.) Nor should the faithful say "enough" to any Heavenly values on earth.

"I have seen everything under the sun", says weary, despairing Ecclesiastes. But no one will ever "have seen everything" beyond the sun. "When we've been there ten thousand years, bright shining like the sun, we've no less days to sing God's praise than when we'd first begun", and we will not even begin to be bored. Because of our charity, we will experience some startlingly new beauty and joy in God every moment. "Every moment mercies new fall as fresh as morning dew."

And this begins in this life, if we had but the wise eyes to see the appetizers of Heaven, the colonies of Heaven, the prophets of Heaven, the spies of Heaven, that are already in our midst. Thus St. Thomas says that "the wayfarer's charity can ever increase more and more." It is like the series of positive integers: there is no highest number, no limit.

And the reason is that charity is an actual participation in, not merely an image of, or an imitation of, or an effect of, God Himself. God the Holy Spirit *is* the eternal charity that unites the Father and the Son; and He is not merely *for* us or *with* us but *in* us and we *in* Him. Charity is like blood; it is the actual life that runs from the heart (God) through the arteries (Christ) of the Mystical Body, and returns through the veins (man). For He is the Heart as well as the Head of His own mystical Body.

Our hearts are finite, but the very capacity to hold love and choose love can be infinitely increased, and therefore our love will be infinitely increased, forever, in Heaven.

This is not the same infinity as the divine infinity. God is *actually* infinite; our participation in Him and His charity is *potentially* infinite, like the number series. God is already perfectly, completely achieved infinite perfection; we grow in perfection forever and ever, always increasing God-ward. We cannot imagine this. But we can believe it, hope for it, and love it.

This process begins in this life, and can be verified in experience. In fact, if it does not begin in this life it will not be continued and perfected in Heaven. God seeds eternal plants in temporal pots.

St. John says that "any one who abides (lives) in Him (God) does not sin" (1 Jn 3:6), and that "any one born of God does not commit sin, for God's seed abides in him, and he cannot commit sin because he has been born of God" (1 Jn 3:9). Yet in the same letter St. John says "If we say we have no sin, we deceive ourselves, and the truth is not in us" (1 Jn 1:8). This sounds like a contradiction, but since it is in the same letter of the same author, he obviously has something else in mind. What?

Charity ... as such ... is incapable of anything that is against its nature. Wherefore charity cannot sin at all, even as neither can heat cool nor unrighteousness do good (II-II,24,11).

An apparent contradiction can be shown to be not a real contradiction if some of the words are used in two different senses. To undo a contradiction, make a distinction.

Part of the explanation depends on a point in Greek grammar. Verbs have many more tenses in Greek than in English, and two different present tenses in Greek are (1) the aorist and (2) the present progressive. The first designates a single action, like "he died" or "he left the city at noon." The second designates an ongoing, repeated, natural or habitual action, like "birds fly" or "intercourse produces pregnancy" or "heavy objects fall." It is the second tense that is used where St. John says that those born of God do not sin: they are born into a divine nature, so they do not sin *naturally* and continually, even though they fall into many one-shot actual sins of the moment.

The single concrete human person who has been "born again" has two dimensions, or two natures, not just one. They have a new, second nature, their participation in the divine nature (2 Pet 1:4), which is also called sanctifying grace, or the presence of the Holy Spirit, the presence of supernatural charity (agape) in their soul; and that new nature is incapable of sin. They also have the old nature, which St. Paul calls "the old man" or "Adam" or "the flesh" as opposed to "the new man", "Christ in you",

and "the Spirit". "Nature" means "the source of its habitual action that flows from and reveals what it is." So the sin nature sins but the new nature does not. More exactly, we sin because we are sinners by our old nature and we love because we are lovers by our new nature. We sin only insofar as we are moved by our old nature, and we practice charity only insofar as we are moved by our new nature.

A single person can have two natures. Christ has two natures: perfect divinity and also perfect humanity. The redeemed have imperfect, fallen, sinful humanity ("the flesh") and also a participation in the nature of Christ, which is perfect and which is charity rather than selfishness.

St. Thomas explains it with the key phrase "as such". Charity as such is incapable of sin. Insofar as what moves our actions is charity, we cannot sin.

The same single concrete thing can both heat and cool other things because there is some heat and some cold in it. If you blend ice cubes and fire, you produce warm water, which will both cool fire and melt ice.

The practical point of this distinction is that whenever we sin, we should not think that is our true identity, but the "old man" still in us, the albatross around our neck. St. Paul says in Romans 7 that when he sins, the source of that is no longer himself but the sin that dwells within him. That does not mean that he is not responsible for it or that he does not choose it. It means it is his false identity that he is choosing to follow. And whenever we practice charity, we should not think that that is our natural human self doing it all by itself; that is God's supernatural grace changing our human nature to conform to the nature of Christ.

Perhaps we can use the analogy of the person with deformed and dehumanized desires (e.g., lust—or homosexuality). That is not his true identity, though he may be deceived into thinking it is, in order to escape responsibility for changing it, and he may passionately resist this truth, which the Church offers him not as a condemnation but as liberation.

By nature we love our own bodies for giving us all kinds of pleasures, of course. But can we love our own bodies out of charity? We are commanded to love our neighbors as we love ourselves; and this love, the love that is *commanded,* must be charity, which is an act of will and free choice and can therefore be commanded, rather than any of the natural instincts, which are not acts of will and free choice and cannot therefore be commanded. But our neighbor, like ourselves, consists of body and soul. It would seem to follow that we can love our own body with charity since we can love our neighbor, body and soul, with charity. But what does this mean? How should we love our own body?

Whether a man ought to love his body out of charity?

Objection 1: **It would seem that a man ought not to love his body out of charity. For we do not love one with whom we are unwilling to associate. But those who have charity shun the society of the body, according to Romans 7:24:** *Who shall deliver me from the body of this death?* **and Philippians 1:23:** *Having a desire to be dissolved and to be with Christ....*

Reply: **The Apostle did not shrink from the society of his body as regards the nature of his body; in fact in this respect he was loth to be deprived thereof, according to 2 Corinthians 5:4:** *We would not be unclothed, but clothed over* **... (for) the nature of our body was created not by an evil principle, as the Manicheans pretend, but by God.... He did, however, wish to escape from the taint of concupiscence, which remains in the body and.... weighs down the soul.**

Objection 2: **Further, the friendship of charity is based on fellowship in the enjoyment of God. But the body can have no share in that enjoyment. Therefore the body is not to be loved out of charity.**

Reply: **Although our bodies are unable to enjoy God by knowing and loving Him, yet by the works which we do through the body we are able to attain to the perfect knowledge of God. Hence from the enjoyment in** **the soul there overflows a certain happiness into the body.... Hence, since the body has, in a fashion, a share of happiness, it can be loved with the love of charity** (II-II,25,5).

St. Thomas first refutes the heresy that the body is of negative value and to be shunned. This is Manicheeism or Gnosticism or Neoplatonism, not Christianaity. For (1) God willed and created our body. He made us bodily creatures and called that creation "very good" (Gen 1:31). (2) He incarnated Himself in a human nature, body and soul. (3) He saved us by bodily death, not by spiritual advice. (4) He rose in His body. He did not leave it behind in the tomb. (5) In His Ascension He took His human nature, body and soul, hypostatically united with His divine nature in His single divine Person, with Him to Heaven forever. (5) He continues to feed us with His own Body in the Eucharist. (6) And He will give us immortal resurrected bodies in Heaven. Thus St. Paul, in the passage St. Thomas quotes, longs for a more perfect body in Heaven, not for bodilessness; "not to be unclothed but clothed over". The body therefore is to be loved; it has high and holy value. And this all men instinctively know, for the oldest records and evidences of human habitation are funerary. Even dead bodies are always treated with reverence. What the saints shun is not the body but concupiscence, which is a disorder that begins in the soul, not the body. Concupiscence is disordered desire, and desires are powers of the soul, though only in souls united to and expressed in bodies. Dead bodies, without souls, have no desires.

St. Thomas then refutes the notion that our bodies play no part in our Heavenly joy or our vision of God. Elsewhere (I,12,3) he even says that we will see God face to face not only with our souls but even with our bodily eyes, as happiness—a state of the spiritual soul—is seen with the bodily eyes *in* a face and in a smile. For this joy, like concupiscence, "flows over" into the body from the soul.

A person is one, though human nature is two-dimensional, body and soul. Charity is not the love of a soul to a soul but the love of a person to a person. It not only can but must include the body.

How do we reconcile all the cursing psalms with the command to love our enemies?

Two things may be considered in the sinner: his nature and his guilt. According to his nature, which he has from God, he has a capacity for happiness, and charity is based on the fellowship of happiness ... wherefore we ought to love sinners out of charity ...

On the other hand, their guilt is opposed to God and is an obstacle to happiness. Wherefore ... it is our duty to hate, in the sinner, his being a sinner, and to love in him his being a man capable of bliss; and this is to love him truly, out of charity ...

... [H]atred of a person's evil is equivalent to love of his good....

... [W]hen our friends fall into sin, we ought not to deny them the amenities of friendship, so long as there is hope of their mending their ways; and we ought to help them to regain virtue more readily than to recover money if they had lost it, in as much as virtue is more akin to friendship than money is....

Objection: **The saints ... desire evil things for the wicked, according to Ps. 9:18:** *May the wicked be turned into hell....*

Reply: **Such imprecations which we come across in Holy Writ may be understood in three ways: first, by way of prediction, not by way of wish, so that the sense is:** *The wicked shall be turned into hell.* **Secondly ... so that the desire of the wisher is not referred to the man's punishment but to the justice of the punisher ... since, according to Wisdom 1:13, not even God** *hath pleasure in the destruction of the wicked....* **Thirdly, so that this desire is referred to the removal of the sin ... to the effect that the sin be destroyed but that the man may live** (II-II,25,6).

We are to love our neighbors—all of whom are sinners. (Ever since Christ's Ascension and Mary's Assumption, we have never seen any other kind of human being on this earth.) Therefore we are to love sinners, i.e., love the concrete persons who are sinners. "Love the sinner, hate the sin." That's clear—so clear that St. Thomas takes it for granted.

But *in* the sinner we find different aspects or dimensions. His *nature* was designed, willed, loved, and created by God and is destined for Heaven as part of the communion of saints, so it is to be loved. But his sin and guilt is not any of those things, and is not to be loved.

Not only is there no contradiction or even tension between the two parts of "love the sinner and hate the sin", but we are to hate the sin precisely *because* we love the sinner, as we are to hate the cancer because we love the bodily life it is killing. Thus "hatred of a person's evil is ... love of his good."

Therefore we, like Christ, should not shun sinners but seek them out, even when they fall into sin—*especially* then—as the good shepherd seeks out the lost sheep, or a parent a lost child. If we should help our neighbors to recover lost money, all the more should we help them to recover lost virtue. We are Doctor God's nurses, and this world is His hospital.

How can we pray the cursing psalms, which call down curses on our enemies? They do *not* mean that we should wish evil to sinners. Sins, not sinners, are our enemies. St. Thomas shows us three ways we can use them: (1) as warnings and prophetic predictions rather than wishes— warnings to ourselves first of all (remember the splinter and the log in Matthew 7:3–5); (2) as praise of God's justice and goodness, not man's evil, and (3) as a curse on the sin (our own!), not on the sinner (ourselves!).

This third way is the most useful one. These "sinners" and "enemies" are allegories, personifications of our own sins, which are our own worst enemies. They are also allegories for demons, evil spirits who tempt us to sin. *These* two are our true enemies, our only enemies, and they alone should be hated and willed to destruction. We do indeed wrestle (fight) against evil, but our enemies are not "flesh and blood but principalities and powers of wickedness in the heavenly places" (Eph 6:12).

Jesus told us, "Love your neighbor as yourself." Should we love ourselves? If so, how? In what way? Did Jesus mean we are to love our neighbors as we already do love ourselves or as we ought to love ourselves? Does everyone love themselves or do some not?

Love of self is common to all in one way. In another way it is proper to the good....

For it is common to all for each one to love what he thinks himself to be. In this way ... all men, both good and wicked, love themselves in so far as they love their own preservation.

Secondly ... all do not think themselves to be what they are. For ... the good look upon their rational nature or the inward man as being the chief thing in them, wherefore in this way they think themselves to be what they are. On the other hand, the wicked reckon their sensitive and corporeal nature, or the outward man, to hold the first place. Wherefore, since they know not themselves aright, they do not love themselves aright, but love what they think themselves to be. But the good know themselves truly, and therefore truly love themselves.

The Philosopher proves this from five things that are proper to friendship. For in the first place, every friend wishes his friend to be and to love; secondly, he desires good things for him; thirdly, he does good things to him; fourthly, he takes pleasure in his company; fifthly, he is of one mind with him, rejoicing and sorrowing in almost the same things. In this way the good love themselves, as to the inward man, because (1) they wish the preservation of it in its integrity; (2) they desire good things for him, namely spiritual goods; (3) indeed, they do their best to obtain them; and (4) they take pleasure in entering into their own hearts, because they find there good thoughts in the present, the memory of past good, and the hope of future good, all of which are sources of pleasure. (5) Likewise they experience no clashing of wills, since their whole soul tends to one thing.

On the other hand, the wicked (1) have no wish to be preserved in the integrity of the inward man, (2) nor do they desire spiritual goods for him, (3) nor do they work for that end, (4) nor do they take pleasure in their own company by entering into their own hearts, because whatever they find there, present, past and future, is evil and horrible; (5) nor do they agree with themselves, on account of the gnawings of conscience (II-II,25,7).

And you thought the modern mind was more psychologically sophisticated than the medieval?

Everyone loves the apparent good. We can't love what appears evil, just as we can't believe what appears false. For "lovable" means "desirable", i.e., "apparently good", just as "believable" means "apparently true".

But we can err. Appearance does not always coincide with reality. We need discernment to distinguish the only-apparently-good from the really-good.

This applies to the self as well as anything else. We all love the apparent self, what we seem to ourselves to be. But we can err. We can feed the false self (e.g., by addictions). This is why prudence, or practical wisdom, is such an absolutely essential virtue. Wisdom judges appearances as real or fake.

Fools, who do not know themselves, do not love their true selves but their false selves. The thief who identifies himself with his money, or the material things money can buy, or the pleasures these things give him, sees theft as desirable, psychologically good (advantageous) for himself. Of course he knows his theft brings pain rather than pleasure to his victim, but he judges his own moral good, the good of his soul, to be less important to himself, less a part of himself, than the physical pleasures of his body and the satisfaction of his selfish passions. He thinks money will make him happy. He is a fool. He does not really love himself, even though he is selfish! Only the wise can truly love themselves because only they know themselves. St. Thomas lists five dimensions of this, five ways in which the fools (the wicked) lack true self-love. Love your neighbor as yourself, but first "know thyself"!

We are commanded to love our enemies. What does this mean? What kind of love is this?

Love of one's enemies may be understood in three ways. First, as though we were to love our enemies as such; this is perverse and contrary to charity, since it implies love of that which is evil in another.

Secondly, love of one's enemies may mean that we love them as to their (human) nature.... [I]n general; and in this sense charity requires that we should love our enemies, namely that in loving God and our neighbor we should not exclude our enemies from the love given to our neighbor in general.

Thirdly, love of one's enemies may be considered as specially directed to them ... charity does require this, namely that we should be prepared in mind ... that we should be ready to love our enemies individually if the necessity were to occur. That man should actually do so without it being necessary for him to do so, belongs to the perfection of charity (II-II,25,8).

Our true enemies are tempting demons, our own sins, and the foolishness that mistakes enemies for friends and friends for enemies (e.g., thinking that yielding to these temptations will at least give us happiness, or thinking that the prophets who make us feel guilty for our sins are our enemies because they make us feel bad).

So if we know our true enemies, i.e., that which really works for our harm, it is impossible to love them, for it is impossible to love what we know to be unlovable.

And if we know other people's sins, we know these sins harm them, so if we love them we cannot love their sins, any more than a doctor who loves his patient can love the patient's disease.

So we can't love our enemies (or the enemies of others we love) "as such", qua whatever evil in

them makes them our enemies. We cannot love evil. That is St. Thomas' first point.

Second, we can and should love sinners even while hating sins, because God created all persons and their common human nature, and declared it (ontologically) good. We are to love all men, and since some men are our enemies (in at least some real ways: they work us real harm, physical or spiritual), therefore we are to love our enemies—qua men, qua human, qua creatures of God, not qua enemies. This "qua human" means that we love their universal human nature, not their concrete individual persons insofar as they are working us real harm. Even if we have to disarm a murderous aggressor with lethal force, we should pray for his salvation.

Third, we can and should go beyond this and love our concrete individual enemies because we are Christians and conduits of the charity of Christ, Who did (and continues to do) exactly that, on the Cross and in the Church. Jesus loved Judas, who committed the greatest crime in history, even in the very act of committing that crime: as Judas was targeting Christ for execution in the Garden of Gethsemane, Jesus called him "*Friend*" (Mt 26:50).

This is not necessary injustice. Christian charity is not *less* than justice but goes far *beyond* justice. That is what makes it so Godlike.

"Love" here means, of course, not warm feelings of personal affection but the genuine will to the true good of this enemy. We do not wish him harm. Sometimes this good will necessarily includes the wish that he suffer pain—not out of vengeance but for instruction, that he may see his evil and repent. That is why we put people in prison. (That *should* be our motive, at least, if we are Christians.)

It is also not an evil, hateful, or vengeful motive to want justice to be done out of love of justice. Love of justice is a good thing. Love of mercy is another good thing, and even better.

162. Love's two dimensions, objective and subjective

Is perfect love (charity) subject to reason? If so, it should be limited. But if love should not be limited, if you can't have too much of it, then it should not be limited by reason either, right?

Every act should be proportionate both to its object and to the agent (subject, actor). **But from the object it takes its species** (nature, definition, form, "what"), **while from the power of the agent it takes the mode of its intensity; thus movement has its species from the term** (end) **to which it tends, while the intensity of its speed arises from the ... power of the mover. Accordingly, love takes its species from its object, but its intensity is due to the lover** (II–II,26,7).

What St. Thomas means by this technical distinction can perhaps be put more clearly if we use many more words.

I may love you, or sunsets, or ice cream; but my love for you is very different from my love of sunsets or ice cream. My love for you is personal because you are a person. My love of sunsets is a love of beauty, not of persons, and that is a different kind ("species") of love. My love of ice cream is a still different kind of love because its object, ice cream, makes the act of love an act of desire to eat and taste this food, not a desire to talk with you or live with you, or a desire to contemplate a sunset or paint a sunset. I don't want to paint you or ice cream, I don't want to talk with sunsets or ice cream, and I don't want to eat you or sunsets. The object of love gives the love its "species", form, character, nature, or "whatness". "What kind of love is this?" You must know love's object to answer that question. Thus the object is the "formal cause" of the love. It determines, specifies, defines the love. This object is also the "final cause" or intended purpose of the love: what my love of you seeks is conversation or life together, what my love of the sunset seeks is appreciation of beauty, what my love of ice cream seeks is the pleasure of taste.

The "efficient cause" of the love, the power that originates the love, is my personal will or desire. That sends the love forth, "creates" (or rather makes) the love, as the sun makes sunlight and storms make rain. There can be more or less energy in the sunlight or the rain, but sunlight can't be more or less sunny, and rain can't be more or less rainy. The quantity comes from the efficient cause but the quality comes from the formal cause. Thus the efficient cause of the love—the person who loves—determines the quantity of love, how much energy, how much passion is in it. And the person who causes the love is the loving subject. Thus passion is subjective. But the object of the love gives it its species or form or nature, and that is objective. (Of course the subject is subjective and the object is objective!)

One application of this distinction is that God loves good men more than bad men, as He loves angels more than men and men more than animals—in terms of the distinctions between the objects of love. God discriminates. He loves angels into angel nature and humans into human nature and animals into animal nature. If God did not discriminate thus in His love, there would be no hierarchy, no superiority of angels over men and men over animals; for God's love does not conform to the hierarchy but creates it. So God loves angels more than men, and good men more than bad men, in terms of *what* they are. For there is more goodness in angels than in men and more goodness in good men than in bad men, more goodness in the object loved. Angels are greater than men as men are greater than animals.

But God loves men more than angels in intensity, because He became one of us, and because our need is greater. And thus God may also love the wicked more than the good in intensity of care, as the shepherd left the ninety-nine good sheep to search for the one lost one, and as the father of the prodigal son worried more passionately about his prodigal than about his loyal son. A mother loves her child more than her dog, but she may have more intense passion and compassion for a dog suffering great pain *at that moment* than she has for her own child's tiny scratch, which is all he has at that moment.

Should we love our parents or our children more?

The degrees of love may be measured from two standpoints. First, from that of the object. In this respect, the better a thing is, and the more like to God, the more it is to be loved; and in this way a man ought to love his father more than his children, because he loves his father as his principle (origin), in which respect he is a more exalted good, and more like God.

Secondly, the degrees of love may be measured from the standpoint of the lover; and in this respect a man loves more that which is more closely connected to him, in which way a man's children are more lovable to him than his father (II-II,26,10).

It is natural, and therefore right, to love your parents more in one way and your children more in another.

Your parents are more like God to you. They gave you life, time ("lifetime"), nourishment, education, etc. You can't possibly pay them back; you can only "pay it forward" to your children. In fact your parents mediated God to you. God invented parents to do his work, beginning with "pro-creation", then continuing in "pro-education," "pro-nourishing", "pro-loving", and all the rest. It is God Who is the First Cause. Augustine begins the story of his life in his *Confessions* by confessing that it was not first of all his mother but God Who nourished him at the breast, using his mother's breast as His medium. Everything is a means by which God comes to us or we come to Him. Everything.

On the other hand, your children are dearer to you than your parents are. Similarly, God loves us more than we love Him. You are united to your children in a way that is more intimate and more free than the way in which you are united to your parents. Similarly, God is united to us in a more intimate and free way—the Incarnation—than the way in which we are united to Him. He loves us more than we love Him—infinitely more.

It is much easier to fail to love your parents than to fail to love your children. That is why there is a commandment that commands love and respect to parents, but not to children. In an age of abortion, there ought to be an eleventh commandment against neglecting, harming, abusing, or even murdering your own children. The instinct to love your parents is strong but easily broken, especially at two times of life: by teenagers who are "feeling their oats" and naturally desiring their independence, and by middle-aged children of physically and especially mentally enfeebled aging parents who appear burdensome. The instinct to love your children is much stronger. It is one of the strongest instincts in nature. Our handicapped children are naturally loved more than our handicapped parents. It is astonishing that the abortion culture could override this deepest instinct so quickly and so easily and with so few apparent qualms of conscience. Our ancestors would not have believed it.

If human life becomes cheapened, it becomes cheapened at both ends. Parents are killed, by euthanasia, when they become a "burden" to their children; and children are killed, by abortion, when they become a "burden" to their parents. All societies in history would regard these two sins as two of the most heartless and inhuman possible sins. To kill your parents is to kill yourself, your own past; and to kill your children is to kill yourself, your own future. Poor, naïve St. Thomas had no idea that a "civilized" society could ever become so heartless. He only lived in a "violent" society where professional soldiers freely contracted to risk being killed by or killing each other for ostensibly just and honorable reasons. But of course we "civilized" people have "progressed" beyond such "primitive violence" today.

The most powerful way to combat this "culture of death" that we live in is to deliberately renew and strengthen and practice our own love for both our parents and our children. Love must begin at home. This is also one of the most effective paths to our own sanctification. For whatever we do to those who are ours, we do to ourselves, just as whatever we do to Christ's brothers, we do to Him.

164. LOVE OF SPOUSE COMPARED WITH LOVE OF SELF

Should you love your spouse more than you love your parents, or less?

Should you love your spouse more than yourself, or "as" you love yourself? If the latter, what does this "as" mean? As much as? As if your spouse were yourself? Or because your spouse in some way is in fact yourself?

On the part of the good which is the object loved, a man should love his parents more than his wife because he loves them as his principles.... But on the part of the union, the wife ought to be loved more, because she is united with her husband as one flesh ... the Apostle says (Eph 5:33) that a husband should *love his wife as himself* ... a man's love for himself is the reason for his love of his wife, since she is one with him.... [T]he principal reason why a man loves his wife is her being united to him in the flesh (II-II,26,11).

As with the previous question, St. Thomas distinguishes the object of love (the beloved) from the subject of love (the lover), and answers the question differently for each of these two aspects of it. Not only do you owe more to your parents than you owe to your children, you even owe more to your parents than you owe to your spouse. They gave you more. They gave you life.

But "on the part of the union", i.e., the lived relationship, your relationship with your spouse and your love to your spouse is by nature, and should be by choice, greater than the relationship to your parents, because it is a closer relationship. Before you were born you were in a very intimate biological relationship with your mother (and, more indirectly and causally, your father), but once you were born you grew more and more biologically and even psychologically independent of her and of your father. But the intimacy with your spouse is meant to keep increasing, for it is greater, and is unique: you are "one flesh".

"One flesh" in Scripture means not merely "participating in sexual intercourse" but "becoming one person, body and soul, without ceasing to be two persons". Thus sex is a remote but real and holy image of Trinitarian life. (See John Paul II's "Theology of the Body".) "Flesh" in Scripture does not mean merely "body" but "whole natural mortal person." It is composed of two dimensions, "body" and "soul". "Flesh" is contrasted not to "soul" but to "spirit", i.e., "the whole person as inhabited and inspired by the Holy Spirit, participating in immortal supernatural life".

St. Paul says that the husband should love his wife "as himself". What does this mean? The next sentence says that what follows from this is that the man's love of himself is the reason for his love of his wife. This means that the union is more than sexual and more than psychological, it is ontological. The man and his wife really are one flesh, one natural person. When you love your wife you are loving yourself, just as when you love your body (or your soul) you are loving yourself because you do not *have* your body (or your soul), as you *have* your possessions; you *are* your body (as well as your soul), and when you love your wife you are loving yourself because you do not *have* your wife, as you *have* your possessions, you *are* your wife (as well as yourself). The two really become one. It's literal.

So if you hate your spouse you are hating yourself, just as when you hate your body (or your soul) you are hating yourself.

This is a radical, life-transforming vision that even the Christian world today has yet to fully appreciate and understand. God raised up a great prophet in Pope St. John Paul II to unfold and explore this precious mystery in a profoundly new and personalist yet profoundly old and Thomistic way, exactly at the time when the mystery of marriage, sex, and family (the one most indispensable foundation for all human society) is being trashed and violated in a historically unprecedented way.

All love has some order, including the highest love, charity, the divine and Heavenly love. On earth it is natural and therefore right to love some people more than others, and this preferential treatment is true of all forms of love, including charity. We should give our family more of all kinds of love than we give strangers. Will this order remain in Heaven, or will we love all with equal charity?

Nature is not done away, but perfected, by glory. Now the order of charity (self, spouse, children, parents, family, friends, strangers, and good men more than bad men) **... is derived from nature.... Therefore this order of charity will endure in heaven....**

The degree of love may be distinguished either in respect of the good which a man desires for another, or according to the intensity of love itself. In the first way, a man will love better men more than himself, and those who are less good, less than himself; because by reason of the perfect conformity of the human to the divine will, each of the blessed will desire everyone to have what is due to him according to divine justice.... But in the second way a man will love himself more than even his better neighbors, because the intensity of the act of love arises on the part of the person who loves (II-II,26,13).

Nothing good in nature will be destroyed in Heaven, but preserved, transformed, and perfected. "Grace perfects nature." Therefore not only the existence of charity but also its order will be preserved in Heaven. Nature is the starting point for grace; therefore natural love of self is the starting point for supernatural charity, which is self-forgetful, self-sacrificing, and self-giving. If you don't have a self, you can't give it away. If it's not worthy to be loved, it's not worthy to be given to another. We are not commanded to love others instead of ourselves but to love others as we love ourselves. Self-love is the seed, other-love is the plant. The seed is preserved and transformed and perfected and multiplied in the plant.

How will we love some more than others in Heaven? We will love everyone maximally, i.e., we will love everything lovable in all of them.

But not all will have the same amounts or kinds of lovability and intimacy with us. We will maintain these differences in Heaven, both objective (lovability, goodness) and subjective (personal passion). Therefore we will love some (the more lovable and the more intimately related) more than others. Like God, we will love the better more because there is more for us to love in them. The flood of love will fill all the containers to the fullest, but some containers will be larger than others. We will love the Blessed Virgin Mary more than Mary Smith because Mary Smith, however saintly and beautiful she is in Heaven, is not the immaculately conceived Mother of God; and this will cause absolutely no envy or resentment on the part of Mary Smith, who will also love the Mother of God more than any other woman. Part of Heaven's joy will be having heroes and heroines to look up to.

Hierarchy is natural, and will remain in Heaven. Hierarchy means superiority in something, but not necessarily in everything. Each of us has more of some good and lovable quality than others have, and each is therefore unique and irreplaceable. This will certainly remain in Heaven. The number of different value-hierarchies will be not just one but many, in fact perhaps literally innumerable. Everyone will be the very best at one thing: being his or her unique self, a goal no one else can ever achieve.

St. Thomas again distinguishes love's objective and subjective dimensions. The objective dimension is who is loved and how much value (lovability) there is in this person. The subjective dimension is the personal subjective passion (intensity) of the love. We love more intensely those who are closer to us, starting with ourselves. This hierarchy too will remain in Heaven, since it is natural. We naturally love ourselves most passionately because we feel ourselves, our own pleasures and pains, most intensely. This will remain in Heaven. It is an essential part of human nature. It is not evil, or selfish, or competitive by nature, only by perversion. We will be wholly human in Heaven, as Christ was wholly human on earth. In fact we will succeed there for the first time in being wholly human, more human than we ever were before.

Failing to love friends is more blameworthy than failing to love enemies; does that mean that loving enemies is more meritorious than loving friends? Or is it less?

Whether it is more meritorious to love an enemy than to love a friend?

These two loves may be compared in two ways: first, on the part of our neighbor whom we love; secondly, on the part of the reason for which we love him.

In the first way, love of one's friend surpasses love of one's enemy because a friend is both better and more closely united to us, so that he is a more suitable matter for love, and consequently the act of love that passes over this matter is better, and therefore its opposite is worse, for it is worse to hate a friend than an enemy.

In the second way, however, it is better to love one's enemy than one's friend, and this for two reasons. First, because it is possible to love one's friend for another reason than God, whereas God is the only reason for loving one's enemy. Secondly, because if we suppose that both are loved for God, our love for God is proved to be all the stronger through carrying a man's affections to things which are furthest from him, namely to the love of his enemies, even as the power of a furnace is proved to be the stronger according as it throws its heat to more distant objects....

Yet just as the same fire acts with greater force on what is near than on what is distant, so too charity loves with greater fervor those who are united to us than those who are far removed; and in this respect the love of friends, considered in itself, is more ardent and better than the love of one's enemy (II-II,27,7).

You will have noticed by this time, of course, that St. Thomas almost always solves a dilemma by making a distinction. That is not a quirk of his personality or even of his method, but a reflection of the nature of reality. Reality is complex: it has many dimensions, "there are more things

in Heaven and earth than are dreamed of in your [always-simplistic and abstracted] philosophy" (*Hamlet*). This is the source of nearly all dilemmas and apparent contradictions, and therefore the key to their resolution.

Assuming that you are a good and moral person, and that you select good people as your friends and bad ones as your enemies, friends are better persons than enemies and therefore to be loved more.

Also, self-love is natural and proper and the starting point of love, and friends are closer to ourselves than enemies, therefore they are to be loved first. This is also proved by the universally admitted truism that hating your good, close friends is more wicked than hating your enemies.

That is so on the one hand; but on the other hand (that typical Greek expression "*men ... de*" is as natural to St. Thomas as it was to Aristotle) loving enemies is better in that it is harder, more heroic, and more Godlike. Also, the only possible motive for loving enemies must be the highest one: love of God.

St. Thomas' analogy of fire being stronger in one way insofar as it reaches out farther from its source (thus only the greatest love can reach out to enemies) yet stronger in another way insofar as it burns most intensely when it is closest to its source (thus we love friends more ardently than enemies) shows how fruitful analogies can be—not in proving points but in illustrating them, showing spiritual truths by means of material images. Indeed, that is the reason God created matter in the first place, according to that great Thomist philosopher John Paul II.

The practical "payoff" for the drive toward sanctity is to choose *both* of two opposite good things, if possible (in this case loving friends and loving enemies) rather than dismissing one because it has in one respect less good in it than the other. For there is another respect in which it has more good in it. This is almost always the case, and the Devil loves to seduce us into comparing two goods (or two evils) and choosing only one of them because it is better, forgetting that this is so only in one aspect. Reality is like a work of art rather than a mathematical formula: its aspects are gloriously many.

As St. Thomas says, "no man can live without joy" (II–II,35,4). All seek joy. But can it possibly be true that there is a single, simple secret of joy? that love (charity) always and infallibly brings you joy rather than sorrow? Isn't that impossibly simplistic?

The joy of charity ... has no admixture of sorrow, according to Wisdom 8:16: *Her conversation hath no bitterness....*

A twofold joy in God arises from charity. One, the more excellent, is proper to charity (alone), and with this joy we rejoice in the divine good considered in itself. This joy of charity is incompatible with an admixture of sorrow, even as the good which is its object is incompatible with any admixture of evil; hence the Apostle says (Phil 4:4): *Rejoice in the Lord always.*

The other is the joy of charity whereby we rejoice in the divine good as participated by us. This participation can be hindered by anything contrary to it, wherefore in this respect the joy of charity is compatible with an admixture of sorrow in so far as a man grieves for that which hinders the participation of the divine good, either in us or in our neighbor, whom we love as ourselves (II-II,28,2).

One can prove the truth of this "simplistic" philosophy of life simply by experiment. Live a life of love, especially the love of God, and observe the joy of it. Live a life of lovelessness and observe the joylessness of it. The experiment has a 100% success rate. If anyone doubts its infallible conclusion, he infallibly shows that he has never really performed the experiment.

In itself, charity has no admixture of sorrow. Insofar as it is charity, it is joyful. And this refers to charity toward God but also toward neighbor. Sorrow comes from other sources, never from charity.

The essence of charity is not supplying others' needs. If that were so, we could not have charity toward God, since He, being perfect has no needs. The essence of charity is the will's affirmation, or "yea-saying", of willing the good of the other, whether the other already has it (as is always the case with God) or whether they do not (as is the case with men). The will both desires the good when absent and rejoices in it when present.

However, there is an "on the other hand" also. (No surprise!) Creatures' participation in divine good is always finite and often mixed with its contrary (harm, evil, pain, or sin). Insofar as the objects of our charity (the ones we love) experience evil, our love experiences sorrow as well as joy, since we love them "as ourselves", and therefore we internalize their sorrows as well as their joys. We multiply both our sorrow and joy by two factors: the number of people we love and the intensity of our love for them. Not only is love compatible with sorrow, but it makes sorrow inevitable. The only way to avoid sorrow is to avoid love.

And we can't avoid sorrow by loving God only and not our neighbors, for two reasons. (1) If we love God, we must love our neighbors, since that is God's absolute command. (2) Since God became incarnate, God became one of our neighbors—in fact all of our neighbors: "As you did it to one of the least of these my brethren, you did it to me" (Mt 25:40).

This principle—that love of neighbor multiplies sorrows as well as joys—is the reason why the sorrows of Christ on the Cross are infinite, and of infinite merit in paying for all our sins. He experienced all the sorrow that we deserved, and more. Even though God qua God has no needs and no vulnerability, God qua man has them. By the Incarnation, God, the Second Person of the Trinity, the single divine Person Who took a human nature into His person without losing His divine nature, only His divine privileges, is enabled to experience sorrow and pain by His love. Eternal Divine love does not change in its own essential nature, but it now experiences the same foreign element (pain) added to it that *our* love does.

This principle is also the reason why we have only two choices in life: (1) embracing both the agony and the ecstasy, the bitter and the sweet, the depths and the heights, by living a life of charity, or (2) avoiding both and crawling into the safe little "control freak" cave called the ego. That is also called Hell.

This highest joy that proceeds from charity—is it finite or infinite in Heaven? If it is only finite, we can always desire more of it than we have, and then, it seems, we will be frustrated forever, since the gap between desire and complete satisfaction will remain. But if joy is infinite, then we can eventually get to the top of the mountain of joy, and then we will be bored and lament that there are no more mountains to climb.

Also, if we and our joys are finite forever, even in Heaven, then one person's joy must be greater than another's. (This conclusion also follows from the principle of justice, which demands unequal rewards for unequal loves.) But how can I be content with my lesser joy, if I know it is lesser?

Whether the spiritual joy which proceeds from charity can be filled?

Our Lord said to His disciples (Jn 15:11): *That My joy may be in you and your joy may be filled.* . . .

Joy is compared to desire as rest to movement . . . rest is full when there is no more movement. Hence joy is full when there remains nothing to be desired. But as long as we are in this world the movement of desire does not cease in us. . . . However, when once perfect happiness has been attained, nothing will remain to be desired because then there will be full enjoyment of God, wherein man will obtain whatever he had desired, even with regard to other goods, according to Psalm 102:5: *Who satisfieth thy desire with good things.* **Hence desire will be at rest, not only our desire for God but all our desires; so that the joy of the blessed is full to perfection—indeed, over-full, since they will obtain more than they were capable of desiring, for** *neither hath it entered into the heart of an, what things God hath prepared for them that love Him* (1 Cor 2:9). . . .

Yet . . . this perfectly full joy is not taken into man but, on the contrary, man enters into it, according to Matthew 25:21: *Enter into the joy of thy Lord* . . .

Each one's joy will be full with regard to himself because his desire will be fully set at rest. Yet one's joy will be greater than another's on account of a fuller participation of the divine happiness (II-II,28,3).

Yes, our joy will be total, totally fulfilled. Yet it will be finite.

The will has two relations to its object, the good: desire for it, insofar as this good is not yet present, and enjoyment of it when the good is present. All desire for good will be fulfilled and quieted in Heaven, because God is our whole good, and God will be perfectly present to us in Heaven. Everything desired and desirable will be present in God. Our desire will be at rest. However, our will's enjoyment of this totally present good will continue and increase forever. This is possible because its object, God, is infinite and inexhaustible, while our appreciation of it is finite.

Courtship and marriage is an analogy. Courtship seeks a good not yet present (marriage, union). Marriage enjoys a present good, and this love and appreciation of the spouse can continue to increase forever, like the series of positive integers. It is potentially infinite. Only God is actually infinite.

Thus, since all desire will be satisfied by God's presence, there will be no frustration, no unsatisfied desire. But there will be no boredom either because enjoyment will be constantly new. And enjoyment, unlike desire, is not frustrated by absence but blessed by presence.

We are finite but the object of our joy, God, is infinite. Thus, in the bull's-eye accuracy of the words of Scripture quoted by St. Thomas, this joy does not enter into us but we enter into it. (See the last two chapters of St. Anselm's *Proslogium* for a beautiful meditation on this.)

Since our joy, like ourselves, will be finite, each one's joy will be different in quantity as well as quality. But there will be no envy (the world's stupidest sin, the only sin that never causes even fake joy), but only perfect charity's rejoicing in each other's joy.

What is peace and how do we attain it?

Peace implies a twofold union.... The first is the result of one's own appetites being directed to one object, while the other results from one's own appetite being united with the appetite of another. And each of these unions is effected by charity: the first, in so far as man loves God with his whole heart, by referring all things to Him, so that all his desires tend to one object; the second, in so far as we love our neighbor as ourselves, the result being that we wish to fulfill our neighbor's will as though it were ours (II–II,29,3).

As St. Augustine famously said over 800 years before St. Thomas, peace is not merely the absence of war. Its essence is positive, not negative. It is the satisfaction of desire ("appetite"). Augustine called it "the tranquility of order", i.e., the perfect order or relation (1) between our desires and their proper object, the Good, which is first and last of all God, (2) among our desires themselves, and (3) between our desires and those of others. Thus peace is the unity (1) between ourselves and God, (2) within ourselves, and (3) between ourselves and others.

The first two go together as inseparable parts of what St. Thomas calls "the first" half of the "twofold union" that is peace. They necessarily go together because there is only one God. Only if there is only one object of desire (will, appetite, longing) can there be one will. Monotheism is a psychological revolution as well as a theological one, because it unifies all human desires. As Kierkegaard titled one of his books: *Purity of Heart Is to Will One Thing*.

The fruit of this unity is unity with neighbors, who also will this same Good, the true God. Thus Thomas Merton unifies and orders these three kinds of peace in the same way St. Thomas does when he says that "we cannot be at peace with others because we are not at peace with ourselves, and we cannot be at peace with ourselves because we are not at peace with God."

Love is the essential act of the will. Only love (charity) can effect these three unions.

The summary of all the commandments, of God's will for us, is to love God with our whole heart and our neighbors as ourselves. In this life we only partly, not fully, attain to this love, and also, therefore, to this peace. When, in Heaven, we have learned to love God with absolutely our *whole* heart, with nothing left over; when we will have exorcised absolutely all selfishness and fear from our hearts; when we have learned to hold nothing whatsoever back from God, "referring *all* things to Him", even the smallest detail; and when we have learned to want our neighbor's will not only as *much* as our own but *as* our own; then we will experience a revolutionary transformation within our consciousness that we can hardly imagine now. "What no eye has seen, nor ear heard, nor the heart of man conceived, what God has prepared for those who love him" (1 Cor 2:9).

To our present sin–darkened minds, "peace" often seems dull. (After all, war is the most interesting thing in life. Surely that is one reason why war has always been so popular. No one is bored when they are about to kill or be killed.) But this illusion is the exact opposite of the truth: true, Heavenly peace is the only thing in human life that is never boring, even in eternity, because this peace is caused by love, the true love of charity; and that love, even in this life, is the only thing that never gets boring. And that is not merely a matter of faith but is proved by experience.

T. S. Eliot says that the profoundest line in all of human literature is Dante's: "In His will, our peace."

Is virtue our end? Or is it peace? Or is it love?

Virtue is not the last end but the way thereto. But peace is the last end, in a sense, as Augustine says (*The City of God*)....

Since, then, charity causes peace precisely because it is love of God and of our neighbor ... there is no other virtue except charity whose proper act is peace (II-II,29,4).

Virtue is not our last end, yet its practice is necessary both before and after we attain our last end (which is God, and peace in God) in the real but imperfect way it is attained in this life. Virtue is necessary *before* this peace because the will to virtue, good will, must exist before repentance for sin can make any sense, and repentance is one of the prerequisites for union with God. It is necessary *after* peace because faith, which together with repentance is our prerequisite for union with God, necessarily produces good works, the works of virtue: "faith by itself, if it has no works (the works of virtue), is dead" (Jas 2:17).

C. S. Lewis says: "The road to the Promised Land runs past Sinai." At Mount Sinai God's chosen people received the world's most perfect tenfold definition of virtue. It was their road map. It was a means, not an end. The righteous (or self-righteous!) pagan, Platonist or Stoic, says that "virtue is its own reward"; but there are greater rewards than this. No one can be saved, and attain eternal joy, without all of the following: (1) a morally honest acceptance of the demands of virtue, (2) a serious effort to practice it, (3) an intellectually honest confession of failure, (4) repentance, and (5) at least an implicit faith and hope in God as Savior. In that sense, virtue (the acceptance of the demands of virtue) is the way, or an essential part of the way, to the last end. But no one can attain the last end (Heaven) by sufficient virtue, but only by honesty, goodwill, confession, repentance, faith, and hope in God's forgiveness.

Charity then proceeds from faith and hope because faith and hope let the very life of God, which is charity, into our souls. Our attempts at charity without God, our attempts at charity *before* faith and hope, all fail because they are based on ourselves and our own false sufficiency and our own righteousness as their foundation and cause. But the charity that comes *after* faith is God's own work in and through us, and is part of our own salvation.

The last end is peace, the peace that consists in perfect unity with God and His will.

This last end, this peace, is attained only by charity, which is "the fulfilling of the Law" (Rom 13:10).

Charity transcends mere virtue. Yet once this charity exists, it fulfills all virtue, as the New Law fulfills the Old and as grace fulfills nature. Charity is the heart and soul of all virtue.

Charity to our neighbor is desiring our neighbor's good; charity to God is rejoicing in God's good. That means the conformity, submission, and surrender to His good will which is the heart and essence of all true religion. This is the point of the word "Islam", which means "surrender or submission" to God and His will. But "islam" also means peace ("shalom"), the peace that is the immediate and infallible effect of this surrender. The saints of all religions, despite their theological errors and disagreements, all know this central fact from experience: that "In His will, our peace."

This peace is not merely the subjective feeling of contentment. It is the objective state of the real attainment of our last end. If we could have a feeling of peace without real peace, it would be worthless: "They have healed the wound of my people lightly, saying 'Peace, peace' when there is no peace" (Jer 6:14).

What is the relation between love (charity) and the works of love (almsgiving)?

It is written (1 Jn 3:17): *He that hath the substance of this world and shall see his brother in need, and shall put up his bowels* (shut up his compassion) *from him, how doth the charity of God abide in him?*

External acts belong to that virtue (charity) **which regards the motive for doing those acts. Now the motive for giving alms is to relieve one who is in need. Wherefore some have defined alms as being** *a deed whereby something is given to the needy out of compassion and for God's sake....*

Almsgiving can be materially without charity (material things can be given for non-loving motives) **but to give alms formally** (essentially), **i.e., for God's sake, with delight and readiness, and altogether as one ought, is not possible without charity** (II-II,32,1).

The first and most practical answer to the question is that love is not just an inner feeling; love always shows its presence by external, visible deeds; love *works*. Indeed, Kierkegaard says that in the Bible love *is* "the works of love" (in his book by that title). Love works; and if we do not see the works of love (in places where they obviously ought to be) then we can be sure that love is not present. Love is the invisible but real cause of visible works of love. The visible reveals the invisible, and the absence of the visible reveals the absence of the invisible.

St. Thomas means by "alms" not merely money but "to relieve one who is in need". There has never been a human being in the history of the world without needs—and that includes even Jesus

Christ, God incarnate. St. Thomas defines love as both motive and deed when he says that "external acts *belong to* that virtue (charity) which regards the motive for doing those acts."

The motive is double: human and divine, natural and supernatural, horizontal and vertical, "out of compassion (for the needy) *and* for God's sake". St. Thomas habitually avoids false and harmful either/ors by gravitating toward both/ands, toward an inclusive "big picture".

In the last paragraph St. Thomas observes that although love (as inner motive) cannot exist without its external works (which is the point of the first paragraph), nevertheless its works can exist without it. St. Paul, in the most loved chapter in the Bible (1 Cor 13), even says that one could even give up his body, his bodily life, without love. We see this in terrorist suicide bombers.

Two inner properties of charity, two marks of its presence, are (1) "for God's sake" and (2) "with delight and (therefore) readiness" (since we are always ready for delight).

Charity is not confined to Christians. Since all men have an innate, natural knowledge of God (as St. Paul says in Romans 1), all men are capable of charity, i.e., "something is given to the needy with (human) compassion *and for God's sake*".

Since (1) charity is supernatural, and comes only from the real presence of God in the soul (St. Thomas' paragraph 3), and since (2) all men, and not only Christians, are capable of charity (as has been proved in the paragraph above), it follows that (3) all men are capable of accepting the real presence of God in their souls, even if they have defective or mistaken concepts of God. (Do you really think *you* don't have any?) Karl Rahner calls these men "anonymous Christians".

172. ALMS

What are "almsdeeds," i.e., the works of love, if not just giving away money?

We reckon seven corporal almsdeeds, namely,
   (1) to feed the hungry,
   (2) to give drink to the thirsty,
   (3) to clothe the naked,
   (4) to harbor the harborless,
   (5) to visit the sick,
   (6) to ransom the captive,
   (7) to bury the dead....

Again, we reckon seven spiritual alms, namely,
   (1) to instruct the ignorant,
   (2) to counsel the doubtful,
   (3) to comfort the sorrowful,
   (4) to reprove the sinner,
   (5) to forgive injuries,
   (6) to bear with those who trouble and annoy us, and
   (7) to pray for all (II-II,32,2).

Traditional lists like this are helpful because (1) they make the general concept very concrete and unavoidable instead of a safe abstraction, and (2) because they do not leave it up to us to make our own lists, which would probably fit our own inclinations more than others' needs.

Cultural conditions have changed very little since St. Thomas' day. The most important human needs are constant. (We don't literally *need* a single one of the many inventions that have made our lives easier since the Middle Ages.) There is not a one of these fourteen deeds that does not have its contemporary equivalent. And all are major needs, crying needs. For instance, "to clothe the naked" is not confined to literally naked people, who were rare in the Middle Ages, as they are now, but it moves us to share the many pieces of clothing that we do not really need and use with people who do really need and can use them. For most of us who are not desperately poor, this almsdeed, like most of the others, costs us very little sacrifice, and only a little time and effort. "To harbor the harborless" refers not merely to boats but to unwanted children and orphans and the homeless, especially victims of natural disasters and pregnant women who need support to be encouraged keep their babies. There are many excellent Catholic organizations devoted to such needs. And literally millions of "the sick" pine away in loneliness in nursing homes. Yet we tend to minimize our visits even to our own extended family.

Some of these works require special authorization, e.g., "to ransom the captive" and "to bury the dead"; and others require discretion and timing to be effective, e.g., "to reprove the sinner." (See #174, below.) But everyone should pick at least one from each list and make it a habit, not just a one-shot, temporary conscience-relief pill. Teachers have the advantage of getting paid for "instructing the ignorant". They also have the disadvantage of a stricter judgment on themselves: see James 3:1.

"To forgive injuries" is necessary for everyone at all times, and is so important that Our Lord made a point of repeating only that one petition in the Lord's Prayer, and making it a condition for salvation! For He commanded us to pray for our own damnation if we do not forgive those who sin against us: "forgive us our trespasses *as* (to the extent that) *we forgive those who trespass against us.*" The commonest examples of "forgiving injuries" is the very next almsdeed, "to bear with those who trouble and annoy us", usually unwittingly—a habit as (obviously) useful as it is (surprisingly) difficult.

1. Is giving alms (helping others in some concrete material or spiritual ways) necessary for salvation?

2. How much are we bound we give?

(1) **No man is punished eternally for omitting to do what is not a matter of precept** (commandment). **But some are punished eternally for omitting to give alms, as is clear from Matthew 25:41–43. Therefore almsgiving is a matter of precept.**

As love of our neighbor is a matter of precept, whatever is a necessary condition to the love of our neighbor is a matter of precept also. Now the love of our neighbor requires that not only should we be our neighbor's well-wishers, but also his well-doers, according to 1 John 3:18: *Let us not love in word, nor in tongue, but in deed and in truth.* **And in order to be a person's well-wisher and well-doer, we ought to succor his needs. This is done by almsgiving. Therefore almsgiving is a matter of precept.**

(2) **On the part of the recipient it is requisite that he should be in need, else there would be no reason for giving him alms.**

Yet since it is not possible for one individual to relieve the needs of all, we are not bound to relieve all who are in need, but only those who could not be succored if we did not succor them....

Accordingly, we are bound (1) to give alms of our surplus, and also (2) to give alms to one whose need is extreme; (3) otherwise almsgiving, like any other greater good, is a matter of counsel (II-II,32,5).

St. Thomas always gives reasonable answers to hard questions.

There is no love (charity) without the works of love (alms); and Christ and the saints tell us we will be judged by God on our charity; therefore we will be judged on our alms. To refuse alms (help) to the needy neighbor is to refuse Christ. So almsgiving (the works of love) is "a matter of precept (commandment)", not a matter of "counsel" (advice). In fact it is a requirement for salvation, since we are *not,* according to Scripture, "justified by faith alone" (Jas 2:24). "Faith by itself, if it has no works, is dead" (Jas 2:17); it is not live faith, not faith that gives us eternal life, not saving faith.

But how much are we to give? This can mean three things: (1) How much must we give if we are to be saved? (2) How much ought we to give? (3) How much would be the ideal to give? There is obviously no exact quantitative answer to any one of these three question which is the same for everyone, e.g., "$1,000", or "exactly 10% of your net income". The very question "How much?" is suspect: it sounds like the questioner is trying to squeak by with the minimum. If so, that proves the questioner does not have charity at all, because charity never does that. There *is* no quantitative minimum or maximum. It's love, not math.

Obviously the interior motive and honesty counts more than the exterior quantity. Yet the quantity counts too, and the quantity is dependent on others' needs and on our own generosity.

St. Thomas' last three paragraphs (his answer to question 2) can hardly be made any clearer. (1) Our "surplus" is by definition *not* our need, so we are obligated to use it to relieve others' needs. Of course, our first "others" are members of our own family. (2) Common sense requires us to practice a kind of triage, prioritizing the greatest needs. (3) And how much we go beyond these commanded necessities is a matter of "counsel" (good advice, ideals) rather than "commandment" (obligations). The more generosity, the merrier, both for the receiver and also for the giver. If you are surprised to hear that, you've never practiced sacrificial giving and experienced its inevitable deep joy. Try it, you'll like it.

Shouldn't we avoid offending people? Should we pester them and bother them about good and evil? "Fraternal correction" sounds nice but nobody is grateful for it. Tell them they're sinning? You may as well tell them they're fat and ugly and smell bad.

Augustine says: *You become worse than the sinner if you fail to correct him.... Fraternal correction is a matter of precept.*

We must observe, however, that while the negative precepts of the Law forbid sinful acts ... always and for all times ... (the positive) acts of virtue must ... be done ... by observing the due circumstances ... namely that it be done where, when, and how it ought to be done ... (we do not) have to correct our erring brother at *all* places and times.... For Augustine says: *If a man refrain from chiding and reproving wrongdoers because he awaits a suitable time for so doing, or because he fears lest if he does so they may become worse ... or turn away from the faith ... this* (is) *to be counseled by charity....*

(But) *when* (as he says in the same passage) *one fears what people may think, or lest one may suffer grievous pain ... one commits a ... sin.*

Since the admonition which is given in fraternal correction is directed to the removal of a brother's sin.... this admonition is chiefly an act of charity ... but secondarily an act of prudence....

Fraternal correction is not opposed to forbearance with the weak, on the contrary it results from it. For a man bears with a sinner in so far as he is not disturbed against him and retains his goodwill towards him, the result being that he strives to make him do better (II-II,33,1).

One ought to forego fraternal correction when we fear lest we may make a man worse.... When it is deemed probable that the sinner will not take the warning and will become worse, such fraternal correction should be foregone, because the means should be regulated according to the requirements of the end.... Whatever is directed to an end becomes good through being directed to the end. Hence whenever fraternal correction hinders the end, namely the amendment of our brother, it is no longer good (II-II,33,6).

Once again, St. Thomas is the voice of reason and common moral sense, avoiding two extreme and opposite errors. On the one hand, to "reprove the sinner" is a "precept", a commandment. And as Augustine says, we share the sinner's guilt if we fail to speak. (For "silence betokens consent" is a maxim of law.) Fear for our own comfort, and worry about "human respect", are no excuse for silence. On the other hand, we are not commanded to be bull-headed, stupid, obtuse, pesty, or self-righteous. Timing is important, and "forbearance" is a virtue too when needed. Fear that our speaking will make the sinner worse is a legitimate fear, and it is possible to pay too little attention to it. But fear of emotional pain is not. Fear of sin should trump fear of pain. (See point #27 on which is the greater evil, pain or sin.)

Today, much more than in St. Thomas' day, the sins that are by far the most commonly approved are sexual. Many Catholics have been so badly educated that they have never been taught, and do not believe, that contraception, fornication, and sodomy are sins at all. They do not know that it is not just the Church's "opinion" or "ideology" but God Himself Who forbids them. This situation calls for far *more* "fraternal correction" than in the past.

But because sexual sins are so attractive and addictive, it is more likely that their "fraternal correction" will be met with anger and the breaking of friendships than the correcting of these sins.

Neither of these two truths contradicts or removes the other.

There's no avoiding the risk of making a prudential judgment call about the sinner's needs and likely reaction to correction, both immediate and long-range. (They may hate you today and thank you tomorrow for correcting them. Or they may thank you today but hate you tomorrow for *not* correcting them!) The one thing we must always keep in mind is the end, which is not our comfort or convenience *or* that of our neighbor, but our neighbor's true good, both temporal and eternal.

The words of the 20th-century Catholic phenomenologist Dietrich Von Hildebrand so perfectly flesh out St. Thomas' advice concerning fraternal correction that I here make an exception to my rule of one page only for each point so that you can receive and profit by these moral and psychological gems of wisdom from his *Transformation in Christ*: It deals not with sin in general, but how to deal with sins, harms, or offenses against yourself.

"The attitude of rancorous enmity is not the only antithesis to the Christian spirit of forgiveness. Another attitude opposed to it is that of simply ignoring the wrong inflicted upon us, as though nothing had happened. This aberration may result from laziness, from faintness of heart, or from a sickly, mawkish clinging to outward peace. We hold our comfort too dear to 'fight it out' with our aggressor; or again, we feel terrified at the thought of any tension or hostility, and fear lest a sharp reaction on our part should exasperate the adversary; or perhaps we yield just out of respect for the abstract idol of peace.

"This is a kind of behavior far remote from the genuine love of peace or from a genuine spirit of forgiveness. It can never achieve the true harmony of peace, but at best a superficial cloaking of enmity, a mood of false joviality which drags our souls towards the peripheral.

"Also, people who behave thus fail to consider the moral damage that their supineness is likely to inflict on others. It is very often necessary to draw a person's attention to the wrong he has done us—in fact, necessary for his own good. To pass over it in silence may easily encourage him in his bad dispositions. But we cannot reproach him to good purpose—that is, without provoking strife—unless we have ourselves attained to that serene attitude cleansed of all impulsive resentment, in other words, unless we have truly forgiven him....

"When we have risen above the mood of regarding his awareness or admission of his wrong as a satisfaction to ourselves, then only shall we be able to ponder judiciously and to decide pertinently whether or not it is necessary for us to remonstrate with him for his good....

"Our admonition should not bear, properly speaking, the note of a reproach. It should rather be in the character of a humble and amicable exposition of our grief, a gentle invitation to our friend to consider the matter in a valid perspective and to collect himself anew" (San Francisco: Ignatius Press, 2001), pp. 341–43.

Is it my place to correct my priest when he clearly sins or teaches error?

(1) **A subject is (a) not competent to administer to his prelate the correction which is an act of justice through the coercive nature of punishment; but (b) the fraternal correction which is an act of charity is within the competency of everyone in respect of any person towards whom he is bound by charity, provided there be something in that person which requires correction....**

(2) **Since, however, a virtuous act needs to be moderated by due circumstances, it follows that when a subject corrects his prelate, he ought to do so in a becoming manner, not with impudence and harshness but with gentleness and respect....**

(3) **To withstand anyone in public exceeds the mode of fraternal correction, and so Paul would not have withstood Peter then (Gal 2:11), unless he were in some way his (apostolic) equal as regards the defense of the faith. But one who is not an equal can reprove privately and respectfully. Hence the Apostle in writing to the Colossians (4:17) tells them to admonish their prelate:** *Say to Archippus: Fulfill thy ministry.*

(4) **It must be observed, however, that if the faith were endangered, a subject ought to rebuke his prelate even publicly. Hence Paul, who was Peter's subject, rebuked him in public on account of the imminent danger of scandal concerning faith....**

(5) **To presume oneself to be simply better than one's prelate would seem to savor of presumptuous pride, but there is no presumption in thinking oneself better in some respect, because in this life no man is without some fault** (II-II,33,4).

(6) **But if we find that we are guilty of the same sin, we must not rebuke him, but groan with him, and invite him to repent with us ... correction becomes unseemly ... when ... a man thinks lightly of his own sins and in his own heart sets himself above his neighbor** (II-II,33,5).

In St. Thomas' day clergy were no more perfect than they are today and sometimes needed "correction". The difference today is that it is sometimes *theological* correction as well as moral: the congregation sometimes believes more than the preacher does!

(1a) A priest can be punished only by his pastor, a pastor by his bishop, a bishop by the pope. But (1b) any Christian can fraternally correct any other Christian, if it is done out of charity (all charityless motives are suspect), but only if the correction is objectively correct and necessary and (2) if it is done with respect for the office and with gentleness to the person (honey gathers more flies than vinegar), and (3) in private, (4) unless innocent people would be harmed if not done in public; (5) and it must be done without presumption and pride (for one can be in the right about one particular thing—the error or sin of the other—without being in the right about everything else); (6) and it must be done without the hypocrisy of being guilty of the very same sin or error oneself.

Notice how much moral common sense St. Thomas has. He constantly avoids easy opposite errors, e.g., laxity or judgmentalism.

Notice how intuitively we say "Aha! That's obviously the right answer!" when we read St. Thomas. There is in each of us a little St. Thomas, sitting there at the heart of our reason, conscience, and common sense, that recognizes right reason, good conscience, and common sense when we find it. We wouldn't have come up with his answers ourselves, yet when we hear his, we instantly say "Of course!"

While we're on the dangerous topic of playing the prophet, what about public sins, that are clear to everyone? If no one denounces them, people will assume it's OK. So we have some responsibility not only toward the spiritual good of the sinner but also to the public, don't we? How should we discriminate when to speak (and where and how) and when to keep silent? For instance, what about Catholic politicians (or, worse, priests or theologians) who publicly support abortion, fornication, or homosexual sex?

With regard to the public denunciation of sins, it is necessary to make a distinction, because sins may be either public or secret. In the case of public sins, a remedy is required not only for the sinner, that he may become better, but also for others, who know of his sin, lest they be scandalized. ("Scandalized" means not just shocked but being spiritually harmed by bad example. See below.) **Wherefore such like sins should be denounced in public, according to the saying of the Apostle** (1 Tim 5:20): *Them that sin reprove before all, that the rest also may have fear,* **which is to be understood as referring to public sins, as Augustine states ...** (II-II,33,7).

The Greek *skandalon* **may be rendered offense, downfall, or a stumbling against something. For when a body, while moving along a path, meets with an obstacle, it may happen to stumble against it, and be disposed to fall down; such an obstacle is a** *skandalon.* **In like manner, while going along the spiritual way, a man may be disposed to a spiritual downfall by another's word or deed, in so far as one man, by his injunction, inducement, or example, moves another to sin; and this is scandal properly so called** (II-II,43,1).

Our Lord said (Mt 18:16): *Take with thee one or two more, that in the mouth of two,* **etc. The right way to go from one extreme to another is**

to pass through the middle space. Now Our Lord wished the beginning of fraternal correction to be hidden, when one brother corrects another between this one and himself alone, while He wished the end to be public, when such a one would be denounced to the Church. Consequently it is befitting that a citation of witnesses should be placed between the two extremes, so that ... thus his sin be amended without dishonoring him before the public (II-II,33,8).

"Scandal" has come to mean anything that elicits a large number of strong negative emotional reactions when made public. But in traditional moral philosophy "scandal" meant something quite different: something more specific, something moral rather than emotional, and something not relative to publicity. As with many other words, we have changed it to something more shallow, subjective, and relative.

St. Thomas' advice follows Christ's. Christ was personally very sensitive to scandal (in the old sense) because He was very sensitive to others being harmed spiritually; and this made Him unafraid to speak out against evil even when it made Him unpopular (in fact so unpopular that He was martyred!). On the other hand, St. Thomas is also following another, complementary aspect of Christ's character: Christ was gentle and reasonable. Christ's recommended treatment of public scandal was private, gradual, and incremental, with no rancorous attempt to dishonor the sinner in public.

This was especially remarkable when we remember that pre-modern cultures, especially Jewish culture, were capable of great moral outrage and simple passion against evil, unlike our current "live and let live" relativistic culture. The same Christ Who seems "judgmental" to our modern sophists must have seemed "soft" to the Pharisees.

Like Christ, St. Thomas would have made a very poor Spanish Inquisitor.

Many people hate the Church, and many atheists passionately hate religion. Do they hate God? Is that possible? How can anyone hate the only absolutely, perfectly good, and lovable being?

Whether it is possible for anyone to hate God?

God can be apprehended by man in two ways: first, in Himself, as when He is seen in His essence; secondly, in His effects.... Now God in His essence is goodness itself, which no man can hate, for it is natural to the good to be loved. Hence it is impossible for one who sees God in His essence to hate Him.

Moreover some of His effects are such that they can in no wise be contrary to the human will, since *to be, to love, to understand,* which are effects of God, are desirable and lovable to all. Wherefore again God cannot be an object of hatred if we consider Him as the Author of such effects.

Some of God's effects, however, are contrary to an inordinate will, such as the infliction of punishment, and the prohibition of sin by the divine law. Such effects are repugnant to a will debased by sin, and as regards the consideration of them God may be an object of hatred to some in so far as they look upon Him as forbidding sin and inflicting punishment (II-II,34,1).

The best is the opposite of the worst, according to the Philosopher. But hatred of God is contrary to the love of God, in which man's best consists. Therefore hatred of God is man's worst sin.... (However,) not everyone who hates his punishment hates God the author of punishments. For many hate the punishments inflicted on them and yet they bear them patiently out of reverence for the divine justice. Wherefore Augustine says that God commands us to bear with penal evils, not to love them. On the other hand, to break out into hatred of God when He inflicts those punishments is to hate God's very justice, and that is a most grievous sin (II-II,34,2).

St. Thomas assumes that there is such a thing as human nature and that that nature is "by nature" attracted to whatever appears good. That may not seem to be a very controversial assumption, but many philosophers today deny it, because they deny either the existence of any such things as universal natures (Nominalism), or that we can know them, or that they are teleological (purposively ordered to a natural good). These assumptions cannot be proved by science, only by philosophy.

Some "effects" of God are as impossible to hate as God is, for they are to God as sunlight is to the sun; they are made of the same realities, so to speak: truth and goodness, understanding and love. To meet these realities is to love them, unless one is demon-possessed and has lost his essential humanity.

What is hated by people who say they hate God is His commandments, and the obligation they place on the human will to obey them rather than our own will, i.e., to stop playing God, to admit that God is God and we are not—that is, to obey the first commandment, to worship God alone.

When we are addicted to sin (and we all are!), God's commandments appear as unwelcome as a family intervention appears to a drug addict. What is hated especially is the punishment that sin must entail, for all punishment, by the very nature of punishment, is unpleasant rather than pleasant.

St. Thomas distinguishes, in his last paragraph, between hating our just punishments, which is a fault but quite natural given our present fallen state, and hating God and justice itself because of these punishments, which is contrary to our very nature. Yet free will enables us to do just that. Nothing else can hate its own nature because nothing else has free will.

Think of two convicts in prison. Both hate prison, but one admits his fault and serves his time as his just desserts, while the other hates the very system of justice itself and would sooner enthrone injustice in power than justice, in order to justify himself. That attitude is more dangerous than the sin that put the prisoner in jail in the first place.

178. HATING SINS WITHOUT HATING SINNERS

What is the key to understanding, accepting and practicing the old adage, "Love the sinner, hate the sin"?

It is lawful to hate the sin in one's brother ... but we cannot hate our brother's nature ... without sin. Now it is part of our love for our brother that we hate the fault and the lack of good in him, since desire for another's good is equivalent to hatred of his evil (II–II,34,3).

One wonders why this adage, "love the sinner, hate the sin", is so often disputed; for it would seem obvious that the only two possible alternatives would be either (1) to hate the sinner as well as the sin or (2) to love the sin as well as the sinner, i.e., to love the sin that is harming the sinner (and that too would be hating the sinner rather than loving him, for it would be loving his harm). Both of these alternatives are forms of hating the sinner instead of loving him.

The analogy is often made with cancer. If sin is to the soul what cancer is to the body, then to love someone's body is necessarily to hate the cancer that is killing it.

The reason this is disputed is that the sinner is so addicted to his sin that he cannot or will not distinguish himself from it. He says that he is what he does, that his very identity consists in his sin, so that to hate his sin is to hate him.

This is an extremely dangerous attitude. It hardly ever attaches to any other sin except one, and is never heard from any organized group of people except one.

And if we refuse to speak the truth to them, out of human respect, that proves that we do *not*

really love them, just as they accuse us of not loving them, but for another reason (because we do not accept their sin).

St. Thomas notes that "it is part of our love for our brother that we hate the fault ... in him." If we accepted the self-justifying sinner's demand to stop hating his sin, we would have to stop loving him. Moral relativists cannot understand this, for they do not believe that there is such a thing as a natural law, or natural vs. unnatural acts, or sins against human nature itself, or often even any sin at all (for if there is no absolute moral law to sin against, how can there be any such thing as sin?). They reject the analogy with cancer because they think of the soul as wholly different from the body, or even nonexistent; or because they reject all natural analogies. But such analogies are so commonsensical and obvious that the reason for rejecting them is almost always moral rather than intellectual: the will not to be judged, not to be wrong, not to have to feel guilty about or give up one's precious sins.

So the strife between us who judge and our brothers who sin is a strife between two loves: Do we love our brothers more than they love their sins, or do we love them less than they love their sins? The strongest love will always win in the end.

This applies to ourselves as well as to our brothers, for when our conscience speaks against our own sins, our conscience is to us what we are to our sinning brothers. And this self-condemnation, rather than the condemnation of a brother's sin, is always the primary situation, and the only one that is safe from dangers of self-righteousness. (Yet even that danger is sometimes worth risking for the sake of brotherly love.)

179. "Hate crimes" vs. adultery: which is worse?

Is hatred the worst of sins against our neighbor?

There are sins by which a man hurts his neighbor more than by hatred, e.g., theft, murder and adultery....

Sins committed against our neighbor are evil on two counts: first by reason of the disorder in the person who sins; secondly by reason of the hurt inflicted on the person sinned against. On the first count, hatred is a more grievous sin than external actions that hurt our neighbor because hatred is a disorder of man's will, which is the chief part of man; and in this is the root of sin, so that if a man's outward actions were to be inordinate without any disorder in his will, they would not be sinful, for instance if he were to kill a man through ignorance.... On the other hand, as regards the hurt inflicted on his neighbor, a man's outward sins are worse than his inward hatred (II-II,34,4).

As usual, St. Thomas answers a difficult and controversial question by making a basic distinction which, once we see it, we know is commonsensical. (But common sense is not very common.)

Traditional or "conservative" morality evaluates crimes primarily by the objective harm they do. Thus murder and adultery are great crimes. Modern, more subjective and psychological, morality evaluates crimes primarily or even wholly by the inner state of soul of the criminal. This subjective perspective is a legitimate and important one, but it should not lead to subjectivism and a denial or ignoring of the traditional, objective dimension. Jesus did not compromise on either of these two dimensions. It is a mistake to specialize when it comes to morality.

Since love (charity) is the greatest spiritual and subjective and personal good, it logically follows that the greatest subjective and personal evils are love's opposites, which are both positive hate and negative indifference or lovelessness. So if "hate crimes" means not merely whatever words happen to offend a certain class of people but the crime

of harming your own soul by deliberately and actively hating other people, then hate crimes are the worst of crimes. However, they may not issue in deeds, or even words, against another person, and thus may not harm others. The one who is hated may not even know that he is being hated.

But a sneer can be a greater crime than a murder subjectively, for a sneer means "You are beneath contempt, you are sub-human, you are worthless scum, you are not even worth taking the trouble and time to kill", while a murder may mean "You are important and formidable and you are my enemy, and thus I must kill you." That can be a compliment, compared to a sneer.

Today, especially in "advanced" places like Canada and Scandanavia, where "adultery" is almost equated with "adult", "hate crimes" mean merely offending groups of people who demand to adulterate sex without being labeled and judged as adulterers. (For instance, it is a "hate crime" to quote certain politically incorrect verses from the Bible, especially the Old Testament, in any public arena.) That morality does not deserve much more than a sneer.

The unbridgeable gap between the old, traditional morality and the new politically correct one is almost wholly about sex. If sex is merely a biological fact that can afford great pleasure, then the old morality is ridiculously superstitious and oppressive: superstitious because it saw sex as part of the image of God (Gen 1:27), as a foretaste of mystical, self-forgetful Heavenly love, and as divinely ordered toward the greatest ongoing miracle in the world, the creation of billions of new, eternal, and intrinsically valuable things called persons; and oppressive because this myth was superimposed onto the simple biological fact and psychological opportunity for pleasure, which was made by the Church to carry a weight of meaning and purpose and responsibility that it did not really have—as if the Church forbade us to cut down trees because she believed that Tolkien's mythical Ents, the talking trees in *The Lord of the Rings*, were literally true. But if sex is the high and holy mystery that the Church sees it as ...

What is the difference between the capital sin of sloth and mere laziness?

Sloth, according to Damascene, is *an oppressive sorrow* which ... is always evil ... For sorrow is evil in itself when it is about that which is ... good in reality, even as ... pleasure is evil if it is about that which ... is in truth evil. Since, then, spiritual good is a good in very truth, sorrow about spiritual good is evil ...

Passions are not sinful in themselves, but they are blameworthy in so far as they are applied to something evil, just as they deserve praise in so far as they are applied to something good. Wherefore sorrow in itself calls neither for praise nor for blame, whereas moderate sorrow for evil calls for praise, while sorrow for good and immoderate sorrow for evil call for blame (II-II,35,1).

Sloth is a far greater problem in our advanced, sophisticated, complex, bored, and jaded time than in St. Thomas' simpler, more natural and primitive time. There are few heroes today. There is little need for courage in our comfortable technological paradise. There is little passion for anything except pleasure and comfort and security. Indeed, passion is confused with fanaticism.

Our society is so afraid of "fanaticism" that it is our F-word. We fear terrorist Muslims without more than we fear relativists within.

The thing St. Thomas characterizes as "an oppressive sorrow" reigns in the most "advanced" places, such as Scandanavia and Harvard, where clinical depression and suicide abound.

Paradoxically, sloth reigns most in our technologically busy world where leisure has been abolished and life has been programmed and scheduled down to the last detail.

Though sloth is "always evil," people may be more the passive victims than the active perpetrators of this spiritual disease, because their culture encourages them to it.

Sloth is more than laziness. Laziness may be (1) physical, due to genetic predispositions and biologically determined temperament, or (2) emotional, a felt preference for relaxation rather than exertion, or (3) moral, a freely chosen attitude of avoidance of exertion even when exertion is a duty or at least would be of more moral value than relaxation. Only insofar as (3) is involved is laziness sinful. For as St. Thomas says, "passions (emotions) are not sinful in themselves" but only when "applied," i.e., deliberately directed, to good or evil. When directed by the will to the good, emotions become good; when to the evil, evil.

Evil consists of both sins of commission and sins of omission. Sloth is a sin of omission: the refusal to exert oneself, to rouse oneself, to move toward the good even when the good is present and recognized. For instance, not jumping in the pool to save a baby from drowning. Or not getting out of your warm, comfortable bed on a cold winter morning to go to Sunday Mass. Or not inquiring of God what He wants you to do. Or, stupidest of all, not inquiring whether or not God even exists. "Drifting."

Not inquiring means not caring, and not caring means not loving, and not loving means not willing, and not willing is a choice, and a choice is praiseworthy or blameworthy.

There is a word in modern languages that is very similar to "sloth." It is a word that did not exist in any pre-modern language. The word is "boredom." I mean not boredom with a particular thing but objectless, generalized boredom, emptiness. We are the first culture in history in which boredom is so common that there is a word for it. (See Walker Percy's *Lost in the Cosmos* for a hilariously incisive treatment of this. See also the section of Pascal's *Pensées* entitled "Indifference".) Boredom (sloth) has invented a new evil word: the word "whatever". It is really a curse word, because it means "the Hell with it" or "I don't give a damn."

181. When Sloth Becomes a Mortal Sin

Granted that sloth is a sin; how can it be a mortal sin?

Mortal sin is so called because it destroys the spiritual life which is the effect of charity, whereby God dwells in us. Wherefore any sin which by its very nature is contrary to charity (which is the very life of God in us) **is a mortal sin by reason of its genus. And such is sloth, because the proper effect of charity is joy in God ... while sloth is sorrow about spiritual good in as much as it is a divine good. Therefore sloth is a mortal sin in its genus.... (But) the movement of sloth is sometimes in the sensuality alone, by reason of the opposition of the flesh to the spirit, and then it is a venial sin; whereas sometimes it reaches to the reason, which consents in the dislike, horror, and detestation of the divine good ... (and) in this case it is evident that sloth is a mortal sin** (II-II,35,3).

"A mortal sin" is not simply a "big" sin, like murder or genocide. A mortal sin is any sin that kills the supernatural life of the soul. ("The supernatural life of the soul" is another way of saying "the life of God in the soul"; and "the life of God", both in Himself and in human souls, is the life of agape, charity, supernatural love, divine love; therefore "the supernatural life of the soul" is charity.)

Sloth is not a spectacular sin. It is a sin of omission rather than commission. The person who is committing the sin of sloth may be doing nothing visible that is wrong. Yet he is rejecting the presence of God, refusing the joy of love.

"Joy" is not merely a passive feeling. It is an act of the will. It is rejoicing. The will freely chooses not only to desire the good when absent but also to accept it, affirm it, and rejoice in it when present. Both are active choices, not just passive feelings. Both are affirmations, so negation is also possible. We can say *to God* what Rhett Butler says to Scarlett O'Hara: "Frankly, my dear, I don't give a damn." And that is in fact damnation if meant with the whole heart.

When we are just too lazy emotionally (or physically) to exert effort toward the good that is present and perceived, that is the sin of sloth, but it is only venial, not mortal. It is a kind of cowardice, an unreasonable fear of difficulties and pains.

But even venial sin can be eternally dangerous, for it habituates us toward mortal sin; and that habituation is a slow, imperceptible sinking, whose point of no return is not clearly marked. It's the "frog in the pot" principle. Turn up the water temperature gradually so the frog doesn't notice he's being boiled until it's too late, and he's dead.

"Dislike, horror, and detestation of the divine good" is mortal sin because it is Hellish. That is probably what makes Hell Hell: that God, and what God is made of (truth, goodness, beauty, holiness), is hated. Christ described damnation this way: "The Light has come into the world and men loved darkness rather than light" (Jn 3:19).

In that way, Hell is not so much punishment for sin as sin itself. As perfect virtue is its own reward, perfect vice is its own punishment.

Dante made the lowest region in Hell icy rather than fiery. He understood how dangerous sloth was. Many saints were made out of passionate sinners—the angry, the hating, the lustful, the cynical; but none were ever made out of the slothful. It takes much more force to overcome inertia and make a heavy object to start moving than it does to change its direction when it's moving the wrong way.

Whether for good or evil, people seemed more passionate in the past, in more primitive times and cultures, e.g., in Christendom in the past and in Islamic cultures today. We moderns are the masters of sloth. Yet our culture specializes in lust more than any culture in history. Can lust come from sloth instead of from passion?

Since, according to the Philosopher, *no man can be a long time in company with what is painful and unpleasant,* **it follows that something arises from sorrow in two ways: first, that man shuns whatever causes sorrow; secondly, that he passes to other things that give him pleasure: thus those who find no joy in spiritual pleasures have recourse to pleasures of the body** (II-II,35,4).

Fr. Thomas Gilby translates this passage, loosely but correctly, "Man cannot live without joy. That is why one deprived of spiritual joy goes over to carnal pleasures."

Lust is the favorite sin of our culture. Indeed, the culture has deemed it not a sin at all, but almost a virtue. But the epidemic of lust is destroying society, through destroying families. And it destroys souls, just as any addiction does. Here is its source—sloth—and its cure—true passion and joy, spiritual passion and joy. Saints are not addicted to lust because they know something even more passionate, more exciting. They know God.

In #180 above, St. Thomas defined sloth as sorrow in the presence of spiritual good. "Sorrow" here does not necessarily mean sorrow about some specific object, like the death of a loved one, but simply lack of joy even when a great spiritual good is present. Now St. Thomas adds the psychological principle that we escape sorrow in two ways, which correspond to what the Scholastics called the "irascible" (averting) and "concupiscible" (attracting) emotions. When our sorrow arises from the positive presence of pain, like a wound, it arouses our "irascible" anger and hatred of the pain. But when our sorrow arises from sloth and boredom, we seek some "concupiscible" diversion from our joylessness. And this is the hidden source of lust.

It also explains something all perceptive observers of modern culture have noticed (e.g., Kierkegaard, T.S. Eliot, C.S. Lewis): that our lusts are far less "lusty" than those of our ancestors. Kierkegaard says "even their lusts are sleepy", and Lewis says that "they simply hop out of and into beds in obedience to sexy advertisements." We are J. Alfred Prufrock, not Henry VIII. (That's why we find Henry VIII so fascinating.)

The deeper reason for this is that, as St. Augustine famously said, "Thou hast made us for Thyself, and [therefore] our hearts are restless until they rest in Thee." Augustine's restlessness, unlike ours, was more passionate than slothful, more sharp than dull. But the principle holds true universally: God made us with a God-shaped vacuum in our hearts ("man cannot live without joy") and that is why if we don't have God we have to stuff that hole full of idols. But it's like stuffing your mouth full of cardboard when you're starving.

Freud thought God was a substitute for sex. He thought just about everything was a substitute for sex. It was a brilliant insight, because it was exactly the truth upside down (like Sartre's "Hell is other people"). In fact, sex is very often a substitute for God. Everything is a substitute for God if pursued as our *summum bonum,* our greatest good. That's why all sins are sins against the First Commandment.

Why isn't true Christianity pacifism? "War is Hell." I can't imagine Jesus with a gun.

Augustine says in a sermon on the son of the centurion (Lk 3:14): *If the Christian religion forbade war altogether, those who sought salutary advice in the Gospel would rather have been counseled to cast aside their arms and to give up soldiering altogether. On the contrary, they were told: "Do violence to no man ... and be content with your pay." If he commanded them to be content with their pay, he did not forbid soldiering.*

In order for a war to be just three things are necessary. First, the authority of the sovereign by whose command the war is to be waged. For it is not the business of a private individual to declare war, because he can seek for redress of his rights from the tribunal of his superior. Moreover it is not the business of a private individual to summon together the people, which has to be done in wartime. And as the care of the common weal is committed to those who are in authority, it is their business to watch over the common weal of the city, kingdom or province subject to them. And just as it is lawful for them to have recourse to the sword in defending that common weal against internal disturbances, when they punish evildoers, according to the words of the Apostle (Rom 8:4): *He bears not the sword in vain, for he is God's minister, an avenger to execute wrath upon him that doeth evil,* so too it is his business to have recourse to the sword ... in defending the common weal against external enemies....

Secondly a just cause is required....

Thirdly, it is necessary that the belligerents should have a rightful intention, so that they intend the advancement of good or the avoidance of evil. Hence Augustine says: *True religion looks upon as peaceful those wars that are waged not for motives of aggrandizement or cruelty, but with the object of securing peace, or punishing evildoers, and of uplifting the good.* For it may happen that the war is declared by the legitimate authority, and for a just cause, and yet be rendered unlawful through a wicked intention (II–II,40,1).

War is not Hell. Only Hell is Hell. Don't exaggerate when it comes to Heaven or Hell!

War is a great evil, but there are many things worse than war. Auschwitz was far worse than war. Hitler's conquest of the world, with an Auschwitz in every country, would have been far worse than the 55 million deaths (often noble deaths) caused by World War II.

If immortal souls are more important than bodies, then hatred in the soul is more evil, and does the person more harm, than death in the body. When one soldier kills another out of duty, not hatred, the deed is harmful physically but the motive can be pure spiritually. It is bad, but it is not the worst thing in the world—except to a materialist.

The idea of resolving conflicts by killing people (which is what war is) is not a just thing, a just idea. In that sense there is no such thing as "just war". But to wage a given war may be a just action. A forest fire is bad for a forest, but a backfire to stop it may well be good for the forest, better than letting it all burn down. Hard and painful deeds, like amputations, may be necessary in a world of sin.

If Jesus had been a pacifist He would never have called John the Baptist the greatest of prophets, for when soldiers asked John for advice he did not tell them to leave their profession.

Since the natural moral law can be added to by additional social circumstances, but never subtracted from (ST I,94,5), other qualifications for a just war need to be added today to the three commonsensical ones mentioned by St. Thomas. For instance, weapons of mass destruction, whether biological, nuclear, or even conventional, cannot avoid slaughtering tens of thousands of innocent noncombatants and are probably intrinsically immoral.

You can't imagine Jesus with a gun—what follows from that? Muslims can't imagine a prophet on a cross; that's why they deny the crucifixion. Our imaginations are not infallible. God's Word is.

184. Sinning a Little Sin to Avoid a Big Scandal?

Whether spiritual goods should be foregone on account of scandal?

Objection: It seems that one ought sometimes to commit a venial sin in order to avoid scandalizing one's neighbor, for instance, when by sinning venially one would prevent someone else from committing a mortal sin; because one is bound to hinder the damnation of one's neighbor as much as one can without prejudice to one's own salvation, which is not precluded by a venial sin....

Reply: Some have said that one ought to commit a venial sin in order to avoid scandal. But this implies a contradiction, since if it ought to be done, it is no longer evil or sinful....

He whose duty it is to teach should not teach what is contrary to the truth ... on no account ought he to suppress the truth and teach error in order to avoid any scandal that might ensue (II-II,43,7).

For any act to be morally right, three things are necessary: (1) right act, (2) right motive, and (3) right circumstances. If any one of these factors is not right, the act is wrong.

Motives and/or circumstances can never make an intrinsically wrong act right. E.g., if all torture is wrong (St. Thomas does not think it is, by the way), then it is wrong even to torture a terrorist who has planted a ticking nuclear time bomb in the middle of Manhattan. A sin is a sin. No is no, and never yes. As St. Thomas says so simply, to say that sometimes one "ought" to commit a sin is a contradiction, for what we "ought" to do is good, not evil. "I ought to sin" means "I ought to do what I ought not to do."

But what if the harm done by not sinning is spiritual instead of just physical? What if the scandal (spiritual harm) done by not sinning is eternal? What if someone who is in a state of mortal sin threatens to kill not me but himself if I do not blaspheme? I believe he will go to Hell forever if I do not sin reluctantly, and thus not mortally (for "full consent of the will" is one of the conditions of a mortal sin). Should I imperil his eternal salvation to save my moral purity?

This is a tricky question, and most tricky questions are solved only by changing the perspective, backing up and remembering "the big picture". The "big picture" here is that we are not God, and God has issued clear commandments to the whole human race for all times and circumstances. We are to obey our Commanding Officer. That is more certain than our calculation of the probable consequences of bodily and spiritual harm, temporal and eternal harm, to our souls and the souls of others.

But isn't it wrong to lie? And didn't the Dutchmen rightly lie to the Nazis about where the Jews were hiding? And wasn't that good? That was obviously good, but it was not a lie. Not all deceptions are lies, just as not all forcible taking of personal property is theft (e.g., kicking his gun out of a madman's hand). We can explain why in two ways. Either (1) the Nazis had given up their right to the truth, as a lethal aggressor gives up his right to life (after all, the commandment does not say never to utter false propositions but never to *bear false witness against your neighbor*), or else (2) this deception was not a lie but precisely the truth—the truth of keeping your promise to the Jews you were hiding.

How you explain this case may be tricky, but what is not at all tricky is the principle that we should never do evil even for the sake of good. If we could do that, then it would be all right for nine of ten people on a lifeboat to murder one innocent person so that the nine could eat him and survive rather than all ten dying of starvation. And once that camel's nose is under the tent....

Some twentieth-century theologians actually taught that we should not send out missionaries because fewer pagans would go to Hell if they had the excuse that they had never heard the gospel. (They didn't put it that plainly, but that was their point.) That is an example of suppressing the truth (a sin of omission) or even lying (a sin of commission) in order to avoid scandalizing (harming) souls. That's just dishonest. Back up. Look at the obvious: What are our marching orders? Who is our Commanding Officer? Where did the Great Commission come from? Are we the General or His soldiers?

God gives us commandments to be kept. But how can we fallen fools and selfish sinners possibly keep the commandment that includes all the other ones, "the first and greatest commandment", namely, to love God with our whole heart?

To love God with one's whole heart has a twofold signification. First, actually, so that a man's whole heart be always actually directed to God: this is the perfection of Heaven. Secondly, in the sense that a man's whole heart be habitually directed to God, so that it consent to nothing contrary to the love of God; and this is the perfection of the way. Venial sin is not contrary to this latter perfection, because it does not destroy the habit of charity (II-II,44,4).

The category of "habit", prominent in Aristotle but absent from most modern moral philosophers, is necessary to answer this question. A habit is a stable disposition to act in a certain way, good or evil. Virtues are good habits; vices are bad habits. Habits are not actions but states of character; they tell us who a person is. Habits are halfway between mere potentialities and actualities. A man has the potentiality to turn somersaults, but not the habit (unless he is a gymnast). But a man has a habit of charity, or of uncharity; and this defines his character, his soul.

Habits, good or bad, are not deterministic. They can be disobeyed. An alcoholic can have a fit of sobriety, and a moral monster can suddenly decide to sacrifice for his friends. Also, a saint can sin, and frequently does, against the habit of charity that defines his soul. Venial sin weakens the habit of charity but does not remove it. Mortal sin removes it. Venial sin is like an argument between spouses, mortal sin is like a divorce.

Charity is the habit that God infuses (spiritually causes) in us when we receive Him, by faith and Baptism. When St. Thomas refers to "charity" (as he does constantly) he does not mean merely "doing good deeds" or "acting unselfishly" or "helping others". He means agape, which is the very life of God in the soul, the state of grace. By nature we are capable of all human loves, but agape is a participation in divine love, which comes from God alone. So "charity" means "the presence of God in the soul." One can do good deeds (philanthropy, altruism) without agape. One can have what the world calls "charity" without having what St. Thomas calls "charity". But one cannot do the reverse; one cannot have charity (agape) without doing good deeds. Charity enters the soul by faith, but it is not confined there: "faith by itself if it has no works is dead" (Jas 2:17). "You will know them by their fruits" (Mt 7:16).

186. ANGER

Is anger sinful?

To be angry is not always an evil....

The Stoics designated anger and all the other passions as emotions opposed to the order of reason, and accordingly they deemed anger and all other passions to be evil.... But according to ... Aristotle ... anger is not always evil.

Anger may stand in a twofold relation to reason. First, antecedently (anger *before* reason); in this way, it withdraws reason from its rectitude, and has therefore the character of evil. Secondly, consequently (anger *after* reason), inasmuch as the movement of the sensitive appetite is directed against vice and in accordance with reason. This anger is good and is called *zealous anger.*

This latter anger, although it hinder somewhat the judgment of reason in the execution of the act, does not destroy the rectitude of reason.... Nor is it incompatible with virtue that the deliberation of reason be interrupted in the execution of what reason has deliberated, since (practicing an) art also would be hindered in its act if it were to deliberate about what has to be done while having to act.

It is unlawful to desire vengeance considered as evil to the man who is to be punished, but it is praiseworthy to desire vengeance as a corrective of vice and for the good of justice (II-II,158,1).

Anger is properly the name of a passion. A passion of the sensitive appetite is good in so far as it is regulated by reason, whereas it is evil if it set the order of reason aside.... Wherefore if one desire revenge to be taken in accordance with the order of reason, the desire of anger is praiseworthy and is called *zealous anger.* On the other hand, if one desire the taking of vengeance in any way whatever contrary to the order of reason, for instance if he desire the punishment of one who has not deserved it, or beyond his deserts, or contrary to the order prescribed by law, or not for the due end, viz. maintaining justice and correcting faults, then the desire of anger will be sinful, and this is called *sinful anger....* Anger should not be immoderately fierce, either internally or externally, and if this condition be disregarded anger will not lack sin even though just vengeance be desired (II-II,158,2).

Chrysostom says: *He who is not angry when he has cause to be angry, sins. For unreasonable patience is the hotbed of many vices; it fosters negligence and incites not only the wicked but even the good to do wrong* (II-II,158,8).

(However,) In the case where anger is contrary to charity, it is a mortal sin (II-II,158,3).

Jesus got angry! He was "like us in all things except sin". Therefore anger is not sin.

Wrath (anger) is ascribed to God, by analogy, in the Old Testament. Even though this is only an analogy, since God has no passive passions, yet nothing evil can be an analogy for anything good. Therefore anger can be good.

Common sense tells us that someone who does not get angry even in the presence of gross evil is not morally superior but morally inferior. He is slothful. He does not care about justice.

Since anger is a passion (emotion), what is true of all the passions is true of anger too: that it is neither good nor evil in itself. The Stoics failed to see that the passions could be good, could participate in the good of reason. They did, however, correctly see that reason is the standard. Anger that destroys reason is evil. Anger that comes from and is justified by reason is good. (Please remember always that "reason" for St. Thomas and the ancients means not cold calculation but wisdom and understanding.)

Sloth is a capital sin. (See above, ##180–82). Sloth makes anger impossible. Thus "he who is not angry when he has (right) cause to be angry, sins."

Anger is, however, dangerous: first, because it tends to paralyze the reason (although this is sometimes necessary) and second, because it can drive out charity (which is always inexcusable).

187. WHY GOD DOES NOT GIVE YOU GRACE TO OVERCOME LUST

Why do the sins of the flesh seem to be so much more common than the sins of the spirit today? Why are most of the ordinary people we know victims of lust but not Phariseeism or hypocrisy or cruelty? In Jesus' day more people seemed to be victimized by the hard, cruel sins. Does our preference for the soft, warm, comfortable sins mean that we are worse or better? Can a divine perspective shed any light on this mystery? What is God doing with us? Why is He abandoning us to lust?

In order to overcome their pride, God punishes certain men by allowing them to fall into sins of the flesh, which, though they be less grievous, are more evidently shameful.... From this indeed the gravity of pride is made manifest. For just as a wise physician, in order to cure a worse disease, allows the patient to contract one that is less dangerous, so the sin of pride is shown to be more grievous by the fact that as a remedy God allows men to fall into other sins (II-II, 162,6).

It's not the flesh but the spirit that's at the root of the problem of lust.

Here is a parallel (but not identical) case: Why does God allow so much pain? He could reduce the amount of pain in the world by 90%, either by miracles, or by providence, or by having made the world less full of toxic germs, cancers, dangerous animals, hurricanes, and earthquakes. The answer is that He has to keep us humble and weak so that we yearn for Heaven and perfection. The more Heavenly earth becomes, the less dissatisfied we would be with it. We fall easily into addiction to earthly goods, so He can't give us too many of them. If we never suffer, we become spiritually stupid.

What's true of physical humility (weakness, pain, disease, vulnerability) is also true of spiritual humility. He has to keep us humble. If He gave us the grace to overcome all our more obvious moral weaknesses, we would become self-righteous Pharisees. And that is far more dangerous than becoming alcoholics or sex addicts, because pride is much more self-deceptive than the sins of the flesh—except today, when the sins of the flesh no longer confess themselves to be sins. That is the greatest danger of the "sexual revolution"—not new practice but new thought, new rationalization—and new pride. "Gay pride" parades—the name says it all. The "pride" is by far a worse problem than the "gay".

Pride is the greatest spiritual danger in the world. It was the sin of Satan. If comes from not the world or the flesh but the Devil. It comes from Hell, and it leads to Hell.

We never have to do evil so that good may come, but we may have to tolerate the lesser of two evils in order to avoid the greater one. Thus many moral evils are tolerated by civil law to avoid a government-enforced morality that would be dictatorial and totalitarian. No one wants government agents in their bedroom monitoring their sex lives. Doctors follow this toleration principle when they use chemotherapy: they tolerate lesser ills like hair loss, weight loss or nausea in order to cure a greater ill like cancer. God also does this: He never does evil, but He tolerates lesser evils in us to avoid greater ones. And the greatest one is pride.

A practical corollary: if we were humble, we would get more grace. God "opposes the proud but gives grace to the humble" (Jas 4:6)—not for Himself, because our pride threatens His ego, but for us, because He gives us only the graces that He foresees we will use well, not those He foresees we will misuse.

Bad doctors treat symptoms; good doctors diagnose the root cause of the symptoms and treat the disease. If we want to overcome the sins of the flesh, we should concentrate more on the sins of the spirit. For they are either themselves the cause of the sins of the flesh (e.g., sloth is a cause of lust: see #182 above), or at least they prevent God from giving us the grace to overcome the sins of the flesh. That is why the habitual, prayerful contemplation of God—His holiness, His beauty, His quiet, tidal love—is a great antidote to the loud, crashing waves of lust.

188. Pride

What is pride and why is it so bad?

The greatest sin in man is pride (II-II,162,6).
Pride is the beginning of all sin (II-II,162,7).
Man's first sin was pride (II-II,163,1).

Gregory says: *There are four marks by which
every kind of pride of the arrogant betrays itself:
either when they think that their good is from themselves, or if they believe it to be from above yet they
think that it is due to their own merits, or when
they boast of having what they have not, or despise
others and wish to appear the exclusive possessors of
what they have* (II-II,162,4).

All sins may arise from pride, in two ways.
First ... through other sins being directed to
the end of pride which is one's own excellence, to which end anything that is inordinately desired may be directed. Secondly ...
pride makes a man despise the divine law
which hinders him from sinning....

It must, however, be observed that this
generic character of pride ... does not imply
that all vices originate from pride always.
For though one may break the commandments of the Law by any kind of sin through
contempt, which pertains to pride, yet one
does not always break the divine commandments through contempt but sometimes
through weakness ... (II-II,162,2).

The root of pride is found to consist in man
not being in some way subject to God and
His rule. Now it is evident that not to be
subject to God is of its very nature a mortal
sin, for this consists in turning away from
God; and consequently pride is, of its genus,
a mortal sin.

Nevertheless just as in other sins which are
mortal by their genus (for instance fornication and adultery) there are certain motions
(of the soul) that are (only) venial by reason of
their imperfection through forestalling the
judgment of reason, and being without its
(free) consent, so too in the matter of pride
it happens that certain motions of pride are
venial sins, when reason does not consent to
them (II-II,162,5).

Pride is essentially an attitude toward God, not
just toward oneself. "I will not serve"—that was
Satan's sin, and that is the pride that is in all sins:
refusal to surrender and obey.

Pride is really very simple. It is the attitude of
the spoiled brat: "I want what I want when I want
it, and if you say No to me, I hate you." "Thy will
be done" is the essential prayer of the saint; "my
will be done" is the essential demand of the sinner.
C. S. Lewis says that "there are only two kinds of
people, in the end: those who say to God, 'Thy
will be done' and those to whom God says, in the
end, '*Thy* will be done.'" By giving us free will,
God says to all of us "Thy will be done," but only
some of us return to Him this compliment.

As bad as pride is, St. Thomas keeps his balance, and points out that (1) not all sins are explicitly sins of pride, some are sins of weakness; and
that (2) not all pride is mortal sin, some is only
venial, because sometimes there is not the full
knowledge of the reason and the full consent of
the will. There is a great difference between the
freely willed "contempt" for God's will and the
struggled-against weakness of a divided will.

Yet even though it is often diluted, pride is
always toxic.

What's the difference between an unfallen, innocent woman (Eve) and a fallen, sinful one?

Objection 1. **It would seem that the particular punishments of our first parents are unsuitably appointed in Scripture. For that which would have occurred even without sin should not be described as a punishment for sin. (1) Now seemingly there would have been *pain in child-bearing* even had there been no sin, for the disposition of the female sex is such that offspring cannot be born without pain to the bearer. (2) Likewise the *subjection of woman to man* results from the perfection of the male and the imperfection of the female sex. (3) Again, it belongs to the nature of the earth *to bring forth thorns and thistles*, and this would have occurred even had there been no sin....**

Reply. **(1) In the state of innocence child-bearing would have been painless.... (2) The subjection of the woman to her husband is to be understood as inflicted in punishment of the woman, not as to his headship (since even before sin the man was the *head* ...) but as to her having now to obey her husband's will even against her own. (3) If man had not sinned, the earth would have brought forth thorns and thistles to be the food of animals but not to punish man, because their growth would bring no labor of punishment for the tiller of the soil, as Augustine says. Alcuin, however, holds that before sin the earth brought forth no thorns and thistles whatever, but the former opinion is the better (II-II, 164, 2).**

Three punishments are mentioned in Scripture that are gender-specific: (1) woman's pain in childbirth, (2) the relation of male dominance and female subjection, and (3) man's pain in work. All three are not natural, as they seem, but unnatural, or fallen. They are not ontologically necessary, and were not present before the Fall. Nor will they be present in "the new heavens and the new earth".

(1) Even now some mammals bear offspring without pain. It is biologically possible. Pain is even now largely psychosomatic (hypnosis can remove it), and it could have been totally so before the Fall. This result of the Fall, then, is due to the fallen relation between soul and body: when the soul no longer conforms to the will of God, the body no longer conforms to the will of the soul. When the prince rebels against the King, the prince no longer has authority over his King-appointed servant.

(2) It is remarkable how little St. Thomas' common sense and justice is skewered by his primitive Greek biology ("male = perfect, female = imperfect"). For him, the relation of "submission to headship" and "obedience to authority" does *not* mean the relation of inferiority in nature or worth, for in his Christian theology the Son *submits* to the Father and obeys His will in all things, yet He is equal to Him in nature and worth. The result of the Fall is the contrariety of wills (his vs. hers), not the order of headship in itself. It not authority itself that is a result of the Fall, but the *kind* of authority—authority that is based on power—that is now typical of the fallen world rather than the kind of authority that Christ commands among His disciples, namely authority that is based on love. See Jn 13:12–16; Mt 20:25–26.

If submission and surrender necessarily meant inferiority, then the very essence of Christianity would be false; for Christ, Who came into the world not to do His own will but to submit and surrender totally to His Father's will, would by that token be inferior to the Father, thus falsifying the first and most fundamental of all Christian creeds, "Jesus is Lord" (1 Cor 12:3). *Kyrios,* the word translated "Lord", does not mean any merely human lord, but God, as the later Nicene creed specifies, "fully God of fully God".

In Christianity, women are ontologically equal in value to men, children to adults, and citizens to rulers. These three fundamental human relationships were all skewered by the Fall, yet preserved for the sake of social order, which, even in its fallen form, is better than chaos.

(3) Notice how St. Thomas, in preferring Augustine's interpretation to Alcuin's, instinctively chooses the interpretation that does not depend on the science of his age. A lesson for our own age. The up-to-date science of one century soon becomes the primitivism of the next.

Primitive people, including our remote ancestors, seem shockingly cruel to us. (And we probably would seem shockingly weak, soft, and self-indulgent to them.) Is this because they are closer to the animals, since "brutality" means "like brute animals"? Do we become less cruel as we evolve farther from animals (if we do)? But then a pure spirit would be least cruel of all; yet Satan is the *most* cruel. Are "savagery", "brutality", and "cruelty" the same?

Savagery and *brutality* **take their names from a likeness to wild beasts ("brutes") which are also described as savage. For animals of this kind attack man that they may feed on his body, and not for some motive of justice, the consideration of which belongs to reason alone. Wherefore properly speaking, brutality or savagery applies to those who in inflicting punishment have not in view a fault of the person punished but merely the pleasure they derive from a man's torture. Consequently it is evident that it is comprised under bestiality, for such pleasure is not human but bestial. It results either from evil custom or from a corrupt nature.... On the other hand, cruelty not only regards the fault of the person punished, but exceeds in the mode of punishing; wherefore cruelty differs from savagery or brutality as human wickedness differs from bestiality ...** (II-II,159,2).

There is a significant difference between the violence of a wild man who has lost his reason and the cold, calculating cruelty of a tyrant. To derive pleasure simply from another's pain, whether that pain is deserved or not, is "not human but bestial", for the beasts know nothing of justice or injustice. On the other hand, cruelty is a form of human injustice, an excess of vengeance. Cruelty wants to exceed the amount of punishment deserved. But punishment *is* deserved, so there is an almost-redeeming feature in cruelty: justice, though it is justice perverted.

In one sense savagery or bestiality is worse, for it does not even participate in the good of justice in a perverted way, but sacrifices human reason entirely to animality. In another way it is cruelty that is worse, since that proceeds from deliberate reason and free choice. This does not exonerate the sin of bestiality, of course, in a human being, since a human being is not a beast and therefore must have become bestial through some fault, without or within, social or individual ("either from evil custom or from a corrupt nature").

As our civilization becomes more sophisticated and rationalistic and less "animal", it probably tends more to cruelty than to bestiality, which is why the bestiality of our early ancestors seems more shocking to us than it did to them.

Or perhaps our civilization is *not* becoming less "animal" but more. It would only be practicing what it preaches. For materialists now proliferate in academic and scientific buildings like cockroaches.

Why does God allow us to be tempted?

Christ commanded us to pray, "Lead us not into temptation." Does God ever lead us into temptation? Isn't that the Devil's work?

It is written (Sir 34:11): *He that hath not been tempted, what manner of things doth he know?*

God's wisdom *orders all things sweetly* **(Wis 8:1), inasmuch as His providence appoints to each one that which is befitting it according to its nature. For as Dionysius says,** *it belongs to providence not to destroy, but to maintain, nature.* **Now it is a condition attaching to human nature that one creature can be helped or impeded by another. Wherefore it was fitting that God should both allow man in the state of innocence to be tempted by evil angels, and should cause him to be helped by good angels....**

Augustine says: *It seems to me that man would have had no prospect of any special praise if he were able to lead a good life simply because there was none to persuade him to lead an evil life, since both by nature he had the power, and in his power he had the will, not to consent to the persuader* (II-II,165,1).

There is an analogy between temptation and pain. Temptation affects the spirit as pain and suffering affect the body. Both are tests, challenges, to be met either well or badly. Therefore both are useful. As Rabbi Abraham Heschel says, "The man who has never suffered—what can he possibly know, anyway?" The author of Ecclesiasticus (Sirach) quoted by St. Thomas says the very same thing about temptation.

As suffering can strengthen or weaken the body, temptation can strengthen or weaken the soul. Because we have free will, life is a drama of good vs. evil. It is interesting because it is like a game—a serious game, of course—and not like a formula or a guarantee. If any kind of game is played, it must be possible to lose it as well as to win it.

Temptation comes from something outside the will, either within our being (like the passions) or from other beings (other men or fallen angels). God could have made us autonomous and impervious individuals, like the angels. Instead, he made us vulnerable to both help and harm from others. If we object to this choice of His, we object to our very human essence.

To be tempted is not necessarily to be compromised, to fall, to sin. Innocent Adam and Eve were tempted. Christ was tempted. To be tempted is to be human.

Arnold Toynbee summarizes all of human history in the formula "challenge and response". God allows challenges, including moral challenges, which are temptations, in order to provoke us to our own free moral responses, to make us strong and heroic.

God also allows temptation to preserve the providential order by which we are helped and harmed by each other; for if we could not be harmed by others, we could not be helped by others either; and if we could not be helped by others, we could not help others; and if we could not help others, charity would be impossible.

God does not tempt us to sin; the Devil does. "Let no one say when he is tempted, 'I am being tempted by God.' For God ... tempts no one" (Jas 1:13). But God allows this evil for the sake of greater good.

When we pray "Lead us not into temptation" we do not mean "Stop tempting us" but "Please do not allow great temptations to assail us, because we are weak and without Your special grace we will fail." It is a prayer of humility.

192. CURIOSITY

The ancients ranked curiosity as a sin. Isn't it an intellectual good, and the mother of education?

Curiosity ... may be sinful....

The knowledge of the truth, strictly speaking, is good, but it may be evil accidentally ... either because one takes pride in knowing the truth, according to 1 Corinthians 8:1, *Knowledge puffeth up,* or because one uses the knowledge of truth in order to sin....

There may be sin by reason of the appetite or study directed to the learning of truth being itself inordinate; and this in four ways.

First, when a man is withdrawn by a less profitable study from a study that is an obligation incumbent on him....

Secondly, when a man studies to learn of (from) one by whom it is unlawful to be taught, as in the case of those who seek to know the future through the demons. This is superstitious curiosity....

Thirdly, when a man desires to know the truth about creatures without referring his knowledge to its due end, namely the knowledge of God ... (II-II,167,1).

To employ study for the purpose of knowing sensible things may be sinful ... when the knowledge of sensible things is directed to something harmful, as looking on a woman is directed to lust; even so the busy inquiry into other people's actions is directed to detraction (gossip)....

One may watch other people's actions or inquire into them with a good intent, either for one's own good, that is, in order to be encouraged to better deeds by the deeds of our neighbor, or for our neighbor's good, that is, in order to correct him if he do anything wrong, according to the rule of charity and the duty of one's position. This is praiseworthy, according to Hebrews 10:24, *Consider one another to provoke unto charity and to good works.* But to observe our neighbor's faults with the intention of looking down upon them or of detracting them ... is sinful.

Sight-seeing becomes sinful when it renders a man prone to the vices of lust and cruelty on account of things he sees represented. Hence Chrysostom says that such sights make men adulterers and shameless (II-II,167,2).

Fourthly, when a man studies to know the truth above the capacity of his own intelligence, since by so doing men easily fall into error: wherefore it is written (Sir 3:22): *Seek not the things that are too high for thee, and search not into things above thy ability ...* (II-II,167,1).

"Corruptio optimi pessima." The corruption of the best things are the worst things. The desire to know the truth is a very great good, and therefore its perversions have great potentialities for evil. But the thing itself—the desire to know truth—is a very good thing.

Actually, St. Thomas mentions no less than ten such perversions:

(1) Pride ("Look how much I know!").

(2) Pragmatic misuse of knowledge for sin ("I've figured out when the cops are sleeping").

(3) Using this good thing to avoid a better thing ("I can't pray now, I'm studying").

(4) Seeking knowledge from forbidden supernatural sources ("Whee! Ouija!").

(5) Idolizing natural knowledge and scorning supernatural knowledge ("Science *versus* religion").

(6) Curiosity directed to lust ("peeping Toms").

(7) Curiosity directed to gossip ("Did you hear what Mabel did?").

(8) Curiosity directed to detraction and libel ("Let's get the dirt on this guy").

(9) Curiosity that makes one shameless ("Let's invent new ways to torture people").

(10) Seeking knowledge beyond your capacity ("I've got to figure out the math of the Trinity").

It shouldn't be surprising that there are so many perversions of one good thing. As Chesterton noted, there is one angle at which you stand upright but many different angles at which you can fall.

Is St. Thomas so serious that he ignores or down-plays the need for physical and verbal games?

Augustine says: *I pray thee, spare thyself at times, for it becomes a wise man sometimes to relax the high pressure of his attention to work.* Now this relaxation of the mind from work consists in playful words or deeds. Therefore it becomes a wise and virtuous man to have recourse to such things at times ... the Philosopher assigns to games the virtue of ... *pleasantness.*

Just as man needs bodily rest for the body's refreshment because he cannot always be at work, since his power is finite and equal to a certain fixed amount of labor, so too is it with his soul, whose power is also finite and equal to a fixed amount of work. Consequently when he goes beyond his measure in a certain work, he is oppressed and becomes weary, and all the more since when the soul works, the body is at work likewise, in so far as the intellective soul employs forces that operate through bodily organs.... Now just as weariness of the body is dispelled by resting the body, so weariness of the soul must needs be remedied by resting the soul; and the soul's rest is pleasure. Consequently, the remedy for weariness of soul must needs consist in the application of some pleasure, by slackening the tension of the reason's study. Thus ... it is related of Blessed John the Evangelist that when some people were scandalized on finding him playing together with his disciples, he is said to have told one of them who carried a bow to shoot an arrow. And when the latter had done this several times, he asked him whether he could do it indefinitely, and the man answered that if he continued doing it the bow would break. Whence the Blessed John drew the inference that in like manner man's mind would break if its tension were never relaxed.... [W]herefore Tully says that *when the audience is weary, it will be useful for the speaker to try something novel or amusing* ... (II-II,167,2).

Play is necessary for the intercourse of human life. Now whatever is useful to human intercourse may have a lawful employment ascribed to it. Wherefore the occupation of play-actors, the object of which is to cheer the heart of man, is not unlawful ... (II-II,167,3).

The Philosopher reckons the lack of mirth to be a vice. In human affairs whatever is against reason is a sin. Now it is against reason for a man to be burdensome to others by offering no pleasure to others and by hindering their enjoyment.... Now a man who is without mirth is not only lacking in playful speech but is also burdensome to others, since he is deaf to the ... mirth of others. Consequently they are ... said to be boorish or rude, as the Philosopher states (II-II,167,4).

There are some people who simply do not like jokes, games, or play. These people have suppressed something in their humanity. "Lack of mirth" is "a vice", just as lack of seriousness is.

It is not merely the practical need for relaxation and recreation, which is necessary for the serious work of life (though it is that too). Play and mirth is also "necessary for the intercourse of human life" and "to cheer the heart of man". This is why God invented not just water but also wine (Ps 104:15). They are aids to the works of charity, to making others happier. (Of course this too can be perverted into sinful or fake happiness.)

St. Thomas does not mention this, but jokes also express and produce a kind of insight or wisdom about life that nothing else quite does. Life is many things, but one of them is A Great Joke.

That doesn't mean it's not also serious. The distinction between the humorous and the serious is not absolute. Proof of that is the greatest joke in history, the one God played on the Devil in the Incarnation. (See Ps. 2:4.)

C. S. Lewis says that "Joy is the serious business of Heaven."

If play, games, jokes, and mirth are in themselves good, how can they go bad?

Nevertheless ... the pleasure in question should not be sought in indecent or injurious deeds or words. Wherefore Tully says that *one kind of joke is discourteous, insolent, scandalous, obscene ... just as we do not allow children to enjoy absolute freedom in their games but only that which is consistent with good behavior, so our own fun should reflect something of an upright mind ...*

There may be excess in play through lack of due circumstances, for instance when people make use of fun at undue times or places or out of keeping with the matter at hand ... (II–II,167,3).

Now these things are directed according to the rule of reason, and a habit that operates according to reason is virtue. Therefore there can be a virtue about games. The Philosopher gives it the name of wittiness, and a man is said to be pleasant through having a happy turn of mind, whereby he gives his words and deeds a cheerful turn.... Hence Tully says: *It is indeed lawful to make use of play and fun, but in the same way as we have recourse to sleep and other kinds of rest, and only when we have done our duty by serious matters ...* (II–II,168,2).

Mirth is useful for the sake of the rest and pleasures it affords ... since in human life pleasure and rest are not ... for their own sake but for the sake of operation (action, living).... **Hence the Philosopher says:** *a little sweetness suffices to season life just as a little salt suffices for our meal* (II–II,168,4).

Once again, as with curiosity, St. Thomas lists some of the many ways this intrinsic good can be perverted:

(1) Indecency (jokes that provoke lust or manifest scorn).

(2) Personal injury.

(3) Discourtesy (a vice almost completely forgotten in our barbarian, vulgar culture).

(4) Insolence (sneering).

(5) Scandal (leading others into sin).

(6) Obscenity (it exists, and we still know it even though we rarely admit it).

(7) Excess ("all play and no work").

(8) Impropriety of time (playing when we should be serious or working).

Tully's point that St. Thomas quotes, about playing *after* we've done our serious duty rather than before it, is a very practical one: it makes our play more free and our work less hurried.

The last paragraph is true but only half the truth. Rest exists for work, yes, but work also exists for rest, as war exists for peace. Or perhaps we should say that work exists for the sake of *leisure*. Leisure is not merely rest or lack of work but non-pragmatic activity, what we usually call "culture." (See Josef Pieper's classic *Leisure, the Basis of Culture*.) Prayer, for instance, is not work. This fact is reflected in the "and" that separates the two in the famous Benedictine summary of monastic life: "pray and work" (*ora et labora*).

Here is a virtue that almost *nobody* mentions any more. Isn't it ridiculous to call modesty in dress a virtue, (1) because it's merely external and (2) because it's subject to culturally relative fashion? What's considered modest in one time or place is considered immodest in another.

Whether there can be virtue and vice in connection with outward apparel?

I answer that **It is not in the outward things themselves which man uses that there is vice, but on the part of man who uses them immoderately. This lack of moderation occurs in two ways. First, in comparison with the customs of those among whom one lives ... Secondly, the lack of moderation in the use of these things may arise from the inordinate attachment of the user ... this inordinate attachment occurs ... when a man seeks glory from excessive attention to dress ... Hence Gregory says ...** *No one seeks costly apparel* **(namely such as exceeds his estate)** *save for vainglory....*

Contentedness is the habit that makes a man satisfied with what is suitable and ... becoming in his manner of life **according to the saying of the Apostle, 1 Timothy 6:8:** *Having food and wherewith to be covered, with these let us be content;* **and** *simplicity,* **which excludes excessive solicitude about such things; wherefore he says that** *simplicity is a habit that makes a man contented with what he has....*

(However,) **those who are placed in a position of dignity, or the ministers of the altar, are attired in more costly apparel than others, not for the sake of their own glory but to indicate the excellence of their office or of the divine worship....**

There may (also) **be sin on the part of deficiency, although it is not always a sin to** **wear coarser clothes than other people. For if this be done through ostentation or pride, in order to set oneself above others, it is a sin** (II-II,169,1).

Although St. Thomas mentions both of the two objections listed in the question, he does not mention the thing that we probably think would occur to him first when speaking of "modesty in dress", namely obscenity and provocation to lust. This is not because he minimizes it, but—quite the opposite—because he gives it another whole question to itself (#196). Here he is thinking only of pride and ostentation.

That was much more of a vice in his time, when society was both hierarchical and formal and when one's clothes reflected one's position in the hierarchy. In our egalitarian and informal society, *everyone* wears jeans, Presidential candidates as well as garage mechanics, women as well as men. Only at Hollywood parties or awards ceremonies are they expected to show off ridiculously expensive clothes. And even then it's only women. Men usually wear dull, standard uniforms, exactly reversing the order of nature (look at the birds). Therefore this passage will probably be of much more interest to women than to men.

Vices mentioned here are of two opposite kinds, excess and defect (as usual with vices), though one of these vices is more common than the other (as is also usual). Vices of excess or ostentation include (1) immoderateness, (2) contempt for custom, (3) inordinate affection for clothing, (4) vainglory, and (5) discontent with simplicity. Two vices of deficiency, i.e., motives for wearing clothes that are "too coarse (cheap)", are also mentioned: (1) a lack of pride in and a disrespect for one's office and its proper glory (rather than your own personal glory), and (2) pride in one's humility, "showing off" one's voluntary poverty.

What can this old celibate monk possibly tell us about women's clothing and cosmetics?

As regards the adornment of women, we must bear in mind that ... a woman's apparel may incite men to lust.... Nevertheless a woman may use means to please her husband....

But those women who have no husband nor wish to have one, or who are in a state of life inconsistent with marriage, cannot without sin desire to give lustful pleasure to those men who see them, because this is to incite them to sin..... And the same applies to men in this respect....

Yet in this case some might be excused from sin when they do this not through vanity but on account of some contrary custom, although such a custom is not to be commended....

Objection: Cyprian says: *I hold that not only virgins and widows but also wives and all women without exception should be admonished that nowise should they deface God's work and fabric, the clay He has fashioned, with the aid of yellow pigments, black powders or rouge, or by applying any dye that alters the natural features.... This is an assault on the divine handiwork, a distortion of the truth....*

Reply: Cyprian is speaking of ... a kind of falsification.... Wherefore Augustine says: *To dye oneself with paints in order to have a rosier or a paler complexion is a lying counterfeit. I doubt whether even their husbands are willing to be deceived by it....* It must, however, be observed that it is one thing to counterfeit a beauty one has not, and another to hide a disfigurement arising from some cause ... For this is lawful....

Accordingly, since women may lawfully adorn themselves, whether to maintain the fitness of their estate, or even by adding something thereto, in order to please their husbands, it follows that those who make such means of adornment do not sin in the practice of their art ... (II-II,169,2).

Reason and common sense prevail again (surprise, surprise). Which of the following opinions of St. Thomas is unreasonable?

(1) "A woman's apparel may incite men to lust." (That's precisely their purpose!)

(2) "A woman may use means to please her husband." (On some occasions, sexual desire is deficient rather than excessive and needs to be aroused. No natural passion is of itself always morally good or bad.)

(3) Marriage is the only proper place where this deliberate arousal of erotic desire is right.

(4) "The same applies to men in this respect." (There is no double standard.)

(5) Some do wrong here not deliberately but out of thoughtlessly following bad social customs.

(6) Such customs are bad. (It is social customs and institutions, not only individuals, that are to be judged morally good or bad.)

(7) Cosmetics are not intrinsically wrong. "Women may lawfully adorn themselves."

(8) They are good when they hide disfigurements or ugliness.

(9) They are deceptive when they are "false advertising".

(10) Respect for their social estate (e.g., queenship) justifies special adornments.

(11) The motive of pleasing their husbands does this too.

There is obviously much more to be said today on this subject. But not less.

What can we learn from heretics, liars, and false prophets, theologians, and philosophers? Should we pay them serious attention for any other reason than to refute their errors?

As the good is in relation to things, so is the true in relation to knowledge. Now in things it is impossible to find one that is wholly devoid of good. Wherefore it is also impossible for any knowledge to be wholly false, without some mixture of truth. Hence Bede says that no teaching is so false that it never mingles truth with falsehood. **Hence even the teaching of the demons with which they instruct their prophets contains some truths whereby it is rendered** (apparently) **acceptable. For the intellect is led astray to falsehood by the semblance of truth even as the will is seduced to evil by the semblance of goodness** (II-II,172,6).

A true prophet is always inspired by the Spirit of truth, in Whom there is no falsehood, wherefore he never says what is not true; whereas a false prophet is not always instructed by the spirit of untruth, but sometimes even by the Spirit of truth (II-II,172,6).

Yes, we should often expect to learn important truths from heretics. And the reason is found in the very metaphysical structure of reality. Truth and error, good and evil, are not equal and opposite forces, as Manicheeism and Zoroastrianism claim. Error is perverted truth, evil is perverted good. All that exists is metaphysically true and metaphysically good. So it is always possible to find something true beneath something false, and something good beneath something evil. Even Hitler had a sense of patriotism and honor and courage, however perverted; if not, he could never have succeeded in doing the harm he did. Even Satan had to speak some truth to deceive Eve in Eden. To see that, carefully compare Genesis 3:5 with Genesis 3:22.

Satan used "know" ambiguously, but every ambiguity is a half-truth. The ambiguity was that God "knows" evil as a free and sober man understands an addiction, but man "knows" evil as an addict does.

Poor Satan! Metaphysical necessity requires him to use some truth to persuade us of any error, and some good to tempt us to any evil. Pure truth is possible, but pure falsehood is not. Satan cannot exclude God totally from his false prophets' deceptions and evils, but God can exclude Satan entirely from His prophets, and render them infallible. This is precisely what He does to the magisterium, or teaching authority of His public prophet, His Church.

(God does not grant her *moral* perfection in practice ("indefectibility"), only infallibility in her public, authoritative teachings in theology and morality.)

The practical corollary of this metaphysical principle is (1) the opportunity to learn some truth from every error, however egregious, and (2) the need for discernment and critical thinking ("Test everything, hold fast to that what is good"—1 Thess 5:21).

Obviously, part of this discernment is judging the two parties involved, (1) the party you are listening to and (2) yourself. (1) You should judge how likely it is that you will find something true and profitable in a compromised source. Reading brilliant heretics can be like hunting for treasure in a dump. *Sometimes* it works. (2) You also have to factor in your own maturity and susceptibility to deception. This is why exorcists do not listen to demons during exorcisms.

We can often learn more from false prophets than from true ones. For instance, the difference God makes can sometimes be appreciated better by reading atheists like Nietzsche and Sartre than by dull, safe, conventional religious writings. Especially honest and (therefore) unhappy atheists (real or fictional) like Albert Camus and Samuel Beckett and Ivan Karamazov.

Is divine grace always invisible and inaudible, or does it also sometimes attach to words?

The knowledge a man receives from God cannot be turned to another's profit except by means of speech. And since the Holy Ghost does not fail in anything that pertains to the profit of the Church, He provides also the members of the Church with speech to the effect that a man not only speaks so as to be understood by different people, which pertains to *the gift of tongues* **(or, more exactly, the interpretation of tongues), but also speaks with effect, and this pertains** *the grace of the word.*

This happens in three ways.

First, in order to instruct the intellect, and this is the case when a man speaks so as *to teach.*

Secondly, in order to move the affections ... This is the case when a man speaks so as *to please* **his hearers, not with a view to his own favor but in order to draw them to listen to God's word.**

Thirdly, in order that men may love that which is signified by the word and desire to fulfill it, and this is the case when a man so speaks as to *sway* **his hearers. In order to effect this, the Holy Ghost makes use of the human tongue as of an instrument; but He it is Who prefects the work within. Hence Gregory says:** *Unless the Holy Ghost fill the hearts of the hearers, in vain does the voice of the teacher resound in the ears of the body* **(II-II, 177, 1).**

God created us as psychosomatic unities. Except for miraculous graces, our souls learn only through our bodies and sensory experience, and they communicate what they learn only through bodily and sensory means, usually words. (And, of course, deeds!)

Scripture targets the tongue as the most powerful of all the organs of the body, for evil or for good. (James 3 is a chapter-long essay on this one organ.) Words are weapons, for good or evil.

And God provides good weapons.

St. Thomas here seems to be thinking primarily of spoken words, but what he says applies equally to writing. He divides these graces into (I) the gift of tongues, which is a supernatural "charismatic" gift of the Holy Spirit, and (II) "the grace of the word", which is a natural gift ("gift" and "grace" are almost identical terms) which comes in three forms corresponding to three good purposes of speech: (1) teaching the mind, (2) attracting and pleasing the affections, and (3) moving the will.

When he uses the term "heart", St. Thomas follows scriptural rather than modern usage and usually means something closer to "will" than to "feelings" or "emotions", for emotions fit into his category #2 rather than #3 above. The "heart" is that power whose characteristic act is to love, and St. Thomas defines love as an act of will: to love is to will the good of the other.

Words can influence all three powers of the soul—thinking, feeling, and willing—to either good or evil. Words are most *adequate* to their purpose in category #1, teaching the intellect; but words usually have the most *powerful* effect on the emotions and the will, because we are usually moved more by the emotions and the will than by the intellect.

The practical "bottom line" is this: be careful how you use these powerful weapons! God gave us two eyes and two ears but only one mouth, so that we could see and hear twice as much as we say.

Are there apparent miracles that are not real? Can evil men work apparent miracles? Can they work real miracles?

The Apostle says (1 Cor. 13:2): *If I should have all faith, so that I could remove mountains, and have not charity, I am nothing.* **Now whosoever has not charity is wicked.... Therefore it would seem that even the wicked can work miracles.**

I answer that **Some miracles are not true but imaginary deeds, because they delude man by the appearance of that which is not; while others are true deeds yet they have not the character of a true miracle because they are done by the power of some natural cause....**

True miracles cannot be wrought save by the power of God....

God works them for man's benefit, and this in two ways: in one way for the confirmation of the truth declared, in another way in proof of a person's holiness, which God desires to propose as an example of virtue (II-II, 178, 2).

The answer to the first two questions is yes. The answer to the third question is no.

The cause of a miracle, properly speaking, is not just preternatural (above the normal powers of nature alone) but supernatural and divine.

St. Thomas does not explicitly mention here what demons can do, but elsewhere he says that they can sometimes, by God's permission, perform preternatural deeds, as did the magicians of Pharaoh in response to Moses and Aaron.

However, the powers of Hell are never equal to the powers of Heaven; our imagination is deceived by picturing angels and demons as equal and opposite forces.

St. Thomas here speaks of two kinds of apparent but not real miracles: those that do not really happen at all, but only seem to happen (e.g., hallucinations or tricks), and those that really happen but do not really have a supernatural cause, as they seem to, but some natural cause. These may be either deliberately deceptive, like the words or deeds performed at séances, or simply events that are wrongly attributed to supernatural causes, as comets were to a superstitious age.

Three things distinguish true miracles from apparent miracles. (1) They are done by God, and therefore for man's good. (2) This good may be man's knowledge of the truth (e.g., Eucharistic miracles that show to the senses the true Body and Blood of Christ). (3) Or it may be confirmation of personal holiness (e.g., the miracles wrought by the intercession of holy persons who have died and are to be canonized as saints).

Discerning true miracles can be tricky—for instance, apparitions and private visions. One principle that is very helpful here, as everywhere, is that "you will know them by their fruits" (Mt 7:16). Another is that God has provided us with a Church to investigate and evaluate these things authoritatively. No private revelations, even to canonized saints, are infallible.

How can the contemplative life be the highest life, as classical pre-modern philosophers like Aristotle and Aquinas believe, if contemplation is an act of the intellect, while love is an act of the will, and the love of God is the highest thing? Doesn't Christianity correct that pagan intellectualism?

Gregory says that *the contemplative life is to cling with our whole mind to the love of God and our neighbor, and to desire nothing beside our Creator.* **Now desire and love pertain to the affective or appetitive power. Therefore the contemplative life has also something to do with the affective or appetitive power....**

Theirs is said to be the contemplative life who are chiefly intent on the contemplation of truth. Now intention is an act of the will. Consequently, although the contemplative life, as regards the essence of the action (of contemplation), **pertains to the intellect, as regards the motive cause of the exercise of that action it belongs to the will, which moves all the other powers, even the intellect.... Wherefore Gregory makes the contemplative life to consist in the love of God, inasmuch as through loving God we are aflame to gaze on His beauty.**

And since everyone delights when he obtains what he loves, it follows that the contemplative life terminates in delight (II-II, 180, 1).

The answer to the question is to correct the question: it's not an either/or. It's a both/and. The point of the quotation from St. Gregory the Great is that contemplation is a "clinging" as well as a seeing, and thus an act of the will as well as of the mind. Indeed, it is the will that commands the mind. And what is "clung" to is not merely the understanding of God but "the *love* of God and our neighbor, and to *desire* (i.e., to will) nothing beside our Creator."

In the second paragraph St. Thomas points out that the attention which is an act of the intellect is commanded by the will. He then goes farther and says that Gregory not only makes contemplation

causally dependent on love, as the act of the will, but also "makes the contemplative life to *consist in* the love of God." The "material cause", in the Aristotelian sense, of the contemplative life is the love of God. It is an intrinsic cause. The causality is not from without but from within; the cause does not stand apart from its effect, as a carpenter stands apart from a house.

When St. Thomas says that "we are aflame to gaze on His beauty" in the contemplative life, he mentions all three powers of the soul, including the emotions, which are indicated by "aflame" and "beauty". This is made even clearer by the last sentence, which says that the fruition ("termination") of contemplation is joy ("delight"). So love is (1) the efficient cause, the motive that moves the intellect to contemplate God, (2) the material cause or content of it, what it "consists in", and (3) the final cause, good, goal, end, or purpose of it. Only the formal cause, the intrinsic essence of it, is intellectual.

The contemplative life is not a withdrawal away from the rest of the life of the soul, especially the will and the emotions, but the fulfillment of all three of its powers. The contemplative withdraws from the world in a way but not from his own humanity; indeed, he withdraws from the world precisely in order to enter more deeply and completely into his own humanity.

This is not a description by a scientist who stands outside his subject but a testimony from a great contemplative saint which is corroborated by his experience and by that of all contemplatives.

If contemplation is the highest of joys, and if it is joy that we always seek, even, and especially, when we sin (for if sin did not seem like joy, we'd all be saints), it follows that the contemplation of God is a powerful weapon against sin because of the joy it yields. As St. Thomas says in II-II, 35,4, "man cannot live without joy; that is why one deprived of spiritual joys goes over to carnal pleasures." If you doubt that spiritual joys are greater, it is clear which of the two joys you've missed. Ask anyone who has tasted both and you will always get the same answer. Try it, you'll like it.

Does this principle (the last paragraph of the preceding page) mean that there is a strong and necessary connection between chastity (sexual virtue) and contemplation, and between lust and ignorance? And if so, does this connection work both ways causally? Does chastity foster contemplation and contemplation foster chastity, just as lust fosters ignorance and ignorance of contemplation fosters lust?

Beauty ... consists in a certain clarity and due proportion. Now each of these is found ... in the reason, because both the light that makes beauty seen and the establishing of due proportion among things belonging to reason. Hence since the contemplative life consists in an act of the reason, there is beauty in it by its very nature and essence; wherefore it is written (Wis 8:2) of the contemplation of wisdom: _I became a lover of her beauty_.

On the other hand, beauty is in the moral virtues by participation, in so far as they participate in the order of reason; and especially is it in temperance, which restrains the concupiscences which especially darken the light of reason. Hence it is that the virtue of chastity most of all makes man apt for contemplation, since venereal pleasures most of all weigh the mind down to sensible objects (II-II, 180, 2).

The answer to all of the questions above is yes.

It was Plato who first made the point, in _The Republic_, which all contemplatives after him have corroborated from their own experience, that spiritual beauties and joys are greater than merely physical ones. To argue that the opposite is true does not prove it is; it proves that the arguer has never experienced the higher beauties and joys, that he has not been scientific and gathered all his data.

St. Thomas' focus on "clarity and due proportion" is only a partial and incomplete definition of beauty. But it is a minimum, at least; a necessary, even if not sufficient, cause. And these features of beauty are found more clearly and strongly in "things belonging to reason" (in St. Thomas' ancient, broad meaning of "reason") than in subrational things. From these two premises it necessarily follows that there is more beauty, and thus more joy, in contemplation than in anything less rational. However beautiful the contemplation of a sunset may be, it can't hold a candle to the contemplation of God.

Between the beauty of God and the beauty of physical things lies the beauty of moral virtues, which are rational "by participation" even though not acts of reason directly. A saint is more beautiful than a beauty queen.

Among the moral virtues the one that most clearly possesses and produces the two attributes of beauty that St. Thomas mentions, "clarity and due proportion (order)", is temperance. Correlatively, disordered desires cause not the most joy but the least. The denial of this truth is one of the Devil's most effective lies and one of our most inexcusable stupidities, for it is refuted time after time. Ask any addict.

St. Thomas himself was given a supernatural grace of chastity on the occasion of his total refusal to be tempted by the prostitute inserted into his prison cell by his brothers to deter him from becoming a Dominican monk; and this is surely part of the secret of his incomparably luminous and clear-sighted rationality in every word he ever wrote. Reason and love are friends but reason and lust are enemies.

It should not be necessary to mention this, but please notice that when St. Thomas says that venereal pleasures "weigh the mind down to sensible objects" he is not denying the beauty or power or even the ontological goodness of physical objects or of the pleasure they naturally cause, but merely reminding us of the obvious and embarrassing fact that it is significantly more difficult to think clearly in the bed than in the pew.

Are art and science compatible with the contemplative life, or even part of it? Or do they too "weigh the mind down to sensible objects" and interfere with it?

That which belongs principally to the contemplative life is the contemplation of divine truth.... This contemplation will be perfect in the life to come, when we shall see God face to face, wherefore it will make us perfectly happy; whereas now the contemplation of divine truth is ... *through a glass and in a dark manner* **(1 Cor 13:12). Hence it bestows on us a certain inchoate beatitude, which begins now and will be continued in the life to come (II-II,180,4)....**

The highest degree of contemplation in the present life is that which Paul had in rapture, whereby he was in a middle state between the present life and the life to come (II-II,180,5). (See 2 Cor 12:1–4.)

Since, however, God's effects show us the way to the contemplation of God Himself, according to Romans 1:20, *The invisible things of God ... are clearly seen, being understood by the things that are made,* **it follows that the contemplation of the divine effects also belongs to the contemplative life, inasmuch as man is guided thereby to the knowledge of God (II-II,180,4).**

There are three degrees of contemplation. The highest, most complete degree never happens in this life, even to the greatest mystic, but only in Heaven, where we see God as He truly is, "face to face".

(1) "Face to face" means "person to person". The divine nature has no physical face. However, we will see Christ literally and physically face to face, since His human nature is now eternally united to His divine nature.

(2) A middle state, halfway between natural contemplation and Heavenly contemplation, is the supernatural gift of "rapture", or ecstasy, in which we are literally taken out of ourselves (out of all self-consciousness and out of the natural powers of our minds as well as our bodies) by divine miracle.

There are many remote prefigurings and suggestions of this rapture and ecstasy in many little ways in which we find ourselves wholly self-forgetful, even now. Great natural beauty, art or music, or the beauty of human love can provoke this. St. Thomas would probably classify these under the third and lowest form of contemplation rather than under the "middle state" of "rapture", since they rest on natural and material things; but they are remote prefigurings of Heavenly contemplation, so we might call them a middle state between what he calls the "middle state" and the lowest, commonest state.

Such experiences are never attained by deliberate effort (we have to be "surprised"), and they are always brief, all *too* brief, and suggestive of much, much more. They are like a few tiny drops of a delicious appetizer or apertif to a great meal that we are waiting for. They make us hungrier than ever for the meal, and that is one of the purposes God has in mind in giving us these gifts.

The best examples of this are moral and religious: when we do a deed of great love and sacrifice, sometimes suddenly or surprisingly; or when we give ourselves up entirely to God, heart and soul and mind and strength, during prayer or when participating in the sacraments. Needless to say, even these happen only by divine grace, never by human strength, planning, or control.

(3) The third, lowest, commonest, and most natural mode of contemplation is the understanding of something of God through His creatures—any of His creatures. People who are not "contemplatives" in their state of life (e.g., monks) can do this kind of contemplation too, e.g., when contemplating the beauty and order in nature or the goodness in acts of human charity, or in looking-along rather than just looking-at religious symbols (like icons) or sacraments to the God they symbolize or sacramentalize.

(1) Most people say contemplation does not "turn them on". Is this because they are missing a joy that is available to everyone? If so, what is it in human nature that makes contemplation joyful? Does the joy come from the exercise of the contemplator's power to know, or from the object known?

(2) Why does St. Thomas say this is the highest of joys and delights?

(3) Isn't love more joyful than knowledge?

(4) And if contemplation in this life is so imperfect compared with that in Heaven, how can there be more joy in imperfect knowledge of perfect things (theology) than in perfect knowledge of imperfect things (natural science)?

(1) **There is delight in contemplation ... in two ways. First by reason of the operation itself, because each individual delights in the operation which befits him according to his own nature.... Now contemplation of the truth befits a man according to his nature as a rational animal, the result being that** *all men by nature desire to know,* **so that consequently they delight in the knowledge of truth....**

Secondly, contemplation may be delightful on the part of its object, in so far as one contemplates that which one loves, even as bodily vision gives pleasure not only because to see is pleasurable in itself, but because one sees a person whom one loves. Since, then, the contemplative life consists chiefly in the contemplation of God, of which charity is the motive, it follows that there is delight in the contemplative life not only by reason of the contemplation itself but also by reason of the divine love (which is the object contemplated).

(2) **In both respects** (mentioned in (1) above) **the delight thereof surpasses all human delight, both because spiritual delight is greater than carnal pleasure ... and because the love whereby God is loved out of charity surpasses all love....**

(3) **Although the contemplative life consists chiefly in an act of the intellect, it has its beginning in the appetite** (desire or will), **since it is through charity that one is urged to the contemplation of God. And since the**

end corresponds to the beginning, it follows that the ... end of the contemplative life has its being in the (will, i.e., the rational) **appetite, since one delights in seeing the object loved, and the very delight in the object seen arouses a yet greater love....**

(4) **The contemplation of God in this life is imperfect in comparison with the contemplation in heaven, and in like manner the delight of the wayfarer's contemplation is imperfect as compared with the delight of contemplation in heaven, of which it is written** (Ps 35:9): *Thou shalt make them drink of the torrent of Thy pleasure.* **Yet, though the contemplation of divine things which is to be had by wayfarers is imperfect, it is more delightful than all other contemplation, however perfect, on account of the excellence of that which is contemplated. Hence the Philosopher says: ...** *though we grasp them but feebly, nevertheless so elevating is the knowledge that they give us more delight than any of those things that are round about us* (II–II, 180, 7).

(1) Even contemplating a star gives joy (try it!), simply because it exercises one of the two greatest powers of our human nature (the other being love). But the greater the object contemplated, the greater the joy. Test that too: when you pray, just look at God's light, love, and life (truth, good, and beauty) and look at Him looking at you with love, like two lovers smiling into each other's faces.

(2) If you doubt this, review #200, above.

(3) At their highest, contemplation (of the mind) and love (of the will and emotions) become one. The closer two mountain climbers approach the summit, the nearer they are to each other.

(4) Since we can't have perfect knowledge (science) of perfect things (God), we must choose between less perfect knowledge (faith) of perfect things (God) or more perfect knowledge (science) of imperfect things (nature). We need both, but which is best? Their different values are indicated by their different joys. This choice is perhaps the deepest difference between medieval and modern man.

Why is contemplation higher than action? Isn't action better for most people?

The contemplative life is ... more excellent than the active life, and the Philosopher proves this by eight reasons.

The first is because the contemplative life becomes man according to that which is best in him, namely the intellect, and according to its proper objects, namely things intelligible; whereas the active life is occupied with externals....

The second reason is because the contemplative life can be more continuous, although not as regards the highest degree of contemplation ... wherefore Mary, by whom the contemplative life is signified, is described as *sitting* all the time *at the Lord's feet.*

Thirdly, because the contemplative life is more delightful than the active; wherefore Augustine says that *Martha was troubled, but Mary feasted.*

Fourthly, because in the contemplative life man is more self-sufficient, since he needs fewer things for that purpose; wherefore it was said: *Martha, Martha, thou art careful and art troubled about many things.*

Fifthly, because the contemplative life is loved more for its own sake, while the active life is directed to something else. Hence it is written (Ps 26:4): *One thing have I asked of the Lord, this will I seek after: that I may dwell in the house of the Lord all the days of my life, that I may see the delight of the Lord.*

Sixthly, because the contemplative life consists in leisure and rest, according to Psalm 45:11, *Be still and know that I am God.*

Seventhly, because the contemplative life is according to divine things, whereas active life is according to human things; wherefore Augustine says: *'In the beginning was the Word': to Him was Mary hearkening; 'The Word was made flesh': Him was Martha serving.*

Eighthly, because the contemplative life is according to that which is most proper to man, namely his intellect, whereas in the works of the active life the lower powers also, which are common to us and brutes, have their part....

Our Lord adds a ninth reason (Lk 10:42) when He says: *Mary hath chosen the best part, which shall not be taken away from her,* which words Augustine expounds thus: *Not 'Thou hast chosen badly' but 'She has chosen better.' Why better? Listen: 'because it shall not be taken away from her.' But the burden of necessity shall at length be taken from thee, whereas the sweetness of truth is eternal.*

Yet in a restricted sense and in a particular case one should prefer the active life on account of the needs of the present life. Thus too the Philosopher says: *It is better to be wise than to be rich, yet for one who is in need it is better to be rich....*

Sometimes a man is called away from the contemplative life to the works of the active life on account of some necessity of the present life yet not so as to be compelled to forsake contemplation altogether Hence Augustine says: *The love of truth seeks a holy leisure, the demands of charity undertake an honest toil....* Hence it is clear that when a person is called from the contemplative life to the active life, this is done by way not of subtraction but of addition (II-II,182,1).

"Contemplation" here includes love (see #203, (3)), while "action" means "external action." "The works of love" in external action derive their greatest value from their source and motive, which is always at least implicitly and unconsciously based on the contemplation of God and His nature as love.

As usual, St. Thomas' reasons for his profoundly countercultural and controversial position are irrefutably logical, clear, commonsensical, and conversant with "the other side" of the coin (last two paragraphs). The Christian life is one coin, but contemplation of God, or "the practice of the [personal] presence of God" is its head, or face.

205. Comparing the Merit (Worth) in the Two Lives, Contemplative vs. Active

Even if contemplation is more joyful than action, that does not prove it is more morally meritorious. Isn't it selfish to prefer the cultivation of one's own spiritual joy to the needs of others? It is love, after all, that is the first and greatest commandment. Mustn't "thy will be done" rather than "my intellect be perfected" be our most fundamental desire?

Whether the active life is of greater merit than the contemplative?

That which pertains more directly to the love of God is generically more meritorious than that which pertains directly to the love of our neighbor for God's sake. Now the contemplative life pertains directly and immediately to the love of God.... Wherefore the contemplative life is generically (abstractly, in itself, by its own essential universal nature) **of greater merit than the active life....**

Nevertheless it may happen (concretely, in a given situation, individually) **that one man merits more by the works of the active life than another by the works of the contemplative life. For instance through excess of divine love a man may now and then suffer separation from the sweetness of divine contemplation for the time being, that God's will may be done and for His glory's sake ...** (II-II,182,2).

The story is a common one of the monk rapt in the contemplation of God and interrupted by a beggar at the door. If he does not turn from his contemplative joy and open the door to the beggar, it is not God that he is contemplating, but himself. For the beggar is Christ. If, on the other hand, he does turn from his contemplative joy and open the door to the beggar, his joy is increased, for the same reason: because the beggar is Christ, and Christ loves us and wills for us the greatest joy.

The merit of both contemplation and action comes from charity. The primacy of contemplation does not exclude or contradict the primacy of charity:

It is written (Col 3:14): *Above all things have charity, which is the bond of perfection,* **because it binds, as it were, all the other virtues together in perfect unity.**

A thing is said to be perfect in so far as it attains its proper end, which is the ultimate perfection thereof. Now it is charity that unites us to God, Who is the last end of the human mind, since *he that abideth in charity abideth in God, and God in him* (1 Jn 4:16). **Therefore the perfection of the Christian life consists radically in charity** (II-II,184,1).

The contrast between love and contemplation, and between God and neighbor as the object of these two acts, is a false contrast.

The loving contemplation of God is the greatest joy and has the greatest merit (1) because love is indeed the greatest thing, and the greatest commandment, (2) but love and contemplation imply or include each other. For (2a) we contemplate out of love and we contemplate the God of love. And (2b) loving God and loving neighbor are inseparable. Loving action toward our neighbor can and should be contemplation's own extended hand. We can do the works of Martha in the spirit of Mary.

The last point—uniting Mary and Martha—seems impossible. It's difficult to contemplate God when you have to contemplate a practical business decision, and it's equally difficult to make a practical business decision when you are contemplating God. St. Thomas admits that there are two *different* lives, the active and the contemplative. They may both be good, but they are so different that not only is one better than the other ("Mary has chosen the better") but each one seems to hinder the other.

Whether the contemplative life is hindered by the active life?

Gregory says: *Those who wish to hold the fortress of contemplation must first of all train in the camp of action* (II-II,182,3).

In other words, the contemplative life not only does not exclude, but requires, the active life. For if we have not cultivated the moral virtues, especially the virtue of self-control, in the arena of action (which is the only place the moral virtues can be cultivated), our selfishness and self-indulgence will hinder our contemplation.

Yet it is also true that action and contemplation have different objects and are different psychic states, so that it is impossible or at least difficult to practice both at the same time. St. Thomas, as usual, solves this apparent contradiction with a commonsensical distinction:

I answer that, **The active life may be considered from two points of view. First, as regards the attention to and practice of external works; and thus it is evident that the active life hinders the contemplative life, in so far as it is impossible for one to be busy with external action and at the same time give oneself to divine contemplation. Secondly,** (in contrast,) **active life may be considered as quieting and directing the internal passions of the soul** (by cultivating the moral virtues); **and from this point of view the active life is a help to the contemplative, since the latter is hindered by the inordinateness of the internal passions** (II-II,182,3).

(A consequence of the difference between action and contemplation is that) **He that is prone to yield to his passions on account of his impulse to action is simply more apt for the active life by reason of his restless spirit. Hence Gregory says that** *there be some so restless that when they are free from labor they labor all the more, because the more leisure they have for thought, the worse interior turmoil they have to bear.* **Others, on the contrary, have the mind naturally pure and restful, so that they are apt for contemplation....** (yet) **those who are more adapted to the active life can prepare themselves for the contemplative by the practice of the active life** (II-II,183,4).

Those unfortunate "restless souls" Gregory speaks of here need not be *satisfied* with their aversion to contemplation if, as all the saints say, contemplation is for everyone, even though a life devoted to it most of the time is only for the few. St. Thomas resolved a dispute among the theologians of his time on the issue of whether the contemplative or the active life was the highest by saying that it was the mixed life which was the highest, since that was the life of Christ. That was also St. Benedict's reason for describing the life of the complete monk as *ora et labora*, prayer *and* work.

It is quite in the spirit of St. Thomas to add that there is also a third relationship between action and contemplation, in addition to (1) action preventing contemplation because attention is required for an external work and (2) action preparing for contemplation by the cultivation of the moral virtues which are a precondition for the intellectual virtues; and that is (3) what Brother Lawrence called "the practice of the presence of God" *in* the active life. This is the typically Jesuit spirituality of "seeing God everywhere", especially in others and in your duties. When you go to the Church's rich variety of religious orders and saints for advice about the spiritual life, you always find one emphasis perfecting or adding to another rather than rivaling it.

Can we be perfect in this life?

(Objection:) **The divine law does not prescribe the impossible. Yet it prescribes perfection, according to Matthew 5:48, *Be you ... perfect, as also your heavenly Father is perfect*. Therefore seemingly one can be perfect in this life....**

(Reply:) **We may consider a threefold perfection. One is absolute, and answers to a totality not only on the part of the lover, but also on the part of the object loved, so that God be loved as much as He is lovable. Such perfection as this is not possible to any creature, but is competent to God alone....**

Another perfection answers to an absolute totality (only) **on the part of the lover, so that the affective faculty always actually tends to God as much as it possibly can; and such perfection as this is not possible so long as we are on the way, but we shall have it in heaven.**

The third perfection answers to a totality neither on the part of the object served nor on the part of the lover.... Such perfection as this can be had in this life, and in two ways. First, by the removal from man's affections of all that is contrary to charity, such as mortal sin. Secondly, by the removal from man's affections not only of whatever is contrary to charity but also of whatever hinders the mind's affections from tending wholly to God. (This is rare. However charity is required of all Christians and) **charity is possible apart from this perfection....**

Those who are perfect in this life are (still) **said to *offend in many things* with regard to venial sins ... Now in the love of our neighbor we may observe a ... perfection ... as to the extent of love, through a man loving not only his friends and acquaintances but also strangers and even his enemies.... Secondly as to the intensity of love, which is shown by the things which man despises** (turns from or sacrifices) **for his neighbor's sake, through his despising not only external goods for the sake of his neighbor but also bodily hardships and even death, according to John 15:13, *Greater love than this no man hath, that a man lay down his life for his friends*** (II-II,184,2).

It becomes increasingly clear the more we read St. Thomas how necessary and effective is his method of answering questions by beginning with relevant distinctions.

One meaning of "be you perfect as your heavenly Father is perfect" is unattainable except in Heaven, by a radical transformation of consciousness. But we can and should cultivate here the desire for that Heavenly transformation. As Robert Browning wrote, "A man's reach must exceed his grasp, or what's a Heaven for?"

We cannot aspire to attain Heaven on earth. But the way in which we *can* aspire to be perfect (*perfectum*, "completely made, finished") in this life is to aspire to the freedom from sin and from all impediments to total charity. Except for pre-fallen Adam and Eve and the Blessed Virgin Mary, none of us attains this total freedom from sin in this life. But the *will* to remove all sins and obstacles can be also be perfect in hope and intention even in this life, though not in actuality and in execution. Imperfect charity is still genuine charity. ("Charity is possible apart from this perfection.")

The test of love's intensity is sacrifice. That is why martyrdom is the supreme test of love, for the martyr gives up literally everything for the thing he loves more than life itself. It's not so much how much you give as how much you have left that measures your generosity. Remember the widow's mite (Mk 12:41–44).

("Intensity" of charity here does not mean merely "emotional heat or passion", since that is not charity's essence but only its accident. It means quantity of love, and thus of will, especially the willingness to sacrifice.)

If everything's perfection consists in achieving its own proper form perfectly, and if form is finite and has limits, so as to give the thing its nature and identity, then does this principle apply to love also? Is love to be limited, measured, moderated, and finitized by something?—by anything at all? Or is the perfection of charity beyond measure?

The perfection of charity, in respect of which the Christian life is said to be perfect, consists in our loving God with our whole heart and our neighbor as ourselves.... [T]he love of God and of our neighbor is not commanded according to a measure so that what is in excess of the measure be a matter of counsel (rather than commandment). **This is evident from the very form of the commandment, pointing as it does to perfection, for instance in the words** *Thou shalt love the Lord thy God with thy whole heart,* **since the** *whole* **is the same as** *the perfect....* **The reason for this is that** *the end of the commandment is charity,* **according to the Apostle** (1 Tim 1:5), **and the end is not subject to a measure, but only such things as are directed to the end** (only the means are subject to a measure), **as the Philosopher observes; thus a physician does not measure the amount of his healing, but how much medicine or diet he shall employ for the purpose of healing....**

Augustine says: *Whatever things God commands, for instance, 'Thou shalt not commit adultery,' and whatever are not commanded yet suggested by a special counsel, for instance, 'It is good for a man not to touch a woman,' are then done aright when they are referred to the love of God and of our neighbor for God's sake, both in this world and in the world to come.* Hence the abbot Moses says: *Fastings, watchings, meditating on the Scriptures, penury and loss of all one's wealth, these are not perfection but means to perfection, since not in them does the school of perfection find its end, but through them ... we endeavor to ascend by these steps to the perfection of charity....*

Augustine says: *The perfection of charity is prescribed to man in this life* (even though it is not achieved in this life) *because one runs not right unless one knows whether to run* (II-II,184,3).

Jesus says (Jn 3:34) that God "gives the Spirit without measure". That is the paradigm for charity, and charity is the standard for perfection. We are to give as God gives, "without measure".

The alternative is: "I give you this much of my heart, my love, my life, my time." That is right for other loves, for merely natural loves. That is wrong for the love of God. We are to love our neighbor only "as ourselves", and there is a measure here, for we are finite: we are not to adore or idolize ourselves, but to love ourselves reasonably and according to the finite measure of our human nature. But we are to love God with our "*whole* heart and soul and mind and strength". The central dimension of Christianity is not "classical" but "romantic", not reasonable and limited but wild and unlimited. In every other field perfection is measured by some finite measure; in loving God, it is not. And the reason is that in God loving us it also is not.

This is the absolute end that measures all other things as means. The principle of "the golden mean" applies to means but not to the final end.

And this is not the icing on the cake, so to speak; it is the cake. It is the heart of the Christian life. If you are not a wild and crazy fanatic when it comes to giving yourself to God, you are not practicing the heart of Christianity. (If you are a fanatic about anything else, you are an idolater.)

Human married love is a finite image of this infinite love. Spouses give their whole selves, hearts, and bodies (including their fertility, their children, future as well as present) to each other forever. (That's why contraception is wrong by nature: it's a limit, a "Wait! Hold! No! Not quite! We won't give each other *Everything*!") It is a unique human relationship, the favorite symbol of the mystics; it is the one relationship that comes the closest to the ultimate and eternal relationship with God in Heaven.

209. HOW THE INCARNATION COMPLETES THE PURPOSE OF THE CREATION

Although he clearly labeled this a mere theological opinion or probability (what the Greeks call a "theologoumenon"), St. Thomas thought that if Adam had not fallen Christ would not have become incarnate. (See #211.) If he was wrong in this "theologoumenon," would that have skewered his understanding of the fittingness of the Incarnation? Why didn't it mean that he thought of the Incarnation as a kind of desperate emergency afterthought?

Whether it was fitting that God should become incarnate?

It would seem most fitting that by visible things the invisible things of God should be made known; for to this end was the whole world made, as is clear from the word of the Apostle (Rom 1:20): *For the invisible things of God ... are clearly seen, being understood by the things that are made.* **But, as Damascene says, by the mystery of the Incarnation are made known at once the goodness, the wisdom, the justice, and the power or might of God— His goodness, for He did not despise the weakness of His own handiwork; His justice, since, on man's defeat, He caused the tyrant to be overcome by none other than man, and yet He did not snatch men forcibly from death; His wisdom, for He found a suitable discharge for a most heavy debt; His power or infinite might, for there is nothing greater than for God to become incarnate....**

To each thing, that is befitting which belongs to it by reason of its very nature; thus, to reason befits man since this belongs to him because he is of a rational nature. But the very nature of God is goodness. Hence what belongs to the essence of goodness befits God. But it belongs to the essence of goodness to communicate itself in the highest manner to the creature, and this is brought about chiefly by His *so joining created nature to Himself that one Person is made up of these three, the Word, a soul and flesh,* **as Augustine says. Hence it is manifest that it was fitting that God should become incarnate....**

As Augustine replies, *The Christian doctrine nowhere holds that God was so joined to human flesh as either to desert or lose or to transfer and as it were contract within this frail body, the care of governing the universe.... God is great not in mass, but in might. Hence the greatness of His might feels no straits in narrow surroundings. Nor, if the passing word of a man is heard at once by many, and wholly by each, it is incredible that the abiding Word of God should be everywhere at once* (III,1,1).

The most important event that ever happened was not the creation but the Incarnation, in which divinity and humanity united forever. In fact, St. Thomas says (first sentence) that it was the reason for the creation in the first place! God created matter, as Pope St. John Paul II says in his "Theology of the Body", to make the invisible visible, to express eternal spirit in temporal matter.

What was expressed was His goodness, and, correlatively, His freedom; for ultimate goodness is love, and love is free. Since love's effects resemble their cause, and since love is free, love respects and enhances the freedom of the beloved rather than suppressing it and using force. In St. Thomas' words, "He did not snatch men forcibly from death" but assumed man's nature so that man's sin could be overcome by the free choice of man himself (i.e., by Christ, the new Adam).

What the Incarnation showed about God was simultaneously His goodness, justice, wisdom, and power (see Augustine's quotation above). Notice how many abstract truths (at least four here) can be understood by right reason from a single concrete event! Notice also that "understanding" here is part of "reason", but it is not logical proof, deductive demonstration—a typically modern confusion. As Augustine points out in the last line, it was rationally as well as morally fitting.

The Incarnation was not "necessary" rather than free (see the next quotation); but it was "necessary" in the sense of "needed" and "fitting", not arbitrary. It flowed from and revealed God's essential nature as measurelessly self-giving love (see #208 above).

Most Christian theologians agree that the Incarnation was "fitting". But what does this mean? There seems to be three answers to this question. In "Why God Became Man" St. Anselm tried to show that the Incarnation was "necessary" and therefore could be rationally proved, demonstrated deductively. Other theologians interpret its "fittingness" to mean that it could be understood as good and right and proper afterwards, but that since it was a totally unpredictable free choice of God's will, it was not "rational" or "necessary" in any sense. St. Thomas seems to take a middle position: he says that the Incarnation, like the Trinity, is one of the truths of Faith that cannot be demonstrated by natural reason alone, yet he speaks of its rational and moral "fittingness". Does this mean that he agrees with St. Anselm that it was "necessary"? If so, in what sense?

A thing is said to be necessary for a certain end in two ways. First, when the end cannot be without it, as food is necessary for the preservation of human life. Secondly, when the end is attained better and more conveniently, as a horse is necessary for a journey. In the first way it was not necessary that God should become incarnate for the restoration of human nature. For God of His omnipotent power could have restored human nature in many other ways. But in the second way it was necessary that God should become incarnate for the restoration of human nature. Hence Augustine says: *We shall also show that other ways were not wanting to God, to Whose power all things are equally subject, but that there was not a more fitting way of healing our misery.*

Now this may be viewed with respect to our *furtherance in good.*

First, with regard to faith, which is made more certain by believing God Himself Who speaks; hence Augustine says: *In order that man might journey more trustfully toward the truth, the Truth itself, the Son of God, having assumed human nature, established and founded faith.*

Secondly, with regard to hope, which is thereby greatly strengthened; hence Augustine says: *Nothing was so necessary for raising our hope as to show us how deeply God loved us. And what could afford us a stronger proof of this than that the Son of God should become a partner with us of human nature?*

Thirdly, with regard to charity, which is greatly enkindled by this; hence Augustine says: *What greater cause is there of the Lord's coming than to show God's love for us? ...*

Fourthly, with regard to well-doing, in which He set us an example; hence Augustine says: *Man who might be seen was not to be followed, but God was to be followed Who could not be seen. And therefore God was made man that He ... Whom man might follow might be shown to man.*

Fifthly, with regard to the full participation in the divinity, which is the true bliss of man and the end of human life; and this is bestowed upon us by Christ's humanity; for Augustine says: *God was made man that man might be made God.*

(6) Also was this useful for our *withdrawal from evil....* because we are thereby taught how great is man's dignity, lest we should sully it with sin.... Pope Leo says in a sermon on the Nativity: *Learn, O Christian, thy worth, being made a partner of the divine nature....*

(7) (And also) because *man's pride, which is the greatest stumbling-block to our clinging to God, can be convinced and cured by humility so great,* as Augustine says (III,1,2).

These seven reasons for the "fittingness" of the Incarnation show what St. Thomas means by this category better than the correct but abstract definition in the first paragraph. They are also a good example of that pre-modern notion of "reason" that consists in wisdom rather than proof. It is half-way between rationalism and irrationalism.

Are there any reasons to believe Christ would or would not have become incarnate if man had not sinned? Or, to change the question from a contrary-to-fact conditional to a real possibility, suppose there are rational beings on some other planet (which is *possible*) and suppose they passed the test we failed in Eden, and remained innocent (which is also possible, since free choice follows upon reason); would Christ incarnate Himself in them too? Obviously we do not know, but can we intelligently guess?

Whether, if man had not sinned, God would have become incarnate?

Augustine says, expounding what is set down in Luke 19:10, *For the Son of Man is come to seek and to saved that which was lost:*—*Therefore, if man had not sinned, the Son of Man would not have come. . . .*

I answer that, **There are different opinions about this question. For some say that even if man had not sinned, the Son of Man would have become incarnate.**

Others assert the contrary, and seemingly our assent ought rather to be given to this opinion. For such things as spring from God's will and beyond the creature's due can be made known to us only through being revealed in the sacred Scripture, in which the divine will is made known to us. Hence, since everywhere in the sacred Scripture the sin of the first man is assigned as the reason of the Incarnation, it is more in accordance with this to say that the work of the Incarnation was ordained by God as a remedy for sin, so that had sin not existed, the Incarnation would not have been. For God allows evils to happen in order to bring a greater good therefrom; hence it is written (Rom 5:20): *Where sin abounded, grace did more abound.* **Hence too in the blessing of the Paschal candle we say:** *O happy fault, that merited such and so great a Redeemer!* (III, 1, 3).

And yet the power of God is not limited to this; even had sin not existed, God could have become incarnate. . . .

Even when St. Thomas may be wrong, his principles are right.

Christ came for a purpose: to die for us. This we know. What we do not know is what other purposes may have led Him to come in incarnate form if He had not needed to die.

It is possible that Christ did in fact come in non-incarnate and pre-incarnate forms throughout Old Testament history: in the burning bush; in the three persons who visited Abraham at the oaks of Mamre (they are called "men," "angels", and "lords"); in "the Angel (messenger) of the Lord"; and/or in Melchizedek (see Heb 7:1–10). If so, these may be clues to a second purpose for His coming: not merely to set right sin but also to reveal Himself to man and for intimacy and closer union, which is the aim of love. And that is a purpose that stems from His essential nature.

St. Thomas almost always accepts the opinions of St. Augustine; and Augustine wrote that "if man had not sinned, the Son of Man would not have come." However, the very first thing St. Thomas says in his answer is that "there are different opinions about this question." And the most important point in his answer (which Augustine would certainly agree with) is that we do not know, since such things "spring from God's will and beyond the creature's due (deservingness)" and therefore are "made known to us only through being revealed". St. Thomas modestly keeps the options open, for "the power of God is not limited" and "even had not sin existed, God *could* have become incarnate."

God's Word clearly says that the reason for the actual Incarnation was (a) our sin and (b) God's love and grace, but does not say whether (b) without (a) would have motivated an Incarnation. We know what we know, and we don't know what we don't know. But what we do know about the reason for the Incarnation is a profound and mysterious answer to the "problem of evil": St. Thomas' quote from Romans 5:20. God turned our greatest evil (sin) into the occasion for our greatest good (salvation); in fact He turned the greatest sin ever—deicide—into the very instrument of our greatest good, "Good" Friday.

If other planets contain rational but non-human creatures, could Christ have assumed their nature as well as human nature, whether to redeem them if they fell or for any other reason?

Could Christ have become incarnate on earth more than once? If two species of rational animals had evolved on earth, rather than just one, could Christ have become incarnate in both? Would He then have three natures rather than two, viz. divine, human, and the other rational species? (Such concrete, pointed questions are those that an imaginative, thoughtful child would ask, and they are more typical of medieval theologians than modern theologians, who tend to think in safe abstractions.)

Whether one divine person can assume two human natures?

Whatever the Father can do, that also can the Son do. But after the Incarnation the Father can still assume a human nature distinct from that which the Son has assumed, for in nothing is the power of the Father or the Son lessened by the Incarnation of the Son. Therefore it seems that after the Incarnation the Son can assume another human nature distinct from the one He has assumed....

The power of the divine person is infinite, nor can it be limited by any created thing. Hence it may not be said that a divine person so assumed one human nature as to be unable to assume another (III,3,7).

The short answer is yes, because the power of God is unlimited. God can do anything that is intrinsically possible, i.e., anything that is meaningful, anything that is not self-contradictory.

(A self-contradiction is not anything at all. The omnipotent God cannot make a rock bigger than He can lift because those words "a rock bigger than omnipotence can lift" mean nothing; they are like "a round square". Only one who is weak can make a rock bigger than he can lift, just as only one who is weak can die.)

The Incarnation did not lessen the divine power. Divinity and its attributes, including omnipotence, was not subtracted from the divine nature, but humanity was added to it, by the Incarnation. And the divine nature, with all its powers, is present in all three of the divine Persons. What was set aside in the Incarnation was some of the *operations* of the divine powers by the Second Divine Person. Thus Christ "learned obedience", like any child (Heb 5:8), and He said that even He did not know (while He was on earth) the time the Father has set for the end of the world (Mt 24:36). Yet He performed miracles and said He could call down twelve legions of angels (Mt 26:53).

St. Thomas explains why he does not give a simple "no" answer to the question. It is because "with God all things are possible" (Mt 19:26).

An extraordinarily practical application of this principle of the divine omnipotence is the total trust preached by St. Paul in Romans 8:18–30. If God is (a) all powerful as well as (b) all-good, all-loving and (c) all-wise, then it logically and necessarily follows that "all things work together for good for those who love God" (Rom 8:28).

Meditate often on the divine omnipotence, especially when you deeply feel the pain of the many evils that God wisely and lovingly allows to enter your life. His reason is always love. And He always wins. And He makes no mistakes. We do not see this. Of course not: we are not infinite wisdom. (Stop the presses!)

When we turn to a crucifix and bow and pray, we not only use it to remind us of Christ, but we direct our adoration for Christ to *it*, even though we know it is only made of wood. We adore only Christ, but we honor images of Him with not just human honor, as we would honor a picture of the President, but with divine honor, i.e., with adoration. Is it idolatry to "adore the image" in this sense?

Damascene quotes Basil as saying: *The honor given to an image reaches to the prototype,* **i.e., the exemplar. But the exemplar itself, namely Christ, is to be adored ... therefore also His image.**

As the Philosopher says, there is a twofold movement of the mind towards an image: one indeed towards the image itself as a certain thing; another towards the image in so far as it is the image of something else ... the latter movement, which is towards the image as an image, is one and the same as that which is towards the thing....

As Damascene observes, *It is the highest absurdity and impiety to fashion a figure of what is divine.* **But because in the New Testament God was made man, He can be adored in His corporeal image** (III,25,3).

Protestants who protest the adoration of images usually misunderstand what an image is or does. An image is more than just a picture which functions as a nonverbal *label* for the real thing, like a bar code in a store. Nor is it merely a memory prod, for words can also prod the memory, but no one adores words. It is an image of a real person. Even a Protestant, if he is a romantic lover, will kiss a photo of his beloved. He is not kissing photo ink on paper, he is kissing his beloved.

When we see an image, we experience two acts of the mind, as even "the Philosopher" (Aristotle) noted. (1) We look *at* the image, (2) but we also, and primarily, look *along* it, as we look along a sign. Let's say it is an image of Socrates. (1) When we look at the image, we say "It is wood." We do not seek philosophical wisdom from wood. (2) But when we look along it, we say "It is Socrates", and we seek philosophical wisdom from him. And insofar as the image directs our thoughts to Socrates, we seek philosophical wisdom from the image. Not that we expect wood to talk, of course, but we expect it to direct our attention to Socrates, who did talk, and very wisely. But the Christ we adore via images not only talked but continues to talk to His people through His Spirit.

This natural, secular principle thus applies all the more to supernatural, religious images. When we adore a crucifix, we do not adore the wood, but the Person. For this Person is human as well as divine. He has a body made of atoms, like ours. He bled to death for us, literally. Therefore we can direct our worship not merely to the divine and invisible Person but also to His incarnate human nature. We adore the Body and the Blood because it is the Body and Blood of God.

Jews and Muslims are forbidden to make images of God, and rightly so, since they do not believe in the Incarnation. But ever since the Incarnation, God has become visible to us in human flesh. "God is spirit" (Jn 4:24). But God is also flesh (John 1:14). Thus what is not permitted for a Jew or a Muslim is permitted for a Christian: to have literal, physical images of God. God in fact had (and still has!) a human body and soul. The soul is seen in and through the body, as happiness is seen in a smile, and in the eyes, "the windows of the soul". God has a corporeal shape—it is a human shape, made of flesh and bones, it is male and young and Jewish—and therefore it can be imaged, as the Father cannot, in another corporeal matter (e.g., wood).

If this is not true, the heart and essence of Christianity is a lie: this literal, physical, corporeal man is not God. Thus the issue of "iconoclasm", the issue whether images are to be abolished or used, is central, not peripheral, to Christianity.

Do Catholics worship Mary?

Why is this usually the most passionate objection Protestants have to Catholicism?

The Mother of God is a mere creature. Therefore the worship of *latria* (adoration) is not due to her. Since *latria* is due to God alone, it is not due to a creature.... (Only *veneration* [*dulia*, respect] is due to creatures, even the holiest.)

Though insensible creatures are not capable of being venerated for their own sake, yet the rational creature is capable of being venerated for its own sake. (But) **the worship of *latria* is not due to any mere rational creature for its own sake. Since, therefore, the Blessed Virgin is a mere rational creature, the worship of *latria* is not due to her, but only that of *dulia*; but in a higher degree than to any other creatures, inasmuch as she is the mother of God. For this reason we say that not any kind of *dulia* is due to her, but *hyperdulia* (III,25,5).**

St. Thomas, following the Church, is very clear that worship (adoration, *latria*) should be given to God alone, and not Mary or any other creature.

Veneration (*dulia*) is very different from worship or adoration. Veneration means two things: first the respect due to all persons because they are made in God's image and have intrinsic value (as Kant's famous formula puts it, all persons are ends, not means, and must be treated as such); and second, among human persons some are to be venerated more than others: the good and wise and holy more than the evil and foolish and unholy. The reason the highest degree of veneration is due to Mary is that she was the holiest merely human being who ever lived, the greatest saint.

Because she was the Mother of God, it was very fitting that God did this, i.e., made her the greatest saint. He totally filled her with His grace, as much as a merely human creature could hold. Thus she is "*full* of grace". The angel called her not just "favored" by grace but super-favored (Lk 1:28). That's in the Bible!

All this is very reasonable, and part of unbroken Church tradition. It is not explicitly taught in the Bible, but it is taught implicitly. It is an interpretation of the data in the Bible by the Church Christ authorized to teach in His name and with His authority. There are many other Catholic doctrines and practices that are not explicitly taught in the Bible. Some of them, like the doctrine of the Trinity, Protestants accept, while rejecting others, like Purgatory, which are also based on principles taught in the Bible (that we are sinners; that in Heaven we are perfect; and that there is a very great gap between sin and perfection). But Protestants typically single out the veneration of Mary as the most objectionable one. Why?

I can only confess that this is a great puzzle to me, even though I remember once sharing this prejudice as a Protestant; now, as a Catholic, I simply cannot understand it. Mary is the most beautiful mere creature that God ever made; to exalt her is to exalt her divine Creator, Whose spiritual daughter she was, and to exalt her divine Son Whose human mother she was and Whose humanity she procreated, and to exalt her divine Spouse the Holy Spirit Who conceived Him in her womb. We look at her as the supreme merely human handmaid of the Trinitarian God (Lk 1:38). We look along her at her divine Father, her divine Son, and her divine Husband.

215. RELICS

What justifies the veneration of relics of the saints?

As Augustine says: *If a father's coat or ring, or anything else of that kind, is so much more cherished by his children as love for one's parents is greater, in no way are the bodies themselves to be despised, which are much more intimately and closely united to us than any garment, for they belong to man's very nature.* **It is clear from this that he who has a certain affection for anyone venerates whatever of his is left after his death, not only his body and the parts thereof but even external things such as his clothes and such like. Now it is manifest that we should show honor to the saints of God as being members of Christ, the children and friends of God, and our intercessors. Wherefore in memory of them we ought to honor any relics of theirs in a fitting manner: principally their bodies, which were temples and organs of the Holy Ghost dwelling and operating in them, and are destined to be likened to the body of Christ by the glory of the Resurrection. Hence God Himself fittingly honors such relics by working miracles at their presence....**

Jerome says: *We do not adore, I will not say the relics of the martyrs, but either the sun or the moon or even the angels*—**that is to say with the worship of** *latria*—**but we honor the martyrs' relics, so that thereby we give honor to Him Whose martyrs they are.** *We honor the servants, that the honor shown to them may reflect on their Master* (III,25,6).

The veneration of relics comes neither under *latria* (adoration) nor *dulia* (the kind of veneration due to persons alone); they deserve a lesser veneration but a real one.

The practice of venerating relics of the saints goes back to the earliest Christian times. St. Thomas' first reason justifying it is the analogy with merely human veneration. It is an a fortiori argument: if even the veneration of a beloved father's relics after he dies is a good thing, how much more the veneration of a saint's?

A second reason is that the practice is justified by two things in combination: by (1) the veneration of persons by a motive of love—the more we love someone, the more we venerate him—and by (2) the metaphysical fact that human bodies are not just instruments of persons but the embodiment of persons. What you do to my body, you do to me.

This is true even in the secular world. It is even more true for a Christian, for whom the body while on earth is the temple of the Holy Spirit, and destined to be resurrected and eternalized in Heaven.

This applies to physical possessions like clothes as well as, but to a lesser degree than, actual body parts. The same is true in the secular world: even Protestants who oppose the veneration of relics still venerate the bodies of their beloved dead. They bury them, with great ceremony, and visit and care for their gravesites. And they venerate their possessions and their clothing, but less. (They do not bury these or care for their grave sites.)

Another argument is taken from the miracles God works through the relics of the saints.

Jerome's point is similar to the point about images in #213 above: our love and attention, like a rubber ball, bounces off the image or relic and onto the person. The relic, like the image, is looked-along rather than just looked-at. Thus when we see the King's servant, we see the King. When a Roman soldier saw his commander, he saw Caesar, Lord of the world. (See Mt 8:5–13.)

216. The Immaculate Conception

In St. Thomas' day Mary's Immaculate Conception was a long-believed popular theological opinion, but not yet a Church-defined dogma. Mary had always been venerated as the holiest of creatures, but the dogma that she was conceived in her mother's womb without Original Sin by a miracle of divine grace was not defined until seven centuries after St. Thomas. His opinion was that her holiness was best explained in other ways than that. This opinion was shown to be wrong; but what can we learn from him here?

Nothing is handed down in the canonical Scriptures concerning the sanctification of the Blessed Virgin Mary as to her being sanctified in the womb; indeed, they do not even mention her birth. But as Augustine, in his tractate on the Assumption of the Virgin, argues with reason, since her body was assumed into heaven and yet Scripture does not relate this, so it may be reasonably argued that she was sanctified in the womb. For it is reasonable to believe that she, who brought forth *the only-begotten of the Father, full of grace and truth,* **received greater privileges of grace than all others; hence we read (Lk 1:28) that the angel addressed her in the words:** *Hail, full of grace!* **(III,27,1).**

The angel said to her: *Hail, full of grace* **(Lk 1:28), which words Jerome expounds as follows, in a sermon on the Assumption:** *Full indeed of grace; for to others it is given in portions, whereas on Mary the fullness of grace was showered all at once* **(III,27,5).**

St. Thomas begins by mentioning the fact that Scripture does not mention anything about Mary's birth or conception. This is one of the premises of the Protestant argument against this Catholic doctrine, the other premise being that nothing that is not explicitly taught by the Bible can be an infallible dogma of the Church and divine revelation. But St. Thomas does not accept this second premise. So the first premise alone did not lead to his conclusion that Mary was not immaculately conceived.

Indeed, St. Thomas explicitly contradicts the Protestant principle, as does St. Augustine, who, together with the Church as a whole, believed in Mary's Assumption into Heaven even though that was not mentioned in Scripture either. Both saints also believed, together with the whole Church until the Reformation, that Mary "received greater privileges of grace than all others". For this is indeed taught in the Bible when the angel called her "full of grace". (See St. Thomas' last paragraph.)

So the basic principles behind the dogma of the Immaculate Conception were in place for many centuries before the dogma was defined. The newly defined dogma only explained the old, traditional principles: it explained the *how* and the *why* of Mary's holiness: that it was a miracle of divine grace whereby Christ's merits, which are necessary for every human's salvation, including Mary's, were applied to her in a different way and at a different time in her life than to others: in her mother's womb before she ever sinned, to prevent her from sinning, rather than after sinning. There are two ways to save someone from falling into a pit: before their fall, by preventing it, and after their fall, by getting them out. God saved Mary before she could fall into sin and saved us after we fell into it. But she, like us, needed a Savior.

Did Mary know she was sinless? Wouldn't it make one proud, and thus sinful, to know that?

Whether the Annunciation took place in becoming order?

To a humble mind nothing is more astonishing than to hear its own excellence. Now wonder is most effective in drawing the mind's attention. Therefore the angel, desirous of drawing the Virgin's attention to the hearing of so great a mystery, began by praising her (III,30,4).

Mary was astonished at the angel's praise in hailing her as "full of grace"—not because she doubted angels, grace, or miracles, but because she was humble.

Humility is unaware of its own excellence— not because it is deceived, and has an unrealistically low opinion of itself, but because it does not think about itself and its own degree of excellence at all.

If humility were not self-forgetfulness, any virtuous person would have the practical dilemma of either directing his attention to his own virtue, which naturally leads to pride, or denying it, which would be a lie. Or, to put the same point in a trilemma instead of a dilemma, if we insist on judging ourselves and our level of virtue, we must either (1) think we are very good, and become proud, or (2) think we are very bad, and despair, or (3) think we are average, and be bored and wishy-washy.

The solution is to deny the common assumption of all three, that we must judge ourselves. It is God Who judges all men, both ourselves and our neighbors. (See 1 Cor 4:3.) We are to keep our eyes on Him (and on our neighbors' needs) rather than on ourselves. "Ingrown eyeballs" are a spiritual disease. God made eyes to see everything *but* themselves. (Although we do need occasionally to make an "examination of conscience", mainly to become aware of our sins so that we can confess them and repent of them.)

The very best possible object for our eyes to focus on instead of ourselves is Christ. For Christ is both fully God and fully man. As God, He is total perfection. As man, He is all our neighbors ("As you did it to one of the least of these my brethren, you did it to me"—Mt 25:40). Thus, focusing on Him is the key to obeying the two great commandments. And Mary had Christ to focus on, both physically and spiritually, more totally and intimately than any other human being ever did. He was the key to her humility, and her humility was the key to her sanctity.

Nothing is more practical in the Catholic religion than Mary, because the whole purpose of this religion is what Dietrich von Hildebrand called "Transformation in Christ", and Mary is our most perfect concrete model and heroine for this *summum bonum* ("greatest good"), i.e., for "the meaning of life".

Since St. Thomas did not believe Mary was immaculately conceived without Original Sin, did he believe she was a sinner during her life and committed actual sins, if she had Original Sin? How close did he come to believing what the Church later defined?

Whether by being sanctified in the womb the Blessed Virgin Mary was preserved from all actual sin?

Augustine says: *In the matter of sin, it is my wish to exclude absolutely all questions concerning the holy Virgin Mary on account of the honor due to Christ. For since she conceived and brought forth Him Who most certainly was guilty of no sin, we know that an abundance of grace was given her that she might be in every way the conqueror of sin ...*

We must therefore confess simply that the Blessed Virgin Mary committed no actual sin, neither mortal nor venial, so that what is written (Song 4:7) **is fulfilled:** *Thou art all fair, O my love, and there is not a spot in thee* (III,27,4).

Both St. Augustine and St. Thomas extol Mary above every creature.

When Augustine says he will "exclude absolutely all questions" about Mary, he means all doubts about her perfection. She was "in every way the conqueror of sin", he says. This cannot be said of any other merely human being who ever lived.

St. Thomas' answer to his original question (his first paragraph) is yes. Mary was sinless. The earliest Fathers of the Church called her the "new Eve", meaning a new innocence. Mary never committed any sin throughout her life. St. Thomas is very clear on that. And that was not controversial in his day or in Augustine's.

St. Thomas also believed that Mary was "sanctified in the womb" of her mother. That is in essence the doctrine of the Immaculate Conception, though not in the way the Church formulated it (which was Blessed Duns Scotus' way rather than St. Thomas' way).

The only controversy in St. Thomas' mind about Mary's sinlessness is whether it was because God prevented her from contracting the spiritual disease of Original Sin at the moment of her conception in her mother's womb, or in some other way, some slightly different. He thought that the *explanation* of her sinlessness which later was called the doctrine of the Immaculate Conception was not certain. But the *fact* it explained, the fact of Mary's total sinlessness, the concrete objective reality of Mary as full of grace and unsurpassably beautiful among creatures—this was utterly certain to him.

Theologically stated, the principle is that saints receive *dulia*, Mary receives *hyperdulia*, and God alone receives *latria*. (See #214, above.) *Dulia* is like a high but finite number; *hyperdulia* is like the highest number out of a finite number of finite numbers; *latria* is like infinity.

The practical "payoff" of the dogma of the Immaculate Conception for us is this: the degree of our faith and hope and trust should correspond to the power of grace in the one we pray to. No merely human person deserves more of our trust when we entrust our needs to her in prayer; no one more rewards our hope of receiving divine grace through human intercession; no one deserves more love and awe-filled, joyful wonder; and no one is a more perfect model, than this most beautiful creature ever created, who is Queen of Angels and Queen of Heaven.

What's in a name?

A name should answer to the nature of a thing.... Now the names of individual men are always taken from some property of the men to whom they are given: either in regard to time—thus men are named after the saints on whose feasts they are born— or in respect to some blood relation—thus a son is named after his father or some other relation. And thus the kinsfolk of John the Baptist wished to call him *by his father's name Zachary,* not by the name John, because *there was none of his kindred that was called by this name,* as related in Luke 1:59–61. Or, again, from some occurrence; thus Joseph *called the name of the first-born Manasses, saying: God hath made me to forget all my labors* (Gen 41:51). Or, again, from some quality of the person who receives the name; thus it is written (Gen 25:25) that *he that came forth first was red and hairy like a skin, and his name was called Esau, which is interpreted red.*

But names given to men by God always signify some gratuitous gift bestowed on them by Him; thus it was said to Abraham (Gen 17:5): *Thou shalt be called Abraham because I have made thee a father of many nations;* and it was said to Peter (Mt 16:18): *Thou art Peter, and upon this rock I will build My Church.* Since, therefore, this prerogative of grace was bestowed on the Man Christ that through Him all men might be saved, therefore He was becomingly named Jesus, i.e., Savior, the angel having foretold this name not only to His mother but also to Joseph, who was to be his foster-father....

The name Jesus could be suitable for some other reason to those who lived before Christ—for instance, because they were saviors in a particular and temporal sense. But in the sense of spiritual and universal salvation this name is proper to Christ, and thus it is called a *new name* (III,37,2).

Devotion to the "Holy Name" is devotion to Jesus because the name is not just a label. "In the name of" means "in the real presence and power of". Think of your name signed onto your checks.

"What's in a name?" Everything: reality, identity, and destiny.

Reality is in a name because God, the creator of reality, also names it, and He gives us the right to name the things in nature that He has designed to serve us. Thus Adam named the animals.

Identity is in a name because since God invented us, we have no more identity outside Him than Frodo Baggins has any identity outside Tolkien.

Destiny, because our Author writes the story of our lives. When God changed someone's name in Scripture, He changed their destiny: Abram to Abraham, Jacob to Israel, Simon to Peter.

Names are not arbitrary labels. Names are meanings. We grow into our names, or we fail to grow into them; we live out our names, or we fail to live them out.

Jesus (the name which means "Savior" or "God saves") really *is* the Savior. That is His reality, that is His true identity, and that is His destiny, the reason He came into the world.

Explore your name. It is no accident that you have it. History (His story) has no accidents.

When we name someone, the name should, as St. Thomas says, "answer to the nature of the thing", but sometimes it fails to do that. It can be a wrong name. But when God names someone, it is never a wrong name, because His names, and words, and thoughts do not *correspond* to pre-existing things, as ours do (thus they cannot *fail* to correspond either), but they *create* the things He names. Thus according to the creation story in Genesis He created everything in the world by naming it. ("Let there be ... and it was.")

This applies to both (1) Christ's "old name", the name He had from before the beginning of time, which is the *Logos* or "Word (speech, discourse, language, communication, revelation, expression, truth, mind, thought, reason, wisdom, understanding, plan) of God" and to (2) His "new name", "Jesus", when He became our Savior through His Incarnation, death, and Resurrection.

Why did God arrange for John the Baptist to baptize before Christ came?

And why did Christ want to be baptized by him? It seemed quite right for John to protest, "I need to be baptized by you, and do you come to me?" (Mt 3:14).

It was fitting for John to baptize for four reasons:

First, it was necessary for Christ to be baptized by John in order that He might sanctify Baptism....

Second, that Christ might be manifested ...

Thirdly, that by his baptism he might accustom men to the Baptism of Christ....

Fourthly, that by persuading men to do penance, he might prepare men to receive worthily the Baptism of Christ....

John was not only a prophet but *more than a prophet,* **as stated in Matthew 11:9; for he was the term** (end) **of the Law and the beginning of the Gospel** (III,38,1).

St. Thomas' first point is the most fundamental one. Christ by His Baptism transformed the spiritual power of water in Baptism. John's baptism did not have the power to give grace or salvation; but Baptism into Christ does. (See Mt 3:11, Acts 10:46–48, and 1 Pet 3:21). Christ "sanctified" Baptism when He was baptized: He charged it with the power to actually sanctify, to give "sanctifying grace". Before Christ, the water of Baptism could not give us any new power or righteousness, but could only express our spiritual intention of repentance. But Christ gave the water a new power rather than the water giving Him any new power: the power to communicate His grace, His salvation. He baptized the water rather than the water baptizing Him.

The second reason was to make public and visible an invisible spiritual reality. This is the purpose of all the sacraments. Indeed, it is the fundamental purpose of matter itself. It is why God created matter, most of all the human body, which has the greatest power to make spirit visible. (Thus the philosopher Wittgenstein, asked what a human soul could possibly look like, answered, "Like a human body.")

The third reason was to be a preparation, a kind of fertilizer.

The fourth was to focus on repentance as a necessary part of salvation.

A fifth reason could be given: Baptism signifies death, and thus Christ's death. Going down into the water, which is symbolically the most complete and perfect form of Baptism, signifies death by drowning. Christ would descend first and most completely into death for us, for (1) He suffered the most agonizing death; (2) He truly and literally died physically; (3) He died spiritually in being totally forsaken by His Father, thus experiencing not only the physical agony of being crucified but also the spiritual agony of Hell; (4) He was buried; and (5) He descended into the realm of the dead (1 Pet 3:18–20) to liberate the righteous souls who had been waiting there.

John's privilege among prophets is somewhat analogous to Mary's privilege among women. No prophet is closer to Christ than John. Christ did not call him the greatest of all the prophets and more than a prophet (Mt 11:9) because he was more complete in his eloquence, his wisdom, or even his sanctity, than any other prophet, but because he completed the whole era of prophets, the Old Law, or Old Covenant, in introducing Christ to the world. As Mary's womb gave Christ to the world ontologically, John's baptism gave Christ to the world epistemologically. John was the first of Christ's paparazzi.

Christ was sinless, so He did not need Baptism to wash away His sins, or even to symbolize that. So what did His being baptized by John mean?

Christ was baptized not that He might be cleansed, but that He might cleanse....

First, because, as Ambrose says on Luke 3:21, *Our Lord was baptized ... to cleanse the waters, that, being purified by the flesh of Christ that knew no sin, they might have the virtue* (power) *of Baptism,* and, as Chrysostom says, *that He might bequeath the sanctified waters to those who were to be baptized afterwards.*

Secondly, as Chrysostom says, *although Christ was not a sinner, yet did He take a sinful nature and 'the likeness of sinful flesh.'* Wherefore, *though He needed not Baptism for His own sake, yet carnal nature in others had need thereof.* And, as Gregory Nazianzen says, *Christ was baptized that He might plunge the old Adam entirely in the water.*

Third, He wished to be baptized, as Augustine says, *because He wished to do what He had commanded all to do.* And this is what He means by saying: *So it becometh us to fulfill all justice* (Mt 3:15). For, as Ambrose says, *this is justice: to do first thyself that which thou wishest another to do, and so encourage others by thy example ...* (III,39,1).

As stated above, Christ wished to be baptized in order to consecrate the Baptism wherewith we were to be baptized.... For which reason, when Christ was baptized, heaven was opened.... [T]he entrance to the kingdom was opened to us by the Baptism of Christ ... which entrance had been closed to the first man through sin. Hence, when Christ was baptized the heavens were opened to show that the way to heaven is open to the baptized (III,39,5).

Sacraments derive from their institution the power of conferring grace. Wherefore it seems that a sacrament is then instituted when it receives the power of producing its effect. Now Baptism received this power when Christ was baptized. Consequently Baptism was truly instituted then (III,66,2).

When we are baptized we actually receive the life of God (Lk 3:16; Gal 3:27) and are saved (1 Pet 3:21). A Baptism is infinitely more powerful than a hurricane or a tsunami. We should bring lifeboats and lifejackets to baptisms.

The Devil must have thought to surprise and trick Christ when he tempted Him, as he surprised and tricked Adam and Eve. But Christ must have known the Devil's plot; in fact He must have even planned and willed to be tempted. Why?

Christ wished to be tempted, first, that He might strengthen us against temptations. Hence Gregory says: *It was not unworthy of our Redeemer to wish to be tempted, Who came also to be slain, in order that by His temptations He might conquer our temptations just as by His death He overcame our death.*

Secondly, that we might be warned, so that none, however holy, may think himself or free from temptation....

Thirdly, in order to give us an example: to teach us how to overcome the temptations of the devil....

Fourthly, in order to fill us with confidence in His mercy. Hence it is written (Heb 4:15): *We have not a high priest who cannot have compassion on our infirmities, but one tempted in all things like as we are, without sin* (III,41,1).

The meaning of life is to become a saint. This involves spiritual warfare, struggle against temptation. In our struggle, it is enormously important to know that Christ too was tempted. It's not only that we have a more complete example to follow and to psychologically "identify with" (though it is that too), but also that Christ is actually present in us enduring our temptations, as He suffers in all our sufferings. He is not a deistic, distant God merely encouraging us to climb a mountain on our own power (though He does encourage us); nor does He merely give us some external assistance, like a more experienced mountain climber pulling us up by the hand (though He does that too); but He is actually in us and we in Him, especially because of Baptism and the Eucharist; and therefore He has come down into our very lives, in their deepest depths, even temptation to sin, which is the closest thing to sin itself. He is really present in our temptations.

Thus when Scripture says that "he made him to be sin who knew no sin" (2 Cor 5:21), this refers not only to His being punished for our sins (though that is true too), but this also refers to His assuming all the weaknesses of human flesh, including temptability. His temptations were not play-acting, they were real. In fact, they continue to be real in our temptations, because He is really *in* us and we are really *in* Him. He suffers in us when we suffer, He rejoices in us when we rejoice. If theologians only knew all the levels of meaning of the word "in" in the New Testament, they would understand all the mysteries of theology.

Notice that all four of the reasons St. Thomas gives are divine actions with human effects: strengthening, warning, exemplifying, and encouraging. When God gives us these things, we really have them. They change us. They actually give us new strengths, new fears, new examples, and new confidences. He really *does things to us* when we ask Him and trust Him. As soon as we open our souls, He fills them. The more we open the door of faith, hope, and love to Him, the more He barges in. Be careful what you ask for, because you will probably get it. Prayer is as dangerous a force as there is anywhere in the universe. It is like nuclear power.

The fact that St. Thomas almost always gives more than one reason or argument for his point does not mean that he thinks of his first reason as weak and in need of support from others. It means that he sees that God's providential wisdom and economy are perfect in every way, and therefore in many ways; that they are like music, a harmony rather than a solo, with many resonances and overtones; or like a painting, with many shadows and colors in perfect unity.

Why do the Devil's temptations work so well? You'd think we would be smarter than to fall for his advertisements. We know where they come from and where they lead to. We know, from repeated and uniform experience, that succumbing to sin always produces misery in the end, and that choosing to obey God's will always produces joy. We know that by faith, by reason, and by experience. So why are we so incredibly stupid? Why is the Devil so successful in deceiving us into looking at the fake fat worm on his fishing hook instead of the hook? He must have many clever plays in his playbook.

The devil does not straight away tempt the spiritual man to grave sins, but he begins with lighter sins, so as gradually to lead him to those of greater magnitude....

Thus too did the devil set about the temptation of the first man. For at first he enticed his mind to consent to the eating of the forbidden fruit, saying (Gen 3:1): *Why hath God commanded you that you should not eat of every tree of paradise?* **Secondly he tempted him to vainglory by saying:** *Your eyes shall be opened.* **Thirdly, he led the temptation to the extreme height of pride, saying:** *You shall be as gods, knowing good and evil.* **This same order did he observe in tempting Christ. For at first he tempted Him to that which all men desire, however spiritual they may be— namely, the support of the corporeal nature by food. Secondly, he advanced to ... vainglory. Thirdly, he led the temptation on to ... holding God in contempt....** (Note this order in the three temptations in Mt 4:1–11.)

And Christ resisted these temptations by quoting the authority of the Law, not by enforcing His power, *so as to give more honor to His human nature ... since the foe of the human race was vanquished not as by God but as by man,* **as Pope Leo says** (III,41,4).

St. Thomas' first paragraph identifies one of the Devil's most successful temptation principles as the "frog in the pot" principle: turn up the water temperature so gradually that the frog doesn't notice that he's being boiled. Evil spirits can do this because, being spirits, they look at things in our time from a point of view outside our time, so that they do not have the weakness of impatience as we do. They are dispassionate.

The distinction between mortal and venial sin is necessary but dangerous, because it tempts us to discount the importance of venial sins. Their chief power is their ability to gradually habituate us to the point of mortal sin, which is the greatest danger there is, the only danger there is, ultimately.

St. Thomas' second paragraph identifies another principle demons use in spiritual warfare: multiple attacks, from many directions at once, or with many different weapons at once. Adam in Eden was tempted by mental doubt, by curiosity, by greed, by vainglory, and by pride. Thus the mind, the will, the imagination, and the passions are all attacked.

Our greatest defensive weapon against temptation is Christ, the perfect Word of God in flesh, and His example in quoting the perfect Word of God in print, as St. Thomas notes in his last paragraph. By not using the divine force that He could have used against His temptations (He could have called down "twelve legions of angels"—Mt 26:53), He gave us an example that we could follow. For we do not have the power to call down angels at our will (though God does send them, at His will), but we do have the power to call out in faith to a far greater power, God Himself, Who became man and was tempted like us so that He could be *in* our spiritual warfare, not just *above* it. Of course we should *use* all our powers, of mind and will and imagination, but not *trust* in them, for that is trusting in ourselves. Our most powerful weapon against temptation is not our own power, whether of mind or will or imagination, but our faith—not because of its subject (us) but because of its object (Christ). And that is well within the power of our human nature. In fact, often the weaker we are, if we are humble and honest enough to admit it, the stronger our faith is, because we know it *has* to be, we know we are hopeless by ourselves.

If Christ was the perfect man as well as God, why did so many people hate Him? The whole world conspired to murder Him: the common people, who shouted "Crucify him!" and their leaders, both religious and secular. (The accusation sign on the Cross was written in Hebrew, Latin, and Greek: the three ruling cultures and languages of the time. The whole world crucified Christ.) Were the leaders of the people more evil then and there than they are now and here? If He came back, would we crucify Him again, as in Dostoyevski's parable "The Grand Inquisitor"? Why was He so offensive?

The salvation of the multitude is to be preferred to the peace of any individuals whatsoever. Consequently, when certain ones, by their perverseness, hinder the salvation of the multitude, the preacher and the teacher should not fear to offend those men, in order that he may insure the salvation of the multitude. Now the Scribes and Pharisees and the princes of the Jews were by their malice a considerable hindrance to the salvation of the people.... For which reason our Lord, undeterred by their taking offense, publicly taught the truth which they hated, and condemned their vices....

A man ought so to avoid giving offense as neither by wrong deed or word to be the occasion of anyone's downfall. *But if scandal arise from truth, the scandal should be borne rather than the truth be set aside,* **as Gregory says** (III,42,2).

St. Thomas could easily have added one more point here: that the leaders who conspired to kill Christ were not the only guilty ones, for the masses too let themselves be swept up into their plan to "Crucify Him!" Christ may have offended the leaders the most, but He offended ordinary people too. And He continues to do so, for He is the same "Christ, yesterday and today and forever" (Heb 13:8).

People were not fundamentally different then and there than they are here and now. More of the common people loved Him than hated Him, but there was deep hate and fear too—and there still is. "The powers that be" arranged His murder (for "all power tends to corrupt and absolute power corrupts absolutely"). He did not give offense to these ruling powers just for the sake of giving offense, but for the sake—for the salvation—of the many.

In every culture in history, the saints, who most resemble Christ, give the most offense to all cultures because all cultures, like all individuals, are fallen and sinful, in many different ways. Cultures, like individuals, have their specially cherished sins. Ask which ideas and beliefs, which values and commandments, most offend those people who are not Christ's disciples in our culture, and you will find the central battlefields and flash points of spiritual warfare today. You will also find the battlefields where we should suffer the most hate and rejection, as He did. If you are not giving offense to these people, as He did, you are not doing His work.

These areas vary from one culture to the next. Few non-Christians are offended today by Christ's call to mercy and forgiveness and by His attack on cold-hearted Phariseeism, just as few Jews in Christ's day were offended by Christ's support of sexual purity. No one in ancient Israel defended contraception, abortion, sodomy, or fornication, even though sinners practiced them; just as no one today defends cruelty and lack of personal compassion, even though sinners practice them.

Other cultures have been obsessed with power, or honor, or victory; ours is obsessed with feelings and with sexual "freedom". Therefore the part of the gospel that gives offense to our culture is almost always the sexual morality of 4,000 years of Judaism and 2,000 years of Christianity.

"Offense" means merely making someone angry; "scandal" means spiritual harm to others. If even *scandal* (to a few) is sometimes necessary for the sake of the salvation of the many, as St. Thomas says, how much more is offensiveness often necessary!

But the motive must be love as well as truth. Our marching orders are to always be "speaking the truth in love". It must be truth, not lovelessness, that gives offense.

Whom did St. Thomas admire as the greatest philosopher who ever lived?

It was fitting that Christ should not commit His doctrine to writing ... for the more excellent the teacher, the more excellent should be his manner of teaching. Consequently it was fitting that Christ, as the most excellent of teachers, should adopt that manner of teaching whereby His doctrine is imprinted on the hearts of His hearers; wherefore it is written (Mt 7:29) **that** *He was teaching them as one having authority.* **And so it was that among the Gentiles, Pythagoras and Socrates, who were teachers of great excellence, were unwilling to write anything** (III,42,4).

St. Thomas, like many of his medieval contemporaries, called Aristotle simply "The Philosopher", and he used the fundamental commonsense concepts of Aristotle's logic, physics, metaphysics, anthropology, epistemology, and ethics more than anyone else's (though with important corrections and additions). But there was someone he ranked even higher than Aristotle, at least personally.

· St. Thomas quoted and approved the words of St. Augustine more than those of any other writer outside Scripture (although he corrected a few key Augustinian ideas, especially in epistemology, as Aristotle corrected Plato). But there was someone he ranked even higher than St. Augustine—not in theology, or in technical philosophy, or in personal sanctity, but in "philosophical sanctity", so to speak.

Erasmus, writing three centuries later, voiced this evaluation when he called this philosopher "Saint Socrates".

St. Thomas' ultimate standard for ranking philosophers was the same as his ultimate standard for ranking anything: Jesus Christ. Socrates is ranked highest among the philosophers because of his resemblance to Christ.

The clue that led St. Thomas to this conclusion was not primarily anything in the content of his teaching (which he sometimes explicitly disagreed with, especially the notion that "all evil is due to ignorance") but his method of teaching. Among philosophers Socrates most resembled Christ because alone among philosophical "teachers of great excellence", Socrates wrote nothing. (St. Thomas had to mention Pythagoras too in this regard, but I suspect that was merely an afterthought or a concession.)

St. Thomas says that Christ's manner of teaching without writing anything is more, not less, excellent than the method of other philosophers.

Lao Tzu says the same thing: he wrote his severely laconic masterpiece the *Tao Te Ching* only under duress, when the gatekeeper at the Great Wall would not allow him to pass and exit from the civilized and (he thought) corrupt civilization of China and enter the Mongolian wilderness until he had given his wisdom to the world in writing; so he quickly wrote down 81 amazingly wise, laconic little poems. It begins with "The Way that can be spoken is not the eternal Way." And later, "Those who know, do not say; those who say, do not know." This is close to Socrates' conviction that what is most worth teaching is not teachable (in words).

More important, it is also close to *God's* conviction that made Him express Himself most definitively not in words, not even in the infallible words of His inspired prophets and saints, but in The Word, Who is a Person—both eternally, in the Trinity, and temporally, in the Incarnation.

St. Thomas is careful, however, to sharply distinguish Socrates from Christ in pointing to the heart of the uniqueness and absolute superiority of Christ's teaching method, which was the direct implanting of eternal Truth in the hearts of His disciples. No man could do that, not even Socrates. For what was implanted by Christ was (and is) not just truth in concepts but truth in Person. The eternal Truth that Christ implants in human hearts is not truths *about* God but God Himself.

Many people wonder why God does not perform more miracles, and use power to save us from our problems. The answer to that question hangs on the Cross, refusing to call down the twelve legions of angels that He had at His beck and call. And our being "in" Christ and therefore "in" His work of redemption is our answer to why we too must "fail" and suffer and die like Him: we are participating in His actual work. This is why God does not miraculously rescue us as a *policy* (only as an instructive exception).

But the opposite question is seldom asked: why God performs any miracles at all in our world and through human agencies. The question here is not why there are so few miracles but why there are so many.

God enables man to work miracles for two reasons. First and principally, in confirmation of the doctrine that a man teaches ... so that when a man does works that God alone can do, we may believe that what he says is from God, just as when a man is the bearer of letters sealed with the king's ring it is to be believed that what they contain expresses the king's will.

Secondly, in order to make known God's presence in a man by the grace of the Holy Ghost, so that when a man does the works of God we may believe that God dwells in Him by His grace....

Now both these things were to be made known to men concerning Christ, namely that God dwelt in Him by grace, not of adoption but of union, and that His supernatural doctrine was from God. And therefore it was most fitting that He should work miracles. Wherefore He Himself says (Jn 10:38): *Though you will not believe Me, believe the works;* **and (vs. 36):** *The works which the Father hath given Me to perform ... give testimony to Me....*

Chrysostom says ... that *He worked signs not for the sake of those whom He knew to be hardened, but to amend others....* **Miracles lessen the merit of faith in so far as those are shown to be hard of heart who are unwilling to believe what is proved from the Scriptures unless they are convinced by miracles. Yet it is better for them to be converted to the faith even by miracles than that they should remain altogether in their unbelief** (III,43,1).

The first strategy behind miracles mentioned by St. Thomas is certification, like a king's signet ring, the seal that is unique and proves that the letter is from the king alone. Jesus came into the world not to give mankind miracles but to give them Himself; but He performed miracles that only God could perform (most especially His own Resurrection) to prove His claim that He was not just man but God, so that mankind could believe this almost unbelievable claim.

The second purpose St. Thomas mentions is almost identical to the first: "to make known God's presence". Pope Benedict begins his book on Jesus by asking: What did Jesus give the world? When He left our world, it remained full of war, sin, suffering, disease, and death. The stunningly simple answer is that He gave us God.

St. Thomas then answers a serious objection to miracles: that they "lessen the merit of faith". And they do; for Christ said to "Doubting Thomas", "You have believed because you have seen (My resurrected body), but more blessed are those who have not seen and yet have believed" (Jn 20:29). And his reply to this objection is both very practical and very compassionate. It is that many of us need miracles to persuade us to belief and conversion; that although this weaker kind of belief, the "Doubting Thomas" belief that depends on miracles, has less *merit*, it has more popularity and thus more population. God wants to maximize the population of Heaven. Imperfect belief is at least much better than unbelief. Because God is love and love will stoop to conquer, God will stoop to conquer. We get miracles only because we are so stupid and hard-hearted that we need them.

If you want to know the reason God performs miracles, look into your own foolish heart.

What are we supposed to learn from Christ's miracles?

Our Lord said (Jn 5:36): *The works which the Father hath given Me to perform ... themselves ... give testimony to me....* **The miracles which Christ worked were a sufficient proof of His Godhead in three respects. First, as to the very nature of the works, which surpassed the entire capability of created power and therefore could not be done save by divine power. For this reason the blind man, after his sight had been restored, said** (Jn 9:32,33): *From the beginning of the world it has not been heard that any man hath opened the eyes of one born blind. Unless this man were of God, he could not do anything.*

Secondly, as to the way in which He worked miracles, namely because He worked miracles ... of His own power, and not by praying (petitioning), **as others do....**

Thirdly, from the very fact that He taught that He was God; for unless this were true it would not be confirmed by miracles worked by divine power ... (III,43,4).

The Greek word for "miracle" (*semeion*) means literally "sign". They are meant to be looked-along, not just looked-at.

The main thing these miracles are designed to teach is Christ Himself, His divine identity. They are "sufficient proof of His Godhead".

Lesser minds would leave it at that, but St. Thomas explores three different aspects of this:

(1) The inference that since only the supernatural God had supernatural power that exceeded all the power of nature, and since Christ had this power, that this logically proved that Christ was God;

(2) That His miracles showed not merely that supernatural power was at work from God but that He was the very source of this power, not merely its instrument, as is the case when a man prays to God for a miracle because he cannot perform one himself (e.g., Elijah on Mount Carmel confronting the priests of Baal: 1 Kings 18:20–40).

(3) The clearest and most direct argument of all is not just His deeds as thought-about by our words and thoughts (= points (1) and (2)), but His own words, i.e., the match between His deeds and His words. He *said* He was God, in many ways and at many times in the Gospels. If this was not true, that would make Him either an insane fool, if He believed it, or a blasphemous liar, if He didn't. His miracles, like His holiness, His love, and His wisdom, make it impossible to call Him a lunatic or a liar; therefore we must call Him Lord. This is the "Lord, liar, or lunatic" argument made famous by C. S. Lewis and Josh McDowell. It goes back to St. Thomas, to the early Christian apologists like St. Justin Martyr, and, as St. Thomas shows here, implicitly to Christ Himself.

We can only marvel at the power and completeness of His teaching strategy, and at St. Thomas' penetration into this power and completeness. The argument He gave us for the most important thing in the world (Himself) is also the strongest argument in the world. That was needed because this most important thing in the world is also the most startling thing in the world, and in that sense the hardest thing in the world to believe. You don't need strong arguments or shocking miracles to prove that $1+1=2$.

If the omnipotent God can do anything, couldn't He have arranged for Christ to have saved the world without suffering and dying?

Augustine says: *We assert that the way whereby God deigned to deliver us by the man Jesus Christ, Who is mediator between God and man, is both good and befitting the divine dignity; but let us also show that other possible means were not lacking on God's part, to Whose power all things are equally subordinate* ... **it was possible for God to deliver mankind otherwise than by the Passion of Christ, because** *nothing shall be impossible with God* (Lk 1:37) (III,46,2).

(But) **St. Augustine says:** *There was no other more suitable way of healing our misery than by* **the Passion of Christ....**

In the first place, man knows thereby how much God loves him, and is thereby stirred to love Him in return....

Secondly, because thereby He set us an example of obedience, humility, constancy, justice, and the other virtues displayed in the Passion....

Thirdly, because Christ by His Passion not only delivered man from sin but also merited justifying grace for him and the glory of bliss....

Fourthly, because by this man is all the more bound to refrain from sin, according to 1 Corinthians 6:20: *You are bought with a great price: glorify God in your body.*

Fifthly, because it redounded to man's greater dignity that as man was overcome and deceived by the devil, so also it should be a man that should overthrow the devil ... (III,46,3).

The answer to the original question is certainly yes. "Other possible means were not lacking on God's part." One drop of blood—from Christ's circumcision at the age of eight days—would have been sufficient to purchase all mankind's salvation. Why then did He give us twelve quarts instead of one drop?

The simple and stunning answer, from Monica Miller's book on the movie "The Passion of the Christ", is: Because He had twelve quarts to give.

The strategy of war and of games is to win with the minimum possible expense and sacrifice. Love does not seek the minimum but the maximum. Love seeks what is most "good", "befitting", and "suitable", not just what works most efficiently.

What was added by those twelve quarts of Passion? St. Thomas gives five clear and simple answers. The first is the most important. For Love, which motivated the Passion, always seeks what is best for the beloved; and what is best for us is to love God with *all* our heart and soul and mind and strength. Nothing elicits this more than *being loved* by God with all of *His* heart and soul and mind and strength.

The fact that St. Thomas can find no less than five strong reasons for God's unpredictable and amazing deed shows the profundity and power of divine Providence. There are no less than five, but there are surely many more. There is always *more* rather than less in the divine strategy, which proceeds from the divine wisdom and love, which are infinite. And this example is a little appetizer or foretaste of Heaven, where we will find more love and wisdom in the mind of God every time we explore it, without any limit, end, or boredom, forever. It is, in St. Augustine's words, the "Beauty ancient yet ever new."

Was even the specific mode of Christ's suffering and death—crucifixion, the most agonizing and feared punishment in the world—part of the divine strategy and plan?

It was most fitting that Christ should suffer the death of the cross.

First of all, as an example of virtue. For Augustine thus writes ... *it is part of righteous living not to stand in fear of things which ought not to be feared.... In order, then, that no kind of death should trouble an upright man, the cross of this Man had to be set before him because, among all kinds of death, none was more execrable, more fear-inspiring, than this.*

Secondly, because this kind of death was especially suitable in order to atone for the sin of our first parent, which was the plucking of the apple from the forbidden tree against God's command. And so to atone for that sin it was fitting that Christ should suffer by being fastened to a tree, as if restoring what Adam had purloined....

The third reason is because, as Chrysostom says in a sermon on the Passion, *He suffered upon a high rood and not under a roof in order that the nature of the air might be purified; and the earth felt a like benefit, for it was cleansed by the flowing of the blood from his side....* (This was shown graphically in the movie "The Greatest Story Ever Told" and also in "The Passion of the Christ," in which His blood ran down His legs, down the Cross, over the ground, into the rivulets and rivers and oceans of the whole earth, purifying them.)

The fourth reason is because by dying on it, He prepares for us an ascent into heaven ... Hence it is that He says in John 12:32: *If I be lifted up from the earth, I will draw all things to Myself.*

The fifth reason is because it is befitting the universal salvation of the entire world. Hence Gregory of Nyssa observes that *the shape of the cross, extending out into four extremes from their central point of contact, denote the power and the providence diffused everywhere of Him Who hung upon it.* Chrysostom also says that *upon the cross He dies with outstretched hands in order to draw with one hand the people of old and with the other those who spring from the Gentiles.*

The sixth reason is because ... this kind of death responds to very many figures. For as Augustine says in a sermon on the Passion, an ark of wood preserved the human race from the waters of the deluge; and the exodus of God's people from Egypt, Moses with a rod divided the sea, overthrew Pharoah, and saved the people of God; the same Moses dipped his rod into the water, changing it from bitter to sweet; at the touch of a wooden rod a salutary spring gushed forth from a spiritual rock; likewise, in order to overcome Amalec, Moses stretched forth his arms with rod in hand; lastly, God's law is entrusted to the wooden Ark of the Covenant, all of which are like steps by which we mount to the wood of the cross (III,46,4).

Few modern theologians would dare to be so polyvalent and so specific! St. Thomas finds six simple, clear, specific, beautiful, and inspiring reasons, not just one (and six Biblical examples of the sixth reason!); and surely there are many more, if we had only the eyes of a saint as well as of a theologian.

The sixth reason should inspire all carpenters to new respect for their holy medium.

The fifth reason should inspire all global, cosmopolitan, cross-cultural outreaches, which run the danger of getting lost in thin universal abstractions instead of this most concrete source of unity.

The fourth reason should inspire the dying.

The third reason should inspire all naturalists and ecologists.

The second reason should inspire all grocers, fruit growers, arborists, and herbalists.

The first reason should inspire all warriors (and we are all spiritual warriors) to fearlessness.

What did Christ suffer, actually?

He did endure every human suffering....

First of all, on the part of men: for He endured something from Gentiles and from Jews, from men and from women ... from the rulers, from their servants, and from the mob.... He suffered from friends and acquaintances, as is manifest from Judas betraying and Peter denying Him.

Secondly, the same is evident on the part of the sufferings which a man can endure. For Christ suffered from friends abandoning Him, in His reputation from the blasphemies hurled at Him, in His honor and glory from the mockeries and the insults heaped upon Him; in things, because He was despoiled of His garments; in His soul, from sadness, weariness, and fear; in His body, from wounds and scourgings.

Thirdly, it may be considered with regard to His bodily members. In His head He suffered from the crown of piercing thorns; in His hands and feet from the fastening of the nails; on His face from the blows and spittle; and from the lashes over His entire body.

Moreover, He suffered in all His bodily senses: in touch, by being scourged and nailed; in taste, by being given vinegar and gall to drink; in smell, by being fastened to the gibbet in a place reeking with the stench of corpses, *which is called Calvary*; in hearing, by being tormented with the cries of blasphemers and scorners; in sight, by beholding the tears of His mother and of the disciple whom He loved....

The very least one of Christ's sufferings was sufficient of itself to redeem the human race from all sins; but as to fittingness, it sufficed that He should endure all classes of sufferings (III,46,5).

There is nothing subtle or hidden or difficult to understand here. What can we add?

First, that it is helpful to be very concrete and specific and detailed when meditating on Christ. (St. Ignatius Loyola emphasized this in his *Spiritual Exercises*.) For Christ was very concrete and specific and detailed—like you. We tend to etherealize Him, to keep Him at an unearthly distance, to worship a distant, deistic Savior, or (even worse) an abstraction, a set of "values". Stay grounded. Smell the blood. Watch that painful movie again.

Second, that His love for us is infinite. When He spread His hands out on the Cross, He embraced everything He had created, and said to us: "See? This is how much I love you!" It is not measured, not "rational" (in the small, pragmatic sense of the word). His love is *crazy!* Its reason is nothing higher than itself.

Third, he did this so that when we suffer in any one of these many ways in which He suffered, He is there. He is very specific and concrete: He entered not just into injuries in general but into lacerations and head injuries and painful sights and sounds and even smells. He did not leave anything bereft of His presence. He did not will to be present only in beauty and peace and power and joy, but also in ugliness and horror and weakness and pain, so that we could find Him there too. He did not come only into some kinds of suffering and not others, but into every one, so that we could find him there. He fulfilled the prophecy in Psalm 139:12: "Even the darkness is not dark to you."

His absence turns the most pleasant places in life into Hell. His presence turns the most painful places in life to Heaven. For where He is, is Heaven. Heaven does not define Him, He defines Heaven.

One may suffer in as *many* ways as possible, qualitatively, without suffering as *much* as possible, quantitatively. How did Christ suffer "to the max"?

There was true and sensible pain in the suffering Christ, which is caused by something hurtful to the body; also, there was internal pain....

The death of the crucified is most bitter, because they are pierced in nervous and highly sensitive parts, to wit the hands and feet; moreover, the weight of the suspended body intensifies the agony; and besides this there is the duration of the suffering because they do not die at once like those slain by the sword.

The cause of the interior pain was, first of all, all the sins of the human race, for which He made satisfaction by suffering....

The magnitude of His suffering may be considered, secondly, from the susceptibility of the sufferer as to both soul and body. For His body was endowed with a most perfect constitution, since it was fashioned miraculously by the operation of the Holy Ghost, just as ... other things made by miracles are better than others, as Chrysostom says respecting the wine into which Christ changed the water at the wedding-feast. And consequently, Christ's sense of touch, the sensitiveness of which is the reason for our feeling pain, was most acute. His soul likewise, from its interior powers, apprehended most vehemently all the causes of sadness....

Christ grieved not only over the loss of His own bodily life, but also over the sins of all others. And this grief in Christ surpassed all grief of every contrite heart, both because it flowed from a greater wisdom and charity, by which the pang of contrition is intensified, and because He grieved at the one time for all sins (III,46,6).

This latter pain was probably what caused Him such agony in the Garden of Gethsemane that He sweat blood (Lk 22:44): He saw all the sins of the world, and all the people who would reject Him despite all His sufferings, and *their* eternal sufferings in Hell. Love suffers far more for the pains of the beloved than for its own pains.

Death by crucifixion is the most painful death mankind could possibly invent (that was its point, its deliberate purpose). St. Thomas gives three very specific reasons for that unique painfulness of crucifixion in his second paragraph. He is not an "absent-minded professor"; he is shockingly concrete.

Christ's body was also uniquely sensitive to these pains because he was the most perfect, and therefore the most sensitive and vulnerable, man who ever lived, both in body and soul. One proof of this is from Chrysostom: what God does is perfect, and Christ's body is perfect because it is made by God, by the Virgin Birth; God the Holy Spirit, not Joseph, was the Father of His body as well as His soul. Similarly the tastiest wine ever tasted on earth was no wine ever made by man but the wine Christ made at the wedding feast in Cana. Christ's body was perfect in all aspects, including His senses, including the sense of touch. Perfection in the sense of touch means sensitivity, and sensitivity means sensitivity to pleasure and pain, and therefore it means sensitivity to pain.

His internal pain was also unparalleled because He felt the weight of all the sins ever committed, as the reason for His pain and the spiritual cause of His pain. The more a parent loves a child, the more pained he or she is by the child's sins, for sins are always self-harms, little soul-suicides. No love feels no pain, a little love feels a little pain, great love feels great pain, infinite love feels infinite pain.

Was there a reason why Christ died so young, at thirty-three? Was that accidental?

Christ willed to suffer while yet young for three reasons. First of all, to commend the more His love by giving up His life for us when He was in His most perfect state of life. Secondly, because it was not becoming for Him to show any decay of nature nor to be subject to disease.... Thirdly, that by dying and rising at an early age Christ might exhibit beforehand in His own person the future condition of those who rise again (III,46,9).

Nothing in God's world is an accident and random from the viewpoint of the divine Author, although some things are accidental rather than essential to other things. In a work of art there is a reason for everything, and everything is a work of divine art.

St. Thomas discovers three of these reasons. (There are usually more than one in the divine economy. In fact, there are always more than we discover: "There are more things in heaven and earth than are dreamed of in your philosophy, Horatio.")

(1) To give Himself maximally, He gave Himself when He was in the best state of life, with the most power and freedom to give, so that there would be the most human value in both the subject (the Giver) and the object (the Gift), as compared with, e.g., infancy, childhood, or decrepitude. He always gives maximally, not minimally.

(2) His soul so ruled His body that He never fell into disease, although the Gospels say He did get tired and hungry. He was "like us in all things except sin" (Heb 4:15). He assumed "flesh", i.e., fallen, mortal human nature, not human nature with perfect preternatural gifts such as it was in unfallen Adam. But it was perfect flesh. The lambs and oxen that were sacrificed in the Old Testament as a foreshadowing and symbol of Christ, Who was the only perfect offering, had to be perfect and "without blemish" (Ex 12:5; 1 Pet 1:19). Once again, He is a maximalist, not a minimalist.

(3) In the resurrection every one of the blessed in Heaven will have a perfect body. ("Perfect" does not mean "identical", of course; individuality will be preserved and enhanced, not abolished or diminished.) St. Thomas opined that this perfection means that our resurrection bodies will be like the body of a thirty-three-year-old, since thirty-three is the time of perfect maturity without the beginning of decrepitude. He realized, of course, that years are not measured in Heaven, so he knew that his number was symbolic rather than literal.

All that we know about our future bodies, we know through Christ's Resurrection. He showed us not only perfect God but also perfect Man, and He showed us a full, concrete example of perfect Man in His own resurrected self. That is the glory that awaits us. C. S. Lewis writes that "these small, perishable bodies are given to us as ponies are given to schoolboys. We must learn to manage—not that we may be free from bodies altogether but that we may be trained to ride those stallions which await us even now, impatiently neighing in the King's stables" (*Miracles*).

How is the place as well as the time of Christ's death and resurrection significant?

Christ died most appropriately in Jerusalem. First of all, because Jerusalem was God's chosen place of the offering of sacrifices to Himself; and these figurative sacrifices fore-shadowed Christ's Passion, which is the true sacrifice.... [T]o Jerusalem He came five days before the Pasch, just as, according to the legal precept, the Paschal lamb was led to the place of immolation five days before the Pasch, which is the tenth day of the moon.

Secondly, because the virtue of His Passion was to be spread over the whole world, He wished to suffer in the center of the habitable world, that is, in Jerusalem ... which is called *the navel of the earth* **(III,46,10).**

Once again, we find that in God's providential plan nothing is accidental, that everything is perfect, and that God's gift of Himself is maximal.

Christ fulfilled everything in Judaism, the one and only directly and divinely revealed religion in the world, including the place of His death and Resurrection. Jerusalem was the divinely appointed site of the one and only Temple at which all the sacrifices commanded by God in Leviticus were offered. All of them without exception in some way pointed to Christ as their fulfillment. No detail is accidental, not even the numbers of days, as St. Thomas mentions. Christ fulfills *everything*: "Behold, I make all things new" (Rev 21:5).

Second, not only is Jerusalem the center of Judaism but it is also the center of the world, and Christ came not only for the Chosen People, but also for all their students, for He chose them to teach the whole world. Jerusalem is the spiritual center not only of Judaism but of the world

because the world's Creator lived and died there; but it is also in a real sense the literal, physical, geographical center of the world, exactly at the crossroads of East and West, North and South geographically, culturally and historically, then as now. All three continents of the Old World touch and meet there: Asia, Europe, and Africa. World events still center there today. If there is to be a global nuclear war, very likely it will be provoked by Israel's enemies' envy of the existence of Israel and especially of Jerusalem.

Many different ancient tribal peoples, by themselves and independently, conceived the idea that their central place of worship, wherever it was, was at "the navel of the earth", the center of all things. Once this place is (supposedly) discovered, they erect their tent there, sticking its central pole into the very navel of the earth, literally as well as symbolically, so that they can move around it and do everything that they do in relation to it as the Absolute, as the whole solar system moves around the Sun (or around the earth, according to the old geocentric model).

And it was not only the *center* but the "*navel*", i.e., the birth-center, the center of new life, new birth (Cf. Jn 3:3). Pagan religions too have a prophetic and apocalyptic dimension.

Thus Christ fulfilled not only the authoritative Jewish prophecies but also the confused but profound dreams of pagan religions, which He had whispered into their imaginations and hearts, which Jungians call the "collective unconscious". (How significantly similar they are throughout place and time!) That is why He commanded His gospel to be preached in concentric circles, first in Jerusalem, then in all Judea and Samaria, and then to the ends of the earth (Acts 1:8). He was harvesting His seeds.

What is the significance of the two thieves who were crucified with Christ?

Pope Leo observes: *Two thieves were crucified, one on His right hand and one on His left, to set forth by the very appearance of the gibbet that separation of all men which shall be made in His hour of judgment.* **And Augustine on John 7:36 says:** *The very cross, if thou mark it well, was a judgment-seat; for the judge being set in the midst, the one* (thief) *who believed was delivered, the other who mocked Him was condemned* (III,46,11).

Another example of divine providence. Non-miraculous as well as miraculous events are "signs" to be read. The literal and the symbolic are not mutually exclusive categories. In God's world everything has significance, i.e., is a sign as well as a thing. St. Thomas, unlike ourselves, has not lost the art of sign-reading. (Cf. ST I,1,10 on the fact that things are signs being the basis for symbolic interpretations of Scripture.)

The most obvious significance of the two thieves is the two ways of life (Psalm 1), leading to salvation and damnation, Heaven and Hell; the free will we all have to choose between them; and the wonderful and terrifying responsibility this gives us. Even the atheist Samuel Beckett saw this. In *Waiting for Godot* he has one of his hopeless characters see hope there: "One of the thieves was saved ."

Going deeper into this sign, we find Christ at the center. He is the great divider ("I have not come to bring peace but a sword"—Mt 10:34) both of men and of ages. He divides history into B.C. and A.D., splitting time in two as an axe splits a coconut.

As Augustine saw, there is irony here too, for the One Who is dying because He was judged by men to be guilty is really the Judge of all men. Christ pointed out this irony to Pilate in John 19:10–11. His position as Judge of all men is shown even physically, by his being in the center between the two thieves, like the king at the Last Judgment who has the sheep on His right and the goats on His left (Mt 25:32). Jesus is not to the right or to the left of either thief; one is to *His* right and the other is to His left. (Perhaps that can apply even to politics!)

Does this mean that the most decisive question in the world is what we think of Christ? Almost but not quite. The most decisive question in the world is what He thinks of us.

It is that same reversal of perspective that is the key to the "solution" to the so-called "problem of evil" at the end of the Book of Job. (See Job 38:1–4.)

God is not passive, but "pure act". We cannot change Him, He changes us. And suffering is a change. Therefore it seems that God cannot suffer. God is also immortal and cannot die, yet Christ is God, and Christ suffered and died. Is this not a contradiction and therefore impossible?

The union of the human nature with the divine was effected in the Person ... yet observing the distinction of natures; so that it is the same Person ... while each nature retains that which is proper to it. And therefore, the Passion is to be attributed to the suppositum (Person) **of the divine nature** (i.e., the single divine Person Who has a divine nature as well as a human nature) **not because of the divine nature, which is impassible** (i.e., the divine nature cannot suffer, because it is not passive, vulnerable, and changeable) **but by reason of the human nature. Hence in ... Cyril we read:** *If any man does not confess that the Word of God suffered in the flesh and was crucified in the flesh, let him be anathema.* **Therefore Christ's Passion belongs to the suppositum of the divine nature** (the single Person Who possessed the divine nature as well as the human nature) **by reason of the passible** (human) **nature assumed.... As is said in ... the Council of Ephesus,** *Christ's death being ... God's death ... destroyed death, since He Who suffered was both God and man* (III,46,12).

The Second Person of the divine Trinity is one Person, but by the Incarnation this one Person has two natures, divine and human, and thus can be both impassible (not passive, not changeable) and passible (changeable). That is not a contradiction. Even you, though you are only one person and have only one nature (human), have opposite attributes: you are invisible, immaterial, and immortal because your soul is invisible, immaterial, and immortal, but you are also visible, material, and mortal because your body is visible, material, and mortal. The same person—you—is both visible and invisible. This is a paradox but not a contradiction. A paradox is only an apparent contradiction. A real contradiction is impossible. It is unthinkable. It is meaningless. It is nothing. It would be a contradiction to say that God did become incarnate and that God did not, or to say that you had an immortal soul and that you did not. But to say that the same person has two opposite attributes, like us, or even two opposite natures, like Christ, is not a contradiction, even though it is a paradox. It is possible. "With God all things are possible" (Mt 19:26). Contradictions are not things at all.

Since Christ is a divine person, His divine impassibility acts on and changes His human passibility rather than vice versa. Just as when Christ was baptized, it was He Who changed the water (giving it the power to give new spiritual life in Baptism) rather than the water that changed Him (see #221 above), so when He suffered and died, He changed suffering and death rather than suffering and death changing Him. His death was active, not passive. He entered death, and conquered it. Death did not enter Him and conquer Him.

St. Thomas explains how this is metaphysically possible by referring to the Church's infallible Christological creedal formulations about the relationship between His single divine *Person* and his two *natures,* human as well as divine. The categories that the Church uses to express this divine mystery are only human, rational, philosophical categories, but they are the best we have and the most commonsensical, once they are understood.

Bottom line: Christ, the single divine Person, really suffered and died, because He really had a human nature. He lacked nothing we had. He was "in *all* things like us, except for sin" (Heb 4:15). He was not a puppeteer and His humanity was not a puppet. He came all the way down so that we could be lifted all the way up.

If Christ's death was not imposed upon Him but freely chosen, why wasn't it suicide?

He says Himself (Jn 10:18): *No man taketh My life from Me, but I lay it down of Myself....*

A thing may cause an effect in two ways. In the first way by acting directly so as to produce the effect; and in this way it was Christ's persecutors who slew Him.... In another way someone causes an effect indirectly, that is, by not preventing it when he can do so.... For He could have prevented His Passion and death.... Therefore, since Christ ... willed His corporeal nature to succumb to such injury, He is said to have laid down His life, or to have died voluntarily (III,47,1).

We can understand martyrs best by looking at the supreme martyr, Christ. The same answer to our question about Christ must apply to all martyrs.

Like the suicide, the martyr freely offers his life. Yet martyrdom is not only not the same as suicide, it is the polar opposite of suicide, since the suicide loves nothing in life enough to keep living, while the martyr loves something so much that he gives up everything for it, even life. The suicide sees less value and meaning in life than anyone else, while the martyr sees more.

Christ freely *offers* His life. It was not an accident, or a "tragedy". He did what we do in the Mass.

But it was not a suicide (and neither is any martyrdom) because, as St. Thomas explains, this offering is not the direct efficient cause, the necessary-and-sufficient cause, of His death. The people who shouted "Crucify Him!" and Judas and Pilate and Caiaphas and Herod and the Roman soldiers were the direct cause of His death, both physically, by nailing Him to the Cross, and legally, by setting in motion the legal and military forces to kill Him, and also spiritually and morally, by wanting Christ dead rather than alive.

A second, and morally different, way of bringing about an effect is not to stop it. God does not (usually) miraculously stop evil from happening, either physical evil or moral evil, by interfering with physical laws or with human free will. His providence allows evil so as to bring about a greater good by it—but indirectly, not directly.

This is morally different from directly causing evil, as choosing to endure, tolerate, or suffer the lesser evil is morally different from choosing to *commit* an evil, even a lesser one. We should never do anything that is intrinsically evil, and we never need to choose to do so; but sometimes we need to choose to endure or suffer an evil, when it is a question of suffering a greater or a lesser one, e.g., choosing to endure painful side effects of chemotherapy in order to save one's life from cancer, or choosing not to criminalize many private moral evils, such as alcoholism or sodomy, because to do so would require the greater evil of tyranny and totalitarianism.

A concrete example of this allowing evil for a greater good can be found in *The Lord of the Rings*. Sauron, the Satan figure, is allowed to fight the last battle, in fact "egged on" to do so, by the warriors of the Fellowship; and his very force is used against him, as in judo, by distracting him from his true peril, Frodo's mission of destruction of the Ring of Power. As in judo, the enemy's own force is made to recoil against him. This is what God providentially did with Judas and the others who directly killed Christ. God is the great judo master.

Thus the martyr, like Christ, actively chooses to endure death (which is caused by others, not self-inflicted) when he could prevent it. Christ could have prevented His death, but that would have made void the whole purpose of the adventure of His Incarnation; and the early Christian martyrs could have avoided death by blaspheming, apostasizing, and worshipping the emperor, but that would have made void the whole purpose of their adventure of faith.

Was Christ's death a free choice of His own, or was it an obedience to His Father's will?

If the answer is that it was both, why do we tend to contrast free choice and obedience if obedience is an act of free choice?

It is written (Phil 2:8): *He became obedient to the Father unto death.*

It was befitting that Christ should suffer out of obedience. First of all, because it was in keeping with human justification that *as by the disobedience of one man many were made sinners, so also by the obedience of one many shall be made just*, as is written in Romans 5:19.

Secondly, it was suitable for reconciling man with God; hence it is written (Eph. 5:2): *He delivered Himself for us an oblation and a sacrifice to God for an odor of sweetness.* Now obedience is preferred to all sacrifices, according to 1 Kings 15:22: *Obedience is better than sacrifices.* Therefore it was fitting that the sacrifice of Christ's Passion and death should proceed from obedience.

Thirdly, it was in keeping with His victory whereby He triumphed over death and its author, because a soldier cannot conquer unless he obey his captain. And so the Man-Christ secured the victory through being obedient to God.... Christ received a command from the Father to suffer. For it is written (Jn 10:18): *I have power to lay down My life, and I have power to take it up again ... this commandment have I received of My Father*—namely, of laying down His life and of resuming it again....

Objection: **Charity is a more excellent virtue than obedience. But we read that Christ suffered out of charity, according to Ephesians 5:2: *Walk in love, as Christ also has loved us and delivered Himself up for us.* Therefore Christ's Passion ought to be ascribed rather to charity than to obedience.**

Reply: **For the same reason Christ suffered out of charity and out of obedience, because He (1) fulfilled even the precepts of charity out of obedience only, and (2) was obedient out of love to the Father's command** (III,47,2).

St. Thomas' last paragraph answers the question about free choice and obedience. The subjective, personal motive for the external act of obedience can be love (charity), and love is always free. The fact that we usually take as our model for obedience the servile submission of a slave to a tyrant rather than the trusting surrender to a lover says more about the subjective effects of our fallenness upon our unconscious minds than it does about the objective nature of love and obedience.

The value of obedience depends on the nature of the person and the commands obeyed. When that person is God, the value of obedience is absolute. Thus "Thy will be done" is the essential formula for obedience *and* for charity, for "God *is* charity." That is also the whole meaning of life in one sentence. The meaning of life = sanctity = "Thy will be done" = charity. It's so simple that it's hard.

When I was about ten years old, the Holy Spirit put into my mind the most brilliant idea I ever had in my life. I asked my father, "Dad, all the stuff we learn in church—it's all only one thing, right?" "Just one thing? What do you mean?" he asked, suspiciously. "I mean, all we have to do, about *everything*, is just ask Jesus what *He* wants us to do and then do it, right?" I will never forget his surprised look of approval. It's all been pretty much downhill from there, I think.

Notice how St. Thomas connects these two in the last paragraph: obedience motivates love and love motivates obedience. Like acorns and oaks, each grows from and into the other. It's an intrinsic cause-effect relation. The reason why "obedience is better than sacrifice" is that obedience is the interior reason and motivating cause for sacrifice. In turn, love is the reason and motivating cause for interior obedience, as well as for the exterior obedience of sacrifices. Motives can be arranged in a causal hierarchy just as physical events can. Let God's love be the First Cause of everything in you.

Christ's death saved us; but how? What did He save us from? What did He save us for? Obviously, from sin and for Heaven; but how does this work?

The Apostle says in Hebrews 10:19: *We have confidence in the entering in to the Holies*—that is, of the heavenly places—*through the blood of Christ.*

The shutting of the gate is the obstacle which hinders men from entering in. But it is on account of sin that men were prevented from entering into the heavenly kingdom, since, according to Isaiah 35:8: *It shall be called the holy way, and the unclean shall not pass over it.* **Now there is a twofold sin which prevents men from entering into the kingdom of heaven. The first is common to the whole race, for it is our first parents' sin, and by that sin heaven's entrance is closed to man. Hence we read in Genesis 3:24 that after our first parents' sin God** *placed ... cherubim and a flaming sword, turning every way, to keep the way of the tree of life.* **The other is the personal sin of each one of us, committed by our personal act.**

Now by Christ's Passion we have been delivered not only from the common sin of the whole human race, both as to its guilt and as to the debt of punishment, for which He paid the penalty on our behalf, but furthermore from the personal sins of individuals, who share in His Passion by faith and charity and the sacraments of faith (III,49,5).

The ideas of Heaven as a place, of sin as a door or gate that is shut, and of ourselves as outside that door, are all material analogies or images of spiritual truths. They enable these invisible truths to enter our visible imagination, as meaningful analogies, signs, images, or pointers.

One of the best images for God and for goodness is light. It was the very first thing God created, and God created the whole material universe to make visible to us some of the truths, some of the realities, that are in Him. Sin prevents us from

entering Heaven because sin is a kind of darkness. It is anti-God and anti-light. No darkness can enter Heaven because Heaven is defined by God, not God by Heaven, and "God is light, and in Him is no darkness at all" (1 Jn 1:5).

Sin is of two kinds: in our nature and in our choices, in what we are and what we do, Original Sin and actual sins. The first is involuntary. We are born with it. We can call it Original Selfishness. Its cause was the first actual sin of our first parents, Adam and Eve. It was like a disease that spread by heredity, for heredity is not just biological but also spiritual, since souls and bodies are not related as two separate things, like a captain and a ship, but like two inseparable aspects of one thing, like the meaning and the words of a book. A baby can be born addicted to drugs, through no fault of its own, if its mother freely chose to take drugs during her pregnancy. We are born addicted to sin because Adam and Eve trusted the Devil instead of God. The Devil is a drug dealer, and the drug he sells is selfishness and mistrust.

The second kind of sin, "actual sin", is voluntary. We will it, we choose to sin. We are not personally, individually responsible for our Original Sin, as a brain-damaged baby is not responsible for his brain damage, but we are responsible for our own actual sins, as a drug addict is responsible for the brain damage he inflicts upon himself by taking drugs. And we are born addicted (to sin) because Adam and Eve bought the Devil's drug.

Christ saves us from both kinds of sin by "incorporating" us *into* His passion and death. We are not punished for another's sin; we sinned "in" Adam. And we are saved "in" Christ, by "incorporation", not by education; by "This is My Body", not by "This is My Mind." It's all in that little word "in".

Both kinds of sin are anti-God. Both are separations from God, like locked doors. Both are darknesses. These are two of many natural images Christ uses for this supernatural mystery: "I am the light of the world" (Jn 8:12) and "I am the door" (Jn 10:9). No image or concept exhausts the mystery.

How was Christ's Resurrection a necessary part of our salvation? Wasn't His death enough?

It behooved Christ to rise again, for five reasons.

First of all, for the commendation of divine justice, to which it belongs to exalt them who humble themselves for God's sake, according to Luke 1:52: *He hath put down the mighty from their seat and hath exalted the lowly.* **Consequently, because Christ humbled Himself even to the death of the Cross, from love and obedience to God, it behooved Him to be uplifted by God to a glorious resurrection** ...

Secondly, for our instruction in the faith, since our belief in Christ's Godhead is confirmed by His rising again....

Thirdly, for the raising of our hope, since through seeing Christ, Who is our Head, rise again, we hope that we likewise shall rise again....

Fourthly, to set in order the lives of the faithful, according to Romans 6:4: *As Christ is risen from the dead by the glory of the Father, so we also may walk in newness of life*; **and further on,** *Christ rising from the dead dieth now no more; so do you also reckon that you are dead to sin but alive to God.*

Fifthly, in order to complete the work of our salvation. For just as He endured evil things in dying so that He might deliver us from evil, so was He glorified in rising again in order to advance us toward good things ... (III,53,1).

It is very clear from Scripture that Christ's Resurrection is absolutely necessary. "If Christ has not been raised, then our preaching is in vain and your faith is in vain ... and you are still in your sins. Then those also who have fallen asleep in Christ have perished. If for this life only we have hoped in Christ, we are of all men most to be pitied" (1 Cor 15:14–19). But why?

St. Thomas, as usual, gives more reasons than one. (For there usually *are* more reasons than one in God's infinitely commodious mind. He is always *more.* Cf. Ps 139:1–6, 17–18.)

First, because Christ rose, justice, not injustice, has the last word.

Second, because Christ rose, our faith is based on solid literal fact.

Third, because Christ rose, our hope is stronger than death.

Fourth, because Christ rose, He can now act in our souls and make us saints. We can't do that ourselves! (Put straps under your boots and then try pulling yourself up by your own bootstraps.) It's not just that "Christ rose" (past tense) but that "Christ is risen" (present tense). The practical point about the Resurrection is that He's alive and acting right now. Imagine seeing what you took to be a stuffed animal in a museum come alive and charge at you.

(The reason He's charging at you like a lion is not to eat you but so that you can eat Him.)

Fifth, because Christ rose, the work of our salvation is a full story, not just half a story: the comedy as well as the tragedy, light as well as darkness.

The reason you can't be saved without the Resurrection is that you can't be saved by a dead Savior. Corpses and memories don't act. Corpses may scare you, but that's all in your imagination. Memories may inspire you, but that's all in your own mind. Christ doesn't come to you from your own mind and imagination; He comes to you from *His.*

When we go to Church, there should be warning signs posted, and sudden shouts: "Look out! He's alive!"

I once heard a holy priest say that every time he prays "Thy will be done" and remembers the Resurrection, he ducks.

Why did Christ rise when He did? Is there some significance to the number three?

If He had risen directly after death, it might seem that His death was not genuine, and consequently neither would His Resurrection be true. But to establish the truth of Christ's death it was enough for His rising to be deferred until the third day, for within that time some signs of life always appear in one who appears to be dead whereas he is alive.

Furthermore, by His rising on the third day, the perfection of the number *three* is commended, which is *the number of everything*, as having *beginning, middle, and end....* Again, in the mystical sense we are taught that Christ *by His one death* (i.e., that of the body), which was light by reason of His righteousness, *destroyed our two deaths* (i.e., of soul and body), which are as darkness on account of sin; consequently He remained in death for one day and two nights, as Augustine observes.

And thereby is also signified that a third epoch began with the Resurrection. For the first was before the Law, the second under the Law, and the third under grace.

Moreover the third state of the saints began with the Resurrection of Christ, for the first was under figures of the Law, the second under the truth of faith, while the third will be in the eternity of glory, which Christ inaugurated by rising again (III,53,2).

There were both literal, physical reasons and symbolic, spiritual reasons for Christ choosing to rise on the third day. (He *chose* this: He is the *Logos*, the eternal Mind of God, Who planned everything, with His Father and Their Spirit. No Person of the Trinity ever acts alone.) The literal and the symbolic are not alternatives with God, as they often are with us: see ST I,I,10, where St. Thomas gives us the basis, in the very nature and activity of God, for this principle of hermeneutics (interpretation). The basis for the oneness of literal and symbolic is ultimately Christ Himself, for He is both the perfect, complete symbol, the *Logos* or "Word" of God, and the perfect, complete fact, God Himself (Jn 1:1).

St. Thomas actually mentions *three* reasons: one biological, one symbolic, and one historical, for Christ rising on the third day. The first reason is to give us just enough time to refute the skeptical objection to the Resurrection that would attempt to explain it medically, by something like a cataleptic fit. An earlier resurrection might cast doubt upon the death. A later one would not be necessary, for three days is quite sufficient. Cell decay, and its smell, are quite evident by then.

Christ, like St. Thomas, is very practical! E.g., when He raised Jairus' daughter (Lk 8:41–42, 49–56), He had to remind the amazed onlookers to give her something to eat. In contrast, Peter's mother-in-law, also miraculously healed, herself plunged into the practical task of "serving" (Lk 4:38–39). Women are more practical about such things than men. Christ, Who invented both, has all the perfections of both.

St. Thomas' numerology, in his second reason, should be seen as playful rather than demonstrative—playful on God's part as well as St. Thomas'. Why should *we* be able to find more meanings in numbers than God does? Even here, we have multiple meanings, as in other symbolisms, rather than only one correct one, as in allegory, and as there is only one correct answer to a mathematical equation. We are not in the realm of equations here. Equations are in the realm of reasoning and proof. Here we are in the realm of contemplation and artistic appreciation of analogies. It is the realm of play.

Obviously the primary symbolic meaning of the number three is the Trinity. Threeness goes all the way up into ultimate reality, as equally does Oneness. (A typical divine both/and to surprise and transcend our human either/ors.)

It also suggests a number of different ways of classifying human history into three eras from God's point of view (which is, of course, the primary point of view!): (1) before the Mosaic Law, (2) the era of Law, and (3) the era of Grace; or, alternatively, (1) Law, (2) Grace, and (3) Heavenly glory. Once again, it is both/and rather than either/or: both schemas are true and useful. Symbols are not exclusive.

If Christ was perfect man and rose in a perfect body, why did His scars remain? ("Doubting Thomas" was invited to touch them: Jn 20:24–29.)

It was fitting for Christ's soul at His Resurrection to resume the body with its scars ... for Christ's own glory. For Bede says on Luke 24:40 that He kept His scars not from inability to heal them but *to wear them as an everlasting trophy of His victory.* **Hence Augustine says:** *Perhaps in that kingdom we shall see on the bodies of the martyrs the traces of the wounds which they bore for Christ's name: because it will not be a deformity, but a dignity in them; and a certain kind of beauty will shine in them* (III,54,4).

The scars of the martyrs are like Purple Hearts, or Congressional Medals of Honor.

There are numerous examples of saints and mystics, in many different eras of church history, who have had visions of the blessed in Heaven. When these blessed saints were martyrs, their scars were still visible. (I do not know whether St. Thomas knew of such cases or not. I suspect he did.)

Why do they keep their scars? Because Jesus did. But why did He keep His scars? Because they are now beautiful, not ugly, like the Passion itself. Christ transformed the meaning of suffering.

Only love can do that.

Let us dare to ask what is the ultimate meaning of our scars, our sufferings, both physical and emotional, when we suffer in union with Christ and offer up all our sufferings to Him, including our death, which seems to be the ultimate, the total loss. The answer is that they are the ultimate glory and victory. They are like His death: great evil transformed into great good. The greatest evil in the history of the world, the brutal murder of God incarnate, is what Christians call "*Good* Friday": our salvation.

This paradox will be true of all martyrs, even little martyrs. All Christians are little martyrs. Whatever was true of Christ's Resurrection body will be true of ours as well, including the signs of suffering love. I suspect Mother Teresa will have her wrinkles as well as her twinkles. For some of the very things which seem in this world to be the most terrible and ugly will be seen in Heaven to be the most beautiful, because they contained the most love. Already we anticipate this Heavenly transformation when we cover crosses with gold and make them into beautiful icons. Think of what the sight of crosses meant to those who lived under the Romans, who used this instrument of exquisite torture to terrify and intimidate the population.

The body shows forth the soul. It is always the soul that experiences the suffering, even if the injuries are bodily injuries. (Corpses cannot suffer.) The transformation of Christ's bodily scars into badges of glory shows us what happens, *even in this life*, to our souls when we lovingly and trustingly offer our sufferings to Christ and unite them to His. He turns "deformity" into "dignity".

The true meaning of "death with dignity"— the slogan that advocates of "mercy killing" often use to mean "death without suffering"—is "death with Christ". Suffering is not undignified! For the Lord of the Universe, God Himself, embraced it to its depths. In the movie *The Passion of the Christ*, on the road to crucifixion Christ literally embraced His cross like a child hugging a teddy bear—not because He was a masochist but because the Cross was the skeleton key that opened the doors to eternal bliss for all of His beloved children.

In his autobiography *A Severe Mercy*, Sheldon Vanauken relates how his recently deceased wife Davy appeared to him with a cheerful and peaceful face but with the same dark circles under her eyes that had been the results of the disease that had killed her. But she had offered up her sufferings and death to Christ for her husband; and Christ gave him a glimpse of the dark glory. When Sheldon asked her about them, she did not explain but just smiled, and sparkled. (Read the book! But have a handkerchief at hand. Tears are guaranteed.)

Why was it good for us that Christ left us and ascended back to Heaven?

Although Christ's bodily presence was withdrawn from the faithful by the Ascension, still the presence of His Godhead is ever with the faithful, as He Himself says (Mt 28:20): *Behold, I am with you all days, even to the consummation of the world.* **For** *by ascending into heaven He did not abandon those whom He adopted,* **as Pope Leo says. But Christ's Ascension into Heaven, whereby He withdrew His bodily presence from us, was more profitable for us than His bodily presence would have been.**

First of all, in order to increase our faith, which is of things unseen....

Secondly, to uplift our hope: hence He says in John 14:3: *If I shall go and prepare a place for you, I will come again and will take you to Myself, that where I am you also may be.* **For by placing in heaven the human nature which He assumed, Christ gave us the hope of going thither....**

Thirdly, in order to direct the fervor of our charity to heavenly things. Hence the Apostle says in Colossians 3:1–2: *Seek the things that are above, where Christ is sitting at the right hand of God. Mind the things that are above, not the things that are upon the earth;* **for as is said (Matt. 6:21):** *Where thy treasure is, there is thy heart also.* **And since the Holy Ghost is love drawing us up to heavenly things, therefore our Lord said to His disciples** (Jn 16:7): *It is expedient to you that I go; for if I go not, the Paraclete will not come to you; but if I go, I will send Him to you* (III,57,1).

He did not leave us when He ascended. He is present. In fact He is *more* present. For He is love, and what love seeks is always maximum presence, intimacy, closeness, union. And the presence of the Holy Spirit is even more intimate, more interior, than the physical presence of Christ when He was on earth. It was the third and consummating stage in Divine Love's journey toward His goal of intimacy with us:

(1) All ancient peoples had gods. But no Gentile god was even remotely as present to, as intimate with, and as active in the lives of his people as the God of the Jews. No other people knew the wondrous intimacy of the covenant, which was like a spiritual marriage; and therefore no other people knew the intolerable burden of sin, which was like a divorce. If you do not know how great marriage is, you cannot know how terrible divorce is.

(2) But God was even more intimately present by the Incarnation. He became not just God above us but God beside us, not just our Father but our Brother.

(3) Even this was not intimate enough. Therefore He sent His Spirit to haunt our souls. The God Who is transcendent, the God above us and *outside* us, first became God *beside* us, God-with-us (the meaning of "Emmanuel"), and then became God *inside* us, by sending the Holy Spirit so that He could be with us "from the inside out" as well as from the outside in. The three eras of divine revelation are three stages of intimacy, because God is love and love seeks ever more intimacy.

St. Thomas gives three reasons why this is best for us. They correspond to faith, hope, and love. First, His spiritual and invisible presence requires more faith than physical, visible presence did; and faith is intimacy because it is trust.

Second, the withdrawal of His physical presence also elicits our hope, for He went away to prepare our Heavenly mansions for us. (He is Heaven's interior decorator.) Our spirit is where He is more than where we are. ("This world is not my home, I'm just a-passin' through.") In this world we are all like E.T.—aliens. When we pray, we "phone home". We all unconsciously recognize ourselves in E.T.; that is the hidden reason why we love that movie so much.

Finally, since "where your treasure is, there will your heart (love) be also" (Lk 12:34), we now love Heaven more than earth because our Beloved is there. The Holy Spirit is the very energy of love that draws our hearts to Christ's Heaven because He draws our hearts to Heaven's Christ.

There are three properties of a sacrament according to the Church's classic definition: a sacrament is "instituted by Christ", "gives grace", and "effects what it signifies". What does the Eucharist signify?

In the Sacrament of the Altar, two things are signified, viz. Christ's true Body and Christ's mystical body....

A sacrament properly speaking is that which is ordained to signify our sanctification.

In which three things may be considered, viz. the very cause of our sanctification, which is Christ's passion; the form (essence) of our sanctification, which is grace and the virtues; and the ultimate end of our sanctification, which is eternal life. And all these are signified by the sacraments. Consequently a sacrament is a sign that is both (1) a reminder of the past, i.e., the passion of Christ; and (2) an indication of that which is effected in us by Christ's passion, i.e., grace; and (3) a prognostic, that is, a foretelling of future glory (III,60,3).

As usual, St. Thomas' answer is bigger than ours.

In modern Catholic theology there has been a dispute, or at least a tension, among sacramental theologians, between the "conservatives", who emphasize St. Thomas' first answer—that the Eucharist points to the Real Presence, to "Christ's true (literal) Body"—and the "liberals", who emphasize St. Thomas' second answer—that the Eucharist points to the "Mystical Body", the Church, "the People of God". This tension is analogous to the one among Biblical scholars between the "conservatives", who emphasize the literal, historical meaning of passages, especially those that narrate miracles, and the "liberals", who emphasize symbolic or "spiritual" meanings. Just as St. Thomas' answer to that hermeneutical

question was a both/and rather than an either/or (ST I,1,10), so here.

St. Augustine says: "By receiving the (sacramental) Body of Christ, we become the (mystical) Body of Christ." This is how we are saved: "He who eats this bread will live forever" (cf. Jn 6:51).

We are not saved by reading and trying to live the Sermon on the Mount, i.e., by *imitation*, as the Modernist moralists say. God gave us not just words but The Word; not just a philosopher but a martyr; not just His mind but His Body.

Nor did He save us by legal fiat, as Lutheran theology says (the "forensic" theory of justification). God is a Father, not a lawyer. He saved us by making us His children, by becoming our Father, by incorporating us into His family, the Mystical Body of Christ. And we enter that family by receiving Baptism and the Eucharist in faith. In other words, we enter into the Mystical Body by means of Christ's true sacramental Body, the Body that died on the Cross for our salvation. That very Body enters into our bodies and our souls by our receiving the Eucharist in faith. (If we receive without faith, He does not enter into our souls, only our bodies; and that is sacrilege.) For the Eucharist not only symbolizes Christ, it *is* Christ.

Thus it fulfills the third part of the definition of a sacrament: it signifies what it does, namely sanctification, Christification, transformation into Christ.

St. Thomas then finds three inseparable but distinguishable aspects of this sanctification: its origin, or efficient cause (the passion and death of Christ), its essential nature, or formal cause (grace, the very life of God), and its end, or final cause (our eternal life). Thus what is signified is both past, present, and future.

(Incidentally, see how natural and necessary, how useful and commonsensical Aristotle's "four causes" are.)

Why must sacraments be visible and material rather than invisible and spiritual?

Sensible (sensory, visible, material) **things are required for the sacraments.**

Divine wisdom provides for each thing according to its mode.... Now it is part of man's nature to acquire knowledge of the intelligible from the sensible. But a sign is that by means of which one attains to the knowledge of something else. Consequently, since the sacred things which are signified by the sacraments are the spiritual and intelligible goods by means of which man is sanctified, it follows that the sacramental signs consist in sensible things.... [H]ence it is that sensible things are required for the sacraments (III,60,4).

The answer to the question is very simple: because *we* are visible and material creatures. The sacraments are for us, provided for us by divine Wisdom, which "provides for each thing according to its mode (nature)". God gives to His angels light (His mind), to His animals food, and to us sacraments.

For we are not pure spirits who happen to be trapped in bodies. We are not even spirits who only *have* bodies, for we do not have bodies as we have possessions. We *are* bodies as well as souls. We can't take our body off as we can take our clothes off. Between our death and the resurrection of the body we are incomplete, like a program stored in a computer or like music on a sheet of paper, or like a poem in the poet's mind.

("Souls" are not the same as "spirits", though both are something other than bodies. A soul is a spirit that is the life of a physical body. Angels are spirits but not souls, because they have no bodies. Animals are not spirits; they have living souls but not rational souls, not intellectual and moral souls, because they are not spiritual beings. They are only biological beings, angels are only spiritual beings, and we are both. A spirit is intellectual and moral, i.e., an intellect and will. Animals have non-intellectual and non-moral souls, which are the life of their bodies; angels are spirits but not souls, since they have no bodies; and we have both intellectual and moral souls and physical bodies.)

Because we have bodies as well as intellects, our intellects acquire truth through the experiences of our body and its senses. These sensations are *signs* of intelligible truths. A sign is not itself the truth known by the mind, but points to it, directs the mind to it. For instance, an image is a sign. The image of a star twinkling in earth's atmosphere is a sign that there is a real star far above the atmosphere. The image of a human body reflected in a mirror is a sign that a real human being, body and soul, is there. The image or figure of a triangle drawn on paper is not a triangle but only a sign of a triangle, since a triangle is composed of three one-dimensional lines, whereas all the lines that we draw on paper are visible and therefore two-dimensional, not one-dimensional. Angels understand trigonometry without any such physical signs.

"Sensible things are required for the sacraments" because sensible things are required for all human knowledge. Without sensible images to begin with, we could know nothing.

In a broad sense, all the miracles God performed to reveal His supernatural power, justice, wisdom, and mercy, are sacramental signs. In a narrower sense, Christ instituted seven special sacramental signs to communicate divine grace directly to the faithful, and these are "*the* seven sacraments of the Church". They are to the soul what food is to the body.

In the Old Testament, prophets, priests and kings were the three holy offices instituted by God for His chosen people. When Christ came, the separate class of prophets ended (John the Baptist was the last), and so did the temple liturgies of animal sacrifice (after the temple was destroyed in A.D. 70), and so did the elaborate laws of the political system God set up in Leviticus, all for the same reason: they all pointed forward to Him and He fulfilled them all. Since sacraments also all point to Christ, why did they not cease too when Christ came? (Indeed, some Protestants argue that they should.)

Whether there was need for any sacraments after Christ came?

Objection: **It seems that there was no need for any sacraments after Christ came. For the figure should cease with the advent of the truth. But** *grace and truth came by Jesus Christ* **(Jn 1:17). Since, therefore, the sacraments are signs or figures of the truth, it seems that there was no need for any sacraments after Christ's Passion.**

Reply: **As Dionysius says, the state of the New Law is between the state of the Old Law, whose figures are fulfilled in the New, and the state of glory, in which all truth will be openly and perfectly revealed. Wherefore then there will be no sacraments. But now, so long as we know** *through a glass in a dark manner* **(1 Cor 13:12), we need sensible signs in order to reach spiritual things; and this is the province of the sacraments** (III,61,4).

Christ came, and Christ is not incomplete, but His coming was, for it needs to be supplemented and fulfilled by His "Second Coming" at the end of time. There is indeed a radical difference between the age of the Old Law and the age of the New Law of the gospel; but there is also a radical difference between this second age, the age of the New Law, and the third and final age, the age of eternal Heavenly glory. In one sense Heavenly glory has already come to earth, for Christ is the essence of Heavenly glory. But in another sense Heavenly glory still awaits. We're not in Heaven yet!

Sacraments are for this "between" time, as extensions of the Incarnation, to channel the life of Christ to us, to leap the 2000 year gap in time between us and Christ, to bring us to Christ and Christ to us.

This is the age of the gospel, of the Incarnation, of the Church and her sacraments, of the Mystical Body of Christ; and it is far more glorious than the age of the Mosaic Law, which in turn was far more glorious than the age between the Fall and God's visible chosen people, His revelation to Abraham and Moses. The age of glory will be far more glorious than even this age. In fact, the excess of the glory of the age of glory over the glory of the age of the gospel will be even greater than the excess of the glory of the age of the gospel over the glory of the age of the Old Law. The excess is itself exceeded exponentially. To use a mathematical analogy, think of the age of paganism as 3, the age of the Old Law as 9, the age of the gospel as 81, and the age of glory as 6,561.

The whole truth came with Christ. But though the One Who came is complete, and there is no more in God than there is in Christ (Col 1:19), yet the mode of His coming to us is not complete. We live in the "already and not yet". He is completely present but we are not; we can meet Him fully face to face only after we have full faces. He is completely present but we have not yet completely assimilated Him, for we now see Him "through a glass, darkly", through sensible signs. That is why we need sacraments.

In glory we will all be mystics. We will see Him face to face. Incredible as it sounds, His Word tells us that "we will know even as we are known," we will know Him as He knows us (1 Cor 13:12), since we will participate in His knowing, in His very subjectivity. Here, we know Him as personal object of our subjectivity, and this knowing is limited by our human nature. We must not be so proud or impatient as to quarrel with our need for sacraments. The only way to grow is to kneel.

The essential Protestant objection to the Catholic theology of the sacraments is this: How can material sacraments cause spiritual grace? The effect seems greater than the cause.

Sacraments are sacred signs. Signs are symbols, which are formal causes. But to say that the sacraments actually give grace makes them efficient causes. Is this not a confusion between two different kinds of causality? Is it not superstitious to mistake the sign for the thing signified? Isn't that like loving a person's picture instead of the person? Isn't it *faith* that makes us one with Christ?

The power of Christ's Passion is joined to us through faith and through the sacraments, in different ways; for the contact which is through faith takes place through the act of the soul, but the contact which is through the sacraments takes place through the use of material things (III,62,6).

Objection: **It seems that the sacraments are not the cause of grace. For it seems that the same thing is not both sign and cause.... But a sacrament is a sign of grace. Therefore it is not its cause.**

Reply: **The sacraments of the New Law are both cause and signs. Hence too it is that, to use the common expression,** *they effect what they signify....* **[T]hey perfectly fulfill the conditions of a sacrament, being ordained to something sacred not only as a sign but also as a cause.**

Through the sacraments of the New Law man is incorporated with Christ; thus the Apostle says of Baptism (Gal 3:27): *As many of you as have been baptized in Christ have put on Christ.* **And man is made a member of Christ by grace alone.**

Some, however, say that they are the causes of grace not by their own operation but in so far as God causes grace in the soul when the sacraments are employed. And they give as an example a man who on presenting a leaden coin (the ancient version of a modern check) **receives, by the king's command, a hundred pounds: not as though the leaden coin, by any operation of its own, caused him to be given that sum of money,** **this being the effect of the mere will of the king ... For the leaden coin is nothing but a sign of the king's command that this man should receive money.... Hence, according to this opinion the sacraments of the New Law would be mere signs of grace, whereas we have it on the authority of many saints that the sacraments of the New Law not only signify but also cause grace.**

We must therefore say ... that none but God can cause grace, since grace is nothing else than a participated likeness of the divine nature, according to 2 Peter 1:4: *He hath given us most great and precious promises, that we may be partakers of the divine nature.* **But the instrumental cause** (as distinct from the principal cause) **works not by the power of its form** (its own nature), **but only by the motion whereby it is moved by the principal agent, so that the effect is not likened to the instrument but to the principal agent.... And it is thus that the sacraments of the New Law cause grace; for they are instituted by God to be employed for the purpose of conferring grace ...** (III,62,1).

If we hold that a sacrament is an instrumental cause of grace, we must needs allow that there is in the sacraments a certain instrumental power of bringing about the sacramental effects (III,62,4).

The New Testament explicitly says that Baptism saves us (1 Pet 3:21). Baptism (and the other sacraments) must therefore be an effective instrumental cause. The sacraments are symbols, of course—signs—but they are also more than signs or symbols, as the words "I take you for my lawful wedded wife/husband" are signs and symbols of the actual marriage that is taking place but also more than that: they actually effect the marriage. There are other "performative" words like that, e.g., the King or Queen saying "I dub thee knight" or the sheriff saying "I hereby deputize you."

In the different sacraments God uses different sensory instruments to give grace: words in Matrimony and Confession, bread and wine in the Eucharist, water in Baptism, laying on of hands in priestly consecration, and oil in Confirmation and Extreme Unction or the Sacrament of the Sick.

Is it simply God's arbitrary will, like magic, that gives the sacraments their power? Does He just snap His fingers and say "Be" and it is? That's how He works His miracles in Muslim Ash'arite theology, but that doesn't sound like the way God works in the sacraments, which are a unique kind of miracle. What is the difference, since both religions agree that God works miracles through created instruments? How does Christ make the difference between Muslim and Christian theology here?

As stated above, a sacrament in causing grace works after the manner of an instrument. Now an instrument is twofold: the one, separate, as a stick, for instance; the other, united, as a hand. Moreover, the separate instrument is moved by means of the united instrument, as a stick by the hand. Now the principal efficient cause of grace is God Himself, in comparison with Whom Christ's humanity is as a united instrument, whereas the sacrament is as a separate instrument....

Christ delivered us from our sins principally through His passion.... Wherefore it is manifest that the sacraments of the Church derive their power specially from Christ's Passion, the virtue (power) of which is in a manner united to us by our receiving the sacraments. It was in sign of this that from the side of Christ hanging on the Cross there flowed water and blood, the former of which belongs to Baptism, the latter to the Eucharist, which are the principal sacraments (III,62,5).

Most of the Church's dogmas have been attacked by, not just one but, two kinds of heretics. For even in the natural order, as Aristotle says, there are usually two equal and opposite errors about what is true and what is good. Each practical moral virtue has two opposed vices, a "too much" and a "too little" (e.g., cowardice and foolhardiness, or insensitivity and self-indulgence). Theoretical truth also usually contrasts with two opposite errors, e.g., angelism vs. animalism regarding human nature, or deism vs. pantheism in theology, or the denial

of free will vs. the denial of predestination. And so too here, with the sacraments. On the one hand, superstition ascribes supernatural powers to the natural things themselves, not as instruments; and on the other hand, in the typically Muslim Ash'arite theology, God does everything Himself and acts not by using natural things as active instruments but only as accidental occasions. Thus the technical term "occasionalism".

In Catholic theology, grace is, on the one hand, absolutely sovereign and also, on the other hand, it uses, perfects, and respects nature. Thus divine grace comes to us through the sacraments in a way which perfects their natural matter in giving it the power to actually cause the increase of grace in souls. It is not like the mind of a writer using a pen to make words on paper but like the love in a man's soul giving his body the power to procreate a baby in a woman's body. The pen is only accidentally and externally connected with the writer, but the body is essentially and internally one with the soul.

What is like the human body in the sacraments is Christ's Body, Christ's incarnate humanity, which won grace for us by His Passion (and death and Resurrection). Christ, divine and human, acts as what St. Thomas calls a "united instrument", as a man's soul and body act as a "united instrument" in sexual intercourse. Thus somewhat as a man really unites to a woman in intercourse (so much so that they procreate new human life), Christ really unites to His faithful in the sacraments.

If you stood on Calvary under the Good Thief's cross, mistakenly believing it to be Christ's cross, and the blood of the Good Thief fell on you, you would not receive any sacramental grace, despite your faith. If you stood under Christ's cross, you would. Sacraments are that literal, that physical. Salvation is very physical. If the woman with the hemorrhage had touched the hem of St. Peter's garment instead of Christ's, her faith alone would not have healed her until it was joined to His body by her touch.—Unless God had willed to heal her that way, of course. God can work outside his sacraments, and often does. There is much "back-door grace", so to speak. But the sacraments are the front door to Heaven, to divine life.

Do the sacraments actually *do things to us*? Do they change our very being?

Whether the sacramental character is the character of Christ?

Some define character thus: *A character is a distinctive mark printed in a man's rational soul by the eternal Character.... But the eternal Character is Christ Himself....*

A character is properly a kind of seal, whereby something is marked, as being ordained to some particular end; thus a coin is marked for use in exchange of goods....

Now the whole rite of the Christian religion is derived from Christ's priesthood. Consequently, it is clear that the sacramental character is specially the character of Christ, to Whose character the faithful are likened by reason of the sacramental characters, which are nothing else than certain participations in Christ's priesthood, flowing from Christ Himself.... [T]hus soldiers who are assigned to military service are marked with their leader's sign, by which they are in a fashion likened to him ... by the military character a soldier of the kind is distinguished from the enemy's soldier, in relation to the battle. In like manner the character of the faithful is that by which the faithful of Christ are distinguished from the servants of the devil, either in relation to eternal life or in relation to the worship of the Church that now is (III,63,3).

The sacraments produce in us "the sacramental character", and "the sacramental character" is "the character of Christ". Therefore the sacraments produce in us the character of Christ.

But what does this mean?

It means that the sacraments are not merely like light, which lights up whatever objects it meets, but like a movie in a projector, which reproduces itself, its own peculiar face, on the screen.

Your species, your humanness, is *what* you essentially are. Your character is *who* you are. It is your "personality", in the deeper and more spiritual sense of that word rather than in the superficial sense of individual quirks, likes and dislikes, and "lifestyle". You are not responsible for your species but you are responsible for your character, because every free choice you make shapes your character, as a paint brush shapes a picture.

But "do-it-yourself" character building has two basic limitations: the species or nature with which we make our choices is fallen, sinful, selfish, and stupid; and we cannot by our own power attain the deepest and final end of our desires, union with God, eternal happiness. Thus, unless we received grace from God, we would all be living tragedies and comedies, as it is depicted in Samuel Beckett's *Waiting for Godot*. It would be "vanity of vanities", as in Ecclesiastes (until the last few verses, which answer the despair of the rest of the book).

George MacDonald says that God, like a good father, is "easy to please but hard to satisfy". He will not be satisfied with us if we are merely justified, saved, guaranteed Heaven. We must also be sanctified. Christ was called "Savior" not merely because He would save us from the punishment due to our sins, but because "He shall save us from *our sins*" (Mt 1:21). Christ tells us we must "be perfect, as your Heavenly Father is perfect" (Mt 5:48). This is what the sacraments gradually do in us: they make us Christlike.

To update St. Thomas' medieval image and analogy, by them we are branded with the face of the Lord of the ranch. Even Calvin calls sacraments more than symbols: they are "signs *and seals*" of grace. The King alone could seal his documents with his unique signet ring. This is what Christ does to us in the sacraments. (He does it gradually but powerfully, like the tides.)

This is why the single most practical answer to the question: How can I become a saint? is frequent and passionate reception of the Eucharist and Confession. If you want to get wet, go out into the water.

Is it just an accident that the number of sacraments is seven?

It is becoming that there should be seven sacraments. For spiritual life has a certain conformity with the life of the body, just as other corporeal things have a certain likeness to things spiritual. Now a man attains perfection in the corporeal life in two ways: first, in regard to his own person; second, in regard to the whole community of the society in which he lives, for man is by nature a social animal. With regard to himself man is perfected in the life of the body in two ways: first, directly, i.e., by acquiring some vital perfection; secondly, indirectly, i.e by the removal of hindrances to life such as ailments or the like.

Now the life of the body is perfected directly in three ways. First, by generation, by which a man begins to be and to live: and corresponding to this in the spiritual life there is Baptism, which is a spiritual regeneration, according to Titus 3:5: *By the laver of regeneration,* etc.

Secondly, by growth whereby a man is brought to perfect size and strength: and corresponding to this in the spiritual life there is Confirmation, in which the Holy Ghost is given to strengthen us. Wherefore the disciples who were already baptized were bidden thus: *Stay you in the city till you be endued with power from on high* (Lk 24:49).

Thirdly, by nourishment, whereby life and strength are preserved to man; and corresponding to this in the spiritual life there is the Eucharist. Wherefore it is said (Jn 6:54): *Except you eat of the flesh of the Son of Man, and drink His blood, you shall not have life in you....*

But since man is liable at times to both corporeal and spiritual infirmity, i.e., sin, man needs a cure from his infirmity, which cure is twofold. One is the healing that restores health: and corresponding to this there is Penance, according to Psalm 11:5: *Heal my soul, for I have sinned against Thee.*

The other is the restoration of former vigor by means of suitable diet and exercise: and corresponding to this in the spiritual life there is Extreme Unction, which removes the remainder of sin and prepares man for final glory. Wherefore it is written (Jas 5:15): *And if he be in sins they shall be forgiven him.*

In regard to the whole community, man is perfected in two says. First, by receiving power to rule the community and to exercise public acts: and corresponding to this in the spiritual life there is the sacrament of (Priestly) Orders, according to the saying of Hebrews 7:27, that priests offer sacrifices not only for themselves only but also for the people.

Secondly, in regard to propagation. This is accomplished by Matrimony both in the corporeal and in the spiritual life, since it is not only a sacrament but also a function of nature.

We may likewise gather the number of the sacraments from their being instituted as a remedy against the defect caused by sin. For Baptism is intended as a remedy against the absence of spiritual life; Confirmation, against the infirmity of soul found in those of recent birth; the Eucharist, against the soul's proneness to sin; Penance, against actual sin committed after Baptism; Extreme Unction, against the remainders of sins ... Orders, against divisions in the community; Matrimony, as a remedy against concupiscence in the individual and against the decrease of numbers that results from death.

Some, again, gather the number of sacraments from a certain adaption to the virtues.... They say that Baptism corresponds to Faith ... Extreme Unction to Hope ... the Eucharist, to Charity ... Orders, to Prudence ... Penance, to Justice ... Matrimony, to Temperance ... Confirmation, to Fortitude (III,65,1).

Most of God's works are neither necessary nor accidental but befitting, like great art. And as in art there are more schemas than one. The sacraments fit man's basic needs both in general (the correspondence between the spiritual and the material) and in particular (the seven sacraments corresponding to man's seven basic needs, both material and spiritual, in at least these three different ways).

Which is the greatest sacrament?

The Eucharist is the greatest of the sacraments....

First of all because it contains Christ Himself substantially, whereas the other sacraments contain a certain instrumental power which is a share in Christ's power....

Secondly, this is made clear by considering the relation of the sacraments to one another. For all the other sacraments seem to be ordained to this one as to their end. For it is manifest that the sacrament of Orders is ordained to the consecration of the Eucharist, and the sacrament of Baptism to the reception of the Eucharist.... And Matrimony, at least in its signification, touches this sacrament in so far as it signifies the union of Christ with the Church, of which union the Eucharist is a figure: hence the Apostle says (Eph 5:32): *This is a great sacrament: but I speak of Christ and the Church* **(III,65,3).**

Modern man has a strange temptation to resist hierarchical ordering because he fears insulting or doing injustice to anything ranked inferior on the hierarchy simply because something is superior to it. This can stem from the sin of envy, the most foolish of all sins, since it is totally incapable of giving any pleasure, even illicit pleasure. In human politics equality before the law is a necessity even in non-democratic regimes, and democracy is probably intrinsically the best form of government, not because all men are equal in wisdom and virtue, or because all men are so good and wise that they should be given as much power as possible, but because all men are so foolish and wicked that no one should be given very great power over others. But this is an earthly necessity caused by sin. God's works do not fall under these principles. There is hierarchy throughout the creation, life being superior to non-living creatures, man to animals, one species to another (are fleas really equal to dogs?), and even within a species one individual is superior and/or inferior to others at various things.

Thus it is no insult to the other sacraments to rank the Eucharist greatest. Especially because the standard is Christ. The other sacraments are great because they "contain a certain instrumental power which is a share in Christ's power" and the Eucharist is greatest because "it contains Christ Himself substantially." We do not adore the other sacraments; we adore the Eucharist.

Vatican II called the Eucharist "the summit and substance of the Christian life", because it really contains Christ, the whole Christ, Who is the meaning of all things. Pascal says that "without Jesus Christ man cannot know the meaning of his life, or of his death, of God or of himself."

There is nothing in Catholicism that more offends Evangelical Protestants than the Catholic doctrine of the Real Presence of Christ in the Eucharist. For if this is not true, Catholics are the most absurd idolaters in the world, worshipping wine and bowing to bread, thinking it is God! (And the commandment against idolatry is the very First Commandment.) On the other hand, there is nothing in Catholicism that is more winning to Evangelical Protestants than the Eucharist, at least in its intention, because it is totally Christocentric, and this (Christocentrism) is the heart and essence of Evangelicalism. Evangelicals can reject the Catholic doctrine while admiring the Catholic motive of total adoration of Christ alone. And Catholics can reject the Protestant rejection while respecting *their* motive, which is exactly the same one!

St. Teresa said she learned more from contemplating water (the second thing God created, after light) than from all the books in the world. Is there some deep meaning in water that God used in making it the material vehicle of Baptism? What was in God's mind and intention when He created water?

By divine institution water is the proper matter of Baptism, and with reason.

First, by reason of the very nature of Baptism, which is a regeneration unto spiritual life. And this answers to the nature of water in a special degree; wherefore seeds, from which all living things ... are generated, are moist.... For this reason certain philosophers (Thales) **held that water is the first principle of all things.**

Secondly, in regard to the effects of Baptism, to which the properties of water correspond. For by reason of its moistness it cleanses; and hence it fittingly signifies and causes the cleansing from sins. By reason of its coolness it tempers superfluous heat; wherefore it fittingly mitigates ... concupiscence....

Thirdly, because it is suitable for the signification of the mysteries of Christ, by which we are justified. For, as Chrysostom says on John 3:5, *Unless a man be born again,* etc., *When we dip our head under the water as in a kind of tomb, our old man is buried, and being submerged is hidden below, and thence he rises again renewed.*

Fourthly, because by being so universal and abundant, it is a matter suitable for our need of this sacrament; for it can easily be obtained everywhere (III,66,3).

At the very beginning of Western philosophy we find the West's first philosopher, Thales of Miletus, saying that "everything is (made of) water". He probably said this because the ancients thought of everything as alive in some way and he noticed that everything alive needs water, nothing can live without water. St. Thomas would not say everything real is literally alive but that everything real *acts*: "first act" (existence) reveals itself in "second act" (characteristic activity). Even a "dead" rock resists pushing. Wholly passive matter is an abstraction. Only merely mental realities do not act in any way.

Thales put water at the beginning of philosophy just as God put it at the beginning of creation and at the beginning of life, both globally (life began in the seas) and individually (all plants and animals die without water). This makes water fitting to be the first instrument also of supernatural life in Baptism.

This is the first reason St. Thomas sees for the correspondence. The second is that as water both cleans and cools, so the grace of Baptism both justifies and sanctifies, washes us from Original Sin and strengthens us against actual sin by cooling the heat of our selfish desires.

Third, submersion in water drowns us; thus water naturally symbolizes death as well as life. Noah's flood killed the world. Many primitive tribes have a terrifying story of a universal flood, which wipes out all life and even all form and order in nature, for water is formless. This makes it fit for Baptism since Baptism kills our "old man" so that Christ our "new man" can rise from the tomb. Christ is a killer—to the works of Satan. He heals by death and resurrection: of bodies, egos, desires, thoughts. Nothing that has not died will be resurrected to eternal life.

This is why total immersion is the preferred and most perfect symbolic form of Baptism, because it most obviously symbolizes death by drowning—although the Church approves sprinkling too, since this also signifies the washing away of the dirt of sin. (See the next page.) However, it must be with water. The quantity of the water is accidental, the quality is essential.

St. Thomas' fourth reason shows that he understands God's motherly practicality as well as His theological and poetical profundity.

Why do Baptists insist on total immersion as the only valid form of Baptism and why do Catholics and most other Christians disagree?

Whether immersion in water is necessary for Baptism?

On the contrary, It is written (Heb 10:22): *Let us draw near with a true heart in fullness of faith, having our hearts sprinkled from an evil conscience and our bodies washed with clean water.*

I answer that, **In the sacrament of Baptism water is put to the use of a washing of the body, whereby to signify the inward washing away of sins. Now washing may be done with water not only by immersion but also by sprinkling or pouring. And therefore, although it is safer to baptize by immersion because this is the more ordinary fashion, yet Baptism can be conferred by sprinkling or also by pouring, according to Ezechial 36:25:** *I will pour upon you clean water,* **as also Blessed Lawrence is related to have baptized. And this especially in cases of urgency, either because there is a great number to be baptized, as was clearly the case in Acts 2 and 4, where we read that on one day three thousand believed and on another five thousand; or through there being but a small supply of water, or through feebleness of the minister, who cannot hold up the candidate for Baptism; or through feebleness of the candidate, whose life might be endangered by immersion. We must therefore conclude that immersion is not necessary for Baptism** (III,66,7).

One answer to the question is that Baptists concentrate merely on the symbolic sign of Baptism and do not believe that it communicates actual sacramental grace—in other words, to them it is only a symbol—and therefore they are more sensitive to and "picky about" the symbol, since it is all they've got. (This is, of course, an answer St. Thomas could not have given simply because there *were* no Baptists in his day, nor any other kind of Protestant.) It's the same reason why most Protestants know the Bible better than most Catholics do and have better sermons: it's pretty much all they've got, so they concentrate on it and do it really well. (God loves them and gives them great gifts through the relatively few doors they leave open to Him.) Above all, they concentrate on one's individual, subjective "personal relationship with Jesus" because they suspect or minimize the objective and visible Church. Too bad they tend to think it's either/or rather than both/and, but there is much there, in what is positive rather than negative in them, for Catholics to admire and emulate.

Even St. Thomas admits that the "Baptist" way of baptizing, total immersion, is "safer," i.e., more perfect. It was also "more ordinary" even in his day, at least for adult converts. But Mother Church, like any practical and compassionate human mother, is as "liberal" and "tolerant" and "pluralistic" and "practical" as she can be with her children, without sacrificing anything substantial or necessary; and therefore she allows sprinkling or pouring, since it signifies the same thing: the washing away of sin.

Her rule has always been the one said to have been formulated by St. Augustine: "In essentials, unity; in inessentials, diversity; in all things, charity." This is also a good principle for parents, rulers in government, and leaders in business, especially if no one of its three principles is sacrificed for the sake of maintaining either of the other two.

Two sacraments are received many times: the Eucharist and Confession. The others are usually received only once: Baptism, Confirmation, Holy Orders, Matrimony, and Extreme Unction. Why is Baptism in the second class?

Baptism cannot be reiterated.

First, because Baptism is a spiritual regeneration.... Now one man can be begotten but once. Wherefore Baptism cannot be reiterated, just as neither can carnal generation....

Secondly, because *we are baptized in Christ's death,* by which we die unto sin and rise again unto *newness of life* (Rom 6:3–4). Now *Christ died* but *once (vs. 10).* Wherefore neither should Baptism be reiterated....

Thirdly, because Baptism imprints a character which is indelible.... Augustine says: ... *We see that not even apostates are deprived of Baptism* (after their apostasy), *since when they repent and return they are not baptized anew* (III,66,9).

The suffering of the passion of Christ is communicated to the one who is baptized inasmuch as he becomes a member of Christ, as if he himself had borne that pain, and therefore all his sins are remitted through the pain of Christ's passion (III, 69, 2 ad 1).

As God created the world only once, "in the beginning", we are physically born only once. This applies both to physical birth (to *bios,* or natural life) and spiritual birth (to *zoe,* or supernatural life). In Baptism we are "born again" "of water and the (Holy) Spirit" (Jn 3:5). This happens just once because the spiritual life we are born into is forever. It needs to be strengthened many times by Eucharistic food, and cleansed many times by sacramental Confession, but it comes into existence once and for all at Baptism. Beginnings are unique.

St. Thomas' second reason concerns how Baptism conforms us to Christ, Who died once for all and rose once for all. We are baptized not just in *imitation* of Christ but we are baptized "into" Christ. So we too die (spiritually, to sin) and rise (into new life, into the very life of Christ in our soul) once for all.

St. Thomas' third reason—that "Baptism imprints a character which is indelible"—should give us great hope for baptized Catholics who have "lost the Faith". Since once you are baptized you are always baptized; since Baptism really changes you forever; since it "imprints a character which is indelible"; there remains even in the apostate who has been baptized a reality that is not present in one who has not been baptized. This "mark" that Baptism has placed indelibly on the soul is like a magnet drawing us home. For Christ promised that He would "draw all men to Myself" (Jn 12:32).

One might say that this mark is like a brand on cattle, if this analogy did not sound insulting. It is insulting because cattle have no free will. Christ "draws" men to Himself, but He does not force them. It's not magic. Free will is preserved. But real drawing power remains there. To use a slightly better image than the owner's brand on a cow, Baptism is like our Owner's name on our dog tag. Even when we are lost, something in us tells us where our home is. For once we are baptized, the identity of Christ, if not the life of Christ, is forever in our soul in some way. Christ is not only outside us but also inside us, even when we are outside Him. Even mortal sin, which is the rejection of Him, is defined by Him and points back to Him as the One rejected. It is His negative image, like a silhouette, that remains in the soul even when He is rejected. The road map is still in the car even when the car is off the road.

254. How God's grace is not confined to His physical sacraments

Protestants often criticize Catholic sacraments as magical "salvation pills", since they work *ex opere operato*, not *ex opere operantis*, i.e., "from the work of the one who is working" rather than "from the work of the one who is being worked on". They are God's work, not ours. They work from themselves, objectively, not just subjectively, from our own personal faith and piety. Most Protestants say this is magic, superstition, materialistic, externalistic, and "unspiritual". Why is that a mistake? Can we be saved without them? Without Baptism?

Three kinds of Baptism are fittingly described. viz. Baptism of water, of blood, and of the Spirit.... (1) **Baptism of water has its efficacy from Christ's passion....** (2) **Now although the effect depends on the first cause, the cause far surpasses the effect, nor does it** (the cause) **depend on it** (the effect). **Consequently a man may, without Baptism of water, receive the sacramental effect from Christ's Passion in so far as he is conformed to Christ by suffering for Him. Hence it is written** (Rev 7:14): *These are they who are come out of great tribulation, and have washed their robes, and have made them white in the blood of the Lamb.* (3) **In like manner a man receives the effect of Baptism by the power of the Holy Ghost not only without Baptism of water but also without Baptism of blood, forasmuch as his heart is moved by the Holy Ghost to believe in and love God and to repent of his sins; wherefore this is also called Baptism of repentance....** (2) **Wherefore Augustine says:** *The Blessed Cyprian argues with considerable reason from the thief to whom, though not baptized, it was said: "Today shalt thou be with Me in Paradise" that suffering can take the place of Baptism.* (3) *Having weighed this in my mind again and again, I perceive that not only can suffering for the name of Christ supply for what was lacking in Baptism, but even faith and conversion of heart, if perchance on account of the stress of the times the celebration of the mystery of Baptism is not practicable.* **The other two Baptisms are included in the Baptism of water.... Consequently**

... the unity of Baptism is not destroyed (III,66,11).

The shedding of blood for Christ's sake, and the inward operation of the Holy Ghost, are called Baptisms in so far as they produce the effect of the Baptism of water (III,66,12).

Whether a man can be saved without Baptism? ... Augustine says that *Some have received the invisible sanctification without visible sacraments, and to their profit....* **Since, therefore, the sacrament of Baptism pertains to the visible sanctification, it seems that a man can obtain salvation without the sacrament of Baptism, by means of the invisible sanctification ... whereby God, Whose power is not tied to visible sacraments, sanctifies man inwardly** (III,68,2).

St. Thomas, and the Church, affirms everything positive that Protestants say about Baptism, all that is not simply a denial of the positive points the Church teaches. (1) Baptism's whole power derives from Christ and His passion. (2) The cause vastly exceeds the effect. God can and does work outside His sacraments. You can't keep God in a box, whether a church building or a sacrament. (3) One can be saved without water Baptism. The Baptism of the Spirit, by "faith and conversion of heart", also saves us. (4) It is the inner Spirit, not the external material water, that is the first cause that saves us even in water Baptism. (5) Baptism and the other sacraments *without* inner faith and conversion are unprofitable and worthless.

The Church negates only the negative things Protestants say about Baptism: (1) that it does not save us, (2) that it is not the Christ-instituted normal initiation to salvation, the front door of Heaven's mansion, (3) that it works from our poor subjective faith and goodwill, not from God's infinite power (*ex opere operato*), (4) that it is only a symbol, not a sign that also effects what it signifies.

Not only the Church but also the Bible teaches a more positive doctrine than that. Look up "Baptism" in a complete concordance. Read all the verses. See why the Church has always taught what she teaches about it.

Should Baptism be given to everybody indiscriminately?

Whether sinners should be baptized?

A man may be said to be a sinner in two ways. First, on account of the stain and the debt of punishment incurred in the past; and on sinners in this sense the sacrament of Baptism should be conferred, since it is instituted specially for this purpose, that by it the uncleanness of sin may be washed away, according to Ephesians 5:26: *Cleansing it by the laver of water in the word of life.*

Secondly, a man may be called a sinner because he wills to sin, and purposes to remain in sin; and on sinners in this sense the sacrament of Baptism should not be conferred.

First, indeed, because by Baptism men are incorporated in Christ, according to Galatians 3:27: *As many of you as have been baptized in Christ have put on Christ.* Now so long as a man wills to sin, he cannot be united to Christ, according to 2 Corinthians 6:14: *What participation hath justice with injustice?* Wherefore Augustine says that *no man who has the use of free will can begin the new life except he repent of his former life.... Augustine says: He Who created thee without thee will not justify thee without thee ...*

Secondly, because there should be nothing useless in the works of Christ and of the Church. Now that is useless which does not reach the end to which it is ordained; and ... no one having the will to sin can at the same time be cleansed from sin, which is the purpose of Baptism; for this would be to combine two contradictory things.

Thirdly, because there should be no falsehood in the sacramental signs. Now a sign is false if it does not correspond with the thing signified. But the very fact that a man presents himself to be cleansed by Baptism signifies that he prepares himself for the inward cleansing; while this cannot be the case with one who purposes to remain in sin. Therefore it is manifest that on such a man the sacrament of Baptism is not to be conferred (III,68,4).

Baptism is not to be given automatically and indiscriminately, for it is not magic. It is not like putting fluoride in everyone's water supply.

Who then should not be baptized? Should sinners? We are all sinners, so if sinners should not be baptized, no one should be baptized. Baptism is precisely *for* sinners, as soap is for dirty people.

On the other hand, there are two kinds of sinners: reluctant, repentant sinners and willing, deliberate sinners. Everyone in the world belongs to one of those two classes. That is the dividing line between the blessed and the damned. Baptism is not for the damned. For the only reason anyone is damned is that their conscious, deliberate will is anti-God. They do not *want* God and what God is: righteousness. They do not want Heaven and what Heaven is: the place where God's will is done. They want what Hell is: the place where their own will is done. So Baptism should not be imposed on them for the same reason Heaven should not, indeed cannot, be imposed on them. God Himself does not impose Himself on us. He seduces souls, He does not rape them.

This is only a more unusual way of stating the doctrine of free will. Augustine said: "He Who created thee without thee will not justify thee without thee." For although Augustine was as strong as Calvin on predestination and divine sovereignty, he was also, unlike Calvin, equally strong on free will.

Because the sacraments are not magic and do not work against our will, Baptism given to deliberate sinners would be a waste, like watering a rock. And because of free will, this would be an attempted contradiction: cleansing from sin those who refuse cleansing from sin.

Contradictions cannot exist. The law of non-contradiction is not just a logical law, it is a real, metaphysical law. Truth and falsehood are also in real things, not just in ideas; that is what is behind St. Thomas' third reason: unwilling Baptism would be false Baptism: fake, unreal. Honesty demands reality.

Baptists seem to have a point: shouldn't Baptism be freely chosen? If so, infants should not be baptized because they cannot yet exercise personal free choice. It isn't automatic and impersonal.

Whether children should be baptized?

Dionysius says: *Our heavenly guides,* i.e., **the Apostles,** *approved of infants being admitted to Baptism.*

I answer that, **As the Apostle says** (Rom 5:17): *If by one man's offense death reigned through one,* namely Adam, *much more they who receive abundance of grace and of the gift and of justice shall reign in life through one, Jesus Christ.* **Now children contract original sin from the sin of Adam, which is made clear by the fact that they are under the ban of death, which** *passed upon all* **on account of the sin of the first man, as the Apostle says in the same passage (vs. 12). Much more, therefore, can children receive grace through Christ so as to reign in eternal life.**

But our Lord Himself said (Jn 3:5): *Unless a man is born again of water and the Holy Ghost, he cannot enter into the kingdom of God.* **Consequently it becomes necessary to baptize children so that, as in birth they incurred damnation through Adam, so in a second birth they might obtain salvation through Christ....**

The spiritual regeneration effected by Baptism is somewhat like carnal birth in this respect, that as the child while in the mother's womb receives nourishment not independently but through the nourishment of its mother, so also children before the use of reason, being as it were in the womb of their mother the Church, receive salvation not by their own act but by the act of the Church (III,68,9).

It is true, as the question assumes, that Baptism is not automatic and impersonal. It is not imposed without free choice. It is also true that infants do not exercise free choice. However, there is a third assumption that is not true: that infants are autonomous individuals and that their relation to their parents is like the relation between two adults. The objection forgets the mystery of heredity. The parents freely choose to ask the Church for Baptism for their children.

The Bible does not clearly and explicitly approve *or* disapprove of infant Baptism. The early Church had to decide this issue (and many others), and did so, not as an addition to the Bible but by appealing to its texts, by interpreting it.

St. Thomas' first argument deduces that infants have Original Sin from the premise that they can die. (Before sin, there was no death. "The wages of sin is death": Rom 6:23.) He then appeals to St. Paul's parallel between Adam and Christ: as all die "in" one man, Adam, all can be made alive "in" one Man, Christ (Rom 5:12–19). Since infants are humans, they too can "be made alive" or saved in Christ. But Baptism is the cause and beginning of this new life. (That is the point of his second paragraph: Christ's own words in Jn 3:5.) Therefore infants can be baptized.

St. Thomas' final paragraph reminds us of the infant-mother relationship, which is very different from the relationship between two free, autonomous adults. The infant is dependent on its mother for life in the womb; and analogously the born infant is still dependent on its parents both physically and mentally, educationally, emotionally, psychologically. There is a womb outside the womb. It is called early childhood.

Mother Church is to parents spiritually what parents are to children both physically and spiritually. The faith of the parents, nourished by the faith of the Church, supplies the free will needed.

This mystery of spiritual heredity, or "in-ness", was one that pre-modern cultures understood better than our modern post-"Enlightenment" culture does. Perhaps we appreciate individuality and freedom more than our ancestors, but they appreciated solidarity and "in-ness" more than we do.

257. The need for the parents' will in infant Baptism

Should infants ever be baptized without their parents' will, or even against it?

Whether children of Jews or other unbelievers should be baptized against the will of their parents?

It is written in the Decretals, quoting the Council of Toledo: *In regard to the Jews the holy synod commands that henceforward none of them be forced to believe ... for such are not to be saved against their will but willingly....*

I answer that **the children of unbelievers either have the use of reason or they have not. If they have, then they already begin to control their own actions in things that are of divine or natural law. And therefore of their own accord and against the will of their parents they can receive Baptism, just as they can contract marriage....**

If, however, they have not yet the use of free will, according to the natural law they are under the care of their parents as long as they cannot look after themselves. For which reason we say that even the children of the ancients *were saved through the faith of their parents.* **Wherefore it would be contrary to natural justice if such children were baptized against their parents' will, just as it would be if one having the use of reason were baptized against his will. Moreover under the circumstances it would be dangerous to baptize the children of unbelievers, for they would be liable to lapse into unbelief by reasons of their natural affection for their parents. Therefore it is not the custom of the Church to baptize the children of unbelievers against their parents' will** (III,68,10).

St. Thomas' "no" answer to this question is based not only on his respect for free will but also on his respect for Baptism.

Scripture tells us that we must "believe and be baptized" to be saved (Acts 18:8). As faith cannot be forced, neither should Baptism.

In fact, faith *cannot* be forced. That is why the attempt should not be made: it would be a lie. The Koran too teaches that: "There must be no compulsion in matters of religion." Behaviors can be forced, beliefs cannot.

We have seen in #256, above, that the faith of the parents is the necessary free ingredient in infant Baptism. If this ingredient is not there, the Baptism is false. The attempt to baptize by force mistakes Baptism as a kind of magic.

If, however, a child of unbelieving parents is of the age of reason, and can make intelligent and free choices, he should be baptized if he asks for it, even against the will of his parents, for the very same reason that he should *not* be baptized if he is *not* of the age of reason: because of respect for free will. St. Thomas says this also applies to Matrimony, which must also be free and not forced. (Parentally arranged marriages, by the way, can be either forced, and therefore false marriages, or freely consented to and thus true marriages.) If there is no real "I" in "I do", there is no real "do" either.

(It is not clear when the "age of reason" begins, but it is clear that a two-year-old has not attained it and that a ten-year-old has. It probably begins around the time schooling begins, at about five.)

Notice the presence of the same idea of "spiritual heredity" that was spoken of in #256 also in St. Thomas' very Biblical saying that the children of the ancients "were saved through the faith of their parents". This is the principle he appeals to in condemning the baptizing of infants against their parents' will no matter what their parents believe.

Thus we have arguments (1) from principles of the revealed theology of Baptism, (2) from principles of natural law (the dependence of children on parents), (3) from a principle common to both (free will), and (4) from the likely practical consequences later in the lives of the unwillingly-baptized children. Principles come first but practical consequences count too.

St. Thomas said that the Eucharist is the greatest sacrament. But Baptism "saves you" (1 Pet 3:21), and is first in time. Why is the Eucharist first in value?

The Church's sacraments are ordained for helping man in the spiritual life. But the spiritual life is analogous to the corporeal life, since corporeal things bear a resemblance to spiritual. Now it is clear that just as generation is required for corporeal life, since thereby man receives life, and growth, whereby man is brought to maturity, so likewise food is required for the preservation of life. Consequently, just as for the spiritual life there had to be Baptism, which is spiritual generation, so there needed to be the sacrament of the Eucharist, which is spiritual food....

A sacrament is so termed because it contains something sacred. Now a thing can be styled sacred from two causes: either absolutely or in relation to something else. The difference between the Eucharist and other sacraments having sensible matter is that whereas the Eucharist contains something which is sacred absolutely, namely Christ's own Body, the baptismal water contains something which is sacred in relation to something else, namely the sanctifying power....

The water of Baptism does not cause any spiritual effect by reason of the water, but by reason of the power of the Holy Ghost, which power is in the water. Hence on John 5:4, *An angel of the Lord at certain times,* etc., Chrysostom observes: *The water does not act simply as such upon the baptized, but when it receives the grace of the Holy Ghost, then it looses all sins.* But the true Body of Christ bears the same relation to the species (natural appearances) **of the bread and wine as the power of the Holy Ghost does to the water of Baptism; hence the species of the bread and wine produce no effect except from the virtue** (power) **of Christ's true Body** (III,73,1).

Biological life and spiritual life are analogous. Thus just as we need both birth (or, more properly, conception) and food for biological life, we also need both for spiritual life. Because of this analogy, we might think Baptism more important than the Eucharist because it is like birth—the beginning of life—while the Eucharist is like growth of a life already there; and physical birth is more important, more radical, than growth because it (or rather conception) gives existence itself.

But the sacredness of the Eucharist is greater not just in degree but in principle, because it is sacred absolutely, in itself: it is the very Body of Christ, and *not* bread or wine, after the Consecration. Catholics *adore* the Eucharist, which is the most outrageous idolatry if it is *not* Christ Himself but only sacred bread and wine. They do not adore Baptism or any other sacrament. The water of Baptism is sacred only because it *carries* God's saving power, like St. Christopher carrying the Christ child incognito. The water of Baptism is only water. But the bread and wine of the Eucharist are not merely sacred bread and wine, they are not bread and wine at all. They are the real Body and Blood of Christ.

St. Thomas makes the difference clear with a startling analogy. Reread his last sentence. God the Holy Spirit *uses* the water of Baptism as a mere instrument; and God the Son uses the appearances of bread and wine as a mere instrument, preserving them as appearances to test our faith. For if we saw with our eyes what was really there, we would see Jesus as clearly as the apostle Thomas did after His Resurrection, and we would instantly fall to the ground and exclaim, "My Lord and my God!" as he did. And then He would say to us what He said to Thomas: "You have believed because you have seen me" instead of saying to us, as He does, "Blessed are those who have not seen and yet believe" (Jn 20:29).

It is a great grace that the Eucharist does not look like Christ or perform constant visible miracles, or give us spiritual "highs" whenever we receive it. That would give us a spiritual sweet tooth instead of being a faith-muscle-exerciser. Visit Him there often! It's like visiting a sickbed rather than a movie: it's not a passive turn-on, it's an active deed of love. The grace of Baptism can be received passively, by an infant, but the grace of the Eucharist cannot. Only faith lets it through, like a faucet handle.

The relationship between Baptism and the Eucharist in terms of their essence, or nature or form (formal causality) is, as we have seen above, the superiority of the Eucharist, which is sacred absolutely, over Baptism, which is sacred only relatively. What is the relationship between these two sacraments in terms of final causality, or end and purpose?

Baptism is the beginning of the spiritual life and the door of the sacraments, whereas the Eucharist is, as it were, the consummation of the spiritual life and the end of all the sacraments ... for by the hallowings of all the sacraments preparation is made for receiving or consecrating the Eucharist. Consequently the reception of Baptism is necessary for starting the spiritual life, while the receiving of the Eucharist is requisite for its consummation ... by Baptism a man is ordained to the Eucharist (III,73,3).

The analogy between Baptism being like birth (or conception) and the Eucharist being like growth through eating food, like all analogies, is limited. Its limit is both in terms of value or importance (birth is more important or more valuable than growth, but the Eucharist is more important and more valuable than Baptism) and also in terms of final causality, end, or purpose. For eating and growth is not the end and purpose of birth, but the Eucharist is the end and purpose of Baptism.

For this reason, we might want to turn to another analogy to supplement the first one (though of course this analogy too is only an analogy and has its limits): Baptism is like accepting a marriage proposal and the Eucharist is like the actual wedding. Or we might even say that Baptism is like saying "I do" in the wedding ceremony and the Eucharist is like consummating the marriage by actual spousal union. For the Eucharist is an actual union between Christ and our souls. As the mystics are bold to say, especially when commenting on their favorite book of the Bible, the "Song of Songs", and as Pope St. John Paul II has echoed in his "Theology of the Body", Christ becomes the husband of our soul. This is a real union, in fact a real spousal union, though it is spiritual rather than physical.

Thus the Church has called the Eucharist "the source and summit" of the whole Christian life. For the source and summit, the beginning and the end, the Alpha and Omega of literally the whole Christian life is Christ Himself ("I am the Alpha and Omega"—Rev 1:8); and it is Christ Himself Who meets us and unites us with Himself in the Eucharist.

The other sacraments are, in different ways, ordered and ordained to this end: Baptism as its beginning, Confirmation as its strengthening, Holy Orders as empowering its priests, Confession as its restoration and spiritual healing, Matrimony as its most complete natural analogy, Extreme Unction as its physical healing or the preparation for its great transition to Heaven, where there will be no sacraments for the same reason there will be no churches, temples, or church services. To find out this reason, read Revelation 21:22.

All the sacraments are sacred signs. Of what is the Eucharist a sign?

This sacrament has a threefold significance: one with regard to the past, inasmuch as it is commemorative of our Lord's Passion, which was a true sacrifice ... and in this respect it is called a *Sacrifice.*

With regard to the present it has another meaning, namely that of ecclesiastical unity ... and in this respect it is called *Communion.* **For Damascene says that** *it is called Communion because we communicate with Christ through it ... and are united to one another through it.*

With regard to the future it has a third meaning, inasmuch as this sacrament foreshadows the divine fruition which shall come to pass in heaven; and according to this it is called *Viaticum* **because it supplies the way of winning thither. And in this respect it is also called the** *Eucharist,* **that is,** *good grace,* **because** *the grace of God is life everlasting* (Rom 6:23) (III,73,4).

As Christ is the eternal Word of God made temporal, so the Eucharist, the sacrament which is the eternal Christ Himself, branches out into all three dimensions of time like a single white light passing through a prism into different colors. Thus St. Thomas mentions three meanings, or significances, to this sacred sign: one past, one present, and one future. Once again, we see his both/and rather than either/or mind. Modern theologians often argue about whether the Eucharist is primarily a sacrifice (of Christ on the Cross in the past for our salvation) or a communion (with Christ and each other in the present). St. Thomas' answer is that it is both, and more.

The three meanings are dependent on each other. If we separate them from each other in our own minds, we pervert each one, making the past meaning (sacrifice) a "salvation pill", the present one ("communion") a piece of self-serving ecclesiastical celebratory auto-eroticism, or the future one ("viaticum") an eternal fire insurance policy. But if we remember their oneness, we will see the past meaning, the sacrifice, as a means to our spiritual marriage to Christ which must begin in this life and be consummated in Heaven; we will see the present meaning, the communion, as union with the divine, not just the human Christ, and thus as union with the Christ of the Cross and the Christ of Heaven; and we will see the future meaning, the viaticum, as the fulfillment of the same relationship that began on the Cross and is presently being lived and grown in the Church and her sacraments, which pour out on us the grace already won on the Cross, the grace which alone can win Heaven for us in our future.

Therefore, when we receive the Eucharist, we are with Christ on the Cross and in Heaven. We are bilocating, not just in space but in time. The Eucharistic Christ is like a time machine. It brings us back to Calvary, into the present Christ, and forward to Heaven, because it makes us to be together with Christ, Who is in all three places and times. Remembering all three of these things vastly enriches our understanding and appreciation and gratitude for what we are doing each time we receive Him in the Eucharist.

Nothing more passionately separates Catholics from most Protestants is the doctrine of the Real Presence of Christ in the Eucharist. Couldn't this be a sign only?

Whether the Body of Christ be in this sacrament in very truth or merely as in a figure or sign?

The presence of Christ's true Body and Blood in this sacrament cannot be detected by sense, nor understanding, but by faith alone, which rests upon divine authority. Hence, on Luke 22:19, *This is My Body, which shall be delivered up for you,* **Cyril says:** *Doubt not whether this be true, but take rather the Savior's words with faith, for since He is the Truth, He lieth not . . .*

This belongs to Christ's love, out of which for our salvation He assumed a true body of our nature. And because it is the special feature of friendship to live together with friends, as the Philosopher says, He promises us His bodily presence. . . . Hence (Jn 6:57) **He says:** *He that eateth My flesh and drinketh My blood abideth in Me and I in him.* **Hence this sacrament is the sign of supreme charity and the uplifter of our hope, from such familiar union of Christ with us. . . .**

Some men accordingly, not paying heed to these things, have contended that Christ's Body and Blood are not in this sacrament except as in a sign—a thing to be rejected as heretical since it is contrary to Christ's words. . . .

No body can be in several places at one time . . . (But) Christ's Body is not in this sacrament in the same way as a body is in a place, which by its dimensions is commensurate with the place, but in a special manner which is proper to this sacrament. Hence we say that Christ's Body is on many altars . . . (III,75,1).

Many Protestants also believe in some way in Christ's presence this sacrament, but all these ways are different from the Catholic doctrine by being in some way a less complete presence. These range from (1) the merely symbolic (as an absent person is present symbolically in a picture of him, which is a kind of sign), to (2) the subjective (as the Holy Spirit is present in the faith and hope and love of the believer whenever any religious activity is performed, such as reading the Bible), to (3) the "occasional" (as God uses many religious things as *occasions* for directly energizing the human soul with grace, but He is not actually *in* those things, as a holiday is an occasion for giving gifts, but the giver is the person, not the day), to (4) the instrumental (as the power of divine grace is present effectively in the other sacraments as instruments, so that the water of Baptism is used as a means of Christ's spiritual cleansing but Christ is not personally present in the water, so that it is not worshipped, and the water remains water and is not transubstantiated into Christ), to (5) the Lutheran alternative to the Catholic doctrine of transubstantiation which is called consubstantiation, in which the bread and wine are not changed but added to, so that Christ becomes really present along with them but they remain.

Why do Catholics believe the astonishing doctrine that what looks and feels and tastes and shows itself under a microscope as merely bread and wine are in fact not bread and wine but Christ Himself, the whole Christ, "Body and Blood, soul and divinity"? There is no physical, scientific evidence for it, nor is there any logical proof of it. Catholics believe it because Christ said so. St. Thomas wrote: "I believe all the Son of God has spoken; than Truth's own word there is no truer token." God said it, that settles it.

If Christ had meant His words only symbolically, He would not have allowed those of His disciples who could not stomach this nearly incredible teaching to leave him (John 6) but would have corrected their too-literal misunderstanding, as He often did to His disciples. But He did not do that here.

Christ can be in Heaven and on earth, on one altar and another, at the same time because His presence is not subject to the laws of nature. A merely natural body cannot be simultaneously in more than one place, and cannot be greater in size ("dimensions") than the place it is in. Christ can. In other words, a miracle literally happens every time He says "This is My Body" through the lips of a priest. Christ never lies.

Why isn't the Catholic doctrine of "transubstantiation" impossible and illogical?

Whether bread can be converted (changed) **into the Body of Christ?**

Eusebius Emesenus says: *To thee it ought neither to be a novelty nor an impossibility that earthly and mortal things be changed into the substance of Christ.*

Since Christ's true Body is in this sacrament, and since it does not begin to be there by local motion, nor is it contained therein as in a place.... [I]t must be said then that it begins to be there by conversion of the substance of the bread into itself.

Yet this change is not like natural changes, but is entirely supernatural, and effected by God's power alone. Hence Ambrose says: *See how Christ's word changes nature's laws, as He wills: a man is not wont to be born save of man and woman; see therefore that against the established law and order a man is born of a Virgin; and: It is clear that a Virgin begot beyond the order of nature ... Why, then, do you look for nature's order in Christ's body, since the Lord Jesus was Himself brought forth of a Virgin beyond nature? ...*

God is infinite act (actuality); **hence His action** ("second act," activity) **extends to the whole nature of being. Therefore He can work not only formal conversion** (change), **so that diverse forms** (natures, essences, species) **succeed each other in the same** (material) **subject, but also the change of all being, so that the whole substance** (being, reality) **of one thing be changed into the whole substance of another. And this is done by divine power in this sacrament; for the whole substance of the bread is changed into the whole substance of Christ's Body, and the whole substance of the wine into the whole substance of Christ's Blood. Hence this not a formal but a substantial conversion; nor is it a kind of natural movement, but, with a name of its own, it can be called** *transubstantiation....*

Form cannot be changed into form, nor matter into matter, by the power of any finite agent. Such a change, however, can be made by the power of an infinite agent, which has control over all being, because the nature of being is common to both forms and to both matters; and whatever there is of being in the one, the Author of being can change into whatever there is of being in the other ... (III,75,4).

This change is effected by a power which is infinite, to which it belongs to operate in an instant.... Thus it is written (Mk 7:34) **that when Christ had said,** *"Ephata,"* **which is** *"Be thou opened,"* **immediately his ears were opened and the string of his tongue was loosed** (III,75,7).

The Eucharist is no more impossible than the Incarnation. Indeed, it is the extension of it.

"With God all things are possible", and only what is self-contradictory and therefore meaningless is not possible even for God because it is not a thing at all. "A round square" or "a good sin" does not suddenly become meaningful because you add the words "God can do this" to it. But "with God all things are possible" because His power is unlimited. If not, God would not be God, but a creature. It takes finite power to effect a finite change, but infinite power to effect the infinite change from absolute nonexistence to existence, i.e., to create a universe not from something but from nothing.

If by command God can change nothingness into the universe without any previously existing physical cause, He can certainly change bread and wine into His Son's Body and Blood. If He can change corpses into living persons, He can change bread into Christ's Body. If He can feed five thousand people with five loaves and two fishes, He can feed a billion Catholics with His Son's Body. If He can change water into wine, He can change wine into His own Blood, and He can change our blood into something "eye has not seen, ear has not heard, nor has it entered into the heart of man" in the resurrection.

("Substance" does not mean "chemical element" in St. Thomas' Aristotelian, pre-modern, pre-scientific language. It means "*what* the thing essentially is", its essential nature.)

263. REAL PRESENCE: "BODY AND BLOOD, SOUL AND DIVINITY"

What are the limitations on Christ's Real Presence in the Eucharist? Is it perhaps just His divinity that is present? Or just His humanity? Or just His Body? Or just His soul?

It is absolutely necessary to confess according to the Catholic Faith that the entire Christ is in this sacrament.... [W]herever the Body of Christ is, there of necessity must the Godhead be....

On the other hand, His soul was truly separated from His body (when He died). **And therefore had this sacrament been celebrated during those three days when He was dead, the soul of Christ would not have been there ... But since** *Christ rising from the dead dieth now no more* (Rom 6:9), **His soul is always really united with His Body. And therefore in this sacrament the Body indeed of Christ is present by the power of the sacrament, and His soul by real concomitance** (III,76,1).

"The entire Christ" is present in the Eucharist.

His divinity existed without His humanity before the Incarnation, but ever since the Incarnation His humanity is joined forever to His divinity. His Ascension was not the undoing of His Incarnation. And since the Eucharist is after His Ascension, His humanity is always fully present in it as well as His divinity.

His humanity never existed without His divinity, so it does not exist without His divinity in the Eucharist either.

His body and soul, like ours, existed together, as the matter and form of His humanity, rather than as two separate substances, as Descartes' anthropology mistakenly describes human nature. But death unnaturally separates the body and the soul; and He really died; therefore St. Thomas says that "had this sacrament been celebrated during those three days when He was dead, the soul of Christ would not have been there" because His body was there and the soul was not in the body. (How concrete and realistic St. Thomas is!)

His human soul did not exist before His human body was conceived in Mary's womb. Some people confuse His soul either with a pure spirit, which could exist in Heaven before the Incarnation, or with His divinity. But a soul is just as created, as natural, as human, and as finite as a body. In fact a soul is the life *of* a body. It is not a pure spirit, like an angel. Christ was never an angel. Before the Incarnation He had neither a human soul nor a human body. After the Incarnation He had both a human soul and a human body at every moment and forever. When He died, His human body was still His human body, in the tomb; and His human soul was still His human soul, when it went to the realm of the dead and preached to the Old Testament saints who were waiting there. (See 1 Pet 3:18–20.)

His body and blood were separated whenever he bled, beginning with His circumcision. At His death, His blood was separated from His body in a fatal way. The Eucharist has two elements, bread and wine, not just one, in order to signify this death, by the separation of His Body and His Blood.

Nearly all ancient cultures so connect "life" with either "blood" or "breath" or both that the same word in most ancient languages means both "life" and "blood" or both "life" and "breath" (*ruach* in Hebrew, *pneuma* in Greek). Ancient peoples noticed that without blood a body dies, so they naturally connected the blood with the life, or the soul, of the body. (Remember that "soul" means not "pure spirit" but "the life of a body".) They also connected the breath with the life, for the same reason. It was not bad science because it was not science at all, it was a common-sense concrete identification which was more than just symbolic (if a body loses its blood or its breath it really does literally die) but less than scientific.

So how much of Christ is present in the Eucharist? What do we receive when we receive Him there? (1) His divinity as well as His humanity. (2) Within His humanity, both His Body and His soul. (3) And within His Body, both His Body and His Blood, in the two elements of the sacrament, which remain hidden behind the appearances of bread and wine when they are transubstantiated.

Is the Church right to give us the Eucharistic bread without the wine? When she offers Communion under both species, is it right to receive the bread only, if this is necessary for practical purposes such as avoiding infections or not risking spillage?

If the bread and the wine signify His broken, bloodless Body and His spilled Blood (outside His body), do we receive just the Body when we receive the "bread" and just the Blood when we receive the "wine"? Or is the whole Christ present in each of the elements or, as the theological formula puts it, "under each sacramental species (kind)"?

The whole Christ is under each sacramental species ... because now Christ's Blood is not separated from His Body, as it was at the time of His Passion and death. Hence if this sacrament had been celebrated then, the Body of Christ would have been under the species of the bread but without the blood, and under the species of the wine the Blood would have been present without the Body....

In Christ's Passion, of which this is the memorial, the other parts of the body were not separated from one another, as the blood was, but the body remained entire, according to Exodus 12:46: *You shall not break a bone thereof*. And therefore in this sacrament the Blood is consecrated apart from the Body, but no other part is consecrated separately from the rest (III,76,2).

As Augustine says: *Each receives Christ the Lord, Who is entire under every morsel, nor is He less in each portion, but bestows Himself entire under each* (III,76,3).

Once again, St. Thomas shows how concrete and realistic the Faith is, when he says that if we had received the Eucharist between the time of Christ's death on the Cross and the time of His Resurrection, we would have received the Body without the Blood, just as we would have received the Body without the soul. But now "the whole Christ is under each sacramental species."

His body and blood were separated on the Cross, but His body was not broken in any other way. (See John 19:31–37.)

As Christ is wholly present in each of the millions of consecrated Eucharistic wafers around the world, even though the wafers are separated from each other physically in time and space; and as He is wholly present in each drop of consecrated wine in all the Eucharists around the world, so He is wholly present in the bread alone without the wine, or in the wine alone without the bread.

Therefore when we receive only the bread, we are not receiving any less of Christ in any way than when we receive both the bread and the wine.

The advantage of receiving under both species instead of only one is that the death that is signified is signified more completely, dramatically, and perfectly. The sign aspect of the sacrament, relative to our subjective human consciousness, especially our imagination, is more complete; but the objective reality of the Presence is not.

The practical "bottom line" is a sort of "best of both worlds" situation: on the one hand, receiving under one species is receiving not one iota less of Christ's reality, yet on the other hand receiving under both species is a special privilege too because it is receiving Him in a more symbolically complete way. It is like the difference between Baptism by pouring and Baptism by immersion.

265. How Christ is "here" in the Eucharist

(1) When the priest moves the consecrated Host from his hand to our tongue, or to our hand, Christ's Body is moved from one place to the other. For a hand and a tongue are places, and different places, and Christ's Body is moved from the priest's hand to our tongue or hand. That follows logically.

(2) But no place can contain Christ's Body, for it is present simultaneously and fully in many different places. It is larger, not smaller, than any place, even the entire universe.

Therefore, since both of these statements are true, Christ's Body must be in the Eucharist in a very different way than we usually think of when we say one body is "in" another, or in a place. How does that work?

Whether Christ's Body is in this Sacrament as in a place?

The place and the object placed must be equal (in size), **as is clear from the Philosopher. But the place where this sacrament is is much less than the Body of Christ. Therefore Christ's Body is not in this sacrament as in a place ... because then it would be only on the particular altar where this sacrament is performed; whereas it is in heaven under its own species and on many other altars under the sacramental species** (III,76,5).

St. Thomas does not answer this question by "spiritualizing" Christ's Body or His real Eucharistic Presence. He is really there in this physical place in a way He is not present in other physical places. For instance, He is not in the pews of the church with His Real Presence as He is in the consecrated Host, and we do not adore Him there. If He were really in the pews, it would be sacrilege to sit down.

This sounds as if His sacred Body, since it is really present in some places but not others, must be smaller than the sum of all places, or the universe. Yet this is not so. The very opposite is so: the Body of Christ is larger than the universe. When you swallow the Eucharist, you are swallowing more than the entire created universe. You are swallowing the Creator. When we physically encompass Him in our bodies, He ontologically encompasses us in His Body.

When the Lady Julian of Norwich was given the vision of a tiny hazel nut held in the hand of God, she asked what it was and God answered: "It is all that is made." The universe is much smaller than its Creator. Christ is the Creator of everything, the "Pantocrator" ("all-creator") typically found in Eastern Orthodox icons, and therefore infinitely larger than all that is created. But He is "larger" not in physical size but in being. The Eucharist is not physically larger than the universe, but it is ontologically larger, somewhat as the soul is larger than the body, not physically (since souls, like God, are not physical chunks of matter) but ontologically, in being.

"But I cannot comprehend this." Quite right. If we could, it would fit into the categories of nature and natural reason. Its incomprehensibility is exactly what we should expect if it is the true supernatural miracle as claimed by the Church that teaches it in His name and with His authority ("he who hears you, hears Me"—Lk 10:16).

The last question was about space. This one is about time.

As Christ is really present in some places (the consecrated Host) and not others, He is also really present there at some times (after the words of Consecration) and not others (before the Consecration). And when He is eaten by the recipient of the Eucharist, He ceases to be present once all the molecules of the bread are digested and its nature ("species") as bread ceases to exist there due to physical or chemical changes in the body. But how can physical or chemical changes have an effect on Christ? How can the eternal God, Who transcends time, be dependent on time and change in any way?

Whatever possesses unfailing existence of itself, cannot be the principle (source) **of failing. But when something else fails, then it** (i.e., existence) **ceases to be in it** (i.e., in the thing that fails), **just as God, Whose existence is unfailing and immortal, ceases to be in some corruptible creature because such corruptible creature ceases to exist.**

And in this way, since Christ has unfailing and incorruptible being, He ceases to be under this sacrament not because He ceases to be, nor yet by local movement ... but only by the fact that the sacramental species ceases to exist....

The Body of Christ remains in this sacrament ... so long as the sacramental species remain; and when they cease, Christ's Body ceases to be under them, not because it depends on them but because the relationship of Christ's Body to those species is taken away, in the same way as God ceases to be the Lord of a creature which ceases to exist (III,76,6).

God is everywhere and everywhen. When a place or time ceases to be, God ceases to be in it. The nature of bread ceases to be in the body once it is fully digested (about fifteen minutes after swallowing it). So the supernatural nature of Christ ceases to be in or behind the species of bread when there is no species of bread any more. God Himself cannot die. When He says "Be!" to anything, that thing cannot fail to be. But when a thing ceases to be the instrument for His presence, it can cease because He ceases to say "Be!" to it. Two examples of this are (1) the soul that loses sanctifying grace by mortal sin and (2) the consecrated bread and wine of the Eucharist about fifteen minutes after receiving them, when the "sacramental species", i.e., the nature ("species") of the physical appearances, namely the chemical structures, are transformed by the body's digestive juices. (We miss a great opportunity for grace if we leave our prayers less than fifteen minutes after receiving Communion. We also disappoint our Lord, Who came an infinite distance, from Heaven to earth, for this intimate encounter. It is a spiritual tryst.)

These two things are the holiest things in the world, for the same reason: Christ is really personally present in the Eucharist and in the soul that accepts Him by faith, hope, and charity. The presence is not the same in the two cases—we do not adore our Christian neighbor—but it is real in both cases. As C. S. Lewis says in *The Weight of Glory*, "It is a serious thing to live in a society of possible gods and goddesses, to remember that the dullest and most uninteresting person you talk to may one day be a creature which, if you saw it now, you would be strongly tempted to worship, or else a horror and a corruption such as you now meet, if at all, only in a nightmare. All day long we are, in some degree, helping each other to one or other of these destinations. It is in the light of these overwhelming possibilities, it is with the awe and circumspection proper to them, that we should conduct all our dealings with one another, all friendships, all loves, all play, all politics. There are no *ordinary* people. You have never talked to a mere mortal. Nations, cultures, arts, civilization— these are mortal, and their life is to ours as the life of a gnat. But it is immortals whom we joke with, work with, marry, snub, and exploit—immortal horrors or everlasting splendours.... Next to the Blessed Sacrament itself, your neighbour is the holiest object presented to your senses."

Christ's presence in the Eucharist is invisible, imperceptible except by faith. Is this for the same reason that I (i.e., my soul, my personality) am invisible to you, or is it for another, different reason?

Do angels and demons perceive Him in the Eucharist as we cannot?

Christ's Body as it is in this sacrament cannot be seen by any bodily eye ... because Christ's Body is substantially present in this sacrament; but substance as such (as distinguished from accidents) **is not visible to the bodily eye, nor does it come under any one of the senses, nor under the imagination, but solely under the intellect, whose object is** *what a thing is* (substance). **And therefore, properly speaking, Christ's Body, according to the mode of being which it has in this sacrament, is perceptible neither by the sense nor by the imagination, but only by the intellect, which is called the spiritual eye.**

(But) **it is perceived differently by different intellects. For since the way in which Christ is in this sacrament is entirely supernatural, it is visible in itself to a supernatural intellect, i.e., (1) to the divine intellect, and ... (2) to a beatified** (in Heaven) **intellect, of angel or of man, which through the participated glory of the divine intellect sees all supernatural things in the vision of the divine essence. But (3) it can be seen by a wayfarer through faith alone, like other supernatural things.**

And not even the angelic intellect of its own natural power is capable of beholding it; consequently the devils cannot by their intellect perceive Christ in this sacrament except through faith, to which they do not pay willing assent. Yet they are convinced of it from the evidence of signs, according to James 2:19: *The devils believe, and tremble* (III,76,7).

"Substance", in St. Thomas' traditional and commonsensical Aristotelian terminology, means not "chemical element" but a thing, an entity, a being—linguistically, a noun. "Accidents" means not "mistakes" but "attributes of substances", whether essential and permanent (these are called "properties" or "proper accidents") or temporary and changeable. "Accidents" include qualities, quantities, relations, times, places, actions, and passions (receptions). They exist only in substances, not in themselves. I can give you blue socks at 3:00 P.M. but I cannot give you blue or 3:00 P.M.

We can see some accidents, but not substances as distinct from accidents. We see substances only in and through their accidents—e.g., we see socks under the appearances of shape and color. When Christ's contemporaries perceived His body, they perceived it by His accidents: bearded, white skin, etc. We do not perceive any such accidents in His Body in the Eucharist. But it is the same Body, the same reality, the same substance.

The philosophical category of "substance" is so essential to the Catholic faith that it is used to express the central, most important, and most distinctively Christian doctrine of all, the divinity of Christ, in the Nicene Creed, in which we confess that Christ is "consubstantial" (of one substance, or "one in being") with the Father.

We cannot perceive Christ's Body in the Eucharist by the senses (whether or not they are amplified by microscopes or other scientific instruments) or the imagination, which is the mind's power to form sense images when the senses are not sensing them. We "perceive" (are aware of) His Body only by faith. Faith is not a feeling; faith is a knowing—a knowing not by sensation or by logical proof but by divine revelation. God said it and therefore we believe it, because God is God.

Angels cannot perceive His presence there either, though God can supernaturally enlighten angels to see it. He can even do that to us, and in fact did, very rarely, by miracle, to a few saints.

Devils (fallen angels) cannot perceive Him there either, by senses (they have none), by faith (they have none), or by their own intellect, directly; "yet they are convinced of it from the evidence of signs", as St. Thomas says, because they are not stupid. They see the life-changing effects of Eucharistic Adoration better than many parish administrators do! And they tremble.

268. Eucharistic *APPEARANCES* OF BREAD AND WINE WITHOUT THEIR *REALITIES*

How can the accidents (appearances) of the Eucharist exist without a subject (substance) for them to be the accidents *of*? Isn't this logically impossible, even by miracle?

Whether the accidents remain in this sacrament without a subject?

The accidents continue in this sacrament without a subject. This can be done by divine power; for since an effect depends more upon the first cause than on the second, God, Who is the first cause both of substance and accident, can by His unlimited power preserve an accident in existence when the substance is withdrawn ... just as without natural causes He can produce other effects of natural causes, even as He formed a human body in the Virgin's womb *without the seed of man* (III,77,1).

The Eucharist is not logically impossible, but it is physically impossible, like any other miracle. What is *logically* impossible is self-contradictory and meaningless, and cannot happen even by infinite, supernatural force. God cannot make 2 plus 2 to equal 3 rather than 4 even by infinite power, not because any *power* is lacking, but because it is meaningless. So if it is logically impossible for accidents to exist without a substance, then even God cannot do this.

But it is not logically impossible. God can certainly create the appearances of a fire, or water, without there being any actual fire or water, so that our senses are deceived. Even we can do something similar (though not identical) by hypnosis. God could even make the apparent fire to burn up something real, for He could create the effects (burning) of a natural substance directly, without using the intermediate cause of that natural substance (fire). So it is not logically impossible. It is only impossible physically, impossible by any power in nature.

But God created nature, and God's power is unlimited by anything in nature. If He could become a temporal man without ceasing to be the eternal God; if He could create the entire universe out of nothing; if He could conceive a baby without a human father; then He certainly can maintain accidents in being directly without their usual substance being present. For God "is the first cause both of substance and accident". He can bypass natural causes, as He did with the Virgin Birth.

How arrogant to limit God by our imagination! God has to keep reminding us over and over again of those two important facts of our existence, as He said to St. Catherine (and also, implicitly, to Job): (1) "I'm God" and (2) "You're not." The fact that we keep forgetting these two most obvious facts in our lives, and need to be constantly reminded of them, is proof of the fallenness of our minds, and of the loving patience of our Heavenly Father to His severely forgetful children.

And if He can do the miracles of the Creation and the Incarnation, He can do any miracles. How foolish to believe in the Big Bang from the Maker of the Big Bang but deny the possibility of any later little bangs from the same Source.

Therefore, when you deeply desire some good, and pray earnestly for it, do not think for one moment that God cannot do it, either by natural or supernatural causes. He is limited by nothing: not by the past, not by history, not by other things in the world, as if He had to coordinate all things in such a way that the good of each was compromised for the good of all. "He's got the whole world in His hands." If He does not do the good thing you pray for now, either He will do it later, or in another way, or He will do something better. "We know that in *everything* God works for good with those who love him" (Rom 8:28) in ways we seldom can foresee. "What no eye has seen, nor ear heard, nor the heart of man conceived, what God has prepared for those who love him" (1 Cor 2:9). His wisdom exceeds ours as much as His power does. It is utterly *ir*rational to limit His reason and wisdom by what *we* take to be rational.

269. How complete is Christ's disguise in the Eucharist?

If we put consecrated bread or wine under a microscope, or in a test tube, will it look and act exactly like ordinary unconsecrated bread and wine? Will the "appearances" act as if they had a natural subject (real bread and wine) under them? Will the "bread" (which is not bread any more!) go moldy? Will the "wine" intoxicate?

Whether the species (appearances) **remaining in this sacrament can change external objects?**

If they could not change external bodies, they could not be felt, for a thing is felt from the senses being changed by a sensible thing . . .

Because everything acts (activity, operation, "second act") **in so far as it is an actual being** (actuality, existence, "first act"), **the consequence is that everything stands in the same relation to action as it does to being. Therefore, because . . . it is an effect of divine power that the sacramental species** (appearances) **continue in the being which they had when the substance of the bread and wine was present** (before the change, before the transubstantiation), **it follows that they continue in their action. Consequently they retain every action which they had while the substance of the bread and wine remained, now that the substance of the bread and wine has passed into the Body and Blood of Christ. Hence there is no doubt but that they can change external bodies** (III,77,3).

The consecrated elements of the Eucharist behave in every way exactly like unconsecrated bread and wine physically. The bread nourishes the body. The wine satisfies thirst. If a large amount is drunk, it will intoxicate.

There are at least two reasons, two causes, for this. One is an efficient cause—an ontological origin—and the other is a final cause—an end, a good, a purpose.

The efficient cause is that the accidents—the appearances of bread and wine—continue to act according to their nature ("species") since no miracle intervenes to stop them. The nature of any thing is the efficient cause of its characteristic activities. "Fish gotta swim, birds gotta fly" because fish are fish and birds are birds. That's the nature of Nature. God does not perform *two* miracles in the Eucharist, only one, at the Consecration.

The final cause is that Christ deliberately hides Himself, disguises Himself, gives no physical sign of His Real Presence in the Eucharist, for a crucially important purpose: to test and elicit and strengthen our faith. If we saw miraculous signs in every Eucharist, or if the Eucharistic bread and wine had no taste, like other bread and wine, or even if we felt unique feelings each time we received the Eucharist, our faith would be less strong because it would have sensible or emotional crutches to lean on. Like Christ on the Cross, where there was no miraculous rescue and not even any comforting feeling of His Father's presence ("My God, My God, why hast Thou forsaken Me?"), we believe and receive in blind faith, pure faith.

What He does in the Eucharist is like wearing a disguise, or like holding up a shield in front of Himself (the shield is the appearances of bread and wine) so that we cannot see Him there behind it. He deliberately hides from us so that we may pursue Him. It is like foreplay among the higher animals, especially dogs and cats. They will run away from each other so that they can be chased. Paradoxically, part of the strategy of the "Hound of Heaven" Who chases us is to make us chase Him.

We should thank God that He so rarely gives us special graces of pious and loving feelings during the Eucharist. The essence of love is not a feeling but a choice, a willing. We must learn to live by this deepest of the muscles of our soul. And to do that, we must exercise it. All Christians, not just great mystics, must live through a "dark night of the soul".

In this life, outside of supernatural mystical experience, do we ever hear Christ speak to us in words, as distinct from hearing a fellow creature reading and repeating the words He spoke when He was on earth, by reading the Gospels?

Whether this is the form of this sacrament: "This is My Body" and "This is My Blood"?

Ambrose says: *The consecration is accomplished by the words and expressions of the Lord Jesus. Because by all the other words spoken praise is rendered to God, prayer is put up for the people, for kings and others; but when the time comes for perfecting the sacrament, the priest uses no longer his own words but the words of Christ. Therefore it is Christ's words that perfect this sacrament....*

In the other sacraments the consecration of the matter consists only in a blessing, from which the matter consecrated derives instrumentally a spiritual power, which through the priest who is an animated instrument can pass on to inanimate instruments. But in this sacrament the consecration of the matter consists in the miraculous change of the substance, which can only be done by God; hence the minister in performing this sacrament has no other act save the pronouncing of the words....

The forms of the other sacraments are pronounced in the person of the minister ... as when it is said, *I baptize thee* or *I confirm thee*.... But the form of this sacrament is pronounced as if Christ were speaking in person, so that it is given to be understood that the minister does nothing in perfecting this sacrament except to pronounce the words of Christ (III,78,1).

St. Thomas calls the words of Consecration the "form" of this sacrament. "Form" does not mean "external shape" or "appearance," but almost the opposite: the essence, the essential nature.

The words are creative words, like the words God spoke to create the world in Genesis 1. They were spoken then by the Word of God, the pre-incarnate Christ. And the things in the creation came to be out of their words. These words were not labels given to pre-existing things, but the words that made the things. The same kind of creative word is spoken by Christ in the Eucharist. "This is My Body" and "This is My Blood" perform a similar miracle as "Let there be light." Every time you are present at Mass, you witness a miracle as great as or even greater than the Big Bang that created the universe.

When the priest utters these words, He is Christ's mouth. When Father Smith says, "This is My Body", he does not mean "This is Father Smith's body." Notice that Father Smith does not say "This is *Christ's* Body" but "This is *My* Body." It is Christ Who speaks. When we hear these words we literally hear the literal words that the literal Christ, Who is literally present, literally speaks. As St. Thomas says in his last paragraph, these words are pronounced in the person of Christ Himself, not in the person of the minister (priest). The words of Baptism are: "I baptize you"; and the "I" here is the priest. But the "My" in "This is My Body" is Christ Himself.

St. Thomas' next to last paragraph shows how no other sacrament is like this one in the immediacy of God's presence and action. In Baptism, for instance, the matter of the sacrament, the water, is used as an instrument, and so is the priest. God uses these two links in a chain—the priest and the water—to give sanctifying grace to the baptized. But in the Eucharist God Himself performs this miraculous act directly.

This makes altars and wombs the two most sacred places on earth, because there God repeatedly performs His two greatest miracles, transubstantiation and the creation of immortal souls. He enters our world whenever we open these two sacred doors. That is the deepest reason why contraception is a sacrilege: it locks the door against His presence and creative activity. It is like a priest celebrating Mass and only pretending to pronounce the words of consecration because he does not want Christ actually to come. But it is Christ Who invented both of those doors, for that very purpose.

What is the greatest sentence ever spoken?

Owing to Christ's infinite power, just as through contact with His flesh the regenerative power (of Baptism) entered not only into the waters which came into contact with Christ but into all waters throughout the whole world and during all future ages, so likewise from Christ's uttering these words ("This is My Body") they derived their consecrating power, by whatever priest they be uttered, as if Christ present were saying them....

This sentence ("This is My Body") possesses the power of effecting the conversion of the bread into the Body of Christ. And therefore it is compared to other sentences, which have power only of signifying and not of producing, as the concept of the practical intellect, which is productive of the thing, is compared to the concept of our speculative intellect, which is drawn from things ... as the concept of the practical intellect does not presuppose the thing understood but makes it, so the truth of this expression does not presuppose the thing signified but makes it (III,78,5).

The terms St. Thomas uses are technical but the point is simple and commonsensical. The "practical intellect" makes something new to be (like a story); the "theoretical intellect" only knows what is already there (like a theory in physics). It is the difference between art and science. Art creates truth, science discovers truth. We discover giraffes but we create hobbits. Our concept of a giraffe is true if it conforms to real pre-existing giraffes; but this is not true of hobbits. Tolkien says, "In a hole in the ground there lived a Hobbit"—and lo and behold, Hobbits come into being. God says "Let there be light"—and there is light. That is the work of the practical (making, doing) intellect: to make a thing, to know it into existence. The theoretical intellect only copies, transmits, signifies, informs, labels, or communicates what is already there. The difference between our practical intellect and God's is that God actually creates the objective reality of what He knows, while we only create ideas, stories, fictions, forms of subjective thought rather than forms of objective reality.

When the priest pronounces the words of Christ, "This is My Body," over the bread on the altar, something happens that is greater than the creation of the universe. When God said "Let there be light", it was only light that was created, though it was created out of nothing; but when He says "This is My Body", using the priest as His instrument, the Second Person of the eternal Triune God is made present out of bread. The change from nothing to something is very great, but the change from something to God is greater. The gap between God and something is even more infinite than the gap between something and nothing. Therefore, every day, millions of times, all over the world, on every Catholic altar, something is said that is greater than the word that created the universe out of nothing. The Mass is a greater event than the Big Bang.

Why did He do it? He does it in the Mass for the same reason He did it on Calvary. It is the same deed and the same Christ; only the manner is different: bloody vs. unbloody. My candidate for the greatest line ever spoken in a movie is Christ's answer, in *The Passion of the Christ*, to His Mother's agonized question, "Why do you have to do all this?" on the horrible, bloody way to Calvary: "See, Mother, I make all things new." He had made all things by giving the universe His mind at the Creation, and now He made all things new by giving us His Body in the Redemption. The Creation cost Him nothing. The Redemption cost Him everything.

If what we drink in the Eucharist is not wine, as it appears to be, but Christ's own Blood, where does it come from? From nothing? Or from Christ's own Body on the Cross? Is this sacrament something like a 2,000-year-long straw that enables us to drink the actual Blood of Christ that is the cause of our salvation? Or is it, as Protestants say, much less shockingly, merely a holy symbol?

Whether grace (sanctifying grace, saving grace) **is bestowed through this sacrament?**

Our Lord says (Jn 6:51): *The bread which I will give is My flesh for the life of the world....*

Christ ... by coming sacramentally into man, causes the life of grace, according to John 6:58: *He that eateth Me, the same also shall live by Me....*

And therefore this sacrament works in man the effect which Christ's Passion wrought in the world. Hence Chrysostom says on the words, *immediately there came out blood and water* **(Jn 19:34):** *Since the sacred mysteries derive their origin from thence, when you draw nigh to the awe-inspiring chalice, so approach as if you were going to drink from Christ's own side.* **Hence our Lord Himself says** (Mt 26:28): *This is My blood ... which shall be shed for many unto the remission of sins....* **And hence our Lord says** (Jn 6:55): *My flesh is meat indeed, and My blood is drink indeed* (III,79,1).

Do St. John Chrysostom's words shock you? Do they shock you into sanity, into realism, into reality, into truth? Or into exaggeration and even blasphemy? When did you see the Eucharist more truly: before or after you first read those words? Will you ever be able to see it in the old way again?

Grace is not merely a gift given gratuitously by God, though it is that too: it is the very life of God, "eternal life", supernatural life, *zoe*, in the soul. The Eucharist gives us grace; *i.e., it gives us God.*

St. Bernard of Clairvaux writes that when he contemplates the crucifix, he sees the five wounds of Christ as *lips*, speaking to us in their bleeding. What are they saying? They are saying, with eloquence far beyond any written words, "I love you." His wounds are kisses.

There are also other ways to interpret the image of Christ's blood flowing from His body, other meanings in this image (which is both a reality and an image, both a thing and a sign). For images and symbols, whether they are merely verbal or whether they are historically real events, as is the case here, do not have only one correct meaning, but many—unless they are allegories, which artificially and deliberately restrict the many possible meanings of a symbol to only one, like a finger pointing at one specific object. Symbols, in contrast, are like lights that illumine many objects.

One such "other way" to interpret the image is by contrast to Dracula. Dracula is a reverse of Christ, an anti-Christ. Dracula sucks your blood, your life, and makes you one of the living dead, one of the damned. Ghouls (as in *Night of the Living Dead* do the same thing to your body: they eat it and make you a ghoul, make you one of the living dead, the damned. But Christ gives you His Body and Blood, His life, to make you one of the saved. Salvation is a blood transfusion. So in the Eucharist we literally *eat His Body and drink His Blood.* Our lips are to be applied to His five wounds as the mouths of starving lions are applied to the blood of the animals they eat, and as the mouths of suckling babies are applied to their mother's breasts. He gives us supernatural life not just symbolically but literally, by giving us His literal Body and Blood. "Unless you eat the flesh of the Son of man and drink his blood, you have no life (*zoe*, supernatural life) in you"—Jn 6:53). Nothing He could possibly have said would have shocked the Jews more than that.

And then He adds that "my flesh is food indeed and my blood is drink indeed"—or "This is real meat and real drink. This is what meat really means: My Body. This is what drink really means: My Blood. They are not symbols. What you eat and drink three times a day is the symbol, and this is the reality. You see things upside down."

Yes, it is shocking. When the real God, and His real love appears, we are always shocked.

If there are no sacraments in Heaven, what is the connection between the sacrament of the Eucharist on earth and our own Heavenly destiny?

Whether the attaining of glory is an effect of this sacrament?

It is written (Jn 6:51): *If any man eat of this bread, he shall live for ever.* **But eternal life is the life of glory. Therefore the attaining of glory is an effect of this sacrament....**

The refreshment of spiritual food and the unity (with Christ) **denoted by the species of the bread and wine are to be had in the present life, although imperfectly; but perfectly in the state of glory....**

As Christ's Passion, in virtue whereof this sacrament is accomplished, is indeed the sufficient cause of glory, yet not so that we are thereby forthwith admitted to glory, but we must first *suffer with Him in order that we may also be glorified* **afterwards** *with Him* (Rom 8:17), **so this sacrament does not at once admit us to glory but bestows on us the power of coming into glory. And therefore it is called** *Viaticum*, **a figure whereof we read in III Kings 19:8:** *Elias ate and drank, and walked in the strength of that food forty days and forty nights unto the mount of God, Horeb* (III,79,2).

The connection is causal. The Eucharist causes our eternal salvation, our Heavenly, eternal glory, because the Eucharist is Christ Himself.

But what kind of cause is it?

It is not a formal cause of our Heavenly glory, because the formal cause of anything is that thing's very essence, which can never be distinct from the thing of which it is the form or essence. But in our Heavenly glory there will be no sacraments, so sacraments and this glory are distinct.

It is not a material cause, although sacraments are always material. For the matter of the Eucharist is the bread and the wine; and these substances do not remain, even on earth, in the Eucharist.

The Eucharist is not a final cause (purpose, or end) of Heaven, but Heaven is the final cause of it.

It is, however, an efficient cause, the real power that effects the change. As the Word of God in Heaven, the eternal *Logos*, the pre-incarnate Christ, was the means or efficient cause by which God the Father created the universe ("God said ... and it was"), so this same Word of God in the flesh on the Cross effects our salvation.

He Himself clearly said that. "If any man eat of this bread, he shall live forever." And He cannot lie because He is Truth Himself: "I am the Truth" (Jn 14:6). Thus St. Thomas writes in his "Adoro Te Devote", "I believe all the Son of God has spoken / Than Truth's own word there is no truer token."

As St. Thomas points out in his third paragraph, this effect of the Eucharist, namely eternal life, begins not in Heaven but on earth. It is perfected in Heaven, but if the seed is not planted here, it cannot flower There.

Christ warns us to "count the cost" (Lk 14: 28). The road to Heaven involves suffering. "If any man would come after me, let him deny himself and take up his cross and follow me. For whoever would save his life will lose it, and whoever loses his life for my sake will find it. For what will it profit a man if he gains the whole world and forfeits his life?" (Mt 16:24–26). No man in history ever uttered a more practical sentence about the subject of practical economics (the science of profit and loss) than that one.

Since the obstacle to our goal of Heaven is sin—mortal sin eternally and permanently, if not repented of, venial sin temporally and temporarily—does God remove this obstacle in the sacrament of the Eucharist, or only in the sacrament of Confession? If in Eucharist He does remove sin, why does the Church forbid anyone in mortal sin to receive this sacrament?

Whether the forgiveness of mortal sin is an effect of this sacrament?

Whoever is conscious of mortal sin has within him an obstacle to receiving the effect of this sacrament ... because he is not alive spiritually, and so he ought not to eat the spiritual nourishment, since nourishment is confined to the living, and because he cannot be united with Christ, which is the effect of this sacrament, as long as he retains an attachment to mortal sin.... Hence, in him who is conscious of mortal sin, this sacrament does not cause the forgiveness of sin ... (III,79,3).

Whether venial sins are forgiven through this sacrament?

The reality of this sacrament is (divine) charity ... which is kindled in this sacrament; and by this means venial sins are forgiven.... The power of charity, to which this sacrament belongs, is greater than that of venial sins (III,79,4).

The Eucharist is not a substitute for Confession. That would make Confession superfluous. It can do no good, either to us individually, or to anyone else, or to the Kingdom of God on earth, to receive the Eucharist into a soul that is in a state of mortal sin, i.e., a soul deprived of the life of Christ (*zoe*, eternal life, supernatural life, sanctifying grace, divine charity). Food can't nourish a dead body.

Thus if we are conscious of mortal sin, or if we believe we are in a state of mortal sin, we should not receive the Eucharist but go to Confession as quickly as possible. Our own judgment of ourselves is fallible, of course, but it is all we have to rely on. God does not give us infallible divine revelations about the state of our own individual souls.

Imperfect contrition (motivated by fear of punishment) without Confession is insufficient to remove mortal sin, but perfect contrition (motivated by justice, honor, and love of God) is. We often do not know whether we have perfect contrition or not, and in this case again we must act according to our own best honest judgment, avoiding scrupulosity and indifference equally.

If our habitual error is scrupulosity, we should worry more about being too scrupulous than about indifference, and be more bold to receive the Eucharist, trusting in God's grace. For over-scrupulosity is an insult to God's mercy, and, as St. Thomas says, "the power of this sacrament is (divine) charity ... and by this means venial sins are forgiven.... (for) the power of charity ... is greater than that of venial sins." Venial sins are not an obstacle to reception of the Eucharist, and the Eucharist, through the infusion of charity, can forgive venial sins. (We do not know exactly which, when, or how many, just as we do not know exactly which, when, or how many germs are removed by soap, light, or medicines.)

If our habitual error is indifference, which is the much more common contemporary error, we should worry more about that than about scrupulosity, and be less bold, or rather less thoughtless and automatic, in choosing to receive the Eucharist. For indifference is an insult to God's holiness. And the consecrated Host in the Eucharist is the holy God Himself.

We may judge whether we are more prone to scrupulosity or indifference, if we honestly ask ourselves this question: Which of these two divine attributes is the more obvious to us, and which is the one we most easily forget or minimize?—His holiness or His mercy?

Venial sins, like inevitable germs on us, do not make us unfit for the banquet table. But we should wash them away by the sacrament of Confession when we notice them.

If the Eucharist is the offering of Christ's sacrifice, and if this has infinite merit and power to forgive all sins, does that mean that no one who receives the Eucharist while in a state of grace will have to experience any punishment for sin in Purgatory? If not, how can sin's guilt be totally purged by this sacrament and yet the need for Purgatorial punishment remain?

Whether the entire punishment due to sin is forgiven through this sacrament?

This sacrament is both a sacrifice and a sacrament. It has the nature of a sacrifice inasmuch as it is offered up, and it has the nature of a sacrament inasmuch as it is received.

Through the power of the sacrament, it produces directly that effect for which it was instituted. Now it was instituted not for satisfaction (for sins) **but for nourishing spiritually the union between Christ and His members ... But because this union is the effect of charity, from ... which man obtains forgiveness, not only of guilt but also of punishment, hence it is that as a consequence and by concomitance with its chief effect, man obtains forgiveness of the punishment—not of the entire punishment but according to the measure of his devotion and fervor.**

But in so far as it is a sacrifice, it has a satisfactory power. Yet ... although this offering suffices of its own quantity to satisfy for all punishment, yet it becomes satisfactory for them for whom it is offered, or ... for the offerers, according to the measure of their devotion, and not for the whole punishment (III,79,5).

The purpose of Purgatory is to completely *internalize*, in your own individual soul, what Christ has completely *accomplished* in objective reality in His Passion. Nothing at all is lacking in Christ's work and in its extension in the Eucharist objectively, in itself. It has total and infinite power to forgive sins. The only thing lacking is the measure of our personal, subjective appropriation of it. To whatever degree that is lacking, Purgatory completes it.

The Eucharist prepares us for Purgatory by plunging us into Christ's Passion sacramentally. In Purgatory our own passion (suffering) will be perfectly united with Christ's. That is why according to St. Catherine of Genoa, in her *Dialogues on Purgatory*, even though its pains will be very great, its joys will be even greater. It will be like taking off filthy rags and putting on Christ's white robe. Like childbirth, the pain will be great but it will be swallowed up in the joy.

When St. Thomas speaks of the Eucharist from the perspective of objective reality—and its objective reality is Christ Himself sacrificed and offered to the Father for our salvation—he says its power to forgive all punishment for sin is unlimited.

("Forgiveness", by the way, is not merely a subjective mental attitude in one person toward another. It is a real transaction, a changed objective relationship. It is remission of a debt. The debt is forgiven. It has been paid by Another and we need not pay it ourselves. We are free.)

But when St. Thomas speaks of the Eucharist from the perspective of our own personal reception of the sacrament, he notes that we do not obtain remission (forgiveness) fully if our charity and devotion is not full. We drink the living Water, and are made really clean by it, not just legally clean; but only in proportion to how much we open the faucet of our faith and love. In other words, although the sacraments work *ex opere operato*, i.e., from the working of the God Who is at work in them rather than from our own subjective devotion as the efficient cause of their grace, yet, though we cannot originate that grace, we can limit its effects or frustrate it by the weakness of our faith and hope and love That is why we need Purgatory: to fulfill the prayer "Lord, I believe, help my unbelief."

We do not know how many of us will need Purgatory (though the saints usually say it will be most of us), because we do not know the point at which our faith and love is enough to bypass that need, and it is not helpful to ask that question. Much better to keep our eyes on Christ rather than on ourselves.

276. How the Eucharist keeps us from sin

Does the Eucharist keep us not only from future punishments but also from future sins? In other words, does it sanctify us as well as justify us?

Whether man is preserved by this sacrament from future sin?

Sin is the spiritual death of the soul. Hence man is preserved from future sin in the same way as the body is preserved from future death of the body; and this happens in two ways. First of all, in so far as man's nature is strengthened inwardly against inner decay, and so by means of food and medicine he is preserved from death. Secondly, by being guarded against outward assaults; and thus he is protected by means of arms by which he defends his body.

Now this sacrament preserves man from sin in both of these ways ... first of all, by uniting man with Christ through grace ... secondly, inasmuch as it is a sign of Christ's Passion, whereby the devils are conquered, it repels all the assaults of demons....

The effect of this sacrament is received according to man's condition. Such is the case with every active cause in that its effect is received in matter according to the condition of the matter. But such is the condition of man on earth that his free will can be bent to good or evil. Hence, although this sacrament of itself has the power of preserving from sin, yet it does not take away from man the possibility of sinning (III,79,6).

Sin is the worst thing in life, because it separates us from God, Who is the Best Thing.

Nothing is a more powerful enemy of sin than God Himself.

Hidden behind the appearances of the Eucharist is God Himself, in person.

Therefore the Eucharist is the most powerful enemy of sin, which is the worst thing in life.

Whatever is the most powerful enemy of the worst thing in life, is the best thing in life.

Therefore the Eucharist is the best thing in life.

St. Thomas explains that Christ in the Eucharist preserves us from sin both inwardly and outwardly, both positively and negatively, both by strengthening the soul as food strengthens the body, and by giving the soul the most powerful weapon against the attacks of our enemies.

We do have real enemies; the word is used literally hundreds of times in the Psalms. They are demons. If there are really no demons, or if they are not the formidable enemies that the Bible, the Church, the saints, and Christ Himself tell us they are, then Christ, the saints, the Bible, and the Church are all fools or liars. True, modern science and modern psychology know nothing of demons. But what logically follows from that? Why would you expect them to?

Is your faith weak? Is your hope and courage weak? Is your love weak? The Eucharist is the Food that will strengthen you. Nothing can compare with it—no efforts on our part, no psychological techniques, no matter how good they are—can possibly compare with Jesus Christ Himself in person.

When assailed by temptations from your spiritual enemies, do you succumb easily, without a great struggle? Do you seldom win? Here is the answer. It will not end your struggles, but it will end your habitual defeats. Demons may laugh at your powers and your virtues; they do not laugh at Christ.

Do you want to become strong? Do you want to become a saint? Put all your trust in Him, in His Real Presence in the Eucharist and in your soul after you receive Him there, rather than in yourself. Ask yourself: Do I really believe that Jesus Christ Himself is really, fully, personally there, when I receive Him, in my body and my soul? If I do, how can I fear the assault of mere creatures, however formidable?

Protestants can put all their trust in Christ too, and become holy and strong, but not as easily, concretely, simply, and objectively as Catholics. What a power we have! How simple it is! He is *really there*! If you believe that, though you will not become perfect *instantly*, your life will be transformed.

Does my reception of the Eucharist, like intercessory prayer, help those I love as well as myself?

Whether this sacrament benefits others besides the recipients?

Prayer is made for many others during the celebration of this sacrament, which would serve no purpose were the sacrament not beneficial to others. Therefore this sacrament is beneficial not merely to them who receive it.

As stated above, this sacrament is not only a sacrament but also a sacrifice ... to others who do not receive it (as a sacrament), **it is beneficial by way of sacrifice, inasmuch as it is offered for their salvation. Hence it is said in the Canon of the Mass:** *Be mindful, O Lord, of Thy servants, men and women ... for whom we offer, or who* (themselves) *offer up to Thee, this sacrifice of praise for themselves and for all their own, for the redemption of their souls, for the hope of their safety and salvation.* **And our Lord expressed both ways, saying** (Mt 26:28, with Lk 22:20): *Which for you,* **i.e., who receive it,** *and for many,* **i.e., others,** *shall be shed unto remission of sins* (III,79,7).

There are numerous prayers for others in the liturgy of the Eucharist: both the dead and the living, both those outside the Church and all ranks in the Church. These are not extra additions, like icing on a cake or costumes on a body. They are part of the Eucharist and its power.

We tend to think that on the one hand there is the Real Presence of Christ given to us as we receive the sacrament, and on the other hand we offer prayers for others as we would do in other religious ceremonies. But there is no such "on the one hand" and "on the other hand." These prayers are not added to the Eucharist; they are parts of it.

Therefore the prayers we offer in the Mass for the world are far more powerful than the prayers we offer outside the Mass, even if the prayers we offer outside the Mass are the same prayers, and even if there are more of them, and even if they are offered for the same people, or for more people, and even if they are offered with the same faith and devotion on our part, or even with a little more faith and devotion on our part.

How big a difference does the Mass make to intercessory prayer for our loved ones? The difference between the intercessory prayers for those we love prayed outside the Mass and the same prayers prayed in the Mass is the difference between prayers prayed by you and prayers prayed by Christ. It's the difference between you and Christ. How big a difference is that?

Here is why, here is the explanation of how that works: Even though those we pray for in the Eucharist do not receive the Eucharist as a sacrament, they can receive great benefits from it because the Eucharist is not only a sacrament that is subjectively received but also a sacrifice that is objectively made. Christ Himself prays for them in this sacrifice, for their salvation and sanctification; for that was the whole purpose of His sacrifice: their salvation and sanctification! Christ's Passion and death were the most powerful prayer ever offered; and that is what is made really present in the Eucharist, in an unbloody manner. The Eucharist is a time machine. It collapses 2,000 years of time and brings the most important event that ever happened, 2,000 years ago on Calvary, into the present.

At the very heart of the Mass we pray the words of Christ quoted by St. Thomas (in the last paragraph) that unite the "you" and the "many", those who are physically present receiving the sacrament and those who are absent but prayed for.

How much, or how badly, do our venial sins (of which we all have many, as the saints are the first to admit) block the power of the Eucharist in our souls and our lives?

Whether the effect of this sacrament is hindered by venial sin?

Venial sins can be taken in two ways: first of all as past, secondly as in the act of being committed. Venial sins taken in the first way do not in any way hinder the effect of this sacrament. For it can come to pass that after many venial sins a man may approach devoutly to this sacrament and fully secure its effect. Considered in the second way, venial sins do not utterly hinder the effect of this sacrament, but merely in part. For ... actual refreshment of spiritual sweetness is indeed hindered if anyone approach to this sacrament with mind distracted through venial sins. But the increase of habitual grace or of charity is not taken away (III,79,8).

St. Thomas gives a surprisingly light, or "liberal", or "optimistic" answer to our question. All sins are sins, and sins are the worst things in the world, so we would expect him to tell us that we usually underestimate the hindrance our venial sins make to the effects of the Eucharist. Instead, he tells us that:

(1) the past venial sins that are repented of "do not in any way hinder the effect of this sacrament"; and that

(2) present venial sins hinder it "merely in part"; i.e., that

(3) even when we are distracted when receiving the sacrament—even when our foolish minds choose to think about something else that is not even to be compared with Christ, when Christ Himself is really present—even then, habitual grace and charity are not taken away,

(4) and even *their increase,* i.e., the increase of graces, is not taken away! In other words, we profit spiritually, we gain in holiness, in every Eucharist even if we are distracted by our own faults!

(5) The experience of "spiritual sweetness" is removed by distractions and venial sins, but the increase of habitual grace is still given. The feeling is much less important than we think. God often withholds this gift even to great saints, to strengthen their will and purify their faith, training us to rely less on our own feelings and more on Him. So do not think that your degree of "spiritual sweetness" is an indicator of your piety. It isn't.

It is not magic. It is not automatic. It is not impersonal. We can and do block grace, and we receive grace only in proportion to our openness, our receptivity, our faith, and our hope and our charity. Yet the power of Christ in this sacrament overshadows all our faults to a far greater extent than we can imagine or easily believe. How could it be otherwise?—it is the infinitely compassionate and infinitely powerful Savior Himself Who is operating here. We cannot overestimate His generosity.

How is our reception of grace in the Eucharist affected by sins of our recent or remote past which we have forgotten, but which remain in our unconscious memory and in their harmful influence on our character? Since sin penetrates to all areas of our being, it must penetrate also to our unconscious; so how do these sins affect our reception of the Eucharist? Or was St. Thomas perhaps so naïve and pre-modern that he did not recognize the existence of the unconscious?

Objection. **It happens sometimes that the sinner is unconscious of his sin. Yet such a one does not seem to sin by receiving the Body of Christ, for according to this** (if unconscious sin prevents reception of the Eucharist) **all who receive it would sin, as exposing themselves to danger, since the Apostle says** (1 Cor 4:4): *I am not conscious to myself of anything* (sinful), *yet I am not hereby justified....*

Reply. **The fact of a man being unconscious of his sin can come about in two ways. First of all through his own fault, either because through ignorance of the law (which ignorance does not excuse him) he thinks something not to be sinful which is a sin, as for example if one guilty of fornication were to deem simple fornication not to be a mortal sin; or because he neglects to examine his conscience ... in this way ... the sinner who receives Christ's Body commits sin, although unconscious thereof, because the very ignorance is a sin on his part.**

Secondly, it may happen without fault on his part, as for instance when he has sorrowed over his sin but is not sufficiently contrite; and in such a case he does not sin in receiving the Body of Christ, because a man cannot know for certain whether he is truly contrite. It suffices, however, if he find in himself the marks of contrition, for instance if he *grieve over past sins and propose to avoid them in the future* **(Rule of St. Augustine). But if he be ignorant that what he did was a sinful act through ignorance of the fact which excuses, for instance if a man approach a woman whom he believed to be his wife whereas she was not, he is not to be called a sinner** on that account. **In the same way if he has utterly forgotten his sin, general contrition suffices for blotting it out** (III,80,4).

Freud was not the first to discover the unconscious. It is commonsense experience. Plato anticipated many of Freud's theories about the unconscious in the *Republic*; and St. Thomas, like all classic spiritual masters, knew its extent and power quite well. So he begins with the assumption that "it happens sometimes that the sinner is unconscious of his sin."

The question then is: Since it is wrong to receive the Eucharist when we have unrepented sin in our soul, and since it is not possible to be consciously repentant of sins that we are not conscious of, and since most people have sins they are not conscious of most of the time, and therefore not repentant of, why is it not therefore wrong for most people to receive the Eucharist most of the time?

The answer is that unconscious sins do not of themselves prevent us from receiving the Eucharist. General contrition for all sin suffices. What does not suffice is when the reason we are unconscious of these sins is not merely ordinary human forgetfulness, inattention, or ignorance, but either deliberate refusal to examine our conscience or inexcusable ignorance of what is and is not a sin. The first of these two reasons is obviously blameworthy. A word must be said today about the second.

Many Catholics today in the West actually believe that "simple fornication", or what used to be called "living in sin" (sex outside marriage), is OK because "everyone's doing it." They know the Church and the Bible forbid it (even the secular world knows that!), so they don't have excusable ignorance. Either they do not believe that the Ten Commandments and the Church's moral teachings are divine revelation and the will of God (in which case they are not really Catholics), or they don't care (in which case they are very bad Catholics). In either case they should not receive Communion until they repent and confess. This demands not just adjustment but *conversion* of heart and mind to the Catholic Faith, i.e., to the mind and will of Christ.

The priest administering Communion cannot know the state of soul of the person seeking to receive it. Is there any justification, then, for his ever denying Communion to any Catholic?

Whether the priest ought to deny the Body of Christ to the sinner seeking it?

A distinction must be made among sinners. Some are secret, others are notorious, either from evidence of the fact, as public usurers or public robbers, or from being denounced as evil men by some ecclesiastical or civil tribunal. Therefore Holy Communion ought not to be given to open sinners when they ask for it....

But if they are not open sinners but occult (hidden), the Holy Communion should not be denied them if they ask for it. For since every Christian, from the fact that he is baptized, is admitted to the Lord's table, he may not be robbed of his right except from some open cause. Hence on 1 Corinthians 5:11, *If he who is called a brother among you,* **etc., Augustine's gloss remarks:** *We cannot inhibit any person from Communion except he has openly confessed or has been named and convicted by some ecclesiastical or lay tribunal.*

Nevertheless a priest who has knowledge of the crime can privately warn the secret sinner, or warn all openly in public, from approaching the Lord's table, until they have repented of their sins and have been reconciled to the Church; because after repentance and reconciliation Communion must not be refused even to public sinners, especially in the hour of death (III,80,6).

It is true that priests cannot read souls; only God can. But some sins are open and public, like being a Mafia hit man or an abortionist or a drug dealer or a professional thief. Someone who is an open and public sinner in a grave matter, and continues to perform the public sin for all to see, can and should be denied Communion. It would be a scandal for the Church implicitly to approve such a person's lifestyle by giving him the all-holy Body of Christ.

What constitutes a grave matter is to some extent a prudential judgment and up to the local priest or bishop. There are some "grey areas" that are matters of degree. Habitual drunkenness is often public and open, but it is not grave enough for the Church to deny Communion to alcoholics, if they are sober at the time. What about a famous person who is married but living openly with a mistress? This is a much more deliberate public sin, and the Church would give scandal (harm to souls) if she acted as if that was acceptable to Christ, by offering Christ in the Eucharist to such public adulterer. What of politicians who publicly support the slaughter of the unborn innocent by abortion? This might seem to be a borderline case, but canon law is quite clear that they should be denied Communion, for their own sakes as well as the sake of public witness, though few bishops dare to enforce this.

But when the sin is not open and public, then the Church does not deny Communion to the sinner even if the sin is grave and the individual is wrong in seeking Communion. Since the sin is not open and public, there is no scandal (harm to souls) in giving them Communion. But when a priest knows of this sin, he should privately warn the individual to repent and confess before receiving.

In fact, even public and grave sinners, if they repent and confess, must be given Communion. This is true even if the priest suspects that the repentance and confession are not genuine, because he cannot be sure, and they must be given the benefit of the doubt, like a suspect who is innocent until proven guilty. Like God, the Church prefers to err on the side of compassion rather than on the side of strictness when it comes to pastoral work. She judges actions strongly and clearly; people much less so.

Especially "at the hour of death". Death has a great way of provoking repentance. Samuel Johnson says "I know no thought that more wonderfully clarifies a man's mind than the thought that he must hang tomorrow morning."

281. EUCHARIST FOR THE MENTALLY DISABLED?

Should Communion be given to the severely mentally disabled?

Whether those who have not the use of reason ought to receive this sacrament?

We read in the First Council of Orange, Canon 13, and the same is to be found in the Decretals (26:6): *All things that pertain to piety are to be given to the insane;* **and consequently, since this is the** *sacrament of piety,* **it must be given to them.**

Men are said to be devoid of reason in two ways. First, when they are feeble-minded, as a man who sees dimly is said not to see; and since such persons can conceive some devotion towards this sacrament, it is not to be denied them.

In another way men are said not to possess fully the use of reason. Either, then, they never had the use of reason and have remained so from birth; and in that case this sacrament is not to be given to them because in no way has there been any preceding devotion towards the sacrament; or else they were not always devoid of reason; and then, if when they formerly had their wits they showed devotion towards this sacrament, it ought to be given to them in the hour of death....

Those lacking the use of reason can have devotion towards the sacrament: actual devotion in some cases, and past in others (III,80,9).

We might argue that Communion should not be given to anyone who is not able to exercise a conscious act of faith, since the Eucharist is not magic, or impersonal, and its effects, though they come *ex opere operato* from God rather than from the soul of the recipient, are increased or decreased by the degree of faith and devotion of the recipient. But this argument is wrong. There are many kinds and degrees of faith and devotion, and we must err on the side of compassion rather than caution in allowing as many people as possible, and as many kinds of people, access to the greatest privilege on earth, real sacramental union, in body and soul, with Jesus Christ, God incarnate.

What, exactly, do we mean by calling some people "insane", "mentally retarded", "mentally defective", "mentally handicapped", "feeble-minded", or "lacking the use of reason"? The first honest answer is that we do not know, exactly. The terms are meaningful but vague, as uncertain as we are. There are many true stories of surprisingly rational things said and done by supposedly non-rational persons (using the ancient, broader and deeper concept of "rational" here: not just "clever" but "understanding").

St. Thomas distinguishes two kinds of lack of reason in human beings, and both kinds may be given Communion. The "feeble-minded", those who have from birth always had a very low IQ, are quite capable of deep and real and precious devotion, as all caregivers to such persons are profoundly aware. Down syndrome persons are beautiful examples. And those who once had a normal use of reason and are now deprived of it (e.g., those in coma, or with Alzheimer's) are still the persons they once were, they are not ex-persons; so if they once had faith and devotion to the Eucharist they must be given Communion— not because we fantasize about what they "would have wanted" if they were now in possession of full reason but because they are in fact now the same person they once were when they expressed a faith and desire for Communion. This is so especially (but not only) at the hour of death.

Devotion as such, in the abstract, assumes reason as such, in the abstract. Rocks and birds cannot have it. But devotion in actual practice is often present but hidden, and admits of many degrees, like reason itself. For instance, even an embryo is a "rational" animal, i.e., a human person, even though its brain and nervous system have not yet developed; for that is a *human* embryo which is growing a *human* brain which will be the instrument of *human* consciousness, i.e., "reason". It is human and therefore "rational" already, actually and not just potentially; that's why it's growing a *human* brain. It's the human soul that's doing that. We have one soul, not two. The same human soul that first grows brains, later thinks with them.

Is daily Communion good, natural, and normal? Wasn't it initiated by Pope Pius X only about 100 years ago? Doesn't it cheapen the Eucharist to make it so common?

Augustine says: *This is our daily bread; take it daily, that it may profit thee daily.*

I answer that, There are two things to be considered regarding the use of this sacrament. The first is on the part of the sacrament itself, the virtue (power) of which gives (spiritual) health to men; and consequently it is profitable to receive it daily so as to receive its fruits daily. Hence Ambrose says: *If, whenever Christ's blood is shed, it is shed for the forgiveness of sins, I who sin often should receive it often: I need a frequent remedy.*

Since man has daily need of Christ ... he may commendably receive this sacrament every day....

Just as bodily food is taken every day, so it is a good thing to receive this sacrament every day. Hence it is that our Lord (Lk 11:3) teaches us to pray, *Give us this day our daily bread....*

The second thing to be considered is on the part of the recipient, who is required to approach this sacrament with great reverence and devotion. Consequently, if anyone finds that he has these dispositions every day, he will do well to receive it daily. Hence Augustine, after saying, *Receive daily, that it may profit thee daily,* adds: *So live as to deserve to receive it daily.* But because many persons are lacking in this devotion, on account of the many drawbacks both spiritual and corporeal from which they suffer, it is not expedient for all to approach this sacrament every day; but they should do so as often as they find themselves properly disposed. Hence it is said: *I neither praise nor blame daily reception of the Eucharist....*

Reverence for this sacrament consists in fear associated with love; consequently reverential fear of God is called filial fear ... because the desire of receiving arises from love, while the humility of reverence springs from fear. Consequently, each of these belongs to the reverence due to this sacrament, both as to receiving it daily and as to refraining from it sometimes. Hence Augustine says: *If one says that the Eucharist should not be received daily, while another maintains the contrary, let each one do as according to his devotion he thinketh right; for Zaccheus and the Centurion did not contradict one another while the one received the Lord with joy whereas the other said: "Lord, I am not worthy that Thou shouldst enter under my roof",* since both honored our Savior, though not in the same say. But love and hope, whereunto the Scriptures constantly urge us, are preferable to fear. Hence too, when Peter had said, *Depart from me, for I am a sinful man, O Lord,* Jesus answered: *Fear not* (III,80,10).

First the historical point: Pius X appealed to authorities among the early "Church Fathers" and medievals in recommending daily Communion. From the beginning it was the norm, or the ideal. St. Thomas clearly recommended it. If God had wanted infrequent Communion instead of daily, "common" Communion, He would have used caviar instead of bread and champagne instead of wine.

Our need for "bread" (food) is an every-day thing; therefore "bread" (food) should be an every-day thing. Our need for "our daily bread" (Christ) is also every day, and should be met every day. The sin that we need to combat is with us every day; therefore the strongest weapon with which to combat it should be every day. Faith and devotion are the prerequisites for receiving Communion, but these also should be with us each day, therefore Communion should too.

This is the ideal. There are two kinds of reasons for accepting something less than the ideal. We may find our devotion weakening and "cheapening" by daily Communion (this is possible but not likely), or our secular responsibilities may simply make it logistically impossible or nearly impossible.

Love and respect ("filial fear") for the Eucharist should be the common motive for both receiving and not receiving daily Communion.

What justifies the Church in offering the laity only the bread and not the wine in the Eucharist?

On the part of the sacrament it is proper for both the Body and the Blood to be received, since the perfection of the sacrament lies in both, and consequently, since it is the priest's duty both to consecrate and to finish the sacrament, he ought on no account to receive Christ's Body without the Blood.

But on the part of the recipient the greatest reverence and caution are called for, lest anything happen which is unworthy of so great a mystery. Now this could especially happen in receiving the Blood, for if uncautiously handled it might easily be split. And because the multitude of the Christian people increased, in which there are old, young and children, some of whom have not enough discretion to observe due caution in using this sacrament, on that account it is a prudent custom in some churches for the Blood not to be offered to the reception of the people, but to be received by the priest alone.

The perfection of this sacrament does not lie in the use of the faithful but in the consecration of the matter. And hence there is nothing derogatory to the perfection of this sacrament if the people receive the Body without the Blood, provided that the priest who consecrates receive both (III,80,12).

The first answer to the question is that it is *not* bread, nor is it bread and wine, that is received in the Eucharist. It is the Body and Blood of Christ under the appearances (or "species") of bread and wine.

The justification of the practice of many Catholic churches in not offering the laity the Precious Blood but only the Body is that it is a matter of practical prudence, not doctrine, just as with the last question, the question about frequent or daily Communion. The doctrine says that the whole Christ is received wholly under both species; therefore one who receives Christ only under the species of bread receives no less than one who also receives Him also under the species of wine.

The reason for the priest receiving under both species is that only thus is the sacramental symbol complete. The lay recipient may also find that his devotion is increased by this more complete symbolism if he receives under both species, and this may be a reason for doing so. But it is not necessarily or automatically better for devotion. Sometimes it is the rarity of a thing that sparks our devotion by sparking our interest, and this interest may lessen once the rarity ceases.

The reason for the laity not receiving the Blood is logistical and practical: the danger of spillage. If we fully understand what (or rather Who) is really there under the appearance of wine, this will be not merely a matter of mere impropriety vs. worldly prudence but a matter of sacrilege vs. worship.

The priest, however, must always receive the Blood as well as the Body, since he consecrated both elements. Therefore he is always under strictest obligation to be extremely careful with these most precious things in the world. A drop from the consecrated chalice is not a drop of wine. It is a drop of God's own Blood. A crumb that falls off the consecrated bread is not a crumb of bread but a particle of God's own Body. For anyone, priest or laity, to treat these things in a common way is a very serious lack of faith as well as of love and respect. For this reason, it is contrary to canon law to use ordinary bread, which often does flake off crumbs. This misuse, which occurs in some Catholic parishes, does not make the sacrament invalid and the consecration ineffective, however. It is precisely because it does not make the consecration invalid, precisely because it is still Christ Himself Who is there, that the Church forbids the use of ordinary bread, except under special circumstances and permission.

These issues may seem technical and legal minutiae about which the Church is being "picky", but they are not that at all, as is clear to anyone who understands the "big picture", the holiest thing the world has ever seen, the very Body of God incarnate.

What are the essential parts of the Mass? What is the reason for each one? Were they the same in St. Thomas' day as they are today?

Since the whole mystery of our salvation is comprised in this sacrament, therefore it is performed with greater solemnity than the other sacraments.

Therefore the celebration of the mystery is preceded by a certain preparation in order that we may perform worthily that which follows after.

(1) The first part of this preparation is divine praise, and consists in the *Introit....*

(2) The second part contains a reference to our present misery, by reason of which we pray for mercy, saying *Lord, have mercy on us,* thrice for the Person of the Father, and *Christ, have mercy on us* thrice for the Person of the Son, and *Lord, have mercy on us* thrice for the person of the Holy Ghost....

(3) The third part commemorates the heavenly glory, to the possession of which, after this life of misery, we are tending, in the words, *Glory be to God on high,* which are sung on festival days, on which the heavenly glory is commemorated, but are omitted in those sorrowful offices which commemorate our unhappy state.

(4) The fourth part contains the prayer which the priest makes for the people (the Collect), that they may be made worthy of such great mysteries.

There proceeds, in the second place, the instruction of the faithful....

(5) The Lectors ... read aloud in the church the teachings of the prophets and apostles;

(6) After this *lesson,* the choir sing the *Gradual,* which signifies progress in life;

(7) Then the *Alleluia* is intoned, and this denotes spiritual joy; or in mournful Offices the *Tract,* expressive of spiritual sighing....

(8) But the people are instructed perfectly by Christ's teaching contained in the *Gospel....*

(9) **After the Gospel has been read, the Creed is sung, in which the people show that they assent by faith to Christ's doctrine....**

So then, after the people have been prepared and instructed, the next step is to proceed to the celebration of the mystery, which is both offered as a sacrifice and consecrated and received as a sacrament....

First we have the oblation;

Then the consecration of the matter offered;

And thirdly, its reception.

In regard to the oblation, two things are done, namely

(10) the people's praise in singing the *Offertory,* expressing the joy of the offerers,

(11) and the priest's prayer asking for the people's oblation to be made acceptable to God....

Then, regarding the consecration, performed by supernatural power,

(12) The people are first of all excited to devotion in the *Preface,* hence they are admonished to *lift up their hearts to the Lord,*

(13) And therefore when the Preface is ended the people devoutly praise Christ's Godhead, saying with the angels: *Holy, holy, holy;* and His humanity, saying with the children: *Blessed is he that cometh.*

(14) In the next place the priest makes a *commemoration* first of those for whom this sacrifice is offered, namely, for the whole Church....

(15) Secondly, he commemorates the saints, invoking their patronage ...

(16) Thirdly ... to them for whom it is offered.

(17) Then he comes to the Consecration itself.

Then follows the act of receiving the sacrament:

(18) First of all, the people are prepared for Communion, first by the common prayer of the congregation, which is the Lord's Prayer ...

(19) **Secondly, the people are prepared by the** *Pax* **(Peace) which is given with the words,** *Lamb of God,* **etc.**

(20) **Then follows the reception of the sacrament, the priest receiving first and afterwards giving it to others....**

(21) **Finally, the whole celebration of Mass ends with the thanksgiving, the people rejoicing for having received the mystery (and this is the meaning of the singing after the Communion)** ... (III,83,4).

The question is answered so directly, fully, and clearly by St. Thomas' description that it would be superfluous to add to it.

This is a summary of the world's greatest philosophy, the world's greatest song, the world's greatest story. Heaven itself looks with awe at each Mass on earth as it looks at the event on Calvary 2,000 years ago that the Mass continues and represents.

What happens in the Mass? What happens is the most dramatic thing that ever happened. What happens is that Christ does here in an unbloody manner what He did on Calvary. What He did there was that He made all things new.

If you understand each of these basic parts of the Mass deeply enough, you will see that there is nothing omitted. Nothing. As the simplest and earliest Christian creed, the Apostles' Creed, rightly understood, tells us everything we are to believe; and as the simplest and earliest Christian prayer, the Lord's Prayer, rightly understood, tells us everything we are to hope and pray for; and as the simplest and earliest Law, the Ten Commandments, properly understood as consummated in the Beatitudes, tells us everything we are to love and desire and will and choose, so the Mass, properly understood, tells us all three of these things at once; and not only does it *tell* us these things, it *enacts* them.

The way the Mass may look from Heaven's eyes is one thing, and perfect; but the way it can look from earthly eyes seems very different, not only because subjectively our earthly hearts are far from Heavenly sight but also because very concrete, physical problems, some of them very embarrassing, may arise in this very imperfect world. Did St. Thomas ever consider the effects of such problems?

Objection 1. It sometimes happens that before or after the consecration the priest dies or goes mad....

Objection 2. It sometimes happens that before the consecration the priest remembers that he has eaten or drunk something, or that he is in mortal sin, or under excommunication....

Objection 3. It sometimes happens that a fly or a spider or some other poisonous creature falls into the chalice after the consecration; or even that the priest comes to know that poison has been put in by some evilly disposed person in order to kill him....

Objection 4. It sometimes happens from the server's want of heed that water is not added to the chalice, or even the wine overlooked....

Objection 5. It sometimes happens that the priest cannot remember having said the words of consecration....

Objection 6. It sometimes comes to pass owing to the cold that the host will slip from the priest's hands into the chalice....

Objection 7. Sometimes too it happens, owing to the priest's want of care, that Christ's blood is spilt, or that he vomits the sacrament received, or that the consecrated hosts are kept so long that they become corrupt, or that they are nibbled by mice, or lost in any manner whatsoever; in which cases it does not seem possible for due reverence to be shown towards this sacrament, as the Church's ordinances require. It does not seem then that such defects or dangers can be met by keeping to the Church's statues.

On the contrary, Just as God does not command an impossibility, so neither does the Church.

I answer that, Dangers or defects happening to this sacrament can be met in two ways: first, by preventing any such mishaps from occurring; secondly, by dealing with them in such a way that what may have happened amiss is put right, either by employing a remedy or at least by repentance on his part who has acted negligently regarding this sacrament (III,83,6).

Notice

(1) that St. Thomas takes these questions quite literally and seriously and realistically;

(2) that his answer is first to emphasize prevention rather than cure (a good general principle for all problems in all areas of life, including politics, business, and warfare both physical and spiritual);

(3) that cures or remedies are assumed always to be findable, so that even in these unusual, bizarre, and extreme cases we need not despair, for "God does not command an impossibility";

(4) and that St. Thomas does not dictate exactly what the remedy is in each case, but leaves it up to common sense and personal prudence and imagination. Perhaps he (or the people of the Middle Ages generally) had too great a confidence in these qualities; or perhaps, more likely, we lack it!

Are we really forgiven by God when the priest pronounces absolution in the Sacrament of Reconciliation?

As our Lord said to His disciples (Mt 28:19): *teach all nations, baptizing them,* etc., so did He say to Peter (Mt 16:19): *Whatsoever thou shalt loose on earth,* etc. Now the priest, relying on the authority of those words of Christ, says: *I baptize thee.* Therefore on the same authority he should say in this sacrament: *I absolve thee.*...

The sacraments of the New Law accomplish what they signify....

God alone absolves from sin and forgives sins authoritatively. Yet priests do both ministerially, because the words of the priest in this sacrament work as instruments of the divine power, as in the other sacraments....

When he says: *I absolve thee,* he declares the man to be absolved not only significatively but also effectively.... [H]e does not speak as of something uncertain, because just as the other sacraments of the New Law have, of themselves, a sure effect through the power of Christ's passion (which effect, nevertheless, may be impeded on the part of the recipient), so it is with this sacrament (III,84,3).

To deny that we are really forgiven by God in this sacrament is to deny that God has the power and the authority to use a human instrument to forgive sins. But Christ explicitly gave that power to His Apostles.

One of the definitions of a sacrament is "a sacred sign instituted by Christ to give grace, that actually effects what it signifies". As the Eucharist both *signifies* the death of Christ, by separating His Body and His Blood—the death that gives us eternal life—and also thereby actually communicates to us that gift of the grace of salvation, or eternal life; and as Baptism both *signifies* the washing from sin and *actually communicates* to us that grace; so the words of the priest in the Sacrament of Penance actually effect what they signify. They are performative words, not descriptive words. They are like "I dub thee knight" or "I hereby make you my deputy", or the "I do" in the marriage ceremony. We are allowed here to participate in a privilege God alone has: His words do not merely speak the truth, they create. When He said "let there be light", light was created. And when He says, through His appointed ministers and instruments, that we are forgiven, these words actually effect our forgiveness. St. Thomas expresses this point by saying that we are absolved (forgiven) "not only significatively but also effectively". The words are not merely formal causes but efficient causes.

Not that the words themselves have this power, but only "through the power of Christ's passion". It is Christ Who is the first cause of all sacramental grace; and the same authority that can give grace can also authorize human and verbal instruments to carry it. To deny that is not to exalt God by demeaning natural causes, or second causes, as His instruments; it is the opposite: it is to limit God's power and authority to use these instruments if He wills to do so.

And He *does* will to do so, for our sake. How much more certain we are when we receive these words from the priest authorized by Christ than when we have only our own soul's testimony, our own faith and conscience, to rely on! How much more effectively our faith and hope is directed beyond ourselves to Christ Himself when He comes to us not only subjectively and spiritually but also objectively and sacramentally, especially, in the Eucharist!

It is true that "spiritual" does not necessarily mean "subjective" and "objective" does not necessarily mean "material", and it is true that He is objectively real whether or not He uses material instruments. But it is much harder for us to escape ourselves when He does not do this, because our natural model for what is objectively real is a material thing. This may be a human weakness, but He teaches us according to our weaknesses, according to our needs.

Should we sacramentally confess frequently, as we should receive the Eucharist frequently?

Man is induced to be merciful by the example of divine mercy, according to Luke 6:36: *Be ye ... merciful, as your Father also is merciful.* **Now our Lord commanded His disciples to be merciful by frequently pardoning their brethren who had sinned against them; wherefore, as related in Matthew 18:21, when Peter asked:** *How often shall my brother offend against me, and I forgive him? Till seven times?* **Jesus answered:** *I say not to thee, till seven times, but till seventy times seven times.* **Therefore also God over and over again, through Penance, grants pardon to sinners....**

The Novatians went to so far as to say that he who sins after the first Penance ... cannot be restored again through Penance.... [T]hey erred in their estimation of the gravity of sin. For they deemed a sin committed by a man after he had received pardon to be so grave that it could not be forgiven. In this they erred not only with regard to sin ... but much more did they err against the infinity of divine mercy, which surpasses any number and magnitude of sins.... Where-fore the words of Cain were reprehensible when he said (Gen 4:13): *My iniquity is greater than that I may deserve pardon.* **And so God's mercy, through Penance, grants pardon to sinners without any end....**

As Augustine says ... *What sort of a physician is he who knows not how to heal a recurring disease? For if a man ail a hundred times it is for the physician to heal him a hundred times....*

A man is a mocker and not a penitent who, *while doing penance,* **does what he repents having done, or intends to do again what he did before.... But if a man sin afterwards ... this does not destroy the fact that his former penance was real, because the reality of a former act is never destroyed by a subsequent contrary act; for even as he truly ran who afterwards sits, so he truly repented who subsequently sins** (III,84,10).

God Himself answers our question by commanding us to forgive over and over again. ("Seventy times seven" means, to a pre-scientific culture where mathematical competence was rare, "so many times that you can't count them".) In fact, He emphasized this unlimited demand for forgiveness so strongly that He commanded us to pray, in the Lord's Prayer, for our own damnation if we did not so forgive our neighbor: "Forgive us our debts *as we forgive our debtors.*" In other words, "If I forgive my neighbor only some sins, not all, then please forgive me only some sins, not all." Since God gives us his mercy repeatedly, we should repeatedly pass on that mercy received to all who offend us; but also, first of all, we must *receive* that repeatedly given mercy repeatedly. That is the basis for frequent Confession. (For most people, "frequent" does not mean "daily", but perhaps weekly, and at least monthly.)

Augustine's parallel is apt: a doctor who healed only one occurrence of a disease and not subsequent occurrences would be a poor doctor. God is not a poor doctor. Therefore He heals the disease of sin in us whenever it occurs, if it is repented.

If you feel God cannot be that merciful; if you think there are some sins that are too great to be forgiven even by God; if like the Novatians you say that sinning again after Confession and forgiveness is inexcusable and unforgivable; then you are not exalting God but demeaning Him. To overestimate the gravity of sin in relation to the mercy of God is to underestimate the mercy of God in relation to the gravity of sin. God Himself says that even Cain can be forgiven; who are you to say God is wrong?

This "liberality" does not make a mockery of Penance. What makes a mockery of Penance is the intention to sin while confessing sin, or actually committing the sin while confessing. You cannot will to sin and will not to sin at the same time; it is a psychological contradiction and impossibility. You may *fear* you will sin again when you are repenting, but you cannot *will* to sin again when you are repenting.

St. Thomas calls it "penance". We call it "repentance." But what is repentance? How can I be sure I have truly repented of all my sins? Sometimes I feel deep contrition and sorrow for my sins and sometimes I do not. How can I find the dividing line between true repentance, repentance that actually "works", and something less? If repentance is the will not to sin, can I truly repent if I am not sure I have this will, deep down? Perhaps I have only the will to will not to sin. Is that true repentance? Or is this whole question mistaken in treating repentance as if it were a feeling?

We can speak of penance in two ways: first, in so far as it is a passion (emotion, feeling), **and thus, since it is a kind of sorrow, it is in the concupiscible** (desiring) **part ... secondly, in so far as it is a virtue, and ... is ... in the rational appetite, which is the will. Therefore it is evident that penance, in so far as it is a virtue, is ... in the will, and its proper act is the purpose of amending what was committed against God** (III,85,4).

The feeling of contrition (sorrow for sin) is a very good and natural and holy thing, but it is not the essence of repentance, nor is it an absolutely essential part of it. We are judged on what depends on our "we", our "I", our personal center, our "heart" in the Biblical sense of that term, which means not merely the source of our feelings or sentiments or emotions (St. Thomas calls them "passions"), but the source of our fundamental choices, which we make by our will rather than by our feelings. Feelings don't *choose*. They just feel.

The emotions are related to the will somewhat as clothing is related to the body. They are not the body itself, but a healthy person always has them (at least in public). Lack of appropriate emotions is not a strength but a weakness, a problem. Yet emotions are not the essence, they are "proper accidents". When we will to repent, we repent, because repentance is an act of the will, not an act of the feelings. We can feel sorrow for sin without repenting of sin in our will (for instance when we

regret a drunken spree yesterday because of the pain of the present hangover, but plan to get drunk again tomorrow). We can also repent without feeling anything. We can will and act without the additional motivation of feelings, as we can love a stranger whom we never met and have no personal feelings for. In fact we can love him so much that we risk our life to save him from a burning building. We can even act *against* our feelings, as in this example, where we will certainly feel fear of fire. Well-integrated healthy emotions are great helpers, like shoes, but they are not the legs that run the journey.

Repentance is a moral virtue. We are responsible for it. We are to blame for lacking it. We must, therefore, be in control of it. We are in control of our will's choices, but not (at least directly) of our emotions and feelings. Repentance is commanded; but it is impossible to command a feeling. (How foolish for me to *command* you to *feel* differently about me!) Therefore repentance is not essentially a feeling.

Therefore if we lack the feeling of repentance but nevertheless want to repent; if we choose repentance with the will; we *are* then repenting, since repentance *is* that choice of the will. We can also want to have the feeling of sorrow for sin when we do not have it and should have it; and this mere wanting, this willing, this choice to have the right feeling as well as the willing "counts" with God as full repentance.

If we are still unsure whether or not we have repented, the test is simple: do we choose to make amends, to change, to undo the wrong we did? For instance, if the sin is adultery, do we break with and say no to the illicit other person? If the sin is lust, do we destroy every form of pornography we had? If not, we are not repenting, but willing to keep sinning. We may fail and fall again after sincere repentance; but if we are really repenting, we must get on the right horse first, before we can either stay on it or fall off it again. We cannot be off it and on it at the same time. And if we are planning and intending to fall off it, we are already off it.

Is fear the origin of repentance? If so, doesn't that make repentance a feeling, or dependent on a feeling?

Whether penance originates in fear?

Objection 1. **It would seem that penance does not originate from fear. For penance originates in displeasure at sin. But this belongs to charity** (since hating sin and being displeased with sin comes from loving and being pleased with God and His goodness).... **Therefore penance originates from love** (charity) **rather than fear.**

Reply 1. **Sin begins to displease a man, especially a sinner, on account of the punishments which servile fear regards, before it displeases him on account of its being an offense against God or on account of its wickedness, which pertains to charity** (III,85,5).

The best motive for repentance is filial fear, which is the fear of offending God, since this stems from charity or the love of God and what God is (goodness, holiness), for His sake rather than our own; yet servile fear (selfish fear of punishment) suffices as a prod to repentance. God accepts this as a beginning but not an end. He is "easy to please but hard to satisfy" (George MacDonald).

Objection 2. **Further, men are induced to do penance through the expectation of the heavenly kingdom, according to Matthew 3:2 and 4:17:** *Do penance, for the kingdom of heaven is at hand.* **Now the kingdom of heaven is the object of hope. Therefore penance results from hope rather than from fear.**

Reply 2. **When the kingdom of heaven is said to be at hand, we are to understand that the king is on his way, not only to reward but also to punish** (III,85,5).

Hope is somewhere between servile fear and filial fear or charity as a motive for repentance. Hope of reward can be either selfish and mercenary or unselfish and idealistic. In other words hope can stem from, or take the form of, either servile fear, the fear of punishments from the King, or filial fear, the fear of offending Him due to our love of Him (charity). Or it can stem from both. (We usually have mixed motives, and progress in the life of the Spirit consists largely in purifying our motives.) In other words, there are better and worse, higher and lower forms of and motives for repentance. St. Thomas distinguishes the two different motives in the passage that follows:

I answer that, ... (Penance includes) (1) **a movement of servile fear, whereby a man is withdrawn from sin through fear of punishment** ... (2) **a movement of charity, whereby sin is displeasing to man for its own sake and no longer for the sake of the punishment** ... (this is) **a movement of filial fear whereby a man, of his own accord, offers to make amends to God through fear of Him.**

The act of penance (both internal repentance and external amends) **results from servile fear as from the first movement ... and from filial fear as from its ... proper principle** (motive) (III,85,5).

The distinction St. Thomas makes above between "a movement of charity" and "the act of penance" is not a distinction between higher and lower *motives*, like the distinction between (1) servile fear and (2) charity, but a distinction *within* filial fear between the internal cause or motive and the external act (going to Confession). He classifies all three as "movements" of the soul, which change our spiritual state in the right direction.

The purpose of servile fear, and the reason God uses it in religion, is wholly to lead us to filial fear. God will accept selfish motives at first ("Pascal's Wager" actually works for many people!) if it moves us from rebellion or unbelief to belief; and He will purify our motives (and the deeds they motivate) later, and gradually.

Are there any sins that are not taken away and forgiven by penance (repentance)? Is there such a thing as "the unforgivable sin"?

Whether all sins are taken away by Penance?

The fact that a sin cannot be taken away by Penance may happen ... because of the impossibility of repenting of sin.... [T]he sins of the demons and of men who are lost cannot be blotted out by Penance because their will is confirmed in evil, so that sin cannot displease them as to its guilt, but only as to the punishment which they suffer, by reason of which they have a kind of repentance (the feeling without the choosing), **which yet is fruitless.... Consequently such Penance brings no hope of pardon, but only despair.**

Nevertheless no sin of a wayfarer can be such as that, because his will is flexible to good and evil. Therefore to say that in this life there is any sin of which one cannot repent, is erroneous: first, because this would destroy free will; secondly, because this would be derogatory to the power of grace, whereby the heart of any sinner whatsoever can be moved to repent....

It is also erroneous to say that any sin cannot be pardoned through true Penance ... because this is contrary to the divine mercy ... for in a manner God would be overcome by man....

Therefore we must say simply that in this life every sin can be blotted out by true Penance.

(The "unforgivable sin" of) **blasphemy against the Holy Ghost (Mk 3:29) is final impenitence, as Augustine states, which is altogether unpardonable because after this life is ended there is no pardon of sins** (III,86,1).

St. Thomas' answer to the question above is essentially this: Because of the limitless divine mercy, there is no sin that is not taken away by repentance on earth, during life. Only those who are already dead both physically and spiritually, i.e., only those in Hell, both humans and demons, have no hope of forgiveness, because they have no hope of repentance because they are no longer in time, or at least the kind of time which allows change of state and repentance.

Since those in Hell hate their punishment, they have sorrow, and regret, and this may be called a kind of "repentance" or "penance", but it is only the feelings associated with repentance rather than true repentance. True repentance is not a feeling (see #288) but a change of will. But "their will is confirmed in evil" forever. As St. Thomas puts it, "such 'penance' brings no hope of pardon, but only despair." Dante hit the bull's eye when he put these words on the sign over the door to Hell: "Abandon all hope, ye who enter here."

No one in time, no "wayfarer", can ever be so evil that he is hopeless, even if he *feels* hopeless. For "his will is flexible to good and evil" because it is a free will. That freedom is lost in Hell.

Thus St. Thomas gives two very strong reasons for his radically optimistic conclusion that there can be no sin that is unforgivable in this life: to say the contrary would deny free will and it would rank our sin greater than God's mercy. The first is the greatest possible insult to man and the second is the greatest possible insult to God, Who then "would be overcome by man".

Therefore when Christ (Mt 12:32) and later St. John (1 Jn 5:16) spoke of an unforgivable sin, this could only possibly mean final impenitence, the refusal to the end to repent and accept God's forgiveness which is always offered. In other words, singing "I did it my way" as you enter Hell.

"After this life is ended there is no pardon of sins" only because the will is no longer in time, no longer "flexible to good and evil", no longer able to change. At death, we all hear the referee say "Time's up." Einstein proved that time was relative to matter, so once the soul has left the world of matter by leaving its body, it is no more in time either—at least the time we now experience, the "space-time continuum".

Why can't God pardon sins even without our repenting, if He is all-powerful?

It is impossible for a mortal actual sin to be pardoned without penance (repentance)....

The difference between the grace of God and the grace of man is that the latter does not cause, but presupposes, true or apparent goodness in him who is graced, whereas the grace of God causes goodness in the man who is graced, because the goodwill of God, which is denoted by the word *grace,* is the cause of all created good. Hence it is possible for a man to pardon an offense for which he is offended with someone, without any change in the latter's will; but it is impossible that God pardon a man for an offense without his will being changed (III,86,2).

God can do everything, i.e., everything that is meaningful, everything that is not a self-contradiction. So if God cannot pardon sins without our repenting, that must be an inherent self-contradiction, like "a virtuous sin" or "a nonexistent existent".

This does not *seem* to be self-contradictory, because it is possible for a *man* to pardon a sinner who does not repent—for instance, a king or the governor or the President could stop the execution of an unrepentant mass murderer and even free him. So why isn't what seems to be the same thing possible for God if it is possible for man?

Because God's grace and pardon and love (which are the same objective reality) is what *creates* goodness in us who are pardoned, while man's grace and pardon presupposes and responds to, or hopes for, goodness in the person pardoned. Thus David prays in Psalm 51: "*Create* in me a clean heart, O God", using the distinctive and unique Hebrew verb *bara'* for the act that only God can perform. No other people had such a word because no other people knew such a God, Who could create something radically new by His infinite power.

So paradoxically, it is the very power of God that is the reason why He cannot do what man can do. There are other such things that He cannot do and we can, not because He is too weak but because He is too strong: He cannot die, or sin, or err, or lie, or break His promises, as we can.

We can pardon sins without the sinner's will being changed, but God cannot, because when God pardons a sinner, the sinner's will is changed by that very pardon. God is more like an author here than a judge. The judge responds to the prisoner on trial; the author makes him what he is.

(This does not take away our free will because what God makes us to be is, precisely, human beings, i.e., beings with free will, as Shakespeare makes Hamlet human and free and makes other things, like Castle Elsinore and the weather, not human or free.)

Forgiveness of sin can come from God without the sacrament of Penance, but not without the virtue of penance (repentance) **... so that even before the sacraments of the New Law were instituted, God pardoned the sins of the penitent** (III,86,6).

God is not limited to His sacraments, so God can and does pardon our sins even without the sacrament of Penance if there is the act and attitude (virtue) of repentance in us, as He did before Christ instituted this sacrament. Of course, if we do truly repent, we will want to do God's will, and God's will is for us to receive this sacrament.

Our own spiritual insides are mysterious, complex, and obscure to us. How can we know whether our repentance is authentic? Since our motives can be mixed, and often are, can our repentance also be mixed? Can we be partially repentant?

A man cannot be truly penitent if he repent of one sin and not of another. For if one particular sin were displeasing to him because it is against the love of God above all things (which motive is necessary for true repentance), it follows that he would repent of all (III,86,3).

The answer to the question is that indeed the *motives* of our repentance can be mixed—for instance, we may be motivated by both servile fear (fear of punishment) and filial fear (fear of offending the God we love) when we repent—but the *objects* of our repentance cannot. The reason for this is that if we repent of one sin and not another, we are not repenting of sin as such, that is, of the broken love relationship with God that sin consists in. And that is a single thing: it is our single *summum bonum*, greatest good, and final end.

The only reason why any sin is displeasing to God, and ought to be displeasing to us, is that it is contrary to, and harms, and dishonors, the love of God which is the ultimate end and good of all things, especially our own lives.

We habitually think of God in relation to something else (e.g., ourselves, our happiness, or our sins) rather than thinking of everything else in relationship to God. Thus our thinking is not really unified as reality is. That is why St. Thomas says that we cannot really repent of one sin and not another: because sin is relative to God, not God relative to sin.

To truly repent of any one sin is to repent of what sin essentially is—the broken relationship with God—and thus to repent of sin as such, and thus to repent of all sins. (This does not mean that we must be aware of all sins, or that our motives must be totally pure.)

But if our motives are not even mixed—if this right motive is not at all the reason sin displeases us—if we are displeased by sin not because it displeases God but only because of some other reason that has nothing to do with God—then our repentance is not really repentance for sin at all. If our motive is only a purely human motive, like shame before other human beings, or an affront to our own human self-esteem, such motives, since they are not at all because of God, are not really repentance to God at all. And therefore this is not repentance (penance) at all, not even the lowest, servile kind.

Our motive for repentance may be *low* without the repentance being *false*. The motive may be merely the purely selfish and servile fear of God, fear of divine punishments, whether in this life in time or after death in Purgatory for a time or in Hell for eternity. This is a true, though inferior, motive for repentance, and this is true repentance, even though it is from "imperfect contrition" rather than "perfect contrition", for the objective reason that it really leads us back to God; but it is inferior subjectively or psychologically because it does not conform to what God essentially is, namely, love.

And if it is the true God that we return to, then this return to God, even from inferior motives ("imperfect contrition," "servile fear"), will necessarily lead us to a better state, better motives, motives of love rather than fear. The reason this change will necessarily happen, however slowly or gradually, is because the true God, to Whom we really come in repentance, *is* love, and "love casts out fear" (1 Jn 4:18). This better motive of love can in turn either be mixed with servile fear or be pure filial fear.

But when we find ourselves apparently repenting of one sin but intending to commit another, we should go back and question our repentance.

This is not an obscure and technical point but crucial for the only thing in our lives that matters eternally, our soul's relationship to God. That is the one war that is truly "total war", the battle for our very selves. "For what does it profit a man to gain the whole world and forfeit his life?" (Mk 8:36)

Does forgiveness mean that punishment is no longer needed?

Whether the debt of punishment remains after the guilt has been forgiven through Penance?

It is related (2 Kings 12:13) **that when David, penitent, said to Nathan:** *I have sinned against the Lord,* **Nathan said to him,** *The Lord also hath taken away thy sin, thou shalt not die. Nevertheless ... the child that is born to thee shall surely die,* **which was to punish him for the sin he had committed.... Therefore a debt of some punishment remains after the guilt has been forgiven....**

In so far as a mortal sin turns inordinately to a mutable good, it gives rise to a debt of some punishment because the disorder of guilt is not brought back to the order of justice except by punishment, since it is just that he who has been too indulgent to his will should suffer something against his will, for thus will equality (an aspect of justice) **be restored....** (E.g., thieves obviously should not be allowed to keep their ill-gotten gains, but be made to pay them back with interest, as restitution.)

Since, however, the turning to mutable good is finite, sin does not in this respect induce a debt of eternal punishment. Wherefore, if man turns inordinately to a mutable good without turning from God, as happens in venial sins, he incurs a debt not of eternal but of temporal punishment (i.e., not Hell but Purgatory).

The remission of the debt of temporal punishment belongs to cooperating grace in so far as man, by bearing punishment patiently with the help of divine grace, is released also from the debt of temporal punishment ...

(In other words, the more we agree with God's will in willing our just punishments, the less separation from God remains in our will; i.e., the more we want our punishments, the less we need them.)

The remission of guilt and of eternal punishment (justification) **precedes the complete release from temporal punishment** (sanctification)**, since both are from grace but the former is from grace alone** (the "Protestant" point: salvation (justification) by grace alone through faith alone) **while the latter is from grace and free will** (the Catholic point: salvation (sanctification) by good works as well as faith) (III,86,4).

Just as mortal sin cannot be forgiven so long as the will is attached to sin, so neither can venial sin, because while the cause remains, the effect remains (III,87,1).

Even repented sin still leaves its tracks, its effects, in the soul—evil habits and desires—like a wild animal leaving its scent, or its stool, even after it is removed. These effects too must be removed, and that is the purpose of the punishments or penances that remain even after sin is forgiven. They are for the soul's sanctification, even after it has been justified by the Blood of Christ.

In this life we often do not see why we need these sanctifying punishments, and we naturally do not want them, because punishment always involves some sort of pain, some sort of "no" to our own will. But we will see the good of these cleansings and we will *want* them with all our heart in Purgatory, where God's presence will enable us to see ourselves clearly and to willingly purify our motives.

We *must* want our just punishments, because God does. We must freely cooperate with God's sanctifying grace in Purgatory, and we should "rehearse" for this on earth by accepting the humblings and humiliations that come to us in this life. For we do not cease to be human in Purgatory, and therefore do not cease to be active and free there. We must literally *co-operate* with God's grace.

St. Thomas locates the need for punishment even after repented and forgiven sin in the objective debt of justice. This is one aspect, and a true one, of the relationship. Another is the psychological need explained in the previous paragraphs. The pre-modern mind was more sensitive to the objective and the modern mind to the subjective. It should not be an either/or but a both/and.

(*Note*: St. Thomas died before he could finish the *Summa*. The rest of the articles are taken from his earlier works, which his friend Fra Rainldo de Piperno gathered, arranged and integrated into the *Summa* outline and labeled "Supplement" (S).)

294. How can we repay an infinite debt to God?

We are finite, and our sins are finite. How then can we owe an infinite debt to God, so that a punishment infinite in length (though finite in severity) is justly exacted of the damned in Hell?

And even if we repent and are not damned, can we repay such an infinite debt in this world by repentance?

Man becomes God's debtor in two ways: first, by reason of favors received; secondly, by reason of sin committed. And just as thanksgiving or worship or the like (a just gratitude) **regards the debt for favors received, so satisfaction** (a just punishment) **regards the debt for sin committed.**

Now in giving honor to one's parents or to the gods, as indeed the Philosopher says, it is impossible to repay them measure for measure; but it suffices that man repay as much as he can, for friendship does not demand measure for measure, but what is possible.

Yet even this is equal somewhat, viz. according to proportion: so that as (a) the debt due to God is, in comparison with (b) God, so is (c) what man can do in comparison with (d) (man) himself (i.e., c is to d as a is to b), **so that in this other way the form of justice is preserved.**

It is the same as regards satisfaction (for sin).... **Man cannot make satisfaction to God if "*satis*" denotes quantitative equality; but he can if it denote proportionate equality, as explained above. And since this suffices for justice, so does it suffice for satisfaction.**

Just as the offense derived a certain infinity from the infinity of the divine majesty, so does satisfaction derive a certain infinity from the infinity of divine mercy, whereby whatever man is able to repay becomes acceptable (S13,1).

St. Thomas' unstated assumption is that God is not unjust, that justice is necessary and eternal.

Justice demands paying debts. "To give each his due", "to give to each what is owed", is the very definition of justice.

We *owe* our benefactors for positive goods given to us, and we are obliged to pay them what we can. We cannot pay our parents for the gift of our very life, and many years of their lives; so we pay what we can, and pay the rest "forward" to our own children, by passing on this gift.

We owe God even more, so we should do something similar but greater regarding the debt of gratitude we owe to God, namely "pay it forward" to our neighbors, even to the extent of martyrdom.

It is significant that in most languages there is a single word for the essential virtue regarding both of these two relationships, which are the only two relationships where we *cannot* pay all that is owed. The word is "piety" (*pietas*). It means honor to both ancestors and God, the authors of our life.

The second kind of debt is negative: payment for sin, or harm. Here too, as with our parents, we must do what we can, which is much less than what God deserves. With regard to the positive aspect of justice, thanksgiving for benefits, we cannot give God what He deserves, which is everything. ("Were the whole realm of nature mine, / That were a present far too small." "O for a thousand tongues to sing my great Redeemer's praise!") But we can give Him all that is possible: our whole heart, soul, mind, and strength, however poor and finite these are. Similarly, with regard to the negative aspect of justice, punishment for unrepented sins, we also cannot give infinite satisfaction qualitatively; but we can give it quantitatively, that is, for an infinite time, in Hell. What makes an eternal Hell just is the infinity of the goodness of God's mercy against which we sin when we refuse to repent. God forgives all sins. Only the unrepentant refusal to accept this gift damns us. For a *gift* must be freely accepted as well as freely given.

On the one hand, we are told that only Christ can save us from sin. We cannot save ourselves. On the other hand, we are told that we must participate in Christ's saving work, and that we must "bear one another's burdens"—which seems to mean something more, and more spiritual, than merely lifting heavy objects like suitcases. Just what can we do for each other now regarding each other's eternal goods, and how can our prayers and good deeds help the souls in Purgatory?

Whether one man can fulfill satisfactory punishment for another?

(*Objection*:) It is written (Gal 6:2): *Bear ye one another's burdens.* Therefore it seems that one can bear the burden of punishment laid on another.

Further, charity avails more before God than before man. Now before man one can pay another's debt out of love for him. Much more, therefore, can this be done before the judgment seat of God.

I answer that ... Satisfactory punishment has a twofold purpose, viz. to pay the debt and to serve as a remedy for the avoidance of sin. Accordingly as a remedy against future sin, the satisfaction of one does not profit another, for the flesh of one man is not tamed by another's fast, nor does one man acquire the habit of well-doing through the actions of another.... On the other hand, as regards the payment of the debt, one man can satisfy for another ... because punishment derives its power of satisfaction chiefly from charity.... And since greater charity is evidenced by a man satisfying for another than for himself, less punishment is required of him who satisfies for another....

(But) one man does not merit the essential reward for another unless his merit has infinite efficacy, as the merit of Christ....

... [O]ne man can merit for another as regards release from punishment, and one man's act becomes another's, by means of charity whereby we are *all one in Christ* (Gal 3:28) (S13,2).

There are two ways no one can suffer for another's sins. Only Christ can merit "the essential reward", since no one else's merits have "infinite efficacy". So no man can justify another. Second, no man can sanctify another directly, since "the flesh of one man is not tamed by another's fast".

But there is indeed a sense—a beautiful sense—in which we can bear one another's spiritual burdens, i.e., temporal punishments for sins, punishments that are still necessary after the sins have been forgiven. This possibility should give joy and hope to all who love others so much that they would willingly labor and suffer for the ones they love.

To explain how this is possible St. Thomas distinguishes two effects of sin: the objective debt of justice, which must be paid (this is justification), and the subjective effect of spiritual stain on the soul, which must be removed (this is sanctification). Only the Holy Spirit, with the free cooperation of the penitent, can sanctify. But we can participate in Christ's justifying (cf. Col 1:24).

In fact, we can do more for others, out of charity, than they can do for themselves, and more than we can do for ourselves, because charity (unselfish love for others) is more effective than anything else, including even the best self-love. When we row each other's boats, when we feed each other, we accomplish more than when we work only for ourselves, precisely because it is done out of charity, which is most powerful to overcome sins. ("Love covers a multitude of sins"—1 Pet 4:8.)

A king once captured twelve of his enemy's best warriors. They offered to fight for their conquering king, and to find out whether they were trustable he starved them for a week, then sat them down around a food-laden round table with their left arms chained and their right arms able to reach only the plate of the man next to them. He kept only those who fed their neighbors, and executed those who tried to feed themselves.

The basis for our satisfying for others' sins is our unity in Christ: we are "members", organs, in Christ's body (Eph 5:30). There is a spiritual gravity. Why should spirit be less unified than matter?

If God forgives sins, why does He still insist on punishment? Aren't these two things opposites?

God does not delight in our sufferings, as appears from Tobit 3:22....

(But) **though God does not delight in our punishments as such, yet He does in so far as they are just....**

Satisfaction (just punishment) **regards both the past offense, for which compensation is made ... and also future sin, from which we are preserved by it.... [P]unishment preserves from future sin because a man does not easily fall back into sin when he has had experience of punishment. Wherefore according to the Philosopher punishments are medicinal ...** (S15,1)

If the scourges (sufferings) **which are inflicted by God on account of sin** (either in this life or in Purgatory) **become in some way the act of the sufferer, they acquire a satisfactory character. Now they become the act of the sufferer in so far as he accepts them for the cleansing of his sins by taking advantage of them patiently. If, however, he refuse to submit to them patiently, then they do not become his personal act in any way and are not of a satisfactory, but merely of a vindictive character.** ("Vindictive" refers not to a personal hateful *motive* but to objective, impersonal, just "vindication".)

As Augustine observes, even as *the same fire makes gold glisten and straw reek,* **so by the same scourges are the good cleansed and the wicked worsened on account of their impatience. Hence, though the scourges are common to both, satisfaction is only on the side of the good.**

Although these scourges are not altogether in our power, yet in some respect they are in so far as we use them patiently. In this way man makes a virtue of necessity, so that such things can become both meritorious and satisfactory (S15,2).

This passage is about the most popular of all arguments for atheism, namely the "problem of suffering", the apparent contradiction between God's love, compassion, mercy, and forgiveness and His deliberate willing that we suffer. God's love is a matter of faith and our suffering is a matter of experience; so if the two contradict each other, faith must be denied, because it is refuted by experience, which cannot be denied.

St. Thomas begins by affirming the data that God, Who loves us, does not delight in our sufferings as such. So if He punishes, it is out of love, not hate. Yet to love someone is to will his happiness, and suffering opposes happiness. But genuine human love sometimes deliberately tolerates and uses sufferings in other people, for instance in surgery, or lifesaving chemotherapy, or parental discipline, which is painful but necessary. The same is true of divine love. For divine love is not another *kind* of love, another species of love, than the most perfect, honest, deep, passionate and complete human love; it is only that same love, namely the will to the beloved's greatest good, greatest and truest happiness, but (1) raised to infinity, (2) freed of all imperfections, (3) joined with infinite wisdom, which always knows what the beloved needs the most, deep down, in the long run, as only God and not man can know, and (4) having unlimited power to providentially implement this wisdom and to effect what it sees to be best for the beloved.

The (relatively) innocent often suffer terribly in this world. That is undeniable fact. So take your choice: there are only two possible reasons for this fact. Either there is no God, or there is. If there is, God allows these sufferings. He could stop them. And there are only two possible reasons why He would allow them: because He loves us or because He doesn't. One possibility is that God allows these sufferings because He lacks even the love *we* have for each other, for we would not deliberately allow those we love to suffer so. The other possibility is that we are not wiser or more loving than God (what a radical thought!). His answer to Job was essentially that: I'm perfect wisdom and love, and you're not.

Capish?

How could the Church that claims to be the Body of Christ, Who is divine love incarnate, be so cruel as to approve excommunication of anyone? Isn't the Church supposed to show God's love and mercy? Doesn't excommunication show a God of hatred and wrath instead?

Whether the Church should excommunicate anyone?

Objection 1: It would seem that the Church ought not to excommunicate anyone, because excommunication is a kind of curse, and we are forbidden to curse (Rom 12:14)....

On the contrary, The Apostle (1 Cor 5:5) ordered a man to be excommunicated.

Further, it is written (Mt 18:17) **about the man who refuses to hear the Church:** *Let him be to thee as the heathen or publican....*

I answer that, The judgment of the Church should be conformed to the judgment of God. Now God punishes the sinner in many ways in order to draw him to good.... [T]he Church ... imitates the judgment of God in leaving him to himself in order that by humility he may learn to know himself and return to God.

Reply to Objection 1: A curse may be pronounced in two ways: first, so that the intention of the one who curses is fixed on the evil which he invokes or pronounces—and cursing in this way is altogether forbidden. Secondly, so that the evil which a man invokes in cursing is intended for the good of the one who is cursed, and thus cursing is sometimes lawful and salutary; thus a surgeon makes a sick man undergo pain by cutting him, for instance, in order to deliver him from his sickness (S21,2).

Excommunication is a punishment. Punishments, in the Christian "big picture", are not merely for justice (they are that too) but also always for love and mercy. People are rightly punished for one and only one ultimate reason: because they are loved. A father punishes his children more than a grandfather does because a father loves his children more passionately and intimately. Jesus' favorite name for God is "Father". But throughout the whole Bible God is never called a grandfather.

The principle St. Thomas appeals to is that "the judgment of the Church should be conformed to the judgment of God." God punishes the sinner out of love—"to draw him to good"—and that is why the Church does the same. The Church, after all, is the Body of Christ, and Christ is the Son of God. God—Christ—Church: there is no possible space into which a wedge can be inserted there. The Son is authorized by the Father and the Church is authorized by the Son.

In one sense a punishment is a curse and in another sense it is not. Insofar as a curse wills harm to the one cursed, a punishment is not a curse; but insofar as a curse warns the one cursed *away* from harm (by fear and terror, since gentler and wiser persuasions have failed), a punishment is the opposite of a curse, as a prophetic warning against imminent enemies wills the opposite of the will of the enemies. Pain may be necessary to accomplish this loving purpose, for fools learn only by experience, and all of us have often been fools.

Of course, excommunication from the Church "works" only on Catholics who believe in and value the Church. To the unbeliever, the Church-hater, or the apostate, it is a decree of freedom, not bondage.

Excommunication is a warning of imminent damnation, for as St. Thomas says in the first line of the next excerpt (#298), only for mortal sin is one excommunicated. It is like a loving mother's shrill cry to her children who are running near the edge of a cliff.

Is there such a thing as collective guilt? If not, how can a group ever be excommunicated?

No man should be excommunicated except for a mortal sin. Now sin consists in an act, and acts do not belong to communities but, generally speaking, to individuals. Wherefore individual members of a community can be excommunicated but not the community itself.

And although sometimes an act belongs to a whole multitude, as when many draw a boat, which none of them could draw by himself, yet it is not probable that a community would so wholly consent to evil that there would be no dissidents. Now God, Who judges all the earth, does not condemn the just with the wicked (Gen 18:25). Therefore the Church, who should imitate the judgments of God, prudently decided that a community should not be excommunicated, lest the wheat be uprooted together with the tares and cockle (S22,5).

Even when a group acts as a group—for instance, the crowd that shouted "Crucify him!" at Jesus' trial—God does not judge the group, only the individual. Thus their self-curse, "His blood be upon us and upon our children", was not accepted by God, and the centuries-old superstition that the Jewish people as a whole were cursed as "Christ-killers" was a perversion of the truth. It was an idea that came not from the mind and will of God (the ultimate source and standard of all truth) but from the Devil. How outrageous that many Christians in the past sided with that perversion instead of with God's judgment! Why did they? In addition to anti-Semitism, two other reasons were probably the two false ideas of group guilt and of God as accepting self-curses.

The Church has always avoided two opposite yet correlative errors typical of the world: collectivism and individualism. God judges only individual souls; yet He judges them not only on what they have done to themselves but largely on what they have done to others. "Truly, I say to you, as you did it to one of the least of these my brethren, you did it to me" (Mt 25:40). Individuals are supremely valuable, but they were created so that they could fulfill themselves by forgetting themselves and giving themselves away to others, as Jesus did. That is almost the definition of a saint.

If God were a collectivist, He would "condemn the just with the wicked". He did not do that even to Sodom. If there was a single good man left in Sodom, that man was saved from eternal fire. But not from the temporal fire that fell on the city. Our virtue may give us an eternal fire insurance policy, but not a temporal fire insurance policy. In this world the good often suffer because of the sins of the wicked. Our sins harm others—that's the bad news—but the good news is that our virtue also helps others. It is a strange but wonderful justice, appropriate for a world in which we row each other's boat as well as our own.

The Church thus does not have the authority to excommunicate groups, since even God does not do that. Even if she could to it, even if she had the authority, she would not exercise it for a practical, prudential reason: "lest the wheat be uprooted together with the tares and cockle". Even if it *were* within her legal right and authority, it would harm more than help. It might be argued that it is like capital punishment today: the state has the right to use it if necessary, but since it is no longer necessary, it would do more public harm than good in the current war against the culture of death.

The Church does have, however, the authority of *interdict* to a group—that is, the authority to deny the Sacraments to an organized group who are in rebellion. And she exercises that authority not to punish but to reform, to bring them back. This often worked, and therefore was often used, in the Catholic Middle Ages; it does not work well, and has not been used much, in modern times.

Protestantism began with Luther's attack on the sale of indulgences. Protestants continue to protest the very existence of indulgences, even after the Church clamped down on the obvious perversion of selling them. What are indulgences and why are they right?

The universal Church approves and grants indulgences. Therefore indulgences have some value ... for it would be blasphemy to say that the Church does anything in vain....

Indulgences hold good both in the Church's court and in the judgment of God, for the remission of the punishment which remains after contrition, absolution and Confession....

The reason why they so avail is the oneness of the mystical body in which many have performed works of satisfaction exceeding the requirements of their debts.... So great is the quantity of such merits that it exceeds the entire debt of punishment due to those who are living at this moment; and this is especially due to the merits of Christ; for though He acts through the sacraments, yet His efficacy is nowise restricted to them, but infinitely surpasses their power.

Now one man can satisfy for another, as we have examined above (13,2). And the saints in whom this superabundance of satisfactions is found did not perform their good works for this or that particular person who needs the remission of punishment ... but they performed them for the whole Church in general, even as the Apostle declared that he fills up *those things that are wanting of the sufferings of Christ ... for His body, which is the Church* **(Col 1:24).**

These merits, then, are the common property of the whole Church. Now those things which are the common property of a number, are distributed to the various individuals according to the judgment of Him Who rules them all ... (S25,1).

Some maintain that indulgences have not the efficacy claimed for them, but that they simply avail each individual in proportion to his faith and devotion. And consequently those who maintain this say that the Church publishes her indulgences in such a way as, by a kind of pious fraud, to induce men to do well, just as a mother entices her child to walk by holding out an apple. But this seems a very dangerous assertion to make. For as Augustine says, *if any error were discovered in Holy Writ, the authority of Holy Writ would perish.* **In like manner, if any error were to be found in the Church's teaching, her doctrine would have no authority in settling questions of faith (S25,2).**

An "indulgence" sounds like a permission to sin or a surrender to the appetite to sin (e.g., "indulging" in too much alcohol or sweets, or something worse). That is not what the term means at all. It means simply "a remission of punishment due to sin". It is almost a synonym for "forgiveness".

Every Christian is saved by a "plenary (total) indulgence" from Christ. His merits effect our forgiveness. In His Passion He took all the punishments we deserved upon Himself and gave us all the rewards He deserved; that was the holy exchange that was the purpose of the Incarnation itself.

Since the Church is not His organization but His organism, His Body, she does the same. She extends the Incarnation, acts on His authority. The principle behind indulgences—that one person's merits can avail for the forgiveness of the punishments due to another person's sins—is not an alien addition to, but the very central principle of, Christian salvation itself.

And the Church, i.e., Christ's people, Christ's body, the saints (not just canonized saints but all who share in Christ's work) share not just passively in receiving the results of Christ's work, but also actively in doing these works for others. This is part of "the communion (common union) of saints", one of the Church's essential dogmas and one of the twelve articles of the Apostles' Creed.

As Augustine argues, if this teaching of the Church is in error, the Church has not the divine authority she (and Scripture and Christ) claims for herself; she is "a pious fraud". If you jettison any one part of the divinely commissioned cargo, you claim the authority to jettison any other as well.

Is Matrimony a universal natural law institution as well as a supernatural Catholic sacrament?

Whether matrimony (marriage) is of natural law?

Objection 1. It would seem that matrimony is not natural. Because *the natural law is what nature has taught all animals.* But in other animals the sexes are united without matrimony. Therefore matrimony is not of natural law.

Reply to Objection 1. The human species in so far as it is rational overflows its genus ... (i.e.), the generic nature, though one in all animals, yet is not in all in the same way.... [T]he begetting of offspring is common to all animals, yet nature does not incline thereto in the same way in all animals, since there are animals whose offspring are able to seek food immediately after birth, or are sufficiently fed by their mother (alone); and in these there is no tie between male and female.... In those whose offspring need the support of both parents, although for a short time, there is a certain tie, as may be seen in certain birds. In man, however, since the child needs the parents' care for a long time, there is a very great tie between male and female....

Objection 2. Further, that which is of natural law is found in all men with regard to their every state. But matrimony was not in every state of man, for as Tully says, *at the beginning men were savages and then no man knew his own children....*

Reply to Objection 2. ... Holy Writ states that there has been matrimony from the beginning of the human race. (Tully's and Hobbes' and Rousseau's "state of nature" is a myth.)

Objection 4. ... [T]hose things without which the intention of nature can be maintained would seem not to be natural. But nature intends the preservation of the species by generation, which is possible without matrimony, as in the case of fornicators, therefore matrimony is not natural.

Reply to Objection 4. Nature intends not only being in the offspring, but also perfect (completed) **being, for which matrimony is necessary** (S41,1).

I answer that, A thing is said to be natural in two ways. (This is a very important distinction for modern moral arguments about "natural law" and "unnatural" acts.) **First, as resulting of necessity from the principles of nature: thus upward movement is natural to fire. In this way matrimony is not natural, nor are any of those things that come to pass at the intervention or movement of the free will. Secondly, that is said to be natural to which nature inclines, even though it comes to pass through the intervention of the free will: thus acts of virtue and the virtues themselves are called natural. And in this way matrimony is natural, because natural reason inclines thereto in two ways.**

First, in relation to the principal end of matrimony, namely the good of the off-spring. (How often we forget this!) **For nature intends not only the begetting of offspring but also its education and development....** Now a child cannot be brought up and instructed unless it have certain and definite parents, and this would not be the case unless there were a tie between the man and a definite woman, and it is in this tie that matrimony consists.

Secondly, in relation to the secondary end of matrimony, which is the mutual services which married people render to one another.... Among those works that are necessary for human life, some are becoming to men, others to women. **Wherefore nature inculcates that society of man and woman which consists in matrimony. These are the two reasons given by the Philosopher** (S41,1).

Matrimony is (1) the only sacrament which is also part of the natural law, (2) the first sacrament God instituted, in Eden, and (3) the most essential of all human relationships and social institutions. Its breakdown in our day is the surest possible sign of the future doom of our culture. Its restoration is the primary need and vocation in our secular society, and must begin in the Church. There is indeed a crisis of vocations today: there is a desperate need for more holy fathers and mothers.

OK, here's the biggie, the No. 1 reason modern Western civilization hates the Catholic Church. Church: Sex = Sin, Sex = No. Modern World: Sex = Joy, Sex = Yes. Final score: World 1, Church 0. Right?

Objection 6. Excess in the passions corrupts virtue. Now there is always excess of pleasure in the marriage act, so much so that it absorbs the reason, which is man's principal good. Wherefore the Philosopher says that *in that act it is impossible to understand anything.* Therefore the marriage act is always a sin.

Reply. The excess of passions that corrupts virtue not only hinders the act of reason but also destroys the order of reason. The intensity of pleasure in the marriage act does not do this, since though for the moment man is not being directed (by reason), he was previously directed by reason.

On the contrary, It is written (1 Cor 7:28): *If a virgin marry, she hath not sinned,* and 1 Tim 5:14: *I will … that the younger should marry, and bear children.* But there can be no bearing of children without carnal union. Therefore the marriage act is not a sin, else the Apostle would not have approved of it.

Further, no sin is a matter of precept (obedience to law). But the marriage debt is a matter of precept (1 Cor 7:3): *Let the husband render the debt to his wife.* Therefore it is not a sin (S41,3).

Every act whereby a precept is fulfilled is meritorious if it be done from charity. Now such is the marriage act.… Therefore, etc. (S41,4).

I answer that, If we suppose the corporeal nature to be created by the good God, we cannot hold that those things which pertain to the preservation of the corporeal nature and to which nature inclines are altogether evil. Wherefore, since the inclination to beget an offspring whereby the specific nature is preserved is from nature, it is impossible to maintain that the act of begetting children is altogether unlawful and that it is impossible to find … virtue therein—unless we suppose, as some are mad enough to assert,

that corruptible things were created by an evil god, whence perhaps the opinion mentioned in the text is derived. Wherefore this is a most wicked heresy (S41,3). Notice St. Thomas' unusually strong language here.

Objection. The sacraments derive their efficacy from Christ's Passion. But matrimony, since it has pleasure annexed to it, does not conform man to Christ's Passion, which was painful. Therefore it is not a sacrament.

Reply. Although matrimony is not conformed to Christ's Passion regarding pain, it is regarding charity, whereby He suffered for the Church who was to be united to Him as His spouse (S42,1).

Some say that whenever pleasure is the chief motive for the marriage act it is a mortal sin; that when it is an indirect motive it is a venial sin; and that when it spurns the pleasure altogether and is displeasing, it is wholly void of venial sin; so that it would be a mortal sin to seek pleasure in this act, a venial sin to take the pleasure when offered, but that perfection requires one to detest it. But this is impossible, since … pleasure in a good action is good, and in an evil action is evil; wherefore, as the marriage act is not evil in itself, neither will it be … sin to seek pleasure therein. Consequently the right answer to this question is that if pleasure be sought in such a way as to exclude the honesty of marriage, so that … it is not as a wife but as a woman that a man treats his wife, and that he is ready to use her in the same way if she were not his wife, it is a mortal sin …, (i.e., when) a man seeks wanton pleasure in his wife when he sees no more in her than he would in a wanton (S49,6).

A "wanton" is a whore. For a man to treat his wife as if she were a whore is indeed a mortal sin, for it is just as bad as for a man to treat a whore as if she were his wife. But for a man to treat his wife as his wife, to love her honestly, personally, and passionately, is a virtue, not a sin. This is so even by pre-modern, pre-John Paul II standards! The "Theology of the Body" begins with Thomism.

What is marriage other than a legal piece of paper from the state?

Now such is the effect of matrimony (Gen 2:24): *They shall be two in one flesh....*

Now things directed to one purpose are said to be united in their direction thereto. Thus many men are united in following one military calling or in pursuing one business, in relation to which they are called fellow-soldiers or business partners. Hence, since by marriage certain persons are directed to one begetting and upbringing of children, and again to one family life, it is clear that in matrimony there is a joining in respect of which we speak of husband and wife; and this joining, through being directed to some one thing, is matrimony; while the joining together of bodies and minds is a result of matrimony. (Thus these can occur without matrimony, but not matrimony without them) (S44,1).

Three things are to be considered in matrimony, namely its cause, its essence, and its effect. And accordingly we find three definitions given of matrimony. (1) The definition of Hugh (which is the *vow*) **indicates the cause, namely the consent ... (2) The definition given in the text indicates the essence of matrimony, namely** *the union ... between lawful persons* **... (3) The remaining definition indicates the effect to which matrimony is directed, namely the common life in family matters.**

Every community is regulated by some law; the law according to which this community is directed, namely divine and human law, finds a place in this definition, while other communities, such as those of traders or soldiers, are established by human law alone (S44,3).

When St. Thomas, following the Bible and the Church, says that two married people become "one flesh", he is saying that marriage is an ontological transformation. Without ceasing to be two, they become one. "The joining together of bodies and minds is *a result of* Matrimony."

("Flesh" does not mean "body" merely, but "natural, fallen, mortal humanity". Its opposite is not "soul" but "spirit", that is, human nature supernaturalized by the Holy Spirit. There are different words in New Testament Greek for these two distinctions. "Soma" and "psyche" mean "body" and "soul". "Sarx" and "pneuma" mean "flesh" and "spirit".)

The will or consent of the couple is the *cause* of Matrimony, or marriage. Their common life together, including sexual and personal intercourse, and the creating of a family and children, is an *effect* of Matrimony. Matrimony's essence is something more: it is the actual union between persons. It takes place in the sacrament, in a very short time. Its effect lasts for the rest of a lifetime.

A "person" is necessarily individual. Yet two individual persons can become one in marriage, and only in marriage. We might call it a "co-person" or a "double person". A married couple is the only example in all created reality of a communal person. Outside marriage, communities are not real persons and persons are not communities.

There is, however, one other example of a communal person: God. He is one and He is three. Marriage is the closest image or analogy of the Trinity.

Unlike all other human communities, marriage is established not just by human law but by divine law. That is why Christ said: "What *God* has joined together, let no man put asunder."

Therefore Matrimony is the first sacrament, the only natural as well as supernatural sacrament, the most important sacrament for society, and the completest reflection of "the image of God" (Gen 2:7). It is more important than the Church; for a world without the Church can have hope that the Church will appear, and once she does appear she will last until the end of time. In the remote past, before the call of Abraham, there was no Church and no chosen people, no Israel, yet the world was in good Providential hands. But if there is in the remote future a world without marriage, as in *Brave New World*, humanity is doomed.

Is sex part of the sacrament of Matrimony? Does marriage make sex sacred?

In every sacrament there is a spiritual operation by means of a material operation which signifies it. Thus in Baptism the inward spiritual cleansing is effected by a bodily cleansing.... In matrimony there is a kind of spiritual joining together in so far as matrimony is a sacrament, and a certain material joining together in so far as it is directed to an office of nature.... [T]he spiritual joining is the effect of divine power by means of the material joining (S45,1).

"The material joining" St. Thomas speaks of is twofold: it is both the free consent of the will to marry, which is the efficient *cause* of marriage, and also the sexual intercourse that "consummates" the marriage—that is, consummates the sacrament, since marriage is a sacrament. Sexual (and spiritual) intercourse and its natural effect, children, is the end or "final cause" of marriage. Sex is for babies as well as for love. That's a "Duh!" to every culture but our own. The chief effect of modern "sex education" is ignorance: ignorance of the single most obvious and important fact about sex, so that babies are now seen as "accidents". (That's like seeing bodily growth as an "accident" of eating.)

Like every sacrament, in marriage "there is a spiritual operation by means of a material operation which signifies it." By the double material operation of the audible words of consent and the act of sexual intercourse, there is "a spiritual operation", i.e., something really happens: God creates something new, a new person, a new kind of person, a collective person, a double person, a couple, a family. It is a miracle; it is something only God can do. "What *God* has joined together, let no man [claim to] put asunder." This is the reason the Catholic Faith not only *forbids* divorce but claims that it is a superstition, a myth, a lie: there is no such thing.

Marriage, then, is a divine act, a divine miracle, effected at the moment of consent, the "I do", which is the first of the two "material operations"

that constitute this sacrament. Sexual intercourse is the second of these two "material operations" that constitute this sacrament. What happens in sexual intercourse is also a literal miracle, a divine act. For in it God (sometimes) creates, out of nothing, a new human soul that is immortal and destined for infinite and unending ecstasy in union with God in Heaven. Man and woman do not create, but only procreate. They supply the bodies but God supplies the souls. They supply the landing field but God sends the planes down to land. They are like the priest at Mass who supplies the material, audible human words "This is My Body" and "This is My Blood" that become the material instrument of the supernatural miracle of transubstantiation.

This is why sex is holy, and why all cultures in the history of the world except our own have intuitively seen this and surrounded it with sacred rules and taboos. This is the essence of "the sexual revolution": not so much a different practice (that's just a difference in quantity: we've always disobeyed the rules, though not as much as today) as a different vision, a different "big picture" understanding.

Pope St. John Paul II's "Theology of the Body" restores and explicates the old "big picture" of sex as sacred, sacramental. It also shows us (rather than just asserting and proving, as did *Humanae Vitae*) why contraception is not only wrong but sacrilegious: it is like a priest celebrating the Mass but only pretending to say "This is My Body" because he does not want God to come and perform the miracle of transubstantiation. Sex is like the Mass and a woman's body is like the altar. Contraception locks the door against God's miraculous act of creation. It says to God: "We don't want You here, we want to be alone. We don't want You to do Your thing, we just want to do our thing." It forgets that it takes "three to get married". (That's the title of an excellent book about marriage by Fulton Sheen.)

If you don't want to eat, don't sit in the dining room. If you don't want to wash, don't go to the wash room. If you don't want God to come, don't go to Mass. Or to marriage.

Is Heaven a state of mind? Is it "spiritual" in the sense of being "subjective"? Or is it as objectively real a place as Hawaii?

Whether places are appointed to receive souls after death?

Objection 1. It would seem that places are not appointed to receive souls after death. For as Boethius says: *Wise men are agreed that incorporeal things are not in a place.* And this agrees with the words of Augustine: *We can answer without hesitation that the soul is not conveyed to corporeal places, except with a body ... that it is not conveyed locally.* Now the soul separated from the body (by death) is without a body, as Augustine also says. Therefore it is absurd to assign any places for the reception of souls....

I answer that ... after death souls ... are as though in a place, after the manner in which incorporeal things can be in a place, according as they more or less approach to ... God (and thus are in Heaven, Purgatory, or Hell).

Reply to Objection 1. Incorporeal things are not in place after a manner known and familiar to us, in which way we say that bodies are properly in place. But they are in place after a manner befitting spiritual substances, a manner that cannot be fully manifest to us....

The separated soul receives nothing directly from corporeal places in the same way as bodies.... [Y]et these same souls, through knowing themselves to be appointed to such places (as Heaven, Hell, or Purgatory), gather joy or sorrow therefrom, and thus their place conduces to their punishment or reward (S69,1).

In discussing the question whether something is or is not objectively real (moral values, souls, universal truths, Platonic Ideas, God, spirits, etc.) we often assume that "objectively real" means "real out there in space, outside my epidermis". This is implicit materialism, for the only things that can exist in space are material things. Angels, for instance, which are pure spirits without material bodies, are not "here" as we and rocks and planets are "here": they are not limited by space. There is no finite number of angels that can dance on the head of a pin, as there is a finite number of molecules that can.

Materialists believe there is only one kind of reality: matter. Some people believe there are two kinds of reality: objective matter and subjective spirit (minds). But this too is too simple, for there is objective spirit as well as objective matter. There is God, angels, and other human souls. There is also a fourth kind of reality: subjective matter; for there is my own body as well as my own mind.

So if there is objective spiritual reality, there may be objectively real places that are not material places, at least in the same sense that earth, or Boston, are material places.

Heaven is such a real place. It is not subjective. Neither is Purgatory, even though resurrection bodies are not present yet in Purgatory. Therefore disembodied souls too can be in real places.

Our souls are in "corporeal places" now because our bodies are. After death our souls will be in other *kinds* of places, that are nowhere in this corporeal, spatial universe—not because their bodies are there, not because they receive their place from bodies, as they do now, but because God assigns them there, and their "there" gives them joy (Heaven), sorrow (Hell), or both (Purgatory) from their rewards or punishments.

Thus when we say that souls after death go to a "place", the term "place" is neither univocal (only one kind of place) nor equivocal (no real place at all) but analogical. Thus St. Thomas says "after death souls ... are *as though* in a place" but "in a manner befitting spiritual substances".

And if we demand more clarity about this "manner", St. Thomas replies that it is "a manner that cannot be fully manifest to us". Naturally. Why would we *expect* an unborn baby to understand what "places" means after birth? All he knows is the womb, a single place with no edges or contrasts. We are in a similar situation; only after death will we experience it, and only then be able to understand it.

If the saved are assigned to Heaven immediately after death, as soon as they leave their bodies, why do they have to wait until the Last Judgment and the resurrection of the body? If they are in Purgatory, is Purgatory part of Heaven?

Whether souls are conveyed to heaven or hell immediately after death?

Even as in bodies there is gravity or levity whereby they are borne in their own place which is the end of their movement, so in souls there is merit or demerit whereby they reach their reward or punishment, which are the ends of their deeds. Wherefore just as a body is conveyed at once to its place by its gravity or levity unless there be an obstacle, so too the soul, the bonds of the flesh being broken ... receives at once its reward or punishment unless there be an obstacle.

Thus sometimes venial sin ... needing first to be cleansed (in Purgatory), **is an obstacle to the receiving of the reward, the result being that the reward is delayed.... This truth is attested by the manifest authority of the canonical Scriptures and the doctrine of the holy Fathers....**

Objection 4 ... **Hell fire and the joys of heaven will be awarded to all by the sentence of Christ judging them, namely at the last judgment, according to Matthew 25. Therefore no one will go up to heaven or down to hell before the day of judgment.**

Reply to Objection 4. **Gregory proposes and solves this very difficulty:** *If then,* he says, *the souls of the just are in heaven now, what will they receive in reward for their justice on the judgment day?* **And he answers:** *Surely it will be a gain to them at the judgment that whereas now they enjoy only the happiness of the soul, afterwards they will enjoy also that of the body....* **The reason why a distinction is drawn between the time before and the time after the resurrection** (of the body) **is because before the resurrection they are there without the body whereas afterwards they are with the body** (S69,2).

The previous question was about place after death; this one is about time.

St. Thomas says both that (1) the saved are judged and assigned to Heaven or Hell immediately after death, and (2) that for many or most of the saved, there is a delay because of the obstacle of venial sins, sinful habits which remain to be Purgatorially cleansed in the soul that is not yet perfect. This implies that Purgatory, though painful, is more a part of Heaven than a part of Hell and therefore has far more joy than pain. (This is also the teaching of St. Catherine of Genoa in her visionary dialogues on Purgatory.) In a sense "all the way to Heaven is Heaven" (St. Catherine).

St. Thomas begins with a commonsensical principle that is hardly ever adverted to today: that there is spiritual as well as physical gravity. This presupposes at least an analogy between matter and spirit, which certainly seems to follow from the psychosomatic unity, and from the Aristotelian hylomorphic anthropology of soul and body as form and matter of a single substance, as distinct from a Platonic or Cartesian two-substance dualism, *or* simple materialism *or* simple immaterialism or spiritualism. All three alternatives to Aristotelian-Thomistic hylomorphism are logically problematic as well as not in accord with our experience.

If spirit is analogous to matter, there can be such things as spiritual gravity (what St. Thomas is talking about in this excerpt), spiritual beauty (see Plato's *Symposium*), spiritual heredity ("Original Sin"), spiritual places (the previous excerpt) and spiritual time (*kairos* as distinct from *kronos*).

So do we go to Heaven immediately after we die, at the Particular Judgment, or do we have to wait in Purgatory until the end of the world, the resurrection of the body, and the Last Judgment?

"Waiting" in spiritual time, in Purgatory, is different than "waiting" in material time, on earth. The saved disembodied soul in Purgatory is already living in Heavenly time in hope, in anticipation. Heaven is guaranteed to it. Similarly, it is already in its Heavenly "place", the eternal mansion, but in the bathroom taking a painfully hot shower to clean off the dirt, not yet in the dining room eating the feast.

If souls are in Heaven, not on earth, can they come to earth from Heaven, or can they bilocate and be present both in Heaven and on earth at the same time (whatever "the same time" could mean when we refer to both Heaven and earth)? If not, where is "the communion of saints" and the unity of the Church Militant on earth, the Church Suffering in Purgatory, and the Church Triumphant in Heaven?

Whether the souls who are in heaven or hell are able to go from thence?

Jerome, writing against Vigilantius, addresses him thus: *Thou sayest that the souls of the apostles and martyrs ... are unable to visit their graves when they will? Wouldst thou lay down the law for God? Wouldst thou put the apostles in chains ... and forbid them to be with their Lord, them of whom it is written: They follow the Lamb whithersoever He goeth? And if the Lamb is everywhere, therefore we must believe that those also who are with Him are everywhere....*

When he (Jerome) **says that they are everywhere he does not mean that they are in several places or everywhere at once, but that they can be wherever they will.**

Further, Jerome argues as follows: *Since the devil and the demons wander throughout the whole world and are everywhere present with wondrous speed, why should the martyrs, after shedding their blood, be imprisoned and unable to go forth? ...*

Further, the same conclusion may be gathered from Gregory, where he relates many cases of the dead having appeared to the living ...

According to the disposition of divine providence, separated souls sometimes come forth from their abode and appear to men, as Augustine ... relates of the martyr Felix.... **It is also credible that this may occur sometimes to the damned, and that for man's instruction and intimidation they be permitted to appear to the living ... as evidenced by many instances.... This is, however,** the difference between the saints and the damned, that the saints can appear when they will to the living, but not the damned ... unless they be sometimes permitted....

Although the souls of the damned are sometimes actually present where they appear, we are not to believe that this is always so, for sometimes these apparitions occur to persons, whether asleep or awake, by the activity of good or wicked angels in order to instruct or deceive the living. Thus sometimes even the living appear to others and tell them many things in their sleep, and yet it is clear that they are not present, as Augustine proves from many instances ... (S69,3).

St. Thomas gives three reasons for believing that souls from Heaven can be present on earth.

The first, from St. Jerome, is the absurdity of the alternative. To say they cannot, is to forbid them to be with Christ, for Christ is here ("Behold, I am with you always, even to the close of the age"—Mt 28:20). The second, also from St. Jerome, is an a fortiori argument: if even demons can visit earth, why should saints and martyrs not be allowed to do this? The third, from St. Gregory the Great and St. Augustine, is experiential and empirical: there are many credible cases of it having happened. God seems to permit even damned souls from Hell to visit earth to warn us. However, St. Thomas qualifies this by saying that this presence may be only in appearance, vision, or dream, not in reality. And the damned would appear only because God wills it, not because they will it. Souls from Heaven, in contrast, go wherever they will, for in Heaven there is perfect harmony of wills and therefore perfect happiness and therefore no frustration of the will of the blessed.

If you doubt all this, remember Hamlet's wisdom that "there are more things in Heaven and earth than are dreamed of in your philosophy." God's acts and permissions are always more, not less, than our imaginations or expectations.

If Hell is the opposite of Heaven, and if Hell is the apotheosis of evil as Heaven is the apotheosis of good, does this mean Hell is pure evil without any good, as Heaven is pure good without any evil?

It is impossible for evil to be pure and without the admixture of good ... as the supreme good is without any admixture of evil.

Consequently, those who are to be conveyed to beatitude, which is a supreme good, must be cleansed of all evil; wherefore there must needs be a place (Purgatory) where such persons are cleansed if they go hence without being perfectly clean.

But (because of the same principle) **those who will be thrust into hell will not be free from all good ... since those who are in hell can receive the reward of their goods in so far as their past goods avail for the mitigation of their punishment** (S69,7).

In Christian cosmology, everything real is created by God, not by the Devil, as it is in Manichean dualism. The Devil cannot create. He is a mere creature; his opposite is not God but St. Michael the Archangel. God has no opposite; the very name "Michael" means "Who is like God?"

Therefore Hell is not the opposite to Heaven as a cave is the opposite of a hill or as Detroit is the opposite of Honolulu. "Absolute good" is conceivable and real, in God; but "absolute evil" is inconceivable and self-contradictory, and therefore not real even in the Devil.

For the very essence of evil is the perversion of good; therefore evil is like a parasite: it presupposes and needs its good host to pervert. Without innocent victims, Dracula has no blood to suck, and dies.

The very same principle that necessitates Purgatory, namely that in Heaven there can be no evil at all, also necessitates the existence of some good in Hell: at least mitigations of its evils. Although Hell is infinite in time, i.e., unending (a "life sentence without possibility of parole"), it is finite in quality. Its pains and punishments are just, and therefore finite, and can be mitigated. A hater of God who was something of a lover of men on earth would not be punished as severely as a hater of God who was not a lover of men at all. And those whose motives and souls were mixed during their lifetime, if it is impossible to separate the good from the evil in them and purify them from their evil in Purgatory, would still necessarily suffer less than those whose motives and souls were more unmitigatedly evil.

This is a kind of natural justice even in the supernatural order. Just as virtue is its own reward, vice is its own punishment. God does not have to *add* anything eternal and additional, from the outside, so to speak. Perfect justice must be done in the end simply because God, that is, ultimate reality, is perfectly just as well as perfectly merciful. Neither justice nor mercy can be compromised because both are divine attributes. But mercy can be resisted and refused, while justice cannot. That is why there must be a Hell even though divine mercy is infinite.

But Hell is in no way equal to or parallel to Heaven. There must be some good in Hell, but there can be no evil in Heaven. Even the agents of torture in Hell, whether they are physical fire or spiritual hate or despair, have some ontological goodness. Take fire, for instance. Some of the saints doubt that there are physical fires in Hell precisely because fire is good, because fire is a beautiful, innocent creature of God. Some of the saints and visionaries (like Lady Julian of Norwich, in her *Revelations of Divine Love*) say that the damned are tortured not by God's wrath ("for I saw no wrath but on man's part") but by His love, which they experience as wrath because of their perverse spirits, as a hate-filled child who wants only to fight with his parents might feel their hugs as tortures.

After death and before the Resurrection of the Body, will we, as disembodied souls, be able to see or hear anything at all? If not, will it feel like total paralysis?

Whether the sensitive powers remain in the separated soul?

There are many opinions on this question.... Now it is evident that certain operations ... do not belong to the soul properly speaking (in itself) but (only) **to the soul as united to the body, because they are not performed except through the medium of the body, such as to see, to hear, and so forth....** Some operations, however, are performed by the soul without a bodily organ, for instance **to understand, to consider, to will. Wherefore since these actions are proper to the soul** (alone) ... **these powers which use no bodily organ for their actions must needs remain in the separated soul** (but not the actions of the sensitive powers).

Others say that the sensitive and other like powers ... remain in the separated soul ... in a restricted sense ... because there remains in the separated soul the ability to produce these powers if it should be reunited to the body.... This opinion appears to be the more reasonable (S70,1).

St. Thomas ascribes to the disembodied soul a sort of internal, virtual, and teleological sensory ability—we will be able to conjure up memory images of sensations we had on earth and anticipatory images of future sensations which the resurrection body will afford us—but he labels this only a theological *opinion* (the Greeks call it a *theologoumenon*). If the disembodied soul can have sensory anticipations, then surely it can also have sensory memories. In any case, we have something more than total paralysis and sensory deprivation to look forward to.

Whether the acts of the sensitive powers (as well as the powers) **remain in the separated soul?**

Objection 2. Augustine says that *the body feels not, but the soul through the body....* Now that which benefits the body can be in the soul separated from the body. Therefore the soul will then be able to feel....

Reply to Objection 2. **The soul is said to feel through the body not as though the act of feeling belonged to the soul by itself, but as belonging to the whole composite by reason of the soul.... It may also be replied that Augustine is speaking according to the opinion of the Platonists who maintained this ...** (S70,2).

There is a real contradiction between St. Augustine's Platonic, dualistic psychology and St. Thomas' Aristotelian, hylomorphic one. The important issue is not whether St. Thomas was ignorant of this or too charitable to St. Augustine, but what is the truth of the matter; for we will all experience the truth, the reality, but we will not all experience the *philosophy* of St. Augustine or of Aristotle, after we die.

Objection 5. **Further, according to the Philosopher, the irascible and concupiscible** (desires and emotions) **are in the sensitive part. But joy and sorrow, love and hatred, fear and hope, and similar emotions which according to our faith we hold to be in separated souls, are in the irascible and concupiscible** (powers). **Therefore separated souls will not be deprived of the acts of the sensitive powers.**

Reply to Objection 5. **Love, joy, sorrow, and the like, have a twofold signification. Sometimes they denote passions of the sensitive appetite, and thus they will not be in the separated soul.... In another way they denote acts of the will which is in the intellective part; and in this way they will be in the separated soul, even as delight will be there without bodily movement, as it is in God ...** (S70,2).

E.g., separated souls will feel joy in God, virtue, and beauty but not in sex, foods, or colors. This distinction between two kinds of post-mortem emotions also helps us to understand our emotions now.

Can one person's good works help another in this world and/or in Purgatory even if they never meet? If so, how?

Whether the suffrages (good works) of one person can profit others?

All the faithful united together by charity are members of the one body of the Church. Now one member (organ of a body) **is assisted by another. Therefore one man can be assisted by the merits of the Church....**

Our actions may avail (for others) **in two ways: first, by way of merit; secondly, by way of prayer—the difference being that merit relies on justice and prayer on mercy....**

Since ... prayer depends on the liberality of God to Whom we pray, it may extend to whatever is rightly subject to the divine power.... On the other hand ... the work of one may avail another not only by way of prayer but even by way of merit ... on account of their communion in the root of the work, which root is charity in all meritorious works. Wherefore all who are united together by charity acquire some benefit from one another' works....

... [E]ven in heaven each one will rejoice in the goods of others. Hence it is that the communion of saints is laid down as an article of faith (in the Apostles' Creed) **... so that those works become somewhat the works of those for whom they are done, as though they were bestowed on them by the doer ...** (S71,1).

An analogy: In this world, lungs do not directly touch kidneys, yet each helps the other, in fact each is essential to the life of the other. We are united in the communion of saints in this kind of way in the Mystical Body of Christ, the Church, for it is not just a visible organization but a spiritual *organism*. Even if we do not touch, we do touch; even if we are strangers, we are not strangers.

The two spiritual bloodstreams that bring life from and to the different organs (individuals) in this Body are prayer and good works ("alms-deeds"). These appeal to mercy and justice respectively, for prayer asks for and receives mercy, and good works merit just rewards, both for the worker and for others as well if these good works are "extra" ("supererogatory") works, since the works were done for something "extra" over and above justice, namely charity.

The whole idea of indulgences is based on this ontology of the communion of saints. The communion of saints is not an "extra", not optional or disposable; it is one of the twelve basic articles of the Apostles' Creed.

In the communion of saints, even though your soul or body cannot become mine, your works can! The mere philosopher puzzles at this mystery, but the lover rejoices at it.

Objection 4. **It belongs to divine justice to repay good for good in the same way as evil for evil. But no man is punished for the evil doings of another. Indeed, according to Ezechial 18:4,** *The soul that sinneth, the same shall die.* **Therefore neither does one person profit by another's good.**

Reply to Objection 4. **It is directly contrary to justice to take away from a person that which is his due, but to give a person what is not his due is not contrary to justice but surpasses the bounds of justice, for it is liberality.... Consequently it is not becoming that one should be punished for another's sins, as it is** (becoming) **that one should acquire some advantage from deeds of another** (S71,1).

Punishing one man for another's sins is less than just, but rewarding one man for another's good deeds is not. It is more than just. Who would protest this? Only the stingy or the envious.

Does the communion of saints cut across the divide of death? If so, how?

Whether the dead can be assisted by the works of the living?

Objection 3. **It belongs only to one who is on the way** (on earth) **to advance on account of some deed. Now after death men are no longer wayfarers.... Therefore the dead cannot be assisted by a person's suffrages** (good works).

Reply to Objection 3. **Although strictly speaking, after death souls are not in the state of the way, yet in a certain respect they are still on the way in so far as they are delayed a while in their advance towards their final reward** (S71,2).

It would truly be "bad news" to learn that our good works and prayers could not help our beloved dead. That would mean death is stronger than love. That is the point of the next answer: that communal life does not end with death any more than individual life does:

Objection 4. **No one is assisted by the deed of another unless there be some community of life between them. Now there is no community between the dead and the living, as the Philosopher says. Therefore the suffrages of the living do not profit the dead.**

Reply to Objection 4. **Although the communion of civic deeds whereof the Philosopher speaks is impossible between the dead and the living, because the dead are outside civic life, the communication of the spiritual life is possible between them, for that life is founded on charity toward God, to Whom the spirits of the dead live** (S71,2).

St. Thomas next settles the issue by the clear and direct words of Scripture, and then explains why it is so: because charity is not just a subjective feeling, a personal virtue, or a good deed but an ontological union between souls. We the living can remember and help the dead only because God has given us two mental powers that transcend the present time, namely memory and anticipation or hope.

On the contrary **are the words of 2 Machabees** [Maccabees] **12:46:** *It is ... a holy and wholesome thought to pray for the dead that they may be loosed from their sins.* **Therefore the suffrages of the living profit the dead....**

I answer that **Charity, which is the bond uniting the members of the Church, extends not only to the living but also to the dead who die in charity. For charity, which is the life of the soul even as the soul is the life of the body, has no end:** *Charity never falleth away* (1 Cor 13:8).

Moreover, the dead live in the memory of the living, wherefore the intention of the living can be directed to them....

Nevertheless we must not believe that the suffrages of the living profit them so as to change their state from (eternal) **unhappiness to** (eternal) **happiness or vice versa, but they avail for the diminution of punishment** (and/ or the increase of reward) ... (S71,2).

Augustine says: *Suffrages profit those who are not very good or not very bad.* **Now such are those who are detained in purgatory** ... (S71,6).

Venial sins are called sins as being dispositions to sin ... so that the punishment which is awarded to them in purgatory is not a retribution simply, but rather a cleansing ... (S75,1).

The basic purpose of Purgatory is rehabilitation, not retribution: the perfection of characters and habits rather than the punishment of sins. God created Purgatory out of love and mercy, not merely justice.

311. WHO ARE FUNERALS FOR?

Are funerals for the benefit and comfort of the living, or for the benefit of the dead?

Whether the burial service profits the dead?

Augustine says: *The funereal equipment, the disposition of the grave, the solemnity ... are a comfort to the living rather than a help to the dead.*

It was, however, a pagan error that burial was profitable to the dead by procuring rest for his soul, for they believed that the soul could not be at rest until the body was buried, which is altogether ridiculous and absurd.... The dead take no harm if their bodies remain unburied....

We have recourse to burial ... for the sake of the living, lest their eyes be revolted by the disfigurement of the corpse, and their bodies be infected by the stench.... [I]t profits the living also spiritually inasmuch as our belief in the resurrection is confirmed thereby.

(However,) it profits the dead in so far as one bears the dead in mind and prays for them through looking on their burial place, wherefore a *monument* is something that recalls the mind (*monens mentem*), as Augustine observes....

Moreover, that burial in a sacred place profits the dead does not result from the action done (by the living) but rather from ... the patronage of some saint by whose prayers we must believe that he is assisted, as well as from the suffrages of those who serve the holy place and pray more frequently and more specially for those who are buried in their midst.... [T]hey can profit the dead not directly but indirectly, in so far as men are aroused to pity thereby and consequently to pray.... [I]t is in this sense that the burial **of the dead is reckoned among the works of mercy** (S71,11).

Sacramentalism is not superstition, like the pagan superstition mentioned by St. Thomas, that souls could not rest until their bodies were buried. Divinely instituted sacraments can benefit the dead, but humanly instituted ceremonies, however good they may be and however necessary for the living, cannot of themselves benefit the dead. They are "for us, the living".

St. Thomas mentions three benefits to the living of the care of dead bodies in funerals. The first is aesthetic: the covering up of the ugliness of decay. The second is hygienic: the prevention of infection. The third is spiritual: an occasion to remember the hope of resurrection.

He also mentions two possible *indirect* benefits that can accrue to the dead from our care of their dead bodies. First, it reminds us to pray for them. Second, burial in sacred ground is itself a kind of prayer, or an appeal to prayer: both our prayers and the prayers of patron saints. Thus these ceremonies can be sacramental (like holy water) but not sacraments. And therefore they are good works for us to do. In fact they are such an important class of good works that they are mentioned as one of the seven corporal works of mercy.

Prayers at the time and place of death typically carry more spiritual weight because they come from deeper places in the heart, and are more directly and immediately concerned with eternity. Do not miss the opportunity to minister to both the dead and the bereaved on these occasions. Do unto others, both the dead and the bereaved, what you would most want them to do for you when you die and when you are bereaved.

312. Whether suffrages offered for several are of as much value to each one as if they had been offered for each in particular?

Sometimes we offer specific prayers or "suffrages" (good works) tailored to the needs of specific other people (e.g., "Please convert Joe" or "Please cure Zoe's cancer"); but sometimes we offer general prayers, like the Rosary, for others either in general, or for a group of persons, or for more than one named individuals. Is praying for all always best? Would adding many more persons to the list for whom we offer the prayer multiply the power of the prayer, or would it divide it? If I offer a Rosary for Jack and Jill, does it still have as much power for Jack as it would if I offered it for Jack alone?

We seem to have a dilemma here. For if the answer is yes, then it seems we should always pray for the whole world rather than concentrating our prayers on one or a few individuals. And that seems wrong. On the other hand, if the answer is no, then that would seem to make prayer like a material thing, such as food, with a finite, quantifiable value, so that dividing a prayer among two individuals instead of praying for one only would be like dividing a pizza among two eaters, where each eater gets only half of what he would have had if he had had the whole pizza alone. And that seems wrong too.

It is better to assist many than one. If therefore a suffrage offered for several is of as much value to each one as if it were offered for one alone, it would seem that the Church ought not to have appointed a Mass and prayer to be said for one person in particular, but that Mass ought always to be said for all the faithful departed. And this is evidently false.

Further, a suffrage has a finite efficiency. Therefore if it be divided among many, it avails less for each one than if it were offered for one only.

If the value of suffrages be considered according as it is derived from the virtue of charity that unites the members of the Church together, suffrages offered for several persons avail each one as much as if they were offered for one alone, because charity is not diminished if its effect be divided among many; in fact, it is increased. And in like manner joy increases through being shared by many, as Augustine says....

On the other hand ... the suffrage for some person in particular avails him more than that which is offered for him in common with many others, for in this case the effect of the suffrages is divided in virtue of the divine justice (S71,13).

If the suffrages offered for a person do not profit all indifferently but those chiefly for whom they are offered, then there is no doubt that general and special suffrages together avail a person more than general suffrages alone (S71,14).

St. Thomas, very reasonably, eliminates the first horn of our dilemma by noting that the Church does pray for specific named individuals. If prayers for many or for all were as effective as prayers for one, this would squander spiritual goods.

Though prayer is not material, nor can its power be measured mathematically, yet like all creaturely acts it and its power are finite, unlike God, and therefore divisible, unlike God. (The Trinity is not God divided into three parts!)

What increases or decreases the power of a prayer is not the number of persons prayed for but the amount of faith, hope, and above all charity that motivates it.

This means that when charity is multiplied by multiplying the number of persons prayed for, the prayer's power is multiplied; and when the charity is divided by multiplying the number, the prayer's power is divided.

Prayer addresses us in the same way that both human love and God's love addresses us: both individually and as a community. It is, as usual, both/and rather than either/or.

Scripture says we are surrounded by a "great cloud of witnesses" (Heb 12:1). Does this mean the saints in Heaven are in the stands watching us on the playing field, cheering us on and helping us by their prayers as we fight, pray, and work in this world? Is that just comforting mythology or is that really true? Is there a Skype connection as far away as Heaven?

Whether the saints have knowledge of our prayers?

Apparently the chief obstacle to the souls of the saints being cognizant of our prayers and other happenings in our regard is that they are far removed from us. Since, then, distance does not prevent these things ... the souls of the saints are cognizant of our prayers and of what happens here below.

Further, unless they were aware of what happens in our regard they would not pray for us, since they would be ignorant of our needs....

Since the souls of the saints do not *comprehend* the divine essence, it does not follow that they know *all* that can be known by the divine essence ... but each of the blessed must needs see in the divine essence as many other things as the perfection of his happiness requires. For the perfection of a man's happiness requires him to have whatever he will, and to will nothing amiss; and each one wills with a right will to know what concerns himself ... Now it pertains to their glory that they assist the needy for their salvation, for thus they become God's co-operators.... Wherefore it is evident that the saints are cognizant of such things as are required for this purpose, and so it is manifest that they know in the Word the vows, devotions, and prayers of those who have recourse to their assistance....

Although the saints, after this life, know what happens here below, we must not believe that they grieve through knowing the woes of those whom they loved in this world, for they are so filled with heavenly joy that sorrow finds no place in them (S72,1).

The Church assures us that our prayers to the saints are effective, when we ask them to intercede for us to God. St. Thomas argues, very simply, that this presupposes that they hear and understand our prayers; and this presupposes that they see us and understand our needs.

They see this not by their own human powers, but through God's Mind ("in the Word"), through their partial vision of the divine essence, a kind of limited mental telepathy with God. Thus the saints are co-workers with God, co-operators in the work of the salvation and sanctification of human souls still "on the way" on earth. We will join them some day, hopefully, and so we had better practice this work now, by interceding for each other. It is a kind of dress rehearsal for our work in Heaven.

Just as we need to know other persons and their needs in order to pray for them here and now, so the saints in Heaven need to know us and our needs in order for them to pray for us there. St. Thomas Aquinas knows your mind, and probably knows it much better than you know his mind, since he has a direct divine assistance in knowing you, which you do not have in knowing him.

St. Thomas' last point is that the saints' knowledge of us is clearer than our knowledge of them and of each other because they are freed from grief, pain, and worry, since they stand in the presence of God and see all that they see in that light, including us and our lives. If you can know the whole story of some great drama, like *The Divine Comedy* or *The Lord of the Rings,* from the viewpoint of its author, and can see each event of its plot in light of its final end, you are confident and at peace as you read even the most painful and problematic passages, knowing that in the end all will be well.

We can share some of that Heavenly peace even now, though not by sight but by faith. For we *see* only "through a glass, darkly" (1 Cor 13:12) but we can *believe* and trust far beyond what we see, since our Author has told us about the drama that we are in, and has promised us that in it "all things work together for good to those who love God, who are called according to His purpose" (Rom 8:28).

Protestants protest against the Catholic practice of praying to saints. What justifies it?

Whether we ought to call upon the saints to pray for us?

The saints who are in heaven are more acceptable to God than those who are on the way. Now we should make the saints who are on the way our intercessors with God ... Much more, therefore, should we ask the saints who are in heaven to help us by their prayers to God (S72,2).

If it is good to ask each other to pray for us here, and better to ask the most saintly friends to do so, it is best of all to ask the perfected saints in Heaven to do so. If it is not right to ask the saints in Heaven to pray for us, then it is even less right to ask the less saintly on earth to do so.

According to Dionysius, the order established by God among things is that *the last should be led to God by those that are midway between*. Wherefore since the saints who are in heaven are nearest to God, the order of the divine law requires that we, who while we remain in the body are pilgrims from the Lord, should be brought back to God by the saints, who are between us and Him....

God's order is not to micromanage everything Himself but to establish subordinate sovereignties, a hierarchy of helpers. He exalts them by having them exalt us. For "grace perfects nature".

It is not on account of any defect in God's power that He works by means of second causes, but it is for the perfection of the order of the universe, and the more manifold outpouring of His goodness on things, through His bestowing on them not only the goodness which is proper to them, but also the faculty of causing goodness in others. Even so, it is not through any defect in His mercy that we need to bespeak His clemency through the prayers of the saints, but to the end that the aforesaid order in things be observed (S72,2).

Pascal says that "God established prayer in order to communicate to His creatures the dignity of being causes." He established prayer for the same reason He established work: to mature our muscles.

This principle of hierarchy means that we should use and be used by every level of it, not just the highest:

Although the greater saints are more acceptable to God than the lesser, it is sometimes profitable to pray to the lesser, and this for five reasons. First, because sometimes one has greater devotion for a lesser saints than for a greater, and the effect of prayer depends very much on one's devotion. Secondly, in order to avoid tediousness, for continual attention to one thing makes a person weary, whereas by praying to different saints, the fervor of our devotion is aroused anew as it were. Thirdly, because it is granted to some saints to exercise their patronage in certain special cases.... Fourthly, that due honor be given by us to all. Fifthly, because the prayers of several sometimes obtain that which would not have been obtained by the prayers of one (S72,2).

Try imagining a world order where any one of these five reasons is *not* true, and you find that that would be an inferior, flawed order. God knew what He was doing when He set this system up!

Insofar as they pray for us by asking something for us in their prayers, their prayers are always granted, since they will only what God wills ... and what God wills is always fulfilled (S72,3).

The best reason for praying to saints in Heaven is that they, unlike friends on earth, never pray for anything outside God's will, which is always the best thing for us; and since their prayers are thus more conformed to God's will than ours are, they are (1) wiser than ours, (2) more powerful than ours, and (3) always effective, since they are one with God's will, which is omnipotent.

315. THE TIME OF CHRIST'S SECOND COMING AND THE END OF THE WORLD

Christ assured us that He would come again, but He did not tell us when. Are there any clues? Are there more than clues? Can we know the time of the End if we understand Scripture well enough?

Many signs will precede the advent of Christ when He shall come to judgment ... but it is not easy to know what these signs may be, for the signs of which we read in the gospels, as Augustine says, refer not only to (1) Christ's coming to judgment but also to (2) the time of the sack of Jerusalem (A.D. 70) and to (3) the coming of Christ in ceaselessly visiting His Church.... [T]hese signs that are mentioned in the gospels, such as wars, fears, and so forth, have been from the beginning of the human race, unless perhaps we say that at that time they will be more prevalent, although it is uncertain in what degree this increase will foretell the imminence of the advent....

The day of the Lord is said to come as a thief because the exact time is not known, since it will not be possible to know it from those signs ... (S73,1).

That which is unknown to the angels will be much more unknown to men.... Now the angels have no exact knowledge of that time, as appears from Matthew 24:36: *Of that day and hour no one knoweth, no not the angels of heaven.* **Therefore that time is hidden from men....**

As Augustine says, *He scatters the fingers of all calculators and bids them be still* **... wherefore all those who have been misled to reckon the aforesaid time have so far proved to be untruthful.... The falseness of these calculators is evident, as will likewise be the falseness of those who even now cease not to calculate (S77,2).**

The time of the first coming of the Messiah was revealed more clearly, in the Old Testament prophets, than the time of His Second Coming. Many of the Jews around Jesus' time were expecting the Messiah because of a strong (but not universal) consensus about that time, which had not existed at any other time in Jewish history. The *nature and work* of the Messiah, by contrast, was not revealed clearly, in order to test the hearts of His chosen people: those whose hearts were set on earthly goods like power and wealth and autonomy, rejected Christ because He did not seem to them fulfill the prophecy that the Messiah would rescue Israel from her "enemies" since they thought their "enemies" were the Romans, who deprived the Jews of these worldly goods. But those whose hearts were set on what God is, viz. righteousness, accepted Christ as their Savior because they recognized their true enemies as their own sins, and that was what Christ saved them from (Mt 1:21).

In contrast, God left the time of the Second Coming obscure but its nature and purpose clear.

Why did He leave the time obscure? So that we would be ready at all and any times to meet this "thief in the night" (Mt 24:43: what an unflattering and shocking image for Christ!)

If even Christ said that He did not know the time of His Second Coming (Mt 24:36), how incredibly arrogant for any human being to imply that he is wiser than his Lord by claiming that he has figured it out! All the batters who have ever stepped up to the plate on this issue have struck out, for 2,000 years. How much trust should we put in those who are now playing that game? This is a devastating critique of the few Protestant Fundamentalists who still specialize in this ridiculous distraction.

Christ left the nature and purpose of the Second Coming clear for the very same reason He left its time unclear: so that we would be ready at all times for the Last Judgment, for the full presence of the Light of Truth, when nothing more will be hidden.

For if we lived each moment of our lives in that presence; if we practiced the presence of the God Who is Truth every day, we would be well on our way to becoming saints. All evil seeks to hide from the light of truth. We must practice living in the light, for we will do it forever in Heaven.

Where will we live forever after death? Won't we miss the earth?

It is written (Rev 21:1): *I saw a new heaven and a new earth....*

Since the world was in a way made for man's sake, it follows that when man shall be glorified in the body, the other bodies of the world shall also be changed to a better state, so that it is rendered a more fitting place for him ...

Now although properly speaking a corporeal thing cannot be the subject of the stain of sin, nevertheless on account of sin corporeal things contract a certain unfittingness for being appointed to spiritual purposes, and for this reason we find that places where crimes have been committed are reckoned unfit for the performance of sacred actions therein unless they be cleansed beforehand. Accordingly that part of the world which is given to our use contracts from men's sins a certain unfitness for being glorified, wherefore in this respect it needs to be cleansed (S73,1).

This (cleansing) **fire of the final conflagration ... will act as the instrument of divine justice.... [I]t will act differently on different people. For the wicked will be tortured by the action of the fire, whereas the good, in whom there will be nothing to cleanse, will feel no pain at all from the fire, as neither did the children in the fiery furnace** (Dan 3), **although their bodies will not be kept whole, as were the bodies of the children. It is said** (Lk 3:17): *Whose fan is in His hand, and He will purge His floor and will gather the wheat,* i.e., the elect, *into His barn, but the chaff,* i.e., the wicked, *He will burn with unquenchable fire.* **Hence it will be thus with the cleansing of the world, so that all that is ugly and vile will be cast with the wicked into hell, and all that is beautiful and noble will be taken up above for the glory of the elect** (S74,8).

We think a lot about this earth, i.e., this universe, which Scripture calls "the heavens (outer space) and the earth"; and we think a little about Heaven; but we hardly ever think about the new earth, the new universe, the "new heavens and new earth" that Scripture promises.

Our natural expectations for life after death are either nothingness, or Heaven, or Purgatory, or Hell, but hardly ever a new earth. But God did not make a mistake in creating a material world and a material body for us. (Yes, "for us": He made the whole universe for us. Its point is not gases and galaxies but saints. That is its product. It is a large womb, and we are its children. God is our Father but it is our mother.) He will perfect His design for us humans. For "grace perfects nature" rather than destroying it or suppressing it. As C. S. Lewis says, "the old field of space, time, matter, and the senses, is to be weeded and dug up for a new crop. We may be tired of that old field; God is not" (*Miracles*).

The main "improvement" will be the eradication of sin and its effects on the world. Genesis 3 mentions some of these effects: death, pain in childbirth, pain in work, conflict between men and women, and spiritual war between good and evil, between "the seed of the woman" (Christ) and the seed of the serpent (Antichrist). The material world God created is declared, by God Himself, to be good, not evil; matter is not the cause of sin, but it does carry the effects of sin. It is a battlefield, and it needs to be *cleansed*, like the Canaanite Satan-worshippers' valley of Gehenna (2 Kings 23:10, Jer 7:31, Mt 10:28).

St. Thomas opines that the very same purifying fire that cleanses the good will torture the wicked. The fire is divine justice, divine righteousness and truth, which the good love and the evil hate, and which therefore simultaneously blisses the blessed and curses the cursed.

If there is a resurrection body, there must be a resurrected world for that body to inhabit. And just as the new body will be better (more "fitting"), so will the new world. And both will be better in ways we cannot now know or even imagine, just as an unborn baby cannot know or imagine either the better, bigger body or the better, bigger world that awaits him outside the womb. (See 1 Cor 2:9.)

What is God's reason for giving us a resurrected body?

The members should be conformed to the head. Now our Head lives and will live eternally in body and soul, since *Christ rising again from the dead dieth now no more* (Rom 6:8). Therefore men who are His members will live in body and soul; and consequently there must needs be a resurrection of the body....

The soul is compared to the body not only as a worker to the instrument with which he works, but also a form to matter. Wherefore the work belongs to the composite and not to the soul alone, as the Philosopher shows. And since to the worker is due the reward of the work, it behooves man himself, who is composed of soul and body, to receive the reward of his work....

Other things being equal, the state of the soul in the body is more perfect than outside the body, because it is a part of the whole composite.... Because, strictly speaking, a thing is more conformed to God when it has all that the condition of its nature requires ... (S75,1).

The ultimate reason for all things human is Christ, Who is perfect man as well as perfect God, and Who "truly reveals man to himself" (Vatican II). Thus the ultimate reason for the resurrection of the body is that "the members [us] should be conformed to the Head (Christ)"; and Christ has a human body now in Heaven (a material body but not a mortal body), since the Ascension was not the *undoing* of the Incarnation. If we did not have bodies in Heaven, we would not be like Christ. If we had no bodies we could not be "members" of His (Mystical) Body. Angels don't have that privilege! (The Greek word translated "members" means "organs in an organism", not the "members" of a club or a class.)

Our bodies are not merely instruments of our souls, as a tool is an instrument of a worker. We are not spiritual substances, like angels, which merely *use* material bodies. Nor are we two substances, bodies and souls, like ghosts in haunted houses. We are a single though composite substance which is both material and spiritual. The soul is the form of the body and the body is the matter of the soul, somewhat as the meaning of a book is its form or soul and the words are its matter or body. They are not two things but two dimensions.

When I hit you or hug you, it is not just my hand or my arms that do the work. Nor is it just my mind, will, or emotions. It is me, the whole me. And when I hit you or hug you, I do not do that just to your body. I do it to you, the whole you. Since all the good and bad works we do on earth are done by the whole self, their just rewards (and punishments) are whole-self rewards (and punishments), bodily as well as spiritual.

Platonists, Gnostics and Hindus all believe that the soul is better without the body than with it. They are wrong. A human soul without a body is not a complete self, like an angel, but an incomplete self, rather like a program in a computer, or sheet music that is not played. It is physically paralyzed, since it has no body or senses to express itself. So even though the nature of God is spiritual and not material, our souls are more like God when they are in a material body, since "a thing is more conformed to God when it has all that the condition of its (God-designed and God-created) nature requires."

We will succeed in being more fully human in Heaven than we ever were on earth. And that includes our bodies. They will be more *bodily* bodies, not less. We tend to imagine human bodies in Heaven as ghostlike, but it is actually our present bodies that are more ghostlike, more thin and faded, less solid and substantial and real, compared with our Heavenly bodies.

Take care of your body; it is the sketch of something far more real and more glorious than itself. Remember C. S. Lewis' image: he says they are like ponies give to schoolboys to prepare them to manage stallions.

This is why St. Paul says that sins against the body are so serious (1 Cor 6:18–20).

Will I get my same body back in Heaven?

Whether in the resurrection the soul will be reunited to the same identical body?

It is written (Job 19:26): *In my flesh I shall see God....*

On this point the (pagan) philosophers erred ... for they held that when the soul while existing in the body had led a life contrary to the ordering of reason ... it passed after death from the body of a man into the body of some other animal to whose manner of living it had conformed in this life, for instance into the body of a dog on account of lust, into the body of a lion on account of robbery and violence, and so forth....

This opinion arises (because) **they said that the soul is not united to the body essentially as form to matter, but only accidentally, as mover to the thing moved, or as a man to his clothes. Hence it was possible for them to maintain that the soul pre-existed before being infused into the body begotten of natural generation, and also that it is united to various bodies** (S79,1); ("Reincarnation")

Whether it will be identically the same man that shall rise again?

The necessity of holding the resurrection arises from this: that man may obtain the last end for which he was made. For this cannot be accomplished in this life ... otherwise man would have been made in vain if he were unable to obtain the end for which he was made. And since it behooves the end to be obtained by the selfsame thing that was made for that end, lest it appear to be made without purpose, it is necessary for the selfsame man to rise again. And this is effected by the selfsame soul being united to the selfsame body. For otherwise there would be no resurrection properly speaking, if the same man were not re-formed. Hence to maintain that he who rises again is not the selfsame man is heretical, since it is contrary to the truth of Scripture which proclaims the resurrection.

This argument affords a very good proof against those who held a distinction between the sensitive and rational soul in man (i.e., that we had two souls, one animal and one spiritual), **because in that case the sensitive soul in man would not be incorruptible, as neither is it in other animals. And consequently in the resurrection there would not be the same sensitive soul, nor consequently the same animal, nor the same man. But if we assert that in man the same soul is by its substance** (essence) **both rational and sensitive, we shall encounter no difficulty in this question** (S79,2).

This last issue is crucial for abortion. If we have two souls, (1) the animal ("sensitive") soul that keeps the animal body alive and (2) the rational, spiritual soul that makes us more than an animal; and if the animal soul appears in the unborn child before the rational soul does; then it could be argued that abortion does not kill a human being but only an animal if the child is aborted early enough, when there is only the animal soul there.

That's essentially the same as saying that you can't call a fetus human just because it's biologically and genetically human. But you can, because that same single human soul that's causing the biological growth is also the spiritual, immortal, rational soul that is God's image and God's child and destined for eternal union with its Heavenly Father. It's not able to perform rational operations yet, but it's there. It's not a second soul. Even the one-celled zygote, at the moment of conception, before any differentiation into organs that can think or feel pain, before the zygote replicates and explodes into millions of cells, like the universe expanding after the Big Bang—even that single-celled thing is a human person, the same human person you are today. For only a human soul can direct the human growth of a human body, from the very beginning. That's not just "life", that's an individual human being.

Will the resurrection body have all its organs? Will it have sex organs? If not, will it lose its feminine or masculine identity? If so, what will they be for if there's no more biological reproduction in Heaven?

Whether all the members of the human body will rise again?

The works of God are perfect (Deut 32:4). **But the resurrection will be the work of God. Therefore man will be remade perfect in all his members.**

Objection 1. **It would seem that not all the members of the human body will rise again. For if the end be done away, it is useless to repair the means. Now the end of each member (organ) is its act. Since, then, nothing useless is done in divine works, and since the use of certain members is not fitting to man after the resurrection, especially the use of the genital members, for then they** *shall neither marry nor be married* (Mt 22:30), **it would seem that not all the members shall rise again.**

Reply to Objection 1. **The members may be considered in two ways in relation to the soul: either according to the relation of matter to form, or according to the relation of instrument to agent.... If, then, the members be considered in the light of the first relationship** (matter to form), **their end is not operation but rather the perfect being of the species, and this is also required after the resurrection.** (Therefore the resurrection body will be perfectly complete in its sexual identity or form.) **But if they be considered in the light of the second relationship** (instrument to the agent that uses the instrument), **then their end is operation.** (The end of "the reproductive system" is ... reproduction!) **And yet it does not follow that when the operation fails** (no reproduction in Heaven) **the instrument is useless, because an instrument serves not only to accomplish the operation of the agent, but also to show its virtue** (i.e., its goodness; it is for beauty and not just utility). **Hence it will be necessary for the virtue of the soul's powers to be shown in their bodily instruments, even though they never proceed to action, so that the wisdom of God be thereby glorified.** ("See me! I am a woman. I am beautiful." This remains, even when "See what I am useful for: I am a future baby-maker" does not remain. But perhaps "I am a past baby-maker" does remain.)

Objection 2. **Further, the entrails** (bowels, intestines) **are members; and yet they will not rise again. For they can neither rise full, since thus they contain impurities** ("dung"!), **nor empty, since nothing is empty in** (perfect) **nature. Therefore the members shall not all rise again.**

Reply to Objection 2. **The entrails will rise again in the body even as the other members, and they will be filled not with vile superfluities but with goodly humours** (S80,1).

St. Thomas is very careful to distinguish what we know from what we don't. (1) We know that our bodies will be perfect, because they will be God's work, and all God's works are perfect. (2) We do *not* know the answer to our question about sex organs. Which of these two is more important? Would we prefer to know all about sex in Heaven but not know, and doubt, that God's works are all perfect?

Even the body's lowest and grossest members, the intestines, will have a role in Heaven, though not the same role as on earth (the elimination of waste). What that role will be, and what its glory and beauty will be, we cannot know or imagine. "Goodly humours" is not only by modern standards very primitive chemistry but even for its own time is deliberately vague. We have enough knowledge of the future to motivate us but not enough to distract us from our present tasks.

A baby in the womb does not have to know how its nose will look, or what it will be used for, once it is born. We do not have to know what we do not need to know about Heaven. It should be our goal but not our distraction. If the shortstop takes his eyes off the ground ball that is being hit to him, and looks instead at the first baseman's glove, where he will eventually throw the ball, he will misplay the grounder and fail to get the out. One step at a time. "One foot up and one foot down, that's the way to London Town."

Will the resurrected body have everything the present body has, e.g., hair and nails?

Whether the hair and nails will rise again in the human body?

It is written (Lk 21:18): *A hair of your head shall not perish.*

Further, hair and nails were given to man as an ornament. Now the bodies of men, especially the elect, ought to rise again with all their adornment. Therefore they ought to rise again with the hair.

The soul is to the animated body as (the personal virtue or habit of) **art is to the work of art ... Now art employs certain instruments for the accomplishment of the work intended ... and it also uses other instruments for the safe-keeping of the principal instruments; thus the art of warfare employs a sword for fighting and a sheath for the safe-keeping of the sword. And so among the parts of an animated body, some are directed to the accomplishment of the soul's operations, for instance the heart, liver, hand, foot; while others are directed to the safe-keeping of the other parts as leaves to cover fruit; and thus hair and nails are in man for the protection of other parts ... and since man will rise again with all the perfections of his nature, it follows that hair and nails will rise again in him** (S80,2).

Whatever belongs to the integrity of human nature in those who take part in the resurrection will rise again....

Further, our resurrection will be conformed to the resurrection of Christ. Now in Christ's resurrection His blood rose again, else the wine would not now be changed into His blood in the Sacrament of the altar. Therefore the blood will rise again in us also ... (S80,3).

Christ's resurrection body was recognizable: by Mary Magdalene at the empty tomb, by the two disciples on the road to Emmaus, by the Eleven in the upper room, by "Doubting Thomas," and by Peter at the Sea of Galilee. If He had been hairless and nailless, He would not have been recognizable as Himself. The reaction would have been "What weird thing is that?" instead of "It is the Lord!"

Just as with the sexual organs, the practical earthly works of the other bodily organs disappear in Heaven but their beauty remains. (St. Thomas calls this "ornament" and "adornment".) For utilitarian work is earthly and temporal, but beauty is Heavenly and eternal.

The same will probably be true of clothes. On earth they have four purposes: beauty ("adornment") and three utilitarian purposes: to protect the potential victims of sexual lust, to protect against cold weather, and to show the wearer's social status or vocation. In Heaven there will be no lust, no cold, and no earthly social status, so the utilitarian purposes for clothes will disappear. Yet clothes will remain for "adornment". "That's me!" a woman says about a dress. Clothing in Heaven will be as natural to the person as hair and nails.

Notice how wonderfully concrete and specific St. Thomas is about our blood and Christ's blood (in his last paragraph). Most modern theologians do not dare ask such questions, the questions children ask. But Christians have concrete data (in divine revelation) as well as abstract speculation (in philosophizing and theologizing), and the speculation must conform to the data. If it does, it can really prove such things, just as the sciences do with their data. St. Thomas also is careful to humbly distinguish such only-probable arguments, which are only from "fittingness", from certain demonstrations.

Our revealed data tell us that Christ's body, which is our only concrete example of a resurrected body and our model for our own resurrection bodies, (1) has blood, and (2) is immortal. In our present life these two things are contradictory, and we cannot know or imagine how they can be reconciled. But we know that they *can* be reconciled, somehow, by God, for our data source (Christ) tells us that they *are*. If it *is*, it can be.

Will our resurrection bodies be young or old? Will my body be the body of an older man compared with my son's body, and at the same time the body of a young man compared with my father's body? If we will have perfect bodies, will they all be equally young?

Whether all will rise again of the same age?

It is written (Eph 4:13): *Until we meet ... unto a perfect man, unto the measure of the age of the fullness of Christ.* **Now Christ rose again of youthful age, which begins about the age of thirty years, as Augustine says. Therefore others also will rise again of a youthful age....**

I answer that, **Man will rise again without any defect in human nature, because as God founded human nature without a defect, even so will He restore it without defect. Now human nature has a twofold defect. First, because it has not yet attained to its ultimate perfection. Secondly, because it has already gone back from its ultimate perfection. The first defect is found in children, the second in the aged; and consequently in each of these human nature will be brought by the resurrection to the state of its ultimate perfection, which is in the youthful age, at which the movement of growth terminates and from which the movement of decrease begins.**

Objection 1. **It would seem that all will not rise again of the same age, namely the youthful. Because God will take nothing pertaining to man's perfection from those who rise again, especially from the blessed. Now age pertains to the perfection of man, since old age is the age that demands reverence. Therefore the old will not rise again of a youthful age.**

Reply to Objection 1. **Old age calls for reverence not on account of the state of the body ... but on account of the soul's wisdom.... Wherefore in the elect there will remain the reverence due to old age on account of the fullness of divine wisdom which will be in them, but the defect of old age will not be in them** (S81,1).

The question is not as trivial as it seems, since time is hardly trivial, and one essential difference between life now and life after death is the kind of time we will experience. Whatever "eternity" means, it means more than merely "endless time".

St. Thomas' answer to the question is more modest than it seems. We know little with certainty about Heaven, but we know that all is perfect there. Insofar as a healthy body of thirty or thirty-three is more perfect than an undeveloped body of three or an aging body of 103, a youthful body is our best concrete image for the body we will have in Heaven. It lacks the two kinds of defects St. Thomas mentions which come from our present time experience: the not yet perfect or the no longer perfect. In Heaven all the "not yets" will have already arrived and all the "no longers" will no longer be lost. In Heaven nothing good is lost, and therefore somehow all the goods lost to our experience on earth by being past ("no longer") or future ("not yet") will be *present*. The blessed will have simultaneously, in the present, all the perfections of childhood, youth, and age without any of their imperfections. Those born blind will see all the beauties they missed on earth, and the infant who died in the womb will feel all the joys of the life he missed outside the womb. How? God only knows, but God knows.

People (especially children) who catch a glimpse of the blessed in Heaven by near-death experiences, out-of-body experiences, or mystical experiences often say things like this: "When I saw Grandma in Heaven she was an old lady and a young woman and a little girl at the same time." The Heavenly body will not be thirty years old *at the expense of* being three or 103.

There may be a very practical application in this world of this otherworldly truth. We can love and appreciate more than the good we have now, we can love and appreciate also the good things that we or others have no longer (the lost joys and innocences of youth) or not yet (the peaceful wisdom of old age); and insofar as we do this, we come closer to bringing the Kingdom of Heaven to earth.

Many, though not all, of the ancients believed that the female gender was not only socially subordinate to the male but intrinsically inferior. Did St. Thomas share this prejudice? If so, he must have believed that in Heaven just as all would be of the same perfect age (thirty), all will be of the same perfect gender (male).

Whether all will rise again of the male sex?

Augustine says: ... *both sexes will rise again.*

At the resurrection, God will restore man to what He made him at the creation. Now He made woman.... Therefore He will also restore the female sex at the resurrection.

I answer that, **Just as ... a different quantity is due to different** (individual) **men** (in the traditional generic, not gender-specific, sense of "men"), **so also ... a different sex is due to different** (individual) **men. Moreover, this same diversity is becoming to the perfection of the species.... Wherefore just as men will rise again of various stature, so will they rise again of different sex.**

And though there be difference of sex, there will be no shame in seeing one another, since there will be no lust ... (S81,3).

Although both St. Augustine and St. Thomas shared some of the assumptions of their cultures about the social subordination of women, neither believed in the intrinsic inferiority of women. And the deepest reason for their transcendence of that prejudice was their transcendence of society as their standard, and their fidelity to divine revelation instead. Thus St. Thomas answers the question that arises from his semi-male-chauvinist culture by an appeal to God's will to create mankind female as well as male when He created them in perfection (and in His own image!—see Genesis 1:27) in Eden.

St. Thomas also appeals to the principle of diversity that is so rightly dear to modern minds. Perfection does not consist in unison but harmony, and therefore we will be different in Heaven, as we are on earth, not only in trivial accidents but also in important properties like gender. For human perfection, in Heaven as well as on earth, is more properly predicated of the whole human community (the "common-unity") than of the individual. Thus Genesis 1:27 did not say merely that women as well as men were made in God's image, but that that image was, or consisted in "male-and-female" together. Adam and Eve were more Godlike when they were together than when they are alone ("It is not good for man to be alone"), because togetherness is the cause and effect of love, and "God is love."

What will it be like in Heaven to notice and rejoice in sexual differences and sexual beauty but without lust? What was it like in Eden? Perhaps the best way to find out is to try it. Try to look at everything, even sex, as God does and as His perfected, unfallen children did once and will do again.

But are there any concrete examples and models of this lustless love for us in our fallen history, which is *between* Eden and Heaven, between Paradise Lost and Paradise Regained? Yes. There are two: Jesus and Mary. Love and imitate them. That is the way to become more Heavenly, and the way to practice for Heaven.

In Heaven we will have bodies, and therefore, it seems to follow that we will be *able* to perform the activities common to humans and animals, such as eating and copulating. Will we do these things? If not, why not?

Whether all will rise again to animal life so as to exercise the functions of nutrition and generation?

Objection 1. **Our resurrection will be conformed to Christ's. But Christ is said to have eaten after His resurrection (Jn 21, Lk 24). Therefore after the resurrection men will eat....**

Reply to Objection 1. **When Christ partook of that meal, His eating was an act not of necessity, as though human nature needed food after the resurrection, but of power, so as to prove that He had resumed the true human nature which He had in that state wherein He ate and drank with His disciples. There will be no need of such proof at the general resurrection, since it will be evident to all....**

Yes, in our resurrection bodies we will be able to eat, as Christ did, but there will be no need to eat, as there was need for Him to show His disciples that He was not a ghost. With our present bodies we are able to howl like wolves, but there is no need to do so, unless we needed to prove to wolves that we were not ghosts. Will we howl like wolves in Heaven? Probably not, because there will be no good reason to, but we will be able to, and if there were good reason to do so, we would.

Objection 2. **Further, the distinction between the sexes is directed to generation, and in like manner the instruments which serve the nutritive power are directed to eating. Now man will rise again with all these. Therefore he will exercise the acts of the generative and nutritive powers.**

Reply to Objection 2. **The distinction of sexes and the difference of members will be for the restoration of the perfection of human nature both in the species and in the individual. Hence it does not follow that they are without purpose, although they lack their animal operations.**

It is true that generation (reproduction) is one of the essential God-designed purposes of the distinction between the sexes in this world; but the distinction between the sexes also has other purposes than generation, even now. These other purposes, which are spiritual rather than biological, and which are proper to humans rather than common to humans and animals (such as love, appreciation, respect, and understanding of the opposite sex) will be preserved and perfected in Heaven. In preparation for Heaven we should seek out and fulfill these other purposes, as well as the biological purpose, even now.

On the contrary, **It is written (Mt 22:30):** *In the resurrection they shall neither marry nor be married.*

Notice that this presupposes that reproduction is an essential purpose of marriage. If there is to be reproduction, there should be marriage; if there is to be marriage, there should be (at least openness to) reproduction. If there is no reproduction (in Heaven), there is no marriage there, and if there is no marriage there, there is no reproduction there.

Further, generation is directed to supply the defect resulting from death, and to the multiplication of the human race; and eating is directed to make up for waste, and to increase quantity. But in the state of the resurrection the human race will already have the number of individuals preordained by God, since generation will continue up to that point. In like manner each man will rise again in due quantity. Neither will death be any more, nor any waste affect the parts of man. Therefore the acts of the generative and nutritive powers would be void of purpose ... (S81,4).

Sex (i.e., sexual activity, not just gender) is Nature's way of outwitting death. Or, to put the same point backwards, death is the price we pay for sex. If no death, no sex.

If we will have bodies in Heaven, how will we move? On our feet, on wings, on horses, in cars?

The human body and all that it contains will be perfectly subject to the rational soul, even as the soul will be perfectly subject to God. Wherefore it will be impossible for the glorified body to be subject to any change contrary to the disposition whereby it is perfected by the soul.... In the saints after the resurrection, the soul will have complete dominion over the body, and it will be altogether impossible for it to lose this dominion because it will be immutably subject to God (S82,1).

The glorified body will be altogether subject to the glorified soul, so that not only will there be nothing in it to resist the will of the spirit, for it was even so in the case of Adam's body, but also from the glorified soul there will flow into the body a certain perfection, whereby ... by the gift of agility it is subject to the soul as its mover, so that it is prompt and apt to obey the spirit in all the movements and actions of the soul....

The more the power of the moving soul dominates over the body, the less is the labor of movement.... Hence those in whom the motive power is stronger, and those who through exercise have the body more adapted to obey the moving spirit, labor less in being moved. And since after the resurrection the soul will perfectly dominate the body ... there will be no labor in the saints' movements, and thus it may be said that the bodies of the saints will be agile (S84,1).

It is written (Is 40:31): *They shall run and not be weary, they shall walk and not faint;* **and** (Wis 3:7): *(The just) shall run to and fro like sparks among the reeds* (S84,2).

Some say that a glorified body passes from one place to another without passing through the interval, and that consequently it is possible for the movement of a glorified body will be instantaneous.... Others with greater probability hold that a glorified body

moves in time ... but that this time is so short as to be imperceptible (S84,3).

As usual, St. Thomas answers a difficult and uncertain question by beginning with a certain and obvious premise: that the Heavenly body will perfectly obey the will of its soul as the soul perfectly obeys the will of God. Our present body often disobeys its soul (especially by dying!) just as this soul often disobeys God (by sinning). In fact the body disobeys the soul *because* the soul disobeys God, as the nobleman's servant is free to rebel against the nobleman once the nobleman rebels against his king. So in Heaven both rebellions will be reversed. What follows from this principle about the body's agility?

Surely, that the body will do everything the soul wants it to do, both physical and spiritual. Thus its movements both of matter and of spirit will be perfectly conformed to its will because that will will be perfectly conformed to God's will. So if it wants to move somewhere instantly, in conformity with God's will, its body will instantly obey, better than the transporter beam aboard the starship "Enterprise" on *Star Trek*.

Even unfallen Adam's body could not yet do that because it was in training, so to speak. It failed its test and had to take the long, hard, crooked road that we now walk to get to its glorious destiny.

St. Thomas mentions an obvious analogy to this even now: that stronger and healthier people have more obedient bodies. His answer about Heaven is only an extension of what is obvious on earth.

Thus in Heaven many Biblical prophesies, like the one he quotes about running without being weary, will be fulfilled in a way far more literal and concrete than we think.

There are many different ways to move. God moves at infinite speed by being omnipresent, or is omnipresent by moving at infinite speed. Angels move without any time gap between their disappearance from one place and their appearance in another, like electrons changing orbit in quantum physics. We will probably still move through some kind of time, unlike angels—but perhaps not.

A number of saints and visionaries have seen the blessed in Heaven, especially those who were tortured and martyred, with their wounds, as they are pictured in traditional Christian art. Is this a projection of culturally conditioned prejudices? Or is it prophetic?

We seem to have a dilemma here. On the one hand, all bodies in Heaven are supposed to be perfect, and wounds are imperfections. On the other hand, Christ's resurrection body, which is the only certain example we have of a resurrected body and which certainly must be a perfect one, still had its wounds, which "Doubting Thomas" touched (Jn 20:27).

On the one hand, Mother Teresa's wrinkles were obviously cosmetic imperfections, but from a deeper point of view they added to her beauty and glory, in fact they were not imperfections but perfections because they were caused by love and wisdom, and they manifested and radiated that love and wisdom. Will she still have them in Heaven, like badges of honorable warfare, things for which to rejoice after the costly victory is achieved?

Are there two kinds of wounds, some of which will be removed and others of which will not?

The scars or wounds will not be in the saints, nor were they in Christ, in so far as they imply a defect, but as signs of the most steadfast virtue whereby the saints suffered for the sake of justice and faith, so that this will increase their own and others' joy.

Hence Augustine says: *We feel an indescribable love for the blessed martyrs so as to desire to see in that kingdom the scars of the wounds in their bodies which they bore for Christ's name. Perchance indeed we shall see them, for this will not make them less comely but more glorious. A certain beauty will shine through them, a beauty though in the body, yet not of the body but of virtue.*

Nevertheless those martyrs who have been maimed and deprived of their limbs will not be without those limbs in the resurrection of the dead, for to them it is said (Lk 21:18) *A hair of your head shall not perish* (S82,1).

The answer to the long question above is yes to all its parts. And Heaven will resolve the apparent dilemma between the parts. But even now we can partly understand the resolution, if we are wise, when we compare the cosmetically perfect but vapid and empty face of a callow, egotistical movie star with the beauty of Mother Teresa's love-wrinkles. We can actually see in this world, with our eyes (if the eyes of the head line up with the eyes of the heart) a foretaste of the kind of beauty St. Thomas ascribes to the Heavenly bodies.

Notice also how St. Thomas makes Scripture come alive, not by taking it less seriously, as mere metaphor or exaggeration, but by taking it more seriously. Nothing good will perish in Heaven, not even a literal hair.

To what extent will our resurrected bodies in Heaven be real *bodies*? Scripture speaks of "a spiritual body" (1 Cor 15:44); does that mean something like a spirit, ghost, or angel?

It is written (Rev 1:7): *Every eye shall see Him.* **Therefore there will be actual sensation....**

Further, there will be actual movement, since they *shall run to and fro like sparks among the reeds* (Wis 3:7).

All are agreed that there is some sensation in the bodies of the blessed; else the bodily life of the saints after the resurrection would be likened to sleep rather than to vigilance.... But there is a difference of opinion as to the mode of sensation (S82,3).

Certain heretics, as Augustine relates,... said that at the resurrection the body will be transformed into a spirit.... But this cannot be maintained ... because if this were possible, and one's body were changed into a spirit, one would not rise again a man, for a man naturally consists of a soul and body (S83,1).

Certain heretics said ... that human bodies in rising again will be like the air or the wind ... but this again cannot be maintained, because our Lord had a palpable body after the Resurrection, as appears from the last chapter of Luke.... Moreover, the human body will rise again with flesh and bones, as did the body of our Lord, according to Luke 24:39, *A spirit hath not flesh and bones as you see Me to have* (S83,1).

Scripture (1 Cor 15:44) distinguishes "a spiritual body" not from "a physical body" but from "a natural body". It is "spiritual" in the same sense that "the spiritual man" (1 Cor 2:15) is "spiritual" now: not that he lacks a body but that he is moved by the Holy Spirit. The new body will be moved by the soul that is moved by the Spirit.

1 Corinthians 2:15 distinguishes the "spiritual" not from the "physical" but from the "natural": it is supernatural, not non-physical. The "spiritual man" has a body both in this life and also in the next. We are to be re-clothed, not un-clothed (2 Cor 5:2–4). Remember, the Spirit that makes us "spiritual" is the same Holy Spirit that provided a literal physical human body for Christ in Mary's womb at the Annunciation!

Christ took His physical human body with Him to Heaven at the Ascension. Therefore He is now visible in Heaven, just as He was on earth. And since He is visible, we will see Him (Rev 1:7). "Therefore there will be actual sensation." For the absence of physical sensation is a lack, not a gain. It is like mere dreaming, or sensory paralysis. That is why the denial of "the resurrection of the *body*" is a heresy (as Augustine says above).

That, plus the evidence of Jesus' post-resurrection body (St. Thomas' last paragraph), is the theological argument, from the data of divine revelation. The philosophical argument, from reason, is that man is essentially body as well as soul. We are not of the same species as angels. "Men without bodies" are oxymorons, like "squares without sides".

St. Thomas says that it is certain that we will have senses, but it is not certain what their "mode" (nature) will be.

If our bodies are destined for eternal Heavenly holiness rather than the scrap heap; if our present bodies are embryonic forms of something so perfect and holy that they share in the very nature of God by sharing in Christ's body; how much more should we now love and respect our bodies, and those of all others! This casts new light on the seriousness of "sins against the body" (1 Cor 6:18–20). Instead of comparing our own bodily sins with spiritual sins (that's the Devil's trick: A is worse than B, so don't worry about B), we should compare them with God's design for our bodies.

What is the relation between bodies and light in Heaven?

It is written (Mt 13:43): *The just shall shine as the sun in the kingdom of the Father,* **and** (Wis 3:7): *The just shall shine, and shall run to and fro like sparks among the reeds.*

Further, it is written (1 Cor 15:43): *It is sown in dishonor, it shall rise in glory....* **After the resurrection the bodies of the saints will be lightsome....** **[T]his clarity** (brightness) **will result from the overflow of the soul's glory into the body ... consequently, according to the greater clarity of the soul by reason of its greater merit, so too will the body differ in clarity, as the Apostle affirms** (1 Cor 15:41) **...** (S84,1).

The clarity of the glorified body results from the merit of the will and therefore will be subject to the will, so as to be seen or not seen according to its command. Therefore it will be in the power of the glorified body to show forth its clarity or to hide it ... (S84,2).

The glory of the body will not destroy (its) **nature but will perfect it. Wherefore the body will retain the color due to it by reason of the nature of its component parts, but in addition to this it will have clarity resulting from the soul's glory. Thus we see bodies which have color by their nature aglow with the resplendence of the sun ...** (S85,1).

It will be like the clarity which He had in the Transfiguration.... **[I]ntense clarity does not disturb the sight, in so far as it acts by the action of the soul, for thus it rather gives delight ... though the clarity of a glorified body surpasses the clarity of the sun, it does not by its nature disturb the sight but soothes it** (S84,2).

Light was the first thing created, and so light is in some ways the primary example of matter. Since the resurrection body will be a concrete material body, but a transformed one, and have relations to matter and the senses, but a transformed one, it will have a transformed relation to light. What might that be?

When Christ let Peter, James, and John see His Heavenly body at the Transfiguration, they saw light coming from it, not bouncing off of it. We too will shine from within, with His light. Perhaps it will come from the heart, as it did in the movie *E.T.* (Thus the song "HeartLight".)

This light that will pervade the resurrection body, St. Thomas believes (second paragraph), will come from the soul's "glory". This presupposes that spiritual "glory" and physical "light" are one, and not related to each other as a mere image or metaphor is related to something literal, but as two dimensions of a single ontological reality; that in the resurrection body "glory" is not purely spiritual and "light" is not purely physical, for soul and body are not two things but two aspects of a single thing: the human person.

This new light of glory, as in this world, will have different degrees; but these will depend on the "merit" or holiness in the soul. Mary will be the brightest, "clothed with the sun" (Rev 12:1).

And since perfected souls will be incapable of envy, all will rejoice in their lesser level of brightness, because it will be exactly what God wills for the common good; and all will identify with that common good as the fulfillment of their individual good, rather than a rival to it, as we fools do now.

Christ hid the glory of His resurrection body while He was on earth (except for the Heavenly foretaste at the Transfiguration). We will be able to do the same (third paragraph). Since our wills will be perfectly harmonized by the divine will, "hiding" will never be motivated by anything but love and truth.

St. Thomas deduces that bodies in Heaven will have colors, for color is part of beauty and glory, and appropriate to material bodies. Light does not rival colors, but brings them all out. The light of the body will make each color more itself, more beautiful: more perfectly white or black or brown or pink, more intense or subtle.

Like many mystics who have caught a preliminary vision, foretaste, or appetizer of Heaven's light, St. Thomas says that the light of Heaven will be brighter than that of the sun yet will not disturb the sight. God will give us new, vastly superior eyes.

If the resurrection body will be concrete, sensible and touchable, can it walk through walls, as Christ did? (How did He do that?)

Is it "passible", i.e., passive to shocks from outside, or is it "impassible"? Could it be destroyed, e.g., by a rock crushing it? If so, how is it immortal? If not, how is it material, sensible, and touchable?

Whether the bodies of the saints will be impassible after the resurrection?

Everything passible is corruptible.... Now the bodies of the saints will be incorruptible after the resurrection, according to 1 Corinthians 15:42, *It is sown in corruption, it shall rise in incorruption*. Therefore they will be impassible....

We speak of a thing being passive in two ways. First in a broad sense, and thus every reception is called a passion (receptivity), whether the thing received be fitting to the receiver and perfecting it, or contrary to it and corrupting it. The glorious bodies are not said to be impassible by the removal of this kind of passion, since nothing pertaining to perfection is to be removed from them.

In another way we use the word *passive* properly, and thus Damascene defines passion as being *a movement contrary to nature*. Hence an immoderate movement of the heart is called its passion, but a moderate movement is called its (natural) operation.... Accordingly, taking passion in its proper sense there will be no potentiality to passion in the bodies of the saints after resurrection, wherefore they are said to be impassible.

The reason for this impassibility is ... (that) the human body and all that it contains will be perfectly subject to the rational soul, even as the soul will be perfectly subject to God. Wherefore it will be impossible for the glorified body to be subject to any change contrary to the disposition whereby it is perfected by the soul; and consequently those bodies will be impassible (S82,1).

St. Thomas' answer to the question above is that the resurrection body will be made of a different kind of matter: matter that is "impassible", i.e., nothing will be able to harm it. This does not correspond to anything in our present experience of material bodies. But it is necessarily true, because the only alternatives to it are (a) a body that is not concrete and material at all, or (b) a body that can be harmed by other bodies, as everything material in this universe can be.

(1) It is certain, from divine revelation, that our resurrected bodies will be immortal. (2) It is clear, from an understanding of the meaning of the terms, that a body is mortal if it is passible, i.e., subject to passion in the sense of passivity, able to be changed by other bodies, so that when these two bodies touch, the form (nature) of the active body dominates and changes the form of the passive body, e.g., when a rock breaks glass or crushes a tin can, or when fire ignites paper. The destiny of the passive, receptive body is determined not by itself but by the active body that changes it. These two premises logically yield the conclusion that our resurrected bodies must be impassible.

Not all passivity in the sense of receptivity is an imperfection. This principle, quite contrary to Aristotle's metaphysics, has revolutionary consequences: that it is not an imperfection to receive or to obey (as the Son obeys the Father). It is not an imperfection or inferiority for a woman to be more receptive than a man, either in her body (to become pregnant), or her emotions (to be more empathetic), or even in her social roles (to quietly oil the social machine, so to speak, to foster relationships rather than to individually initiate or to fight, as males of nearly every animal species are more prone to do).

Our Heavenly bodies will be perfect, and therefore not subject to any passivities of imperfection such as pain, disease, impotence, or death. An axe could not chop off a limb even if it were swung, because the matter of the new body will be a new kind of matter, impervious to harm, probably not made of atoms. But we will be "passive" (receptive) to the goods we receive from God and each other.

Here is another dilemma: will we remember our sins in Heaven? If so, we must feel some regret and sadness, thus spoiling Heaven's perfect joy. If not, our ignorance would detract from Heaven's total truth. For the joy of Heaven surely cannot depend on the closing of eyes, but on their opening to truth.

Whether after the resurrection every one will know what sins he has committed?

Augustine says that *a kind of divine energy will come to our aid so that we shall recall all of our sins to mind.*

Since the divine judgment is most perfect, it is necessary for the conscience to witness to everything that has to be judged. But all works, both good and evil, will have to be judged (2 Cor 5:10) ... **Therefore each one's conscience must needs retain all the works he has done, whether good or evil....**

According to Romans 2:15–16, *In the day when God shall judge,* **each one's conscience shall bear witness to him, and his thoughts will accuse and defend him....** **[E]ach man's conscience will be as a book containing his deeds on which judgment will be pronounced, even as in the human court of law we make use of records. Of these books it is written in the Apocalypse** (Revelation) **(20:12):** *The books were opened; and another book was opened, which is the book of life; and the dead were judged by those things which were written in the books according to their works ...* (S87,1)

Augustine considers it unfitting that at the judgment a material book should be read containing all the deeds of each individual written therein, for the reason that it would be impossible to measure the size of such a book or the time it would take to read. But in like manner it would be impossible to estimate the length of time one would require in order to consider all one's merits and demerits and those of others if one saw these various things one after the other. Therefore we must admit that each one sees them all at the same time ... in an instant.

This is easily credible with regard to the blessed since they will see all things in the Word (S87,3).

St. Peter, in Heaven, now edifies both himself and others by telling them of his threefold denial of Christ after His arrest. For he sees it in light of his repentance and God's grace in forgiving it. It is now an opportunity for thanksgiving, as is everything in Heaven. Even sins come under Romans 8:28, if brought through the golden doors of our repentance and God's forgiving grace.

Because CPR resuscitates thousands today, it is now a commonly known "NDE" or near-death experience, that at the moment of death your whole life passes before you in an instant, with perfect clarity; and in this "life review" everything is seen truly, nothing is covered up. God is apparently sharing a foretaste of His own vision of our life with us, as He will do completely in Purgatory and/or Heaven; and repented and forgiven sins are part of this bitter yet sweet vision. St. Thomas had no CPR, and therefore few NDEs as his data, as we do, but he knew this anyway, if not inductively from data, then deductively from philosophy.

Although charity is now the cause of sorrow for sin, yet the saints in heaven will be so full of joy that they will have no room for sorrow; and so they will not grieve for their sins, but rather will they rejoice in the divine mercy whereby their sins are forgiven them (S87,1).

At first I found it scandalous that many people who had glimpses of Heaven through out-of-body or near-death experiences said that God (the "being of light") laughed at their past sins, and so did they. I now see that this might conform to St. Thomas' quite correct and orthodox vision of "deep Heaven" (though not, of course, of Purgatory). To get to this infinitely joyful sunlight we must confront and not ignore the incomparably sorrowful dark clouds of sin. But once the clouds are gone ... total joy.

Why must there be two Last Judgments, a "particular judgment" and a "general judgment"? If each of us is judged as soon as we die, why do we need a general judgment? And if all of us are to be judged at the general judgment, why do we need a particular one? Is God a Platonist, who believes in the separate reality of general terms like "humanity"?

It is necessary that there should be ... a general judgment ... in order that just as all things proceeded immediately from God, so at length the world will receive its ultimate complement (completion).... **Hence at this judgment the divine justice will be made manifest in all things, whereas now it remains hidden, forasmuch as at times some persons are dealt with for the profit of others, otherwise than their manifest works would seem to require. For this same reason there will then be a general separation of the good from the wicked because there will be no further motive for the good to profit by the wicked, or the wicked by the good, for the sake of which profit the good are meanwhile mingled with the wicked so long as this state of life is governed by divine providence** (S88,1).

The problem of justice is at the heart of the "problem of evil", which is the strongest argument against the goodness of God. Bad things happen to good people, and good things happen to bad people, and bad people use and abuse good people, and good people often have to lose good things (like life) in order for bad people to be stopped from taking good things from good people.

So there is such a thing as social sin as well as individual sin. The whole system is broken. We are no longer living merely in the world-garden God created—in *gaia*, "earth"—but in the fallen world-culture we create—in *aion* (in Latin, *saeculum*), the "age" or era infected by sin. *Gaia* is a space-word, a matter-world; *aion* is a time-word, a history-word. *Aion*, not *gaia*, is the word Scripture uses for "the world" when it speaks so negatively about it (e.g., 1 Jn 2:15).

This social sin, this fallen world-order, is what needs to be judged and corrected, at the general judgment, as well as individual human souls being judged at the particular judgment, if we are to be happy and perfect in Heaven. If and only if this is done, "at length the world will receive its ultimate complement."

St. Thomas uses the fact that "at times some persons are dealt with for the profit of others, otherwise than their manifest works would seem to require" as the crucial example of injustice. It is not injustice simply; it is the temporary hiddenness of eventual, inexorable divine justice. God uses some people's evil for other people's good. The most glaring example is Judas Iscariot, and even more, the Devil himself, who strategized his own apparent supreme victory in Christ's crucifixion, which was the supreme triumph of evil and yet was also used as the cause of our redemption!

God does not separate the good from the wicked in this world because His mysterious providence keeps using the wicked for the profit of the good in many hidden ways. He did that with Judas and Satan in a revealed way; in the crucifixion He lifted the curtain that usually hides His providential wisdom. He gives us little glimpses under His curtain at other times too, and some are higher "liftings of the curtain" than others (e.g., the Joseph story in Genesis: see Gen 50:20). At the General Judgment, the curtain will be torn from top to bottom. We cannot see that now, but we can believe it, and we can live it. For we are in the same story whose final end and point is that Beatific Vision of perfect divine justice providentially using and judging even the evil for the sake of the good.

In *The Lord of the Rings,* Frodo and Sam wonder "what kind of a story we're in". It is a wonderfully concrete way of asking what is the meaning of life. And the answer is that we are in a perfect story, which is an adventure story, a war story, a detective story, a psychological novel, and above all a love story. That is why God inspired the Bible: to show us the story we are in, to reflect a little of the light of the Last Judgment on our present wayfaring.

All the many predictions about the time of the end of the world—are they all B.S.?

Whether the time of the future judgment is unknown?

Objection 1. It would seem that the time of the future judgment is not unknown. For just as the holy Fathers looked forward to the first coming, so do we look forward to the second. But the holy Fathers knew the time of the first coming ... wherefore the Jews are reproached for not knowing the time of Christ's coming (Lk 12:56)....

Reply to Objection 1. At His first coming, Christ came secretly.... Hence, that He might be recognized by believers, it was necessary for the time to be fixed beforehand with certainty. On the other hand, at the second coming, He will come openly.... Consequently there can be no error affecting the knowledge of His coming....

It is written (Mk 13:32): *Of that day or hour no man knoweth, neither the angels in Heaven, nor the Son, but the Father....*

Further, it is written (1 Thess 5:2): *The day of the Lord shall so come as a thief in the night....* For the world will come to an end by no created cause, even as it derived its existence immediately from God. Wherefore the knowledge of the end of the world is fittingly reserved to God (S88,3).

For good reasons, Christ made the time of His first coming clear but the manner obscure, and the time of His Second Coming unknown but the manner clear.

He made the time of the first coming clear for the same reason He made the manner obscure: to test His people, so that those who loved Him and what He was—righteousness—would recognize Him, and those who did not, would not. He wanted to give enough light for seekers to find Him Whom they loved, but not so much light that non-seekers would find Him Whom they did not love. Thus He made the prophecies of the manner of His coming deliberately obscure: for instance, that the Promised One (the Messiah) would deliver his people from their "enemies". Those whose heart was set on worldly power did not recognize Him because they misidentified their enemies as the Romans, who stole political and financial power from the Jews; and Jesus did not free Israel from the Romans. But those whose heart was set on righteousness recognized Him because they identified their true enemies as their own sins, and His name was Jesus ("Savior") "because he will save his people from their sins" (Mt 1:21). Thus the judgment begins in this world: everyone gets what their heart desires.

For the same reasons, Christ made the manner of His Second Coming clear but the time obscure: so that at all times His people would be ready for Him, for the Truth and Judgment that will leave nothing any more obscure. (See Lk 12:2–3.) It is like death: the reason God arranged that we know *that* it will be, but not *when*, is so that we should be ready always.

Those who claim to know the time of the end not only misunderstand the divine purpose in hiding it but more profoundly and seriously misunderstand themselves. They think they are wiser than the Son of God, Who said that He Himself did not know the time! (Mt 24:36) This prediction is not just a fault of the mind but of the heart. It is the sin of pride. In judging the time, they judge themselves.

We all do that—judge ourselves—in everything we do, both for good and evil. That is how the judgment works. At the Last Judgment we will not be able to argue with the Judge because we will see ourselves as well as God in the judge's seat. We will *know*.

What, exactly, will be judged at the Last Judgment? And how will this explain why there will be three assignments, to Heaven immediately, to Heaven through Purgatory, and to Hell?

The judgment comprises two things, namely the discussion of merits and the payment of rewards. As regards the payment of rewards, all will be judged, even the good, since the divine sentence will appoint to each one the reward corresponding to his merit. But there is no discussion of merits save where good and evil merits are mingled together.

Now (1) **those who build on the foundation of faith** *gold, silver, and precious stones* **(I Cor. 3:12), by devoting themselves wholly to the divine service, and who have no notable admixture of evil merit, are not subjected to a discussion of their merits. Such are those who have entirely renounced the things of the world and are solicitously thoughtful of the things that are of God.... [T]hey will be saved but will not be judged.**

(2) **Others, however, build on the foundation of faith** *wood, hay, stubble*: **they, in fact, love worldly things and are busy about earthly concerns, yet so as to prefer nothing to Christ, but strive to redeem their sins with alms; and these have an admixture of good with evil merits. Hence they are subjected to a discussion of their merits, and consequently in this account will be judged, and yet they will be saved** (S89,6).

(3) **The judgment as regards the sentencing to punishment for sin concerns all the wicked, whereas the judgment as regards the discussion of merits concerns only believers, because in unbelievers the foundation of faith is lacking, without which all subsequent works are deprived of ... perfection ...** (S89,7).

What distinguishes the saved from the damned is their relation to Christ. This is not St. Thomas' opinion, this is Christ's own clear teaching. What is not clear is just what the minimum is for being accounted a "believer"—i.e., how much good will, i.e., a will that seeks God and what God is (goodness), and how much explicit knowledge of God in the mind, there must be to qualify for salvation. Since we do not know the answers to these questions; since only God, and not we, know the secrets of men's hearts; we do not know the comparative population statistics of Heaven and Hell, and should we not claim we do, even implicitly. When His disciples asked Christ "Are many saved?" His answer was simply: "Strive to enter" (Lk 13:24).

We do know, however, that God is perfectly just as well as perfectly loving. He cannot compromise either of these two eternal attributes of His own nature. How He will reconcile the apparently contradictory demands of justice and love, we cannot fathom; but He will. Part of the answer, surely, is that He offers total mercy and forgiveness to all who will accept it by trusting Him and repenting of their sins, but He does not, and cannot, give forgiveness to those who will not receive His gift. Gifts are freely given and freely received. Heaven cannot be forced on a creature with free will.

And since God is perfectly just, therefore we will all be rewarded and punished with perfect justice. This means two things: what St. Thomas calls "rewards", i.e., our eternal destinies (whether we will get a ticket to Heaven's stadium or not, and if so, whether we will need to practice first in the minor leagues of Purgatory); and what he calls "merits", i.e., how high our place will be in the stadium. (The analogy is only barely serious and certainly not to be taken literally.)

Notice that St. Thomas, like Scripture (St. Thomas is always "like Scripture"!), sees faith as the foundation for works; thus we will be judged both on our faith and our works (Scripture clearly teaches both): our faith (i.e., our relation to Christ) will determine what he calls the judgment according to rewards, and our works will determine the judgment according to merits. The first is pure mercy, the second is pure justice.

Scripture tells us there will not only be Heaven but also "new heavens and a new earth". What is that?

It is written (Is 65:17): *Behold I create new heavens and a new earth, and the former things shall not be in remembrance;* and (Rev 21:1): *I saw a new heaven and a new earth. For the first heaven and the first earth was gone.*

Further, the dwelling should befit the dweller. But the world was made to be man's dwelling. Therefore it should befit man. Now man will be renewed. Therefore the world will likewise....

We believe all corporeal things to have been made for man's sake, wherefore all things are stated to be subject to him (Ps 8:5). Now they serve man in two ways: first as sustenance to his bodily life; secondly, as helping him to know God, inasmuch as man sees the invisible things of God by the things that are made (Rom 1:20).... [G]lorified man will nowise need creatures to render him the first of these services, since his body will be altogether incorruptible.... [M]an will not need the second service ... since ... he will see God immediately in His essence. The carnal eye, however, will be unable to attain to this vision of the essence; wherefore, that it may be fittingly comforted in the vision of God, it will see the Godhead in its corporeal effects, wherein manifest proofs of the divine majesty will appear....

Although properly speaking, insensible bodies will not have merited this glory, yet man merited that this glory should be bestowed on the whole universe in so far as this conduces to man's increase of glory.

This disposition of newness will be neither natural nor contrary to nature, but above nature, just as grace and glory are above the nature of the soul; and it will proceed from an everlasting agent which will preserve it for ever (S91,1).

"Heavens" in the plural, in Scripture, means simply what is above the sky, i.e., the rest of the created universe outside the earth. "Heaven" (singular) is the realm of God. As God "bilocates" and is both in Heaven and on earth, because He is everywhere ("omnipresence"), in an analogous way we will also 'bilocate' in that we will be with Him in Heaven and also live in a real material universe, a "new heavens and a new earth" that He will create.

Man is not fully man without a body. And a body needs a world. God would not give us a new body without a new world for it. For "all corporeal things were made for man's sake." Man is the center of the universe. Pre-Copernican astronomy was right symbolically and spiritually, though not physically. The universe is for man. God does not care about gases and galaxies for their own sake; they are only part of the cosmic womb designed to birth the only creature created in His image, "the only creature God loved for his own sake" (Vatican II). This is the true and truly radical "humanism".

Science, of course, knows nothing of this. How would the goldfish know what is outside its bowl, or the intentions of the one who set it up? How would we know what is outside our universe?

As the first universe was our nursing mother, supplying physical needs, the new one will be our art museum, supplying spiritual needs. We will not need food or air or reproductive organs; these will be for beauty and glory. Both universes are works of God and therefore aids to seeing Him in His reflections as in a mirror; but while this one is dark ("through a glass, darkly") the other will be bright.

Animals, plants, and minerals cannot merit eternal life, but man, as the priest of all creation, merits this for them "insofar as this conduces to man's increase of glory". We are creation's priests.

This new world will be neither natural (part of this nature, or caused by it) nor unnatural, but supernatural. It will be not just more than nature but more "natural" than nature.

Isn't "the beatific vision", seeing God face to face, beyond our capacity?

Whether the human intellect can attain to the vision of God in His essence?

Objection 1. It would seem that the human intellect cannot attain to the vision of God in His essence. For it is written (Jn 1:18): *No man hath seen God at any time ...*

Reply to Objection 1: **The words quoted can be explained in three ways, according to Augustine. In one way as excluding *corporeal* vision, whereby no one ever saw or will see God in His essence; secondly, as excluding intellectual vision of God in His essence *from those who dwell in this mortal flesh*; thirdly, as excluding the vision of *comprehension* (as** distinct from apprehension) **from a created intellect....**

Objection 3. **Further, Damascene shows that the most perfect way in which our intellect can be united to God is when it is united to Him as to something unknown. Now that which is seen in its essence is not unknown....**

Reply to Objection 3: **Damascene is speaking there of the knowledge whereby wayfarers (in this life) know God.... He cannot be fathomed by our intellect, but our most perfect knowledge of Him as wayfarers is to know that He is above all that our intellect can conceive, and thus we are united to Him as to something unknown. In heaven, however, we will see Him by His essence, and we shall be united to Him as to something known....**

Objection 6.... **There is no possible proportion between our intellect and the divine essence, since an infinite distance separates them.** (The difference between the infinite and the finite is itself infinite.) **Therefore our intellect will be unable to attain to the vision of the divine essence.**

Reply to Objection 6: **Sometimes ... there is no need for proportion between knower and known.... We may also reply that ... nothing hinders our intellect, although** finite, being described as proportionate to the *vision* of the divine essence, but not to the *comprehension* thereof ... (S92,1). (In fact, this is how we see each other now! Who fully comprehends even his own heart, much less the hearts of others?)

On the contrary, **It is written** (1 Cor 13:12): *We see now through a glass in a dark manner, but then face to face.... Further, it is written* (1 Jn 3:2): *When He shall appear we shall be like to Him, because we shall see Him as He is....*

(So even if we cannot explain *how* it is possible, God Himself assures us that it will be.)

Further, the desire of the saints cannot be altogether frustrated. Now the common desire of the saints is to see God in His essence, according to Exodus 33:13, *Show me Thy glory;* **Psalms 79:20,** *Show Thy face and we shall be saved;* **and John 14:8:** *Show us the Father and it is enough for us.* **Therefore the saints will see God in His essence....**

This is "the argument from desire": no natural desire can be in vain, or meaningless. Every desire in our nature corresponds to some reality we are designed for. And we have a natural desire to see God, i.e., perfect beauty, perfect truth, and perfect love (goodness). Even atheists must admit religion is *desirable*, is a beautiful fairy tale, "too good to be true". If they do not, there is something wrong with either their understanding of what religion is or with their desiring hearts, or with their honesty, i.e., with their tongue in telling us (or themselves) what is in their hearts.

Since understanding is an operation most proper to man, it follows that his happiness must be held to consist in that operation when perfected in him.... [I]f in the most perfect operation of his intellect man does not attain to the vision of the divine essence, but to something else, we shall be forced to conclude that something other than God is the object of man's happiness ... which is absurd.... Consequently ... it must be asserted that our intellect will at length attain to the vision of the divine essence ... and this will be the beatific vision....

We seem to have a dilemma. On the one hand, God is not a body, so our bodily eye cannot see Him. But on the other hand, if our bodily eye cannot see God, what will it be good for in the Beatific Vision? Is all this talk of "seeing God" "face to face" mere metaphor for the kind of abstract intellectual knowledge sought by the philosopher, or the philosopher in us? Doesn't the lover seek more than the philosopher? Doesn't the Bible tell us something more than philosophy tells us about our eternal bliss?

God can nowise be seen with the eyes of the body or perceived by any of the senses, as that which is seen directly, neither here nor in heaven....

Yet it will see it as an object of indirect vision, because on the one hand the bodily sight will see so great a glory of God in bodies, especially in the glorified bodies and most of all in the body of Christ, and, on the other hand, the intellect will see God so clearly, that God will be perceived in things seen with the eye of the body, even as life is perceived in speech. For although our intellect will not then see God from seeing His creatures ("from" here signifies a cause-effect relationship), yet it will see God in His creatures seen corporeally. This manner of seeing God corporeally is indicated by Augustine.... *It is very credible that we shall so see the mundane bodies of the new heaven and the new earth, as to see most clearly God everywhere present . . . as when we see men . . . we do not believe, but see, that they live* (S92,2).

What a fascinating analogy! How is life perceived "in" speech? Not in the same way that sounds or syllables are. How is happiness perceived "in" a smile, even by a month-old baby? How is another person's personality perceived "in" their words? How does a lover recognize his beloved's spirit "in" his or her love letters? How do we perceive the eyes as "the windows of the soul"? By intuition, by wisdom, by "the third eye", by the inner eye, by the eye of the heart. "The heart has reasons which the reason does not know." It does not just feel, it knows.

Jesuit spirituality traditionally focuses on "seeing God in all things". This is an excellent way of rehearsing for one aspect of the Beatific Vision. Of course, it must be based on a "fanatical" love and longing for God and "detachment" from creatures (or at least a willingness to be detached from them for God's sake). Otherwise "seeing God in all things" means merely a religious veneer and excuse for worldliness.

We cannot see "life" as we can see bodies, though life is in bodies. For life has no color, shape, or size, as bodies do. Yet, as Augustine notes, we "see life in" men when we see their bodies. Life is not an object of our *belief* or *opinion*, or of our *faith* or *trust*, but of our *sight*. But it is (what St. Thomas calls) "indirect sight" rather than direct sight. It is what Michael Polanyi calls *The Tacit Dimension*.

God should be the object of our "indirect sight" even now. That would make this life the perfect rehearsal for the next. It is what Brother Lawrence called "the practice of the presence of God".

The key to doing this is very simple. It is love. It is the lover who finds resemblances to his beloved and reminders of his beloved in everything. The non-lover may do it occasionally, when he remembers. But most of the time he forgets, and is distracted. The lover does not forget and is not distracted as much because he does not *want* to be distracted.

But the love that accomplishes this is a choice, not a feeling. This habit of seeing and feeling God in all things is not innate or automatic. It has to be cultivated. It develops gradually, as a plant grows. And the plant food is regular daily prayer. Only by means of many repeated acts of *will*, choosing to pray even when we do not feel like it (which is probably most of the time!), can we reach the goal of seeing and *feeling* God's presence everywhere. Only the love of willing, often in the teeth of contrary feelings, can bring us to the love that sees, feels and enjoys God's presence. Only our continual spiritual warfare against our spiritual ADD, plus His grace, can bring us His peace.

What will we say to each other in Heaven?

Of those who see God in His essence, each one sees in His essence so much the more things according as he sees the divine essence the more clearly. And hence it is that one is able to instruct another concerning these things. Thus the knowledge of the angels and of the souls of the saints can go on increasing (S92,3).

This is why Heaven will never be boring. There is always something new, something more, in God's infinity for our finite minds to know, love, wonder at, and be fascinated with.

C. S. Lewis says in *The Problem of Pain:*

"For doubtless the continually successful, yet never complete, attempt by each soul to communicate its vision to all others (and that by means whereof earthly art and philosophy are but clumsy imitations) is also among the ends for which the individual was created."

There is a practical consequence for our present life in this distant Heavenly ideal. The more we practice this "communion of saints" now, the readier we are for Heaven and the less Purgatory we will need. This casts a new light on our primary practical commandment in this life, to love our neighbors: it is not only for their and our good in time, but also preparation for our and their eternal blessedness. And not only in terms of reward (though that too), but in terms of creating our capacity for greater understanding, appreciation, and enjoyment of God in Heaven.

For it is God Himself, and not just this "communion of saints" in Heaven by which each of the saved will instruct others about God, that is the essence of our Heavenly happiness. The communion of saints is a property of it, a consequence or overflow, so to speak. For if this is not so, if the communion of saints is our end and God our necessary means to it, that reduces God to a means and not our final end. The communion of saints will be a great part of our Heavenly happiness, but it is not *necessary*. Only God is necessary. If without the communion of saints we cannot possibly be happy in Heaven, then God alone is not sufficient for our happiness, then God is only a part, and not the whole, or the essence, of our happiness. In that case God is not God, but *a* god, something more like Zeus. This is St. Thomas' point in the next paragraph:

The desire of the saints to know all things will be fulfilled by the mere fact of their seeing God, just as their desire to possess all good things will be fulfilled by their possessing God. For as God suffices the affections in that He has perfect goodness, and by possessing Him we possess all goods ... so the vision of Him suffices the intellect: *Lord, show us the Father and it is enough for us* (Jn 14:8) (S92,3).

St. Anselm puts the point beautifully in his *Proslogium:*

"If particular goods are enjoyable, consider carefully how enjoyable is that good which contains the joyfulness of all goods.... In fact, all the goods of body and soul will be there such that 'neither eye has seen, nor ear heard, nor the heart of man conceived' (1 Cor 2:9). Why, then, do you wander about so much, O tiny man, seeking the goods of your soul and body? Love the one good in which all good things are, and that is sufficient. Desire the simple good which contains every good, and that is enough. For what do you love, O my flesh, and what do you desire, O my soul? There it is, there it is, whatever you love, whatever you desire."

Why will we need resurrected bodies in Heaven? Why isn't the happiness in the soul enough?

The happiness of the saints will increase in extent after the resurrection, because their happiness will then be not only in the soul but also in the body.... For man's body may be considered in two ways: first, as being dependent on the soul for its completion; secondly, as containing something that hampers the soul in its operations.... As regards the first way of considering the body, its union with the soul adds a certain perfection to the soul, since ... the soul is more perfect in its natural being when it is in the whole— namely, man who results from the union of soul and body—than when it is a separated part. But as regards the second consideration, the union with the body hampers the perfection of the soul, wherefore it is written (Wis. 9:15) that _the corruptible body is a load upon the soul_. If, then, there be removed from the body all those things wherein it hampers the soul's action, the soul will be simply more perfect while existing in such a body than when separated therefrom. Now the more perfect a thing is in being, the more perfectly is it able to operate; wherefore the operation of the soul united to such a body will be more perfect than the operation of the separated soul. But the glorified body will be a body of this description, being altogether subject to the spirit.... Now every imperfect thing desires its perfection. Hence the separated soul naturally desires reunion with the body (S93,1).

Thus St. Paul speaks of desiring not to be "un-clothed" but "re-clothed" (2 Cor 5:1–4). Our divinely designed and created human nature demands a body. We are not angels; that is why we should not be "spiritualists". We are also not animals; that is why we should not be materialists. And since our nature includes a body, the perfection and happiness of that nature includes a body.

In this life the body does two things to the soul: augmentation and diminution, helping and hampering. On the one hand they are cooperating friends. Bodies give souls information and pleasure, through the senses; and souls give bodies life and vitality. But on the other hand they are squabbling enemies. (Think of the time you tried to make your body stay awake all night to study for an exam. Or lust: although it's not just biological but also spiritual, yet the wild hormones certainly contribute.) One of the reasons why we are not perfectly happy is because we cannot do all that our souls want to do, and one of the reasons why we cannot do all that our souls want to do is because our bodies are recalcitrant, weak, or stupid. Body and soul often fight, like most married couples. We are fallen.

But we are wholly healed in Heaven. The positive half of the body-soul relationship—the ways in which our bodies help our souls—will be preserved and extended, in ways we cannot now imagine. St. Augustine says that the glory and joy of the purified soul will overflow into the resurrected body in a "voluptuous torrent" (_torrens voluptatis_).

Between death and the resurrection of the body, we will be separated souls, souls without bodies. That will _not_ be a better condition than Heaven. It will be a time of waiting, of longing, of incompletion. For most of us it will probably be a Purgatory that will consist of a mixture of great pain (because we will fully know our own sins and all their ugliness and harm) and great joy (because Infinite Love will be there holding our hand and showing us these purifying truths). It will be like retraining a pilot (the soul) who used to fly a little single-engine prop plane (the body) that wore out after seventy years or so, in a big new flight simulator (Purgatory), so that he will be able to fly a jumbo jet (the resurrection body) that will last forever. He's a pilot, and he needs a plane. He's a more perfect pilot when he's flying a plane than when he isn't. That's why we will long to be re-clothed (with a body) rather than un-clothed (free from bodies). Purgatory is not Heaven.

But we need Purgatory to prepare us for our new bodies. Human souls need bodies and bodies need souls.

Won't Heaven be perfect equality rather than a hierarchy? Won't everyone's happiness be total, and therefore the same?

The more one will be united to God, the happier will one be. Now the measure of charity is the measure of one's union with God. Therefore the diversity of beatitude will be according to the difference of charity....

For our actions are meritorious not by the very substance of the action but only by the habit of virtue with which they are informed. Now every virtue obtains its meritorious efficacy from charity, which has the end itself for its object. Hence the diversity of merit is all traced to the diversity of charity ... (S93,3).

What St. Thomas says about Heaven is also true of this life: the more charity you have, the more you have of union with God, likeness to God, and appreciation of God. And since God is the source of all happiness, joy, and beatitude, the more charity you have the happier you will be. Charity to neighbor opens the eye of the soul to see God more clearly. And seeing God is our ultimate happiness. Therefore charity is the cause of our happiness.

This is testable very simply. Live for one day, or one hour, with more charity. You will experience more happiness. Live for one day, or one hour, with less charity. You will experience less happiness. It is amazing that in light of this repeated experiment and experience, in light of the fact that the results are always the same, we nevertheless choose to live with less charity, knowing by experience that its results will be less happiness.

The obverse of this truth is that when we are unhappy there is one infallible antidote: forget yourself and live for others. It will always take you out of yourself and out of your unhappiness.

We know this, yet we do not do it. We are not just fools, we are idiots. That is the surest proof of Original Sin and our fallenness. We all know that love is the key to happiness, and we all want more happiness rather than less, yet we love less rather than more.

In Heaven we will have no doubts, no forgetfulness, and no ignorance. We will see God clearly, and we will see sin clearly, and we will have no temptation to choose what we clearly see is misery over what we clearly see is joy. Only because we are ignorant, do we sin. Plato was right in that: all evil is due to ignorance. What he failed to see is that this ignorance is also due to evil, that we not only choose wrongly because we see wrongly but also that we see wrongly because we choose wrongly. Our selfishness blinds us.

St. Thomas, like Christ and unlike the Pharisees, is not a legalist. Our actions and choices merit rewards (in the form of happiness) not by their external physical activity as such, like magic or technology, but by their internal motivations and the habits of character they form. (See the first sentence of St. Thomas' last paragraph.) This is why we do not receive instant feelings of happiness as soon as we perform an external act of charity, but we do experience deep and lasting happiness in proportion as our hearts become like the hearts of the saints in charity.

There will be differences, and inequality, and hierarchy, in Heaven because there are natural differences, and hierarchy, on earth, and Heaven perfects whatever is natural on earth. But this will not be the visible, worldly, always-somewhat-unjust hierarchies that we know now. "But many that are first will be last, and the last first" (Mt 19:30). It will all be perfectly just and necessary and natural. And therefore no one will protest it or hate it. No one will be foolish enough in Heaven to commit the stupidest and saddest sin of all, the sin of envy.

The one hair-raising quotation from St. Thomas that all the anti-Catholic anthologies always reprint is the one where he says that the blessed in Heaven will get some of their joy from beholding with satisfaction the tortures of the damned in Hell. Is there any possible excuse for this horrible lack of charity? How could a canonized saint and a Doctor of the Church possibly teach that? What did he really say, and what did he really mean?

Whether the blessed pity the unhappiness of the damned?

Objection 1. **It would seem that the blessed pity the unhappiness of the damned. For pity proceeds from charity; and charity will be most perfect in the blessed....**

On the contrary, **Whoever pities another shares somewhat in his unhappiness. But the blessed cannot share in any unhappiness. Therefore they do not pity the afflictions of the damned.**

I answer that, **Mercy or compassion may be in a person in two ways: first by way of passion, secondly by way of choice. In the blessed there will be no passion in the lower powers except as a result of ... choice. Hence compassion or mercy will not be in them except by ... choice....**

So long as sinners are in this world, they are in such a state that ... they can be taken away from a state of unhappiness and sin to a state of happiness. Consequently it is possible to have compassion on them both by the choice of the will (in which sense God, the angels and the blessed are said to pity them by desiring their salvation) and by passion, in which way they are pitied by the good men who are in the state of wayfarers. But in the future state it will be impossible for them to be taken away from their unhappiness, and consequently it will not be possible to pity their sufferings (in the passive sense of pity).

Reply to Objection 1: **Charity is the principle of pity when it is possible for us out of charity to wish the cessation of a person's unhappiness. But the saints cannot desire this for the damned, since it would be contrary to divine justice** (and also impossible, once time and choice end) (S94,2).

St. Thomas' first two paragraphs (Objection 1 and the "On the contrary") give us the essential dilemma: we cannot deny either perfect love or perfect happiness in the blessed in Heaven. But on earth, these two goods sometimes contradict each other: the more you love, the more you can suffer because love makes you vulnerable to the sufferings of those you love. Love multiplies your sufferings by the two factors of the extent and the depth of your love: the more people you love and the more you love them, the more you can suffer. (But of course love also multiplies your joys by the same two factors.)

To solve this dilemma something has to change in Heaven. And that is St. Thomas' answer. Love becomes wholly active, not passive. When someone we love does something self-destructive, we say, "How could you do that to yourself?" but we also mean, and feel, "How could you do that to me?" In Heaven, our charity will still say the first thing but not the second. We will still have active charity to the damned, but not passive vulnerability. We won't want them to suffer, but we won't suffer with them.

A second change is also necessary. In this life, when we see a criminal justly punished, we feel both sorrow at his suffering and joy that justice is done. We have a mixed reaction. Better that he be punished, and justice be done; but better still if only he had not committed the crime at all. If only he had chosen differently, we moan. Well, in Heaven we will be able to rejoice in God's justice everywhere, even in Hell, without feeling this sad moaning, this "if only", because time and choice will be finished.

We cannot *imagine* what this will feel like, and we should not try, but we can *know* by reason that it must be so.

This explains how you can be happy in Heaven even if some people you love are in Hell. It's not that God lies to you and tells you they are not in Hell; and it's not that you stop loving them. It's that your love, *like God's love*, is no longer able to be held hostage, as it is now: "I hate your love for me, so I'm going to make you suffer by hurting myself"—we can say that to each other now, but not then. If you don't understand this, just trust that God will solve the problem for you in Heaven, as He solves it for Himself.

The reasoning above (#339) is clear, but the conclusion is still murky. How can the blessed in Heaven rejoice when they see the sufferings of the damned, even if that suffering is necessary and just? They can rejoice in the justice, but not in the sufferings. But the justice is an abstraction, while the sufferings are concrete. Will abstractions be more real than concrete things to the blessed? The previous answer said that we cannot *imagine* this state (because we cannot experience it here); can we at least *explain* it a little more?

Whether the blessed rejoice in the punishment of the wicked?

I answer that **A thing may be a matter of rejoicing in two ways. First, directly** (and concretely), **when one rejoices in a thing as such; and thus the saints will not rejoice in the punishment of the wicked. Secondly, indirectly** (and abstractly), **by reason of something annexed to it; and in this way the saints will rejoice in the punishment of the wicked by considering therein the order of divine justice....**

Objection 1. **It would seem that the blessed do not rejoice in the punishment of the wicked. For rejoicing in another's evil pertains to hatred. But there will be no hatred in the blessed....**

Reply to Objection 1. **To rejoice in another's evil as such** (concretely) **belongs to hatred, but not to rejoice in another's evil by reason of something** (abstractly) **annexed to it. Thus a person sometimes rejoices in his own** (physical) **evil as when we rejoice in our own afflictions as helping us to merit life:** *My brethren, count it all joy when you shall fall into divers trials* (Jas 1:2).

Objection 2. **Further, the blessed in heaven will be in the highest degree conformed to God. Now God does not rejoice in our afflictions. Therefore neither will the blessed rejoice in the afflictions of the damned.**

Reply to Objection 2. **Although God rejoices not in punishments as such** (concretely), **He rejoices in them as being ordered to His justice** (abstractly).

Objection 3. **It is most reprehensible in a wayfarer to take pleasure in the pains of others, and most praiseworthy to grieve for them. Therefore the blessed nowise rejoice in the punishments of the damned.**

Reply to Objection 3. **It is not the same with a wayfarer** (on earth) **as with a comprehensor** (in Heaven), **because in a wayfarer ... such passions are praiseworthy, as indicating the good dispositions of the mind, as in the cases of shame, pity, and the repentance for evil; whereas in a comprehensor there can be no passion but such as follows the judgment of reason** (S94,3).

This is an extension of the previous point. St. Thomas here uses the same key distinction as he used in the previous excerpt. Like God, we will be able to separate in fact what we can only separate in thought now: when we see or know the sufferings of the damned, we will be able to separate the cause for our actively rejoicing (that God's justice is done) from the cause for our passive sorrow (pity at the sufferings of the damned). We will be able to free the first from the second. We cannot do that here.

In Heaven, our active rejoicing in justice, like our active charity and goodwill to all, even the damned, will not cease. But our passive pity and vulnerability and suffering will.

When St. Thomas says that in Heaven all passions will follow the judgment of reason, he is not saying that in Heaven all are Stoics. "Reason" to him means not merely, or even primarily, the teeth-clenching "stiff upper lip" by which passions are fought and overcome, but the joyful vision of God's beauty, the "Beatific Vision". "Reason" means essentially "mental seeing or knowing". What our reason can know only by abstraction here, we will actually see concretely there. Here, we can only "see" the meaning of justice by an act of intellectual abstraction (from just acts or laws or persons); there, we will see it (with our minds) as concretely and fully as we here see colors.

If St. Thomas' answer still does not convince you, what is the alternative? That Hell holds Heaven's happiness hostage forever?

Is Hell a torture chamber, something worse, or something better?

Just as every creature will be to the blessed a matter of joy, so will all the elements conduce to the torture of the damned, according to Wisdom 5:21, *the whole world will fight with Him against the unwise.* **This is also becoming to the divine justice, that whereas they departed from One by sin and placed their end in material things which be many and various, so should they be tormented in many ways and from many sources ...** (S97,1).

The answer to the above question is: Something worse. For the same reason salvation is total and cosmic, its absence and opposite must also be total and cosmic. With God's presence, all things are goods and joys; without God, *nothing* can be good or joyful. If this is not so, God is not God.

It is written (Wis 11:17): *By what things a man sinneth, by the same also he is tormented.* **Now men sin by the sensible things of this world. Therefore it is just that they should be punished by those same things** (S97,6).

This is the basis for many of the details in Dante's *Divine Comedy*. Fitting punishment is not an opinion or an option; it is logically necessary and deducible once the essential nature of justice is understood. The concrete forms in which this justice will be done in Hell are, of course, in Dante merely speculative, imaginary, and almost certainly not literally accurate—but because they are too weak, not too strong. Justice cannot be weakened, even by mercy. Refusing mercy necessarily dooms us to pure justice.

The worm ascribed to the damned must be understood to be not of a corporeal but of a spiritual nature; and this is the remorse of conscience, which is called a worm because it originates from the corruption of sin, and torments the soul, as a corporeal worm born of corruption torments by gnawing ... (S97,2).

If Hell consisted merely of tortures by agents external to ourselves (demons), it might be possible to hope to escape from these external agents of torture, and thus to escape from the torment. But if the agent that tortures you in Hell is also yourself, you can never hope to escape, for you can never escape yourself.

There cannot be a continual dissolution from the bodies of the damned, since nothing is restored to them by food.... [T]herefore the weeping of the damned will not be corporeal (S97,3).

A corporeal (literal, physical) Hell would not be the worst possible, since matter would limit the evil, the harm, the dissolution. Bodies cannot endure torture forever; they die. But souls do not die.

In hell the place must be so disposed for seeing as regards light and darkness that nothing be seen clearly, and that only such things be dimly seen as are able to bring anguish to the heart.... Now seeing is in itself pleasant ... Yet it happens accidentally that seeing is painful, when we see things that are hurtful to us or displeasing to our will (S97,4).

Sights can be beautiful. Even fire can be beautiful. Fire is God's creature, God's invention. Even when it burns you, you can at the same time notice its beauty. A Hell of literal fire would not be as bad as one without it. St. Thomas' refusal to take the imagery about Hell literally (i.e., physically) stems not from the conviction that the reality of Hell cannot be not as bad as we usually imagine it, but from the conviction that our imagination cannot be as bad as the reality of it. Dante got it right when he identified the sign over its door as: "Abandon *all* hope, ye who enter here."

If Hell is not so bad, then Jesus is not so good, because He repeatedly warned us of its horror. If we seek to correct St. Thomas by spiritualizing his quasi-physical descriptions, fine—but this makes it more deeply awful, not less.

Does the previous point mean that there cannot possibly be physical fire and pain in Hell too, but only spiritual pain? Wouldn't both pains be worse than either one alone?

Whether the fire of hell will be corporeal?

Objection 1. It would seem that the fire of hell whereby the bodies of the damned will be tormented will not be corporeal. For Damascene says: The devil and *demons . . . together with the ungodly and sinners, will be cast into everlasting fire, not material fire, such as that which we have, but such as God knoweth. . . .*

Reply to Objection 1. Damascene does not absolutely deny that this fire is material, but that it is not material as our fire, since it differs from ours in some of its properties . . .

Objection 2. Augustine says: *In my opinion the place to which the soul is committed after death is spiritual and not corporeal. . . .*

Reply to Objection 2. We may reply that Augustine is expressing an opinion without deciding the point, as he often does . . . (S97,5).

I answer that There have been many opinions about the fire of hell. For some philosophers, as Avicenna, disbelieving in the resurrection (of the body), thought that the soul alone would be punished after death. And as they considered it impossible for the soul, being incorporeal, to be punished with a corporeal fire, they denied that the fire whereby the wicked are punished is corporeal, and pretended that all statements (in the Koran) as to souls being punished in a future after death by any corporeal means are to be taken metaphorically. For just as the joy and happiness of good souls will not be about any corporeal object, but about something spiritual, namely the attainment of their end, so will the torment of the wicked be merely spiritual, in that they will be grieved at being separated from their end, the desire whereof is in them by nature. Wherefore, just as all descriptions of the soul's delight after death that seem to denote bodily pleasure—for instance, that they are refreshed, that they smile, and so forth—must be taken metaphorically, so also are all such descriptions of the soul's suffering as seem to imply bodily punishment, for instance, that they burn in fire, or suffer from the stench, and so forth. For as spiritual pleasure and pain are unknown to the majority, these things need to be declared under the figure of corporeal pleasures and pains in order that men may be moved the more to the desire or fear thereof. . . .

Avicenna himself added another explanation by saying that the souls of the wicked are punished after death not by bodies but by images of bodies, just as in a dream it seems to a man that he is suffering various pains on account of such like images being in his imagination. Even Augustine seems to hold this kind of punishment. . . .

But this would seem an unreasonable statement, for the imagination is a power that makes use of a bodily organ, so that it is impossible for such visions of the imagination to occur in the soul separated from the body . . . Augustine (in another text) admits that the fire by which the bodies are tormented is corporeal . . . (S97,5).

Those who disbelieve in the resurrection of the body do not believe there can be corporeal fire in Hell because there is no body to experience it. But Christians believe in the resurrection of the body. It is one of the twelve articles in the Apostles' Creed. If justice calls for a corporeal dimension in the *rewards* for corporeal works of goodness, the same justice calls for a corporeal dimension in the *punishments* for corporeal works of evil.

St. Thomas admits this is only human opinion, not certain divine revelation. But how likely is it that Hell, the greatest evil and the deprivation of all good, will be *less* complete and terrible than we can imagine, if Heaven will be much *more* complete and wonderful than we can imagine? (1 Cor 2:9).

Where is Hell? We always picture it as "down" and Heaven as "up." Is this (1) just silly, or is it at least (2) symbolically true? Is it (3) literally true?

Whether the fire of hell is beneath the earth?

Objection 3. **After the day of judgment the bodies of all the damned will be tormented in hell. Now those bodies will fill a place. Consequently, since the multitude of the damned will be exceeding great, for** *the number of fools is infinite* **(Sir 1:15), the space containing that fire must also be exceeding great. But it would seem unreasonable to say that there is so great a hollow within the earth ...**

Reply to Objection 3. **Hell will never lack sufficient room to admit the bodies of the damned.... Nor is it unreasonable that God's power should maintain within the bowels of the earth a hollow great enough to contain all the bodies of the damned.**

I answer that, **As Augustine says,** *I am of opinion that no one knows in what part of the world hell is situated ...* **Gregory, having been questioned on this point, answers:** *About this matter I dare not give a rash decision....*

Heaviness is to the body what sorrow is to the spirit, and joy (of spirit) is as lightness (of body). Wherefore just as in reference to the body all the heavier things are beneath the others if they be placed in order of gravity, so in reference to the spirit, the lower place is occupied by whatever is more sorrowful. And thus even as the empyrean (highest Heaven) is a fitting place for the joy of the elect, so the lowest part of the earth is a fitting place for the sorrow of the damned (S97,7).

Note how modest and reasonable St. Thomas is, both in his objections and in his replies, despite his knowing very little of what we know about the science of the earth and the physical universe.

And most especially in his final judgment ("no one knows"). Sometimes a philosopher's good habits of mind are revealed most clearly in his errors.

We know today that the center of the earth contains not Hell but molten matter. But St. Thomas' analogies ("heaviness is to the body what sorrow is to the spirit, and joy of spirit is as lightness of body") point to at least a necessary symbolic truth to the "down" picture. In Christianity, body and soul, matter and spirit, are not totally separated, as in Descartes. They are two dimensions of the one universe God created, and two dimensions of ourselves. Matter matters! If Christ had physically descended down into the earth instead of ascending up into Heaven, Christianity would have produced a radically different eschatology. To a pre-Cartesian mind "high" meant not just "physically, vertically high" and "low" meant not merely the physical opposite of that. And we still use pre-Cartesian language when we speak of "high ideals", and we still connect these two meanings, the physical and the spiritual, when we place judges, and kings on physically high seats to symbolize their spiritual authority.

Of course, "lowest" had a different meaning physically for a medieval man than it does for us. Medieval men did not spontaneously see the earth as a ball moving through empty and relative space (though the educated knew it was round and not flat); they saw "up" and "down" as absolute reference points rather than as relative.

But the change in science does not affect the analogical meanings of "high" and "low". There is a universal human association between sadness, burial, death, darkness, and "down-ness"; and this does not depend on the level of physical science. It is instinctive. So is the association between joy, freedom, life, light, and "up-ness" or rising. We love to dance, to jump, to climb mountains, and to fly. God designed us that way, and designed Heaven for us as something more *like* the sky than the ground.

Why can't there be any more chance to repent in Hell? Why did Dante's horrible sign over Hell's entrance read "Abandon all hope, ye who enter here"? Won't the damned in Hell regret their present state, and the life that led them to it?

A person may repent of sin in two ways: in one way directly, in another way indirectly. He repents of sin directly who hates sin as such; and he repents indirectly who hates it on account of something connected with it, for instance punishment.... Accordingly, the wicked will not repent of their sins directly, because consent in the malice of sin will remain in them; but they will repent indirectly, inasmuch as they will suffer from the punishment inflicted on them for sin.

The damned will will wickedness but shun punishment; and thus indirectly they repent of the wickedness committed (98,2).

The damned will not repent of *sin* at all. If they did, God would accept it, and take them gladly to Heaven. They will repent only of the pain of their punishment. In a similar way, a jailed criminal may repent only of being caught and of being in jail, without repenting of being the criminal he is or of committing the crime, except for the circumstances that caused him to be caught.

In fact, Hell is not merely punishment for sin; it is sin itself in its consummation in eternity. It is not an external punishment that is added to sin by God's choice; it is the necessary effect of sin. "The soul that sins shall die" (Ezek 18:4). "You shall not eat of the (forbidden) fruit . . . neither shall you touch it lest you die" (Gen 3:3). It was the lying devil who said "Ye will not die" (Gen 3:4).

The punishment is unavoidable, inevitable, natural. It is not like the spanking a child might get for jumping off the roof, but the broken bones he will necessarily get from it. It is like the hangover from intemperate drinking, not like a judgmental sermon from a teetotaler.

Similarly, Heaven is not an external, arbitrary, or artificial reward for goodness, like fame or prize money given to a public hero who saved a life. That is not what he worked for. He worked for the life he saved, and that is his natural reward, plus his own well-deserved satisfaction of being the person who did it. "Virtue is its own reward" and vice is its own punishment.

In this world, punishment is given both out of justice and out of charity, out of the hope that the guilty party who is punished will be improved, rehabilitated, and moved to repentance. But this end of charity is not always attained. In fact, it more often fails to do this than it succeeds, even in this life, where there is still a future and plenty of time to change.

In the next life, time as we know it is no more. You can't change your fundamental character any more. The book is finished and goes home to the printer. As the blessed are safe and fixed in Heaven, with no chance of falling out of it (how un-Heavenly would Heaven be if they could fall out of it?), so the damned, for the very same reason, are fixed in Hell with no chance of changing their character. The time to change is now. After death, the dimension of eternity is added to what we have become in time. Imagine triangles in time becoming pyramids in eternity, and squares in time becoming cubes in eternity. The shape of the foundation is set here, the fullness of the building is added there.

Will the damned in Hell want simply to cease to exist? Is it possible to desire nonexistence? Is nonexistence possible for a soul? Do suicides desire to cease to exist? Is that desire possible? Is its fulfillment possible? If not, does that show the ultimate tragedy of suicide? What is the difference between the state of soul in a suicide and the state of soul in the damned? Are suicides necessarily damned?

Whether the damned ... wish not to be?

It is written (Rev 9:6): *In those days men ... shall desire to die and death shall fly from them.*

The unhappiness of the damned surpasses all unhappiness of this world. Now in order to escape the unhappiness of this world, it is desirable to some to die, wherefore it is written (Sir 41:3 DR): *O death, thy sentence is welcome to the man that is in need and to him whose strength faileth....* **Much more, therefore, is** *not-to-be* **desirable to the damned.**

I answer that Not-to-be **may be considered in two ways. First, in itself—and thus it can nowise be desirable, since it has no aspect of good but is pure privation of good. Secondly, it may be considered as a relief from a painful life or from some unhappiness; and thus** *not to be* **takes on the aspect of good, since** *to lack an evil is a kind of good,* **as the Philosopher says. In this way it is better for the damned not to be than to be unhappy. Hence it is said** (Mt 26:24): *It were better for him if that man had not been born....* **In this sense the damned can prefer** *not to be* (S98,3).

What is not desirable cannot be desired. Simply not to exist, rather than to exist without pain, is not desirable, for there is *nothing there* to be desirable. Therefore simple nonexistence cannot be what either the damned or suicides desire.

However, it is possible even in this world to focus on the pains of life and to desire simply to be free from them, without desiring anything else. In that sense both the damned and suicides do desire not to be, i.e., not to be as they are, in pain.

The great difference between the damned and suicides is that there is still hope for suicides but not for the damned. This is confirmed by the fact that many who attempt suicide come back from near-death with experiences, either Heavenly or Hellish, that convince them that their suicide attempt was a mistake and could not possibly succeed in getting them what they sought, viz. freedom from all pain. Suicides usually see the cause of their pains as external, and want to escape the external world; but if they have near-death experiences, as some do, they usually discover that they made a terrible mistake because the experience of pain is in themselves, and they can never escape themselves, in time or in eternity. When they are given a second chance by coming back from a failed attempt, they are grateful, and rarely attempt suicide again. Some have experiences of the brink of Hell; some of something more hopeful and positive like Purgatory.

It is very wrong to despair of "successful" suicides' salvation because the human heart is complex and many-layered. Many suicides are insane and not fully responsible for the act; all are profoundly confused. God in His tricky mercy will get them to Heaven eventually if it is at all possible, through a Purgatory that will shock but cleanse. Their "fundamental option" may have been for life, not death, but buried beneath more obvious, more conscious layers of fear and reaction to pain that motivated their act. Thus we should never despair of them because we never know whether with their whole heart they despaired of God. We should always hope they had an ember of hope that God could blow into a fire of life.

It remains true, however, that suicide is one of the very worst possible mistakes to make.

Can you still sin in Hell? Don't the damned hate?

Envy reigns supreme in the damned. Therefore they grieve for the happiness of the blessed, and desire their damnation (S98,4).

Whether the damned hate God?

It is written (Ps 73[74]:23): *The pride of them that hate Thee ascendeth continually.*

I answer that The appetite is moved by good or evil apprehended. Now God is apprehended in two ways: namely, in Himself as by the blessed, who see Him in His essence, and in His effects, as by us and by the damned. Since, then, He is goodness by His essence, He cannot in Himself be displeasing to any will; wherefore whoever sees Him in His essence cannot hate Him. On the other hand, some of His effects are displeasing to the will.... [A]ccordingly a person may hate God not in Himself but by reason of His effects. Therefore the damned, perceiving God in His punishment, which is the effect of His justice, hate Him.

Objection 2. No one can hate goodness itself, as neither can one will badness itself. Now God is goodness itself. Therefore no one can hate Him.

Reply to Objection 2. This argument would prove if the damned saw God in Himself ... in His essence (S98,5).

Hell is the worst thing there is. The worst thing there is, is sin itself. (St. Thomas says that "the evil of fault is worse than the evil of punishment or pain.") Therefore Hell is not just the punishment for sin but also sin itself.

What sins can be committed in Hell? At least two, the two that cause the most pain and the least pleasure, even forbidden pleasure, on earth: envy and hate.

It gives us a shock of horror to read, in St. Thomas, that the damned, like the devils, desire the damnation of the blessed. But there is a tiny hope for a "happy" or hopeful spin that it is possible to put on this horror: think of a person you fear might go to Hell, or be in Hell. Could he in this life desire your eternal unhappiness? If not, perhaps he could not do so in the next life either.

A similar hopeful spin could be put on the other Hellish sin, hatred of God. Most unbelievers do not hate God. (Is it possible to hate a being you think does not exist?) They just don't love Him, because they don't believe He's real.

In the long "I answer that" paragraph, and in his reply to Objection 2, St. Thomas explains why Plato was right when he said that if you really know the good, you cannot help but love it. Plato's mistake was to confuse earth with Heaven. Only there will we see God so clearly that it will be absolutely impossible not to love Him. Here, it is possible to hate Him because of His just punishments, just as it is possible to hate your good and loving but just and punishing earthly father.

Will those in Hell remember their lives on earth?

In the damned there will be actual consideration of the things they knew heretofore as matters of sorrow, but not as a cause of pleasure. For they will consider both the evil they have done, and for which they were damned, and the delightful goods they have lost, and on both counts they will suffer torments (S98,7).

In his little masterpiece *The Great Divorce,* a modern version of Dante's *Divine Comedy,* C.S. Lewis says that damnation and salvation both work backwards:

"… [B]oth good and evil, when they are full grown (in eternity), become retrospective. Not only this valley (Purgatory, the beginning of their Heaven) but all their earthly past will have been Heaven to those who are saved. Not only the twilight in that town (the beginning of their Hell), but all their life on earth too, will then be seen by the damned to have been Hell. That is what mortals misunderstand. They say of some temporal suffering, 'No future bliss can make up for it,' not knowing that Heaven, once attained, will work backwards and turn even that agony into a glory. And of some sinful pleasure they say 'Let me have but *this* and I'll take the consequences': little dreaming how damnation will spread back and back into their past and contaminate the pleasure of the sin. Both processes begin even before death. The good man's past begins to change so that his forgiven sins and remembered sorrows take on the quality of Heaven; the bad man's past already conforms to his (present) badness and is filled only with dreariness. And that is why, at the end of all things…. the Blessed will say 'We have never lived anywhere except in Heaven,' and the Lost, 'We were always in Hell.'"

St. Catherine of Siena famously said, "All the way to Heaven is Heaven."

St. Thomas deduces a similar conclusion about the damned, most probably from the two reasonable premises (1) that memory is inherent in the soul and (2) that nothing causes pleasure in Hell, not even memory, but only causes sorrow.

Or, equally, he could deduce this conclusion from the two reasonable premises (1) that they will hate the evil of their punishment, and thus suffer the results of their sins, and (2) that they will suffer the pain of regret at not having attained all the goods of Heaven, and despair at having no hope of ever attaining them.

Bottom line: there is nothing good about Hell, nothing at all, not even the memories the damned have of the pleasures they had on earth. And there is nothing bad about Heaven, nothing at all, not even the memories of the pains the blessed had on earth. For as Heaven is the very best, Hell is the very worst.

This is true even if there were no other pains in Hell than the pain of loss, for that is the eternal loss of God, the total good, the source of *all* goods: happiness, joy, hope, love. St. Thomas' traditional picture of all the positive pains of Hell, something like a torture chamber, may turn out to be only symbolical; but even if so, what it symbolizes is as bad as a torture chamber. Much worse, in fact. Remember Dante's sign. (This is the thing we will explore next.)

Is there any chance or possibility that Hell might end? Shouldn't it end? How is it just for God to punish sinners eternally for sins that were only temporal?

Whether by divine justice an eternal punishment is inflicted on sinners?

Objection 1. **It would seem that an eternal punishment is not inflicted on sinners by divine justice. For the punishment should not exceed the fault:** *According to the measure of the sin shall the measure also of the stripes be* **(Deut. 25:2). Now fault is temporal. Therefore the punishment should not be eternal.**

Reply to Objection 1. **Punishment does not have to be equal to fault as to the amount of duration, as is seen to be the case also with human laws.** (For a murder in one moment of passion we may justly imprison a man for the rest of his life. The punishment must fit the crime in moral ways, not necessarily physical ways.) **We may also reply with Gregory that although sin is temporal in act, it is eternal in will.** (Those in Hell do not repent, so their will is evil eternally.)

Objection 3. **Further, a just judge does not punish except in order to correct ...** (for) *punishments are a kind of medicine.* **Now to punish the wicked eternally does not lead to their correction, nor to that of others, since then there will be no one in future who can be corrected thereby.**

Reply to Objection 3. **The punishments inflicted on those who are not altogether expelled from the society of their fellow-citizens are intended for their correction; whereas those punishments whereby certain persons are wholly banished from the society of their fellow-citizens are not intended for their correction, although they may be intended for the correction and tranquility of others who remain in the state. Accordingly the damnation of the wicked is for the correction of those who are now in the Church.**

In human penology too, sometimes the punishment justly and necessarily, for the protection of the innocent, excludes the criminal from society (by exile) or from human life itself (by capital punishment). And this is for the good of deterrence toward others.

Objection 6. **Further, the justice of God would seem to require that sinners should be brought to naught** (annihilated), **because on account of ingratitude a person deserves to lose all benefits; and among other benefits of God there is being itself....**

Reply to Objection 6. **Although a man deserves to lose his being from the fact that he has sinned against God the author of his being, yet ... being is presupposed to merit and demerit, nor is being lost or corrupted by the inordinateness of sin, and consequently privation of being cannot be the punishment due to any sin.** (Annihilation ("privation of being") would be less just, for sin does not refuse, hate, or lose existence itself, but does that to goodness.)

On the contrary, **It is written** (Mt 25:46): *These shall go into everlasting punishment....* However strong the arguments may seem to be for alternatives to eternal punishment, our supreme authority on the matter could not be more clear. Christ has spoken, the case is closed.

I answer that, **Since punishment is measured in two ways, namely according to the degree of its severity and according to its length of time, the measure of punishment corresponds to the measure of fault as regards the degree of severity.... But the duration of punishment regards the disposition of the sinner ... as regards those who sin in such a way as not to deserve to be entirely cut off from the fellowship of the saints, such as those who sin venially, their punishment will be so much the shorter or longer according as they are more or less fit to be cleansed through sin clinging to them more or less. This is observed in the punishments of this world and of purgatory ...** (But) **Gregory says:** *... those should never cease to be punished who ... never ceased to desire sin ... The wicked only put an end to sinning because their life came to an end; they would indeed have wished to live for ever that they might continue in sin for ever ...* (S99,1). If we are just and rational, though we tremble, we agree.

349. How can God refuse the prayers of the saints for mercy to the damned?

Surely God's goodness, love and mercy is greater than the sinner's evil. Why does it not conquer?

If the saints do not pray for those in danger of damnation, they lack charity. If they do, how can God refuse their prayers of charity? Is His mercy and charity less than the saints'?

How can sin and evil and misery win in the end? If the damned freely choose eternal misery over eternal joy, doesn't that mean that they win and that God and love loses? And that our love for them, as expressed in our prayers for their salvation, also loses?

There are people who do something self-destructive just to upset those they hate. Don't these people win in the sense that they prove by their self-destructive choices that even the love of those who love them does not conquer their own hate, that even the goodness and mercy of those who pray for them does not conquer their own evil? Doesn't God's gift of free will to all persons, even evil persons, give to evil persons a greater power for evil than the prayers of good persons have for good when those prayers are not answered by the conversion of the evil persons?

Whether God's mercy suffers (allows) ... **men to be punished eternally?**

Objection 2. **The charity of the saints in this life makes them pray for their enemies. Now they will have more perfect charity in that life. Therefore they will pray then for their enemies who are damned. But the prayers of the saints cannot be in vain, since they are most acceptable to God. Therefore at the saints' prayers the divine mercy will in time deliver the damned from their punishment.**

Reply to Objection 2. **As Augustine and Gregory say, the saints in this life pray for their enemies that they may be converted to God while it is yet possible for them to be converted ... since for those who depart this life without grace there will be no further time for conversion, no prayer will be offered for them ...** (S99,3).

The prayers and loves and hopes of the saints, and of God Himself, cannot pray for and hope for what is intrinsically impossible, like making $2 + 2$ not to be 4, or the past not to have been, or circles to be square. In fact, it is psychologically impossible to hope and pray for what we know is intrinsically impossible. What we pray for is what is possible.

The conversion of a sinner is always possible in this life, in time. Even Hitler may have repented in the split second between his squeezing his suicide gun's trigger and the effect of that act, namely his death. "While there's life, there's hope."

But where there is no more life, no more time, and therefore no more possibility of repentance, there is no more hope. Therefore we cannot and should not (try to) pray for the damned, either human or angelic (demons, fallen angels). That is like praying that circles be non-circular. It is intrinsically impossible.

We cannot regret and be saddened by what we know is impossible—intrinsically, inherently, necessarily, absolutely impossible. The conversion of the damned is impossible—it is a self-contradictory concept—because after death there is no more time for conversion. Conversion necessarily presupposes time, at least the kind of time necessary for changing your will, since conversion is a change of will, a change of heart. After death, this change is impossible.

For if it were possible in Hell, it would be possible in Heaven too, and in that case Heaven would be as uncertain and as changeable as Hell. If the damned in Hell could change and choose to become saved, then the saved in Heaven could possibly change and choose to become damned. And then Heaven would not be Heaven. In order for Heaven to be Heaven, Hell must be Hell.

There was a medieval legend about "the harrowing of Hell" in which Christ descended into Hell and emptied it, at the end of time. Is there any possible truth to this hopeful story?

Whether by God's mercy all punishment of the damned, both men and demons, comes to an end?

It is written (Mt 25:41): *Depart from Me, you cursed, into everlasting fire, which is prepared for the devil and his angels.* **Therefore they will be punished eternally....**

If the unhappiness of the wicked angels comes at length to an end, the happiness of the good will also come to an end, which is inadmissible.

As Augustine says, *Origen erred in maintaining that the demons will at length, through God's mercy, be delivered from their punishment.* **But this error has been condemned by the Church ... because it is clearly contrary to the authority of Holy Writ** (Rev 20:9–10) ...

Objection 1. It would seem that by God's mercy all punishment of the damned, both men and demons, comes to an end. For it is written (Wis 11:24): *Thou hast mercy upon all, O Lord, because Thou canst do all things.*

Reply to Objection 1. **God, for His own part, has mercy on all.... [H]owever, His mercy ... does not reach to certain people who render themselves unworthy of that mercy** (and *incapable* of receiving it, by rejecting it) **as do the demons and the damned who are obstinate in wickedness ...** (S99,2).

However pleasing they may be, human legends cannot trump clear, direct divine revelation. When there is a contradiction between what man says and what God says, which do we choose? It's a "Duh!" for anyone but an unbeliever. (That's the simple point of St. Thomas' second and fourth paragraphs above.)

We saw above (#349) that if there is time for the most fundamental change possible in our lives after death; if we can change our essential orientation toward God; if there is a "second chance"; then there must be a second chance for apostasy as well as for repentance. If Hell is not secure, neither is Heaven. There is a similar parallel in regard to time's extent after death. If time after death is finite rather than infinite, then Heaven can end as well as Hell. (That's the point of the third paragraph.)

The objection from God's mercy is answered not by mitigating this mercy in any way—it is infinite. There is no possible sin that God will not forgive, willingly and instantly and happily. But forgiveness is a gift, and a gift must be free: freely given and freely received. God always freely gives His mercy, but we do not always freely accept it. If we do not believe Him and trust Him, we keep the hands of our soul closed even though God's hands are open. It is this unbelief and pride that makes us refuse to repent and receive God's forgiveness, rather than the gravity of any sins we have committed, that renders us "unworthy" of His mercy. "Unworthy" does not mean "undeserving", for we are all undeserving! It means "incapable of receiving." To ask for mercy to force itself upon the unwilling is to ask for what is intrinsically impossible and self-contradictory.

Lack of faith (trust) toward the giver causes us to refuse the gift. This is why faith is necessary for salvation. And this is why it is so important for parents to be trustable to their children, by showing them total love and honesty. If children learn to be suspicious, cynical, and mistrustful of others, beginning with their parents (who are inevitably their primary models for the whole human race), it will be much harder for them to trust God when they grow up. Even St. Augustine found it very difficult to call God "Father" because he had such a bad relationship with his own earthly father. This is one way in which we experience "the iniquity of the fathers upon the children" (Ex. 20:5).

There is a Russian story about an evil, nasty, selfish old woman who was being taken to Heaven on an onion because she had once given an onion to a hungry beggar. It was the one and only good deed in her life, but it was real and God honored it. Is something like that possible? If not, will all the good deeds of mercy and love that those in Hell had performed on earth be simply forgotten or erased?

Whether all those who perform works of mercy will be punished eternally?

It is written (1 Cor 6:9–10): *Neither fornicators ... nor adulterers, etc., shall possess the kingdom of God.* Yet many are such who practice works of mercy. Therefore not all of the merciful will come to the eternal kingdom, and consequently some of them will be punished eternally....

Nothing profits unto eternal life in the absence of charity. Now it happens that certain persons persevere in works of mercy without having charity.... Most evident is this in the case of those who lay hands on other people's property, for after seizing on many things, they nevertheless spend something in works of mercy....

Objection 2. Further (Mt 25:3–46) we find a description of our Lord's discussion with the damned and the elect. But this discussion is only about works of mercy. Therefore eternal punishment will be awarded only to such as have omitted to practice works of mercy....

Reply to Objection 2. The reason why the discussion refers only to the works of mercy is not because eternal punishment will be inflicted on none but those who omit those works, but because eternal punishment will be remitted to those who after sinning have obtained forgiveness by their works of mercy... (However "enough" good works *without repentance* cannot save us. We cannot "buy" Heaven.)

Objection 3. Further, it is written (Matt 6:12): *Forgive us our debts as we also forgive our debtors,* and further on (vs. 14): *For if you will*

forgive men their offenses, your heavenly Father will forgive you also your offenses. **Therefore it would seem that the merciful, who forgive others their offenses, will themselves obtain the forgiveness of their sins, and consequently will not be punished eternally.**

Reply to Objection 3. **Our Lord said this to those who ask that their debt be forgiven, but not to those who persist in sin. Wherefore the repentant alone will obtain by their works of mercy the forgiveness that sets them free....**

Objection 4. **Further, a gloss of Ambrose on 1 Timothy 4:8, *Godliness is profitable to all things,* says: ... though he should suffer from the inconstancy of the flesh, without doubt he will be scourged but he will not perish....**

Reply to Objection 4. **Those who while yet in this life fall into sins of the flesh through frailty are disposed to repentance by works of mercy. Wherefore such a one will not perish, that is to say, he will be disposed by those works not to perish, through grace bestowed on him by our Lord, Who is blessed for evermore. Amen** (S99,5).

Once again, divine revelation has to trump human feeling. That is St. Thomas' first reason.

If works of mercy alone were enough to save us, without the life of charity (agape, caritas) in the soul, which is supernatural, and which is the very life (*zoe*) of God, and which must be received by faith, then we could buy Heaven by becoming robbers and then giving away our ill-gotten gains.

Christ made it very clear that repentance and faith, as well as works of love and mercy, are needed for salvation. We must have the right relation to God as well as to our fellow men. They are parts of an organic whole. Each part disposes us to, and leads to, the other parts.

(By the way, Christ did not say just how explicit, clear, conscious, and accurate the repentance and faith had to be. Heaven's doorman judges hearts more than heads.)

And in that Russian story, the old lady eventually went to Hell because she refused to share her onion with another who needed it even as it was taking her to Heaven.

The idea of a Limbo after death was believed by most Catholics in the Middle Ages, though never officially taught by the Church as dogma. But the majority of today's theologians, even the faithful and orthodox ones, are usually of the opinion that it is not true. What did "Limbo" mean, what were the reasons for it, and what are the reasons against it?

Whether those souls which depart with original sin alone suffer from a bodily fire and are punished by fire?

Gregory Nazianzen ... distinguishes three classes of unbaptized persons: namely, those who refuse to be baptized, those who through neglect have put off being baptized until the end of life and have been surprised by sudden death, and those who, like infants, have failed to receive it through no fault of theirs.

Of the first he says that they will be punished not only for their other sins but also for their contempt of Baptism.

Of the second, that they will be punished, though less severely than the first, for having neglected it. (Gregory does not specify whether this punishment is in Hell or in Purgatory.)

And of the last he says that *a just and eternal Judge will consign them neither to heavenly glory not to the eternal pains of hell, for although they have not been signed with Baptism, they are without wickedness and malice, and have suffered rather than caused their loss of Baptism.* **He also gives the reason why, although they do not reach the glory of heaven, they do not therefore suffer the eternal punishment suffered by the damned:** *Because there is a mean between the two, since he who deserves not honor and glory is not for that reason worthy of punishment, and on the other hand he who is not deserving of punishment is not for that reason worthy of glory and honor.... Hence, as his guilt did not result from an action of his own, even so neither should he be punished by suffering himself, but only by losing that which his nature was unable to obtain. On the other hand, those who are under sentence for original sin* (alone) *will suffer no loss whatever in other kinds of perfection and goodness which are consequent upon human nature ...* (Appendix I,1,1).

Limbo was thought to be a kind of eternal Heavenly nursery, where the souls of the unbaptized who died in infancy go to be happy forever but without the Beatific Vision of "full Heaven".

The reason for believing it was this dilemma: No one can enter Heaven without faith and Baptism (at least implicitly, the desire for Baptism, or "the Baptism of desire"). But infants cannot exercise the act of faith, and some of them die unbaptized, so they cannot enter Heaven. On the other hand, no one is sent to Hell for Original Sin but only for his or her own personal "actual sins"; but infants are as incapable of choosing sin as they are of choosing faith. So if they can't go to either Heaven or Hell, yet their souls are immortal, there must be a third place after death. Thus Limbo.

The basic premise of the argument is that God is just. That is a certain premise. Whether the conclusion of Limbo necessarily follows from this premise is not as certain. God has not told us how He solves this dilemma, so we are free to speculate.

Most theologians today believe that since God's love and mercy is as certain as His justice, and since God is incredibly clever, especially in arranging for what He wills most of all, namely, our salvation; therefore it is likely that God somehow gets these infants into Heaven. He is not limited to the "normal" ways; there may well be something like back doors to Heaven small enough for infants to squeeze through.

The bottom line is that no one knows. There may well be no Limbo. And there may well be one.

If there is a Limbo, what do those who are there experience?

Whether these same souls (in Limbo) **suffer spiritual affliction on account of the state in which they are?**

Right reason does not allow one to be disturbed on account of what one was unable to avoid.... Now in these children there is right reason deflected by no actual sin. Therefore they will not be disturbed....

The pain of punishment corresponds to the pleasure of sin; wherefore, since original sin is void of pleasure, its punishment is free of all pain....

On this question there are three opinions....

If one is guided by right reason, one does not grieve through being deprived of what is beyond one's power to obtain, but only through lack of that which in some way one is capable of obtaining. Thus no wise man grieves for being unable to fly like a bird, or that he is not a king or an emperor, since these things are not due to him; whereas he would grieve if he lacked that to which he had some kind of claim ... Hence they will in no wise grieve for being deprived of the divine **vision; nay, rather will they rejoice for that they will have a large share of God's goodness and their own natural perfections** ... (Appendix 1,2).

The innocent souls in Limbo have no kind of pain even though they are not in Heaven, because they are not so foolish and irrational as to wish to have what is not possible for them to have. They are content, as a wise man is content not to be a bird or an emperor.

The premise for this opinion of a painless Limbo is God's justice, which would not consign the innocent to sufferings they did not deserve. And if even justice would not tolerate undeserved pain, how much less would love and mercy! God may be more than justice, but never less. Those who die without having committed sins do not deserve any punishment, and they are not given any.

The premise is certain (that God is just), but it is not certain that the conclusion (Limbo) necessarily follows from it. Even though nearly all Catholics in St. Thomas' day believed in Limbo, he is careful to call this a matter of opinion ("on this question there are three opinions") rather than certainty.

If Limbo is painless, why isn't Purgatory? What are its pains and why are they necessary?

Whether the pains of purgatory surpass all the temporal pains of this life?

Augustine says: *This fire of Purgatory will be more severe than any pain that can be felt, seen or conceived in this world. . . .*

In Purgatory there will be a twofold pain. One will be the pain of loss, namely the delay of the divine vision, and the pain of sense, namely punishment by . . . fire (of some kind). **With regard to both, the least pain of Purgatory surpasses the greatest pain of this life. For the more a thing is desired, the more painful is its absence. And since after this life the holy souls desire the Sovereign Good with the most intense longing—both because their longing is not held back by the weight of the body, and because had there been no obstacle, they would already have gained the goal of enjoying the Sovereign Good—it follows that they grieve exceedingly for their delay. Again, since pain is not hurt, but the *sense* of hurt, the more sensitive a thing is, the greater the pain caused by that which hurts it; wherefore hurts inflicted on the more sensible parts cause the greatest pain . . .** (Appendix I,2,1).

Unlike Limbo, Purgatory is painful, for its whole point is "purgation", like an operation that has no mercy on the cancer (sinful habits of character) that infects the patient (the believer who has been fully justified but not yet fully sanctified).

Why do St. Augustine, St. Thomas, and many other Catholic theologians, as well as mystics who are given actual visions of Purgatory (especially St. Catherine of Genoa in her *Dialogues on Purgatory*)

all say that the pains of Purgatory are more severe than any pain in this life?

For two reasons. One is that we will see and know with certainty, not just believe by faith, how utterly beautiful Heaven is, as the whole point of our existence; and the pain of our temporary loss of this infinite good will exceed anything comparable or imaginable on earth. "For the more a thing is desired, the more painful is its absence." The very longed-for joy of Heaven's distant vision, the joy of the Heaven we will see and long for, a joy that is incomparably greater than any we experience on earth, will be the cause of the pain that is incomparably greater than any we experience on earth.

A second reason is that even though the pains of Purgatory, unlike earthly pains and earthly fires, are never harmful to us but only good for us, yet they will feel more hurtful and "fiery" than earthly pains because we will be more conscious and sensitive. Earthly life is full of soporifics, anaesthetics, pain-dullers. In fact, compared with Purgatory our whole life on earth will appear to have been life only half awake. In Purgatory we will be fully awake, fully sensitive, and fully cognizant of the evil of all of our sins. Our clear knowledge of God's brightness and beauty will make our clear knowledge of our own darkness and ugliness more painful than any similar light that shows up our most terrible defects here on earth. We will fully appreciate how we dishonored God's honor, and we will fully fulfill our repentance. As St. Thomas says, "The more sensitive a thing is, the greater the pain." Like Christ on the Cross, we will have perfected sensitivities.

But we will not regret it. We will *want* the purifying pains, like a filthy tramp taking a hot shower so that he can enter the banquet room of a mansion. Or like a snake shedding his old, dirty skin.

Will Purgatory's pains be inflicted on us or will we freely choose them? If they are inflicted from without, how can they purify our free souls within? If we choose them, won't that make us masochists?

Whether this punishment is voluntary?

No one asks to be freed from a punishment that he suffers willingly. Now those who are in Purgatory ask to be set free. Therefore they will not undergo that punishment voluntarily.

(However,) **a thing is said to be voluntary in two ways. First, by an absolute act of the will; and thus no punishment is voluntary, because the very notion of punishment is that it be contrary to the will. Secondly, a thing is said to be voluntary by a conditional act of the will. Thus cautery** (surgical cutting) **is voluntary for the sake of regaining health.**

Hence a punishment may be voluntary in two ways. First, because by being punished we obtain some good; and thus the will undertakes a punishment, as instanced in satisfaction, or when a man accepts a punishment gladly and would not have it not to be, as in the case of martyrdom. Secondly, when, even if we gain no good by the punishment, we cannot obtain a good without being punished, as in the case of natural death; and then the will does not undertake the punishment, and would be delivered from it, but it submits to it. And in this respect the punishment is said to be voluntary. In this latter sense the punishment of **Purgatory is said to be voluntary** (Appendix I,2,2).

We will not be masochists, even in Purgatory. No one wants pain as such. Of course we will regret that we will have to suffer so much pain in Purgatory. In that sense, the pains will be unfree. As St. Thomas says, "The very notion of *punishment* is that it be contrary to the will." For if I will it, if I desire it, then it is desirable to me, and then getting it is not a punishment but a reward!

Yet it will be free in another sense. We will agree with God's diagnosis and prescription for Purgatory's operations, as we agree with a wise earthly doctor who tells us we need a painful operation to save our life.

The good we will obtain by Purgatory, namely Heaven, will be so great that we will be motivated to greatly desire these pains, since we will see that they are necessary to enable us to enter and enjoy Heaven. They will be like the labor pains of a woman whose whole will is set on the birth of her child. Thus even though death is our "last enemy" and the destruction of all our earthly goods, we can embrace death as the necessary door to Heaven. Artificial immortality by genetic engineering would be the most horrible thing that could possibly happen to the human race on earth. It would lock the door to Heaven.

An old oratorio ("Open Our Eyes") sings: "Thou hast made death glorious and triumphant, for through its portals we enter into the presence of the living God."

356. The amount of time you spend in Purgatory

The Church has attached numbers to the indulgences she grants for specific good works, such as "300 days in Purgatory" for a novena. What is the basis for this? Is does not seem to be purely speculative and imaginary. On the other hand, it cannot be literal, because the souls in Purgatory are no longer in the universe and subject to earthly time. So it must be something between these two. How can this be explained?

Whether one person is delivered from this punishment sooner than another?

Objection 2. **In point of duration, unequal merits receive equal retribution both in Heaven and in Hell. Therefore seemingly it is the same in Purgatory.**

Reply to Objection 2. **Mortal sin, which deserves the punishment of Hell, and charity, which deserves the reward of Heaven, will after this life be immovably rooted in their subject. Hence as to all there is the same duration in either case. It is otherwise with venial sin, which is punished in Purgatory.**

On the contrary, **is the comparison of the Apostle, who denotes the differences of venial sins by** *wood, hay and stubble* **(1 Cor 3:12). Now it is clear that wood remains longer in the fire than hay and stubble. Therefore one venial sin is punished longer in Purgatory than another.**

I answer that **Some venial sins cling more persistently than others, according as the affections are more inclined to them and more firmly fixed in them. And since that which clings more persistently is more slowly cleansed, it follows that some are tormented in Purgatory longer than others ...** (Appendix 1,2,6).

Divine justice is not less than human justice; thus it requires equal punishments for equal sins and unequal punishment for unequal sins. Divine mercy requires the same, for more mercy is needed to forgive great sins than small ones, and more rehabilitation is required for great sinners than lesser sinners. Rehabilitation and education takes time, therefore those who need more of it will spend more time in Purgatory and those who need less of it, less time.

This is true of venial sins, which are relative and finite and can be quantified, at least analogically. In contrast, mortal sin is total loss of Heaven. It is not a matter of degree. And salvation as such is also a simple either/or, an absolute. Both are irrevocable, unchangeable, and eternal. Purgatory is only temporal, temporary.

Its time, however, cannot be literally measured by earthly clocks. Therefore the language about "years in Purgatory" or "days in Purgatory" is true symbolically and analogically, not literally. However time is measured there, "300 days" means simply "twice as much as 150 days". Even if Purgatory is not temporal but instantaneous, like taking a bandage off a wound all at once (which is possible though not likely), its pains are measurable in degrees of severity.

Infinite bliss in Heaven, and infinite misery in Hell, are not matters of degree, as are the pains in Purgatory. Although there will be degrees of bliss in Heaven and degrees of misery in Hell, the difference between bliss and misery is not itself a matter of relative degree but is absolute. A woman is either pregnant or not, though she may be one month pregnant or nine.

Sins to which we are more addicted need longer time for purgation. This is so even in this life. So we should be careful not only to avoid sins that are the most objectively serious (e.g., murder is worse than theft) but also sins to which we are more addicted. A weakly repentant pornography addict may have to spend more time in Purgatory than a sincerely repentant one-time rapist. (Of course, neither will go to Purgatory, and thus eventually to Heaven, unless they repent.)

Why is the existence of Purgatory certain, unlike Limbo?

Whether there is a Purgatory after this life?

Objection 1. It would seem that there is not a Purgatory after this life. For it is said (Rev 14:13): *Blessed are the dead who die in the Lord. From henceforth now, saith the Spirit, that they may rest from their labors....*

Reply to Objection 1. The authority quoted is speaking of the labor of working for merit, and not of the labor of suffering to be cleansed.

On the contrary, It is said (II Maccabees 12:46): *It is a holy and wholesome thought to pray for the dead, that they may be loosed from sins.* Now there is no need to pray for the dead who are in Heaven, for they are in no need; nor again for those who are in Hell, because they cannot be loosed from sins. Therefore after this life there are some not yet loosed from sins, who can be loosed therefrom; and these have charity, without which sins cannot be loosed, for *charity covereth all sins* (Prov 10:12; I Pet 4:8). Hence they will not be consigned to everlasting death, since *he that liveth and believeth in Me shall not die for ever* (Jn 11:26); nor will they obtain glory without being cleansed, because nothing unclean shall obtain it, as stated in the last chapter of the Apocalypse (vs. 14). Therefore some kind of cleansing remains after this life....

Those who deny Purgatory speak against the justice of God ... (Appendix 2,1).

The most serious religious objection to Purgatory, on the part of Protestants, is that the anticipation of the pains of Purgatory detracts from a happy death ("blessed are the dead who from now on die in the Lord"—Rev 14:13).

But that is like saying that the pains of labor detract from the joy of childbirth. Deferred happiness is still happiness.

In Purgatory we will rest from our active labors of making right choices. We are in Purgatory rather than Hell, we are in Heaven's remedial class, only because we have made the right choices on earth while there was still time. That active labor is completed. But we will experience the passive (receptive) labor of being purified and perfected in Purgatory.

Scripture clearly teaches Purgatory. (1) The passage from Maccabees, which praises prayers for the dead, makes no sense if all the dead are either in Heaven or Hell. (2) Purgatory can be proved even to Protestants who do not accept Maccabees and the other deutero-canonical books as Scripture (even though the same Church that canonized the other sixty-six books also canonized these). For Scripture clearly teaches that (1) we are sinners (1 Jn 1:8), that (2) nothing unholy can enter Heaven (Rev 21:27), that there is no sin in Heaven, but perfect sanctity and holiness; and that (3) the gap between sin and perfect holiness is very, very great (Lk 16:26). To believe that an ordinary, sinful believer, immediately after death, can just sashay into Heaven and endure the Beatific Vision, the revealing light of divine holiness, without a radical change in his soul, is radically to underestimate either (1) the badness of badness or (2) the goodness of goodness or (3) the bigness of the difference between them.

What is the difference between the pains of Purgatory and the pains of Hell?

Whether it is the same place where souls are cleansed and the damned punished?

I answer that, **Nothing is clearly stated in Scripture about the situation of Purgatory, nor is it possible to offer convincing arguments on this question** (Appendix II,2).

Obviously, there is an enormous difference between the two because even if the pains are the same in both places (which is doubtful), there are also more important, crucially important, goods that are present in Purgatory and not in Hell in addition to the pains: (1) faith and (2) hope and (3) charity and (4) repentance and (5) the joy of the presence of God and (6) the assurance of salvation.

But the pains themselves seem somewhat similar in that both (1) are after death, (2) are primarily spiritual pains, and (3) are incomparably greater than any earthly pains. These similarities gave rise to the popular picture, especially in the Middle Ages, of Purgatory as a sort of temporary Hell.

St. Thomas, more than most medievals, sits lightly on this picture of Purgatory as a temporary suburb of Hell, and does not insist on it, thus making room for a more positive picture of Purgatory,

which we have implied in some of our comments above.

He did this because he was utterly honest and utterly humble and therefore deeply internalized Socrates' "Lesson One", the "learned ignorance", knowing how little he really knew, especially about God and the next life. If divine revelation (Scripture and the Church's infallible dogmas) do not clearly answer questions like this one (and similar questions about the next life, such as the comparative population statistics of Heaven and Hell), we must be content to know that we do not know. And that is St. Thomas' last word.

It was also the last word of his life, for he refused to finish the *Summa*. These last excerpts are not from the *Summa* but from the "Supplement" which his successors culled from his earlier writings, precisely because St. Thomas refused to answer these questions in his more mature work. And the reason he refused, the reason he said, "I can write no more", was because God showed him, in a supernatural vision, something of Himself and the life of Heaven that St. Thomas was destined to begin a very short time later; and in light of that light, everything he had ever written he called "straw".

You have no right to call theology "straw" until you have written a *Summa Theologiae*.

POSTSCRIPT

What St. Thomas didn't say

Here is what he did say about what he didn't say:

(1) that the most eloquent knowledge of God is to know that He transcends all knowledge;

(2) and therefore, a fortiori, that He transcends all words. All the mystics of all the world's religions agree in that, at least. St. Thomas, the greatest of wordsmiths, sculpted 4,000 pages of profoundly condensed words for his little *Summa* (for "beginners"!), massed together like a neutron star, but he did this for the same reason an artist painting a single star on a dark night would surround one tiny, bright point of light with massive darkness: he wrote all these words ultimately only to frame and to set off by contrast the God Who infinitely transcends all words, since He is *The* Word, in the singular ("Hear, O Israel: the Lord, the Lord your God is one!");

(3) that Socrates, the world's greatest philosopher, is right in assuming that we know very little, and much less than we think we know, and that on many questions we must be satisfied with possibility or probability or "arguments from fittingness";

(4) that the argument from merely human authority, though weighty, is not conclusive; in fact it is "the weakest of all arguments";

(5) that compared with what we will see in Heaven, and compared with what St. Thomas was graciously given the opportunity to see on earth by the mystical vision God gave him shortly before his death, he has to make the shocking judgment about the greatest work in the history of theology that it's only "straw". (To modernize the shock, imagine he said, "It's all bullshit." Straw was often used in the Middle Ages for covering animal dung.) If he had *not* made this shocking judgment about it and had not left it unfinished, it would *really* have been unfinished. "Perfect" literally means "completely made," *per-factum*. The most perfect and finished possible work on earth is to know that all work on earth is imperfect and unfinished. The *Summa*'s capstone is its lack of a capstone.

(6) That the most appropriate commentary on St. Thomas is therefore one that is also unfinished;

(7) and that the demand which this book, like the *Summa* itself, makes on its reader is not merely comprehension, scholarship, or study, but life. Truth in thought is the necessary foundation for truth in life, truth in action—a building without a foundation will not stand—but the foundation is for the sake of the building, not the building for the sake of the foundation. The ultimate purpose of this book, and of the *Summa*, and of all theology, is not just knowing the truth but being the truth and doing the truth.

So do it, already: be a saint. God will not let you go until you are. That is why there is Purgatory, and that is why you will love it.